INTERNATIONAL REAL ESTATE

(Global Real Estate)

By

Dr. Mark Lee Levine, Editor

Professional Publications
P&E
and Education, Inc.

INTERNATIONAL REAL ESTATE (GLOBAL REAL ESTATE)
Authored in part and Edited by

Dr. Mark Lee Levine
BS, JD, PAP, LLM (t ax), Ph.D., CCIM, MAI, CRE, CIPS, Cert. FIABCI, Dipl. FIABCI,
FRICS, GAA, GRI, SREA, CA-C, SRS, CRS, CRB, CPM, ALC, CLU, ChFC, DREI, RECS, TRC

Professor, Prior Director

Burns School of Real Estate and Construction Management
Daniels College of Business
UNIVERSITY OF DENVER

2101 South University Blvd. DCB-380 Denver, Colorado 80208
303.871.2142 FAX: 303.871.2971
E-mail: mlevine@du.edu
https://portfolio.du.edu/pc/port?portfolio=mlevine

Burns School Global website: http://burns.daniels.du.edu

Published by Professional Publications and Education, Inc. (PP&E)
Denver, Colorado 303.871.2142

Caveat

Inasmuch as there are differing opinions on a number of legal, tax and related matters which obviously affect many activities, certainly not limited to those involving international real estate issues, it is important for me to emphasize a general Caveat and Disclaimer. I have no intention of giving legal, tax and/or other advice by means of this text.

The intent is to state general propositions, specific points, and development of case law and other authority. Any opinions or posit ions are limited in this respect, and further are qualified in that they are not necessarily the opinions of any or all parties that might be involved in producing this text or any portion thereof.

All parties are advised that careful planning necessitates consulting with their own legal, tax and other counsel. This text should not be a substitute for that advice, but rather, it should be used as a tool to help inform the user.

Therefore: This publication is designed to provide accurate and authoritative information about this subject. The reader is advised that the material contained herein may be inappropriate in a given situation. The book is sold with the understanding that the publisher and Author are not engaged in rendering legal, accounting or other professional services through this publication. Further, due to the nature of this publication, any of the information contained herein is subject to change without notice. The matters contained herein may be utilized only as consistent with all applicable laws, regulations and restrictions. If legal advice or other expert assistance is required, the services of a competent professional should be sought.

Dedication

To my students—the "special group" and Diane Smith, Assistant.

The special group involves those students over 45 years who have been willing to teach me. Those who are in the teaching field are the real estate beneficiaries; we, as professors, have hundreds–thousands–of strong minds that test our thoughts, guide our deliberations, hone our skills, and often put us back on the right track. This book, with thanks that cannot be expressed in a few lines, is dedicated in honor of Diane and those students who have helped me over 45+ years of teaching. Without the efforts of Diane and my students, this book would not exist. And, a special thanks is owing to Graduate Research Assistant, Jesse Daniel, for his work in this latest edition. THANK YOU.

Preparation for the production of this edition was guided and supported by the efforts of Dr. Abbi Levine Rosenthal, our talented daughter who has worked in this area of preparing manuscripts for publication. Thank you, Dooie!

Dr. Mark Lee Levine

Table of Contents

Preface

As Editor of the materials produced by our authors (noted in the acknowledgments on the following page) and assisted in part by Dr. Jeffrey L. Engelstad, Ph.D., Clinical Professor at the Burns School of Real Estate and Construction Management, Daniels *College of Business*, UNIVERSITY OF DENVER, along with various students, real estate professionals, professors, publishers, as well as others who have supported this endeavor, our goals are to collect, organize, and present materials of interest to those involved in international real estate.

As Editor, I do not claim originality of data. Our "originality" rests in the authors' collecting, formatting, and presenting the data. This includes a template format involving standard sect ions for the book. Such a standard format for each country presented allows the user easy access to the material. It also allows updates for referencing and cross-referencing of materials. Particular focus has been placed on developing a single-source reference tool that can be utilized by those involved in international real estate.

In summary, the emphasis in this Work on international real estate is to:

1. Provide an overview of each country's population, geographic size, demographics, and similar information, including political issues;
2. Provide a focus on key real estate issues, as contained in the Real Property Issues and Real Estate Trends sections of each country;
3. Review factors that impact real estate actions and positions, such as cultural and political issues; and
4. Provide helpful tools, references to various countries, practice problems, case studies, charts, diagrams, International links, and similar materials to aid in the examination of international real estate issues.

General sources of data, in addition to specific sources and data noted in the Selected References section of each chapter, were drawn from:

1. General country data;
2. The World Factbook by the CIA (*U.S. Central Intelligence Agency*), CIA web site at https://www.cia.gov/library/ publications/the-world-factbook/index.html, also referred to herein as the CIA World Fact book, and other sources noted herein;
3. General real estate information provided by the UNIVERSITY OF DENVER, Daniels *College of Business*, Burns School of Real Estate and Construction Management (Burns School), including the Burns School Global Real Estate Web site at http://burns.daniels.du.edu, and real estate experts regarding each country;
4. Real estate law issues, guided by references to Martindale-Hubbell; and 5. The authors of each chapter who are key sources and authorities for this book and the data therein.

This book is a tool that will be periodically updated. As a presentation of important factual and real estate data on each country, it allows the reader to utilize this information to develop a foundation for the decision-making processes in various countries, whether for general analysis, brokerage, consulting, financing, investing, development, construction, property management, governmental use, taxes, and other real estate-related activities.

Acknowledgments

After writing 22 books, over 30 new editions, and related works over the years, I thought assembling this **INTERNATIONAL REAL ESTATE (Global Real Estate)** book could follow the procedural steps used in prior books. However, it became apparent that editing a book, as opposed to writing, takes a great deal of coordination, time, and effort because of the many contributors involved. With this in mind, I cannot say "thank you" enough to the devoted contributors for their efforts and contributions to this book.

A quotation that consistently stays in my mind from President Woodrow Wilson captures the essence of our gratitude to so many people as to this INTERNATIONAL REAL ESTATE (Global Real Estate) project. President Wilson said: "I use not only all the brains I have, but all I can borrow." Certainly that has been the position for this book, especially when no one person has the ability to capture all of the information and considerations of real estate located throughout the world. It was absolutely necessary engage the fine minds with real estate knowledge of the various countries covered.

For the material and content of Chapters, I heartily thank the contributing authors.

For mistakes or errors in format, I must stand responsible for those. (However, should our readers be good enough to inform us of such issues, we will attempt to correct them).

Our thanks are extended to the following people, with my apologies if we have not acknowledged someone. Numerous people have been good enough to aid in this project and/or our Burns School Global Real Estate Web site at http://burns.daniels.du.edu (or http://burns.dcb.du.edu). We encourage others to utilize this book and to consider making contributions to the publication of this Book.

The idea is to provide the most up-to-date, broad scope, practical and useable tools to understand international/global real estate issues that impact the activity of anyone involved in this arena. Obviously, this book is only as good as he material and the organization involved. Therefore, your comments, suggestions and contributions would be greatly appreciated.

UNIVERSITY OF DENVER COMMUNITY: I acknowledge the strong support that we have received from the UNIVERSITY OF DENVER, the *Daniels College of Business* and our Burns School of Real Estate and Construction Management (Burns School). The University is fortunate to have the leadership of Current Chancellor Chopp and prior Chancellors Coombe, and Ritchie. Likewise, we have been guided by the inspiration and remarkable ability of Dean Emeritus James R. Griesemer at the *Daniels College of Business. As* to international issues, we were directed by the extremely capable and talented prior Vice Provost for Office of Internationalization, Dr. Ved Nanda. As Director of the Burns School of Real Estate and Construction Management (Burns School), I have had the benefit of their energy and enthusiasm, as well as that from our outstanding faculty, staff and students through our various programs.

Many members of the faculty are readily recognizable, given their activities throughout the United States in the fields of real estate and construction management.

Dr. Jeffrey L. Engelstad, Ph.D., Professor at the Burns School of Real Estate and Construction Management (Burns School), has been very active in the real estate field. He also holds the designation of Certified Commercial Investment Member (CCIM). Unquestionably, this book would not be what it is without his strong support. I take this opportunity to specifically acknowledge and thank Jeff for his outstanding contribution in aiding the production of this book. He is a bright light in the real estate field that will shine for many years. We are fortunate that he is at the UNIVERSITY OF DENVER.

Dr. Michael J. Crean, Ph.D., retired Professor at the Burns School, is well known for his exciting teaching style, experience and knowledge in the areas of real estate finance and real estate appraisal.

We thank our personnel at the **UNIVERSITY OF DENVER,** *Daniels College of Business,* Burns School of Real Estate, especially Diane Smith. Diane has been the key to the physical preparation of this book and has been very instrumental in compiling and generally editing most of this material. David Dinakar, prior Technology Systems Manager at the *Daniels College of Business,* UNIVERSITY OF DENVER, compiled many of the Burns School charts herein and authored most of the India Chapter. UNIVERSITY OF DENVER student Kevin Sutton also helped edit and update much of the material, as well as Joshua Fine.

UNIVERSITY OF DENVER STUDENTS: We have had the benefit of input from outstanding students at the UNIVERSITY

OF DENVER, *Daniels College of Business*, and specifically in our Burns School of Real Estate and Construction Management, who have been important in development of this material. We commenced this project with a select list of several students who collected material in areas where we focused attention. Our initial group of talented graduate students, and a few undergraduate students, with some modifications (since we added several students after the inception of the project), included Michael Friedman, Lisa Feifer, Warren (Brady) Scott, Andrew Swedenborg, Michael Sunoo, Ben Widjajakusuma, Omar Malik, Eric Marble and others. Since then, many other students have worked on this project, e.g., Jose Ramirez, Samer I. Asafour, Neil Lubar, Adam Berszenyi, Donald E. Cape, Jr., Michael Elliott, David R. Gibson, Kyler Knudsen, Scott Schraiberg, David Griggs, Dillon Joos, Peter Alexander Molnar, Leo Simonavich, David Beach, Tyler Elick, Travis McCain, Jessica Harris, Matt McBride, Daniel Lucchesi, Geoff Burgess, Carlos V., and numerous Authors noted herein. My wife, Ellen H. Levine, also a prior DU student, has contributed immensely. DU student Michelle Weiszmann authored most of the country-specific Case Studies. We especially thank the real estate professionals in our XMRCM Program (Executive Masters In Real Estate and Construction Management), Walter S. Clements, Leslie A. Kramer, Suzanne Miller, Gary Ralston, Ira D. Warshauer, J. Matthew McMullen, and Bob Behrens, who contributed to this work.

In addition to these outstanding students, many who now hold leading jobs in the real estate and construction management industry, we have had the benefit of input in our research from many students who have undertaken education within our real estate program. Specifically, we have had the benefit of input from many students in our INTERNATIONAL REAL ESTATE (Global Real Estate) classes, which I have had the pleasure of teaching.

And, in special support for this edition of the Work, as mentioned earlier, we thank, in particular, the outstanding support work undertaken by recently graduated Masters student, Jesse Daniel. His expertise and professional support were of great value for this edition.

SUPPORT FROM THE NATIONAL ASSOCIATION OF REALTORS® (NAR): Various international organizations have also had valuable comments and input. Focusing on international real estate organizations, one of the most outstanding is the NATIONAL ASSOCIATION OF REALTORS® (NAR), International Section. That Section issues an appropriately earned Designation of the Certified International Property Specialist (CIPS). Many of the CIPS staff and individuals, and those aspiring to such Designation, have been extremely helpful in this Project. Some of those individuals helpful at NAR-International, without attempting to be exhaustive, include: Alejandro Azcona, Georgi Ann Bailey, Gloria Berman, Nathan Boothe, David Bradley, Tanya Carter, Jacob R. Casanova, Manfred Chemek, Allen Decker, Vi Dolman, Don Dowd, Bob Elrod, Ari Feldman, Susan Greenfield, Joe Hanauer, John Hudson, Sandra Hudson, Dave Jennings, Pius Leung, Tom Marquis, Miriam Meyer-Lowe, Roger B. Minkoff, Takashi Misawa, Jean Murphy, Myrl D. Nofziger,

Franc J. Pigna, Bill Powers, Maure Rosol, Therese Salmon, David S. Segrest, Mary L. Sherburne, Scott Sherwood, Jeff Siebold, John M. Stone, Dr. John Tuccillo, Aida D. Turbow, and George Green, among many!

We have had the benefit of many supporters at NAR, via their activities as past Presidents of NAR, including, but not limited to, Dorcas Helfant, Norm Flynn, Nestor Weigand, and Bob Elrod.

We have also had the benefit of other Institutes and councils at the NATIONAL ASSOCIATION OF REALTORS®, relative to their input. Materials that they collected and information on activities in various real estate markets have proven to be invaluable. These include, but are not limited to, COMMERCIAL INVESTMENT REAL ESTATE INSTITUTE (CIREI), (Certified Commercial Investment Member) (CCIM designation, COUNSELORS OF REAL ESTATE (CRE designation), INSTITUTE OF REAL ESTATE MANAGEMENT (IREM) (CPM designation), REALTORS® LAND INSTITUTE (ALC designation), Residential Council (CRS Designation) and others at the NATIONAL ASSOCIATION OF REALTORS®, especially the International Section of NATIONAL ASSOCIATION OF REALTORS® (CIPS Designation), and, specifically, George Green, Miriam M. Lowe, and Heidi Henning.

In addition to the direct support from the NATIONAL ASSOCIATION OF REALTORS®, we have had the benefit of the Herbert U. Nelson Memorial Fund, an organization formed in connection with the NATIONAL ASSOCIATION OF REALTORS® relative to support for research and activities involved in real estate. The Herbert U. Nelson Memorial Fund, through its Board of Trustees, has been kind enough to provide Grants to me to help support some of the financial needs and concerns to produce this INTERNATIONAL REAL ESTATE (Global Real Estate) material. The Trustees of the Foundation have been generous in their financial and personal support for this undertaking. My thanks are also extended to each and every Trustee of the Leonard P. Reaume Memorial Foundation, a/k/a REAUME Foundation, who also contributed to this Work. Those Trustees are: Joe F. Hanauer, Dorcas T. Helfant, Norm Flynn, Bill Lester, Gail Lyons, Phil Smaby, and Nestor Weigand, Jr. SUPPORT FROM OTHERS: We have had wonderful input from numerous publishers and others dealing in the area of written materials, electronic materials and other support materials that benefit pedagogical teaching techniques relative to real estate.

The International Real Estate Federation, FIABCI (Federation Internationale des Professions Immobilieres) has also been extremely helpful with materials and comments from its members. Some of these members overlap with some of the other groups, indicated above. However, certainly we specifically acknowledge members of FIABCI as well as specific individuals, such as Susan Newman, prior Secretary General, Sheldon Good, past President of FIABCI, and Noelle Brisson.

Additional members of FIABCI have also been very helpful, including Bernardo Noriega, past President of FIABCI-Mexico, and Air Feldman.

Without attempting to be exhaustive in this area, we appreciate and acknowledge the materials and/or input from members of: AMERICAN REAL ESTATE SOCIETY (ARES); Bill Endsley of the APPRAISAL INSTITUTE (AI); REAL ESTATE EDUCATORS ASSOCIATION (REEA); and specifically Kristin Wellner of the Real Estate Management Dept. at the UNIVERSITY OF LEIPZIG (Germany); Dr. Karl-Werner Schulte, Professor at the UNIVERSITY OF REGENSBURG (International Real Estate Business School - EUROPEAN BUSINESS JOURNAL) (Germany); and William (Bill) James of JAMES REAL ESTATE SERVICES (Denver, Colorado), also Adjunct Professor at the Burns School of Real Estate and Construction Management, Daniels *College of Business*, at the UNIVERSITY OF DENVER.

We gratefully acknowledge the ability to use various materials that certainly support the activity of this INTERNATIONAL REAL ESTATE (Global Real Estate) text. Such documentation has been extremely helpful in allowing us, in various concise ways, to assemble and assimilate material from various countries.

On the legal side, MARTINDALE-HUBBELL has been extremely generous in allowing us, for part of our legal materials, to utilize some of the Martindale-Hubbell products on international real estate legal aspects. We extend our thanks.

MICROSOFT ®, specifically through Product Manager Alex Simmons, has been good enough to allow us to reproduce certain materials relative to "Customs and Courtesies" through Culture-grams® contained in Microsoft's Encarta.

"Culturegrams" ® are available in the Microsoft ® Encarta ® World Atlas, Copyright 1996 MICROSOFT CORPORATION. All rights reserved. To learn more regarding the Encarta line of products, visit http://www.encarta.com.

In addition to the use of the Microsoft® material, although Microsoft® has acquired the same, we acknowledge and thank BRIGHAM YOUNG UNIVERSITY and KENNEDY CENTER PUBLICATIONS for cooperation on this material relative to cultural matters. We referred to some of this material via Microsoft®, as indicated. On the legal side, the organization of MARTINDALE-HUBBELL has been extremely generous in allowing us, for part of our legal materials, to utilize some of the MARTINDALE-HUBBELL products on international real estate legal aspects. We extend our thanks to this organization, and especially to Stanley Walker, Carl Cooper, and Shawn Clark, Senior Director, Large Law, LexisNexis®

MARTINDALE-HUBBELL. We note that certain items in the Section (text) have been reproduced from Martindale-Hubbell International Law Digest, REED ELSEVIER, INC., with permission from the publisher. All rights are reserved.

We have had the benefit of numerous materials from various organizations relative to current real estate trends and issues. One of the major supporters of this book includes the firm of JONES LANG LaSALLE (JLL). Our thanks are extended to this firm for allowing us to reproduce various materials from their research on current trends in international real estate. Through Mr. A. J. Darwell, Director of Research at JLL, we have received support to utilize various JLL materials. In connection with this, we also thank other members of JLL, such as Nigel Roberts of the London office of JLL. Our thanks are also extended to Helen Arnold at the New York offices of JLL and to our prior student in the Graduate Program, who was a member of JLL, Lisa Feifer.

Other organizations have been very helpful in national and international areas, e.g., CUSHMAN & WAKEFIELD, ERNST & YOUNG, as well as Price Waterhouse Coopers, via Stephen Laposa and Nick Murray.

In helping to publicize the material and give to us input as to other areas that need coverage, we certainly thank and acknowledge the FLORIDA ASSOCIATION OF REALTORS® and specifically Amy Perkins of that organization.

I have had the benefit of input and expertise from various members of the INTERNATIONAL EASTERN EUROPEAN REAL PROPERTY FOUNDATION (IRPF). Our thanks are extended to them. Norm Flynn, Chairman of the IRFP Board of Directors, and Compton Chase-Lansdale, President and CEO for the Foundation, as well as Al Van Huyck, prior Executive Vice President, and Allen Decker, prior Vice President, as well as numerous additional members of the organization have been very helpful in guiding us with materials regarding Eastern Europe.

I acknowledge the help of many members of the INTERNATIONAL REAL ESTATE INSTITUTE (IREI), an organization in Arizona that specializes in activities in international real estate matters.

Many thanks are extended to the myriad number of people who have made contacts as well as assembled and collected this plethora of data that is necessary to attempt to make organized comparisons and analyses of international real estate issues in 33 countries, including C. Scott Thomas.

Most importantly, my thanks are enthusiastically extended to each Author who contributed to this Book. The Authors are the heart and soul of this text. These ladies and gentlemen are noted in the beginning of each Chapter. Each contributed his or her valuable time and energy to this book, only hoping in return that it proves to be a wonderful learning and resource tool.

DEARBORN PUBLISHING COMPANY: We sincerely thank all of the people at DEARBORN PUBLISHING COMPANY who published our prior work, INTERNATIONAL REAL ESTATE, A Comparative Approach (2004). Specifically, we thank Michael Scafuri, Brett Hallongren, Evan Butterfield and Kate DeVivo. We also thank our prior publishers, WHITEHALL PRINTING, especially Kristi LaRiche and Ed Roche, as well as HAMPDEN PRESS, especially Stephanie and Kim. REVIEWERS: We thank all who provided comments and suggestions that greatly improved this work. These reviewers included Dr. Roy T. Black, Associate Professor, Department of Real Estate, GEORGIA STATE UNIVERSITY; Gail G. Lyons, HARLAN, LYONS AND ASSOCIATES, LLC. / BOULDER REAL ESTATE SERVICES, LTD. / REALTY EXECUTIVES; E. Robert Miller, NATIONAL ASSOCIATION OF REALTORS®; David S. Segrest, SEGREST INTERNATIONAL, INC.; Mark Hoven Stohs, CALIFORNIA STATE UNIVERSITY, Fullerton; and Ko Wang, CALIFORNIA STATE UNIVERSITY, Fullerton. We also want to thank Doris Barrell for lending her extremely helpful comments and guidance.

FAMILY: An overriding "thank you" is in order to acknowledge the extraordinary efforts of members of my Family that provided a unique collection of talent for this Work. Libbi (Levine) Segev and Aviv Segev, a team (wife and husband) of attorneys, with special real estate and law training, reviewed and added to the Work in many areas. Ellen, my dear wife, who, among other areas of training, also holds a Masters in Real Estate and Construction Management, added her expertise, including experience in the international arena. And, our daughter, Abbi, brought her formidable training and talent to bear on this Work. With a background in writing, Dr. Abbi (PhD), as we like to call her, made certain that the number of embarrassing grammatical and editing mistakes I made was reduced to a level that one can claim "oversight" when an error pops up now and then. (And, be assured, there are errors in the Work; and, I claim and accept responsibility for the same. Having authored some 52 books, if we include new edit ions, I am positive that each book contains my mistakes.)

Once again, thank you to all!
Dr. Mark Lee Levine
(Jan, 2016)

Dr. Mark Lee Levine is a full Professor and Prior Director of the **Franklin L. Burns School of Real Estate and Construction Management,** *Daniels College of Business,* **UNIVERSITY OF DENVER,** specializing in real estate, international real estate, tax aspects of real estate transactions and real estate liability issues. He is a widely sought consultant in these areas as well. Dr. Levine is a principal in **LEVINE SEGEV LLC,** Attorneys, and Chairman of the Board of Directors of **LEVINE, LTD., REAL-TORS®,** a full-service real estate firm in Colorado.

Dr. Levine is a partner in numerous real estate investments and serves on various publishing and advisory boards. He holds a collection of academic degrees, including a Bachelor of Science in business and economics from Colorado State University; a Doctorate of Jurisprudence from the University of Denver, School of Law (JD); a post- law (JD) degree (LLM) (t ax law) from New York University; he is a graduate from the Professional Accounting Program (PAP) at Northwestern University Graduate School of Management; and Dr. Levine also holds a Ph.D. in Business.

Levine is an active member of various tax, legal and real estate committees. He is a member of the Denver, Colorado, and American Bar Associations as well as several other professional groups. He is admitted to the federal district, circuit, tax, and U.S. Supreme and state courts. A popular lecturer, he is also Author of 22 books (and over 30 revisions of books) in addition to hundreds of articles in many publications.

Dr. Levine holds (or has held) numerous professional designations in real estate, valuation, law, tax and related fields, including CCIM, MAI, CRE, CIPS, Cert. FIABCI, Dipl. FIABCI, FRICS, GAA, GRI, SREA, CA-C, SRS, CRS, CRB, CPM, ALC, CLU, ChFC, DREI, RECS and TRC.

See each country Chapter for contributing authors.

A. Purpose

The general purpose of this book is to provide international real estate comparisons for individuals who might consider international commerce.

Undertaking international real estate business includes both "inbound activities" (investment or activities coming into the United States from outside of the U.S.) as well as "outbound activities" (investments or activities from the United States out to other countries). The model for this book is based on "inbound" activities from other countries to the U.S., and "outbound" from the U.S. to other countries.

B. Structure of the Book

This text is broken down into three parts. Part *One* includes the Introduction, Table of Contents, and Table of Countries. *Part Two* contains country chapters. *Part Three* is the Appendices.

In *Part Two*, country chapters provide the basic information that a business person should consider when evaluating the potential for real estate business in that country. As will be noted by a quick perusal, each chapter is created on the basis of a template with standard sections. This approach allows the user to easily compare and contrast elements across different countries. In addition to this information, some of the chapters contain a small country-specific case study, study questions, and numerous charts and graphs.

Part Two consists of larger case studies that illustrate how the types of information presented in the country chapters can be applied in real-life real estate decisions. These cases present the kind of scenario that a real estate student, professional, or investor could face in the business world, comparing the countries under consideration across a variety of topics.

Finally, the *Appendices* provide further information and comparative charts that the reader may want to use frequently.

Other attributes of this Book include the use of Case Study examples, Study Questions, mini-case studies, as well as the use of charts and graphs to compare various countries throughout this text and in the Appendices.

C. Use of Book

The ideal use of this book would be to consider fundamentally whether to undertake business in a particular country, including considerations when to exit from doing business in that country. This book might be best utilized in a class setting by considering a company that might weigh opportunities of expansion from the initial country, such as the United States, to an outbound country, such as nearby Canada, or to a very distant country such as Australia.

In undertaking this analysis, historical and economic considerations must be examined, including risk and return analyses, and must be augmented by considerations that are more unique to countries outside of the United States. If a businessperson contemplated undertaking business outside of the United States, issues as to currency stability and conversions, cultural aspects, rights and legality to do business in the country in question, political stability and security, and many other issues become paramount, especially the economic stability of a given country. These issues are examined in Case Study sections at the end of most of the country chapters, as well as in the longer Case Studies included in *Part Two*.

For example, a U.S. company may consider expanding into Europe by utilizing the detailed analysis of each European country. Simply comparing the attributes and factors that are noted in each country chapter could include, but not be limited to, literacy of the population, general age of the population, economic stability, etc.

While this book contains a great deal of information necessary to formulate solid international real estate business proposals and decisions, it is in no way meant to be entirely comprehensive. The information presented herein is intended to provide a springboard for a more detailed investigation and analysis into the topics presented. To aid in doing this we have provided a wealth of additional references within each country Chapter and in the Appendices.

Also included in *Appendix C* are charts that can be used to convert different units of measurement between the English and Metric systems. These "Units *of Measurement and Conversion*" charts, in part, are reprinted with permission from the Real Estate Manual, State of Colorado, Colorado Real Estate Commission (2008).

D. Comparative Template

As the user will quickly discover, each country chapter is set up in the same way to facilitate the ability to compare and contrast the countries. Specific elements in the template are important to analyze general global issues. Consider the following:

■ 1. Geography

The country location is important for many reasons. By studying the map of each country, the reader can see its geographic position and possible conflicts with neighboring countries, available transportation, proximity to waters, and other vital issues.

For example, contrast landlocked countries against countries with access to waterways. Geography was, is, and will continue to be an important element in undertaking real estate transactions or other business transactions in any country.

■ 2. History and Overview

The history of each country indicates cultural considerations, conflicting current and past situations between countries, as well as formal or informal affiliations among countries. If a country, such as South Korea, was previously occupied by a country, such as Japan, part of the reasoning behind some covert and/or latent antipathies that may exist between these particular countries is more clearly understood. Prior conflicts may not result in existing animosity, but an overview of each country's history helps to understand relationships between them.

Types of relationships may also have been substantially impacted by prior historical positions. For example, there are many English-speaking countries in Africa and India as a direct result of previous occupancy of those countries, or relationships with those countries, by Great Britain (the United Kingdom).

■ 3. People

The mix of the populace, categorized by male or female demographics, life cycles, birth rates, death rates, etc., can be crucial when undertaking business in each country. For example, knowing that a country that is dominated primarily by a younger population (such as in many African countries) may be very important when undertaking business in that country, especially if the product is marketed to a younger group, or, to contrast, to an older group. Marketing specialty foods, such as pizza, in a country with a predominately *older* population may not have nearly the same market value as it would in a country with a *younger* population.

Ethnic divisions, various religions, and education are also important elements that influence associations and commerce within each country. One should approach positions differently in a mixed population, as opposed to a predominately ethnic or religious majority. Literacy in Africa, for example, is substantially below that in Scandinavian countries. Marketing specific products in a country with a lower literacy rate by relying on the consumer's ability to read can make transactions more difficult.

■ 4. Government

The nature of government, whether it be a republic, democracy, dictatorship, or otherwise, may influence the ability to do business there. Conflicts between or among governments are important considerations. For example, the United States has general prohibitions in undertaking business in Cuba. Issues of human rights, nature of relationships within governments, whether governments have Legislative, Executive and/or Judicial Branches of government, and many other vital concerns must be addressed when interacting between individuals of various countries.

■ 5. Economy

A nation's economy includes its currency fluctuations, the ability of a country or its companies to repay debts, financial stability of the government, financing transactions, unemployment rates, technical ability and training of employees, and the nature of products produced in the country, among other items.

■ 6. Currency

Currency conversions, from one type of currency value to another, vitality of the currency, etc. are briefly examined in this section.

■ 7. Transportation

Companies must depend upon transportation to do business. The ability to utilize navigable inland waterways, shipping ports, airports, and pipelines for natural gas, petroleum, etc., are important issues to move goods and services within and among countries.

■ 8. Communications

The ability to communicate within a country is crucial when undertaking business there. Access to land phone connections, cellular phones, radio, television, Internet, and much more, are linchpins to undertake business in a country.

◼ 9. Real Property Issues

The ability to understand real property issues within a given country, whether by ownership of land, proof of ownership via title insurance, documents evidencing mortgages or other claims on the property, ability and means of transferring real estate, the right to own real estate in each country, and other topics are examined in Section 9 of each country. (See particularly this section in the U.S. chapter as to how each country compares with the United States.) The format to undertake real estate brokerage transactions, appraisals, valuations, sales, and much more, whether through real estate associations or otherwise, is another aspect of the importance of this section. Unfortunately, some countries do not provide much information on real estate issues. Yet, how laws are structured for real estate is an important element when comparing positions of the United States with other countries.

◼ 10. Real Estate Trends

This section focuses on more current issues and includes Internet links with various countries. This section examines real estate leases, apartments, residential structures, single-family homes, condominiums, other retail, industrial and office space, as well as investments, special-use properties including hotels and golf courses, and much more. While this section attempts to focus on general trends, these trends can quickly change. Some countries do not provide much information on real estate trends. Because some countries do not provide detailed information on real estate trends, specifics of current trends can usually be found by using Internet Web site links, noted throughout.

◼ 11. Cultural Issues

Most of us are generally aware of making a bad shot while playing a sport, such as golf, tennis, basketball, etc. However, in the world of international business, real estate or otherwise, we are sometimes not aware of making a blunder—a faux pas. When we lose the real estate transaction, we may not even consider that the transaction was lost as a result of the faux pas that took place. The moral of the story: Learn what is defeating your international transactions, and correct the problems to avoid the faux pas (boo boo).

One cannot stress enough the importance of cultural issues. Utilizing information, in part, from Section 11, as well as from the Burns School Global Real Estate web site at http://burns.daniels.du.edu (or http://burns.dcb.du.edu) in the Cultural Section for each country, and The World Factbook *at the CIA web site* https://www.cia.gov/library/publications/the-world- factbook/index.html, also known herein as the CIA World Factbook, as well as other resources noted herein, may help avoid

cultural faux *pas* when interacting with peoples of various countries. For instance, people in some societies treat certain numbers (e.g., 13) as lucky or unlucky. Wearing the color *black* in the United States can have many meanings (e.g., a clothing color worn at funerals). Contrast wearing *white* clothing as the standard color worn at funerals in many Asian countries. Even the use of flowers (such as giving roses generally denotes *love* in the U.S.) can have different connotations in other countries.

Giving the wrong gifts can result in cultural *faux pas*. For example, giving someone a clock in China can denote death. Concern with impropriety and propriety in giving gifts, how to give gifts, the type of gifts, and value of gifts, are only several issues that can be examined. Different types of dress, greetings, mannerisms, body language, methodology in presenting cards, use of contracts, documents, etc. can be acceptable or not acceptable in business transactions, depending on the country.

◼ 12. Discussion Questions

It is helpful to review questions which could raise additional issues in different situations. Discussion Questions in Section 12 of most countries provide a sampling of concerns that might be raised to help stimulate thinking of whether or not to undertake business between countries.

◼ 13. Case Study

This section allows for raising additional issues in the form of a case approach. These sections, which appear for most countries, follow an Exit Strategy approach that considers when to extricate a business from a country. These chapter Case Studies are examples which are short and concise that focus on several key issues.

More detailed Case Study examples are found in Part Two of the book. These more complex Case Studies compare various attributes using the template approach, and allow for more thorough examinations of several countries.

◼ 14. Selected References

This International Real Estate (Global Real Estate) book directs the reader to other topics and references to consider when undertaking business in other countries. The Selected References section provides for multiple, additional sources beyond those contained in the body of the book. Such resources include Web sites as well as hard copy materials, articles, texts, government sources, and much more.

While this Selected References section could be greatly expanded, as there seems to be a never-ending supply of changing information, we concentrate on some essential international real estate resources.

■ 15. Glossary

Though not actually part of the template, the Glossary allows the user to focus on a few definitions and concepts that were mentioned within the country chapter.

E. Decision-Making Criteria:
(See also *Appendix D.*)

1. LEGAL TO DO BUSINESS: Obviously, if it is illegal to undertake business in a given country, there is no more to discuss. For example, the United States, generally speaking, prohibits its citizens from undertaking business within Cuba. Therefore, there is "nothing to discuss" about the expansion into that country, at least at this time. (Many projections and assumptions indicate that this could change in Cuba in the near future. Such changes have taken place in other Communist countries wherein citizens of the United States were not able to enter into transactions.) Policies change, as illustrated by current trade relations that now exist between China and the United States.

2. ECONOMIC STABILITY/INSTABILITY: A country may be so economically unstable that there is no desire to undertake business there. In some countries, such as Colombia or Argentina, even if it is "legal" for a U.S. citizen to undertake business, many other concerns are quickly apparent.

Citizens of other countries face similar issues when interacting with governments and businesses in countries lacking economic stability. For example, in Argentina business can be legally undertaken, but a businessperson may choose not to undertake such business, due to political and economic instability.

3. CURRENCY ISSUES: Currency issues generally are not "deal killers" that stop business transactions. However, high inflationary considerations and the instability of a country's monetary policies, connected with economic instability, could influence companies to undertake measures to avoid currency problems, or to not undertake business there. Using the Euro, or U.S. dollar, as opposed to the local currency, may solve some of these currency problems.

4. SAFETY RISKS TO INDIVIDUALS: Safety factors may be so important as to actually exclude activities among businesses in certain countries. Lack of safety can be a significant "deal killer," and the risk may be so great that owners and employees of companies may not even consider doing business in certain countries.

5. DIFFICULTIES IN OWNERSHIP: Some countries prohibit non-native (foreign) ownership, or non-native ownership in specific areas, such as along coastlines, in defense areas, etc. The difficulties involved in owning a businesses and undertaking transactions could be so great as to actually eliminate the potential exchange of commerce and business activities. Some governments make citizenship, occupancy, limits on ownership and expansion of businesses so difficult over longer periods of time that doing business there could be unfeasible.

6. ACCESSIBILITY OF GOODS AND SERVICES: The ability to access railroads, waterways, airports, etc., may be too cumbersome so that the result may exclude the potential of operating within that country.

7. RATE OF RETURN: Most companies would choose not to operate outside of the home country, if the rate of return on the investment in another country is not at least equal to, or substantially more, than the businessperson might obtain when operating locally. Additional risks and time considerations complicate doing business among countries. Unless the rate of return is substantially higher in another country, consideration of expansion is often limited. (The rate of return is not necessarily a "deal killer," as long as the rate of return is equal to or greater than that of the home country.) Many companies recognize the need to expand into other countries for additional reasons, such as saturation within a specific market within the domestic, home country. Other reasons, such as diversification, would encourage the business to focus on other countries, outside of the domestic place of business, even when the rate of return is not substantially higher than that of the domestic location. However, normally companies look to a substantial greater rate of return to even consider investing or acting outside the country of origin.

8. RISK-REWARD CONSIDERATIONS: Risk and reward considerations also tie to the rate of return, such as risks that assets of a given company may be confiscated by another government. A company might also suffer appropriation by another country, violence, and damage of business property.

Other factors also must be considered. The issues of SARS (Severe Acute Respiratory Syndrome), and mad cow disease in Great Britain and Canada were not considered in many countries until recently. Consider the tragedies of September 11, 2001 involving the World Trade Center, etc. Other factors may also become extremely important, and they all should be considered when making the decision to expand into markets of other countries.

See the example Case Studies in individual country chapters, as well as *Appendix D*, which illustrate several factors to perhaps consider when weighing whether or not to expand into other countries and markets.

9. WHY EXIT STRATEGIES? The short Case Studies in some country chapters focus on attributes of doing business in a particular country and when to consider getting out of a country. Changes in circumstances of the business, sudden political instability, economic factors, outbreaks of war or other confrontations, repatriation issues, return on investment, and many more factors must be considered when evaluating conditions that might arise, as well as opt ions and plans for a formal exit strategy from a country. One major factor to contemplate entering the country to do business is whether a country does or does not have benefits for compensating individuals if property could be confiscated by the government. If assets could be appropriated or taken by the government, with or without compensation, what rights could a businessperson have as a non-citizen? Changes in governmental politics and economics, formal laws, allowing or disallowing certain investments, restrictions on visas, citizenship, and related issues must be analyzed initially on whether to undertake business, while contemplating the possibility of subsequent events that might necessitate terminating business activities in the country.

To cope with these potential problems, several exit strategies should be developed in a formal plan, allowing for either a reasonable exit time frame to exit or an immediate withdrawal strategy because of the exigencies of current events.

Some alternative exit strategies, if time allows, could include orderly selling, merging, closing, or otherwise dealing with businesses, selling off assets, liquidating portions of the business, leasing out property owned by the entity, providing for partnerships or other joint venture arrangements.

There are no exact answers to many of the exit issues raised in these short sample Case Studies. However, the overall benefit for the user is to focus on necessary planned or unplanned exit issues that may become very important later.

The Impact of Cultural Mistakes on International Real Estate Negotiations

BY MARK LEE LEVINE, PH.D., CRE, FRICS, CIPS

This article has been reprinted from *Real Estate Issues* with the permission of The Counselors of Real Estate of the National Association of REALTORS®, Vol. 31, No. 2, Fall, 2006. © by Dr. Mark Lee Levine, Denver, Colorado, 2007. All Rights Reserved.

WHEN CONDUCTING BUSINESS, INDIVIDUALS often focus on how they think, not how the other party views the situation. This built-in bias is generally very detrimental and highly toxic for international real estate transactions, and can contribute to the possibility of making cultural blunders that have a negative impact on business relations. Those who fail to be cognizant of cultural differences and concerns will frequently destroy what could have been a successful transaction. More important, the injured party—often the real estate consultant, investor or broker—typically is not aware of the blunder that spoiled relations and caused the loss of the transaction.

■ Illustrations of Typical Cultural Blunders

Numerous elements form the foundation of etiquette in various cultures. They are crucial to conducting business successfully in countries with different traditions and communication norms than those in Western culture. Though many blunders can be humorous or simply embarrassing in some situations, others could be highly volatile—and could even destroy a business relationship. Following are some of the more common cultural sensitivities that anyone conducting business on an international level should know.

Family and Gender

Recognize the importance of the family structure and authority within the business structure. Addressing the wrong person in the family—asking the son rather than the father to make a decision, for example—may destroy the transaction. This scenario exists in many South American countries. In other areas such as South Korea and Japan, it may be extremely difficult to undertake business transactions with women, because they are not readily accepted in certain business settings.

Financial Issues

A focus on only net financial benefit s, such as a rate of return analysis, may be extremely short sighted. Though a return on investment is crucial in most business circumstances, other issues such as family relationships or prestige may be of more import at least in the short term. This is especially true in most Asian countries.

Legalities

In the United States it is generally not an insult or unusual for a long legal document to outline real estate acquisitions. However, in many Eastern European and Asian countries, it could be considered an insult to have an extremely detailed document, which could imply that the person presenting it doesn't trust the other. In the United States, Canada and England, for example, the contract is the document that ultimately defines the transaction. But elsewhere, it can be the starting point of the discussion.

Proper Names, Titles and Addresses

Familiarity and the use of first names may be popular in the U.S., but that is not the case in many other countries. In Asia and even many European countries, addressing people by their first name is an insult until or unless the relationship grows to a level where such familiarity is proper. Note, too, that many Asian countries list surnames first and given names last. Make a point to confirm surnames in advance whenever possible. Similarly, failing to address someone by his or her proper title—such as a doctor, professor, prince or chief executive officer—can have a devastating effect.

Touch

Business people in the United States tend to be more inclined to touch a person or move into their personal space. Touching in many countries, especially in the Middle East, is not acceptable, whether through a handshake or otherwise. In many cultures or religions, one example is the Jewish orthodox community, it is improper for men and women to touch members of the opposite sex other than their spouses or close family members.

Introductions and Business Cards

Formal introduction—using surnames, not first names, of the parties being introduced—is usually a sign of proper respect and etiquette. Presentation of business cards often accompanies this practice. It's common in the United States for professionals to casually hand out cards with one hand. But in many Asian countries including Korea, Japan and Indonesia, it's customary to hand the business card to the recipient with two hands and, in many instances, also give a slight bow.

Present the business card so that the recipient can read the name on The card, and make sure it includes a proper title such as chief executive officer, president, doctor, professor or manager.

When on the receiving end, accept the card, acknowledge the card, review the card and perhaps even compliment the card. In some countries, it's poor taste to put the card away during the business meeting; instead the card should remain on the table in front of the recipient, until the meeting concludes. Above all, never place the card in a back pants pocket.

Professionals who practice in different countries should have cards that are printed in multiple languages. When working in Hungary, for example, a card with Hungarian on one side and English on the other can be very helpful.

Don't write on a business card while that individual is present. Doing so would likely be considered disrespectful.

Inappropriate Exposure

Certain parts of the body can be off limits. Touching the head of a young child in most Asian countries is not acceptable behavior. Likewise, women should be careful about exposing their arms, legs or even faces in many Muslim countries. Often, the degree of exposure deemed acceptable depends on the culture, age of the woman and religious doctrine. Showing the bottom of a shoe when crossing the legs also is an affront in many Muslim countries as well as in Thailand. Know whether custom requires removing shoes and socks when entering religious areas and homes. Some countries even have specific traditions for washing hands and feet upon entering the home.

Wearing shorts or other types of casual clothing is not acceptable in many cultures.

The most sensitive situations apply to women in orthodox settings in the Middle East, where proper attire for women does not include shorts or short skirts.

Colors

Colors are import ant in many settings and can convey positive or negative messages. For example, black often symbolizes mourning in many western countries. But in Asia, red or white typically are worn to funerals. So wearing what might be considered light, cheerful hues in the West could have a much different impact in China, for example.

Numbers

Certain numbers are considered lucky or unlucky in various countries and in various settings. Labeling a house or office with an unlucky number may prevent the lease or sale of a property. For example, in the United States it is quite common for many buildings and hotels to avoid a numbered 13th floor; elevator buttons jump from 12 to 14.

The number 4 signifies death in some Asian countries. Therefore avoiding this number in addresses and documentation can improve chances of success.

Gifts

Types of gifts, timing in giving gifts and the setting for gift-giving are all very important in various cultures. Don't make mistakes such as giving alcohol in Muslim countries, where drinking is prohibited, or giving pork products in Muslim or conservative Jewish communities.

On the other hand, gifts could be considered bribes in some countries. The United States Foreign Corrupt Practices Act and similar laws in other countries often make giving money or other expensive gifts illegal. A thorough understanding of laws and practices is necessary before giving gift s, especially when they are valuable or involve money.

Eating and Etiquette

The choice of foods and manner of eating foods is another important consideration. For example, it is quite acceptable in Indonesia to eat with knives and forks or chopsticks, but eating meals with the fingers also is common. In Asian countries, proper etiquette calls for diners to lift the rice bowl toward the face when eating,

whereas Western cultures may consider moving plates rather than utensils uncouth. Placing chopsticks to the side of the bowl is proper; do not leave chopsticks sticking up or out of the food. Eating with one end of the chopsticks and using the other end for picking up food from a central dish is often considered proper in Japan and other countries where chopsticks are the main eating tools. On the other hand, in Singapore and many other countries, taking food from a central plate without turning the chopsticks is quite common and acceptable.

The order and method of the consuming foods also is important. Some cultures forbid mixing certain foods, such as milk and meat in a traditional orthodox Jewish setting. Other cultures limit or prohibit alcohol. In addition, formal or ceremonial meals must not be rushed; they often take several hours.

Gestures

Gestures such as pointing, especially with the index finger, are taboo in many Asian countries, though directing with the full hand usually is acceptable. And a kiss on the cheek in Central and South American countries, France and Mexico often is proper and perhaps even necessary to avoid insult. But in countries such as Korea and Japan, a slight bow would often be proper etiquette. Placing the hands together and bowing slightly would be an acceptable gesture of welcome in countries such as India and Thailand.

Shaking hands is an acceptable practice in many jurisdictions, especially in the United States and other Western cultures. Yet it is unacceptable in many countries where contact between nonrelated men and women is restricted. Using the left hand for any public purpose usually is unacceptable in many Middle Eastern countries. And tipping or removing a hat, meanwhile, may be a respectable action in many countries, but inappropriate in Jewish and Muslim cultures, for example, which require head coverings.

Be sure to know what topics of discussion are inappropriate. In Central and South America as well as Asia, talking about some business topics during meals is rude. Instead, some cultures discuss business only after the meal is finished; others limit such discussion to formal business meetings.

Timing for Business Discussions

The timing of business discussions should consider numerous issues. For example, in most Muslim settings, Friday is not a day for conducting business. Many other cultures do not discuss business on Saturdays or Sundays. Thus, setting the meeting date is crucial.

Timeliness

In many jurisdictions, timeliness is not of great concern; in other settings, it is an insult to be late. In Germany, for example, one normally schedules a meeting for a specific time. Arriving late would be an insult. But in some situations in Central and South America, Thailand, Indonesia and elsewhere, some degree of tardiness is typical. Because of adverse traffic conditions— such as those in Jakarta, Indonesia; Bangkok, Thailand; Cairo, Egypt; Dubai, United Arab Emirates; Mexico City; and many other cities—some delay is almost expected.

Proper Dress at Meetings

General dress codes in many societies dictate proper attire for general business meetings, meals or other situations. Yet in many Asian and Middle Eastern countries where the temperature is quite hot for a majority of the year, omitting a coat and tie is common.

Topics of Discussion

Be cognizant of proper topics to discuss. For example, the recent conflict between Pakistan and India would be a topic to avoid in those two countries. Be aware of sensitive political and social issues; do not bring them up in formal, and even informal, business settings. It would normally be impolite in the United States to ask someone his or her age. But asking someone's age in most Asian countries is usually acceptable and often important to determine the individual's status and degree of respect he or she expects.

The status of the family is an acceptable topic in many societies. However, asking about personal information may not be acceptable until one reaches a greater state of comfort in business dealings. This situation is especially true in a several African nations, where inquiring about a colleague's wife would often be considered forward. In most Asian countries, discussing the family isn't considered small talk, as it is in United States; it is part of getting to know the person, before undertaking business transactions.

Saying No

In many western societies tactfully saying "no thank you" to a business proposition is usually acceptable. In other societies— such as most Asian societies, especially Japan and Korea— saying "no" outright is unacceptable. Instead, other approaches to avoid the absolute "no," such as using body language or postponing the decision, show sensitivity to the society's typical practices.

Accepting or Rejecting an Offer

During a meeting, the process of requesting an immediate answer to determine whether a position is accept able—if the price is acceptable when discussing a property sale, for example —is common in the United States. Yet this practice would be poor etiquette in many Asian countries. It not only could compromise the purchaser's standing among peers, but it also fails to recognize that a group or high- level executive must often make the decision. Attempting to "force" a decision is frequently considered an affront and is unacceptable behavior.

Negotiations

The method of negotiating is substantially different in many countries. For example, people in the United States often attempt to present a win-win situation that shows how all parties benefit from the transact ion. But this practice may be considered a sign of weakness elsewhere. Similarly, giving in on a point and expecting a reciprocal good faith position by the other side is an acceptable practice in many cultures, but don't expect this tactic to work in settings such as Russia, Eastern Europe and many Asian countries.

Calm, non-threatening, friendly negotiations are the common approach in Asia. Patience is necessary because the time needed to structure an undertaking in places such as in Japan and Korea—as well as many South American countries—is relatively long when compared to transact ions undertaken in the U.S. and Western Europe. Another key difference is that directly involving professionals other than the principals in business meetings often is inappropriate. Lawyers, account ants and other specialists often provide support, but shouldn't be mentioned in the early stages of negotiation. They can consult with the parties outside of business meetings, then prepare documents only after the parties have reached a final agreement.

■ Learn from Mistakes to Ensure Future Success

If one is not aware of the cultural nuances and differences, it is entirely possible that the transaction will not bear fruit and will not conclude positively. Even more unfortunate, the parties may lack an understanding about what caused the relationship to deteriorate.

Many U.S. brokers and principals are not aware of cultural elements that can effectively terminate a transaction with a buyer or seller from outside the United States. Failing to acknowledge cultural requirements or unknowingly insulting a potential colleague can spell doom for a business transaction. Losing the transaction is a disappointment; but even more important, the broker, principal or investor may not realize that it was his or her actions that ruined the deal.

Individuals who are unaware or unconcerned about other parties' cultural concerns will likely not complete many international business transactions. Learning what caused the affront, however, and adopting culturally sensitive communication methods could lead the way to future success. When examining the overall issues, the knowledge and personal interaction of those involved in the transaction often are just as import ant as the financial aspects. Both are necessary for a successful transaction to take place. As are respected colleague said:" People don't care how much you know—until they know how much you care." Showing an understanding of the lifestyle, culture and social norms of people across the global market is part of that caring.

COUNTRIES

Afghanistan

INTERNATIONAL REAL ESTATE (GLOBAL REAL ESTATE)
Authored by *Samer Ismail Asfour* and *Joshua Fine*

Dr. Mark Lee Levine, **Editor**

1. Geography

Afghanistan is a landlocked country in Southeast Asia. It is bound by Pakistan to the east and south, Iran to the west, Turkmenistan to the northwest, Uzbekistan and Tajikistan to the north, and a short border with China to the northeast. The Hindu Kush mountain range runs diagonally through the country from southeast to northwest and separates the northern provinces from the rest of the country.

The Hindu Kush and mountainous central highlands occupy the bulk of Afghanistan and are a component of the Himalayan Range. The forbidding terrain reaches heights of over 7,400 meters (24,000 feet). North of the mountains lay the fertile northern plains with elevations of up to 600 meters (2,000 feet). The southwestern plateau, on the other side of the Hindu Kush, accounts for 25% of the land area and is an arid region vegetated mostly by scrub with an average elevation of about 900 meters (3,000 feet). Just over 12% of the country is arable land.

Afghanistan has a continental dry climate with large differences between day and night temperatures as well as quick seasonal transitions. Summer temperatures in the plains can reach 46 degrees Celsius (46°C) (115 degrees Fahrenheit) (115°F), while in the higher plateaus winter temperatures can fall to -26°C (-15°F). The *Winds of 120 Days* which occur between June and September can have velocities of up to 180 kph (108 mph), and the rainy season is from October to April, although rainfall is very irregular. Average temperature ranges in Kabul are from -8°C to 2°C (18°F to 36°F) in January to 16°C to 33°C (61°F to 91°F) in July.

Afghanistan has deposits of natural gas, crude oil, and other minerals. The country suffers from a lack of fresh water, soil degradation, overgrazing, deforestation and desertification.

2. History and Overview

The country of Afghanistan was formed from the unification of various Pashtun tribes in the 18th century. A constitutional monarchy was established in 1964, but was overthrown by a 1973 coup. On April 27, 1978, pro-Soviet leftists took power in a bloody coup known as the *Great Saur Revolution*. The Soviet Union invaded in 1979 to support the nascent communist regime. Soviet troops remained in the country for ten years, fighting a long and protracted guerilla war with Muslim *Holy Warriors* or *Mujaheddin*. The Soviets finally withdrew from the country in 1989. With the power vacuum created by the Soviet withdrawal, Afghanistan descended into a bloody civil war. The Taliban, a hardline Islamic force supported and trained by Pakistan, came to power in 1996 and imposed harsh Islamic rule throughout the country. Following the terrorist attacks

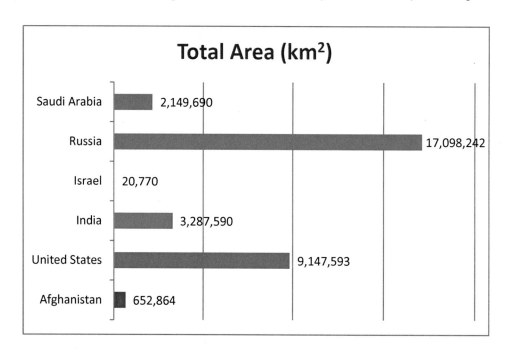

Total Area (km²)

Country	Total Area (km²)
Saudi Arabia	2,149,690
Russia	17,098,242
Israel	20,770
India	3,287,590
United States	9,147,593
Afghanistan	652,864

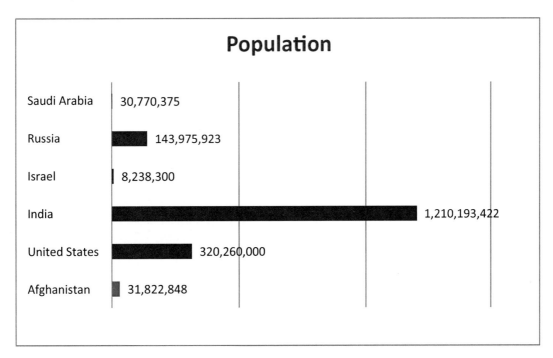

of September 11, 2001, the United States led an invasion of Afghanistan because the country was believed to have harbored terrorist groups.

A United Nations-sponsored conference in Bonn, Germany, in 2001 led to the adoption of a Constitution and establishment of a democratic government. Afghanistan held elections on December 7, 2004, and Hamid Karzai was elected the first President of the country.[4]

■ 3. People

Out of Afghanistan's total population of **31,822,848,** about 42% are age 14 or younger. Approximately 55.5% of the population is between 15 to 64 years of age. Only 2.5% of the population is 65 years of age or older The population is also growing rapidly. The population growth rate is 2.29% (2014 est.) The birth rate

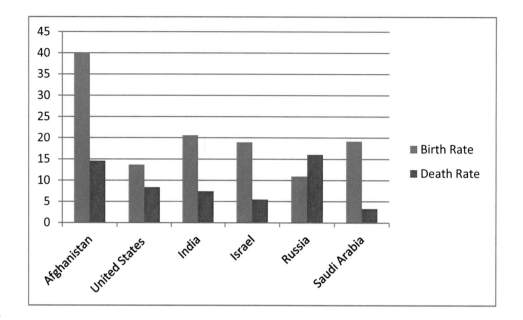

at 38.84 per 1,000 population is more than double the death rate at 14.12 per 1,000. Infant mortality is the very high at 117.23 deaths per 1,000 live births, but has been slowly improving over the past five years. The life expectancy in Afghanistan is only approximately 50.49 years.

The official religion is Islam. Approximately 80% of the population is Sunni Muslim, and 19% are Shi'a. The official languages are Dari (Afghan Persian), spoken by half of the population, and Pashto, spoken by 35% of the people. Turkic languages are spoken by just over 11% of the population, and 30 distinct minor languages are spoken by members of Afghanistan's diverse ethnic groups. Much of the population speaks at least two languages. Only about 31.7% of the population of age 15 and over can read and write, and the literacy rate has been slowly improving over the past five years.

4. Government

Afghanistan is an Islamic Republic with its capital in Kabul. The country is divided into 34 provinces. Afghanistan celebrates its Independence Day on August 19, marking the date in 1919 when the country attained independence over foreign affairs from the United Kingdom. Following the U.S.-led invasion and fall of the Taliban, Afghanistan adopted a new Constitution on January 16, 2004. The new constitution retains the country's Islamic roots, which states that no law should be "contrary to Islam."

The Executive Branch is led by the President, currently Hamid Karzai. There are two vice presidents and a cabinet of 25 ministers appointed by the President. The Legislative Branch consists of a bicameral Legislature of the *Wolesi Jirga* (House of People) and the *Meshrano Jirga* (House of Elders). In extraordinary circumstances (such as for issues of independence or national sovereignty) the government may convene a *Loya Jirga* (Grand Council).

The Judicial Branch is led by the *Stera Mahkama* or Supreme Court and subordinate High Courts and Appeals Courts. Afghanistan and the United States maintain diplomatic relations, and each country maintains an embassy in the other's capital.

5. Economy

Although the Afghan economy has improved considerably and the real Growth Domestic Product (GDP) growth rate exceeded 14% in 2012, Afghanistan remains a poor country, highly dependent on foreign aid, farming and raising livestock (sheep and goats). Economic considerations have played second fiddle to year Soviet military occupation (which ended February 15, 1989). During that conflict, one-third of the population fled the country to neighboring Pakistan and Iran, who sheltered a combined number of six million refugees at the war's peak. In early 2000, 2 million Afghan refugees remained in Pakistan and about 1.4 million in Iran. GDP has fallen substantially over the past 20 years because of the loss of labor and capital, as well as disruption of trade and transport; and severe drought added to the nation's difficulties especially from 1998-2000.

The majority of the population continues to suffer from insufficient food, clothing, housing, and medical care. Inflation, at 7.6% (2013 est.), remains a serious problem throughout the country. Trafficking in narcotics is a major policy concern for the government. International aid, while substantial, can deal with only a fraction of the humanitarian problem, let alone promote economic development.

6. Currency

The Afghan currency is the *Afghani (AFA)*. For current conversion rates, see the Global Real Estate Web site at the Burns

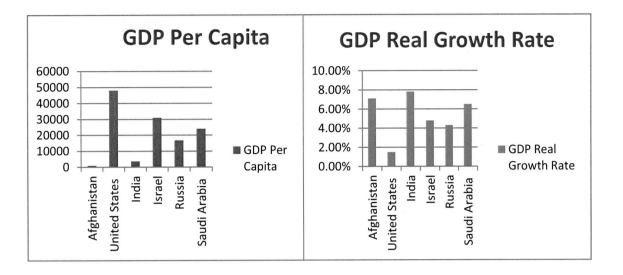

School, *Daniels College of Business,* UNIVERSITY OF DENVER at http://burns.daniels.du.edu.

■ 7. Transportation

Although Afghanistan has about 42,150 kilometers (km) of roadways, generally the highway system requires almost total reconstruction, and regional roads are in a state of disrepair. The poor state of the Afghan transportation and communication networks has further fragmented and hobbled the struggling economy. Of Afghanistan's 52 airports (2013 est.), only 23 have paved airport runways. Afghanistan has about 1,200 km of waterways.

■ 8. Communications

There approximately 13,500 (2012 est.) main line telephones in Afghanistan for a **population** of over **30 million,** with limited main line telephone service. However, there are 18,000,000 (2012 est.) cellular phones in use. Afghanistan has one state-owned radio system with 150 private radio stations, 50 TV stations, and 12 international broadcasters (2010). There are 223 Internet service providers (hosts), and approximately 1,000,000 (2009 est.) Internet users in Afghanistan.

■ 9. Real Property Issues

Property right protection is weak in Afghanistan due to the turmoil following decades of war, the displacement of millions of refugees, and a lack of clear property registries. Organizations like the United States Agency for International Development (USAID) are seeking to stabilize the situation by helping to establish mapping and registry records. USAID has recently completed aerial mapping of two districts in Kabul and helped reorganize land records in 16 land registry offices throughout the country, representing 3.8 million land records, or 85 percent of all property records in Afghanistan.[8]

The nascent Afghan government has also sought to stabilize property rights by enacting laws protecting property ownership and foreign investment. Foreigners are not permitted to own land, but the Private Investment Law grants registered foreign organizations the right to lease real property for terms of up to fifty years. Despite these developments, the United States Department of State warns that investing in real estate interests in Afghanistan is difficult and even hazardous. According to the State Department, returning Afghan nationals seeking to recover property or foreigners seeking to invest have become embroiled in complicated real estate disputes and have faced threats of retaliatory action, including kidnapping for ransom and death.[10] In part because of these difficulties, the United States Army has deployed a specialized real estate unit, known as the Contingency Real Estate Support Team (CREST), to assist the military in securing and negotiating real property leases for its operations. Private investors should proceed with great caution. Real estate transactions that are successfully negotiated are generally cash only. Access to banking facilities is extremely limited. Credit card transactions and international bank transfers are unavailable or very limited. There is only one ATM machine in Kabul, but the U.S. State Department reports that travelers have complained of difficulties using it.[11]

■ 10. Real Estate Trends

According to the U.S. State Department, land disputes are quite frequent in Afghanistan, due to lack of clear title enforcement, allowing multiple ownership of property. In general, real estate contracts are unenforceable, which means that foreign investors should exercise great due diligence when attempting to purchase property in Afghanistan. See the Global Real Estate Web site at the Burns School, Daniels *College of Business, University* of Denver at http://burns.daniels.du.edu.

■ 11. Cultural Issues

Any nation's culture is complex and vibrant in its diversity.

While broad cultural characterizations such as those presented here can be generally accurate, following such generalities too strictly may be dangerously misleading. To conduct business effectively and profitably in a country, it is vital to have a thorough understanding of its culture's complexities.

Dress in Afghanistan is traditional and conservative. Women are rarely seen in public, but if they are, they wear a head-to-toe covering over their clothing. For more information, see the Global Real Estate Web site at the Burns School, Daniels *College of Business*, UNIVERSITY OF DENVER at http://burns.daniels.du.edu.

12. Discussion Questions

1. Does the adoption of a constitution and the democratic election of a president increase the likelihood that Afghanistan will attract investment capital?

2. How long will it take – in your opinion – for Afghanistan to become an attractive country relative to investments?

3. What is the influence on Afghanistan from its mix of neighbors?

13. Case Study

Afghanistan Rugs Exporting Kabul, Afghanistan

Memo

To: Board of Directors
From: Consultants
Re: Exporting of Rugs in Afghanistan

I. Problem

With the elimination of the Taliban in Afghanistan, Afghanistan Rug Exporting (ARE) was to begin exporting rugs from Afghanistan to the United States. Because the Taliban had been removed from power, the assumption was that many Afghan refugees would begin to return to Afghanistan and work as weavers to create the magnificent rugs. The thought was with the return of these refugees, the factories would also move back to Afghanistan. Then ARE would provide the exporting services.

So far there have been plenty of rugs to export, but in the last month ARE has seen factories going out of business, because the work force is not adequate. With the rebuilding and reconstruction of Afghanistan, the parents of the young boys who are the weavers of the rugs want them back doing other things. The carpet industry in Afghanistan needed a company, such as ARE, to get the carpets on the market without the need to have buyers come to the country. Prior to ARE arriving with its business in Afghanistan an, the carpet industry was under Pakistani control. The problem, now, is the lack of a workforce for the looms in Afghanistan. With the limited workforce, not as many rugs will be made. That will lower ARE's profits. The question is: Will the workforce continue to dwindle; or will there be a resurgence of Interest as more people come back to Afghanistan?

II. Initial Exit Strategy

The initial exit strategy was simple. Because of the war threats that could instantly arise in this country; ARE was working from a shoestring budget, with limited assets. The office space for ARE is currently a hotel room. ARE is using fax, email and phones to take orders. The reason for the office in the hotel was to be able to leave the country "on a moment's notice." Because of the possibility of violence, war and other hazards, ARE did not enter into Afghanistan without an immediate exit plan. Although ARE was able to function relatively simply, the exit plan did not contain a time frame for exiting the country. ARE's directors never considered an exit plan in the regular course of business. With the market and the lack of a labor force, ARE must put in place some guidelines to exit the business.

III. Contingency Exit Plan

As the rugs become less readily available for export, ARE must re-evaluate the opportunity to export them. The first step would be to look at the market outside of Afghanistan. With the war and international attention on the events in Afghanistan, the demand increased for high quality hand woven rugs. As the rugs become harder to come by, it might be justifiable to raise the price of rugs that are exported. ARE has already established a successful network of carpet industry people. Once ARE has undertaken a market study to determine if it can raise the prices of the rugs, this will determine how quickly ARE should exit. The hope would be that the spotlight on Afghanistan, and some advertising that the rugs will not be as easy to obtain, might be just enough to support

the continued operation. If ARE is able to create a human- interest story, such as what has been seen about *tanzanite*, the stone, "that there is no longer any more of coming out of the mines," then we might be able to increase demand. If ARE cannot increase the prices and continue to make a profit, the Company will have to "check out" of the hotel.

IV. Conclusion

An immediate market study needs to be prepared to see if there is the demand to support a raise in the cost for carpets. Because of the difficulty of undertaking a market study on the specific services,

the study will need to be based, in part, on the demand of Afghanistan rugs in other countries. Once this has been completed, the ARE Board of Directors will be able to make the decision on whether ARE should stay, exit hastily, or slowly exit the Afghanistan business.

Refer to: Newnations.com. Homepage. http://www.newnations. com/headlines/af.html. International Real Estate Digest. Homepage: www. ired.com. X- rates.com. Homepage. http://www.x-rates.com/.

U.S. Embassy. Homepage. http:// usembassy.state.gov.

14. Selected References

American Business Bureau, American Embassy. Amman (August 2000) U.S. Bureau of Census at http://www.census.gov.

U.S. Department of Commerce at http://www.statusa. gov. U.S. Bureau of Economic Analysis at http:// www.bea.gov.

U.S. Department of State Homepage. http://www. state.gov. U.S. Embassy.

Homepage. http://usembassy.state.gov. World Trade Centers Institute at http://www.wtci.org.

World Trade Organization at http://www.wto.org. World Bank. *Adult Illiteracy Rates*. The Economist. Personal information; field research

15. Glossary

Afghan Transit Trade Agreement – Allows Afghanistan to have access to the sea and to undertake trade and commerce with the international community to the extent required by Afghanistan's economy.

Dari – One of two official languages considered (Afghan Persian).

Durand Line – Drawn in 1893 by Sir Mortimer Durand to create a border between Pakistan and Afghanistan.

ECO: Economic Cooperation Organization promotes regional cooperation in trade, transportation, communications, tourism, cultural affairs, and economic development.

Frontier Constabulary – A Para-military force of the Interior Ministry of Pakistan. This is the force that trained the Taliban.

Harakat-I-Islami – Islamic Movement, one of the political parties; this is of The United Front.

IDB: Islamic Development Bank fosters the economic development and social progress of member countries and Muslim communities individually as well as jointly in accordance with the principles of Islamic Law.

Loya Jirga – means "grand council". The institution, which is centuries old, is a similar idea to the Islamic "shura", or consultative assembly.

Loya Jirga – A traditional Grand Assembly. This group will meet to decide on a transitional authority, including a broad-based transitional administration. The permanent and elected government is expected to be

in place no more than two years from the emergency Loya Jirga.

OIC: Organization of the Islamic Conference promotes Islamic solidarity in economic, social, cultural, and political affairs.

United National and Islamic Front for the Salvation of Afghanistan (UNIFSA) – composed of various political parties brought together in their common struggle against Taliban rule.

WFTU: World Federation of Trade Unions promotes the trade union movement.

"Winds of 120 Days" – Occurs between June to September and can have speeds up to 108 mph.

About the Authors

Samer I. Asfour, Chief Operating Officer of Design Jordan in Amman, Jordan. Mr. Asfour was The General Manager of the Amman World Trade Center in Amman, Jordan.

Joshua Fine, graduated from Harvard Law and the Burns School of Real Estate and Construction Management, *Daniels College of Business,* UNIVERSITY OF DENVER.

Argentina

INTERNATIONAL REAL ESTATE (GLOBAL REAL ESTATE)
Authored by *Jose Ramirez* and *Gary L. Harder*

Dr. Mark Lee Levine, Editor

1. Geography

Argentina is at the southern part of South America. It borders Bolivia to the north; Paraguay to the northeast; Brazil, Uruguay, and the Atlantic Ocean to the east; Chile to the west.[14]

Argentina has an area of **2,780,400** sq km (square kilometers) and is slightly less than three-tenths the size of the United States. The coast on the Atlantic Ocean is 4,989 km long from the mouth of the Río de la Plata River down to Tierra del Fuego.

Border disputes exist with United Kingdom on the Falkland Islands, Islas Malvinas (1982). Other territory claims exist with United Kingdom on South Georgia and theSouth Sandwich Islands. Argentina also has territorial claim in Antarctica.

A temperate climate predominates in Argentina, with an arid climate in the southeast and a sub Antarctic in the southwest. Terrain includes the Pampas plains in the northern half, the mountainous Patagonia area to the south, and the Andes Mountains along the western border. The average temperature in Buenos Aires during summer (December to February) is roughly 24°C (75°F) and during the winter (June to August) is roughly 11°C (52°F).

Argentina has natural resources in the form of fertile plains in the pampas, lead, zinc, tin, copper, iron ore, manganese, petroleum, uranium and gold.

Land use includes 13.68% for arable land and permanent crops of only 0.36%, with the balance in other uses, including meadows and pastures.

Environmental problems include urban pollution, as well as deforestation, soil degradation, and water pollution. There has been erosion from inadequate flood controls and degradation from irrigated soil problems. Air pollution and water pollution exist in major cities, such as Buenos Aires. Water pollution and other pollution in the rivers persist as a result of inadequate controls, use of pesticides and fertilizer runoff. Argentina is a signatory party to a number of international environmental agreements. Conservation efforts attempt to control nuclear testing, ozone levels, desertification, biodiversity, endangered species and marine life, and pollution relative to wetlands and other related areas. Argentina is prone to natural hazards such as earthquakes and violent storms.

2. History and Overview

Argentines are a fusion of diverse national and ethnic groups. Descendants of Italian and Spanish immigrants predominate. Immigrants from Europe arrived in the late eighteenth and

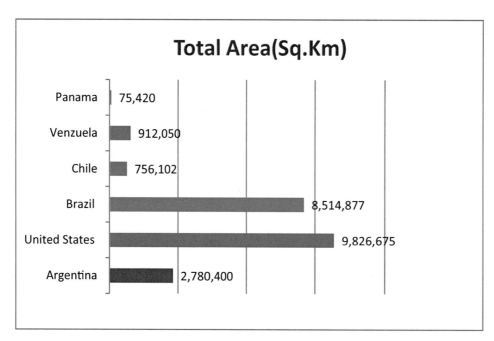

early nineteenth centuries. In the recent past there was an influx of immigrants from other countries in Latin America. Argentina has the largest Jewish population in Latin America. Buenos Aires declared independence from Spain on July 9, 1816. National unity was established and the constitution was promulgated in 1853. Conservative forces dominated Argentine politics until 1916, when Hipolito Yrigoyen, a member of the liberal force, was elected for office through democratic election. He remained in office until 1930. He was ousted from office by a coup d'etat that marked the beginning of a turbulent time in this country, during the Infamous Decade and Revolution of '43. After World War II, Juan Domingo Perón won the presidential elections of 1946 and 1951. Parodist dictatorship was followed by a military junta, which took power in 1976. Democracy returned on October 30, 1983, when Rail Alfonse received 52% of the popular vote for president. In 1989, Carlos Saul Menem won presidential elections. Menen was re-elected in 1995. In December 1999, Fernando De La Rua took office. De La Rua resigned on December 20, 2001 following violent riots that stemmed from his administration's inability to curb falling production and rising unemployment. A legislative assembly then elected Adolfo Rodriguez Saa on December 23, 2001. Saa's inability to rally support from his own party and continued violence led to his resignation on December 30, 2001. Yet another legislative assembly elected Peronist Eduardo Duhalde president on January 1, 2002. Duhalde-differentiating himself from his three predecessors-quickly abandoned the peso's 10-year-old link with the U.S. dollar, a move that was followed by currency devaluation, inflation, poverty and social unrest. In the face of rising poverty and continued social unrest, Duhalde also moved to bolster the government's social programs. Argentina celebrated early elections, after the Duhalde resignation in April 2003. Thus, on May 25, 2003, Néstor Carlos Kirchner became president. He was replaced in office by his wife, Cristina Fernández de Kirchner, who became Argentina's first female president elected, on December 10, 2007. She was elected with 45% of the votes. In 2011, Cristina Fernández de Kirchner was re-elected, for a second term, with 54% of the votes.

■ 3. People

Argentina's population is **43,131,966** (2015, est.) with 25.1% under 14 years old, 64.1% in the 15-year-old through 64-year-old category, and 10.8% in the 65 years age and older group (2015 est.)

As with many other countries in South America, Argentina boasts much of its population in its urban areas such as Buenos Aires, Córdoba, Rosario, Mar del Plata, and Mendoza. Most of the population, close to 90%, lives in urban areas, with close to one-third (1/3) of the population living in the greater or metro Buenos Aires.

Life expectancy for the male population is 73.72 years. The female life expectancy is 80.33 years (2015, est.) Population growth rate change for 2015 is estimated to be -0.94% (2015, est.), with a modest declining pattern from its 1995 rate of 1.3%. Argentina has a birth and death rate per 1,000 of population of 17.52 and 7.14 respectively (2015, est.) Both birth and death rates have shown little change since 1995. Overall, these statistics indicate that Argentina has a stable population growth. There are approximately 0.29 migrants per 1,000 populations (2015, est.) As opposed to the overall death rate, as noted above, the infant mortality rate is 9.87 deaths for every 1,000 live births (2015, est.)

Ethnic divisions in Argentina include white (mostly Spanish and Italian) at 97%, and 3% Mestizo, Amerindian, or other. The dominant religion in Argentina is Roman Catholic, which is approximately 92% of the population, although less than 20% of those designated as such are practicing Roman Catholics. The remaining religions consist of 2% Protestant, 2% Jewish, and 4% other. The dominant language is Spanish, as the official language, but French, English, German, and Italian are also spoken.

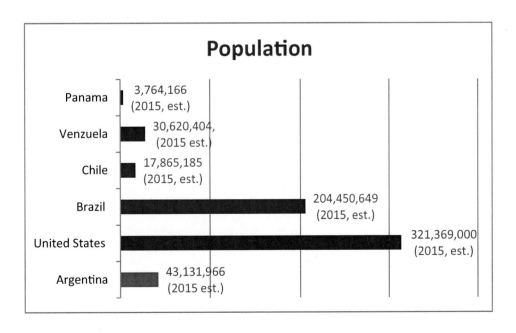

Population

Panama	3,764,166 (2015, est.)
Venezuela	30,620,404, (2015 est.)
Chile	17,865,185 (2015, est.)
Brazil	204,450,649 (2015, est.)
United States	321,369,000 (2015, est.)
Argentina	43,131,966 (2015 est.)

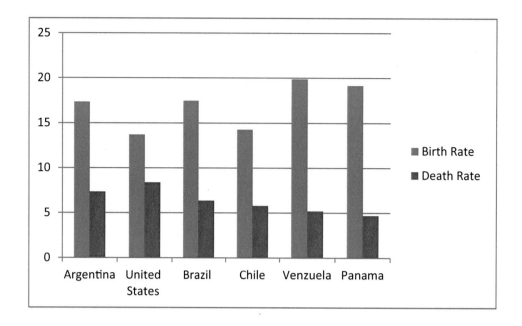

Literacy is 97.7% (2011, est.), which is one of the highest in South America. There is no statistical difference regarding literacy as between men and women.

4. Government

The government of Argentina is a republic with its capital in Buenos Aires. There are 23 provinces of administrative-type divisions known as *Provincias,* and one Federal District, *Distrito Federal.* The United States does not recognize Argentine claims to Antarctica.

Independence Day for Argentina is July 9, 1816, when Argentina gained its independence from Spain. The national holiday of Argentina is the revolution date of May 25, which occurred in 1810.

The Argentine Constitution was first passed in 1853 and revised in 1994.It has provisions similar to those in the Constitution of the United States of America. The legal structure in Argentina is a mixture of US and West European legal systems. It is constructed on civil law that relies on compiled codes such as Commerce and Civil Codes. Judiciary decision processes are based on code rather than on past precedents in prior judicial decisions. Because of Argentina's Spanish, Italian and other ancestral ties, laws are derived from other sources that include: Roman law, French Napoleonic Code, and Spanish and Portuguese laws. Because of the strong Italian ancestral influence, Italian law is an important Commercial Code source. Each province passes its own constitution in compliance with the federal government system.

Judicial Power is exercised by the Supreme Court of Justice, or *Corte Suprema,* and by other lower courts. The Corte Suprema has creditability problems and is considered weak because of its organizational problems and the influence from the executive branch. Voting in Argentina is universal and commences at 18 years of age.

The Legislative Power, or *Poder Legislativo,* is vested in the Congress, which consists of two powers: the Senate and the Chamber of Deputies. Senators are elected for a period of 6 years, and deputies are elected for a period of 4 years. Both senators and deputies can be reelected indefinitely. The Chief of State, the *Presidencia De La Nación,* is the President. The Vice President is the next executive. The head of the government is also the same as the Chief of State, i.e., the President. There is a bicameral National Congress, known as the *Congreso Nacional,* consisting of a Senate, the *Senado de la Nación,* as well as a second branch or chamber known as the Chamber of Deputies. There are 257 members in the Chamber of Deputies. Elections are held for half of the Deputies every two years. There are 72 members in the Senate, representing the 23 provincial provinces. Elections are held for one-third of the Senators every two years. The *Congreso Naciónal* is considered to have low prestige due to years of cronyism and corrupt politics. This unfavorable status was further heightened when in mid-2000 a bribery scandal was exposed that included a number of Senators. Argentina's President Fernando de la Ruá, of the *Alianza por el trabajo, la Justicia y la Educación* (Alianza Part y), took office in December, 1999, but was forced to resign in December 2001. Appointed interim president was Rodíquez Adolfo Saá (Peronist Party). The fifth president, Eduardo Duhalde (Peronist Party), served in the two weeks following the resignation of Fernando de la Ruá. He remained in the office, until Nestor Kirchner took office in May, 2003.

There are a number of political parties in Argentina. In addition to the Front For Victory party, party of the current President, Cristina Fernández de Kirchner, there are other the parties, such as: *Frente Grande* (Broad Progressive Front), *Partido Solidario* (Solidarity Party), Partido *Demócrata Cristiano* (Democratic Christian Party), *Partido Demócrata Progresista* (Democratic Progressist Party), *Partído por la Dignidad y la Independencia* (For Dignity and Independence Party), *Partído Intransigente* (Intransigent Party), *Partído Justicialista (o*

Peronista) (Peronist Party), *Partido Obrero* (Workers' Party), *Unión del Centro Democrático* (Democratic Center Union), Partido Socialista (Socialist Party), and a few smaller provincial parties. There are other political groups that impact the governmental operations. These organizations include business organizations, students, the Roman Catholic Church, and the military. Labor unions have strong political and cultural influence in Argentina. They have rallied its labor membership in support of a number of national strikes in 2000 and 2001. The major union groups are the General Confederation of Labor (CGT), Central Argentine Workers (CTA), Argentine Industrial Union, and Argentine Rural Society.

Diplomatic representation exists with the United States with Argentina's office in

Washington, D.C. The United States diplomatic representation exists with an embassy in Buenos Aires.

Argentina has defense branches, including an Army, Navy, Air Force, and National Gendamerie (National Guard).

■ 5. Economy

The Argentine economy is dominated by agricultural, mining, petroleum, manufacturing, and service sectors. The fertile plains of the pampas have created an export-oriented Agricultural sector in this country.

The Gross Domestic Product (GDP) per capita was approximately $14,715.2 (2013, est.) - it had decreased to approximately $7,500 in 2000 during Argentina's economic crisis. Argentina GDP growth rate is 2.9% (2013, est.) The (unofficial) inflation rate in 2013 was around 20%, yet the officially reported was around 10%. When Carlos Menem took office in 1989, inflation was problematic with 1989's and 1990's inflation rate at 4,900% and 1,300%, respectively. The inflation rate was 22% in 2010. Menem's economic shock reforms to curb inflation and economic problems were twofold: First, the selling of state-owned enterprises, and second, to stop the runaway inflation, the adoption of currency convertibility (April 1, 1991) by pegging

the peso to the U.S. dollar at a 1 to 1 ratio. By the time that Fernando De La Rua took office in 1999, inflation in Argentina was close to negative 3%. Gains made in the 1990s faltered in the latter part of 2001 and early 2002 with inflation sharply increasing to 38.5% by the third quarter of 2002 (http://www.latinfocus.com/countries/argentina/argcpi.htm). Argentina's GDP per capita (measured in US dollars) enjoyed a strong increase in the 10 years following convertibility, an impressive growth outcome when compared to Brazil's for the same period.

Beginning in September 1998, Argentina faced its first major recession in a decade. This recession increased unemployment to 15% by August 1999, and increased further to approximately 21.5% by December 2001. Reports in Buenos Aires newspapers (May 2002) reported unofficial unemployment rate to have reached 25%. A long-standing goal by Argentina's policy makers has been to employ economic structural reforms to allow for sustainable growth, keep in check inflationary pressures, and to encourage foreign investment. The government wanted to encourage exports and realize sustainable growth. These policy reforms were thwarted by economic policy failures, resignation of President Fernando de la Ruá, and the introduction of banking laws that prohibited savings withdraw, *el corralito*, resulting in social unrest in the streets.

The total labor force in Argentina is about 19,092,526. Unemployment has been a historical problem for Argentina and had posed additional problems because of depressed economic conditions. The effects from default on international loans, liquidity problems, account imbalances, decline of exports, and business failure resulted in the return of unemployment problems since the fourth quarter of 2001. An unemployment rate of **7.5%** was reported for 2013, an improvement from the 17.5% in 1995, but in 2002 unemployment was reported at almost 21.5%. The dominant occupation is (72%) in services . Industry follows with approximately 23%, and the balance flows to the agricultural sector (2009, est.)[19]

Argentina's economic bearing was extremely shaky the end of 2001, with Argentina falling into an economic depression in the first quarter of 2002.In 1991, an economic reform policy was implemented that pegged the peso to the US dollar on

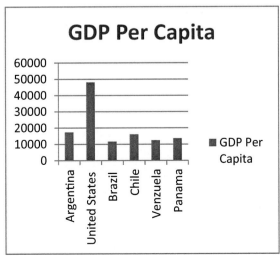

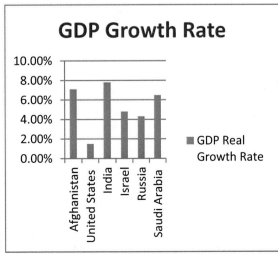

a 1 to 1 exchange rate. The monetary base policy shifted to a growth policy with monetary reserves set by law. Inflation fell, following the new policy, but it was disrupted by the Mexican crisis in 1995. The Mexican peso crisis resulted in Argentina attempting to hold off capital flight, losses in banking deposits, and a recession. Real GDP in 1997 achieved 8%; this was attributed to banking system reforms shortly after the 1995 recession onset. In 1998, concerns over Russia, Southeast Asia, and Brazil altered investor confidence that resulted in driving Argentina's interest rates up to a three-year high. These opposing economic forces reduced the growth rate by half. By 1999, an improvement was not in sight as the GDP declined by 3%. After taking office in December 1999, President Fernando de la Ruá implemented tax increases and a deficit reduction plan. The new government arranged for a contingency standby facility with the International Monetary Fund (IMF) in the amount of over $7 billion. By December 2000 economic conditions moved the government to accept the IMF's $14 billion structural program so it could meet its debt obligations. Early in 2002, Argentina defaulted on its loan obligations and the peso was permitted to float for the first time since 1991. A scheduled payment to the IMF of under $11.0 million is due by December 2003, and with inadequate reserves for this payment, credibility with the IMF, World Bank, and institutional investors was traumatized. However, the economy recovered dramatically under the presidencies of Eduardo Duhalde and Nestor Kirchner. The government restricted its defaulted debt in 2005 and paid off its IMF (International Monetary Fund) obligations in full in 2006.

As stated earlier, the unemployment rate is approximately 7.5% (2013, est.). However, unemployment reached 25% in 2001, which was an increase from its nearly 13% rate in 1998. The combination of high unemployment, negative productivity, and sagging consumer participation in the marketplace resulted in approximately 23.4% Argentines to be considered at the poverty level (2007). 2/

Industries in Argentina include food processing, motor vehicle, consumer durables, textiles, chemical and petro chemical, printing, metallurgy and steel. Argentina exported, in 2013, a total of $76.634 billion. Argentina imported, in 2013, $73.655 billion, mostly in motor cars and other vehicles, petroleum oils obtained from bituminous minerals, natural gas, parts of electrical apparatus for line telephony and line telegraphy. With the recent change of the peso's ability to float and the resulting value of the peso, Argentina's ability to compete in the export market has suffered and has caused an increase in the cost of imports, resulting in inadequate supplies of some key products along with inflationary pressures.

Argentina's major trading partners were Brazil, China, Chile, United States and European Union (EU). Argentina is attempting to increase its exports to the United States, Brazil, Netherlands and other countries. Argentina exports agricultural goods, especially maize, soy beans, wheat, and meat products. Concomitant with exports are the imports for Argentina, with its major trading countries, as indicated earlier.

6. Currency

The currency is the *peso*, consisting of 100 centavos in one (1) peso. See the Burns School Global Real Estate Web site for the UNIVERSITY OF DENVER at http://burns.daniels.du.edu for currency conversions.

7. Transportation

Argentina has 36,966 kilometers (km) of railroad lines and 231,374 km of roadways, with about 30% of the roadways being paved. There are about 11,000 km of navigable inland waterways in Argentina. Pipelines to transport gas, oil and refined products are 29,930km, 6,248 km,and 3,631km, respectively (2013, est.).

Argentina has numerous ports for shipping, such as Bahia Blanca, Buenos Aires, Comodoro Rivadavia, Concepción del Uruguay, La Plata, Mar del Plata, Necochea, Rio Gallegos, Rosario, Santa Fe, Ushuaia Amuay, Bajo Grande, Puerto Cabello and Puerto La Cruz.

Over 1,138 airports are utilized in Argentina, and 161 airports have paved runways. Many airports are able to handle major jets. Of those airports with paved runways, approximately 94% have runways that range in length from 914 (m) to over 3,000 m.

8. Communications

In 2012, Argentina had approximately 10 million main telephone lines in use and 58.6 million mobile cellular telephones. Current expansion includes fiber-optic cable trunk lines between all major cities. However, the communication system in Argentina is below the standards of the United States. This number is nowhere comparable to the United States, but they do show a strong position relative to many other countries. The microwave system is widely used, but it suffers from interruption as a result of frequent rainstorms. This is true even in Buenos Aires. The government owns a TV station and radio network, in addition to over 24 TV stations and hundreds of privately-owned radio stations. There were 11.232 million Internet hosts in 2012 and approximately 13.694 million Internet users.

9. Real Property Issues

Property ownership information can be obtained from the Property Register. Because the Property Register is public, anyone can verify the status of a certain property (ownership, burdens, mortgages, etc.)

In Argentina, deeds are the contracts that are notarized and recorded with the Property Register within 15 days of signature. Deeds in the common law sense do not exist in Argentina.

Contracts involving the conveyance of, or the encumbrance of, real property must be in the form of public documents and must be duly authenticated and registered.

Title documents evidencing ownership are recorded in the Property Register corresponding to the location of the property. Recordation gives full right to the ownership of real property.

Under law, all documents must be recorded that constitute, transmit, declare, modify, or extinguish rights upon real estate; impose attachments and any other injunctions; and any other document required by law, which law can vary by province.[20]

The Civil Code governs the nature, form, objects and obligations of contracts. To constitute a contract there must be an offer and acceptance, express or implied. The offer is void if the offeror dies or becomes incapacitated before acceptance is received. Offers may be retracted any time before acceptance, if the offeror has not renounced his right to retract. Verbal offers must be accepted immediately. The offeree may retract his acceptance any time before it reaches the offeror. A contract which should be in the form of a public instrument, that is, notarized, but one that is drawn up as a private document constitutes an obligation to reduce the same to a public instrument.[21]

Also, the seller may not set the conditions that the property may be reclaimed through the return of the price of purchase. It is recommended that the parties retain a lawyer familiar with these local matters.

Property listings are available by main networks in the city of Buenos Aires, some of which consist of groupings of other smaller systems (e.g. the SOM System (http://www.som.com.ar), a pioneer in the sector, is active mainly in the northern district of the city of Buenos Aires. Some 200+ agents belong to this network.)

In all cases, the broker provides its clients with a listing of properties available for sale or rent, and information is updated daily using computer systems. There is still a possibility to establish a national network to link the various networks in the interior of the country with the city of Buenos Aires. This will be part of a program for regional integration and possible links with other countries as the real estate market becomes internationalized. Inroads to what this globalization may look like in the future can be seen at realtors.com, in its international website (http://www.realtor.com/international/) or at world-properties.com (http://www.worldproperties.com).

The Real Estate Federation of Argentina has various computerized systems that are used for multiple listing services (MLS).

Residential sales commissions are generally 6%, with 3% paid by the buyer, and 3% paid by the seller. Commercial sales commissions are up to 10%, again split equally between the buyer and seller. For the residential broker who rents residential income properties, commissions are usually either one-month's rent or 5% of the total amount of the contract. For the commercial/retail broker who rents commercial establishments, commissions are received from the tenants and range between 3% and 5% of the total amount of the contract. Real estate

agents are paid by commission. Both the seller and the buyer typically pay the commission.

Real estate trade associations include the Real Estate Federation of Argentina, *Federación Inmobiliaria de la Argentina* (http://www.fira.org.ar), Argentina Real Estate Chamber, *Cámara Inmobiliaria de Argentina* (http://www.cia.org.ar), Real Estate Entrepreneurs Association, *Asociación de Ejecutivos de la Vivienda*, and FIABCI (http://www.fiabci.com/ar), an international association of real estate Professionals, based in France. FIABCI stands for *Fédération Internationale des Professions Immobiliéres* or *International Real Estate Federation*, a non-governmental organization in consultative status with the Economic and Social Council of the United Nations.

Auctioneers or brokers usually take part in the real estate transaction. The broker acts as an intermediary between the seller and the buyer. The agent seems to represent both parties; i.e., there is a dual agency relationship. According to the Commercial Code, the real estate broker cannot be part of the contract; he only helps to achieve an agreement between the seller and the buyer.

Real estate salespeople are required to hold a license to conduct a real estate transaction.

The national, state/provincial, and municipal governments make licensing mandatory. Education at the college level is required. There is no requirement for annual or periodic training to keep the license. Requirements for obtaining a real estate license in Argentina are as follows: pass a qualifications exam and, in some provinces, carry out a three-year college course.

Argentine law establishes different ways to acquire the ownership right to a property. All conditions are fulfilled when the title is enrolled in the Property Register. These include promissory sales contract, exchange, grant, inheritance, grant on will, and acquisitive prescription.

The Civil Code states that the maximum lease term allowed is twenty years for residential real estate and fifty years for other real estate. Contracts with a longer term will be considered valid only for the years expressively allowed in the Civil Code. The minimum lease term is two years for residential real estate and three years for commercial properties. Contracts with a shorter term will be considered valid for the term established by law. Some exceptions to the minimum term include embassies, consulates, and real estate owned by the government.

Once the lease contract is signed, the tenant is obliged to leave the amount of monthly rental payment per contract year as a deposit, which will be returned when the lease term ends. This deposit protects the owner against damage to the property.

A tenant may cancel the lease within six months after its origination, upon appropriate notice. If this occurs during the first year, the tenant must pay the equivalent of a month and a half of rent. If this happens after that date, he must pay the equivalent of one month's rent as a penalty. The owner cannot interrupt the lease contract before its end. Contract terms can be re-negotiated when the term is completed. If an agreement is not reached for its renewal, the owner can request restitution. Though the tenant might continue occupying the property after expiration of the lease, Argentina law will not consider it as automatically renewed. If the rent is not paid for two consecutive months, the owner has a right to demand payment within ten days. After ten days, the owner can petition the courts to have the tenant removed. Real property in Argentina may be held in severalty or concurrently. Concurrent forms of Ownership include:

General Partnership:
A general partnership consists of two or more persons with unlimited and joint responsibility engaged or commercial purposes under a firm name that must include *Sociedad Colectiva*. All modifications of partnership agreement require unanimous approval of partners, unless otherwise provided, and all other resolutions shall be adopted by majority vote.

Limited Partnership:
A limited partnership involves two or more persons. Active partners have same responsibilities as partners of a general partnership, while silent partners are liable to the extent of their capital contribution. The firm's name must include words *sociedad en comandita simple*, and names of all active partners should appear therein. Administration of a limited partnership is undertaken by active partners or third parties and is subject to same norms as general partnerships. Resolutions are adopted in same manner as general partnerships. Silent partners have the right to vote in accounting matters and the appointment of administrators. There are three types of limited Partnerships:

1. **Cooperative Societies,** *sociedad de capitaly industria*, are formed by individuals Who supply capital and are subject to unlimited liability, and one or more individuals Who contribute only their personal services and are not personally liable;
2. **Cooperative Societies** which cannot be restricted as to the number of members or Shares, capital or duration; and
3. **Joint Ventures** which typically are formed for one or more specific temporary commercial transactions and are subject to the general laws of contracts. If members knowingly allow their names to be used in business, they incur unlimited and joint liability.

With new banking laws since January 2002, the uses of mortgages have changed substantially. In February 2015, interest rates from banks were between 15.96% (Banco Central de la República Argentina) and 35.00% (BBVA) for a term of no more than fifteen years. With limited money reserves, bank and international liquidity difficulties, equity requirements are high.

Mortgages must be recorded to be valid against third parties. They do not pass title to the mortgagee. Mortgagor retains title subject to lien of mortgage. A mortgage on real property extends to land and buildings, other improvements, rents and insurance proceeds. A mortgage must be in the form of a notarial or public instrument, and the contract to which it is accessory may be in the same document. The instrument constituting the mortgage must contain the following: the names and domiciles of the debtor and creditor; the date and nature of the contract to which it is an accessory and where filed; the situation of the property and its boundaries; and, if rural property, the district, and if urban property, the city or town and street; and the exact amount of the debt.

From the late 1970's to the early 1990's, banks were almost absent from real estate lending. However, nowadays banks have aggressively re-entered the market extending credit to builders and developers, lending on individual purchases and participating in real estate equities. Banks typically require loan-to-value ratios between 70% to 85%, although as this ratio improves the demand will surely increase.

The National Mortgage Bank (NMB) hopes to lead the securitization process in Argentina through a credit line that will purchase loans for new housing and issue mortgaged backed securities in the capital market. The NMB's ability to offer subsidies for the construction of primarily single-family urban homes has been strengthened as well by the new laws permitting the securitization of loans. Residential financing for low-income persons is available through the Fondo Nacional de Vivienda (FONAVI). FONAVI's funds are collected from taxes on gasoline and from employee contributions to the social security system.

The government taxes real property according to its fiscal value. The fiscal value is based on different attributes of the property, such as size of land and/or building, the site, the type of construction, and so forth. Also, the government taxes the net income of the real estate "exploitation" and the benefits obtained through its sale. This tax ranges between 11% and 30%. The value added tax (VAT) is 21% of the building cost if there is new construction. Rental operations and sale of used units are not subject to VAT. The stamp tax is applied on real estate transactions. The stamp tax is based on a percentage of the overall transaction price. It can be from 1% to 4%. The rate varies according to the province.

In the area of commercial real estate, there is great variety across the country in terms of zoning regulations on shopping centers, wholesale stores, and other retail establishments generally. Regulations of commercial developments in some areas of the country are so strict that they discourage investment through the imposition of burdensome, time-consuming procedures.

In Argentina, the forms of ownership are comparable to those in the United States. Rights in real property are based on Roman Law. The ownership right is guaranteed by the National Constitution and ruled by the Civil Code. Argentines and foreigners are treated the same way; the Foreign Investments Law protects both.

In addition, the United States and Argentina signed a bilateral investment agreement in 1992 through which US investors have the right to take disputes to international arbitration when other methods of reaching agreements have failed. Non-Argentines can own real property in Argentina with only one restriction: Only Argentine nationals can own property along the borders of Argentina with another country.

Non-Argentine investors also can be confident in the safety of their investments from governmental expropriation. First, the Argentina government has not engaged in any expropriations since the government established its current and continuing course of economic reform and development in 1989. Secondly, the explicit statement in Article IV of the U.S. and Argentina investment agreement states that investments will not be expropriated at less than fair market value. The U.S.- Argentina agreement can be reasonably regarded as securing the general treatment of international investors in the country.[2]

■ 10. Real Estate Trends

Office Space

Firms continue to show a tendency to reduce both occupied area and administrative staff. This is the result of improvements in communications, banking services, and computers. In addition, the difficult access to downtown attracts firms to more accessible sites in the out skirts or in industrial parts of the area.

Seventy percent (70%) of the economic, financial, and commercial activity of Argentina is concentrated in **Buenos Aires.** Supply has risen in the last years and demand has kept pace, keeping the vacancy rate around 10% since 2009. Total vacancy in for premium office space (A/A+) was 10.63% in 2014. There are over 1,407,667 (2014, est.) square meters of premium office space (A/A+) in Buenos Aires, mainly in the North Zone CABA, Puerto Madero Norte, and Catalinas.

Retail Space

The demand for commercial stores can be divided into two different markets: stores in shopping centers and stores on the streets. Stores on the streets have become a saturated market. Because there are too many street shops, competition is fierce. A clear sign of this is the gradual disappearance of the "key money" for the rent of ships in several commercial zones. Shopping centers remain the most active segment of the construction market. However, while more than 60% of shopping center visitors go there for a walk, only 15% really spend money there. Shopping centers find competition from other shopping centers and from commercial establishments located on the streets. Centers are generally owned by the developer and rented for four- to five-year terms.

Leases are established at the highest amount resulting from a percentage on sales (usually 7%) and a minimum (based on store size). Common area maintenance expenditures and advertising costs are shared among the tenants. At the beginning and the renewal of the lease contract, an additional sum is paid (equivalent to 15% to 20% of the total amount of the lease contract). If the shopping center is successful, store tenants will be willing to pay this "key money."

The broker who rents the commercial establishments receives from the tenants 0.6% of the total amount of the contract.

Industrial Space

The present economic conditions, favoring deregulation and the opening of barriers, are obliging firms to be efficient and to compete with other countries. This policy is adverse to many of the small-size and medium-size industrial firms that continue to employ outdated manufacturing techniques and suffer from a lack of available financing and poorly trained workers.

Residential Space

Government subsidized financing programs are not as available because of economic conditions and the government's inability to maintain payments on public and international obligations. Financial Terms of a local government subsidized program (City of Buenos Aires), in 2015, were: 85% Loan-To-Value, 15-20 years, 7%-14% interest, for up to AR$ 674.262.

■ 11. Cultural Issues

Any nation's culture is complex and vibrant in its diversity. While broad cultural characterizations such as those presented here can be generally accurate, following such generalities too strictly may be dangerously misleading. To conduct business effectively and profitably in a country, it is vital to have a thorough understanding of its culture's complexities.

Argentineans are very fashionable and current on both European and North American styles. However, European styles are considered more fashionable. Greetings are accompanied with a handshake and a slight nod showing respect. Among women there is often a kiss on the cheek if the parties are familiar with each other. It is common that Argentineans use titles, such as *Señor, Señora, Don* or *Doña*, when first introduced or in formal situations.

Visiting, gestures, and social eating activities are similar to those customs followed in the United States. Invited guests, however, are not expected to arrive on time.

Arriving 30-minutes late or more is tolerable. Spanish is used in most business transactions. There is a Spanish variant spoken in Argentina, as well as in other parts of South and Central America, that departs from Spanish in Mexico or Spain.

Visitors will notice, in addition to verb changes, the Italian accent. The conjugated verb form for the informal *you* is *vos* instead of *tú*, and *sos* for the plural. Irregular verb conjugations with stem changes in the *tú* form remain in the infinitive form in Argentina with an accent used on the verb change ending. Care should be taken regarding the use of *tú* since it can convey disrespect. Use formal forms of speech until the individual gives permission to be spoken to in the informal manner, at which point both parties can agree on informal speech. The Argentine people are patient and accepting, and understand that Spanish speakers from Europe, Mexico and the United States are not familiar with their form of Spanish. The Argentines will kindly explain the difference in a manner that will minimize embarrassment to all parties. For more on cultural matters, see the Burns Web site at: http://burns.daniels.du.edu.

12. Discussion Questions

1. What is Argentina's current unemployment rate? Why has this rate been historically high? How could Argentina could reduce and improve this rate?

2. With a history of economic crises in Argentina, how do you think it can attract investors, and to which areas of investment?

3. Considering its vacancy rates, affordability of writs, and cost of mortgages, what are some ideas that would help the housing market in Argentina?

13. Case Study

Management of Argentina Properties for Sale Inc. (MAPS) 121 Plaza del Sol Buenos Aries, Argentina

Memo

To: MAPS Board of Directors
From: Consultants
Re: Argentina Properties

I. Problem

Management of Argentine Properties for Sale, Inc. (MAPS), a subsidiary of Global Office Solutions, Inc. (GOS), expanded into Argentina in 1998. MAPS was doing fine until the recent economic crisis in Argentina. MAPS was hit rather hard. MAPS has borrowed funds, in U.S. dollars, to purchase two office buildings. Because of the collapse of the Argentine Peso, the Board of Directors is concerned that in the near future MAPS will have a difficult time paying its loans. Although MAPS is still collecting rents at the office buildings, the rents are paid in Argentine Pesos. Thus, MAPS is not receiving enough to cover the initial loan payments, which are in U.S. dollars.

In January, 2002, the Argentina Peso was devalued to 1.4 pesos to $1.00, after ten years of trading at a value equal to the U.S. dollar. As of September 16,

2002, the Argentina Peso reached 3.69 to $1.00. Because of this valuation issue, MAPS is rapidly losing money. The loans were structured as nonrecourse loans, which allow MAPS to "walk," but MAPS would like the opportunity to do business in Argentina in the future. If it leaves Argentina now, it may damage any future position there. Because of the change in the market, MAPS has to reevaluate its exit plan.

II. Initial Exit Strategy

When there was first talk of the Peso not being tied to the US dollar, MAPS was not concerned. The Directors of MAPS felt that the market was relatively stable, and that MAPS could continue to do business. The exit strategy was timed for after 5 to 10 years of owning the properties, depending on the market. MAPS would eventually sell the properties, but would try to remain as the manager for one to two years. The hope was to continue to upgrade the properties to a completely Grade A portfolio within Argentina. MAPS was hoping to build the portfolio to approximately five to ten Class A office properties that were owned by the Company, and five to ten managed properties that had been initially purchased, upgraded and then sold. This was a long-term investment

plan as MAPS expected to be in Argentina for the long term, between 20 years and 40 years. If the returns were below what was expected for more than two years, the exit strategy was to sell and get out of the market in Argentina. If MAPS was unable to sell the realty at reasonable prices, and it still wanted to exit, the next plan was to outsource the management, so that MAPS could get its people out of the country. It would just hold on to the investments until it could command a better price. (Of all the projections and forecasting, nothing came close to predicting the economic crisis that has befallen Argentina.)

III. Contingency Crisis Exit Strategy

Due to the economic factors affecting the Argentine market, currently, the Board of Directors has decided to exit this market, immediately. With this as the decision,

MAPS must go through priorities. Each of the buildings owned by MAPS must be placed on the market. The brokers with MAPS have a good working relationship; the brokers have helped MAPS find the properties; they will be contacted and asked for a proposal on each building. In each proposal, MAPS will need to have an explicit out line on what tools, resources and marketing materials are available to them, and how they will go about selling our properties, immediately, at the best prices available.

Although, given the market, MAPS will not be able to profit from the sale of the buildings, the hope is, with the upgrades that were undertaken, that MAPS can at least break even. (The initial pricing to sell the properties will place each of them at a price slightly above the balance on the loan.) Once the properties are listed, MAPS will work towards cutting back on all expenses, except those that are deemed absolutely necessary.

MAPS will also attempt to reduce the employee headcount. (MAPS does not want a reduction so high that it cannot keep the buildings properly maintained and in positive showing condition.) MAPS does not want to sacrifice, safety,

condition, appearance or any other aspect that might affect the marketability of the properties. Once three of the five buildings have been sold, MAPS will begin to attempt to relocate any employees who want to be moved to one of our other offices, throughout the world. If MAPS has a problem and is unable to sell the properties, MAPS will continue to reduce the price, until the buildings sell. If at some point MAPS is unable to continue to make the loan payments, MAPS will attempt to negotiate with the banks that hold the loans. If MAPS must, it can look into one of the other markets where it has property to transfer funds to cover the loans. But, the highest priority at this point is to exit from Argentina. MAPS must cut its losses and make an agreement with any bank, to allow MAPS to exit the country.

IV. Conclusion

As a result of the recent crisis, it is the suggestion that MAPS immediately prepare to exit Argentina. The initial exit strategy, noted above regarding sales, should be attempted. In trying to exit the market without damaging its reputation in Argentina, it will benefit the company in the long run to try to negotiate settlements with the loan holders. But, if at some point we are unable to make the payments on the loan and we cannot settle with the lenders, we must rely on the non-recourse loans that were made to allow us to purchase the buildings.

Refer to: X-rates.com. Homepage. http://www.x-rates.com.

U.S. Embassy. Homepage. http://usembassy.state.gov. U.S. Department of State. Homepage. http://www.state.gov.

14. Selected References

Argentine Secretary of Tourism (2007). *Tourism Investments*. Argentine Secretary of Tourism (Online). Available: http://www.turismo.gov.ar.

CIA World Factbook at https://www.cia.gov/library/publications/the-world-factbook/index.html.

Hodgson, Cullinan and Campbell (1999)."Land *Ownership and Foreigners – A Comparative Analysis of Regulatory Approaches*". Food and Agriculture Organization of the United Nations (Online). Available: http://www.fao.org.

Inter-American Development Bank. "Argentina and the IBD" (2007)."Basic *Socio-Economic Data Report: Argentina*" (2000). Inter-American Development Bank (Online). Available:http://www.iadb.org

La Nacion, Section 2, Page 1, 2 (May, 2002), Buenos Aires and *Wall Street Journal*, page A15, 28 (May, 2002).

National Institute of Statistics and Census (2007). General *Aspects of Argentina Republic* (in Spanish). National Institute of Statistics and Census (Online). Available: http://www.indec.mecon.gov.ar.

Organization of American States at http://www.oas.org.

Richard Ellis International Property Specialists. C.B. Richard Ellis. http://www.cbre.com. Time Almanac. *TIME Almanac*. Boston: Information Please LLC.

United States Department of State. *Background Notes: Argentina*. United States Department of State (Online). Available: http://www.state.gov.

U.S. Bureau of Census at http://www.census.gov. U.S. Department of Commerce at http://www.stat-usa.gov. U.S. Bureau of Economic Analysis at http://www.bea.gov. U.S. Embassy. Homepage. http://usembassy.state.gov. World Trade Centers Institute at http://www.wtci.org. World Trade Organization at http://www.wto.org.

World Bank. *Adult Illiteracy Rates*. The Economist X-rates.com. Homepage. http://www.x-rates.com.

Servicio Meterorológico Nacional, Servicios Climático, Clima en Argentina, Información Gráfica de Temperatura y Precipitación, Valores Medios de Temperatura y Precipitación – Capital Federal, http://

www.smn.gov.ar/serviciosclimaticos/?mod=elclima&id=5&var=capitalfederal

United Nations Data, Country Profile: Argentina, https://data.un.org/CountryProfile.aspx?crName=Argentina

Argentina Histórica, Evolución Política, Retorno del Fraude: Revolución de 1943, http://argentinahistorica.com.ar/temas.php?tema=6&titulo=23&subtitulo=105

Todo Argentina, Historia: La década infame (1930-1943), http://www.todo-argentina.net/historia/decadainf/index.html

Todo Argentina, Historia: El Peronismo (1943-1955), http://www.todo-argentina.net/historia/peronista/index.html

Election Resources on the Internet: National Elections in Argentina – Results Lookup, Elections: October 28, 2007, Provinces: Argentina Totals, http://www.electionresources.org/ar/president.php?election=2007

Election Resources on the Internet: National Elections in Argentina – Results Lookup, Elections: October 23, 2011, Provinces: Argentina Totals, http://www.electionresources.org/ar/president.php?election=2011

Ministerio del Interior, Dirección Nacional Electoral, Elecciones Nacionales, 23 de Octubre de 2011, Escrutinio Definitivo, http://www.elecciones.gov.ar/estadistica/archivos/resultados_nacionales_2011_presidente_vice_total_pais.pdf

Instituto Nacional de Estadística y Censos, Población, Proyecciones Nacionales, Población por sexo y grupos quinquenales de edad. Años 2010-2040, http://www.indec.mecon.ar/nivel4_default.asp?id_tema_1=2&id_tema_2=24&id_tema_3=84

Ministerio del Poder Popular de Planificación, Instituto Nacional de Estadística, Demográficos - Proyecciones de Población: Venezuela. Proyección de la población, según entidad y sexo, 2000-2050 (año calendario), http://www.ine.gov.ve/index.php?option=com_content&view=category&id=98&Itemid=51

Estimaciones y Proyecciones de la Población en la República de Panamá, por Provincia. Comarca Indígena, Distrito y Corregimiento, Según Sexo: Años 2000-2015, Boletín No. 10, https://www.contraloria.gob.pa/inec/Archivos/P2391Boletin10.pdfInstituto Nacional de Estadísticas, Chile, Demográficas y Vitales, Demografía, Población, País y Regiones. Actualización Población 2002-2012 y Proyecciones 2013-2020, http://www.ine.cl/canales/chile_estadistico/demografia_y_vitales/demografia/pdf/poblacion_sociedad_enero09.pdf

Instituto Brasileiro de Geografia e Estatística (IBGE), Diretoria de Pesquisas. Coordenação de População e Indicadores Sociais. Gerência de Estudos e Análises da Dinâmica Demográfica, http://www.ibge.gov.br/home/estatistica/populacao/projecao_da_populacao/2013/default_tab.shtm

Cuadros Estadísticos, Indicadores Demográficos, Esperanza de Vida al Nacer por Sexo. Período 2010-2040, http://www.indec.mecon.ar/nivel4_default.asp?id_tema_1=2&id_tema_2=24&id_tema_3=84

Cuadros Estadísticos, Indicadores Demográficos, Tasa de mortalidad infantil por sexo. Total del país. Período 2010-2040, http://www.indec.mecon.ar/nivel4_default.asp?id_tema_1=2&id_tema_2=24&id_tema_3=84

Ministerio del Interior y Transporte, Dirección Nacional Electoral, Régimen Electoral, http://www.elecciones.gov.ar/articulo_princ.php?secc=3&sub_secc=0#.VQ9YG-Fjaao

Cámara Nacional Electoral, Partidos Reconocidos, Partidos de Orden Nacional, p.2-3, http://www.cuidatuvoto.org.ar/pdf/partidosreconocidos.pdf

World Bank, World Integrated Trade Solution, Trade Stats by Country, Argentina GDP per Capita (Current US$) 2009-2013, http://wits.worldbank.org/CountryProfile/Country/ARG/StartYear/2009/EndYear/2013/Indicator/NY-GDP-PCAP-CD

World Bank, World Integrated Trade Solution, Trade Stats by Country, Argentina Trade Summary 2013 Data, http://wits.worldbank.org/CountryProfile/Country/ARG/Year/2013/Summary

The World Bank, Research, Global Economic Prospects, Country and Region Specific Forecasts and Data, http://www.worldbank.org/en/publication/global-economic-prospects/data?region=LAC

The World Bank, Data, Inflation, Consumer Prices (Annual %), http://data.worldbank.org/indicator/FP.CPI.TOTL.ZG?display=default

The World Bank, Data, Labor Force, Total, http://data.worldbank.org/indicator/SL.TLF.TOTL.IN

The World Bank, Data, Unemployment, Total (% of Total Labor Force), http://data.worldbank.org/indicator/SL.UEM.TOTL.ZS/countries

The Economist, Argentina's New Inflation Index, Pricing Power: Will the Country's Statisticians now be allowed to do their work?, February 22, 2014, http://www.economist.com/news/americas/21597020-will-countrys-statisticians-now-be-allowed-do-their-work-pricing-power

United Nations Data, Country Profile: Argentina, https://data.un.org/CountryProfile.aspx?crName=Argentina#Economic

Cámara Inmobiliaria Argentina, Aspectos Legales, Ley 10.973 – De Los Martilleros y Corredores Públicos, Capítulo IV: De Los Aranceles, http://www.cia.org.ar/aspectos_legales_articulo_ley10973.php

Código Civil, Capítulo 4, Locación, Sección 3: Tiempo de la Locación, http://www.infojus.gob.ar/docs-f/codigo/Codigo_Civil_y_Comercial_de_la_Nacion.pdf

Código Civil, Capítulo 4, Locación, Sección 6: Extinción, http://www.infojus.gob.ar/docs-f/codigo/Codigo_Civil_y_Comercial_de_la_Nacion.pdf

Inversor Global, Hipoteca: Cómo sacar un crédito hipotecario en la Argentina?, Febrero 16, 2015, https://igdigital.com/2015/02/hipoteca-como-sacar-credito-hipotecario-en-la-argentina-2/

Banco Central de la República de Argentina, Monetarias y Financieras, BADLAR - Tasas de interés por depósitos a plazo fijo de más de un millón de pesos o dólares, promedio ponderado por monto, en porcentaje nominal anual, http://www.bcra.gov.ar/index.asp

Taxation and Investment in Argentina 2014: Reach, Relevance and Reliability, Sections:5.5 Stamp Duty and 6.5 Real Property Tax, http://www2.deloitte.com/content/dam/Deloitte/global/Documents/Tax/dttl-tax-argentinaguide-2014.pdf

HG.org, Legal Resources, Articles, Real Estate Purchase Process in Buenos Aires, Argentina, Joffe, K., http://www.hg.org/article.asp?id=30505

San Martin, Suarez y Asociados, Real Estate in Argetina, Buenos Aires, April 2012, http://www.sms.com.ar/imgcomweb/SMS%20Real%20Estate%20April%202012.pdf

Ministerio de Planificación Federal, Inversión Pública y Servicios, Secretaría de Obras Públicas, Subsecretaría de Desarrollo Urbano y Vivienda, FO.NA.VI – Fondo Nacional de la Vivienda, http://www.vivienda.gob.ar/fonavi.php

Banco Central de la República de Argentina, Monetarias y Financieras, Tasas de Interés por Préstamos al Sector Privado No Financiero, http://www.bcra.gov.ar/index.asp

BBVA Francés, Personas, Productos, Préstamos, Préstamos Hipotecarios – Adquisición, https://www.bbvafrances.com.ar/tlal/jsp/ar/esp/individu/producto/prestamos/hipoteca/adquisi/index.jsp#0

CBRE Global Research and Consulting, Buenos Aires, Mercado de Oficinas, MarketView, http://www.gatewaytosouthamerica.com/archivo/buenos_aires_mercado_de_oficinas_3t_2014_espa%F1ol.pdf

Censo 2010, Resultados Definitivos. Variables Seleccionadas, Total del País, Viviendas, Cuadro V1.Total del país. Total de viviendas por provincia. Año 2010 and Cuadro V2. Total del país. Viviendas particulares habitadas, hogares y población censada por tipo de vivienda, según provincia. Año 2010, http://www.censo2010.indec.gov.ar/resultadosdefinitivos_totalpais.asp

Ciudad de Buenos Aires, Red en Todo Estás Vos, Primera Casa BA, http://www.buenosaires.gob.ar/redentodoestasvos/posibildad-de-vivienda/primera-casa

15. Glossary

Congreso Nacional – National Congress, which is bicameral and consists of a Senate and a second branch known as the Chamber of Deputies.

FONAVI's – (National Fund for Housing) Provides residential housing financing.

The funds are collected from taxes on gas and employee contributions to the social security system.

Malvinas – The Falkland Islands. This is the term that the Argentineans use for these Islands. There has been a land dispute over this area.

Povincias – Another term for the provinces. The government has 23 Provinces and 1 Federal District.

About the Authors

José F. Ramirez was born in Caracas, Venezuela, where he earned a degree in civil engineering at the Universidad Central de Venezuela. He later earned a, in the United Stated, a diploma in business administration from the University of California – Berkeley; a master's in real estate and construction management from the Burns School of Real Estate and Construction Management, *Daniels College of Business*, UNIVERSITY OF DENVER; and, in Australia, a Master of Construction Law from the University of Melbourne. At the beginning of his career, he actively appraised residential real estate in Venezuela. A few years later, he actively participated in the design and development of commercial real estate in that country. More recently he has provided consulting construction and real estate services for commercial real estate in Colombia, United States and Venezuela. He currently works as a consultant for the construction and real estate development industries in the United States.

Gary L. Harder, owner and president of Harder, Inc., a real estate valuation firm in Colorado Springs, Colorado. Mr. Harder has specialized in real estate for 20 years. With 25 years of real estate experience, spanning residential and commercial sales, property management, and feasibility and financial analysis, in the past ten years Mr. Harder's interests have been in international economics and international real estate issues, and he has participated in international delegations to exchange ideas with real estate counterparts. A graduate student at the UNIVERSITY OF DENVER, Mr. Harder's research is on the political economy of International Monetary Fund (IMF) structural adjustment programs, and the microeconomic and macroeconomic effects that the Fund's policies and conditional programs have on member countries.

Australia

INTERNATIONAL REAL ESTATE (GLOBAL REAL ESTATE)

Dr. Mark Lee Levine, Editor

1. Geography

Australia is a continent situated between the Indian Ocean and the South Pacific Ocean, with land area (only slightly smaller than the United States) of 7,741,220 sq km (square kilometers), including the Lord Howe Island and the Macquarie Island.

The long coastline is approximately 25,760 km. Australia has very few border disputes, although there are some territorial issues with regard to Antarctica. The climate varies since the continent is so large.

Natural resources include, among others, coal, iron ore, copper, lead, zinc, diamonds, natural gas, and some petroleum. Australia is the world's largest net exporter of coal, accounting for 29% of global coal exports (as of 2015).

Permanent pastures comprise about 54% of the land, with forests and woodlands of about 19%. 6.13% of the land is arable; the balance is mixed use. Environmental issues exist: soil erosion, damage to natural habitats of animals that are threatened with extinction and damage to fresh water resources. Australia has been involved in a number of treaties to protect these areas, including nuclear bans, ozone layer protection, ship pollution controls, wet land laws, and others.

2. History and Overview

Portuguese, Spanish, Dutch, and English explorers observed the island before 1770, when Captain Cook explored the east coast and claimed it for Great Britain.

On January 26, 1788 (now celebrated as Australia Day), the First Fleet under Capt. Arthur Phillip landed at Sydney, and formal proclamation of the establishment of the Colony of New South Wales followed on February 7. Many but by no means all of the first settlers were convicts. The mid-19th century saw the beginning of government policies to emancipate convicts and assist the immigration of free persons. The discovery of gold in 1851 led to increased population, wealth, and trade. The six colonies that now constitute the states of the Australian Commonwealth were established in the following order: New South Wales, 1788; Tasmania, 1825; Western Australia, 1830; South Australia, 1836; Victoria, 1851; and Queensland, 1859.

Australia passed the Statute of Westminster Adoption Act on October 9, 1942, which officially established Australia's complete autonomy in both internal and external affairs. Its passage formalized a situation that had existed for years. The Australia Act (1986) eliminated the last vestiges of British legal authority.

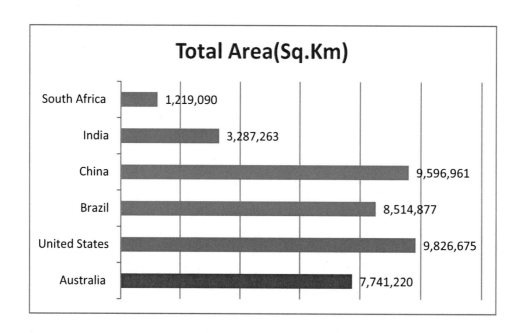

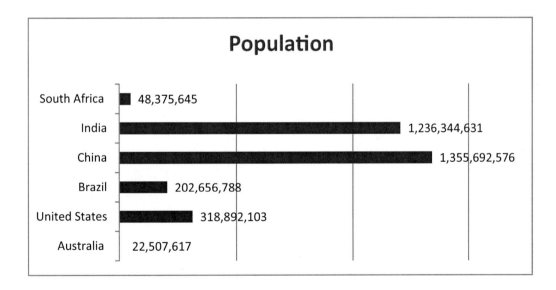

Population

South Africa	48,375,645
India	1,236,344,631
China	1,355,692,576
Brazil	202,656,788
United States	318,892,103
Australia	22,507,617

■ 3. People

Australia's population is 22,507,617 people (2014 est.)

The age structure is 66.9% in the 15-year-old to 64-year-old category. 18% of the population is in the 0 to 14-year-old category, and 15.1% is in the group of over 65 years of age (2014 est.)

The population growth rate was 1.09% in 2014, which is slightly lower than in 2012. The birth rate is 12.19 per 1,000 population, and the death rate is 7.07 per 1,000. Life expectancy is 82.07 years. Literacy is 99% of those who are 15 years of age or older.

■ 4. Government

The government of Australia is a federal Parliamentary state. The capital is Canberra. There are six states and two Territories in Australia. Independence was gained on January 1, 1901, as the Federation of the United Kingdom Colonies; the Constitution was effective on this date. The national holiday is January 26th (commencing in 1788).

The legal system is based on the English common law, as a result of English influence in the entire country.

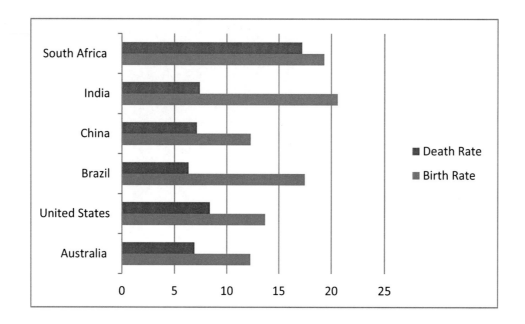

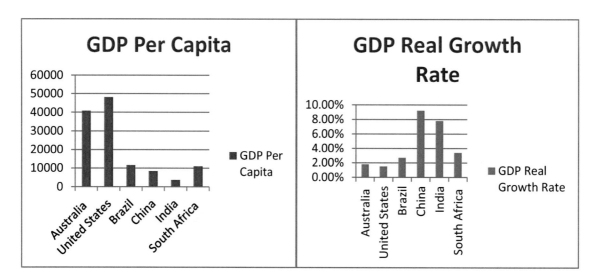

Branches of government include the Executive, Legislative, and Judicial. Within the Executive Branch, the Chief of State is the British Monarch (Queen Elizabeth II of the United Kingdom). However, the head of government is the Prime Minister Anthony John "Tony" Abbott. The Legislative Branch is the bicameral federal Parliament, consisting of a Senate and a House of Representatives. The House selects the head of government, the Prime Minister. The Judicial Branch consists of a High Court with the Lower Courts. The major parties include the Liberal Party, National Party and the Australian Labor Party.

The United States maintains diplomatic relationships with Australia, and has an Embassy office in Canberra. The Australian Ambassador maintains its office in Washington, D.C.

■ 5. Economy

Australia has a typical modern Western economy, encouraging free capitalism. The Gross Domestic Product (GDP)

was $1.483 trillion (2014 est.) The GDP per capita is $46,600 (2014 est.)

Inflation is low at 2.7% (2014), and unemployment is 6% (2014), giving Australia a strong, stable economy. Australia is active in exporting coal, gold, meat, wool, iron ore and other goods. The following figures are built on a comparative basis, showing the per capita earnings in Australia as opposed to the United States and other countries. The following table shows the GDP real growth rate in Australia, 2.8%, as contrasted with the United States and other countries.

■ 6. Currency

The currency is the Australian *Dollar* (AUD). See the Burns School Global Real Estate Web site for the UNIVERSITY OF DENVER at http://burns.daniels.du.edu for currency conversions.

7. Transportation

Australia relies on an extensive rail network for transportation of goods, with 38,445km of rail line; 823,217 km of roadways are also used, with about 40% being paved. Pipelines are used to transport crude oil, petroleum products and natural gas. Australian ships depart from major ports such as Adelaide, Brisbane, Sydney, Melbourne, and additional ports throughout the coastal lines. Australia has 480 airports, with a majority having paved runways.

8. Communications

As a separate continent has fairly isolated, Australia must rely heavily on its communication system, with good domestic and international service. Approximately 10.47 million telephones are used by its population, and 24.4 million cellular phones (2012). Australia utilizes satellite earth stations and other high-tech systems. Numerous radio and television systems broadcast throughout the country.

9. Real Property Issues

Australia has commission-paid agents, although the means of selling real estate often involves an auction process. Additional requirements are imposed on non-Australian residents or citizens when they purchase real estate. The requirements are controlled partly by the Foreign Investment Review Board. These restrictions vary based upon the property type, value and the percent ages of foreign equity involved in the investment. For more information on this, see Martindale-Hubbell *Australia Law Digest, 30* or visit the Foreign Investment Review Board Web site at http://www.firb.gov.au/.

Real estate agents in Australia use a multiple-listing service (MLS) and various real estate trade associations, such as the Real Estate Institute of Australia.

Each state within Australia has its own license law, meaning there is no absolutely uniform countrywide code. Tests for some agents for proper licensing are required in only some jurisdictions. Legal descriptions utilize mostly a metes-and-bounds survey system. Rights of interest of those in land are reflected by proper recording of documents on the public records. The system utilizes a land title registration through the Torrens land registration system. There are real estate property taxes, income taxes, and property transfer taxes. To explore more about real property issues, see the links for the Real Estate Institute of Australia, the Global Real Estate Web site at the UNIVERSITY OF DENVER, the National Association of REALTORS® sites and numerous others noted in the Internet Resources Appendix in this book.

10. Real Estate Trends

Real estate trends in Australia are reflected in the Web sites indicated in the Internet Resources Appendix in this book, and maintained by some of the larger real estate consulting and brokerage firms, such as Jones Lang LaSalle. See also other links noted below in the Selected References section for information on office, industrial, retail, hotel, residential, and multifamily properties. These report the current rates for leasing and for purchase of real estate throughout Australia.

11. Cultural Issues

Any nation's culture is complex and vibrant in its diversity. While broad cultural characterizations such as those presented here can be generally accurate, following such generalities too strictly may be dangerously misleading. To conduct business effectively and profitably in a country, it is vital to have a thorough understanding of its culture's complexities. Australia's customs are similar to those found in the United States and other Western countries, although dress is much more casual. Eating is usually informal, continental style. For more in this area, see some of the other links and Web sites located in the Internet Resources Appendix in this book.

12. Discussion Questions

1. With the strong economy in Australia, where would be some areas of opportunity for investment?

2. Is the location of Australia and advantage or disadvantage for investments from the United States or Europe, or is this not a factor?

3. What are some of the advantages and disadvantages of the additional requirements imposed upon non-residents in regards to purchasing real estate?

4. Auctions are widely used in the sale of real estate in Australia. What are the benefits and pitfalls of the auction to a buyer, the seller, and the real estate agent?

13. Case Study

Ski Company International, Inc. Ski Australia Vacations, LLC

Memo

To: Board of Directors
From: Consultants
Re: Australian Branch Lack of Snow

I. Problem

In 1998, Ski Company International (SKI) branched out from Canada and the United States into Australia. The Company has been providing quality ski vacations that are all inclusive packages. During the first two years the Company had a windfall snow season. It was ahead of all projections. However, during the next two seasons, the Company barely covered expenses. This season is looking to be even worse. The bookings are down 30% from last season. The events in the last year have directly affected the tourism industry. The economy in the United States has affected SKI's numbers. Over 60% of SKI's customers were from the U.S. The marketing by SKI in Australia and Europe has yet to produce much business from those target markets. The projections for the next two years do not look to be improving. The SKI Canada and United States branches have also seen a decline in business. But SKI is well established. With return customers and the long-term marketing, it will be able to last through another bad season. The SKI Australian Branch has just opened; it might not have the capacity to keep operating. If the bookings are not up by 15% in the next month, SKI will have to take some "drastic" measures.

II. Initial Exit Strategy

The initial exit strategy was to first route calls to one of the call centers in the United States after the first year, if there was enough customer base. Then, the operation would be moved. In 1998, the Company leased office space for a lease term of 10 years. In the event that SKI decided to vacate the space or needed more space because of growth, the Board felt that the leased property was in a good location, and it was a class A building so it would not be difficult to sub-lease. (The space would be listed on the market as soon as the decision had been made to exit the market. After this, the Company would begin liquidating any assets which consisted mainly of computers, office furniture etc. Once the assets were liquidated and the space sub-leased, SKI would be able to exit.)

III. Contingency Exit Strategy

The tourism industry, for SKI, does not seem to be coming back from the hit it took in the last year. The U.S. was SKI's main customer base. Travel has been dramatically reduced. The economy and the events of September 11, 2001 hurt the industry, because people are not spending as much money for tourism. And, they are afraid to fly. The outlook does not seem to be improving within the next 6-12 months. We cannot sustain the business without immediately improving profits. Thus, SKI must look at vacating the business in Australia and combining the limited resources to the offices in the U.S. and Canada.

The first step in a hasty exit from this market would be to find a broker to list the property to sub-lease, while, at the same time, begin negotiations with the landlord to terminate the lease. If a capable licensed real estate agent can be found in SKI's jurisdiction, it is highly suggested that we hire the Company to sub-lease the space. SKI needs to find someone with as much leasing experience as possible, to maximize the sub-lease approach. Once the property is on the market, we must look to the other property that will need to be moved, donated, sold, or discarded. The customers that SKI has currently booked must be serviced, and all of the issues solved. No new customers should be Taken after (date). This means that advertising needs to be terminated, and letters sent to SKI's network of colleagues in the tourist industry. (The letter needs to state that the other two offices in the U.S. and Canada will remain open.) SKI also needs to notify all current customers as to this change, and to provide them with the contact information they need if they have questions or concerns. Once these issues have been resolved, the assets need to be sold, moved, donated or discarded. (Computers that cannot be shipped to one of the other offices can be donated to a local school, along with furniture, office supplies and anything else that cannot be moved.) Once the office is cleaned out and the space sub-leased, SKI can easily exit the business in this location and focus its energies on the other two branches. Maybe, at a later date, when tourism picks up again, SKI can branch out again. But, for the current year, it does not look good for SKI.

IV. Conclusion

After looking at the issues facing SKI, with the lack of tourism, it is suggested that SKI close the operation in Australia and refocus its efforts to the other two branches. At this time the cost to stay open, until the market re-bounds, is not worth the risk that the market might not rebound for many years. Thus, SKI should proceed with the Contingency Exit Plan, immediately.

Refer to: U.S. Embassy. Homepage. http://usembassy.state.gov. U.S. Department of State. Homepage. http://www.state.gov.

14. Selected References

http://www.abs.gov.au.

http://www.australia.com (background notes for Australia). http://www.fed.gov.au.

http://www.joneslanglasalle.com (click on "Research"). http://www.state.gov/ (background notes for Australia).

CIA World Factbook at https://www.cia.gov/library/publications/the-world-factbook/index.html.

Richard Ellis International Property Specialists. http://cbre.com. Time Almanac. *TIME Almanac.* Boston: Information Please LLC.

United States Department of State. *Background Notes: Australia.* United States Department of State (Online). Available: http://www.state.gov. U.S. Bureau of Census at http://www.census.gov. U.S. Department of Commerce at http://www.stat-usa.gov. U.S. Bureau of Economic Analysis at http://www.bea.gov.

U.S. Embassy. Homepage. http://usembassy.state.gov. World Trade Centers Institute at http://www.wtci.org. World Trade Organization at http://www.wto.org. World Bank. *Adult Illiteracy Rates.* The Economist. X-rates.com. Homepage. http://www.x-rates.com.

15. Glossary

Aborigines – Australia's native people.

British penal colony – In 1788 this was the name for Australia because convicts were brought to the country.

About the Author

Dr. Mark Lee Levine *is the Editor of this Book.*

Austria

INTERNATIONAL REAL ESTATE (GLOBAL REAL ESTATE)

Dr. Mark Lee Levine, **Editor**

1. Geography

Austria is located in central Europe, just north of Italy. Austria's area is 83,871 sq km (square kilometers). On a comparative basis, it is slightly smaller in size than the state of Maine. Austria is bordered by the Czech Republic, Germany, Hungary, Italy, Liechtenstein, the Republic of Slovakia, Slovenia and Switzerland. It has no coastline and, as such, has no maritime claims.

The climate in Austria is fairly temperate. It has cold winters and frequent rain in the lower areas and snow in the mountains. Summers are fairly cool. The terrain in the west and south is mountainous, including the Alps. Along the eastern and northern areas it is generally flat or slightly sloping.

Natural resources include timber, lead, coal, copper, hydropower, iron ore and others. Austria has fairly strong land use, with arable land of 16.59%. There are few environmental problems in Austria, aside from air pollution caused by air traffic, various vehicles and industrial plants.

2. History and Overview

In ancient times, the area now known as Austria was a Roman province. Many different forces occupied Austria. Austria was also a conqueror of many different lands. Once the center of a great empire, Austria was left in political and economic chaos by World War I. Austria became a Republic in 1918, reduced to its essential Germanic core and only about a quarter of its former size. The 1930s were a time of economic and political unrest in Austria. Prior to World War II, Austria was annexed by Germany. Following the war, Austria was reestablished within its prewar boundaries under a provisional government. The country was re-established within its prewar boundaries under a provisional government. The country was divided into four administrative zones and occupied by U.S., Soviet, French, and British Forces. In 1955, the country regained its independence from the occupying forces and joined the United Nations (UN). Austria has been officially neutral since 1945. The geographical centrality and history of Austria have caused a dual orientation toward Western Europe and Eastern Europe, specifically the Balkans and Hungary. Ethnically and linguistically, Austria's closest ties are with Germany and Switzerland.

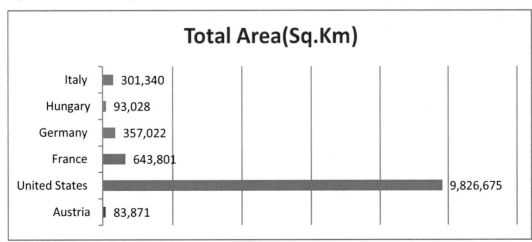

Total Area(Sq.Km)

Italy	301,340
Hungary	93,028
Germany	357,022
France	643,801
United States	9,826,675
Austria	83,871

3. People

The population of Austria is 8,223,062 people (2014 est.) The 15-year to 64-year age group comprises 67.7% of the population. The age groups are approximately split in the group under 15 years old and the group over 64 years of age.

Birth rates are 8.69 per 1,000. Death rates are 10.23 per 1,000 of population. Infant mortality is 4.28 per 1,000 of population; life expectancy is 79.91 years. Males have a 77-year life span, and females, 82.97 years. Dominant ethnic positions are 91.1% Austrians, with a very small numbers of Croatians and other groups. The dominant religion is Roman Catholic, consisting of 73.6% of the populace. Protestants and Muslims are the next largest groups, sharing the remaining percentage points with several other religions. The dominant language is clearly German, although Austrians are sensitive about their independent status is *Austrians*, not Germans.

Literacy is high in the country, with 98% of the population literate, i.e., able to read and write in the age group of 15 years of age or older. The labor force is 3.778 million people (2014). The dominant portion of the labor force is in services and industry (69.8% and 28.6%, respectively), with small portions in agriculture (1.5%).

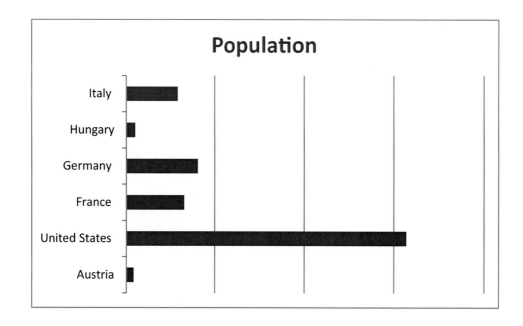

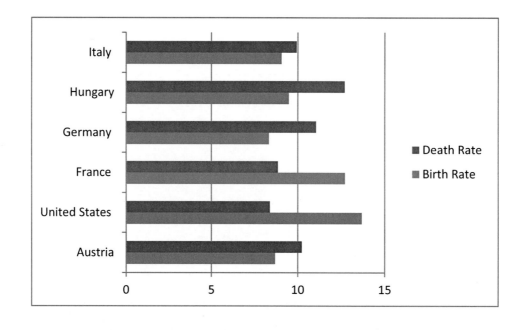

4. Government

The government is a federal republic and is housed with its capital in Vienna. It is administratively divided into nine states. The original *Margravate* of Austria was established in 976 A.D. The modern republic was proclaimed on November 12, 1918 from the Austro-Hungarian Empire. Its national holiday is October 26th, commencing in 1955. Its Constitution was issued in 1920, revised in 1929, and reinstated May 1, 1945. The legal system of the government is based on Roman law, with modifications. There is judicial review by a constitutional court and separate smaller courts. Voting suffrage commences at 18 years of age, applying to men and women. Voting is compulsory for Presidential elections.

The branches of government consist of an Executive Branch, with the President, Chancellor, and appointed Cabinet, a Legislative Branch that is bicameral, known as the Federal Assembly or *Bundesversammlung*, and a Judicial Branch, overseen by the Supreme Judicial Court, or *Oberster Gerichtshof.*

There are numerous political parties in Austria, including the Social Democratic Party of Austria, and the People's Party, among others. Diplomatic representation exists with the United States through its Ambassador in Washington, D.C., as well as the U.S. Ambassador located in Vienna.

The flag of Austria is three horizontal bands. Red is at the top, with white in the middle and red at the bottom.

5. Economy

Austria boasts of a very strong and stable economy. With strong raw material benefits and a strong labor force, Austria is also noted for specialized niches in industry and services, such as tourism and banking.

Austria has a Gross Domestic Product (GDP) per capita of $45,400 (2014). Its GDP is $436.1 billion. Inflation is very low at 1.5%, and unemployment, at 5.6%, is exceptionally low for Western Europe. Austria's GDP real growth rate is 1%.

6. Currency

Currency in Austria is the Euro (was the Austrian *schilling*). Current rates for the Euro (and Austrian schilling) are available in the Wall Street Journal or the Web site indicated in this material.

7. Transportation

Austria is a land-locked country, but is blessed with strong railroads, highways, some inland waterways, pipelines and major river ports in Lienz and Vienna. It also has ample air transportation infrastructure, totaling 55 airports, many of which have paved runways that can handle large jet aircraft and international passengers or freight.

8. Communications

Austria has a well-developed communication system, with 3.342 million telephones in the country and 13.59 million cellular telephone users (2012). It also utilizes satellite, radio broadcasting and television broadcasting stations.

9. Real Property Issues

The following material was drawn from the Burns School Global Real Estate Web site at the UNIVERSITY OF DENVER at http://burns.daniels.du.edu and from the Martindale-Hubbell *Austria Law Digest.* **Acquisition Costs:** Real estate sales commissions in Austria average 3% to 5% for **Acquisition Costs:** Real estate sales commissions in Austria average 3% to 5% for residential sales and are slightly lower for commercial transactions. Real estate sales commissions are typically paid by the seller. There is

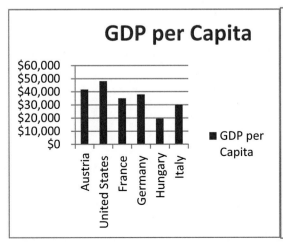

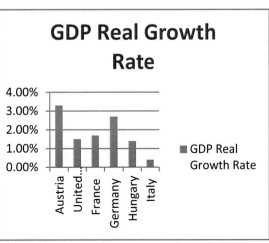

also a 1% notary fee and a 4.5% registration fee. Approximately one-third of all real estate transactions involve agents.

Property and Ownership Information: Property and ownership information is available to the public. Land registers record ownership and encumbrances on specific parcels of real property.

Real Estate Trade Associations: *Bundesinnung der Gebaeudeverwalter, Realitaetenvermittler* und *Inkassoburo,*

License Requirements: A real estate license is required to engage in real estate brokerage. Applicants must meet a minimum age requirement, have experience and be absent of criminal convictions and bankruptcy.

Land Description Meters and Bounds Survey System: The metes-and-bounds survey system is often used.

Rights and Interests in Land: The Austrian government retains certain rights in real property such as the right to levy property taxes, the right of escheat and the right to control the use of private property through zoning.

Forms of Ownership: Corporations and partnerships may acquire, hold, and convey title to real property in Austria. There are two main types of corporations: the *Aktiengesellschaft* or joint stock company, and the *Gesellschaft mit beschränkter Haftung* or limited liability company. Partnership forms existing in Austria include *Offense Handelgesellschaft* or General Partnership; Kommanditgesellschaft– limited partnerships; and there is a special type of partnership, Stille *Gesellschaft,* which is a partnership only between the partners. It does not operate as such against third parties. A *Stille Gesellschaft* has a dormant partner who is not liable to creditors for partnerships debts.

Transfer of Title: Deeds in the common law sense are unknown in Austria. Title to real property is transferred and becomes effective by a declaration of both the grantor and grantee before a notary or recording judge. Transfer of title must be entered in the land register or *Grundbuch.* Conveyance after death can be made by a will. If a property owner dies intestate, property will be distributed among his or her heirs at law. The transfer of real property in rural areas is subject to the approval of a local real property transfer commission.

Recordation and Transfer of Title: Title to land and all real property is recorded in the Land Register. Land Registers are kept open to the public and can be relied upon under Austrian law.

Contracts: Austrian civil code contains essential provisions relating to contracts. In general, continents to be valid must be for a lawful purpose. Contracts can be oral or written; Austria has no statute of frauds provision. Contracts for the use of real property are subject to local laws in effect where the property is situated. **Mortgages:** Real property can be mortgaged as security for a debt in Austria. Mortgage deeds must state the exact consideration and must be entered in the land register.

Priority of mortgages depends upon their date of registration. Mortgages may be foreclosed under power of sale provisions.

Property Taxes: Ad valorem land taxes are levied based upon the standard tax value of the property. This tax is approximately 0.8%, but may vary according to jurisdiction. Additionally, land value taxes of approximately 1% may be levied on vacant land. Land transfer tax is assessed on all conveyances of real property. This tax is usually 3.5% of the price paid for the property. A tax on income is levied in Austria and there are special provisions for capital gains taxes.

Land Use Control: The use of private property is restricted by zoning and subdivision regulations in Austria.

◼ 10. Real Estate Trends

The following material in this Real Estate Trends section was drawn from the Global Real Estate Web site at the UNIVERSITY OF DENVER at http://burns.daniels.du.edu and other reports, as noted. CB Richard Ellis provides a wide variety of local market reports that you could access by going to their Web site at http://www.cbre.com and clicking on "Research Center."

City of Vienna: Typical Lease Length is 5 years. Source: Richard Ellis International Property Specialist s, 1996.

Retail: There is approximately 1.1 million sq m (square meters) of retail space in Austria. The retail market has remained strong and rental rates are fairly stable in Vienna. In Austria, more households occupy multifamily than single-family structures. Just over 50% of all households own their primary residence.[37]

◼ 11. Cultural Issues

Any nation's culture is complex and vibrant in its diversity.

While broad cultural characterizations such as those presented here can be generally accurate, following such generalities too strictly may be dangerously misleading. To conduct business effectively and profitably in a country, it is vital to have a thorough understanding of its culture's complexities. Most Western-style greetings are used, including handshakes and possibly a kiss on the cheek with one who is well known to the party. Professional titles are important and are used in most circumstances. This may include the title herr known as Mister, or fraulein for Miss. Frau is equivalent in the United States of Mrs. or Ms. Use of hand gestures and similar actions are comparable to those used in the United States. See the general cultural discussion for the country of Germany in this book. Much of the same material applies here.

12. Discussion Questions

1. Austria is bordered by countries from the former Soviet blocks. As these countries are building their economies, what could be the impact on Austria's economy?

2. Austria and Japan have similar national products per capita, but Japan's population is almost sixteen times that of Austria. What do you think accounts for this?

3. Do you think the development of more single-family homes would be a wise investment in Austria? Why or why not?

13. Case Study

Real Estate Residential Resort Development Austria (RERRD) (Resort) Innsbruck, Austria

Memo

To: Board of Directors
From: Consultants
Re: Multi-Family Development

I. Problem

Expanding into other countries to develop multi-family housing was an easy decision. The tough part was how to decide which countries to research. After market studies, Austria looked to be a good market, with more households living in multi-family rather than single family homes. The need for some affordable housing in Innsbruck was apparent. There were so many ski areas within a small distance that employees were needed to operate the areas and thus some affordable housing was necessary. We have identified a sight and began the process to purchase the property. We are using a licensed real estate broker, who was recommended by another U.S. company. The problem began when the people living next to our development site began to protest. The properties adjoining our site are higher end condominiums that are owned primarily as second homes. Many of the condominiums owners are foreigners and specifically U.S. citizens. The protest came in the form of attempt to block the purchase. The problem specifically came from the fact that because we are a U.S. company, the U.S. citizens felt they could fight us just as they would in the states. The next roadblock that occurred in the project was the lack of a construction company who was familiar with the techniques that were planned. An American architect did the design and the construction drawings were in English and had not been translated. Although we were able to find a contract or who did speak English, the details of the drawings needed to be translated, so that sub-contractors would be able to read and understand the drawings. The last and most destructive problem was the engineering drawings were completely inept. The engineer who had been hired to do the drawings completely missed the boat. So, we now have a piece of land where people do not want us to build, with drawings that are not only in the wrong language, but also partially unusable.

II. Initial Exit Strategy

The initial exit strategy was to complete the project and then sell the project as a whole or possibly sell each unit off separately, within 5-10 years. When we were ready to sell, a new market study would be undertaken to see which option would work better and provide the most profit. A broker would be hired as well to complete the transactions.

III. Contingency Exit Strategy

Due to the difficulties in starting the project, a exit strategy to vacate sooner might be necessary. The money that has been spent so far on the project is minimal to the money that eventually will be spent to complete the project. At this time, it might be beneficial to cut our losses. The possibility of selling the land and looking elsewhere for a different project might be to our advantage. Considering the opposition and lack of adequate drawings, it might be possible to put the project on the shelf and focus our energies somewhere else until we can have adequate drawings completed by local architects and engineers, working to gain the support of the local community. These two options can give us either a complete exit out of the country or a way to work our way back into the same project at a later date. We have numerous other projects that we can bring to the front for development all over the world and we can afford financially to hold on this one. Some other options might be to find some Austrian investors and get their support to build this project.

IV. Conclusion

At this time, it would be wise to hold off on this project. I would suggest that a new architect and a new engineer are hired to re-draw the plans. That they be hired from the local community, so that the plans are not in English, we can then have them translated to English. After this has been completed, we need to start doing some public relations in the area, to gain support for the project. I suggest we look for some local investors to help provide support. We can begin with the local real estate market. Then we need to get involved in the community, show them how this project is going to add to the community they live in and gain their support. Once we have tried some of these options, we can re-evaluate the need to exit the country or if we have repaired the damage and continue with the project.

Refer to: X-rates.com. Homepage. http://www.x-rates.com.

U.S. Embassy. Homepage. http://usembassy.state.gov. U.S. Department of State. Homepage. http://www.state.gov.

14. Selected References

CIA World Factbook at https://www.cia.gov/library/publications/the-world-factbook/index.html. http://www.austria.gv.at/e. http://www.bmaa.gv.at. http://www.real-estate-european-union.com/english/austria.html. *Richard Ellis International Property Specialists*. C.B. Richard Ellis. http://www.cbre.com.

Time Almanac. *TIME Almanac*. Boston: Information Please LLC.

United States Department of State. *Background Notes: Austria*. United States Department of State (Online). Available: http://www.state.gov.

U.S. Bureau of Census at http://www.census.gov. U.S. Department of Commerce at http://www.stat-usa.gov. U.S. Bureau of Economic Analysis at http://www.bea.gov.

U.S. Embassy. Homepage. http://usembassy.state.gov. World Trade Centers Institute at http://www.wtci.org. World Trade Organization at http://www.wto.org.

World Bank. *Adult Illiteracy Rates*. The Economist.

15. Glossary

Akitengesellschaft – joint stock Company.

Bundesinnung der Gebaeudeverwalter – Real estate trade association in Austria.

Geselleschaft mit beschrankter Haftung – Limited Liability Company.

Grundbuch – The land registry in Austria.

Margravate of Austria – Military governor.

About the Author

Dr. Mark Lee Levine is the Editor of this Book.

Brazil

INTERNATIONAL REAL ESTATE (GLOBAL REAL ESTATE)
Authored by *Jose Ramirez* and *Dr. Mark Lee Levine*, Editor

1. Geography

Brazil is the world's fifth-largest country by land size. It occupies almost half of South America, where it borders every South American country, except Chile and Ecuador. It borders Colombia, Venezuela, Guyana, Suriname, French Guiana and the Atlantic Ocean to the north; Peru, Bolivia, Paraguay and Argentina to the west; Uruguay and the Atlantic Ocean to the south; and, the Atlantic Ocean to the east. Brazil's land area is 8,514,877 sq. km. It is slightly smaller than the United States. Coastlines consist of 7,491 km on the Atlantic Ocean.

Border disputes exist on two short sections of boundary with Uruguay, at the Rincón Artigas, which resulted from what Uruguay's claim was a wrongful determination of the *Arroyo Invernada,* and at the Isla Brasilera, in the confluence of the Cuareim River and the Uruguay River.

The Brazilian climate is mostly tropical. It has noticeable seasonal variations in rain, temperature and humidity, but only the south has extreme seasonal changes. The Brazilian winter is from June to August, with the coldest southern states receiving average winter temperatures of between 13°C and 18°C (55°F and 64°F). The average temperature in Rio de Janeiro is 26°C (79°F) during the summer (December to February) and 22°C (72°F) during the winter (June to August).

Brazil can be divided into four major geographic regions: The Atlantic coastal ranges, the *Planalto Brasileiro,* or central plateau, the Paraguay Basin and the Amazon Basin.

Brazil has natural resources in the form of bauxite, gold, iron ore, manganese, nickel, phosphates, platinum, tin, uranium, petroleum, hydropower, timber, soy beans, sugar cane, meats, and coffee.

Land use includes 8.45% for arable land and permanent cropland of only 0.83%, with the balance in other uses.

Environmental issues include deforestation in the Amazon Basin, air and water pollution, land degradation, solid waste management, and water pollution.

2. History and Overview

In 1500, Pedro Alvares Cabral claimed Brazil a colony of Portugal. In 1808, Brazil became a kingdom under Dom Joao VI, who returned to Portugal in 1821. It was a kingdom until September 7, 1822, when Dom Pedro I, son of Dom Joao VI, declared its independence. He then became its emperor. His son, Dom Pedro II, ruled from 1831 to 1889, when a federal republic was established after a coup by Deodoro da Fonseca, Marshal of the army. From 1889 to 1930, the government was a constitutional democracy. This period ended with a military coup that placed Getulio Vargas in the presidency. He remained as dictator until 1945. Between 1945 and 1946, José Linhares provisionally acted as president. From 1946 to 1961, Eurico Dutra, Getúlio Vargas, `João Café`, Juscelino Kubitschek, and Janio Quadros, respectively, were elected presidents. When Quadros resigned

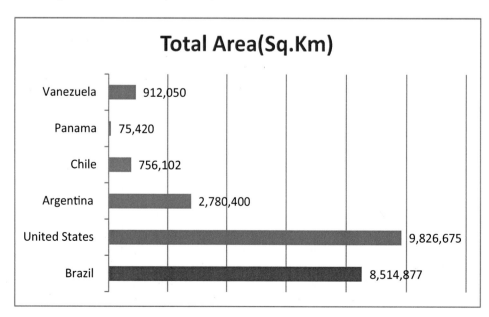

Total Area(Sq.Km)

Vanezuela	912,050
Panama	75,420
Chile	756,102
Argentina	2,780,400
United States	9,826,675
Brazil	8,514,877

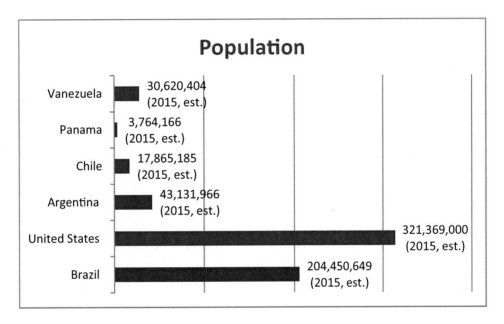

Population

Country	Population
Vanezuela	30,620,404 (2015, est.)
Panama	3,764,166 (2015, est.)
Chile	17,865,185 (2015, est.)
Argentina	43,131,966 (2015, est.)
United States	321,369,000 (2015, est.)
Brazil	204,450,649 (2015, est.)

in 1961, Vice President João Goulart succeeded him. JoãoGoular remained in office until a coup on March 31, 1964. The coup leaders chose Humberto Castelo Branco as president followed by Arthur da Costa e Silva (1967-69), Emilio Garrastazu Medici (1968-74), and Ernesto Geisel (1974-79), all of whom were senior army officers. Geisel began a democratic government that was continued by his successor, Gen. JoãoBaptista de Oliveira Figueiredo (1979-85). In January 1985, Tancredo Neves, the first civilian president since 1964, was elected for office; however, he died on April 21. His Vice President, Jose Sarney, became President upon Neves' death. Brazil completed its transition to a popularly elected government in 1989, when Fernando Collor de Mello won 53% of the vote in the first direct presidential election in 29 years. In 1992, a corruption scandal led to the resignation of President Collor de Mello.

Vice President Itamar Franco took his place and governed for the remainder of Collor's term, culminating in the October 3, 1994 presidential elections, when Fernando Henrique Cardoso was elected President. He took office January 1, 1995 and was re-elected in October, 1998 for a second four-year term. President Cardoso sought to establish the basis for long-term stability, growth and to reduce Brazil's extreme socioeconomic imbalances, with uneq ual income distribution remaining a pressing problem. Cardoso was succeeded by Luiz Inácio "Lula" da Silva who promised to focus his term on land reform, overhaul of the tax and pension systems and minimum-wage increases, as well as Zero Hunger. Lula has been compared to Castro; and he has acknowledged his admiration for Cuba's former leader, Fidel Castro. Luiz Inácio "Lula"da Silva was replaced on January 1, 2011, by his protégé and former Chief of Staff, Dilma Rousseff. She was elected, in a second round of voting, with 56% of the votes, and became Brazil's first female president. In 2014, Dilma Rousseff was re-elected, in a second round, for a second presidential term, with 52% of the votes.

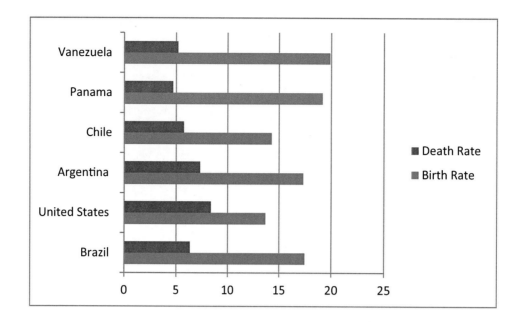

This re-election occurred amid corruption and poor services protests in the country.

Brazil, the largest and most populous country in South America, is a land of diverse culture. Many non-indigenous people are the descendants of Italians, Japanese, Africans, Germans, and the Portuguese. Hence, Brazil is the only Portuguese-speaking nation in South America. Its predominant religion is Roman Catholic (74%). Most of the population, close to 84%, lives in urban areas. The majority of the population lives in the south-central area, in industrial cities, such as São Paulo, Rio de Janeiro, and Belo Horizonte. An estimated 11.895 million people live in São Paulo (est. 2014), which is the biggest city in South America. Many of São Paulo's residents are descendants of Italian and Japanese immigrants. The largest Japanese community outside Japan is in Sao Paulo.

■ 3. People

Brazil has **204,450,649** (2015, est.) people. The age structure is approximately 23.2% in the 0 to 14-year-old category, and 68.9% in the 15-year-old through 64-year-old category. The balance, a small percentage of around 7.9%, is in the 65-year- old and older group.

Life expectancy for the male population is 72.46 years (2015, est.) The female life expectancy is 79.56 years (2015, est.) The population growth rate is 0.83% (2015, est.) Birth rates are about 14.16 in 1,000 of population (2015, est.) The death rate is 6.08 in 1,000 (2015, est.)

Ethnic divisions in Brazil include white for 47.7% of the population, and *mulatto* at 43.1% of the population. The balance is approximately 7.6% black, and the remaining are Japanese, Arab, Amerindian and others.

The dominant religion, Roman Catholic, is 64.6% of the population, and the rest is a mix of other religions, such as Indian animism, African cults, Afro-Catholic syncretism and Kardecism, a spiritualist religion embracing Eastern mysticism. The dominant language is Portuguese. It is the official language, but languages such as Spanish, English, French are also spoken. Portuguese is infused with many words from Indian and African languages. It is spoken with different accents, dialects and slang. Literacy is approximately 90.4% (2011, est.)

■ 4. Government

Brazil is a Federative Republic, with the capital located in Brasilia. There are 26 states or administrative-type divisions, known as *Estados*, and one Federal District, *Distrito Federal*.

Brazil gained its independence from Portugal on September 7, 1822. This date is their national holiday of Independence. The current Constitution was formed on October 5, 1988. The legal system in Brazil follows the Roman Codes. It has not accepted compulsory International Code of Jurisprudence (ICJ) jurisdiction. The government consists of Executive, Legislative, and Judicial Branches.

The Executive Branch consists of a President, a Vice President, and a Cabinet, appointed by the President. The Legislative Branch is a bicameral National Congress, *Congresso Nacional* that consists of the Federal Senate, *Senado Federal*, and the Chamber of Deputies, *Câmara dos Deputados*. The Judicial Branch consists of a supreme Federal tribunal, *Supremo Tribunal Federal*. Diplomatic representation exists with the United States. There is a Brazilian office in Washington, D.C. The U.S. diplomatic representation exists with an Embassy in Brasilia.

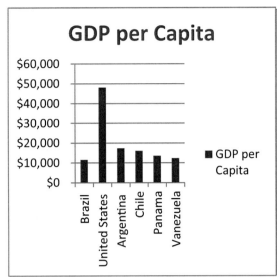

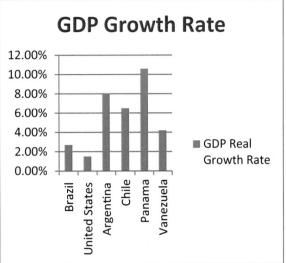

5. Economy

The Brazilian economy, the most diversified economy in South America, is dominated by agricultural, mining, manufacturing, and service products. Although stratospheric inflation rates disrupted the economy in Brazil in 1994, with often 50% monthly and up to 2,000% annual inflation rates, recently Brazil's economy has an inflation rate that is roughly 6.2% on consumer prices (2013 est.) The Gross Domestic Product (GDP) per capita is $11,208.1 (2013, est.) Brazil's GDP growth rate is 2.5% (2013, est.) Unemployment is 5.9% (2013 est.), remaining below 10% during the last few years. Industries include textiles, iron ore, soybeans, coffee, motor vehicles and parts, other machinery and equipment. Brazil exported an estimated $242.178 billion (2013, est.) In 2013, Brazil imported $239.621 billion, mostly in petroleum oils and oils obtained from bituminous minerals, motor cars and motor vehicles, electronic integrated circuits, and natural gas.

Brazil's major trading partners are the China, United States, Argentina, Germany, Netherlands, Japan and Nigeria.

6. Currency

Currency is the *Real* (R$), consisting of 100 cents in one (1) Real. See the Burns School Global Real Estate Web site for the UNIVERSITY OF DENVER at http://burns.daniels.du.edu for currency conversions.

7. Transportation

Brazil has approximately 28,538 kilometers (km) (467 km electrified) of railroad lines, excluding urban rail, and 1,580,964 km of roadways, with 212,798 km of the roadways being paved.

There are 50,000 km of inland waterways in Brazil that can accept larger vessels for shipping. With petroleum being an important export product in Brazil, pipelines are very important to transport crude oil and other petroleum products, along with natural gas. Brazil has numerous ports for shipping, including those such as Belem, Fortaleza, Ilheus, Imbituba, Manaus, Paranagua, Porto Alegre, Recife, Rio de Janeiro, Rio Grande, Salvador, Santos, and Vitoria. Airports number 4,093 in Brazil; 698 have paved runways. Many of the airports are able to handle major jets.

8. Communications

In 2012, Brazil had 44.3 million main telephone lines in use, and 248.324 million mobile cellular phones. It also has an extensive microwave radio relay system and a domestic satellite system with 64 earth stations.

Brazil has numerous radio stations and television stations.

9. Real Property Issues

Real estate professionals share transaction information in a system similar to the United States and the use of the MLS. The first MLS publicly known was launched in 1995, by Secovi-SP (*Sindicato das Empresas de Compra, Venda, Locação e Administração de Imóveis Residenciais e Comerciais de São Paulo*) and *Bolsa Nacional de Imóveis* (BNI), under the *Sistema Integrado de Vendas Autorizadas* (SIVA). Secovi-SP, currently offers MLS services via its *Rede Secovi de Inmóveis* (Secovi's Properties Network). There are also smaller, local services that share the same information. The seller, in general, pays the broker's commission, which is usually between 5% to 6%, or as determined regionally by the *Conselho Regional de Corretores de Imóveis*

(CRECI), Regional Council of Real Estate Brokers, on residential, commercial and land transactions. CRECIs act under the supervision of the Conselho Federal de Corretores de Imóveis do Brasil (COFECI), Federal Council of Real Estate Brokers of Brazil. Although the association to which the broker belongs typically suggests the commissions, commissions are a matter of negotiation. In Brazil, a broker may specialize and expand sales services by including services for development, leasing, and property management. The typical services offered by brokers include showing and advertising the property, negotiating the sale and drawing up legal contracts for sale. Other professionals who might be included in the formation of a sale could include bankers, lenders or appraisers. Real estate trade associations includes *the Sindicato de Emprasas de Compras, Venda, Locacaoe Administracao de Inoveis Residenciaise Comerciais de São Paulo (http://www.secovi-sp.com.br), a/k/a SECOVI- SP, Sindicato da Industria da Construcão Civil do Estado de Sao Paulo (www.sindusconsp.com.br), Federação Nacional dos Corretores de Imóveis (http://www.fenaci.org.br), a/k/a FENACI,* and FIABCI (http://www.fiabci.com), the international association of real estate agents that is based out of Paris, France. SECOVI, founded in 1946, is a non-governmental association of real estate companies, not individual real estate professionals. SECOVI is the most influential real estate trade association in Brazil. SECOVI has a bilateral cooperation agreement with the National Association of REALTORS®. Other affiliations include FIABCI, Urban Land Institute, and the REALTOR® Association of Miami. *Revista Secovi-SP Condomínios* is a real estate trade magazine published by SECOVI in Portuguese, which 25,000 copies are printed and distributed monthly to real estate professionals. Both members and non- members may place ads in *Secovi-SP Condomínios* (http://www.revistasecovicondominios.com.br/). Non- Brazilian investors must rely on the local newspaper to place ads, or in real estate companies with franchises in Brazil (e.g. RE/MAX, Colliers, CBRE, Jones Lang LaSalle). The Brazilian government requires that all real estate brokers and agents have a license to practice, although a high school level education (typically a trade school) is the maximum level of education that is required. There is no requirement for continuing education. The requirement of a license is a fairly recent development. There are approximately 300,000 (2015, est.) real estate practitioners in Brazil. The Brazilian Federation establishes rural real property taxes, and municipalities establish urban real property taxes. Municipalities, under Federal constitution law, also determine eminent domain, escheat, and police power. Taxation of real property transfers is a power of the States of Federative Republic of Brazil. Each state enacts transfer taxation rate, or *Imposto de Transmissão de Bens Inter Vivos* (ITBI). For example, in the Federal District (Brasilia) and Rio de Rio De Janeiro the ITBI is 2% while in São Paulo the ITBI is 3%. The tax is collected from the person acquiring the property or right. Deeds are used to convey real property. They must be signed by both parties, notarized and provide two witnesses. To be valid, the deed is recorded or registered in the public registry. All deeds and mortgages are to be registered in the registries in charge of public officials (registrars) for authentication, conservation, and to establish validity against third parties. Upon death, property is divided equally among married couples with transfer requirements remaining the same. Elements of a contract include two willing and able participants who come together to transfer the title to a specific good or property in consideration of a payment by the other party. A third party may be involved to determine an equitable price. Real estate sales may be recorded. The courts can transfer the property to the purchaser, if the seller refuses to execute any final conveyances.

Performance conditions also often exist for sellers involved with an installment sale.

An individual who is registered and is a notary, with power of attorney, prepares the contracts. More than one power of attorney representing a single individual is not allowed. A typical mortgage is for 30 years. The validity is based on the mortgage being recorded on the books of the notary. The notary is charged with the duty of seeing that all taxes have been paid. All mortgages must be inscribed in the registry of the place where the mortgaged property is located. New mortgage instruments may replace old instruments upon term expiration, prior to being liened. Property can be foreclosed when the debt or is deemed insolvent or has defaulted. Defaults often result in a higher rate of interest and penalty fees, rather than foreclosure. Lenders may not assume ownership of property in a residential mortgage default. They must attempt to sell the property and apply the proceeds towards fulfilling the mortgage amount. Investors who are not Brazilian are allowed to own property in their own name. However, there are limitations on real estate transactions involving non-Brazilian investors. An investor who is not Brazilian must seek the approval of the government when buying, selling, or investing in real estate. Such an investor may also be prohibited from buying large areas of land, ocean-front real estate, and real estate close to the national border. There are no Brazilian restrictions placed upon Brazilian investors who invest in other countries.

Due to the World Cup and Olympic Games, in 2014 and 2016 respectively, Brazil has seen a significant growth in real estate developments. Mostly in its principal cities, such as Rio de Janeiro and São Paulo. As of the third quarter of 2014, it is estimated that Rio de Janeiro has over 1.8 million square meters and São Paulo has over 3.8 million square meters of rentable Class AA & A office space, with a vacancy rate of 16.8% and 20.7% respectively.

In the first quarter of 2015, residential mortgage percent rates for new homes would be around 10%, from private institutions, such as HSBC or Banco Santander, for a 15 year term loan. The loan-to-value ratio for these private institutions would be around 70 to 80%. Public institutions offer subsidized mortgages, in which case the terms are significantly more attractive, but not everyone may qualify. The terms may be: 5% APR, loan-to-value of 90%, and a term of 30 years. Restrictions regarding the maximum value of the property to be financed and the amount on the monthly payments in relation with the beneficiary's monthly income will apply.

10. Real Estate Trends

A number of strong web site links help to acquire information in Brazil, especially those from the National Association of REALTORS®, the Miami Association of REALTORS®, CB Richard Ellis, Jones Lang LaSalle, and the Burns School Global Real Estate Web site, Daniels *College of Business*, UNIVERSITY OF DENVER at http://burns.daniels.du.edu.

11. Cultural Issues

Any nation's culture is complex and vibrant in its diversity.
While broad cultural characterizations such as those presented here can be generally accurate, following such generalities too strictly may be dangerously misleading. To conduct business effectively and profitably in a country, it is vital to have a thorough understanding of its culture's complexities. Brazilians prefer to wear European fashions, specifically Italian and French. The people are very fashion conscious, especially the women. While Brazilians greet each other with a handshake; but, good friends often embrace. Women often kiss each other on alternating cheeks, although they may not actually touch cheeks and only "kiss the air." Common terms are *Tudo bem?* (Is everything fine?) *or Como vai?* (How are you?). Much of the activity when visiting, using gestures and eating are similar to those customs in the United States.

12. Discussion Questions

1. What influence, if any, does the life expectancy in Brazil have on the overall economy?

2. Brazil is the fifth largest country by land size. What are the four larger countries (land size)?

3. What are the considerations a foreigner (non-Brazilian) should have if deciding to invest in Brazil?

13. Case Study

White Elephant Construction, Inc. (Elephant) Rio de Janeiro, Brazil

Memo

To: Board of Directors of White Elephant Construction
From: Consultants
Re: Purchasing new buildings

I. Problem

White Elephant Construct ion, Inc. (Elephant) was formed to purchase office building, apartments and other construction projects that had been partially built, but not completed in Brazil. The buildings are called "white elephants" or *elefante branco*. These buildings were not finished usually due to a lack of funds for construction or development. Elephant entered Brazil and attempted to purchase these types of buildings and then turn around and sell them. Initially, Elephant was able to purchase one building, and it finished the project. There are three current projects that White Elephant Construction is attempting to purchase. So far Elephant has been unable to complete any additional purchases. Elephant has been operating in Brazil for over a year. (Only one project has been completed and the project has yet to sell.) The fact that Elephant hired an interpreter and felt that it could do the selling and purchasing on its own has been a major point of contention within the Company.

II. Initial Exit Strategy

The initial exit strategy for the Company was simple. When the time came for Elephant to exit the market, it would just sell the properties and not purchase any others. This seemed to be a logical approach. However, now, with the roadblocks that Elephant is facing when trying to purchase any new properties, and the fact that the single building it has been able to finish has not sold, the Company is taking a fresh look at its plans.

Options

There seem to be some options if, as a Company, Elephant determines it can hold to its approach. The three options suggested are as follows:

1. Elephant will hold onto the building that it currently owns and go into the management business.
2. Elephant will cease its attempt to sell and purchase on its own. It may hire a Brazilian broker, who can help Elephant market the existing property and possibly help find other properties to purchase.
3. The last option is to get out of the market. With only one building currently owned, Elephant might be able to limit its losses. However, if Elephant continues without assistance, it may be the destruction of the company.

Some of the options may be considered.

Once each of these options has been thoroughly analyzed by members of the Board of Directors, with a more complete audit of the market, the Company will be better able to make a decision.

III. Contingency Exit Strategy

In the event that none of the three options listed above, or any others that are raised, during the next few weeks, are unacceptable, Elephant needs to be prepared as to how it will exit the market. The first step should be to attempt to lease the existing building. Elephant needs to hire a local company from Brazil to oversee lease work on the building. Once the building has been leased, Elephant again can put the property on the market, using a Brazilian agent. A complete market study will need to be completed. If none of the options were successful, the last and least desirable option would be to sell the building as a "white elephant" at any price.

IV. Conclusion

Hiring local real estate professional needs to be Elephant's first step in continuing or exiting the market. The construction business seems to be increasing in Brazil. Elephant needs to look at the effect of working with local experienced agents, If after six months the property does not sell, we will need to re-evaluate the Company's approach. If the property does sell, we will need to re-evaluate the company's approach. If the property does sell, and at a good price, the Company may want to go forward with the plan to purchase other buildings. If the Company does not succeed in selling the one building it now owns, it must look at how long the Company is willing to support this business. It *might be a good idea to get out now, if losses will continue.*

Refer to: *International Real Estate Digest. Homepage.* http://www.ired.com.

U.S. Department of State. Homepage. http://www.state.gov. U.S. Embassy. Homepage. http://usembassy.state.gov.

Communicate.com Inc. Brazil.com. Communicate.com, Inc. (online). Available at http://www.brazil.com.

14. Selected References

Central Intelligence Agency. *World Factbook: Brazil.* Central Intelligence Agency (online) at https://www.cia.gov/library/publications/the-world-factbook/index.html.

International Real Estate Digest. Homepage. http://www.ired.com.

Organization of American States at http://www.oas.org. U.S. Bureau of Census at http://www.census.gov.

U.S. Bureau of Economic Analysis at http://www.bea.gov. U.S. Department of Commerce at http://www.stat-usa.gov.

United States Department of State. *Background Notes: Brazil.* United States Department of State (Online). Available: http://www.state.gov.

U.S. Department of State. Homepage. http://www.state.gov. U.S. Embassy. Homepage http://usembassy.state.gov. World Trade Centers Institute at http://www.wtci.org.

World Trade Organization at http://www.wto.org.

World Bank. World *Bank Brazil.* World Bank (Online). Available: http://www.worldbank.org.

Frontera Uruguay – Brasil. Límites Contestados: Rincón de Artigas and Isla Brasilera, Aguilar, G., http://eva.universidad.edu.uy/mod/resource/view.php?id=160968

Instituto Nacional de Meteorologia, Clima, Normais Climatológicas do Brasil 1961-1990, Mapas: Tem. Méd. Compensada (°C), Planilhas: Temp. Méd. Compensada (°C), Código: 83743, Nome da Estação: Rio de Janeiro, http://www.inmet.gov.br/portal/index.php?r=clima/normaisClimatologicas

United Nations Data, Country Profile: Brazil, https://data.un.org/CountryProfile.aspx?crname=Brazil

Brazil, Brazil Environmental Issues, http://www.brazil.org.za/environmental-issues.html

The World Bank, Projects & Operations, http://www.worldbank.org/projects?lang=en

Instituto Brasileiro de Geografia e Estatística, 2010 Population Census Summary, Tables (in zip), Tabela 1.11 - População residente, por situação do domicílio e sexo segundo as Grandes Regiões e as Unidades da Federação – 2010, http://www.ibge.gov.br/english/estatistica/populacao/censo2010/sinopse/sinopse_tab_brasil_zip.shtm

Instituto Brasileiro de Geografia e Estatística, 2010 Population Census Summary, Tabela 1.6 - População nos Censos Demográficos, segundo os municípios das capitais - 1872/2010, http://www.ibge.gov.br/english/estatistica/populacao/censo2010/sinopse/sinopse_tab_brasil_zip.shtm

Instituto Brasileiro de Geografia e Estatística, **Population estimates for the Brazilian municipalities on 07.01.2014,** Table of estimates by municipality (in zipped xls format), http://www.ibge.gov.br/english/estatistica/populacao/estimativa2014/estimativa_dou.shtm

World Statesmen.org, Nations and Territories: Brazil, http://www.worldstatesmen.org/Brazil.html

Instituto Nacional de Estadística y Censos, Población, Proyecciones Nacionales, Población por sexo y grupos quinquenales de edad. Años 2010-2040, http://www.indec.mecon.ar/nivel4_default.asp?id_tema_1=2&id_tema_2=24&id_tema_3=84

Ministerio del Poder Popular de Planificación, Instituto Nacional de Estadística, Demográficos - Proyecciones de Población: Venezuela. Proyección de la población, según entidad y sexo, 2000-2050 (año calendario), http://www.ine.gov.ve/index.php?option=com_content&view=category&id=98&Itemid=51

Estimaciones y Proyecciones de la Población en la República de Panamá, por Provincia. Comarca Indígena, Distrito y Corregimiento, Según Sexo: Años 2000-2015, Boletín No. 10, https://www.contraloria.gob.pa/inec/Archivos/P2391Boletin10.pdf

Boletín No. 10, https://www.contraloria.gob.pa/inec/Archivos/P2391Boletin10.pdfInstituto Nacional de Estadísticas, Chile, Demográficas y Vitales, Demografía, Población, País y Regiones. Actualización Población 2002-2012 y Proyecciones 2013-2020, http://www.ine.cl/canales/chile_estadistico/demografia_y_vitales/demografia/pdf/poblacion_sociedad_enero09.pdf

Instituto Brasileiro de Geografia e Estatística (IBGE), Diretoria de Pesquisas. Coordenação de População e Indicadores Sociais. Gerência de Estudos e Análises da Dinâmica Demográfica http://www.ibge.gov.br/home/estatistica/populacao/projecao_da_populacao/2013/default_tab.shtm

Congresso Nacional, http://www.congressonacional.leg.br/portal/

Supremo Tribunal Federal, http://www.stf.jus.br/portal/principal/principal.asp

World Bank, World Integrated Trade Solution, Trade Stats by Country, Brazil GDP per Capita (Current US$) 2009-2013, http://wits.worldbank.org/CountryProfile/Country/BRA/StartYear/2009/EndYear/2013/Indicator/NY-GDP-PCAP-CD

World Bank, World Integrated Trade Solution, Trade Stats by Country, Brazil Trade Summary 2013 Data, http://wits.worldbank.org/CountryProfile/Country/BRA/Year/2013/Summary

The World Bank, Research, Global Economic Prospects, Country and Region Specific Forecasts and Data, http://www.worldbank.org/en/publication/global-economic-prospects/data?region=LAC

The World Bank, Data, Inflation, Consumer Prices (Annual %), http://data.worldbank.org/indicator/FP.CPI.TOTL.ZG?display=default

United Nations Data, Country Profile: Brazil, https://data.un.org/CountryProfile.aspx?crName=Brazil

The World Bank, Data, Unemployment, Total (% of Total Labor Force), http://data.worldbank.org/indicator/SL.UEM.TOTL.ZS/countries

"Imobiliárias já têm sistema de venda integrada", Folha De S.Paulo, Mercado, September 21, 1995, http://webcache.googleusercontent.com/search?q=cache:-WusUDuBINAJ:www1.folha.uol.com.br/fsp/1995/9/21/dinheiro/16.html+&cd=2&hl=en&ct=clnk&gl=us

National Association of REALTORS, International Operations Division, The Americas and International Real Estate: Certified International Property Specialist Network Course Manual, 2006, Chapter 6-14, http://www.rebac.net/Teach/CIPS/Americas/2006/2006AmericasStudentManual.pdf

Conselho Federal de Corretores de Imóveis, Sistema Cofeci-Creci, http://www.cofeci.gov.br

International Consortium of Real Estate Associations, World Properties.com, Country Info: Brazil, FENACI-Business-Practices, http://www.worldproperties.com/en/CountryInfo/Brazil/Brazil-Fenaci/Fenaci-Business-Practices.aspx

Jones Lang LaSalle, On Point: Pesquisa Imobiliária|Real Estate Research: Rio de Janeiro, Escritórios AA & A|Class AA & A Offices, 3° trim. 2014|Q3 2014, http://www.jll.com.br/brazil/en-us/Research/On%20point_RJ_3T2014.pdf?d19bac34-9e2c-4550-aabd-d5635937840b

Jones Lang LaSalle, On Point: Pesquisa Imobiliária|Real Estate Research: São Paulo, Escritórios AA & A|Class AA & A Offices, 3° trim. 2014|Q3 2014, http://www.jll.com.br/brazil/en-us/Research/On%20point_SP_3T2014.pdf?6c583325-8819-4cb3-90db-70f62bea4127

Jones Lang LaSalle, Brazil Retail Overview 2013-2014, http://www.jll.com.br/brazil/en-us/Research/JLL%20-%20Brazil%20Retail%20Overview.pdf?7a05a62d-8995-4009-9939-c82e2141031c

Brazil Investment Guide, Taxation for the Brazil Real Estate and Land Investor, 5. Imposto de Transmissão de Bens Inter Vivos (ITBI): Property Transfer Tax, http://www.brazilinvestmentguide.com/information/taxation-for-the-brazil-real-estate-and-land-investor.pdf

National Association of Realtors, The Global View|Blog: How Many Real Estate Professionals Exists Worldwide?, Hornberger, J., January 2015, http://theglobalview.blogs.realtor.org/2015/01/21/how-many-real-estate-professionals-exist-worldwide/

The Brazil Business, How to Become a Realtor in Brazil, Duran, R., April 15, 2013, http://thebrazilbusiness.com/article/how-to-become-a-realtor-in-brazil

Thomson Reuters, Practical Law, Commercial real estate in Brazil: Overview, Moreira, C., Mamprin, C., and Bérgamo, M., http://us.practicallaw.com/5-503-6987

Buying Real Estate in Brazil – Part 1, Locke, F. http://www.gringoes.com/articles.asp?ID_Noticia=896

Buying Real Estate in Brazil – Part 2, Locke, F., http://gringste.nextmp.net/buying-real-estate-in-brazil-part-2/

Buying Real Estate in Brazil – Part 3, Locke, F., http://www.gringoes.com/articles.asp?ID_Noticia=928

HSBC, Crédito Imobiliário, http://www.hsbc.com.br/1/2/br/para-voce/credito/emprestimos-e-financiamentos/credito-imobiliario?WT.ac=HBBR_MMCCC107

Santander, Crédito Inmobiliário, http://www.santander.com.br/portal/wps/script/templates/GCMRequest.do?page=6287

Caixa, Aquisição de imóvel novo, http://www.caixa.gov.br/voce/habitacao/financiamento/aquisicao-imovel-novo/Paginas/default.aspx

15. Glossary

Sindicato de Emprasas de Compras, Venda, Locacao e Administracao de Inoveis Residenciais e Comerciais de São Paulo (SECOVI-SP) – A real estate trade association that has a bilateral cooperation with the National Association of REALTORS®.

Sistema Intergrado de endas Autorizadas (SIVA) – A system similar to the multiple- listing service (MLS) in the United States.

About the Author

José F. Ramirez was born in Caracas, Venezuela, where he earned a degree in civil engineering at the Universidad Central de Venezuela. He later earned a, in the United Stated, a diploma in business administration from the University of California – Berkeley; a master's in real estate and construction management from the Burns School of Real Estate and Construction Management, *Daniels College of Business,* UNIVERSITY OF DENVER; and, in Australia, a Master of Construction Law from the University of Melbourne. At the beginning of his career, he actively appraised residential real estate in Venezuela. A few years later, he actively participated in the design and development of commercial real estate in that country. More recently he has provided consulting construction and real estate services for commercial real estate in Colombia, United States and Venezuela. He currently works as a consultant for the construction and real estate development industries in the United States.

Canada

INTERNATIONAL REAL ESTATE (GLOBAL REAL ESTATE)

Dr. Mark Lee Levine, Editor

■ 1. Geography

Canada is located in the northern part of North America, which borders on the North Atlantic Ocean and the North Pacific Ocean, with the mass of the land structure located north of the United States of America.

The Canadian land area is 9,984,670 km², slightly larger than the United States. It shares common boundaries with Alaska and mostly with the United States. It has a coastline of 202,080 km. There are border disputes, as a result of ownership claims by Canada, especially disputes involving France.

The climate is fairly temperate in the south, and subarctic and arctic in the north. Terrain consists basically of plains and mountain areas in the west, and lowlands in the southeast.[46]

Land use consists of 4.57% arable land, about 3% with meadows and pastures, and over half, approximately 54%, in forests and woodland areas.

There are a number of environmental problems that are typical of larger Western countries considered as "first-world countries." These include air pollution that causes acid rain damage to forests and oceans. Canada is the second largest country in geographic area, after Russia.

■ 2. History and Overview

U.S. and Canadian relations have been very close over many years. The U.S. and Canadian governments work closely on many multilateral issues. Canada is a member of the North Atlantic Treaty Organization (NATO), a member of the Organization of American States (OAS), and it has sought to expand economic ties with numerous other countries. Trade and investment issues between the United States and Canada provide for substantial economic growth for Canada. In fact the amount of goods traded between the U.S. and Canada exceeds U.S. trade with all of the European Union (EU). The Province of Quebec and the separatist movement there remains an important concern. Following the failure of two constitutional initiatives in the last 14 years, Canada is still seeking a constitutional arrangement that will satisfy the aspirations of the French-speaking province of Quebec. The issue has been a fixture in Canadian history, dating back to the 18th century rivalry between France and Britain. For more than a century, Canada was a French colony. Although New France came under British control in 1759, it was permitted to retain its religious and civil code. The early 1960s brought a "Quiet Revolution" to Quebec, leading to a new assertiveness and heightened sense of identity among the French-speaking *Quebecois*, who make up 23.2% of Canada's population. In 1976, the separatist *Parti Quebecois* won the provincial election and began to explore a course of greater independence for Quebec. This led to a 1980 referendum in which the *Parti Quebecois* unsuccessfully sought a mandate from Quebeckers to negotiate a political independence for Quebec. Subsequently, an agreement between the federal government and all the provincial governments except Quebec led to Canada assuming from the United Kingdom full responsibility for its own constitution. Quebec objected to the new arrangement, particularly to a provision that did not require

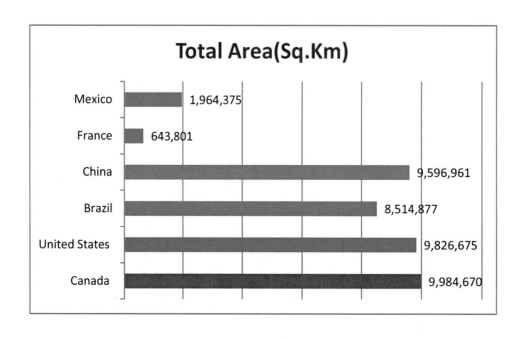

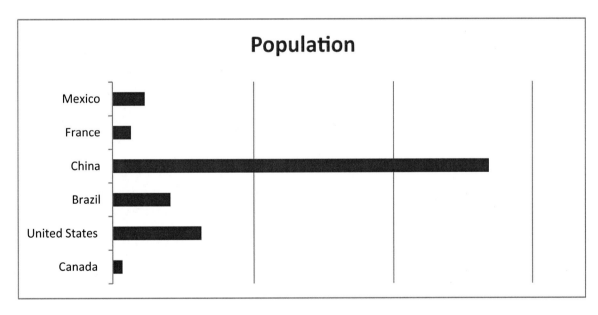

the consent of all provinces for constitutional amendments. Several attempts to find a formula to include Quebec failed, leading in 1995 to another referendum on sovereignty in Quebec. This time the *Parti Quebecois* lost by slightly over 1% in its bid to win a mandate to negotiate political independence. The 1995 referendum proved a high water mark, and since that time support for holding a third referendum has declined. Though the Parti *Quebecois* is still in power in Quebec, sentiment for separatism seems to be declining, and another referendum is unlikely in the near future.[48]

3. People

Canada has a population of **34,834,841** people (2014) and an age structure consisting of 15.5% in the 0 to 14 age group; 67.2% in the 15 through 64 age group; and the balance of the population, 17.3%, is in the age brackets of 65 years of age and older.

The population growth rate is 0.784%, with birth rates being about 10.28 out of every 1,000. The population growth rate is 0.76%, with birth rates being about 10.29 out of every 1,000 population. The death rate is approximately 8.31 per 1,000.

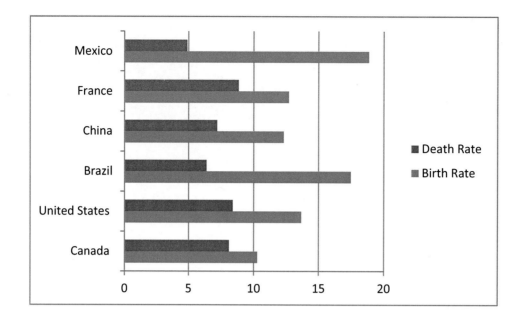

Migration rates have been 5.66 out of 1,000, with infant mortality rates of 4.71out of 1,000. Life expectancy is 81.67 years, including 79.07 years for males, and 84.42 years for females.

Ethnic groups include those of British Isles origin with 19.8%, the French with 15.5%, other Europeans with 15%, and Native American with 4.2%. There is a mix of other ethnic groups, with mostly being Asians. Religious positions include 40.6% of the population practicing as Roman Catholic, 20.3% as Protestants, and the balance practicing other religions.

Official languages are English and French. Literacy is 99% of the populace 15 years of age or older. The labor force consists of 19.21 million people (2014 est.)

4. Government

The government in Canada is a federation of provinces under a parliamentary democracy with a constitutional monarchy. The capital is Ottawa, in the province of Ontario. There are ten Provinces and three Territories. Independence was July 1, 1867, from the United Kingdom. Canadian Day is July 1, (1867). The Constitution is the amended British North American Act of 1867. The legal system is based on the English common law system, with the exception of Quebec, where the civil law system was passed based on the French law. Voting suffrage is 18 years of age and is universal for male and female. The ceremonial branches of government include the Chief of State, Queen Elizabeth II of Great Britain, who is represented by the Governor General. However, the government is led by the Prime Minister, who chooses a Cabinet, the *Federal Ministry*, from among members of the Prime Minister's own Party sitting in Parliament. The leader is of the Majority Party in the House of Commons, who is automatically designated by the Governor General as the Prime Minister.

Branches of the government consist of an Executive Branch, Legislative Branch, and Judicial Branch with a Supreme Court. Diplomatic representation exists between the United States and numerous other countries.

5. Economy

The Canadian economy is a strong, high-tech industrial society resembling the structure of the United States in per capita output, market position, and general production patterns. The Gross Domestic Product (GDP) is $1.794 trillion (2014 est.) The GDP per capita is $44,500. The GDP real growth rate is 2.3%. The inflation rate at 2% (2014) and unemployment rate at 6.9% (2014) have been fairly stable, and are comparable to the United States.

6. Currency

The Canadian currency is the *Canadian dollar (CAD)*. The Canadian dollar rate varies on a daily basis, compared with other countries that fluctuate on the world market. For an examination of currency rates compared with other countries, see the Currency Converter Web link, Burns School Global Real Estate Web site for the UNIVERSITY OF DENVER at http://burns.daniels.du.edu.

7. Transportation

Canada has 46,552 km (kilometers) of railroad tracks as well as a substantial land system, including 1,042,300 km of roadways. However, due to its large landmass, only approximately 40% of

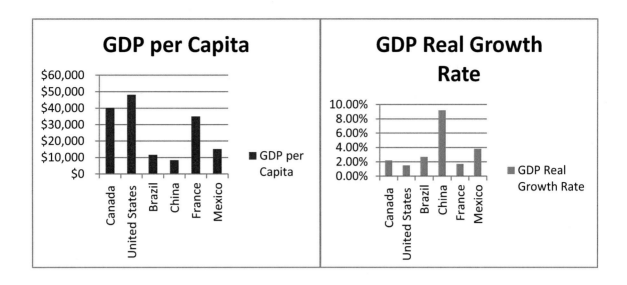

the roadways are paved. Canada has many inland waterways, with emphasis on the St. Lawrence Seaway. Canada uses ports to export and import goods, for cruises and resort activities, and for commercial trade to support the country. Airports are substantial throughout Canada; of the 1,467 airports, 523 have paved runways.

■ 8. Communications

Canada has 18.01 million main telephone lines in use and 26.263 million mobile cellular phones. Modern technology has enabled Canada to develop a sophisticated communications system that utilizes many satellite earth stations, including AM and FM radio stations, shortwave radio broadcast stations, and television broadcast stations. Of the country's population, 26.96 million people use the Internet, with 8.743 million Internet service providers (hosts) (2012).

■ 9. Real Property Issues

Acquisition costs for real property often involve commissions being paid; commissions are normally paid by the seller, although this is negotiable. Legal fees are often shared between buyer and seller, as are numerous other expenses involving closing. The Canadian government maintains strong real estate records, which are available for public review. Fees vary between municipalities as to transfers of real estate as well as transaction information. Numerous real estate boards, or their equivalent, and multiple listing services (similar to those in the United States) exist throughout Canada.

The Canadian Real Estate Association (CREA) is a major real estate trade group, 320 Queen Street Suite2100, Tower A, Ottawa, Ontario, Canada K1R5A3 (http://crea.ca/). Licensing and educational certifications vary throughout the Canadian Provinces and are required for real estate brokers. The land description method is similar to that employed in the United States, using a metes-and-bounds system, among others. Rights and interest in land include related issues, such as property or ad valorem property taxes, eminent domain issues, and *escheat*, where property will flow back to the government if there are no beneficiaries from a decedent. Property is affected by police power positions. A spouse has certain property rights on the death of the spouse's mate. Forms of ownership include owning in severalty, tenancy in common, joint tenancy, entities such as partnerships, joint ventures, corporations and trusts. Corporate ownership can be a federal or provincial ownership. Transfer of title is generally through deeds, whether quitclaim or otherwise. Transfer of title can take place by a will, or other means of transfer. Adverse possession exists in Canada and generally requires a ten-year time frame to establish the time period for meeting adverse possession. Recording evidence of title is on public record, through deeds, mortgages and other items of record that reflect claims on property. The four requirements of a contract are generally consideration, mutual assent, legality and capacity. Many standard real estate contract forms are utilized in Canada, usually in connection with the sale and purchase of residential real estate, leasing of real estate and listing agreements. Mortgage documents or other encumbrances are executed showing the claim by the credit or. Canadian loan positions and financing are often similar in concept to the United States.

Government loans and support are often given to businesses, to encourage relocation and establishment of businesses in given areas. There is no time frame limiting the statutory term for the loan, with many residential loans being ten years. There is no allowable deduction for interest paid on home mortgage loans. Property taxes in Canada are levied on a provincial basis. In many jurisdictions, a transfer tax is also levied when property is conveyed. The amount of that tax depends on the province involved. Closing procedures for sale of property are regulated by the Canadian government. The Closing period generally lasts no longer than 60 days, although in some cases it may last longer because of complexities. Appraisals are not required by law, but they are commonly undertaken. Insurance, by law, is required on mortgages. Most lenders will require additional insurance to protect their interests and protect them on their policies on a co-insurance basis.

Land use controls exist in Canada with regard to zoning, private covenants, deed restrictions and a number of items similar to the United States.[52]

Real estate organizations in Canada include the Canadian Real Estate Association as well as a number of other organizations. See the Selected References section in this book.

◼ 10. Real Estate Trends

For a detailed examination of this area involving commercial, industrial, residential and apartment property, see the links in Selected References in this book. For example, see http://www.royallepage.ca.

Trends for real estate and types of real estate are dynamic and vary throughout Canada. In the office market, vacancies range from as low as 8.9% in Vancouver up to 17% in Montreal. The average, per square foot, rents are just as variable. The Class A rental rates of Montreal are nearly double those of Calgary.

There is some consistency in the industrial markets throughout the country. Vancouver and Calgary, however, deviate significantly from data in Canada's other major cities. In general, the Canadian markets have shown increases in vacancy rates and a decline in the net rental asking price per square foot.

◼ 11. Cultural Issues

Any nation's culture is complex and vibrant in its diversity.

While broad cultural characterizations such as those presented here can be generally accurate, following such generalities too strictly may be dangerously misleading. To conduct business effectively and profitably in a country, it is vital to have a thorough understanding of its culture's complexities. The cultural issues span a broad area. Specific issues involve greetings, gestures and personal appearance. Although the dress is similar to that of the United States, Canadians generally seem to be somewhat more conservative in their attire as compared to the United States. Canadians generally seem to be somewhat more conservative in their attire. Greetings are similar to those used in the United States, although in some areas of Canada there are more greetings that employ a light kiss, cheek to cheek.

12. Discussion Questions

1. What are some of the issues regarding disputes between English and French populations in Canada and how do these disputes affect investment opportunities in Canada?

2. What do you think accounts for Canada's strong gross domestic product in relation to its population?

3. Is Canada part of NAFTA and is this a benefit to Canada? Why or why not?

4. Does Canada's close proximity to the United States help or hinder its abilities to attract investors?

13. Case Study

Heli-Skiing Escapes (HSE) Banff, Alberta, Canada

Memo

To: Board of Director
From: Consultants
Re: Lack of snow

I. Problem

Heli-Skiing Escapes (HSE) expanded, from the U.S.A., just over three years into Banff, Alberta, Canada. The first location was outside of Vail, Colorado. Then HSE opened another operation in Utah. The success prompted HSE

to expand into Canada. The market in Canada seemed to be saturated with other operations, but the Board members felt that HSE could offer day heli-skiing, so that many skiers could afford the adventure. This was accomplished because, when HSE expanded into

Canada, HSE was able to reduce costs by not providing lodging, but providing transportation for day heli-skiing from Banff. The first two seasons were great. There was great snow, and there were many referrals from the other two operations. In fact, the first two years exceeded any of HSE's projections. The first year HSE even managed to have the operation featured in a prominent ski film production. This provided wonderful advertising to attract a large variety of skiers. HSE had reserve capital in case of a bad snow year, but only enough to cover us through one year. However, this past season was a very low snow year. HSE did not meet project ions. It barely had enough funds to cover its operating costs. The other problems for HSE had involved vandalism to the helicopters. This required canceling three weeks of reservations in the high season. Insurance barely covered the cost to repair the helicopters, much less the loss of revenue. Another problem this last season was the negative publicity of the boy who was lost temporarily. During a tour, a 12-year-old boy wandered away. He was stranded over night in the backcountry. (If it had not been for the avalanche beeper, HSE would not have been able to locate him.) This negative publicity also reduced HSE's reservations. The tourist industry as a whole has seen a reduction in business.

Currently, for the upcoming season, HSE has only half of the bookings compared with previous seasons. These issues could have been overcome if HSE had only one event per season; however, these events occurred in the same season. The question now is: Should HSE continue the operation in Canada, or does it exit?

II. Initial Exit Strategy

HSE's exit plan, initially, was to transfer all the assets, including the helicopters and the buses, back to one of the operations in the U.S. Currently the HSE Canadian offices are located in the second home of one of the Board of Directors. This makes exiting the office space easy. This was to be the easy way to exit. After the 4th year of operation, HSE's agreement expires with the Canadian government, to operate on National Forest for skiing. If the agreement is renegotiated, at reasonable terms, we would continue. At that point, HSE is planning to establish permanent roots, by renting or buying office space and looking into buying land to build an economy hotel for our guests. If HSE went that far, exiting would be much more difficult. HSE would attempt to sell the business to a competitor or just close down and sublease office space. The helicopters and the ski gear can be transferred, easily, operations.

III. Contingency Exit Strategy

Because HSE is still within the first four years of its business plan – where no permanent office space has been established, and it has not renewed the lease with the government for the use of the backcountry – HSE is able to exit, relatively painlessly. This means that HSE can transfer assets and cancel the reservations, by returning deposits and redirecting guests to competitors. Once this has been completed, HSE just needs to transfer the employees who want to move and lay off the ones who want to stay in Canada.

IV. Conclusion

In light of the recent difficult events of the past year, and the uncertainty that the government will renew the agreement, it is suggested that HSE close the operation in Canada. Implementing the Initial Exit Plan should cover all of the issues and save

HSE money, allowing it to continue to operate in the U.S.

Refer to: X-rates.com. Homepage. http://www.x-rates.com.

U.S. Embassy. Homepage. http://usembassy.state.gov. U.S. Department of State. Homepage. http://www.state.gov.

14. Selected References

Information about the embassy, state governments, local agencies, and other details worldwide can be located here: http://canada.gc.ca. http://www.canadianembassy.org. http:/www.dfait-maeci.gc.ca.

CIA World Factbook at https://www.cia.gov/library/publications/the-world-factbook/index.html.

Organization of American States at http://www.oas.org.

Richard Ellis International Property Specialists. C.B. Richard Ellis. http://www.cbre.com.

Time Almanac. *TIME Almanac.* Boston: Information Please LLC.

United States Department of State. *Background Notes: Canada.* United States

Department of State (Online). Available: http://www.state.gov.

U.S. Bureau of Census at http://www.census.gov. U.S. Department of Commerce at http://www.stat-usa.gov. U.S. Bureau of Economic Analysis at http://www.bea.gov. U.S. Embassy. Homepage. http://usembassy.state.gov. World Trade Centers Institute at http://www.wtci.org. World Trade Organization at http://www.wto.org. World Bank. *Adult Illiteracy Rates.* The Economist. X-rates.com. Homepage. http://www.x-rates.com.

15. Glossary

CREA (Canadian Real Estate Association) – Real Estate trade group.

"Tu va bien?" – French speakers in Canada use this expression meaning, "How are you doing?"

About the Author

Dr. Mark Lee Levine, is the Editor of this Book.

Chile

INTERNATIONAL REAL ESTATE (GLOBAL REAL ESTATE)
Authored by *Jose Ramirez* and *Dr. Mark Lee Levine*, Editor

■ 1. Geography

Chile is located in the southern part of South America; it occupies half of the western border of South America. It borders Argentina and Bolivia to the east; the Pacific Ocean to the west; Peru to the north; and the Drake Passage to the south.

Chile consists of 756,102 sq. kilometers (km) and is a little larger than Texas. Its coastline runs 6.435 km along its west coast.

Border disputes exist with several countries. Bolivia, for example, has wanted a sovereign corridor to the Pacific Ocean, since the Atacama area was lost to Chile in 1884. Also, disputes existed with Bolivia over Rio Lauca water rights, in 1961, after Chile started testing installations that served to produce hydroelectric power as well as irrigation water in Chile's Azapa Valley. This test diverted waters of the Rio Lauca, waters that otherwise would have emptied in Bolivia's Lake Coipasa. This dispute is now just part of a larger issue, and may ultimately be resolved when these two countries potentially settled on Bolivia's outlet to the sea. Other disputes exist with Argentina and the United Kingdom over the Chilean Antarctic Territory that partially overlaps Argentine and British claims.

Chile features a very diverse climate. The northern region is dry and desert like with average temperature of 28°C (82°F). The central region is temperate with average temperature of 14°C (57°F) in winter and 29°C (84°F) in summer. The southern region is cool and damp with an average temperature of 4°C (39°F) in winter and 18°C (64°F) in summer. The average temperature in Santiago during summer (December to February) is 20°C (68°F) and during the winter (June to August) is 9°C (48°F). Chile's seasonal climates are opposite those in the United States.

The terrain includes the Andes Mountains, the Central Valley, and the Coastal Plains. Chile has natural resources in the form of copper, timber, iron ore and steel, nitrates, precious metals, molybdenum, wood and wood products, transport equipment, cement, textiles, grapes, fish meat, and hydropower. Still, Chile's number one export is cooper, which accounted for over 50% of its total exports in 2013.

Land use includes approximately 1.74% of arable land, 0.6% of permanent crops, and 97.65% in other uses, including meadows and pastures. Environmental problems include deforestation, pollution from industrial and vehicle emissions, and water pollution from raw sewage.

Environmental protection efforts include nuclear test bans, ozone protection, desertification, biodiversity, endangered species and marine life conservation, Antarctic environment modification, climate change, and pollution relative to wetlands and other areas. Chile is prone to natural hazards as earthquakes, tsunamis, and volcanoes activity.

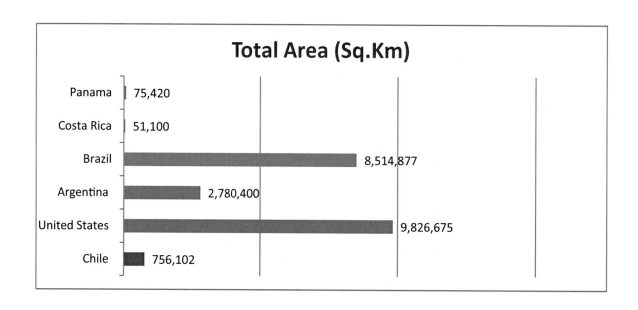

2. History and Overview

Chile's independence from Spain was declared on September 18, 1810, with the creation of a national junta. On February 12, 1818, after a period of eight years, also known as the *Reconquista*, Bernardo O'Higgins formally proclaimed independence. But, it was not until July 14, 1826 when Chile became a fully sovereign country. From 1946 to 1952, Gabriel González Videla served as President. In 1952, General Ibáñez was elected for office until 1958, when Jorge Alessandri Rodríguez was elected to the presidency. Highlight from this period, 1947 to 1958, are that during most of this period the communist party was banned from Chile under the Law for the Defense of Democracy and that Chile broke off diplomatic relations with the Union of Soviet Socialist Republics (USSR).

In 1964 Eduardo Nicanor Frei-Montalva was elected President. He initiated a period of major socioeconomic reforms in Chile that, by 1967, encountered heavily opposition from both the leftist and the conservative parties.

In 1970, Dr. Salvador Allende was elected President. He remained in office until September 11, 1973, when a military coup over threw him. Allende reportedly committed suicide while the armed forces bombarded the presidential palace. After Allende's death, the military took power and ruled by a junta headed by Augusto Pinochet Ugarte. His dictatorial regime continued until December 1989, when Presidential and Legislative elections were held in Chile for the first time in 19 years. In 1990, Patricio Aylwin took office, but Pinochet remained the commander- in-chief of the armed forces. During this period, 1973 to1990, Chile lived one of its darkest moments in history, when many people were tortured, executed, exiled or disappeared, for being opposed to Pinochet's military regime. In 1993, Eduardo Frei Ruiz-Tagle won the elections for President. One of Frei's major steps towards the consolidation of democracy in Chile was in May 1995. Then, the Supreme Court defied Pinochet's coercion and demanded the arrest of the former head of Chile's secret police and his deputy. Previously, Pinochet had challenged the authority of the Supreme Court to sentence them. They were accused, in 1993, for masterminding the assassination, in 1976, of Orlando Letelier, a Chilean opposition leader. In March 2000, Ricardo Lagos Escobar became President. This was one month after the Supreme Court opened the possibility of a trial against Pinochet for human rights violations.[55]

3. People

Chile has **17,865,185** (2015, est.) people with an age structure of 21,0% in the 0 to 14- year-old category and 64.3% in the 15-year-old through 64-year-old category; and, the balance, 14.7%, is in the 65 years of age and older group. Life expectancy for the male population is 76.52 years (2015, est.) The female life expectancy is approximately 81.69 years (2015, est.) The population growth rate is 1.04% (2015, est.) Birth rates are about 13.95 in 1,000 of population (2015, est.) The death rate is 5.84 in 1,000 (2015, est.)

About two-thirds of Chileans are *mestizo*, or mixed Indian and Spanish descents. A small number of Chileans descend from Germans, Swiss, Italians, British, French, and Yugoslavs, who settled in Chile during the 19th and 20th Centuries.[57]

Most of the population, approximately 89%, lives in urban areas (2011). The most populated city in Chile is its capital, Santiago.[58]

Ethnic divisions in Chile include *mestizo*, at about 88.9% of the population. The balance of the population is Mapuche at approximately 9.1% and the balance 2.0% other ethnicities. The dominant religion is approximately 66.7% Roman Catholic, with about 16.4% Protestant, and a negligible percent Jewish. The dominant language is Spanish as the official language, but native dialects also are spoken in the remote interior. Literacy is at 98.6% (2009, est.), one of the highest in Latin America.

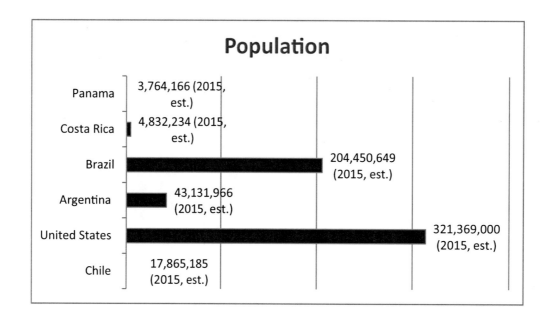

Population

Country	Population
Panama	3,764,166 (2015, est.)
Costa Rica	4,832,234 (2015, est.)
Brazil	204,450,649 (2015, est.)
Argentina	43,131,966 (2015, est.)
United States	321,369,000 (2015, est.)
Chile	17,865,185 (2015, est.)

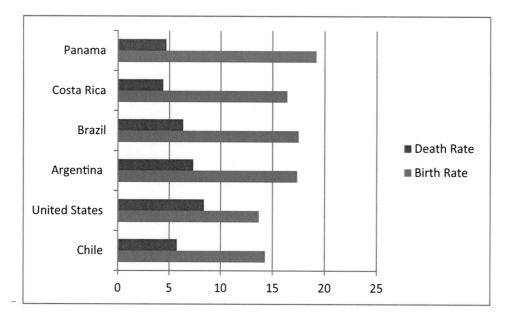

■ 4. Government

Chile is a Republic, with the capital located in Santiago.

There are 15 regions of administrative-type divisions subdivided into 54 provinces. Chile gained its independence from Spain on September 18, 1810, and this date is their national holiday of independence. The current Constitution was formed on September 11, 1980, and has been amended many times. The legal system in Chile is based on the Code of 1857 derived from Spanish law and subsequent codes influenced by French and Austrian law. The government consists of Executive, Legislative, and Judicial Branches. The Executive Branch is vested in the President. A cabinet is appointed by the President. The Legislative Branch is a bicameral national congress, *Congreso Nacional*, which consists of the Senate, *Senado*, and the Chamber of Deputies, *Cámarade Diputados*.

The Judicial Branch consists of the Supreme Court, *Corte Suprema*, and other lower- level Courts. Diplomatic representation exists with the United States, with Chile's office in Washington, D.C. The U.S. diplomatic representation exists with an Embassy in Santiago.

■ 5. Economy

During the last 20 years, Chile has revamped its economy with strong financial institutions and sound policies. Today, it enjoys the strongest sovereign bond rating in Latin America (Standard

& Poor's). It has changed from an economy dominated by a sole product of cooper, into an open and diversified economy. Metals, mineral ores, oil and natural gas constitute much of the export totaling $66.46 billion (2008). Other exports include copper, food product s, paper products and pulp, chemicals and wine. The economy during 1998 to 1999 went into recession, mostly because of tight monetary policies and a severe drought in 1999. Moreover, in 1999, Chile experienced a negative economic growth rate. The Gross Domestic Product (GDP) per capita earning is $15,732.3 (2013, est.) The GDP real growth rate is 4.2%. The inflation rate in 2013 was 1.8%, was 8.2% in 1995 and down from 26.1% in 1990. Unemployment is around 6.0% (2013, est.)

In 2013, Chile exported $77.367 billion of goods and services, and imported $79.616 billion, mostly in energy, communication, and transportation equipment. Chile's major trading partners in 2013 were the China, United States, Japan, Brazil, Argentina, South Korea and Germany.

6. Currency

Currency is the *Chilean peso* (Ch$.), consisting of 100 cents in one (1) Chilean peso. See the Burns School Global Real Estate Web site for the UNIVERSITY OF DENVER, *Daniels College of Business*, at http://burns.daniels.du.edu for rate conversions.

7. Transportation

Chile has 7,082 kilometers (km) of railroad lines and 77,764 km of roadways, with about 23% of the roadways being paved.

There are inland waterways in Chile that can accept larger vessels for shipping.

Chile has 3,160 km of gas pipelines, 781 km of liquid petroleum pipelines, 985 km of crude oil pipelines, and 722 km refined products. Chile has numerous ports for shipping, including those such as Antofagasta, Arica, Chanaral, Coquimbo, Iquique,

Puerto Montt, Punta Arenas, San Antonio, San Vicente, Talcahuano, and Valparaiso. Over 481 airports are utilized in Chile (2013); 90 have paved runways, and 391 have unpaved runways.

8. Communications

In 2012, Chile had 3.276 million main telephone lines in use and over 24.13 million mobile cellular telephones. Current expansion includes a modern system based on extensive microwave radio relay facilities and satellite systems with three earth stations. Chile has AM radio, FM radio, shortwave radio broadcast stations as well as television stations, and a domestic satellite system with 3 earth stations.

9. Real Property Issues

Information on the ownership of real estate and real rights can be found in the Registry of Properties. This information serves as legally binding notice of ownership. Titles, publicly registered at the national Registry of Properties, are open for inspection without a fee and provide a chain of title abstracts and marketability of title.

The Registry of Properties was created by the real property regulations of June 24, 1857. It mandates that all transactions having to do with real estate or real estate transactions must be recorded in the form of a public instrument. A public instrument is one written by a notary in his protocol book from which he issues certified copies. Contracts and deeds require authentication by a notary and are kept by in the office of the notary as official documents. Deeds executed in Chile must remain with the notary who executed the instrument. The notary will then give a copy to the titleholder. This copy will serve as a legal title in a court of law. The following must be recorded in the Registry of Properties: documents conveying or declaring the ownership of real estate and real rights; documents constituting, conveying, modifying or renouncing rights

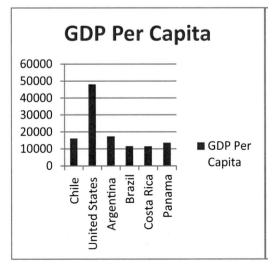

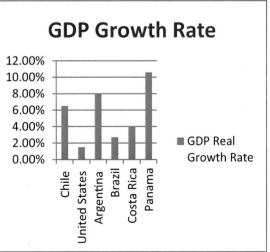

of usufruct, mortgage and certain other rights in real estate; and judgments declaring the ownership of real property. Until such documents are presented for record, the ownership of property is not deemed affected. Other documents relating to real property or rights therein, such as leases, attachments, etc., may be recorded so as to constitute notice to third parties. Contracts for the sale of real property or for an interest in real property must be in writing. There are three essential elements of a contract in Chile. They are: (1) All parties to the contract must be legally competent; (2) there must be mutual agreement or "a meeting of the minds," a mutual willingness to enter into a contract; and (3) the contract must be supported by consideration, i.e., something of value, be it money, a promise, property or services. An attorney or notary must draw real property listing and sales contracts. However, form contracts for leases can be used and notarized. Conveyance of real property, to be recorded at the Registry of Properties, must contain a true statement of consideration because tax on transfers is based on real consideration. In public instrument both grantor and grantee must sign and be present before a notary at the same time in person or by an attorney-in- fact. Transference of title can also be accomplished by documents drawn outside of Chile, but must first be reviewed and authenticated by a Chilean consul or diplomatic agent. Documents in use are mortgage deeds and bargain and sale deeds. Against a title recorded in the Registry of Properties, the adverse possession period does not run except by virtue of another recorded title. Law regulates the closing procedure. Closing takes place, typically, 60 days after the contract of sale. The conveyance of title after death can only be attained via written will or by court action. Adverse possession exists after ten years of continuous, uncontested use.

Chile's Civil Code, art. 1888 (and following), stipulates that in private sales of real property, rescission may be asked within four years, by the vendor, if it is found that the price received is less than one-half the just value of the property; and by the buyer if the value is less than one-half the price paid. If a sale of real property is made at a certain price for a unit of area, the vendor must, if the area is found to be less than that stipulated, make up the difference or refund part of the price paid. If the area is found greater, the buyer must pay more. But in either case, if the difference exceeds 10%, the sale may be annulled. While appraisals are not required in Chile, it is common practice to obtain one. The government regulates the real estate brokerage profession in Chile. However, there are no examination requirements to grant a real estate license. There is an administrative process and a charge for the "privilege license" to obtain his/her license. There is no continuing education requirement to maintain the real estate license.

The buyer and the seller usually equally share the cost of commissions equally, which is of 4% (i.e. 2% buyer and 2% seller). All transactions are closed with an attorney. Costs include transfer fees, attorney fees, document preparation and recording charges. Closing fees are usually paid by the buyer. Special provisions of Chilean Civil Code govern cooperative associations. They require authorization by a special law and

the express permission of the President of the republic. There are multiple-listing service (MLS) systems available on the Internet. These sources provide up-to-date information regarding transfers of real property and transaction prices. Real estate trade associations include theChilean Chamber of Construction (http://www.cchc.cl), *Cámara Chilena de la Construcción*, National Chamber of Real Estate Services (http://www.acop.cl/), *Cámara Nacional de Servicios Inmobiliarios A.G.*, and Chilean Real Estate Brokers Association (http://www.coproch.cl/), *Asociación de Corredores de Propiedades de Chile.*

Land is described in two ways in Chile:

1. Information **reference:** Reference is made to street numbers and place names, e.g., 123 Avenida Juarez or Rancho Juarez.
2. Metes-and-Bounds **Description:** Reference is made to distance (metes) and direction (bounds) and is dependent upon manmade monuments and geographic survey.

Mortgages must be executed before a notary in the form of a public instrument and recorded in the mortgage registry. Their date and effect are from the date of recording. Mortgages that are executed abroad must be recorded in the official register in Chile to be official. Each party must be present before the notary. The document must describe the property in detail and state at what amount the parties are valuing the property. Only real property under ownership or usufruct title can be mortgaged. Personal property is included in mortgages on real property when it forms an inherent part of the realty. Liens are divided into five classes: (1) those for judicial costs in matters favoring all creditors; (2) those of inkeepers and common carriers; (3) those of the government against taxpayers; (4) those of mortgagors on the property mortgaged; and (5) those of common creditors. Typically in Chile the property on a subject loan is held as security for the loan. The loan document must describe the property in detail and state mortgage amounts for each parcel held as security. Mortgages establish preference over other creditors by their date of record. Multiple mortgages on the same property are not allowed. A judge conducts foreclosure sales after a property has been legally attached. Property must first be valued, unless value is agreed upon and undisputed. The property is sold to the highest bidder. Once the sale of the subject property is final, the debt or has no legal recourse. Parties may agree to any interest rate that does not exceed 50% of the current banking interest rate, as determined every month by the central bank.

Fixed rate loans are common in Chile, with the average term being greater than ten years. Private loans are between 75% and 80% of the value, but the borrower's monthly household income must be normally at least four times the monthly loan repayment. Loans are most commonly taken out for 20-year terms. A 20-year loan annual, fixed rate, mortgage rate may vary between 4.10% and 7.70% (2015). The balance of a mortgage is generally indexed by the variation of the Chilean Consumer Price Index. Thus, the interest rate on mortgages, plus the commercial bank's common 3% extra lending rate, are in real terms, indexed against inflation. Both banks and private lending institutions originate loans. Funds are brought into the housing finance market from pension funds by the purchase of a financial security instrument called a *letra hipotecaria* or *LH*. A *hipoteca* is a mortgage; an LH is a security issued on a residential mortgage loan.

Government subsidies are also available to stimulate the growth of home ownership. Since 1994, about 30,000 families took part in the housing subsidy program. This can finance up to 100% of the mortgage loan, but it can be only for natural persons, buying residential properties, with values comprehended between US$40,000 and US$200,000, approximately (2015, est.; UF 1,000 and UF5,000; 1 UF = CLP 24,641.81; CLP 1 = US$0.00162).

A sale is completed and binding when the vendor and vendee have agreed upon the property sold and the price. In the case of real property, the sale is only completed when the property is registered.

Unlimited Partnership, sociedad colectiva, is a partnership in the usual form in which all partners have unlimited and joint liability.

Limited Partnership, sociedad en comandita, is a partnership in which one or more of the partners are subject to unlimited and joint liability for the partnership obligations, and one or more are not responsible for debts and losses, except up to the amount of the capital they have invested **Corporations** are designated by name, accompanied by words *Sociedad Anónima* or abbreviation *S.A.* At least two stockholders are required for the organization and continued legal existence of a corporation. There is no restriction as to nationality or residence of incorporators. The Chilean government maintains certain rights in all privately held property. The government has the right of eminent domain, but only if the property will be used for public purposes or if the owner does not pay property taxes. Property taxes exist; they are based on the value of the subject property. Property escheats to the government, if there is no heir. The Chilean government does not maintain the right of police power in private property. Ownership is unrestricted in fee simple estates. Leasehold estates, granting possessory rights only, exist as a tenancy for years. Dower and curtsey are not recognized in Chile. With community property, spouses are given equal rights in real property, depending on the marital status of the parties.

Estates of decedents pass either through will or by operation of law. Although there is no system of dower, wives of decedents are given certain rights as to shares of intestacy property.

A single rate per mill of assessed value of real property as overall national and municipal territorial taxes, including charges for public light; pavement of streets and certain municipal loan services was established in 1969. Value assessments are made every five years or more often, and at least once every ten years. General assessment as well as individual assessments may also be made.

Real estate taxes are payable in four installments, due in April, June, September, and November, calculated on the valuation in force at the time of payment. Insurance is regulated by *Banco Central de Chile.* In the case of loans on real property, *Seguro de Desgravamen,* life insurance, is required on the debt or as well fire insurance on the property. Otherwise, property insurance is not required, but is common practice to have it.

Environmental impact statements are required for any major infrastructure developments and/or real estate projects. The regional or national environmental commission must approve all projects. Fiscal fees and execution of any instrument of sale are payable by the vendor unless agreed otherwise.

There are controls on how a parcel of real estate may be used. Zoning is used to control growth and to separate land uses that are incompatible. In addition, public subdivision regulations exist to control how land can be converted into buildable lots. Covenants and deed restrictions do not exist in Chile.

Chile has strong legal protection for property rights, including secured investments in real property. Given the small size of the country, U.S. confidence in security of investing in Chile is shown in the figures for overall U.S. investment of $9.5 billion U.S. dollars between 1979 and 1997.

Land ownership in Chile does not have any restriction on foreigners, other than 10 Km. near the border, were this is prohibited. However, there might be rules and restrictions set out in the state's foreign investment code. Similarly, different tax treatment and foreign exchange restrictions and controls may effectively constitute indirect restrictions on foreign ownership or use of land.[62]

■ 10. Real Estate Trends

A number of strong Internet links help to acquire information in Chile, especially those from the National Association of REALTORS®, the Miami Association of REALTORS®, CB Richard Ellis, Jones Lang LaSalle, and the Global Real Estate web site at the UNIVERSITY OF DENVER, *Daniels College of Business,* Burns School of Real Estate and Construction Management (Burns School) (*http://burns.daniels.du.edu*).

■ 11. Cultural Issues

Any nation's culture is complex and vibrant in its diversity. While broad cultural characterizations such as those presented here can be generally accurate, following such generalities too strictly may be dangerously misleading. To conduct business effectively and profitably in a country, it is vital to have a thorough understanding of its culture's complexities.

"The family unit plays a major role in Chilean society. Chileans believe in the extended family. Almost half of the Chilean work force is female. Many women hold distinguished business and political positions in Chile.

"Weekend and holiday gatherings are almost traditional in Chilean society. At these gatherings, Chileans might prepare dishes made up of fish, seafood, chicken, beef, beans, eggs, and corn. Chileans have the main meal of the day at midday. The evening meal is a lighter one. During the afternoon, it is customary for Chileans to take a teatime. The typical Chilean dish is a stew called *'cazuela de ave'. It* consists of chicken, potatoes, rice, and maybe onions and peppers."

12. Discussion Questions

1. How do environmental issues affect the development of real estate in Chile?

2. Are foreigners allowed to own real estate in Chile?

3. Does Chile's border dispute with Bolivia hinder Chile's economic development?

13. Case Study

Wines of the World (WOW) Santiago, Chile

Memo

To: Board of Directors
From: Consultants
Re: Exiting strategy for Blight Eaten Vineyards Chile

I. Problem
Wines of the World (WOW) purchased a vineyard in Chile last year. This was the first purchase of what would have been many vineyards all over the world. The vineyard in Chile had been owned by the same family for over 100 years. The father died the prior year before WOW acquired it. The children did not want to run the vineyard. The last three years, prior to WOW taking over the vineyard, had been produced three good crops of grapes, according to the sellers and the accounting records. (A real estate agent was used in the purchase of the business.) This last season no crop was harvested. The grapes were eaten by "Blights," insects that can destroy a vineyard in no time at all. The goal of the company was to find existing functioning wineries' in other parts of the world, including, but not limited to, Brazil, Italy, France and the U.S.

Chile was the first country on the list for expansion, because WOW found that the winery was available and because of the favorable price.

II. Initial Exit Strategy
The initial exit strategy was to place the vineyard up for sale after 10 years to 20 years of production. WOW wanted this to be a winery to make a mark on the wine world. Once the winery had been well established, internationally, it would be placed up for auction, by an international auction house. This would provide prestige when selling. This would give WOW the opportunity to require a minimum bid, to then hope that the name and the prestige would bring a higher price.

III. Contingency Exit Strategy
Due to the loss of an entire crop from the Vineyard, WOW must look at exiting the wine business altogether. WOW needs to liquidate all of the assets and then put the winery up for sale, using a qualified broker who has access marketing and who would be able to sell the business as soon as possible. If WOW is unable to sell the land, WOW could possibly develop the land, if it could get the property re-zoned.

This option would take more money and effort, but might be a possibility if WOW has no choice.

IV. Conclusion
Because of the destruction of the grapes, WOW has lost an entire year of profits. If WOW can possibly hold on through the year, existing on the sales from the last year and reserve capital, the Consultants suggest that WOW try to hold onto the business. The vineyard is in a perfect location, not only to attract tourists, but also to produce quality wine. The Consultants also suggest that WOW bring in an expert, who can suggest a plan of action to possibly save any grapes that are left and to provide planning for the next year's crops. Once this proposal has been evaluated, the Consultants suggest that WOW work on a new marketing campaign, target markets, work to improve the winery and its processes, while it waits for next year's crop.

Refer to: International Real Estate Digest. Homepage. http://www.ired.com. X-rates.com. Homepage. http://www.x-rates.com.

U.S. Embassy. Homepage. http://usembassy.state.gov. U.S. Department of State. Homepage. http://www.state.gov.

14. Selected References

Armstrong, Kristi (NA). Republic *of Chile: A Guide to the 20th Century,* Historical Text

Archive: Chile (online) at http://www.historicaltextarchive.com.

CIA World Factbook at https://www.cia.gov/library/publications/the-world-factbook/index.html.

Gobierno de Chile (2000).Portal *del Gobierno de Chile.* Gobierno de Chile (online) in

Spanish at http://www.gobiernodechile.cl.

Inter-American Development Bank (2000).Basic *Socio-Economic Data Report: Chile,* Inter-American Development Bank (online) at http://www.iadb.org. Organization of American States at http://www.oas.org.

Richard Ellis International Property Specialists. C.B. Richard Ellis. http://www.cbre.com. Time Almanac. *TIME Almanac.* Boston: Information Please LLC.

United States Department of State. *Background Notes: Chile.* United States Department of State (Online). Available:http://www.state.gov. U.S. Bureau of Census at http://www.census.gov. U.S. Department of Commerce at http://www.stat- usa.gov. U.S. Bureau of Economic Analysis at http://www.bea.gov.

U.S. Embassy. Homepage. http://usembassy.state.gov. World Trade Centers Institute at http://www.wtci.org.

World Trade Organization at http://www.wto.org. World Bank. *Adult Illiteracy Rates.* The Economist.

X-rates.com. Homepage. http://www.x-rates.com.

Latin America Diplomatic History: An Introduction, Davis, H., 1977, p.220, https://books.google.com/books?id=P6-FJzbWFnoC&pg=PA220&lpg=PA220&dq=how+the+river+lauca+dispute+resolve&source=bl&ots=xVkYPm2ZBL&sig=tli4E0C7VkKsE2l0a4M6kKEvAbI&hl=en&sa=X&ei=Ftn8VLK0L8L0oASRp4KYCQ&ved=0CDUQ6AEwBQ#v=onepage&q=how%20the%20river%20lauca%20dispute%20resolve&f=false

Central Intelligence Agency, Office of Current Intelligence, Special Article: The Bolivian-Chilean Dispute, Approved for Release August 2000, http://www.foia.cia.gov/sites/default/files/document_conversions/89801/DOC_0000414138.pdf

Dirección General de Aeronáutica Civil, Dirección Meteorológica de Chile, Departamento de Climatología y Meteorología, Climatología, Climatología Regional (2001), http://164.77.222.61/climatologia/

United Nations Data, Country Profile: Chile, https://data.un.org/CountryProfile.aspx?crName=Chile

World Statesmen.org, Nations and Territories: Chile, http://www.worldstatesmen.org/Chile.html

Instituto Nacional de Estadística y Censos, Población, Proyecciones Nacionales, Población por sexo y grupos quinquenales de edad. Años 2010-2040, http://www.indec.mecon.ar/nivel4_default.asp?id_tema_1=2&id_tema_2=24&id_tema_3=84

Instituto Nacional de Estadística y Censos, Población, Proyecciones Nacionales, Población por sexo y grupos quinquenales de edad. Años 2010-2040, http://www.indec.mecon.ar/nivel4_default.asp?id_tema_1=2&id_tema_2=24&id_tema_3=84

Estimaciones y Proyecciones de la Población en la República de Panamá, por Provincia. Comarca Indígena, Distrito y Corregimiento, Según Sexo: Años 2000-2015, Boletín No. 10, https://www.contraloria.gob.pa/inec/Archivos/P2391Boletin10.pdf

Instituto Nacional de Estadística y Censos (INEC), Población y Demografía – Población – Proyecciones, Resultados Nacionales, http://www.inec.go.cr/Web/Home/GeneradorPagina.aspx

Boletín No. 10, https://www.contraloria.gob.pa/inec/Archivos/P2391Boletin10.pdfInstituto Nacional de Estadísticas, Chile, Demográficas y Vitales, Demografía, Población, País y Regiones. Actualización Población 2002-2012 y Proyecciones 2013-2020, http://www.ine.cl/canales/chile_estadistico/demografia_y_vitales/demografia/pdf/poblacion_sociedad_enero09.pdf

Instituto Brasileiro de Geografia e Estatística (IBGE), Diretoria de Pesquisas. Coordenação de População e Indicadores Sociais. Gerência de Estudos e Análises da Dinâmica Demográfica, http://www.ibge.gov.br/home/estatistica/populacao/projecao_da_populacao/2013/default_tab.shtm

World Bank, World Integrated Trade Solution, Trade Stats by Country, Chile GDP per Capita (Current US$) 2009-2013, http://wits.worldbank.org/CountryProfile/Country/CHL/StartYear/2009/EndYear/2013/Indicator/NY-GDP-PCAP-CD

World Bank, World Integrated Trade Solution, Trade Stats by Country, Chile Trade Summary 2013 Data, http://wits.worldbank.org/CountryProfile/Country/CHL/Year/2013/Summary

The World Bank, Research, Global Economic Prospects, Country and Region Specific Forecasts and Data, http://www.worldbank.org/en/publication/global-economic-prospects/data?region=LAC

The World Bank, Data, Inflation, Consumer Prices (Annual %), http://data.worldbank.org/indicator/FP.CPI.TOTL.ZG?display=default

United Nations Data, Country Profile: Chile, https://data.un.org/CountryProfile.aspx?crName=Chile

The World Bank, Data, Unemployment, Total (% of Total Labor Force), http://data.worldbank.org/indicator/SL.UEM.TOTL.ZS/countries

Biblioteca del Congreso Nacional de Chile, Código Civil de la República de Chile, http://www.leychile.cl/Navegar?idNorma=172986

Biblioteca del Congreso Nacional de Chile, Decreto 1205: Reglamento de Corredores de Propiedades, Published on November 9, 1944, http://www.leychile.cl/Navegar?idNorma=288308

Zona Inmobiliaria: Conoce las Tareas en un Corredor de Propiedades, http://www.zonainmobiliaria.com/zonainmobiliaria/noticias/conoce-las-tareas-en-un-corredor-de-propiedades/2013-10-14/134224.html

ComparaOnline, Crédito Hipotecario, Financiamiento Hipotecario http://www.comparaonline.cl/credito-hipotecario/financiamiento-hipotecario#top

Portalinmobiliario.com, Fuentes de Financiamiento, http://www.portalinmobiliario.com/financiamiento/leer.asp?Mnu=fin_fte&Cuerpo=base_a.cl.asp

Bancafacil, ¿Qué es el Crédito Universal? http://www.bancafacil.cl/bancafacil/servlet/Contenido?indice=1.2&idPublicacion=6000000000000124&idCategoria=5

Superintendencia de Bancos e Instituciones Financieras Chile, Productos Bancarios, Simulador de Créditos Hipotecarios, http://www.clientebancario.cl/simuladorhipotecario/aplicacion?indice=101.2.1

Servicio de Impuestos Internos, Bienes Raíces, Preguntas Frecuentes, ¿Cómo son cobradas las contribuciones?, http://www.sii.cl/preguntas_frecuentes/bienes_raices/001_004_0310.htm

Normas Sobre la Adquisición, Administración y Disposición de Bienes del Estado, Título I: Disposiciones Generales, Artículo 6, Published on November 10, 1977, http://www.leychile.cl/Navegar?idNorma=6778

15. Glossary

Associación Gremial de Corredores de Propiedades y Promotores de la Conctrucción – Association of Real Estate Brokers and Construction Promoters.

Corredores de Propiedades – Real estate professionals.

Hipoteca - a mortgage.

Law for Defense of Democracy – In force from 1947 to 1958, when the communist party was banned from Chile and Chile broke off diplomatic relations with the USSR.

Letra Hipotecaria – Funds are brought into the housing finance market from pension funds by the purchase of a financial security instrument.

Mestizos – Mixed Indian and Spanish decents

Reconquista – The time between September 18, 1810 and February 12, 1818, when Chile declared independence in 1810 and in 1818 Bernado O'Higgins proclaimed independence.

Registry of Properties – Contains info on ownership of real estate and serves as legally binding notice of ownership

Seguro de Desgravamen – life insurance.

Mutuo Hipotecario - mortgage.

About the Author

José F. Ramirez was born in Caracas, Venezuela, where he earned a degree in civil engineering at the Universidad Central de Venezuela. He later earned a, in the United Stated, a diploma in business administration from the University of California – Berkeley; a master's in real estate and construction management from the Burns School of Real Estate and Construction Management, *Daniels College of Business,* UNIVERSITY OF DENVER; and, in Australia, a Master of Construction Law from the University of Melbourne. At the beginning of his career, he actively appraised residential real estate in Venezuela. A few years later, he actively participated in the design and development of commercial real estate in that country. More recently he has provided consulting construction and real estate services for commercial real estate in Colombia, United States and Venezuela. He currently works as a consultant for the construction and real estate development industries in the United States.

China

INTERNATIONAL REAL ESTATE (GLOBAL REAL ESTATE)
Authored by *Professor Jonathan Adelman, Pius Leung* and
Dr. Mark Lee Levine, Editor

■ 1. Geography

China is located in eastern Asia, where it borders the East China Sea, Korea Bay, the Yellow Sea and the South China Sea, between North Korea and Vietnam. China is a huge country of 9,596,961 square kilometers (sq km), slightly smaller than the United States.

China has enormous land borders with Afghanistan, Bhutan, Burma, India, Kazakhstan, North Korea, Kyrgyzstan, Laos, Mongolia, Nepal, Pakistan, Russia, Tajikistan and Vietnam. China has had many border disputes with its neighbors and entities that it considers under its jurisdiction, e.g., Taiwan. It has fought wars and border skirmishes with South Korea (1950 to 1953), Taiwan (1958, 1966), India (1959, 1962), Russia (1969) and Vietnam (1979). Geographically speaking, China is the second largest country in the world, behind Russia **and** Canada, and the United States.

The climate in China is very diverse, given its massive land area and various high and low geographic areas. Northern areas can be very cold, while southern China tends towards a semi-tropical warm climate. With several thousand miles of coastline, China has extensive access to Asian markets through famous ports such as Shanghai, Hong Kong, Guangzhou and Xiamen.

Numerous natural resources in China include extensive deposits of coal, iron ore and petroleum, as well as mercury, hydropower, uranium, lead, zinc, and many other valuable minerals.

With 7% of the world's arable land, China supports 22% of the world's population.

Land for irrigation includes almost 500,000 square kilometers (km). (Deng Xiaoping's family responsibility system, introduced after 1979, dismantled the socialist communes and successfully introduced extensive capitalist incentives, while retaining ultimate state ownership of the land.) Approximately 43% of Chinese territory consists of meadows and pastures; 14% are in woodlands.

China, especially with its rapid industrialization of the last two decades, faces many serious pollution issues, so serious that indices of air pollution appear in the paper every day. These problems include air pollutants, such as high sulfur coal, which produces acid rain that damages the forests. Natural hazards exist in the form of typhoons, floods, tsunamis, earthquakes and droughts. The 1976 Tangshan earthquake claimed 240,000 victims, and other notable earthquakes occurred in the 21st Century.

■ 2. History and Overview

China is the most populous country in the world, with approximately 1,355,692,576 people. Demographers estimate that the one-child policy, enforced vigorously in the cities and more loosely in the countryside in the last two decades, has held down population growth by 300 million people; yet, the Shanghai governments re- evaluate the possibility of allowing two children, even in major cities. Yet, because of the great youth bulge, even a zero population growth policy sees the current population continuing to increase an estimated 15 million additional people per year (almost the entire population Chile

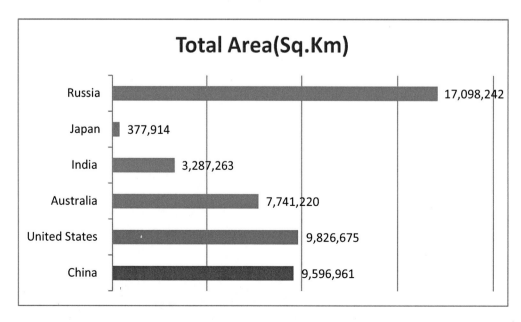

in 2012). China has addressed a possible change to now allow more than one child per family. China is a growing military power, with nuclear weapons, intercontinental ballistic missiles, supersonic jet fighters, and other modern weapons. At the same time, handicapped by its isolation from the world after the Russian withdrawal in 1960, and its historic economic backwardness, China still lags, perhaps 20 years, behind the West in many key areas. Its navy, for example, cannot compete with Western navies for the foreseeable future. The main military focus is to develop smaller, powerful, rapid deployment forces that can establish local dominance over Vietnam, Taiwan or the South China Sea. Challenging the United States is a task that will be left, if at all, to the next generation. China, thus, has a growing military capability, large land mass and a huge population. Since 1971 it has been a permanent member of the United Nations Security Council, which gives it veto power (although it has usually abstained from using it) over United Nations Security Council Resolutions dealing with multilateral issues. China has many disputes with bordering countries, including, for example, India, Vietnam, Russia, South Korea, and Vietnam. Taiwan is now part of China.

Under the impetus of the "Four Modernizations" started by Deng Xiaoping in 1979 and continued by Jiang Zemin after 1990, China has greatly expanded its international trade to a level over $350 billion U.S. dollars. It has received over $350 billion in foreign direct investment. China is one of the largest creditors of the U.S., and roughly 70% of that foreign direct investment has come from overseas Chinese, with Japan in second place. The Chinese economy is closely tied to many of its neighbors and other countries, including European countries and the United States. China is now the largest outside creditor of the U.S. China has been very active in expanding other types of activities with other nations, including scientific activities, technical exchange programs, educational programs and numerous inter- country activities.

■ 3. People

As noted, China has the largest population in the world, with 1,355,692,576 people (2014). The age structure is 17.1% of the population from 0 to 14 years, which makes this segment alone about 4 times larger than the population of the United States. Approximately 73.3% of the population is 15 to 64 years old, while those older than 65 years are 9.6% of the total populace. However, within 30 years, even with medical advances and China's increasing economic prosperity, China will have a rapidly aging population.

Population growth has slowed to only 0.44% a year, due to the one-child policy, first introduced by Deng Xiaoping in the late 1970s. In the countryside, the policy has been less rigorous, with two children frequently allowed. And, on occasion, three children are allowed (if there are two girls). The birth rate is 12.17 per 1,000. The death rate is approximately 7.44 per 1,000. This still leaves a large population growth rate per year. Life expectancy is 73.09 years for males and 77.43 years for females.

There is a notable disparity between the number of people living in urban areas and those that live in rural areas. In 2014, about 45.6% of the population still lives in the countryside, and 54.4% live in the towns or cities. China is experiencing rapid urbanization as the economy continues to grow, with an estimated 3.05% of the population moving to cities every year between 2010 and 2015. There is also a huge gap between Inner China (850 million people) and the more affluent coastal China (400 million people). Unlike many other countries, one ethnic group (Han Chinese) dominates the country. Over 1 billion Han Chinese make up 91.5% of the population. There are over a dozen other major minorities, including Mongolians, Tibetans, Koreans, Uighurs and others. The most severe ethnic conflict has been with Tibet and its Dalai Lama, who fled to India after the failed uprising against Chinese rule in 1959.

Since the end of the Cultural Revolution (1966 to 1976), China has experienced greater religious freedom, especially

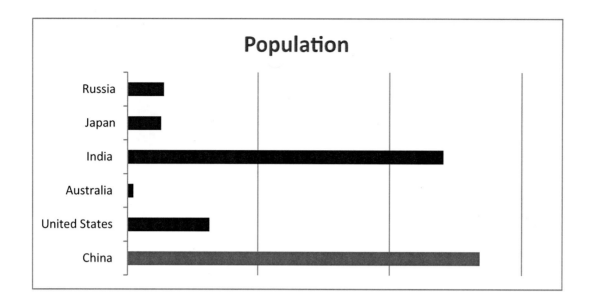

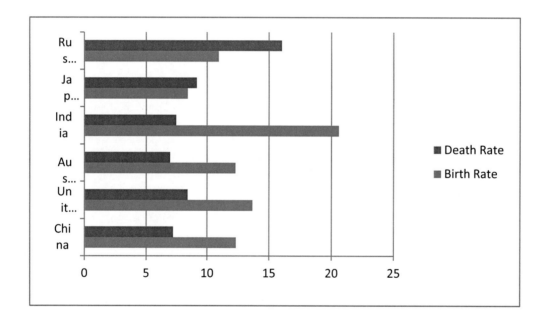

for religions with long-term roots in the country (such as Buddhism, Islam, and Christianity). But, the official policy favors atheism. There remain problems with underground churches that are denied official status by the government. While there are numerous dialects throughout the vast country, the official language used everywhere is Mandarin Chinese (the dialect originally found around Beijing). Literacy is approximately 90.9% of the population, with 99% primary school enrollment.[68]

There are over 5 million university students in China, with six of the top ten universities (such as Peking University, Tsinghua University, People's University and Fudan University), found in Beijing and Shanghai.

■ 4. Government

China is a Communist state, with its capital in Beijing. The government, while becoming more decentralized, remains highly concentrated in Beijing. There are 23 Provinces, five autonomous Regions, and four Municipalities. The People's Republic of China was established by the Chinese Communist Party under Mao Zedong on October 1, 1949. This date remains the National Day in China. The reforms of Deng Xiaoping and Jiang Zemin (1979 to 2000) established a new kind of socio-political-economic system, moving away from state economic control and planning commonly associated with Marxism-Leninism in favor of demand-based economics typically associated with free-market capitalism. (Dr. Mark Lee Levine, professor at the University of Denver, labels the result as "capitalistic *communism.*")

After the end of the Maoist era (1949 to1976), a new Constitution was promulgated under Den Xiaoping in December, 1982. The legal system is an amalgam of customs and statutes. There has been a modified civil code in effect since January 1, 1987, with new codes being passed more recently. President Jiang Zemin proclaimed in 1998 that China was in the process of becoming a nation honoring the rule of law. This is a lengthy process, currently under way. Voting is at 18 years of age and is universal. Current leadership position in China is to continue with the "open type" policy.

The branches of government consist of the Chief of State as the President, Legislative Branches within the National People's Congress, and the Judicial Branch. The latter is the Supreme People's Court, with judges appointed by the National People's Congress.

The Chinese Communist Party has dominated China since the proclamation of the new government in October, 1949. It continues to be the dominant force in China. This separates China from Europe, where Communism vanished following the collapse of the Soviet Union in 1991.

There is U.S. diplomatic representation in China through the American Ambassador, located in Beijing. The large American Embassy (with over 500 Americans) is located there. A corresponding diplomatic representation for China, with their Ambassador and Embassy, is located in Washington, D.C.

China's large defense forces, with spending of roughly 1.99% of GDP per year, includes ground forces (PLA), naval forces (PLAN), air forces (PLAAF), strategic missile forces (Second Artillery Corps), and military police forces (PAP).

■ 5. Economy

The Chinese economy has grown extraordinarily in the two decades since the Four Modernizations were proclaimed

in 1979 by Deng Xiaoping. China has led the world with 9% annual growth rate. Gross Domestic Product (GDP) per capita has quadrupled in the last **20 years;** the *Central Intelligence Agency World Factbook* calculates the GDP per capita at close to $12,900 (2014). The standard of living, while still very modest by Western standards, has grown very rapidly. China's GDP was $17.63 trillion USD in 2014. Note: this measure is calculated by the purchasing power parity method due to large socialist subsidies and its fiat exchange rate. There is a vast gap, often 10 to 20 times, between the far more affluent coastal region (that has attracted much foreign investment) and the poorer, inner China area. Nevertheless, the GDP real growth rate is 7.4% (2014). However, the rate of growth in China has been slowing in the last few years.

Inflation rates in China, once quite high, have sharply declined in recent years (2.1% in 2014). Now deflation, with vast industrial over capacity, looms as a significant problem. Unemployment is relatively low at 4.1% (2014), but the accuracy of this figure is difficult to determine, due to poor rural data, underemployment in state-owned industries and large-scale layoffs in state-owned industries.

■ 6. Currency

The currency in China is the *yuan (CNY)* sometimes referred to in pinyin as the *renminbi (RMB).* For conversion rates, see the Burns School Global Real Estate Web site *at* http://burns.daniels.du.edu.

■ 7. Transportation

Transportation in China has favored more rudimentary approaches over the last several hundred years. In the last decade the government paid serious attention to modernizing its infrastructure. It recently spent several billion U.S. dollars per year on a massive highway project connecting all 30

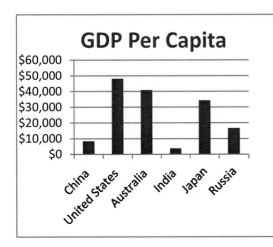

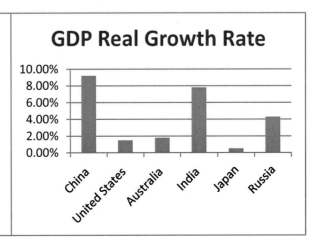

provincial and autonomous regional capitals by 2015. China also has 507 airports throughout the country. China has an extensive railroad network, with 86,000 kilometers (km) of railways. It has over 4,106,387 km of roadways of which 3,453,890 km are paved. China also has very extensive inland, navigable waterways.

China utilizes pipelines to transport crude oil and petroleum products as well as natural gas. It has numerous shipping ports to transport goods, including such famous ports as Shanghai, Hong Kong, and Qingdao. Its 507 airports are being improved to transport goods and peoples. There is a modern air network linking all major cities with regular connections, via jet aircraft.

◼ 8. Communications

The communication system in China is huge. However, given the massive population, as compared with other countries, the infrastructure to support general landline telephones is insufficient to provide for the current populace. The country has 278.86 million landlines in use and 1.1 billion mobile cellular phones in use as of 2012. Satellite communications and fiber optic lines are also prevalent in the country. A powerful Internet revolution is underway. In 2011, 389,000,000 Chinese were on the Internet (in 2002 there were an estimated 45,800,000 Chinese on the Internet, and in 2006 there were 123,000,000 Internet users), with about 19,772,000 Internet service providers (hosts) in 2011. Censorship is generally reserved for political and pornographic sites. All broadcast media are owned by, or affiliated with, the Communist Party of China or a government agency (2008), including AM radio, FM radio stations, short wave stations, and television stations broadcasting in China. China is moving very quickly to improve its total communications systems.

◼ 9. Real Property Issues

Acquisition costs and procedures for acquiring property are developing in China as a result of greater freedom and the transition to capitalism. There is beginning to be something analogous to private property ownership, which may actually be labeled as long-term "leases." New regulations in China require registering documents for ownership of real estate, although details for such transfers are fairly limited at this time. A progressive tax system impacts some transfers of real estate, especially since the recent changes that allow some property ownership or leasing. Property in China is generally divided into the following three types:

1. *Socialist ownership* by the government, somewhat equivalent to ownership by a state in the United States;
2. *Collective ownership,* which may be ownership by an organization or body of companies, or the equivalent;

3. *Private ownership* by individuals or private entities. Transfer of land in China takes place via the transfer of the right to *use* the land, which is actually closer to a *lease* arrangement, although the term used in China is often labeled "ownership." Specific laws exist involving ownership of property between a husband and wife, especially inherited property. Registration and evidence of ownership of property is generally undertaken in the local area, by administrative departments. Contracts are utilized to acquire property, including specific requirements to be included in a contract, such as the subject property description and the time involved for the transfer.

Leasing or mortgages for borrowing with regard to real estate is fairly limited in China. Insurance relative to property ownership and protection of positions does exist, but it is on a very limited basis. This is being modified and reviewed as a result of recent changes in China with regard to certain forms of ownership.

Some land use controls exist in China, although historically these have been controlled by the state. Under Chinese Land Administration Law, those who use land have obtained certain "rights" for that use and the regulations that impact the degree of "private" use of the land under this authority.[70]

See also the links in this Section, noted below, for additional sources of information.

◼ 10. Real Estate Trends

Chinese trends regarding real estate are rapidly changing, aligned toward the concept of "private ownership" (which is more the equivalent of a "lease," as explained above) for different types of property, including office, industrial, retail, residential, etc.

See the major real estate companies, such as Jones Lang LaSalle or CB Richard Ellis, provide useful information about realty activities in China and property that is for sale, for lease or otherwise available. See also the links in "Selected References" below connecting to other sources, such as the Burns School Global Real Estate Web site, *Daniels College of Business,* UNIVERSITY OF DENVER at http://burns.daniels.du.edu , as well as the *International Real Estate Digest* Web site.

◼ 11. Cultural Issues

Any nation's culture is complex and vibrant in its diversity. While broad cultural characterizations such as those presented here can be generally accurate, following such generalities too strictly may be dangerously misleading. To conduct business effectively and profitably in a country, it is vital to have a thorough understanding of its culture's complexities. Cultural issues are important in any country when undertaking business activities. However, in China, given the large population, unique Chinese cultural issues and the previously noted "enclosed community," as a result of Communism, many visitors are trying to learn the intricacies of many of the cultural facets in China. Questions as to personal appearance and dress, special types of greetings, gestures, eating habits, status within a class and numerous other activities must be examined very carefully when attempting to transact business in China.

When visiting the home of a Chinese citizen in China, punctuality is important. Being a few minutes late can be considered impolite. And guests always conduct themselves in a restrained manner. In the past, the Chinese attire has been fairly restrained and conservative as well, but there is an ongoing injection of western styles into the urban culture of China. Most of the older population segments still maintain the traditional dress. Chinese introductions tend to be formal, utilizing a person's full name. Bowing is very common in greetings. Physical contact, other than a handshake should be avoided, particularly when dealing with older people and those in important positions.

12. Discussion Questions

1. Why has China has been able to grow so rapidly under a Communist government? Why were other Communist countries unable to do this?

2. How long will it take Chinese reforms, spurred by membership in World Trade Organization (WTO), to achieve a privatization of real estate, currency reform and protection of private property before non-Chinese investors will be able to participate in these changes?

3. What are the prospects for Chinese commercial and residential real estate development? How will non-Chinese be able to participate in this transformation of China?

4. When will Chinese real estate no longer be divided into two sectors, but unified into one, open to both natives and foreigners?

5. Is the model for Chinese real estate development Taiwan, Hong Kong and/or Singapore? What will this mean for China?

13. Case Study

Memo

To: Board of Directors
From: Consultants
Re: Shut Down of WISE

I. Problem

WISE

Weiszmann Internet Search Engine Inc. Chaoyang District, Beijing, China
Weiszmann Internet Search Engine (WISE) was started in 2000. The search engine has been used all over the world and has produced profits in each of the new markets that were entered. In 2001, after extensive research on entering the market in China, WISE was made aware of additional concerns. The government passed laws in December 2014. These stated:

The National People's Congress passed a new law that criminalizes several forms of online political activity, including using the Internet to 'incite the overthrow of state power, topple the socialist system, or 1/4 destroy national unity,' 'promote cults', or support the Independence of Taiwan. The provisions were part of a general Internet safety law that also bans such activities as hacking into computer networks, linking pornographic Web sites, spreading rumors to manipulate stock prices and creating and disseminating computer viruses." (Digital Freedom Network, http://www.dfn.org/focus/china/shutdown.htm#dec00law.)

Because of these, and certain other laws, the risks to WISE's search engine was higher in China then in other countries, particularly because of open forums on WISE that might have opened up some areas listed in the above stated law. The WISE Directors felt that the risk was worth the investment. But, they may have been very wrong.

The Chinese government recently blocked WISE from operating, for reasons that are not clear. WISE has been unable to continue operating its search engine in China. This has caused WISE to cease collecting any revenue. Because of such actions, advertising dollars and payments had to be refunded. People were unable to access the Web site.

After the recent block on other major search engines, with all of the press received, WISE felt this might be the opportunity to get the block "lifted." However, thus far WISE has had no hint that the block might be lifted soon, if ever. At this point, WISE must look at its exit strategies and decide what is best.

II. Initial Exit Strategy

The exit strategy initially was to shut down the Web site, after the advertisers and the WISE customers had received proper notice. The risks involved in the business did not make it ideal to lease office space for the long-term. WISE hired a local firm to help find office space to rent. (Not all office building owners are allowed to rent office space to foreigners.)

After a search of the market, we rented space from the Consulting Firm in their own building. This service is called "links." "This is a service for individuals and companies starting up, who do not want big overheads." (Beijing Business Online http://www.cbw.com/busbj/issue45/12.html). This gave us some flexibility on vacating, if for some reason WISE ran into problems with the Government, or any other major issues.

Another difficulty that WISE faced was that of housing its employees. (Non-Chinese cannot live wherever they want. They must live in buildings with a special certificate.) WISE housed its employees in hotels for the initial time, until the company was "up and running" for a certain period of time. These decisions, which were made when WISE entered the market, might save costs if it becomes necessary to exit the market. This exit strategy can be executed immediately; or, WISE can slowly exit, depending on the situation. The circumstances that WISE now faces call for *immediate* execution of the exit strategy. Because there is no certainty as to when, and if, WISE will be able to have the search engine released, it must proceed with exiting the market.

III. Contingency Exit Strategy

See Initial Exit Strategy.

IV. Conclusion

The exit strategy plan must be executed, now. It is recommended by the Consultants that WISE exit as quickly as possible. With one month's notice to its customers, and once refunds have been handled, WISE should be in position to exit the market. The offices can be closed quickly and quietly, while moving our employees back to a secure location in the United States. Following through on the exit plan will help WISE to refocus in other markets until China is a more stable market in which to do business.

Refer to: X-rates.com. Homepage. http://www.x-rates.com.

U.S. Embassy. Homepage. http://usembassy.state.gov. U.S. Department of State. Homepage. http://www.state.gov.

14. Selected References

Kolodko, Gregorz, From *Shock to Therapy: The Political Economy of Post socialist Transformation* (New York: Oxford University Press, 2000).

Lloyd, P. J., and Zhu, Xiaoguang, *Models of the Chinese Economy* (Northhampton, England: Edward Elgar, 2001).

Starr, John, *Understanding China: A Guide to China's Economy, History and Political Structure* (New York: Hill and Wang, 2000). For further information, see: *CIA World Factbook*, https://www. cia.gov/library/publications/the-world- factbook/index.html.

U.S. Bureau of Census at http://www.census.gov. U.S. Department of Commerce at http://www.stat-usa.gov.

U.S. Bureau of Economic Analysis at http://www.bea.gov. U.S. Embassy. Homepage. http://usembassy.gov.

World Trade Centers Institute at http://www.wtci.org. World Trade Organization at http://www.wto.org.

15. Glossary

Collective ownership – May be ownership by an organization or body of companies or the equivalent.

Han Chinese – An ethnic group in China that dominates the country with 92 % of the population.

Private ownership – Ownership by individuals or private entities.

Socialist Ownership – Ownership by the government of land, somewhat similar to ownership by a state in the United States.

About the Author

Professor Jonathan Adelman, full professor in the Graduate School of International Studies of the UNIVERSITY OF DENVER. Since receiving his Ph.D. in Chinese and Russian politics from Columbia University in 1976, he has written or edited 10 books. Having visited China numerous times, he is an honorary professor at both Peking University and People's University.

Pius K Leung, CCIM, *Adjunct Professor of the Bauer College of Business at University of Houston and University of International Business and Economic in Beijing*

Costa Rica

INTERNATIONAL REAL ESTATE (GLOBAL REAL ESTATE)
Authored by *Jose Ramirez Dr. Mark Lee Levine*, Editor

■ 1. Geography

Costa Rica is located in Central America. It borders Nicaragua to the north, Panama to the south, the Pacific Ocean to the west, and the Caribbean Ocean to the east. Costa Rica consists of 51,100 square kilometers (km) and is approximately twice the land size of Maryland. Coastlines consist of 1,290 km on the Pacific Ocean and the Caribbean Sea.

The Costa Rican climate is typically tropical, hot and humid, with warm days and cool nights. The temperature varies according to the altitude. The Pacific coast is drier than the Atlantic Coast, where rain falls about 300 days per year. The temperature in San Jose varies from 16°C (61°F) to 26°C (79°F), and rain falls about 183 days per year. The wet season is from May to November. The hottest months are May and June. Terrain includes coastal plains, which are separated by rugged mountains.[72]

Land use includes 31% for forests and woodlands, 6% arable land, and permanent crops of only 5%. Meadows and pastures are 46%, with the balance of the land in other uses.

Environmental issues include deforestation, soil erosion, coastal marine pollution, fisheries protection, solid waste management, and air pollution. Conservation efforts are present relative forest conservation, clean energy/clean technology, climate change prevention, land improvement, biodiversity, endangered species and marine life conservation, whaling, pollution relative to wetlands and other areas, and waste management (industrial waste and municipal solid waste (MSW), hazardous waste, **o**rganic waste and waste agricultural biomass (WAB), waste plastics, **and** e- waste). Border issues with Nicaragua have threatened the country's tourism industry in the area known as the San Juan River. Talks between the two nations regarding this issue began in 1999, and Costa Rica took its case before the International Court of Justice in September, 2005. In this court's opinion, rendered in July 2009, although some rights were reserved for Nicaragua to regulate navigation on the San Juan River common areas, persons travelling on the San Juan River on board of Costa Rican vessels were no longer required to obtain Nicaraguan visas or to purchase Nicaraguan tourist cards.

■ 2. History and Overview

Costa Rica gained its independence from Spain on September 15, 1821. Hence, the background for most Costa Ricans is from Europe, mainly from Spain. According to the 2011 census, whites or mestizos account for roughly 84% of the population, mulattos account for roughly 7%, and afro descendants account for about 1% of the population.

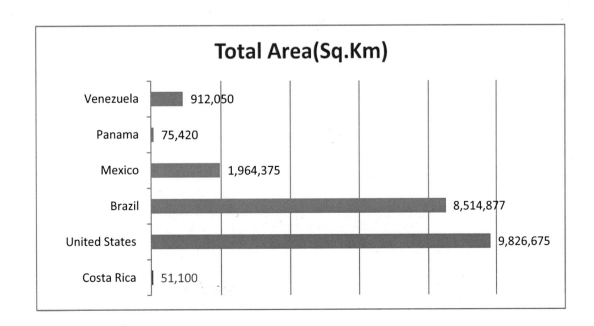

In general, most of the population (73%) lives in urban areas, mainly in the Cetral Valley, where Costa Rica's major cities: San José, Heredia, Alajuela and Cartago, are located.

Cost a Rica, joining other Central American provinces, declared independence from Spain on September 15, 1821. It was part of a Federation from 1823 to 1838, when border disputes among the provinces of the Federation made Costa Rica to withdraw and to proclaim its sovereignty.

In the upper part of the 19th century, democracy in Costa Rica began, with only two lapses between 1917 and 1919, when Federico Tinocoruled as a dictator, and, in 1948, when Jose Figures led an armed uprising in the wake of a disputed presidential election. The constituted junta, after Figures' civil war, drafted a constitution that guaranteed universal suffrage and the abolition of the military. In fact, today Costa Rica remains without a military force. Social order is safe guarded by the police force.[75]

3. People

Costa Rica's estimated population for 2015 is **4,832,234** people with an age structure of 23% in the 0 to 14- year-old category, and 70% in the 15-year-old through 64-year-old category. The balance, a small percentage of 7%, is in the 65 years of age and older group.

Life expectancy for the male population is 77.4 years (2015, est.) The female life expectancy is 82.4 years (2015, est.) The

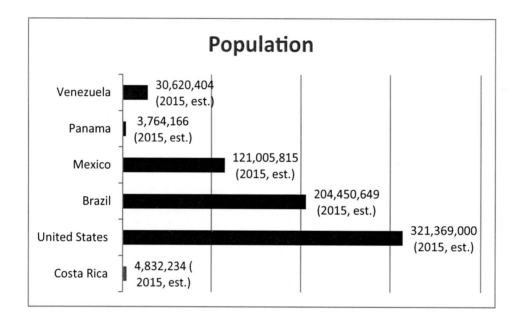

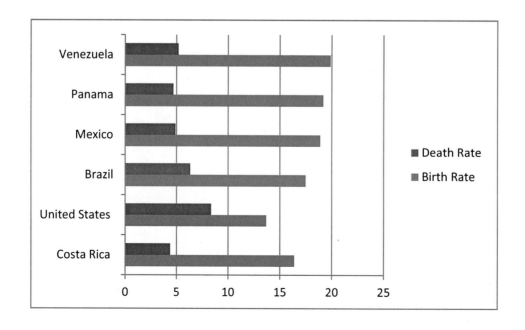

population growth rate is projected to stay at 1.1% in 2015. Birth rates are about 15.3 in 1,000 of population (2015, est.) The death rate is approximately 4.4 in 1,000 of population (2015, est.)

The dominant (and official) religion in Costa Rica is Roman Catholic at 76.3%, with Evangelical at 13.7% as, Jehovah's Wit nesses at 1.3%, other Protestant at 0.7%, and others religions at about 8% other.

The official language is Spanish, but English is understood in tourist areas. The use of French and German is increasing. Many Caribbean Blacks in Costa Rica speak an English dialect, known as *Creole*.

Approximately 98% of the population is literate - defined as the population age 10 and over who can read and write (2015 est.)

4. Government

Costa Rica is a democratic republic, with its capital located in San Jose. The country is administratively divided into seven Provinces, Provincias: San José, Alajuela, Cartago, Heredia, Guanacaste, Puntarenas y Limón.

The current constitution was formed on November 7, 1949. The legal system in Costa Rica follows the Spanish civil law system, with judicial review of legislative acts in the Supreme Court. The government consists of Executive, Legislative, and Judicial Branches. In addition to the three Branches, the Supreme Tribunal of Elections is considered to be a fourth Branch.

The Executive Branch consists of the President, two Vice Presidents, and their ministers. The Legislative Branch is a unicameral assembly, *Asamblea Legislativa*, formed by 57 deputies, *diputados*. The Judicial Branch consists of the Supreme Court of Justice, Corte Suprema de Justicia, composed by 22 magistrates,.The Election Branch is represented by the Supreme Tribunal of Elections, *Tribunal*

Supremode Elecciones.Diplomatic representation, in the form of consulates exists in the U.S., providing services for the majority of U.S. states. Costa Rica also has an embassy in the U.S., which is located in Washington, D.C.

5. Economy

The Costa Rican economy depends on tourism, agriculture, and electronics exports. Electronic exports have been very important since 1998, when high-tech companies, such as Acer, Microsoft®, GE and Intel Corporation, chose Costa Rica to place production and distribution facilities.

The Gross Domestic Product (GDP) per capita earning is approximately $ 10,184.6 (2013, est.) The inflation rate has been between 3.68% (2013) and 5.82% (2010) between 2009 and 2014, which positively reflects the efforts made by the government in Costa Rica, since 2000, to curb inflation amid public service inefficiency and a large government deficit. Unemployment has also been fairly high for the last number of years, exceeding 11%, and although it declined to 6.6% in 2006, this rose again to 8.5% in 2013. Cost a Rica's annual GDP growth rate is projected at 4.1% for 2015.

In addition to tourism, industries include microprocessors, food processing, textiles, clothing, construction materials, fertilizer, and plastic products. Costa Rica exported a total of $11.472 billion in 2013. In that same year, 2013, Costa Rica imported $18.124 billion mostly in petroleum, electronic integrated circuits, printed circuits, medicaments, transmission apparatus, raw materials, consumer goods, capital equipment, and electricity. Costa Rica's major trading partners are the United States, Netherlands, China, Mexico and Japan.

6. Currency

Currency is the *colon* (C.), consisting of 100 cents in one (1) colon See the Burns School Global Real Estate Web site for the UNIVERSITY OF DENVER at http://burns.daniels.du.edu for currency conversions.

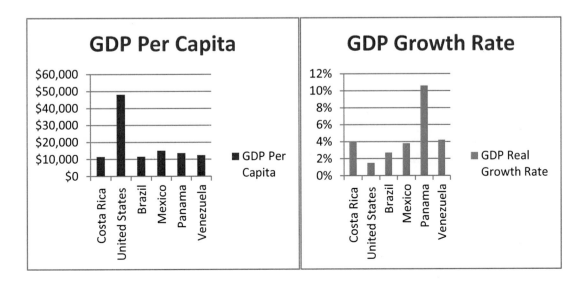

7. Transportation

Costa Rica has approximately 278 kilometers (km) of railroad lines, and 38,018 km of roadways, with about 25% of the roadways being paved. There are about 730 km of inland waterways in Costa Rica that are seasonally navigable. Petroleum products pipelines are 662 km (2010).

Costa Rica has six ports for shipping and harbors: Caldera, Golfito, Moin, Puerto Limón, Puerto Quepos, and Puntarenas.

In 2013, the estimated number of airports in Costa Rica was 161, including 47 with paved runways.

8. Communications

In 2012, Costa Rica had approximately 1.018 million main telephone lines in use, and 6.151 million mobile cellular's. Current expansion includes satellite earth stations, coaxial cables, and interurban, fiber optic networks.

In 2015, Costa Rica had AM radio, FM radio and shortwave radio stations, as well as a number of television broadcast stations.

9. Real Property Issues

In Costa Rica, all properties are registered in the Property Section of the *Registro Público* under the *Registro Nacional*. Condominiums are registered in a special section, called the Horizontal Property, *Propiedad Horizontal*.

Property subject to condominium laws and regulations is registered under a general entry (mother property, fincamadre).Each individual unit is registered as a sub entry, fincafilial. In the *Registro* under property entries, one will find all entries that affect the title. Condominium owners have their own set of regulations. These regulations solve problems relating to commons areas. Many older buildings are being renovated into condominiums and then subjected to the regulations.

This registry should show the legal owners, all liens, encumbrances and related contracts affecting the property. Information on the *Registro Nacional* does notmake reference to the selling prices and terms.

Real estate agents, *agentes*, or brokers, *corredores inmobiliarios*, receive a commission from the seller. The commission ranges between 5% and 10% of the purchase price and is paid when the sale closes. While people acting as real estate agents and brokers are not necessarily licensed, there are rules and regulations governing the process. Almost anyone can act as an agent or broker. The agent or broker has no legal obligation to the buyer, other than helping the buyer reach an agreement with the seller. Most agents will act as intermediaries in the negotiation of price and purchase conditions. Some agents may have studies made of the *Registro*.

After finding property, one needs an attorney. The attorney is responsible for protecting one's interests during the negotiations and the closing. The attorney will also check the property's registration and inform the buyer of the legal status of the property. The counsel's responsibilities also include negotiating conditions and clauses in the contract. It is best to agree on an attorney's fee at the beginning of the relationship. The fee can be a fixed rate, percentage of purchase price, hourly or any combination. One should have the agreement in writing to avoid misunderstandings. Notarial fees must also be paid for the notarization and registration of the closing. These fees have a fixed rate. They are established by executive degree. Other fees include property taxes, stamp taxes and registry fees. All of these fees together represent approximately 5% of the purchase price. Independent appraisals are available. Because the appraised value is usually only a reference, it does not always reflect the "actual" value of the property.

There are two associations that allow membership to licensed real estate agents and brokers: (1) Costa Rican Chamber of Commerce for Real Estate, Cámara Costarricense de *Corredores de Bienes Raices*, and (2) Costa Rica Global Associations of REALTORS (CRGAR).[79]

The Plat Registry, *Catastro*, which is part of the *Registro Nacional*, should have a registered plat or map of the property. The map should include: the owner, location, size, boundaries, reference to the registration and, sometimes, information on surrounding properties.

Contracts are not as comprehensive as in many other western countries. Due to the Costa Rican civil law system, contracts usually cover the items that the law doesnot mandate. Some agents have contracts establishing their right to list your property. This is not common practice. The notary who is also responsible for closing and recording the transaction prepares the contracts.

Before closing, the seller and the buyer must select a notary, notario. The notary is responsible for drafting and registering all purchase documents. Legally, the notary is working for both parties and should look after both parties' interests. This obligation is not always met, since the notary is usually a trusted person of the party selecting the notary. If the buyer is paying in full, he has the right to select the notary. If the seller is financing, he has the right to select the notary. And if a bank is providing the loan, it has the right to select the notary. Notaries have a far greater responsibility under civil law. They must be attorneys before being accepted to act as notaries. Final registration of the property is not possible until all needed documents and all moneys have been given to the notary.

Yearly property taxes are lower, proportionally, than those of comparable property in the United States. Currently this is 0.25% of the registered value of the property. This value of the property is determined every five years, by a board certified engineer, with experience in real estate valuation, and hired by municipality where the property is located. The owner of property would have the right to challenge this determination according to the law. There is a transfer tax of 1.5%, applied to the higher between the (1) registered value of the property and (2) sale price of the property. Currently, there are no capital gains taxes on the disposition of real estate.

If property tax, transfer tax, or any other tax payment is delayed, the property assessed will become security for that payment. The government will then have the right to secure a tax lien against the property.

Article 45 of the Costa Rican Constitution provides protection for private property.

No person can be deprived of their property unless a justified public interest is legally proven to exist. If this is the case, the owner must be justly compensated. In the past, problems arose with foreigners over expropriations. Constitutional amendments have made it difficult for the government to expropriate, especially without compensation.

In Cost a Rica, if a property owner dies and there are no heirs, the property will revert to the government. Fee simple estates are the common way to own property. The leasehold in Costa Rica, is established by a *Contrato de Arrendamiento*, a tenant agreement, which is called in the *Ley General de Arrendamientos Urbanos y Suburbanos*. This law applies to tenant agreements for housing, office space, commercial or industrial purposes. Under current Costa Rican laws, it is almost impossible to evict a tenant. The Costa Rican government passed the Monitorio Arrendaticio law (in 2013) to help expedite tenant evictions, but procedural problems are hampering this latest government effort to alleviate this problem.

Tenat leases is regulated by civil code. These are restricted to what is said in the contract. Registration of the leases are not required, but the leases can affect the property. When purchasing property, one should physically inspect the property and question the person that has possession. Unregistered leases are common in Cost a Rica. To avoid legal issues, one should have tenants evicted *prior* to purchasing a property.

Property can be owned individually, jointly, in trust, as household property, or in the name of corporations, or any combination of the same. For estate planning purposes, the most common way to own property has been through corporations. One individual can own all of the stock in a corporation. Joint property ownership can be a percentage of the property or be physically divided.

Title insurance is not currently available; it should not be necessary if the *Registro* functions properly. Costa Rica's property registration system can be considered a form of the Torrens system. The *Registro Nacional* should have the history of the property with all of its encumbrances. All property registered under Costa Rican Civil law is titled property. Untitled property cannot be registered. It is possible to purchase the rights to untitled property, but there are substantial risks with such purchases. There is no way to be sure that the declared owner is the legal owner. The two most common types of mortgages are the normal mortgage, *Hipoteca Común*, and the bond mortgage, *Cédula Hipotecaria*. A normal mortgage is security for the loan, with the property being sold to collect loan costs if the loan is not paid. The mortgage can be assigned, but transfer costs will be about the same as a new loan. A bond mortgage is in the form of a document. The owner of the document has the right to collect specified payments from the property owner. If payments are not made, the document owner can sell the property through court proceedings and keep the proceeds. The document owner has the right to sue the property owner if proceeds from the sale are not enough to cover the debt.

Buyers can finance single-family homes, townhomes, condominiums, apartment buildings, commercial projects and industrial projects. The real estate mortgage bond market has taken off, with the Costa Rican government passing laws allowing contracts to be conducted in U.S. dollars. People are now able to borrow at much better rates and in a stronger currency. Although private banks, many sponsored by U.S. lending institutions, are becoming more prevalent in Costa Rica, the three state banks are the only banks that are 100% insured. The real estate bond market is international, with a multitude of private investors.

During the past few years, zoning laws have been enforced. These laws are not registered against the property, so buyers should research them, separately. Since most easements are registered, buyers can determine if any easements affect the property. Easements are either apparent (seen on property) or non-apparent.

All mineral rights in Cost a Rica are government owned. Under the Cost a Rican Mining Code, the government has the power to authorize exploration and exploitation of minerals on third- party property. Property owners are paid compensation for any government restrictions on the use of the property.

Most shoreline property is owned by the government and can only be developed through a concession, granted by the government. These concessions are issued for five to twenty years. Yearly payments must be made to the Concession Registry, to keep it current. Non- Costa Ricans have restrictions on these concessions; they must have lived in Costa Rica for five years as a legal resident. If a corporation has title to a concession, it is not allowed to have more than a 50% foreign ownership. With deforestation problems, Cost a Rica is making an effort to preserve its natural forests. If a person's property is near a forestry reserve or ecological buffer zone, one might find ecological restrictions.

Certain building restrictions may be imposed on new construction or renovation. Also, builders should be careful in signing waivers to obtain building permits. The waiver to collect indemnification for improvements allows the government to purchase the land, without taking into account the value of improvements.

A number of strong Web site links help to acquire information on Costa Rican realty, especially the National Association of REALTORS®, Web site, the Miami Association of REALTORS®, Andersen Consulting, and the Global Real Estate Website at the UNIVERSITY OF DENVER, *Daniels College of Business*, Burns School of Real Estate and Construction Management (Burns School) (http://burns.daniels.du.edu).

■ 10. Real Estate Trends

Waterfront property is a highly sought investment by both local and nonlocal investors. The prices for these properties are rising dramatically and many of the properties have become over-priced. There are other types of property available at a slight distance from the waterfront whose prices are much more reasonable. It is currently recommended, due to high interest rates, that potential investors seek financing from institutions outside of Cost a Rica. For the latest trends, see the Selected References section at the end of this Chapter.

■ 11. Cultural Issues

Any nation's culture is complex and vibrant in its diversity. While broad cultural characterizations such as those presented here can be generally accurate, following such generalities too strictly may be dangerously misleading. To conduct business effectively and profitably in a country, it is vital to have a thorough understanding of its culture's complexities.

Western dress is common throughout Costa Rica. Women generally pay more attention to their appearance than men and are generally very fashionably dressed. Women friends or relatives greet each other with a light kiss on the cheek. If women are not yet acquainted, they often pat each other on the arm. Men shake hands. When addressing others, professional titles are used either with or without a surname, depending on the situation. Señor (Mr.) and *Señora* (Mrs.) are also used, especially for people with whom one is not well acquainted.

Hand gestures are common and important to everyday conversation. Eye contact is very important, especially when discussing a serious issue or talking to a superior. It is traditionally understood that the lack of eye contact means the person cannot be trusted. Chewing gum while speaking is very impolite.

Urban Costa Ricans generally prefer that visits be arranged in advance. Dinner guests are usually given refreshments and drinks while they socialize with their hosts for an hour or so before the meal is served. After dinner, coffee and dessert accompany more conversation. Guests generally leave shortly thereafter. Costa Ricans eat rice and beans in various combinations for nearly every meal. Typical at breakfast is *gallo pinto* (which is a mixture of rice and black beans). Casado—made up of rice, black beans, eggs, meat, and plantain—is a common lunchtime (and very heavy) meal.

12. Discussion Questions

1. **How important is it to make eye contact when conducting business in Costa Rica?**

2. **What large industry is being impacted by the labor dispute between Costa Rica and Nicaragua?**

3. **What kind of impact does the environment have on development in Costa Rica?**

13. Case Study

Diving Underwater Guide Services (DUGS) San Jose, Costa Rica

Memo

To: Board of Directors
From: Consultants
Re: I.R.S. Phone Call

I. Problem

Diving Underwater Guide Services (DUGS) has been operating out of Costa Rica for over ten years. DUGS has successfully operated at a profit, and it has had improved profit margins every year since it opened.

Recently a phone call from the I.R.S was received on the Company answering machine, referring to the fact that one of the DUGS' partners is under investigation for tax evasion. This is a highly grave matter. Three members of the Board of Directors own the Company, as a Limited Liability Company. This could affect all of the owners, not just the person being investigated.

DUGS has consulted a Tax Attorney. He suggested that DUGS engage an independent auditor, to audit of all of the books immediately. This is to make sure that everything is correct. If there is a problem, DUGS must find a way to either restructure so that the partner under investigation does not affect the business, or, in the alternative, close the business.

II. Initial Exit Strategy

The initial exit strategy that was planned was to turn over ownership to the owners, once the current owner was ready to retire. When the three parties started the business, they never thought there would be a reason to exit. They were young and did not plan for the future. So, the most that the owners did was to draw up an Limited Liability Company, so that the children would inherit or take over the percentage of ownership when the given owner was no longer with the Company.

III. Contingency Exit Strategy

This was never planned; however, with the current events, DUGS needs to find out what are its options to protect the business. If there is a way to restructure

the Company so that it is protected, this would be a favorable choice. The owners do not want to close or exit. If the owners must close, to protect their own personal assets, it can do so and sell the assets to other dive shops in the area.

A restructure might make more sense, because if DUGS sells the assets, it would not be able to sell for enough to cover the costs of closing and to set up a new company. If DUGS is able to restructure and remain open, it could begin to plan an exit strategy. (If DUGS tries to sell the business at this point, it would be difficult because, with the I.R.S. investigating, it would reduce the value of the Company. (Restructuring and then selling would be a much more favorable option to exit.

IV. Conclusion

A tax attorney should be hired to oversee the audit of the Company, give guidance and help on the restructure.

The remaining two owners could look to buy out the other partner. The cost for the attorney and any other restructuring costs should be deducted from the "defaulting" owner's share, considering that it was the actions of that person which brought the problems to the business. If DUGS must liquidate the assets and sell the shop, DUGS must consider if it should list the property themselves, or find a local expert.

Refer to: International Real Estate Digest. Homepage. http://www.ired. com. X-rates.com. Homepage. http:// www.x-rates.com.

U.S. Embassy. Homepage. http:// usembassy.state.gov. U.S. Department of State. Homepage. http://www.state. gov.

14. Selected References

Britannica.com Inc. Costa *Rica: Statistics.* Britannica. com Inc. (Online) Available: http://www.britannica. com.

CIA World Factbook at https://www.cia.gov/library/ publications/the-world-factbook/geos/cs.html

Costa Rican-American Chamber of Commerce. Publications: *Business Costa Rica.*

Costa Rican-American Chamber of Commerce (Online). Available: http://www.amcham.co.cr.

Cost a Rica Net (2000). *Real Estate in Costa Rica.* Cost a Rica Net (Online) at http://www.crica.com/restate/.

Inter-American Development Bank(2000).Basic Socio-Economic Data Report: Costa

Rica. Inter-American Development Bank(Online).Available: http://www.iadb.org. International Real Estate Digest. Homepage. http://www.ired.com. Organization of American States at http://www.oas.org.

Richard Ellis International Property Specialists. C.B. Richard Ellis. http://www.cbre.com.

Time Almanac. *TIME Almanac.* Boston: Information Please LLC. U.S. Bureau of Census at http://www. census.gov.

U.S. Department of Commerce at http://www.stat-usa.gov. U.S. Bureau of Economic Analysis at http:// www.bea.gov. U.S. Embassy. Homepage. http:// usembassy.state.gov.

United States Department of St at e. *Background Notes: Costa Rica.* United States

Department of State (Online). Available: http://www. state.gov.

World Trade Centers Institute at http://www.wtci.org. World Trade Organization at http://www.wto.org. X-rates.com. Homepage. http://www.x-rates.com/.

United Nations Data, Country Profile: Costa Rica, https://data.un.org/CountryProfile.aspx?cr Name=COSTA%20RICA

International Court of Justice, (Costa Rica v. Nicaragua), Judgment, I.C.J. Reports 2009, p. 213, http:// www.icj-cij.org/

Instituto Meterorológico Nacional, http://www.imn.ac.cr

U.S. Embassy, Costa Rica, Environmental Hub For Central America And The Caribbean, http://costarica.usembassy.gov/envhub.html

Global Issues: Social, Political, Economic and Environmental Issues That Affect Us All: Protecting Biodiversity in Costa Rica's Thermal Convection Dome in the Pacific, http://www.globalissues.org/news/2014/10/20/20190

Global Issues: Social, Political, Economic and Environmental Issues That Affect Us All: Climate Change Legislation Faltering in Costa Rica, http://www.globalissues.org/news/2014/05/21/18715

Global Issues: Social, Political, Economic and Environmental Issues: Carbon-Neutral Costa Rica: A Climate Change Mirage?, http://www.globalissues.org/news/2014/02/05/18196

Global Partnership on Waste Management: Costa Rica, http://www.unep.org/gpwm/Information-Platform/CountryNeedsAssessmentAnalysis/CostaRica/tabid/106562/Default.aspx#organic

World Statesmen.org, Nations and Territories: Costa Rica, http://www.worldstatesmen.org/Costa_Rica.html

Instituto Nacional de Estadistica y Censos (INEC), Censo 2011, Resultados: C 14. Costa Rica Población total por auto identificación étnica-racial, según provincia y sexo, http://www.inec.go.cr/Web/Home/GeneradorPagina.aspx

Instituto Nacional de Estadistica y Censos (INEC), X Censo Nacional de Población y VI de Vivienda 2011: Resultados Generales, http://www.cipacdh.org/pdf/Resultados_Generales_Censo_2011.pdf http://www.cipacdh.org/pdf/Resultados_Generales_Censo_2011.pdf

Naciones Unidas, Cepal: Comité Especial de la CEPAL sobre Población y Desarrollo, Ecuador 2012, Población, territorio y desarrollo sostenible, http://www.cepal.org/sites/default/files/publication/files/s2012034_es.pdf

Ministerio del Poder Popular de Planificación, Instituto Nacional de Estadística, Demográficos - Proyecciones de Población: Venezuela. Proyección de la población, según entidad y sexo, 2000-2050 (año calendario), http://www.ine.gov.ve/index.php?option=com_content&view=category&id=98&Itemid=51

Dirección de Estadística y Censo, Estadística Panameña: SituaciónDemográfica, Estimaciones y Proyecciones de la Población en la República de Panamá, por Provincia. Comarca Indígena, Distrito y Corregimiento, Según Sexo: Años 2000-2015,

Boletín No. 10, https://www.contraloria.gob.pa/inec/Archivos/P2391Boletin10.pdf

Consejo Nacional de Población, Secretaría de Gobernación, Proyeccion de la Población 2010-2050, Datos de Proyecciones, http://www.conapo.gob.mx/es/CONAPO/Proyecciones_Datos

Instituto Brasileiro de Geografia e Estatística (IBGE), Diretoria de Pesquisas. Coordenação de População e Indicadores Sociais. Gerência de Estudos e Análises da Dinâmica Demográfica, http://www.ibge.gov.br/home/estatistica/populacao/projecao_da_populacao/2013/default_tab.shtm

U.S. Census Bureau, Population Division, Projections of the Population and Components of Change for the United States: 2015 to 2060 (NP2014-T1), http://www.census.gov/population/projections/data/national/2014/summarytables.html

Instituto Nacional de Estadistica y Censos (INEC), Población y Demografía – Población – Proyecciones, Resultados Nacionales, http://www.inec.go.cr/Web/Home/GeneradorPagina.aspx

Gobierno fácil, Gobierno y Democracia, http://www.gobiernofacil.go.cr/E-GOB/weblinks/index.aspx

Embassy of Costa Rica to the Kingdom of Belgium, the Grand-Duchy of Luxembourg, and Mission to the European Union, Costa Rica, Government, http://costaricaembassy.be/en/costa_rica/government/

Embassy of Costa Rica in Washington D.C., http://www.costarica-embassy.org

World Bank, GDP per Capita (current US$), Costa Rica, http://data.worldbank.org/indicator/NY.GDP.PCAP.CD/countries/CR?display=graph

Banco Central de Costa Rica, Índice de Precios al Consumidor (IPC), Variaciones Acumuladas, Índice General, http://indicadoreseconomicos.bccr.fi.cr/indicadoreseconomicos/Cuadros/frmVerCatCuadro.aspx?idioma=1&CodCuadro=%209

Instituto Nacional de Estadistica y Censos (INEC), Resultados y Series, Empleo: Series 2003-2009, C6B Fuerza de trabajo condicion de trabajo y tasas 2010-2013, http://www.inec.go.cr/enaho/result/empleo.aspx

The World Bank, Data, Global Economic Prospects – Forecast: Costa Rica, http://data.worldbank.org/country/costa-rica#cp_wdi

World Bank, World Integrated Trade Solution, Costa Rica Trade Summary 2013 Data, http://wits.worldbank.org/CountryProfile/Country/CRI/Year/2013/Summary

Green Condos, Reglamento a la Ley Reguladora de la Propiedad en Condominio en Costa Rica, http://www.greencondoscr.com/2012/reglamento-ley-reguladora-propiedad-condominio-costa-rica/

Viva Costa Rica, Food and Drink, http://www.viva-costarica.com/costa-rica-information/costa-rica-food.html

Asamblea Legislativa de la República de Costa Rica. Ley 7527, Ley General de Arrendamientos Urbanos y Suburbanos, www.asamblea.go.cr

Asamblea Legislativa de la República de Costa Rica. Ley 7933, Ley Reguladora de la Propiedad en Condominio, www.asamblea.go.cr

Asamblea Legislativa de la República de Costa Rica. Ley 7509, Impuesto Sobre Bienes Inmuebles

Asamblea Legislativa de la República de Costa Rica. Ley 9160, Monitorio Arrendaticio.

Imprenta Nacional - Costa Rica, https://www.imprentanacional.go.cr

Is there a Licensing for Real Estate Agents in Costa Rica, Simons, M., June 24, 2013, http://www.tanktopsflipflops.com/is-there-licensing-for-real-estate-agents-in-costa-rica/

Cámara Costarricense de Corredores de Bienes Raíces, http://camara.cr

Costa Rica Global Association of REALTORS®, http://crgar.com/

Impuesto a la Propiedad de Bienes Inmuebles Costa Rica – Exención, D&N Servicios, http://www.dyncr.com/blog/impuesto-a-la-propiedad-de-bienes-inmuebles-costa-rica-exencion/

Ministerio de Hacienda, Dirección General de Tributación, B. Impuesto Sobre el Traspaso de Bienes Inmuebles, http://dgt.hacienda.go.cr/tiposimpuestos/Paginas/Impuestosobrelostraspasodebienesinmuebles.aspx

Justia, Costa Rica, Leyes, http://costa-rica.justia.com/nacionales/leyes/

Karen Real Estate, Costa Rica Taxes, http://karenreal-estate.com/info/taxes-in-costa-rica.16.html

Diario Extra, La Ley y su Alcance, Morales, G., http://www.diarioextra.com/Anterior/detalle/236231/la-ley-a-su-alcance

Properties in Costa Rica, FAQ Property Ownership, http://www.propertiesincostarica.com/faq.html#restrictions

Kiribe S.A., FAQ's, http://kirebe.com/faqs-en

Lang & Asociados, Real Estate, Language: Can Foreign Languages be Validly Used in Binding Documents and Transactions in Costa Rica, http://www.langcr.com/language_real_estate.html

The Real Costa Rica, Carter, J. Buying Beachfront Property in Costa Rica, http://www.therealcostarica.com/realestatecostarica/buy_beachfront.html

The Real Costa Rica, Banking and Currency Costa Rica, http://www.therealcostarica.com/costa_rica_business/banking_in_costa_rica.html

(AMCHAM), Cost a Rican American Chamber of Commerce. "Doing Business in Cost a Rica". Miami,2011.Costa Rican-American Chamber of Commerce.<www.amcham.co.cr>.

Affairs, Bureau of Consular. *International Travel*. Washington: Travel.State.Gov United States Department of State,2012.Print.

15. Glossary

Arrendamiento Civil – Common leasehold, a contractual lease in which the parties agree to their contractual obligations.

Catastro – The plat registry, which is part of the Registro Nacional. Will have a registered plat or map of the property.

Cédula Hipotecaria –Bond mortgage.

Concession Registry – Yearly payments must be made to this registry if one receives a concession to develop specific property owned by the government.

Contrato de Arrendamiento – Tenant agreement;, called in the "Ley General de Arrendamientos Urbanos y Suburbanos", which regulates the leasing of real estate in Costa Rica.

Corredores inmobiliarios – Brokers.

Creole – An English dialect spoken by Caribbean Black in Costa Rica.

Finca Filial: An exclusive property within a condominium, which is an autonomous portion for the independent use and enjoyment, and that is directly communicate with public roads or with a certain common space leading to them.

Finca Filial Matriz: Is any *finca filial* that for its own characteristics, in terms of size, availability of services and access, allows to build a new condominium within the original condominium.

Finca Matriz: Property that originates the condominium, conformed by two or more "fincas filiales" and its corresponding common areas.

Hipoteca Común – Normal mortgage.

Asamblea de Condominio – is the supreme organ of the condominium where under its jurisdiction, matters of common interest are treated and discussed, and disputes, if any, are resolved.

Propiedade Horizontal – Horizontal Property; were condominiums register.

About the Author

José F. Ramirez was born in Caracas, Venezuela, where he earned a degree in civil engineering at the Universidad Central de Venezuela. He later earned a, in the United Stated, a diploma in business administration from the University of California – Berkeley; a master's in real estate and construction management from the Burns School of Real Estate and Construction Management, *Daniels College of Business,* UNIVERSITY OF DENVER; and, in Australia, a Master of Construction Law from the University of Melbourne. At the beginning of his career, he actively appraised residential real estate in Venezuela. A few years later, he actively participated in the design and development of commercial real estate in that country. More recently he has provided consulting construction and real estate services for commercial real estate in the Colombia, United States and Venezuela. He currently works as a consultant for the construction and real estate development industries in the United States.

Czech Republic

INTERNATIONAL REAL ESTATE (GLOBAL REAL ESTATE)

Dr. Mark Lee Levine, Editor

■ 1. Geography

The Czech Republic, a part of former Czechoslovakia, is located in central Europe, southeast of Germany. The Czech Republic has approximately 78,867 sq km (square kilometers) of land. It is bounded by Austria, Germany, Poland and Slovakia. The Czech Republic has no coastline because it is landlocked by the countries noted above. Border disputes existed prior to its separation from Slovakia, and border disputes continue regarding land confiscation from World War II, including with Liechtenstein.

The climate in the Czech Republic is fairly temperate, with cool summers and fairly cold and humid winters. The terrain is generally rolling plains in the west, and some hills and plateaus. In the eastern part in Moravia, the terrain is mainly hills. Environmental issues persist in most of Europe; the Czech Republic is no exception. Air and water pollution issues around Bohemia are prevalent, and acid rain damages the forests. The Czech Republic has made treaties and agreements relative to pollution problems.

■ 2. History and Overview

Czechs lost their independence to the Hapsburgs Empire in 1620. The Czechs were under the rule of the Austrian monarchy for 300 years. The collapse of the monarchy brought independence to the Czechs following World War I. Despite cultural differences, the Slovaks shared with the Czechs similar aspirations for independence from the Hapsburgs and voluntarily united with the Czechs. Slovaks did not share the same economic or cultural development as the Czechs, but the opportunities for freedom enabled the Slovaks to overcome some of these differences. Czechoslovakia fell under German control in March of 1939. At the end of World War II, Soviet troops overran all of Slovakia, Moravia, and much of Bohemia, including Prague. A civilian uprising against the German garrison took place in Prague in May 1945. Following Germany's surrender, some 2.9 million ethnic Germans were expelled from Czechoslovakia with Allied approval under the Benes Decrees.

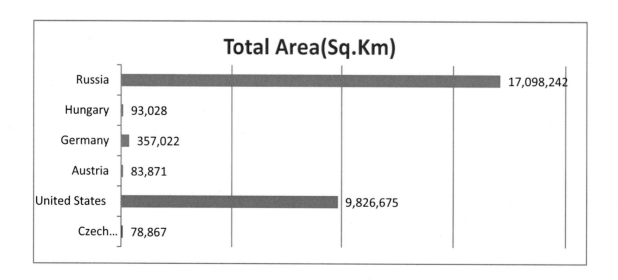

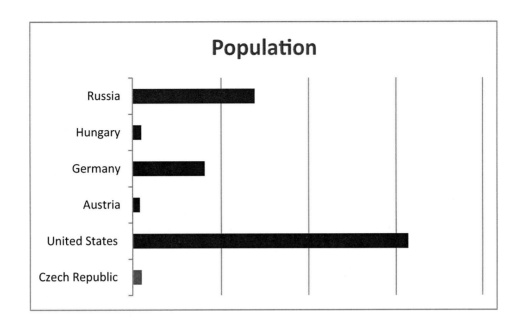

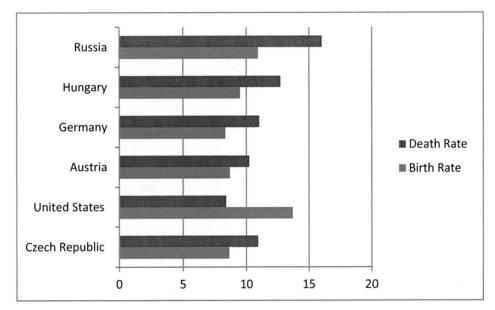

Reunited after the war, the Slovaks and Czechs held national elections in which the majority of the key positions went to the Communist party. This group eventually succeeded in quieting the anti-Communist forces. The Communist party seized power in February 1948. The Communist party remained in control until its almost complete collapse following the Velvet Revolution in November 1989. The Czechs and the Slovaks separated into two (2) countries in 1993, resulting in the Czech Republic and the Republic of Slovakia.

Soviet influence was present with both countries, given that the Communists seized Czechoslovakia in 1948 and continued to control the country until 1989.[83]

■ 3. People

The population of the Czech Republic is 10,627,448 people. The dominant age, 67.6%, is the 15-year-old to 64-year-old category. The 0 to 14-year-old age group accounts for 14.9% of the populace, and the 65-and-older age group accounts for 17.5% of the population.

The birth rate is approximately 9.79 per 1,000. The death rate is approximately 10.29 per 1,000. Life expectancy is approximately 78.31 years, with males living 75.34 years, and females living 81.45 years.

Of the populace, 64.3% is Czech. Moravians account for 5%, while 1.4% is Slovak. The balance is generally made up of other groups.

As a result of control by the Communists for so many years, nearly 34.5% of Czechs are not affiliated with any religious group. About 10.4% are Roman Catholic, and the balance consists of Protestants and other religions.

The language in the Czech Republic is generally Czech, with a fair amount of Slovak being spoken. The two languages are very similar, and Czechs and Slovakians can easily understand one another. A very high literacy rate, 99%, indicates a well-educated populace, especially relative to most of the Eastern European populations.

4. Government

The Czech Republic is a Parliamentary democracy, with its capital in Prague. It has 13 Regions or divisions and one capital city for administrative purposes.

The independence of the Czech Republic was effective January 1, 1993, splitting off from Slovakia, as mentioned. The Constitution was ratified December 16, 1992 and was effective January 1, 1993.

The legal system is a civil law system based on Austro-Hungarian codes. Voting is at age 18 and is universal. Branches of the government include a Legislative Branch, which is a bicameral Parliament, an Executive Branch, and a Judicial Branch, led by its Supreme Court, which is a constitutional court.

Political parties exist in the Czech Republic, including the prior position of the Communist party, or KSCM, the Civic Democratic Party, the Civic Democratic Alliance or ODA, and a number other parties.

Diplomatic representation with the United States exists through an Ambassador housed in Washington, D.C. from the Czech Republic. The United States maintains diplomatic representation with the Czech Republic via an ambassador in Prague.

5. Economy

The Czech Republic has had a strong political and economic system relative to other countries in Eastern Europe, stabilizing after the collapse of the Soviet Union. The Czech Republic has attracted a great deal of foreign aid and foreign investments. There have been numerous changes in the Judicial and statutory positions, favoring more support and greater stability for foreigners investing in the Czech Republic.

The Gross Domestic Product (GDP) per capita is approximately $28,400. Inflation (consumer prices) is around 0.5% (2014 est.) Unemployment is 7.9% (2014 est.) All of this supports the economic expansion in the Czech Republic, with GDP real growth rate at 2.5%.

6. Currency

The currency in the Czech Republic is *koruny (CZK)*. The Czech Republic joined the European Union (EU) in 2004 and aims to replace the *koruny* with the *euro* within the several years. For current exchange rates for the koruny, see the currency Web links at the Burns School Global Real Estate Web site for the UNIVERSITY OF DENVER at http://burns.daniels.du.edu.

7. Transportation

The Czech Republic has 9,469 km (kilometers) of railroad line and has a fairly reasonable roadway system of over 130,671 km of roads, including 730 km of expressways.

There are no major inland waterways, aside from the Elbe (Labe). Several pipelines are utilized in the Czech Republic to move natural gas.

The Czech Republic has 128 airports (2013) to handle air transportation, with large cities like Prague able to handle international jet traffic from throughout the world.

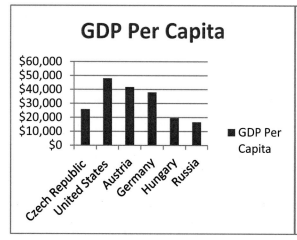

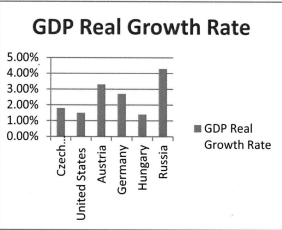

8. Communications

The Czech Republic has 2.1 million landline telephones for its population and 12.973 million cellular phones (2012 est.) International satellite earth stations are used, and AM, FM and short wave radio stations are prevalent, as well as television broadcast stations (2010).

9. Real Property Issues

Given the tumultuous background, the Czech Republic has quickly developed laws involving acquisition, use and disposition of real property.

Along with other former Communist-controlled countries, this country also faces the need to revamp its laws to provide for stability as to title of ownership in real estate, as the prior ownership was generally held by the Communist state.

One must be careful to distinguish the terms of ownership that are common in some Western countries, given that in the Czech Republic the term "ownership" may mean only the "land," and not include other improvements or activities on the land, such as buildings, natural objects such as growing crops, trees, etc.

Forms of ownership in the Czech Republic vary, but generally ownership in severalty and also concurrent forms of ownership exist, as well as ownership by partnerships, limited liability companies and joint stock companies. Ownership is transferred by properly recorded documents in the Real Estate Registrar's office. No title insurance is currently available in the Czech Republic; therefore, some degree of risk is prevalent relative to ownership of property. Prior record keeping under the prior Communist system makes it generally difficult to determine the status of property ownership.

Similar toot her previously cont rolled Communist countries, the Czech Republic continues to make the transition to privatization. Ownership of property often remains the means to determine who actually is and who should be owners of the real estate in question.

In the Czech Republic, a real estate broker is a *relatiní maklér*, and a real estate office is a *realtiní kancelàr*. Records of ownership are kept in the *Cadastre* office, called the *Katastràlni úrad*. Lawyers in these offices are qualified to register sales contracts, which are generally prepared by advocates and notaries. Deeds are also kept here; the Czech word for this type of document is roughly translated as "latest."

Those who wish to work as a broker or an agent must obtain a license, but this document, unlike the United States license, requires no qualifications. By law, licensed brokers may only work for sellers, while an agent can work for both buyers and sellers. Commission is charged to the seller, the buyer, or both. The general rate is 3% to 6%, but there are no legal requirements for rate or payment. In addition to commission, agents working for a broker often also receive a small salary.

Brokers may participate in Internet-based common listing systems, but properties listed on these systems rarely have exclusive rights contracts attached. There is no association of brokers, but the association of Real Estate office has a Code of Ethics that most brokers follow.

Contracts are written by attorneys and notaries, and terms cannot be changed by the buyer or seller once they are signed. The time between contract and settlement may take anywhere between two weeks and six months, with much faster times in Prague than outside of the city.

Settlement procedures are generally conducted by brokers' attorneys.

Financing is available for buyers. The term is up to 30 years, with a rate of around 5%. Some mortgage banks offer loans with no down payment, but at most banks the down payment is 30% of the loan amount. The mortgage contracts are recorded or registered in the Real Estate Registry to be effective.

In the Czech Republic, the government owns approximately one-third of all residential property. There are two types of real estate taxes: **land tax** and **building tax,** a tax on structures.

Land tax is imposed on plots of land that have been entered into the Land Register, and it is payable by the owner or user. The tax on land with building permission is CZK 1 per square meter.

Building tax is calculated according to the registered ground area of the building. It is CZK 1, 5, or 10 per square meter for residential buildings, and an additional CZK 0.75 per square meter for each additional floor.

In heavily populated areas, both land tax and building tax are multiplied by a coefficient that varies according to locality, ranging from 0.3 to 4.5. The highest coefficient is applicable in Prague.

The registered owner of the land or buildings generally pays these taxes on an annual basis, although in some cases the user or the leaseholder is the payer. All taxpayers must file tax returns to their financial authorities by January 31st of the first tax period, according to a calendar year.

Real estate transfer tax is charged at a uniform rate of 5% of the sales price of a property, or the usual market price, whichever is higher. It is payable by the seller, and the buyer is the guarantor.[87]

10. Real Estate Trends

Real property trends have been difficult to determine, given the limited data and time since private property came into vogue after Communist rule. Several consulting companies, such as Jones Lang LaSalle, have published informational reports involving the Czech Republic as to vacancy rates in offices, retail, industrial, investment, residential, multi-family and other types of ownership.

For current detailed rates and information, see the authorities cited below, including such companies as Jones Lang LaSalle, C.B. Richard Ellis, CORFAX International, Colliers International,

DTZ International Property Advisors, Knight Frank, and other sources noted below, including the International Real Estate Digest, http://www.realtor.com, and others.

■ 11. Cultural Issues

Any nation's culture is complex and vibrant in its diversity. While broad cultural characterizations such as those presented here can be generally accurate, following such generalities too strictly may be dangerously misleading. To conduct business effectively and profitably in a country, it is vital to have a thorough understanding of its culture's complexities.

Culture in the Czech Republic is imbued with Eastern European characteristics, mannerisms, morays, and folkways. European customs are prevalent, although the transition and influx of western European populations in dress, mannerisms, food and general activity also co-exist in the Czech Republic.

Greetings that might have tended to be different several years ago are becoming more westernized, utilizing "Hello," shaking of hands and addressing by surnames (last names). Traditional phrases, such as "Pleased to meet you" or "Good day," *Dobry Den*, are commonly spoken. Titles are normally used as a common courtesy. Czechs often eat three meals a day along with a mid-morning snack. Lunch is the main meal of the day for most citizens. Generally speaking, dinner and breakfast are lighter meals.

12. Discussion Questions

1. **What is meant by "ownership" of property in the Czech Republic?**

2. **Does the land locked nature of the Czech Republic have an impact on the economic recovery of the country from its post-Soviet days?**

3. **What are the environmental issues in the Czech Republic?**

13. Case Study

World Wide Souvenirs Czech Republic (WWS)

Memo

To: Board of Directors
From: Consultants
Re: Recent flood damage

I. Problem

World Wide Souvenirs (WWS) was opened 15 years ago. The store in the Czech Republic was WWS's 5th store opened. The Company currently has 22 stores throughout the world, each selling tourist souvenirs for the specific country of location. The floods that occurred in Prague completely destroyed the Company- owned store. All of the merchandise has been destroyed. The store cannot be restored or repaired without extensive work. The store fixtures are completely. The insurance was not kept current due to the lack of communication between the store manager and the headquarters office. (This presents a problem in funding for a new strategy.)

II. Initial Exit Strategy

WWS was opened 15 years ago. At the time the Company had no exit strategy. WWS did not look that far into the future.

III. Contingency Exit Strategy

Due to the lack of insurance and the complete destruction of the inventory and the interior of the store, the Company would be starting from the beginning. To exit now would be ideal if the Company does not wish to continue business in the Czech Republic. The Company-owned store could be put up for sale, and the money could be used to provide for some recoup of the investments made by WWS. There would be no inventory or other assets to consider, because they were all destroyed in the flood.

IV. Conclusion

Due to the damage, lack of insurance and cost to restore, it is suggested that WWS immediately list the property for sale.

Refer to: Kuznik, Frank, "Prague After the Deluge." Page E01, Washington Post (September 1, 2002).(Retrieved

September 16,2002).http://www.washingtonpost.com/ac2/wp- dyn? pagename=article&node=&contentId=A16795-2002Aug30&notFound=true.   U.S.

Embassy. Homepage. http://usembassy.state.gov. U.S. Department of State. Homepage. http://www.state.gov.

X-rates.com. Homepage. http://www.x-rates.com/.

14. Selected References

CIA World Factbook at https://www.cia.gov/library/publications/the-world-   factbook/index.html. http://www.czech.cz/.   http://www.czech-travel-guide.com/default.php3.   Kuznik,Frank,"Prague After the Deluge." Page E01,Washington Post (September 1, 2002). (Retrieved Sept ember 16, 2002). http://www.washingtonpost.com. *Richard Ellis International Property Specialists*. C.B. Richard Ellis. http://www.cbre.com. Time Almanac. *TIME Almanac*. Boston: Information Please LLC.

United States Department of State. *Background Notes: Czech Republic*. United States Department of State (Online). Available:http://www.state.gov.

U.S. Bureau of Census at http://www.census.gov. U.S. Department of Commerce at http://www.stat-usa.gov. U.S. Bureau of Economic Analysis at http://www.bea.gov. U.S. Embassy. Homepage. http://usembassy.state.gov. World Trade Centers Institute at http://www.wtci.org. World Trade Organization at http://www.wto.org.

World Bank. *Adult Illiteracy Rates*. The Economist. X-rates.com. Homepage. http://www.x-rates.com/.

15. Glossary

Ownership – may be only the land and not include other improvements or activities on the land such as buildings, natural objects such as growing crops, trees etc.

About the Author

Dr. Mark Lee Levine, is the Editor of this Book.

Denmark

INTERNATIONAL REAL ESTATE (GLOBAL REAL ESTATE)
Authored by *Kevin Sutton and Dr. Mark Lee Levine, Editor*

■ 1. Geography

Denmark is located in Northern Europe, bordering the Baltic Sea and the North Sea, on a peninsula north of Germany. Denmark also includes the two major islands of Sjaelland and Fyn. Denmark controls the Danish Straits linking the Baltic and North Seas.

Denmark is relatively small with its total land area being approximately equal to twice the size of the state of Massachusetts. The land area totals approximately 43,094 km^2 (square kilometers). Denmark only has only 140 kilometers of land borders, where it abuts Germany. The coastline is about 7,314 kilometers. The climate is temperate with some humidity and overcast skies. Winters tend to be fairly mild, but the area can be subject to high winds. The summers are fairly cool and comfortable.

Natural resources include petroleum, natural gas, fish, salt, limestone, stone, gravel, and sand. The terrain is very flat with no dramatic varieties of elevation. The land use break down is approximately 56.99% for arable land and the remaining 43% going to a variety of uses. Denmark has the highest percentage of arable land of any country in the world.

Environmental concerns exist with air pollution from vehicle and power plant emissions. There is also some concern over nitrogen and phosphorous pollution in the North Sea. Flooding is a threat in many areas of the country where the land is protected from the sea by a system of dikes.

■ 2. History and Overview

During the 9th through 11th centuries, Denmark was a great power. By the 15th century Denmark, Norway, Sweden, Finland, the Faroe Islands, Iceland, and Greenland were all united under the Danish crown. Sweden and Finland left the union in 1520, while Norway remained until the 19th century. The Danish liberal movement gained moment um in the1830s, and in 1849 Denmark became a constitutional monarchy. After the war with Prussia and Austria in 1864, Denmark was forced to cede Schleswig-Holstein to Prussia and adopt a policy of neutrality. Toward the end of the 19th century, Denmark inaugurated important social and labor market reforms, laying the basis for the welfare state. Denmark remained neutral during World War I. Despite its declaration of neutrality at the beginning of World War II, it was invaded by the Germans in 1940 and occupied until liberated by the Allied forces in May 1945. Resistance against the Germans was sporadic until late 1943. By then better organized, the resistance movement and other volunteers undertook a successful rescue mission in which nearly the entire Jewish population of Denmark was shipped to Sweden (whose neutrality was honored by Germany). However, extensive studies are still undertaken for the purpose of establishing a clearer picture of the degree of Danish cooperation—official and corporate—with the occupying power. Denmark became a charter member of the United Nations and was one of the original signers of the North Atlantic Treaty.[91]

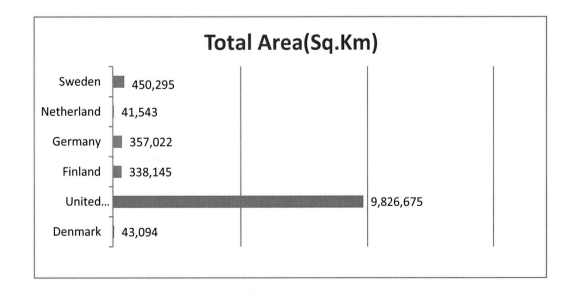

3. People

Denmark has a fairly small population of **5,569,077** residents with the majority (64.7%) falling between 15 and 64 years of age. Approximately 17% of the population is 14 years of age and under with the remaining balance falling in the 65 years and older category. The population growth rate is fairly slow at only 0.22% according to 2014 estimates, and has been slowly falling over the past decade.

Life expectancy in Denmark is fairly high at an average of 79.09 years. A man's life expectancy is 76.68 years, while a woman's life expectancy is 81.64 years. There are 10.22 births per 1,000 population, and there are 10.23 deaths per 1,000 population

Almost everyone in Denmark, 80%, is Evangelical Lutheran. About 16% are other Protestants and Roman Catholic. About 4% are Muslim (2014 est.)

The official and dominant language is Danish with English being a predominant second language. There is a small German-speaking minority located toward the southern part of Denmark. The Faroe Islands have a Nordic population with its own language. The Dutch boast a nearly 100% literate population.

4. Government

Denmark is a constitutional monarchy, with its capital in Copenhagen.

Administrative divisions consist of 14 Counties and 2 Boroughs. Denmark was first organized as a unified state in the 10th century. It became a constitutional monarchy in 1849. There is no designated national holiday, but constitution day on the 5th of June is generally viewed as the national day.

The legal system is a civil law system with judicial review of legislative acts. The Constitution was overhauled in 1953 to allow for a unicameral legislature and a female Chief of State, now Queen Margrethe II (since 1972). The head of government is the Prime Minister. The Legislative Branch consists of a unicameral People's Assembly or *Folketinget*. Following legislative elections, the leader of the majority is typically appointed by the monarch. The Judicial Branch has the Supreme Court, and judges are appointed by the monarch for life.

Diplomatic representation exists with the United States maintaining an Embassy in Copenhagen. Denmark maintains an office for their Ambassador in Washington, D.C.

5. Economy

Denmark possesses a thoroughly modern market economy featuring high-tech agriculture, up-to-date small-scale and corporate industry, extensive government welfare measures, comfortable living standards, a stable currency, and high dependence on foreign trade. Denmark is a net exporter of food and energy and has a comfortable balance of payments

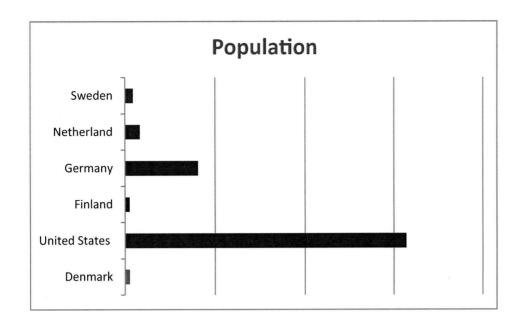

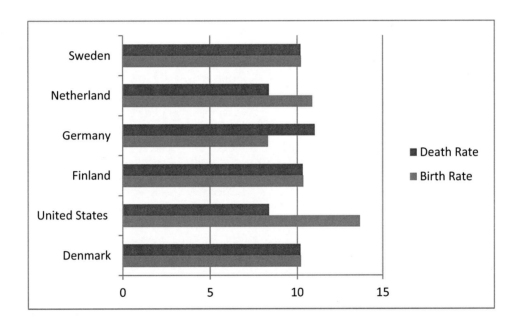

surplus. Government objectives include streamlining the bureaucracy and further privatization of state assets. The government has been successful in meeting, and even exceeding, the economic convergence criteria for participating in the third phase (a common European currency) of the European Monetary Union (EMU), but Denmark has decided not to join the 12 other EU members in the euro economy is extremely strong and developed.

The Gross Domestic Product (GDP) per capita is about $ 44,300 according to 2014 estimates. The Gross Domestic Product (GDP) is $347.2 billion. The economy shows a GDP real growth rate of 1.5% (2014 est.) Denmark has viable exports in machinery and instruments, meat, and dairy.

■ 6. Currency

Danish currency is the *kroner,* with current conversion rates available on the currency conversion Web link at the Burns School Global Real Estate Web site for the UNIVERSITY OF DENVER at http://burns.daniels.du.edu.

■ 7. Transportation

There are 2,667 km (kilometers) of rail lines in Denmark and 73,929 km of roadways (2012). Denmark also utilizes a series of

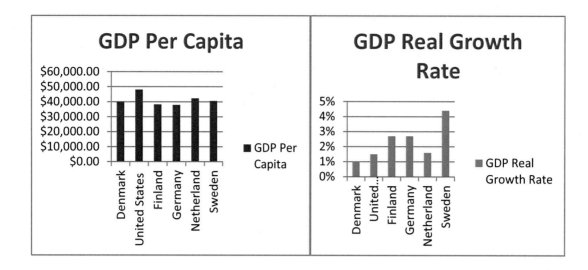

inland waterways totaling 400 km. Pipelines in Denmark transport crude oil, petroleum products and natural gas.

Major ports include Abenra, Alborg, Arhus, Copenhagen, Esbjerg, Fredericia, Kolding, Roenne, and others. There are 80 airport runways within the country with 28 of those being paved.

8. Communications

A highly sophisticated telephone system is widely used throughout the country, relying on buried cables and microwave radio relay. There are four cellular mobile communications systems. There are 2.431 million main telephone lines in use and 6.6 million cellular telephones (2012 est.)

Denmark has television broadcast stations. The country has 4,297,000 Internet service providers (hosts) with 4,750,000 Internet users (2012 est.)

9. Real Property Issues

The national government of Denmark requires real estate practitioners to obtain a license before conducting real estate transactions. To obtain a license, an examination must be passed. In addition, a college education is required, as are four years of evening business courses and two years of experience in the industry. Once the license has been obtained, no continuing education is required to keep it.

Commissions are not regulated by the government and are paid by the seller.

Typically, commission is 2% to 4% of the sale price. The buyer is responsible for paying a transfer tax that amounts to1.2% of the sale price (excludes residential transactions).

Real Estate Practitioners represent either the buyer or the seller, but not both. Multiple listings systems exist in Denmark. The national association of real estate practitioners in Denmark operates an Internet-based multiple listing service. Denmark

has a very high rate of loan-to-purchase financing. Typically, 95% of a home purchase is loan financed. The financing of both private and commercial real estate purchases in Denmark generally comes from the Danish mortgage bond credit system. These mortgage bonds are judged to have roughly the same level of security as Danish government bonds. Real estate mortgages are recorded in the public registers of the local authority in which the purchase was made.

All sectors of the Danish economy operate under a high tax burden, and property ownership is no exception. Besides the high initial transfer tax of 25%, the imputed rent of owner-occupied homes is included in the base for the income tax paid to the central government, counties, and municipalities. The imputed rent is calculated as a percentage of the property's assessed value. Other annual taxes on property include a Land Tax on unimproved land and on improvements to land, and a Service Tax on commercial and government buildings. These latter two taxes are for the benefit of local governments and are not the significant taxes in terms of generating revenue. The government in Denmark has the right to levy property taxes, the right of escheat, and the right to control the use of private property through the exercise of police power and zoning.

A real estate transaction is closed by a notary. The notary is responsible for preparing the tit le deed, *skoeder*, recording the deed, and arranges the final settlement between the parties. In order to be valid, deeds and mortgages are registered. Denmark bases its title records system on the German Title Registry system. The Danish title registry maintains and consistently updates an inventory of properties in the country. In this inventory, all properties can be identified by what is known as their cadastral parcel numbers. Private surveyors provide the subdivision plans and measurements from their work to the registry, which then updates maps and assigns plots a cadastral parcel number. The cadastral number is needed when completing the mandatory reporting of the transfer of property at the registry. Further information on the property transfer, such as the sale price and mortgage details, must be reported to the valuation authority. A high degree of information on any property is publicly available and reliable.

In Denmark, real estate practitioners must obtain a wide variety of information from the local government before closing on a sale. They must find out details on the property ranging from unpaid bills, outstanding taxes, status of utility connections, and any environmental issues. Normally, up to six to eight separate departments of the local government must be consulted to amass all of the required information. Drags holm *Kommune*, a municipality of about 13,500 people, has developed a system that now transfers the inquiries into electronic forms. This allows the different departments to work on an overall request at the same time. This system has cut the time it normally takes for Danish real estate practitioners to get the information they need to legally conclude a sale in half. The next step is to allow the real estate practitioners to submit both their requests and payments electronically. This model is being followed in other local authorities and has the potential to greatly ease a significant bureaucratic time burden on Denmark's real estate sector.

Non-European Union citizens and companies that have been located in Denmark for less than 5 years can only purchase real estate after applying to and receiving permission from the Danish Department of Justice. It commonly takes four weeks to obtain approval for a purchase. And, restrictions are placed on non-Danish European Union citizens that want to purchase vacation homes. This derives from a general unease throughout Scandinavia about the purchase of second homes by mainly German citizens. It is uncertain how long these restrictions against European Union citizens will remain legally enforceable under European Union law.

More than 80% of real property transactions in Denmark involve real estate professionals. Denmark's Real Estate trade association is called The Danish Association of Chartered Estate Agents, Dansk *Ejendonsmaeglerforehing*. The *Dansk Ejendonsmaeglerforehing* was founded in 1912 and has approximately 2,300 individual members. Real estate license requirements are regulated by the Ministry of Commerce. Danes obtain loans from commercial banks and mortgage banks. Interest rates are typically adjustable and loan to value ratios range between 60% and 80%. Appraisals and property insurance are typically required by lenders to secure a loan. Speculative building is uncommon, except where the building is significantly preleased.

Corporations are exempt from paying ad valorem property taxes. A stamp duty is paid on deeds, mortgages, and real property leases. The stamp duty fee ranges from 0.3% to 4% of the property value. All signatories to the transaction are responsible for the payment of the stamp duty.

Central business districts throughout Denmark are subject to stringent land use controls.

10. Real Estate Trends

Real estate trends in Denmark, like in most countries, are continually evolving. Several companies such as Jones Lang LaSalle (http://www.joneslanglasalle.com) and CB Richard Ellis (http://www.cbre.com) provide detailed, current information on the latest industrial, office, and retail real estate market trends.

11. Cultural Issues

Any nation's culture is complex and vibrant in its diversity.

While broad cultural characterizations such as those presented here can be generally accurate, following such generalities too strictly may be dangerously misleading. To conduct business effectively and profitably in a country, it is vital to have a thorough understanding of its culture's complexities.

Denmark tends to be somewhat more casual than other European countries in regards to a person's dress. However business settings still typically call for suits and traditional professional at tire.

Punctuality is important in Denmark. It is also import ant to note that the date is customarily written with the day first, then the month, and followed by the year. The summer is typically set-aside for leisure. It can be considered rude to try and make major business deals during these more relaxed months.

In Denmark, people do not often welcome idle conversation from strangers. When communicating in Denmark it is important to maintain a decent distance between persons, often two arms length.

12. Discussion Questions

1. Where is Denmark located, geographically, relative to its neighbors in Europe?

2. Is the geographic location of Denmark an advantage or disadvantage for Denmark in doing business in Europe – and in the world?

3. From Copenhagen, the city built a major bridge connecting parts of Sweden. How do you think this will impact commerce, relationships with neighbors (Sweden and others), and add to the strategic position of all of Denmark?

13. Selected References

CIA World Factbook at https://www.cia.gov/library/publications/the-world-factbook/index.html. http://www.escapeartist.com/embassy33/denmark.htm. http://www.real-estate-european-union.com/english/denmark.html.

Richard Ellis International Property Specialists. C.B. Richard Ellis. http://www.cbre.com.

Time Almanac. *TIME Almanac.* Boston: Information Please LLC.

United States Department of St at e. *Background Notes: Denmark.* United States Department of State (Online). Available:http://www.state.gov.

U.S. Bureau of Census at http://www.census.gov. U.S. Department of Commerce at http://www.stat-usa.gov. U.S. Bureau of Economic Analysis at http://www.bea.gov. U.S. Embassy. Homepage. http://usembassy.state.gov. World Trade Centers Institute at http://www.wtci.org. World Trade Organization at http://www.wto.org.

World Bank. *Adult Illiteracy Rates.* The Economist. Xrates.com. Homepage. http://www.x-rates.com/.

14. Glossary

Dansk Ejendonsmaeglerforehing – The Danish Association of Chartered Estate Agent s, which is the real estate trade association in Denmark.

Drasgsholm Kommune – **A** Danish municipality. **Skoeder–Title** deed in Denmark.

About the Author

Kevin Sutton, graduate student of the Burns School of Real Estate and Construction Management, *Daniels College of Business,* UNIVERSITY OF DENVER.

Finland

INTERNATIONAL REAL ESTATE (GLOBAL REAL ESTATE)
Authored by *Kevin Sutton and Dr. Mark Lee Levine, Editor*

1. Geography

Finland is located in Northern Europe, bordering the Baltic Sea, Gulf of Bothnia, and Gulf of Finland between Sweden and Russia. The total land area of Finland is 338,145 sq km (square kilometers) making it only slightly smaller than the state on Montana.

Finland borders Norway, Sweden, and Russia. These land borders total 2,563 km. Excluding islands and coastal indentations, Finland has 1,250 kilometers of coast line. The climate is cold temperate bordering on subarctic. The climate is relatively mild, however, because of the moderating influence of the North Atlantic current, Baltic Sea, and more than 60,000 lakes. Due to the climatic conditions the majority of the population is concentrated on small southwestern coastal plains. Natural resources include timber, copper, zinc, iron, ore, and silver.

The terrain is mostly low, flat rolling plains. Elevation changes are not substantial throughout the country with ranges from sea level up to 1,328 m (meters).

Approximately 7.4% of the land is arable while 92.59% of the land has other uses. Environmental concerns exist with air pollution from manufacturing and power plants that contribute to acid rain. There is additional concern over water pollution from industrial wastes and agricultural chemicals. Wildlife populations are threatened by habitat loss.

2. History and Overview

Finland's nearly 700-year association with the Kingdom of Sweden began in 1154 with the introduction of Christianity by Sweden's

King Eric. During the ensuing centuries, Finland played an important role in the political life of the Swedish-Finnish realm, and Finnish soldiers often predominated in Swedish armies. Finns also formed a significant proportion of the first "Swedish" settlers in 17th-century America.

Following Finland's incorporation into Sweden in the 12th century, Swedish became the dominant language, although Finnish recovered its predominance after a 19th century resurgence of Finnish nationalism. Publication in 1835 of the Finnish national epic, The *Kalevala* (a collection of traditional myths and legends) first stirred the nationalism that later led to Finland's independence from Russia.

In 1809, Finland was conquered by the armies of Czar Alexander I. Thereafter, it remained an autonomous grand duchy

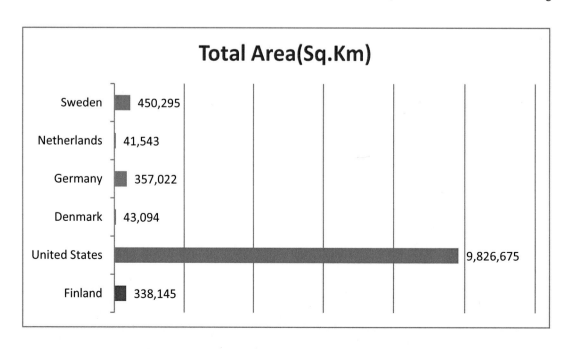

Total Area(Sq.Km)

Country	Total Area (Sq.Km)
Sweden	450,295
Netherlands	41,543
Germany	357,022
Denmark	43,094
United States	9,826,675
Finland	338,145

connected with the Russian Empire until the end of 1917. On December 6, 1917, shortly after the Bolshevik Revolution in Russia, Finland declared its independence. In 1918, the country experienced a brief but bitter civil war that colored domestic politics for many years. During World War II, Finland fought the Soviet Union twice–in the Winter War of 1939-1940 and again in the Continuation War of 1941-1944. This was followed by the Lapland War of 1944-1945, when Finland fought against the Germans as they withdrew their forces from northern Finland. Treaties signed in 1947 and 1948 with the Soviet Union included obligations and restraints on Finland, vis-à-vis the U.S.S.R. as well as territorial concessions by Finland. Both have been abrogated by Finland since the 1991 dissolution of the Soviet Union.[98]

■ 3. People

Given the climatic conditions, it is no surprise that Finland as a relatively small population of **5,268,799** residents. The majority, 64.4%, of Finland's inhabitants fall between 15 and 64 years of age. Approximately 15.8% of the population is 14 years of age and under with the remaining balance falling in the 65 years and older category. The population growth rate is 0.05% according to 2014 estimates.

Life expectancy in Finland is fairly high at an average of 79.69 years. A woman's life expectancy in Finland, on average, is 83.29 years, while a man's is 76.24 years. There are 10.35 births per 1,000 population, and there are 10.51 deaths per 1,000 population.

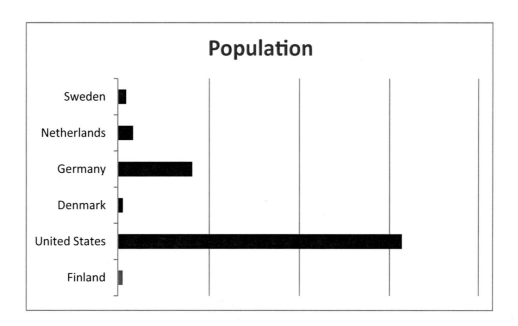

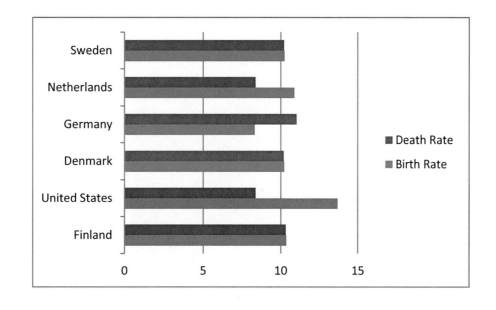

Finns are ethnically predominant at 93.4% with Swedes accounting for 5.6% of the population. Religions are comprised of about 78.4% Lutheran Church of Finland, 1.1% Orthodox Church, and 19.2% claiming no religious affiliation.

Finnish and Swedish are both official languages with 89.3% speaking Finnish and 5.3% speaking Swedish. Literacy rates are approaching 100% for the entire population.

■ 4. Government

Finland is a republic, with its capital located in Helsinki. Administrative divisions consist of 19 regions. Finland gained its independence from Russia on December 6, 1917. The country recognizes its national holiday, Independence Day, on December 6.

The Executive Branch is the Chief of State, the President, and the head of government is the Prime Minister and Deputy Prime Minister. The President is elected by popular vote for a six-year term. The Prime Minister and Deputy Prime Minister are appointed from the majority party by the President following parliamentary elections. The Legislative Branch is comprised of a unicameral Parliament or *Eduskunta*. A Supreme Court, *Korkein Oikeus*, makes up the Judicial Branch with judges being appointed by the President. The legal system is a civil law system based upon Swedish law. The Supreme Court has the ability to request legislation interpreting or modifying laws.

Diplomatic representation exists with the United States maintaining an Embassy in Helsinki. Finland maintains an office for their Ambassador in Washington, D.C.

■ 5. Economy

Finland has a highly industrialized, largely free-market economy, with per capita output roughly that of Austria, Belgium, the Netherlands, or Sweden. Its key economic sector is manufacturing – principally the wood, metals, engineering, telecommunications, and electronics industries. Trade is important,

with exports equaling almost one-third of Gross Domestic Product (GDP). Except for timber and several minerals, Finland depends on imports of raw materials, energy, and some components for manufactured goods. Because of the climate, agricultural development is limited to maintaining self-sufficiency in basic products. Forestry, an important export earner, provides a secondary occupation for the rural population. Rapidly increasing integration with Western Europe, Finland was one of the 11 countries joining the Euro Monetary System (EMU) on January 1, 1999, dominating the economic picture for Finland over the next several years.

The Gross Domestic Product per capita is $40,500 according to 2014 estimates. The GDP is $276.3 billion. Unemployment rests at 8.6% in Finland. The inflation rate has been slowly declining in the last five years, and currently sits at 1.3% (2014). The labor force in Finland is 2,665,000 people who partially contribute to Finland's main exports of machinery and equipment, chemicals, transport equipment, paper, chemicals, metals and timber. The GDP real growth rate is estimated at -0.2% for 2014, largely due to turmoil and following austerity measures employed in the Eurozone economy.

■ 6. Currency

Finnish currency is the *euro*, with current conversion rates available on the currency conversion Web link at the Burns School Global Real Estate Web site for the UNIVERSITY OF DENVER at http://burns.daniels.du.edu.

■ 7. Transportation

There are over 5,994 km of rail lines in Finland and 78,000 km of roadways. Finland also utilizes 8,000 km of inland waterways including the Saimaa Canal of 3,577 km, which can accommodate large ships. Pipelines in Finland are used to transport natural gas.

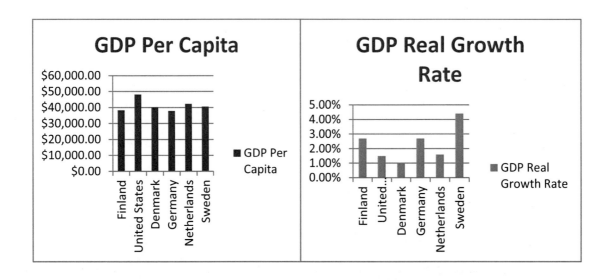

Major ports include Hamina, Helsinki, Kokkola, Kotka, Turku, and others. There are 148 airport runways within the country of which 74 are paved (2013 est.)

■ 8. Communications

Finland possess a modern system with excellent service.

Domestic communication uses cable, microwave relay, and extensive cellular. Submarine cable, satellite earth stations, and a single Inmarsat–shared with Denmark, Iceland, Norway, and Sweden– service international communications. There are 890,000 main telephone lines in use and 9.32 million cellular telephones.

Finland has television broadcast systems and AM radio, FM radio and shortwave radio broadcast stations. The country has 4,763,000 Internet service providers (hosts) with 4,393,000 Internet users (2012).

■ 9. Real Property Issues

Finland has a nationwide multiple listing service, and *Suomen Kinnteistonvalittajain Liitto* of Helsinki is the real estate trade organization in Finland. Licensed real estate agents handle approximately 60% of all property transactions.

Many of the recent commercial developments have been centered in Espoo, which is only a 15-minute drive from Helsinki. The quality of life combined with the highly educated and motivated work force has been a magnet for high-tech companies. Nokia plans to add to its existing 167,225 sq m. Other major corporations, such as, Cisco and Microsoft, have planned expansions in Finland.

The largest new business development in the region is the construction of the telecommunications research center in Ruoholahti, a former wasteland that is being transformed into a high-tech wonderland. The Helsinki High-Tech Center consisting of four eight-story towers, a total of 387,700 sqft (square feet) opened for business in 2001. It is customary to negotiate the sale of real estate through a written contract, but a person's word is also binding. The transfer of title is handled through a registry and there are two types. The Land Register is used to record the location of the land and the Property Register is used to record the ownership interest. Attorneys and licensed real estate agents are used in the majority of transactions.

In some cases ownership of land by either foreign investors or companies may be restricted, but it is not prohibited. Land is transferred by written contracts, with evidence of title being recorded at the Land Registry for the description and the Property Registry for the owner's name. Property taxes are assessed based on the value of the property and range from 0.2% to0.8%.

Over half of the real estate transactions are undertaken with real estate agents, who have to be licensed. They must also meet age and citizenship requirements. The service cost of buying real estate is somewhat higher than in the United States. In addition to sales commissions that range from 4-8% of the purchase price, there is also a 1% notary fee and a 6% stamp duty fee.

■ 10. Real Estate Trends

Real estate trends in Finland, like in most countries, are continually evolving. Several companies such as Jones Lang LaSalle (http://www.joneslanglasalle.com) and CB Richard Ellis (http://www.cbre.com) provide detailed, current information on the latest industrial, office, and retail real estate market trends.

■ 11. Cultural Issues

Any nation's culture is complex and vibrant in its diversity.

While broad cultural characterizations such as those presented here can be generally accurate, following such generalities too strictly may be dangerously misleading. To conduct business effectively and profitably in a country, it is vital to have a thorough understanding of its culture's complexities.

In business dealings in Finland, there is often minimal small talk prior to meetings and negotiations, but casual conversations are often held afterward in a restaurant or sauna. Business attire is comparable to that of the United States. Fashions generally follow the trends of the rest of Europe.

It is very important to be conscious of what is said in conversation as Finns tend to take words quite seriously. Verbal contracts and promises are often binding regardless of the circumstances in which they are made.

When conversing in Finland it is important to maintain an appropriate distance. The only physical contact should be in the form of a handshake.

12. Discussion Questions

1. Finland is known for its technology, specifically cell phones. Why is it that Finland seems so much more advanced in this area than many other parts of Europe?

2. What are the advantages to Finland of being a leader in this area of technology?

3. In what other areas does Finland seem to have an edge (by technology or otherwise) over its neighbors in Europe – or in other parts of the world? That is, what are its strengths?

13. Selected References

CIA World Factbook at https://www.cia.gov/library/publications/the-world-factbook/index.html. http://www.escapeartist.com. http://www.real-estate-european-union.com/english/finland.html. OverseasPropertyOnline.com. http://www.reeu.com.

Richard Ellis International Property Specialists. C.B. Richard Ellis. http://www.cbre.com. Time Almanac. *TIME Almanac.* Boston: Information Please LLC.

United States Depart ment of St at e. *Background Notes: Finland.* United States Department of State (Online).Available:http://www.state.gov. U.S. Bureau of Census at http://www.census.gov. U.S. Department of Commerce at http://www.stat- usa.gov. U.S. Bureau of Economic Analysis at http://www.bea.gov.

U.S. Embassy. Homepage. http://usembassy.state.gov. World Trade Centers Institute at http://www.wtci.org. World Trade Organization at http://www.wto.org. World Bank. *Adult Illiteracy Rates.* The Economist. X-rates.com. Homepage. http://www.x- rates.com/.

14. Glossary

Eduskunta–The Finnish unicameral Parliament.

Kalevala–A collection of traditional myths and legends leading to nationalism and Finland's independence.

Korkein Oikeuso–Finnish Supreme Court.

Suomen Kinnteistonvalittajain Liitto–A real estate trade organization in Finland.

About the Author

Kevin Sutton, graduate student of the Burns School of Real Estate and Construction Management, *Daniels College of Business,* UNIVERSITY OF DENVER.

France

INTERNATIONAL REAL ESTATE (GLOBAL REAL ESTATE)
Authored by *Kevin Sutton Dr. Mark Lee Levine*, Editor

1. Geography

France is located in Western Europe, bordering the Bay of Biscay and the English Channel, between Belgium and Spain, southeast of the United Kingdom, and the Mediterranean Sea between Italy and Spain. France consists of 643,801 sq km (square kilometers) of total land area, slightly more than twice the size of Colorado, with approximately 4,853 km of coastline.

France has had many border disputes with many neighbors. This includes those that are contiguous as well as issues involving islands in a number of areas where France previously had control. These areas include Europa Island, territorial claims in Antarctica and other locations. France's climate is generally cool in the winters and mild in the summers, but it can be very hot in the summers near the Mediterranean. Arable land consists of approximately 33.4% of the land; irrigated land is approximately 1.83% (2014). France has a number of environmental issues, including acid rain, air pollution from industrial vehicle emissions and water pollution from urban waste and agricultural runoff. Natural hazards include flooding issues, among others.

2. History and Overview

France was one of the earliest countries to progress from feudalism to the nation-state. Its monarchs surrounded themselves with capable ministers, and French armies were among the most innovative, disciplined, and professional of their day.

During the reign of Louis XIV (1643-1715), France was the dominant power in Europe. But overly ambitious projects and military campaigns of Louis and his successors led to chronic financial problems in the 18th century. Deteriorating economic conditions and popular resentment against the complicated system of privileges granted the nobility and clerics were among the principal causes of the French Revolution (1789-94). After the Franco-Prussian War (1870), the Third Republic was established and lasted until the military defeat of 1940.

World War I (1914-1918) brought great losses of troops and materiel. In the 1920s, France established an elaborate system of border defenses, the Maginot Line, and alliances to offset resurgent German strength. France was defeated early in World War II, however, and occupied in June 1940. Allied forces liberated France in 1944. A bitter legacy carries over to the present day.

France emerged from World War II to face a series of new problems. After a short period of provisional government initially led by Gen. Charles de Gaulle, the Fourth Republic was set up by a new constitution and established as a parliamentary form of government controlled by a series of coalitions.

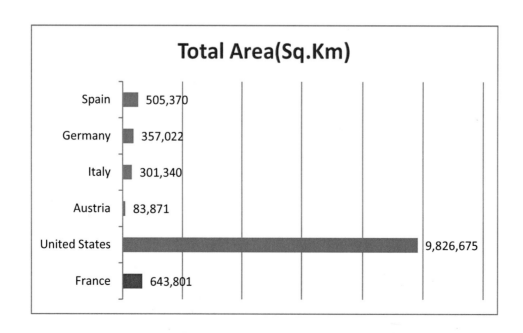

Total Area(Sq.Km)

Spain	505,370
Germany	357,022
Italy	301,340
Austria	83,871
United States	9,826,675
France	643,801

This government structure eventually collapsed as a result of the tremendous opposing pressures generated in the divisive Algerian issue. A threatened coup led the Parliament to call on General de Gaulle to head the government and prevent civil war. He became prime minister in June, 1958 (at the beginning of the Fifth Republic). He was elected president in December of that year. While France continues to celebrate its rich history and independence, French leaders are increasingly tying the future of France to the continued development of the European Union. French leaders have stressed the importance of European integration and advocated the ratification of the Maastricht Treaty on European economic and political union, which France's electorate narrowly approved in September 1992. President Jacques Chirac assumed office May 17, 1995, after a campaign focused on the need to combat France's stubbornly high unemployment rate.[105]

■ 3. People

France's population is **66,259,012.** Approximately 63% are in the 15-year through 64-year age category. On opposite sides of that division, ages are almost equally divided, with 18.7% in the zero to 14 years of age range, and 18.3% are in the 65 and over age category.

The population growth rate is 0.45% (2014 est.) Birth rates are 12.49 per 1,000. Death rates are 9.06 per 1,000. Infant mortality rates are low, at 3.31 per 1,000.

Life expectancy in France is 81.66 years overall, with males at 78.55 years and females at 84.91 years. Ethnic divisions in France include Celtic, Latin, Slavic and North African as well as a number of other, smaller groups. Religious groups include Roman Catholics, at about 63%- 66%, as well as smaller mixes of Protestants, Jews, Muslims and others. Almost 100% of the population speaks French, although English is often spoken in the major cities. The literacy rate is approximately 99% for those aged 15 and older.

The labor force is 29.87 million people out of the total population.

■ 4. Government

France is a Republic, with its capital in Paris. France has 22 regions for governmental control. The national holiday is the taking of the Bastille on July 14, 1789. The legal system is based on a civil law system. Suffrage is at 18 years of age and is universal.

Branches of government include the Executive Branch with the Chief of State as President, and the head of government being the Prime Minister. The Cabinet is a Council of Ministers, appointed by the President on the suggestion of his Prime Minister. The Legislative Branch is bicameral, consisting of a Senate

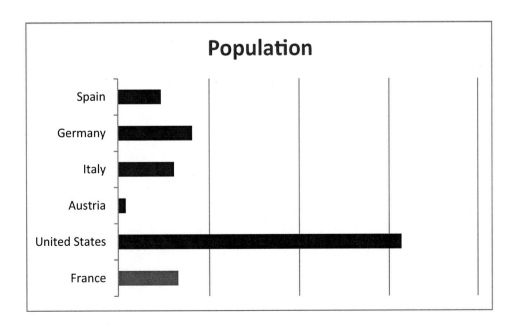

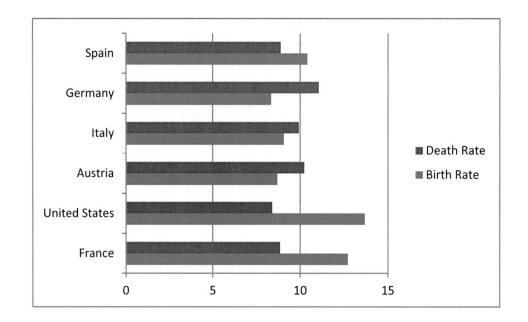

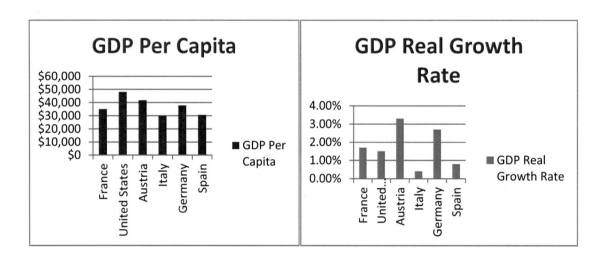

and a National Assembly, known as *Assemblee Nationale*. The Judicial Branch is the Constitutional Court.

Diplomatic representation with the United States from France is in Washington, D.C.; the U.S. Ambassador is located in Paris.

France has a defense makeup of Army, Navy, Air Force, Air Defense, and the National Gendarmerie.

5. Economy

The Gross Domestic Product (GDP) is $2.902 trillion (2014 est.) The GDP per capita is $40,400. Inflation is fairly low, 0.7% over the last several years.

However, unemployment is 9.7% (2014). The GDP real growth rate is 0.4%, slowing in recent years as the Eurozone has experienced economic hardships.

Industries for France include a number activities in textiles, electronics, food processing, automobiles, chemicals, steel, machinery and tourism. France is very active in the agricultural section, being one of the top world producers of wheat.

6. Currency

The currency is now the *euro*. It was previously the *French franc*. For details, see the Burns School Global Real Estate Web site at the UNIVERSITY OF DENVER at http://burns.daniels.du.edu.

7. Transportation

France has approximately 29,640 km (kilometers) of railroads, and 1,028,446 km of highways. It utilizes inland waterways, pipelines to transport crude oil and petroleum products, along with natural gas. And it has numerous ports for importing and exporting. France has 464 airports.

◼ 8. Communications

France uses 39.29 million landline telephones and 62.28 million cellular telephones. It has one of the more sophisticated communications systems in the world. It has a large-scale optical fiber system and utilizes satellites for domestic communication, along with microwave relay and use of domestic satellites along with other earth station satellites. France has numerous AM and FM radio stations (including many repeaters), and shortwave and television broadcast stations. About 17,266,000 Internet service providers (hosts) and 45,262,000 Internet users operate in France (2012).

◼ 9. Real Property Issues

Transaction costs in France for selling real property add up to approximately 25%.France has one of the highest brokerage fees of European countries. Agency listings can be either open or exclusive. The distinctions between real and personal property in France are similar to the definitions in the United States. French law defines real property as immovable by nature. A French real estate brokerage is referred to as an *Immobilier*.

Licensing is required and must be updated yearly in France. In order to hold a license a person must have obtained a University degree, have four years of professional experience, and hold liability insurance. Foreigners have the same rights professionally as natives. Notaries have the exclusive right to prepare deeds of sale, mortgages and other real property instruments.

Deeds in France are subject to numerous laws and taxation rules. The owner and taker sign a *promesse de vente* (sales promise) clearly defining the terms of property transfer. The most common type of sales promise is a unilateral promise of selling. Real property can be acquired by accession, succession, prescription, or contract. Acquisition by contract states that every creation or transfer of real property must be registered by a notary with the *Bureau de la Conservation des Hypotheques* (Registry of Real Estate Mort gages).

A two-year commercial lease type can be used in France, which is defined in the Civil Code in Article 1712. The procedure for this type of lease is called *Usine Relais*.

This lease type is designed for startup companies with good prospects that require a need to expand quickly. Companies in this type of lease have no entitlement to a conventional renewal. Because of its shortcoming, the *Usine Relais* lease is used less frequently than a simple lease in France. The *Tribunal de Commerce* deals with the legalities of the simple lease should any conflicts arise.

The contract of sale may be made by notarial deed or in the form of a private agreement. The property changes possession as soon are there is an agreement on price and the object of that price. The promise to sell or buy is considered void if it is not registered at the tax registry office.

Legal, judicial, and contractual are the three types of mortgages used in France.

Mortgages are given priority based upon their date of registration. If a mortgagor defaults then the property made be sold in order to satisfy the debt. Any liens holding priority over the mortgage must also be registered with the Register of Real Estate.

A three percent (3%) tax on property value is imposed upon legal entities holding property in France while their principal office is located outside France. An exemption would be possible once proper documentation has been obtained. The property value is determined annually and 50% of that value is taxed at a certain rate.

◼ 10. Real Estate Trends

According to the real estate firm *Référencement Immobilier*, almost 50% of sales today come from Internet contacts. Other companies advertising on the Internet are *Laforêt Immobilier*, *Lesite Immobilier— sales* and financing, SeLoger, LeMonde, and many others.[109]

◼ 11. Cultural Issues

Any nation's culture is complex and vibrant in its diversity. While broad cultural characterizations such as those presented here can be generally accurate, following such generalities too strictly may be dangerously misleading. To conduct business effectively and profitably in a country, it is vital to have a thorough understanding of its culture's complexities.

French customs are generally more formal than those of the United States. Attire is somewhat conservative but always fashionable. The French see one's dress as a reflection of social status and success. When communicating, the French will appreciate a sincere effort to speak their language. They will, however, switch to English if they perceive the speaker to be struggling.

Business luncheons are more common than dinners. Punctuality is important, but a person is not considered late should they arrive within ten minutes of the appointment time. Gifts are appreciated, but should be chosen with caution. It is considered improper to include a business card with a gift. The French are very knowledgeable about food and wine. Gifts of this nature should not be given unless the giver is assured of the gift's quality.

Greetings will often involve a handshake or kiss on the cheek. Despite the formal nature of business practices in

France, conversations are often conducted in close proximity. They may even include some physical contact along the lines of a hand on the shoulder, etc.

For additional information in this area, see the Burns School Global Real Estate Web site at the UNIVERSITY OF DENVER at http://burns.daniels.du.edu.

12. Discussion Questions

1. France appears to have a strong economy. It has low inflation, but high unemployment. What would you recommend that France could do to put people back to work?

2. How have border disputes that France has with its neighbors affected its economy, including tourism?

3. Has the adoption of the Euro been beneficial to France?

13. Case Study

Human Trafficking Investigation (HTI) Paris, France

Memo

To: Board of Directors
From: Consultants
Re: Deportation of Sex Workers from Outside the EU

I. Problem

Human Trafficking Investigation (HTI) is a non-profit organization that helps families try to locate loved ones who they have thought were taken from their home country and put into sex slavery. The Company also helps those who have been taken. It provides a safe haven and help to return these victims to home or help them locate legitimate work.

Paris was a prime location. Prostitution is legal, and many of the victims forced into slavery are taken to Paris. The Interior Minister of France wants to deport prostitutes that are not from the EU.

"Now, however, Paris's longtime prostitutes have a new and unlikely champion. Nicolas Sarkozy, President Jacques Chirac's new tough-talking interior minister, has announced plans to introduce legislation this fall that would allow the immediate deportation of prostitutes who are from outside the 15-country European Union. (Prostitution is legal in France, and under EU rules, citizens of other union countries have a legal right to live and work here.)"[110]

This legislation, if it passes, would mean that HTI would have less slave trade. If so, possibly it should relocate to one of the Company's other branches. The Office of Monitor and Combat Trafficking in Persons also considers France a Tier 1 country, according to the Trafficking in Persons Report released. The definition of a Tier 1 country is:

The governments of countries in Tier 1 fully comply with the Act's minimum standards. Such governments criminalize and have successfully prosecuted trafficking, and have provided a wide range of protective services to victims. Victims are not jailed or otherwise punished solely as a result of being trafficked, and they are not summarily returned to a country where they may face hardship as a result of being trafficked. In addition, these governments sponsor or coordinate prevention campaigns aimed at stemming the flow of trafficking." Trafficking in Persons Report, June 5, 2002. Released by the Office to Monitor and Combat Trafficking in Persons.[111]

Because France is listed as Tier 1, they have programs that are beginning to work.

Therefore, HTI might be able to serve people better if it moved to one of our other locations, which are listed as Tier 2 and 3 locations.

II. Initial Exit Strategy

The exit strategy was to stay until HTI ran out of funds, or until the problem was completely eradicated from France. These were the only two exit strategies that were put in place. Most of the funds come from the United States. HTI recently received a grant from the Better World Foundation of the United Nations.

III. Contingency Exit Strategy

With the proposed legislation pending, HTI must develop a plan to consider moving the organization to another country. Because France is doing what they can to help eradicate the problem, the services of HTI will be more productive if it re-locates to a Tier 2 or 3 country.

Research and the HTI network of contacts will help give HTI a good idea as to where the trade might flow, next. Once this is decided, HTI will have to try to work an arrangement with its landlord to sublease or buyout the lease. (The landlord has at times donated the rent value to HTI, because HTI acts for a good cause.) If HTI could work out some way to exit the lease, it would be able to move the Company.

If HTI is unable to find a solution for its office space, it could easily use the current office as a headquarters and branch that, at some point, would become its head-quarters.

IV. Conclusion

With the large grant just received from the United Nations Foundation, the best course of action would be to relocate to one of our other branch offices in another country, one that is close to the France office. This will give HTI the opportunity to work with the governments of Tier 2 and 3 countries.

Refer to: Richard, Keith, "France May Limit Prostitution," August 11, 2002, page A20, Washington Post (September 16, 2002). http://www.washingtonpost.com/wp-dyn/articles/A3846- 2002Aug10.html.

Trafficking in Persons Report. June 5, 2002, released by the Office to Monitor and Combat Trafficking in Persons. (Retrieved September 18, 2002). http://www.state.gov/g/tip/rls/tiprpt/2002/10653.htm.

International Real Estate Digest. Homepage. http://www.ired.com. U.S. Department of State. Homepage. http://www.state.gov.

U.S. Embassy. Homepage. http://usembassy.state.gov. X-rates.com. Homepage. http://www.x-rates.com/.

14. Selected References

CIA World Factbook. https://www.cia.gov/library/publications/the-world- factbook/index.html. http://www.info-france-usa.org. http://www.insee.fr/en/home/home_page.asp.

Richard, Keith, "France May Limit Prostitution," August 11, 2002, page A20, Washington Post (September 16, 2002).http://www.washingtonpost.com/wp-dyn/articles/A3846- 2002Aug10.html.

Trafficking in Persons Report. June 5, 2002, released by the Office to Monitor and Combat Trafficking in Persons. (Retrieved Sept ember 18, 2002). http://www.state.gov/g/tip/rls/tiprpt/2002/10653.htm.

International Real Estate Digest. Homepage. http://www.ired.com. U.S. Bureau of Census at http://www.census.gov. U.S. Department of Commerce at http://www.stat-usa.gov.

U.S. Bureau of Economic Analysis at http://www.bea.gov. U.S. Department of State. Homepage. http://www.state.gov.

U.S. Embassy. Homepage. http://usembassy.state.gov. World Trade Centers Institute at http://www.wtci.org. World Trade Organization at http://www.wto.org.

See the Burns School Global Real Estate Web site at the UNIVERSITY OF DENVER at http://burns.daniels.du.edu.

Richard Ellis International Property Specialists. C.B. Richard Ellis. http://www.cbre.com.

Time Almanac. *TIME Almanac.* Boston: Information Please LLC.

15. Glossary

Baux commerciaux – Commercial leases.

Buerau de la Conservation des Hypotheques – (Register of Real Estate Mortgages) All real estate must be registered.

Promesse de Vente – Owner and taker sign a sales promise which clearly defines the terms and clauses of the property transfer.

Promesse Unilaterale de Vente – Unilateral promise of selling.

Usine Relais – a two-year lease intended for start up businesses with high potential that require the possibility of quick expansion.

About the Author

Kevin Sutton, graduate student of the Burns School of Real Estate and Construction Management, *Daniels College of Business*, UNIVERSITY OF DENVER.

Germany

INTERNATIONAL REAL ESTATE (GLOBAL REAL ESTATE)
Authored by Dr. *Kristin Wellner* and Dr. *Mark Lee Levine*, Editor

1. Geography

Germany is the most populous country in the central Europe's Central Time Zone (CTZ). Germany is bordered by the North Sea, Baltic Sea, Austria, Belgium, the Czech Republic, Denmark, France, Lichtenstein, Luxembourg, the Netherlands, Poland and Switzerland. Germany's land area is 357,058 sq km (square kilometers).

Germany's terrain consists of the northern lowlands, the central hilly land, the alp forelands (highlands), and the high mountains (alps) in the south. Germany's biggest rivers are the Rhine and the Elbe, flowing in the North Sea, and the Danube, flowing from west to east, into the Black Sea.[113]

The climate in Germany is generally temperate, but with cold winters, and fairly warm summers in many areas. There is often rain in all seasons.

In comparison to other countries Germany has roughly natural resources. The most important of them are (have been in former time) coal, lignite, natural gas and oil, salt (potash, calcium chloride), and iron ore.

Land use consists of approximately 30% for forests and woodlands. Approximately 53% is for pastures and agricultural land. There is a mix of other uses. Germany has more than 6,000 natural preserves, with over 8,000 sq km. For environmental preserve, Germany founded 15 national parks and 95 nature parks and several other protected areas.

The environmental area was one topic of significant work during the Unification of Eastern Germany and Western Germany. As a result of decades of neglect, there are several large areas of contaminated land in the states of former East Germany, primarily from industrial pollution. Two of the many URL web sites on this subject include www.destatis.de/EN and http://www.umweltbundesamt.de/en(englisch version).

2. History and Overview

German history has been divided among economic, social and religious lines. From medieval history, the land of Germany was split among many kingdoms, princedoms and different owners. The larger, historical countries include Prussia, Bavaria, Franconia and Saxony. Germany become a union Nation (Monarchy) with Berlin as the capital after the German–French–War in 1871.

In 1914, Germany allied with Austria and Hungary to declare War on Russia, Great Britain and France. World War I ended in 1918, when Germany became a Democratic Republic.

In 1933 Germany supported Adolph Hitler and his vision to revitalize the German economy after the Economic Depression in the 1930s. Under the Third Reich, Hitler gained absolute power and conquered multiple countries throughout Europe, which produced World War II and the destruction of about 55 million people (including 6 million Jewish people, as well as other ethnic groups).

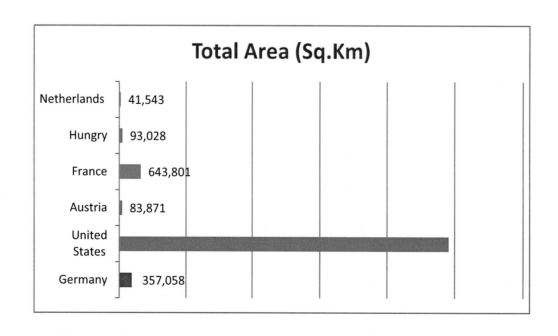

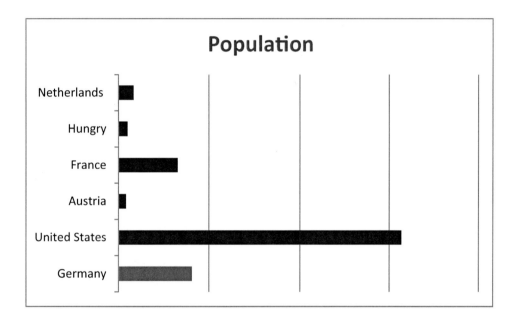

At the end of World War II in 1945, Germany was divided into four allied occupation zones controlled by the Americans, British, French, and Russian armies. Economic prosperity, following the War, led Germany to become the strongest economy in Europe, after several transitional years of economic, political and financial strains. The unification of East Germany and West Germany occurred on October 3, 1990.

■ 3. People

Germany is the most populous country in Europe, with **81,083 Tsd.** inhabitants in 2014. Its age structure is composed of 54.8% in the 20−year−old to 60−year−old bracket, 18.1% under that age group, and 27.1% over that age group. The mean age is 43 years.

Germany had a negative growth rate lately estimated to be only −0.2% (2013). The birth rate is 8.5 per 1,000. The death rate is 11.1 per 1,000.

Life expectancy in Germany is fairly high, at 74.5 years for males, and 81 years for females.

The dominant ethnic positions are Germans at 92.4%, with the balance mainly consisting of Turks, Serbs−Croatians, Italians, Greeks, Italians, Poles, Russians, Asians, Bosnia−Herzegovina, Austrians and the Spanish.

Religion is dominated by approximately 30% Protestants and 30% Roman Catholics. The balance is a mix of those affiliated with other religions, and approximately 40% who are not affiliated with any religion and a very small share of other religions.

German is the dominant language in Germany, although it is not unusual to find multiple languages spoken, especially

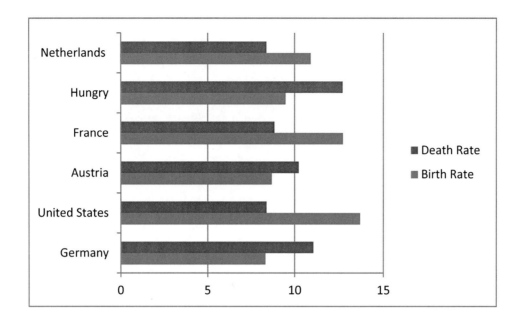

European languages and multiple dialects. Literacy is very high, at approximately 99%. Germany supports a strong educational system.[117]

4. Government

West Germany and East Germany unified on October 3, 1990, after a 40–year division following World War II. Germany contains 16 States (Administrative divisions). It is a Federal Republic, the *Bundesrepublik Deutschland*, with its capital in Berlin. October 3, 1990 is the national holiday, "Tag der Deutschen Einheit" – the German Unity Day, or the Day of Unity.

Germany had a prior unification from dozens princedoms on January 18, 1871as a Monarchy. Monarchy was ended after the World War I and transform in a Republic in 1918. This state had been divided after World War II in a western and eastern part. West Germany, the *Bundesrepublik Deutschland*, was governed by a basic Constitution, *Grundgesetz*, adopted on May 23, 1949, known as the Basic Law. East Germany and West Germany were again re–unified on October 3, 1990, and the "Grundgestez", with modifications, became the Constitution of the United German. This Constitution declared human right s, including human dignity, private liberty, equal rights under the law, freedom of faith and religion, right of free opinion, and rights as to property. The legal system of Germany is a civil law system, with judicial review of legislative acts and a federal Constitution. Germany has a social system and democratic Constitution.

The Executive Branch includes the President and the federal government, including the federal Ministries, and the head of government, who is the Chancellor. The Legislative Branch is a bicameral chamber, with the Lower House of the federal Parliament and the federal Council. However Germany has a federal system, where a determined part of the legislative and executive power is held by the 16 federal state governments. The Judicial Branch of the government is under federal constitutional courts.

Voting in Germany is at 18 years or older and is universal. Political parties existing in Germany include the Christian Democratic Union, *Christlich Demokratische Union Deutschlands (CDU)*, in cooperation with the Christian Social Union, *Christlich- Soziale Union*, now in coalition with the Social Democratic Party, *Sozialdemokratische Partei Deutschlands (SPD)*, the Green Party, *Die Grünen*, the Communist Party, *Die Linke*, the Free Democratic Party, *Freie Demokratische Partei (FDP)*, as well as numerous other political parties and associations.

German diplomatic representation exists between the United States and Germany, with an Ambassador from the United States housed in Berlin. A German Ambassador is housed in Washington, D.C., in the United States.

Defense forces in Germany include an army, navy, air force, border police, coast guard and other units.[118]

5. Economy

The German economy has been generally very strong as a result of its physical location, political setting, stability and open positions on economic trade and development, competing especially with the United States, Japan and other major countries.

Germany promotes open trade, especially within the European Economic Union. Germany has the fifth largest economy in the world, with a Gross Domestic Product (GDP) of US$3.820 trillion (2014), yet has become one of the highest growing economies in the European zone with GDP real growth rate at 1.6%. in 2014 (2% estimated in 2015). Germany's Gross Domestic Product (GDP) per capita is US$ 47,201, in the average of the

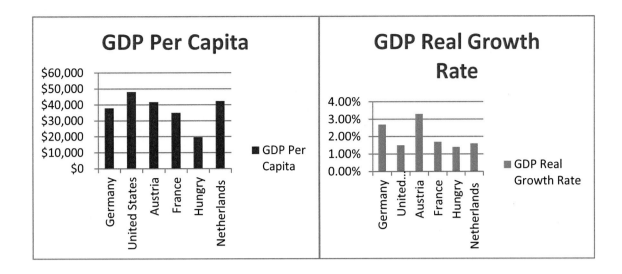

western economies. The unemployment rate is approximately 6.5% (5/2014).

Important sectors in the German economy include engineering, automobile production, chemicals, and electronics.

6. Currency

Since January 1, 2002, Germany formally switched its national currency from the *Deutsche Mark (DM)* to the *Euro (EUR)*, like 12 other members of the European Union (EU). One *Euro* would be equivalent to 100 *Eurocent*. See all Euro banknotes and coins at http://www.euro.ecb.int . See https://www.ecb.europa.eu/stats/exchange/eurofxref/html/index.en.html for daily Euro foreign exchange reference rates.

7. Transportation

Germany has one of the most sophisticated transportation systems in the world, through its nearly 41,981 km (kilometers) of railroads. Germany has a strong highway system (including autobahn), with most of its approximately 644,480 km of highways being paved. Several pipelines move crude oil and natural gas through Germany.

Germany utilizes inland waterways, allowing greater shipping and development, especially along the Rhine and the lower course of the Elbe. There is a strategic canal connection across Northern Germany, between the Baltic Sea (in Kiel) and the North Sea (Hamburg). Germany's larger oversea ports are in Hamburg (waterway to North Sea) and Rostock (Baltic Sea) and among others. The largest port for inland navigation is Duisburg (Rhine).

The German airport system includes over 549 airports, including 330 airports with paved runways (2010). The largest airports are in Frankfurt, Munich, Berlin and Dusseldorf. In Berlin is a new big airport in construction.

8. Communications

Germany has a well–developed communication system and technologically advanced telephone systems, with digital service offered throughout the country including 45,600,000 main line telephones and 105,000,000 cellular telephones. The Internet is regularly used by 20,416,000 Internet service providers (hosts) and 65,125,000 Internet users. Cellular phones are used extensively throughout the country.

9. Real Property Issues

Germany allows free trade, with few restrictions on foreign or domestic business ownership. Non–Germans are allowed to acquire real estate and obtain financing in Germany.

Commissions on sale of property are normally 3-8% of the gross value of the transaction and 3.5-6.5% of property acquisition tax (depending on the 16 state tax law). Notaries (specialized attorneys) are used to register title. This is a most common practice in most European countries.

Property and ownership is recorded in a Land Register (*Grundbuch*). This is a reliable record of property ownership and gives very strong assurance to purchasers as to their right to title of real estate. Valuation groups and municipal bodies collect data on transactions, e.g., information about value, cap rates, ownership, taxes, etc. They are fairly sophisticated and fairly reliable. German real estate broker associations undertake support for German real estate activities. The two major groups are the *Bundesverband Ring Deutscher Makler (RDM)* and the *Verband Deutscher Makler (VDM) unified in 2004 to the Immobilienverband Deutschland (IVD)* http://www.ivd.net/.

In Germany, licensing of real estate practitioners is required, but there is no problem to get this license without an examination. The real estate broker is often labeled as the *Immobilienmakler*. In the future the membership of The Royal Institution of Chartered Surveyors (RICS) will be more and more a quality label in Germany, too. Land descriptions are generally formed through metes–and–bounds descriptions and a survey system. Land may be held as a freehold or may be leased or rented. Statutory dower and courtesy are not existent in Germany, although other forms of rights for spouses exist.

Special forms of ownership interests exist as to fee simple interests or other interests, which are not a total fee position. One of these lesser types of ownership is *hereditary leasehold*. This is used to allow some form of ownership, but it is limited and is not the same broad scope that exists with a fee simple. Other forms are neighboring rights, usufruct (life interest or limited interest), and rights–of–way. Property value can be influenced by pre-emptive rights, rent or lease rights, and by registered mortgages.

Partnerships, whether limited or general, civil law associations and limited liability companies, among other entities, also exist in Germany. Real estate funds (open end and closed end) and real estate investment companies (especially G–REITs) exist. Evidence of title generally follows a register or Torrens type of system.

Contractual positions are similar to that in the United States in that they general require an offer and acceptance (mutual agreement in general), a writing, etc. Property taxes are levied annually and are paid to the municipality; additionally, real estate property transfer taxes are usually required on transfers of direct real estate transactions.

In Germany there exists a strong law of tenancy (supported tenants with special codes for social housings) and a Building Code (BauGB) with many regulations for architects, construction contractors and developers, as well as unlimited other codes mentioned construction and energy saving (HOAI, VOB, and 16 state construction codes).[120]

10. Real Estate Trends

German cities are one of the important locations for commercial real estate investors in Europe. Germany has no one main place for real estate investments, but the five biggest cities –– Frankfurt, Munich, Berlin, Hamburg and Dusseldorf –– are of special interest. After the financial crises Germany is a "safe haven" for domestic and foreign investors because of its strong economy and comparatively low prices with a rising trend. The market is stable and quite transparent. Currently there a two main trends: first are the growing big cities due to urbanization trends with strong gentrification effects in inner city areas. The opposite trend are the abandonment of the little towns and villages far away from cities.

Many new educational opportunities possibilities for professionalization in real estate, valuation, consulting, and trading were introduced in the last twenty years. Within the last three decades, many real estate consultants and real estate management companies have been established in Germany.

The German real estate industry has also been supported well by many real estate, law, and accounting firms, relative to its real estate activities. Many professional offices are located in various German cities. Principally data are difficult to obtain in Germany, but data are available on rent prices, vacancy rates, expenses, and so forth, whether for office, retail, industrial, residential, multifamily or other real estate. Data sources are the real estate research and brokerage firms and the *Gutachterausschuss* (official regional organizations of appraisal experts in each administrative district, Landkreis, and for real estate prices and property interest rates (*Liegenschaftszins*) and land prices (*Bodenrichtwert*).

For current links to determine rates, vacancies and other real estate information, see the sites of such firms as BulwienGesa AG, Jones Lang LaSalle and DTZ Zadelhoff, FERI Research, CB Richard Ellis, and other brokers or investment companies are indicated below in the Selected References section. They provide strong data that is available as to real estate trends in Germany. See the web sites below for details in real estate market and investment information in Germany. A great pool of information and research results is also available by the Society of property researchers, Germany (www.gif–ev.de), as a sister of the ARES (American Real Estate Society)and part of ERES (European Real Estate Society).

11. Cultural Issues

Any nation's culture is complex and vibrant in its diversity. While broad cultural characterizations such as those presented here can be generally accurate, following such generalities too strictly may be dangerously misleading. To conduct business effectively and profitably in a country, it is vital to have a thorough understanding of its culture's complexities.

Germany has a history of deep interests in literature and music. German culture is influenced by famous artists, e.g. Goethe, Schiller, Bach and Beethoven. Germany also has important scientists in medicine, physics, mathematics, and chemistry. Germans follow much of the European fashion and tend to be fairly well dressed, yet more formal than many other Europeans. They tend to be very orderly and exact in business transactions.

Most greetings in day–to–day activities are similar to those of other European nations and Western developed countries. Punctuality and formality are characteristically associated with Germans. Greetings are similar to those utilized in most western countries, although in Western countries the label of "Mr." would generally be referred to in Germany as *Herr*. The equivalent reference to "Mrs." or "Miss" would be *Frau*. The title of "Miss" in the United States would be *Fraulein* in Germany; however, this term is politically incorrect. In business activities, it is usual to use the formal family name, instead of the first name.

Business attire for Germans is fairly conservative. Normally it includes (for men) dark suits or dark coats, white shirts, and fairly conservative dress in general. Eating habits generally follow the Continental style, with fork held in the left hand and knife in the right hand.

12. Discussion Questions

1. What is the major environmental concern in Germany?

2. Is Germany's location beneficial to attracting investors and thus increasing its economy?

3. What has been the economic impact on Germany since its reunification?

13. Case Study

German-American Food Bar (GAFB) Hamburg, Federal Republic of Germany

Memo

To: Board of Directors
From: Consultants
Re: Employees connected to AAMMKK

I. Problem

German American Food Bar (GAFB) was opened 5 years ago, just around the corner from the University of Hamburg. The focus was to serve American dishes, along with great German beer, and attract local college students. The events of September 11, 2001, have given the restaurant some bad publicity. Some people who may have known about planning of the attacks may have worked in the restaurant. A local group near the University often met in the restaurant, which seemed to have diminished the customers. Now, more people do not eat at our restaurant, as the property has been vandalized four times in the last year. The vandalism keeps getting more expensive. The restaurant has very little insurance. There is a high deductible. GBAFB cannot gain a better insurance, because of the vandalism. With any more events of destruct ion, the Company will surely need to close its doors for good.

II. Initial Exit Strategy

When the Company opened its doors, it never envisioned the events that occurred. GBAFB was made up of exchange students who saw a need for a little bit of home in a foreign country. They just took a risk and tried something. For four years it provided a nice profit. The only exit strategy was to make certain that in the event one of the four of the owners wanted out of the business, the others would be able to buy that partner out. (The owners also set up a plan for a buyout if one of the owners died. These were the only exit plans that were currently in place.)

III. Contingency Exit Strategy

Even if the owners are able to hold onto the business, they need a plan that they can implement if something drastic happens again. Currently there is a ten-year lease, with a clause that the Company can terminate the lease with three months' notice. This makes the space easily to exit, but the disproportion of the assets would be more difficult.

If GBAFB could possibly convince the landlord to re-let the property with the current fixtures, or possibly sell the business and all the assets to another party, then GBAFB could vacate. If the Company was able to execute any approaches, it might be able to close the business without losing all of its investments. Because GBAFB did not plan for any exit strategy, it has very little in capital reserve.

IV. Conclusion

The receipts from the restaurant are still covering all of the expenses. It is suggested that the owners close the Company, take out a loan to remodel the restaurant, and change the name. It can undertake some publicity to let potential customers know that it is a new restaurant. Hopefully that will erase the negative aspects. If the owners could encourage the school to have some functions at the restaurant, it might help the image as well. A free pizza and beer party for the re-opening for students with student ID.s should help to change the image and draw in customers who might not normally come into the restaurant. The restaurant should be renamed to see if it can increase profits and erase the negative image. It appears that the location and operators were strong. The problem was the image, post September 11, 2001. A new restaurant, focusing on "students," not countries, may be the key.

Refer to: Finn, Peter, "The Man in the Middle of September 11the Plot," Page A16, Washington Post (September14,2002).http://www.

washingtonpost.com/wp-dyn/articles/ A15602- 2002Sep13.ht ml.

International Real Estate Digest . Homepage. http://www.ired.com. U.S. Department of State. Homepage. http://www.state.gov.

U.S. Embassy. Homepage. http:// usembassy.state.gov. X-rates.com. Homepage.http://www.x-rates. com/.

U.S. Embassy. Homepage. http:// usembassy.state.gov. U.S. Department

of State. Homepage. http://www.state. gov.

14. Selected References

Burns School Global Real Estate Web site at the UNIVERSITY OF DENVER at http://burns.daniels. du.edu.

CIA World Factbook.https://www.cia.gov/library/pub-licistions/the-world-factbook/index.html.

Finn, Peter, "The Man in the Middle of the September 11 Plot," Page A16, Washington Post (September 1, 2002) at http://www.washingtonpost.com/wp-dyn/artices/A15602- 2002Sep13.ht ml.

http://www.bulwien.de/en -> Search for RIWIS Databank.

https://www.msci.com/real-estate -> Search for the German index.

http://www.dtz.com/germany. http://www.dvcs.de/ DVCS/Homepage/index.html http://www.feri.de/ en.

http://www.joneslanglasalle.com/ or http://www. joneslanglasalle.de.(click for the "English" version).

http://www.rreef.com/ (click for the "English" version). http://www.real-estate-european-union.com/

english/germany.html. *Richard Ellis International Property Specialists.* C.B. Richard Ellis. http://www. cbre.com.

Statistical Data: https://www.destatis.de/EN/Homep-age.html.

Time Almanac. *TIME Almanac.* Boston: Information Please LLC.

Unit States Department of State. *Background Notes: Germany.* United States Department of State (Online).Available:http://www.state.gov. U.S. Bureau of Census at http://www.census.gov. U.S. Department of Commerce at http://www.stat- usa. gov. U.S. Bureau of Economic Analysis at http:// www.bea.gov.

U.S. Embassy. Homepage. http://usembassy.st at e.gov. World Trade Centers

Institute at http://www.wtci.org. World Trade Organi-zation at http://www.wto.org.

World Bank. *Adult Illiteracy Rates.* The Economist. X-rates.com. Homepage. http://www.x-rates.com/

15. Glossary

Dauernutzungsrechte - Long-term lease; a lease of over 30 years and recorded as a land encumbrance.

Eigentum - Absolute ownership; common law concept of fee simple ownership. An absolute owner has the right to sell, lease, will, or give away the property. **Erbbaurecht** - Hereditary building right; a legal

estate in land. It is somewhat equivalent to the common law concept of a free holding. The owner has the right to build and use the improvements on the site and sometimes controls the entire site. The land is not owned, and the hereditary building right usually lasts for 99 years or the life of the improvement.

Pfandbrief - Mortgage-backed bonds that fund first loan of up to 60% of house values.

Teileigentum - Part ownership; ownership of a self-contained unit in a nonresidential building.

Wohnungseigentum – Condominium ownership; ownership of a self-contained residential unit.

Gemeinschaftseigentum – Ownership of the common used parts (e.g. stairs, walls, garden etc.) of a building with

Teileigentum and/or Wohnungseigentum.

About the Author

Dr. Kristin Wellner, Chair of Planning and Construction Economics/ Real Estate, Faculty VI Planning Building Environment, Technical University Berlin, Germany.

Hungary

INTERNATIONAL REAL ESTATE (GLOBAL REAL ESTATE)
Authored by *Kevin Sutton, graduate student,*
University of Denver, and Dr. Mark Lee Levine, Editor

1. Geography

Hungary is located in central Europe, northwest of Romania. Its area consists of 93,028 sq km (square kilometers), slightly smaller than the U.S. state of Indiana.

Hungary's borders include those with Austria, Croatia, Romania, Serbia, and Republic of Slovakia.

The country has no coastlines. The terrain is mostly flat. Some limited resources in the form of coal and natural gas comprise most of its natural resources. Land use is 48.57% arable, 20% as meadows and pastures and approximately 18% for forests and woodlands. The climate is fairly temperate, with cold winters and very warm summers. Environmental issues are of great concern as to air pollution, given that most Eastern European countries have not addressed this issue until recently, if at all.

2. History and Overview

Hungary has long been an integral part of Europe.

Following the defeat of the Austro-Hungarian Dual Monarchy (1867-1918) at the end of World War I, Hungary lost two-thirds of its territory and nearly as much of its population. Hungary fell under communist rule in 1945. Forced industrialization and land collectivization soon led to serious economic difficulties. Hungary joined the Soviet- led Warsaw Pact Treaty Organization in 1955. Revolution and reform dominated Hungarian government for the next 30 years, eventually giving way to a Western style parliamentary democracy. This transition was the first and the smoothest among the former Soviet bloc, inspired by a nationalism that long had encouraged Hungarians to control their own destiny.[125]

3. People

Hungary has population of 9,919,128. There are 67.4% of the population in the category of 15 years through 64 years of age; 14.8% in the category of 0 to 14 years, with the balance of 17.8% in the 65 and older age group.

Population growth has been fairly flat of late, however. More recent estimates show a decrease in the birth rate to 9.26 births per 1,000. Death rates hover at 12.72 per

1,000. Infant mortality is 5.09 deaths per 1,000 live births. Life expectancy is 75.46 years for the total population, with 71.73 years for males and 79.41 years for females.

Ethnic divisions include 92.3% Hungarian, Roma at 1.9%, and small percentages total 5.8% for the balance of the population. The dominant religions are Roman Catholic at 37.2%; Calvinists at 11.6%; and Lutherans at 2.2%. A mix of other religions comprise the balance. The Hungarian language is spoken by 99.6% of the people, with English being a strong second language for many in the major cities. Literacy for children age 15 and over for reading and writing is at about 99.4% of the population. The labor force is approximately 4.388 million (2014).

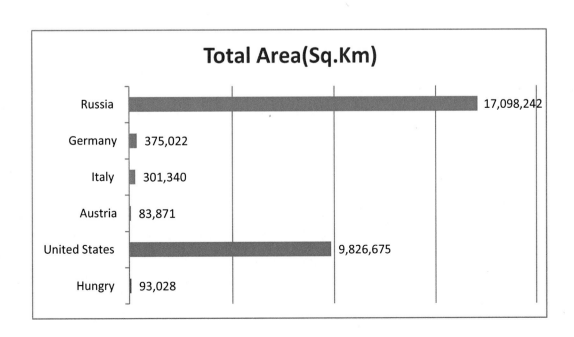

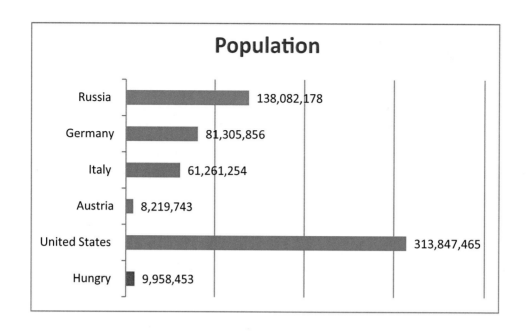

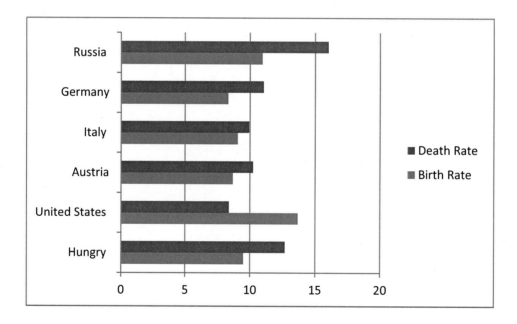

4. Government

The Republic of Hungary is a parliamentary democracy, with the capital in Budapest and 39 counties. The national holiday is August 20, commemorating the founding of the Hungarian state at approximately 1,000 A.D., known as St. Stephen's Day. The Constitution has been modified on several occasions. The legal system is being modified to follow Western cultures. Voting is age 18 and is universal.

The Executive Branch is made up of the Chief of State or the President, the head of government as the Prime Minister, *Miniszterelnöki Hivatal,* and a Cabinet, which is a Council of Ministers and is elected by the National Assembly, *Ország-gyulés,* on recommendation by the President. The Legislative Branch is unicameral, known as the National Assembly. The Judicial Branch is known as the Constitutional Court, *Alkotmánybíróság.* U.S. diplomatic representation with Hungary consists of the U.S. Ambassador located in Budapest, and the Hungarian Ambassador being in Washington, D.C.

5. Economy

The Gross Domestic Product (GDP) is approximately $129.7 billion, with GDP per capita of $24,300 (2014). Inflation was about 0% in 2014, and was very high in 1994 at 21%; in 2008 the inflation rate was around 6.1%; in 2011 the inflation rate was 3.9%. The GDP real growth rate is 2.8% (2014).

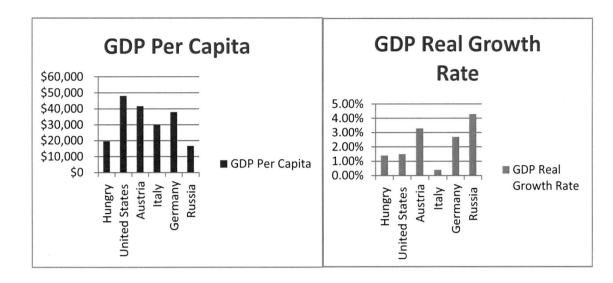

Unemployment was 7.1% in 2014; this is a sharp decline from 9.1% in 2013, fueled by continuing development and expansion in Hungary. A number of industries exist, such as construction materials, processed foods, textiles, chemicals, automobiles and others.

■ 6. Currency

Currency is the *forint* (HUF). See the Burns School Global Real Estate Web site at the UNIVERSITY OF DENVER at http://burns.daniels.du.edu for currency conversions.

■ 7. Transportation

Hungary has 8,057 km (kilometers) of railroads and 199,567 km of total highways. It boasts of inland waterways and pipelines to transport crude oil and natural gas, as well as major ports, such as the one in Budapest. Hungary has 41 airports, 20 with paved runways (2013).

■ 8. Communications

Hungary has 2,960,000 telephones with fiber optic connections to all neighboring countries (2012). Mobile cellular telephones of approximately 11.058 million are in use (2012). Hungary also has sophisticated AM radio and FM radio stations, and short wave radio stations, as well as 95 television broadcast stations (2012).

■ 9. Real Property Issues

Licensing in Hungary is regulated by a separate government decree. The decree defines the content and competence of the brokerage activity; however the details of practice are unregulated. A written contract is often used, but not required. Approximately twenty five percent of all residential real estate transactions are carried out by brokers. This is a result of communist government control over transactions and the public's slow adoption of brokerage services over the last ten years.

There is no legal regulation regarding broker services to be provided to the client.

There is also no law regulating the commission. It is agreed upon in writing and varies depending upon the type, price of property, time limits, and complexity. In most cases the seller or landlord pays the commission, which is due upon signing the deed.

A brokerage license may be obtained by completion of secondary school and then participation in a professional course followed by a written, oral and practical exam.

A license does not need to be renewed.

The majority of brokers work individually with the whole market free to access. There are no local or regional restrictions. The most important multiple-listing service (MLS) source is http://www.ingatlan-buda.hu (free access).

Non-Hungarian ownership is allowed for persons possessing a permit obtained from the local Public Administration Office. This permit will give someone the right to acquire real estate with the exception of arable land and land located in natural reserves. Foreigners can gain property without a permit by right of inheritance. Legal description of property is recorded by a cadastral map. Parcels on the map are cross-referenced with a land registry system. This registry provides parcel size and location; ownership information and history; lien and easement information. Real Estate is registered at the county land office, Foldhivatal. Ownership of and any rights to real estate, including the mortgage are to be entered with this registry. There is no record of selling price. Title search is a relatively easy job, and tit le insurance is not customary. Land registry information is guaranteed by the state. A bona fide purchaser is given clear title to the property even in the case that an unrecorded claim may exist provided that the purchaser has no knowledge of such claim.

■ 10. Real Estate Trends

Increased foreign investment has greatly improved the investment and building opportunities in Hungary. The strongest demand lies around the capitol city and metropolitan areas of substantial population. Quality modern office space has been in demand with the arrival of foreign companies in Hungary. Improvements in telecommunications infrastructure within the country could be the catalyst for further expansion in the office market.

The Hungarian economy is largely export oriented which results in a for warehousing spaces. This market remained largely dormant until the late 90's when the first speculative development was initiated. The rise of demand for logistic and warehouse facilities signals Hungary's emergence as a gateway location for distribution towards Eastern Europe and the Balkans.

For further details in this area, see the Burns School Global Real Estate Web site at the UNIVERSITY OF DENVER at http://burns.daniels.du.edu.

■ 11. Cultural Issues

Any nation's culture is complex and vibrant in its diversity.

While broad cultural characterizations such as those presented here can be generally accurate, following such generalities too strictly may be dangerously misleading. To conduct business effectively and profitably in a country, it is vital to have a thorough understanding of its culture's complexities.

The family name is often used when a person introduces themselves. Introductions and greetings also commonly involve a handshake. Professional attire in Hungary is often conservative, yet stylish. Women pay particular attention to dress. Most visits should be prearranged as only family and close friends will drop by unannounced. Small gifts are common when invited to someone's home.

12. Discussion Questions

1. What are some of the environmental issues in Hungary?

2. What has helped Hungary reduce its unemployment and inflation?

3. How has Hungary's location affected its ability to attract capital?

13. Case Study

Fantasy Real Estate Sales (FRES)

Headquarters in Milan, Italy Offices in Italy, Sweden, Hungary, Spain, Russia, Netherlands, United Kingdom and Greece

Memo

To: Board of Directors
From: Consultants
Re: Downsizing

I. Problem

Overview

Fantasy Real Estate Sales (FRES) was established in Greece in 1995. The idea behind the Company was drawn from a Greek real estate agent, XElvina Greeeelepis, owner of XXEGGG Realty. XElvina's real estate company had many different properties listed, including villas and private islands. The inspiration for FRES came from meeting XElvina.

The Directors felt we would be able to help people find their "fantasy" pieces of real estate, such as castles, villas, ranches, winery's and any unique properties falling into the "fantasy" realm of real estate.

Italy

Recently the headquarters of FRES, located in Milan, Italy, began to grow. It was doing so much business that it had seven full-time agents, and one office manager. FRES needs to hire more people, but it is concerned with hiring too many, because if the Company has more than 15 employees, it will have to "take care of the employees" for a long time. This is based on the employment laws in Italy. See http://www.cmslegal.com/intelligence/cms_news/employment.htm.

Russia

The Russian market is beginning to pick up new business. There are plenty of properties available, but FRES's target buyers are hesitant to purchase property in Russia. (FRES is working on advertising the benefits of realty in Russia. FRES started doing overnight stays at the individual properties, so potential clients can see what it is like to be in Russia.)

Hungary

Currently, in Hungary, the Company has had a reduction in properties available for sale. FRES was been unable to secure properties for sale. It has also had two properties flood in the last two months.

Netherlands

The market is booming. There seem to be enough "fantasy" properties at the current time.

United Kingdom (England, Scotland, Wales)

The United Kingdom, including the **England, Scotland and Wales** markets, has been relatively stable. These markets, for FRES, do not perform extremely well, but they do not go below projected income.

Spain

This market is just beginning to show the growth potential that was projected by FRES for the country. The market had a difficult time because prices were inflated.

As such, it was not a good investment to purchase a fantasy property here; however, prices are beginning to come inline. Thus, with other European markets, the general market is beginning to pick up in sales.

Sweden

Currently the Swedish market is booming. The agents cannot keep up with the market.

II. Initial Exit Strategy

Exiting these countries would be relatively easy, except for Italy, where the headquarters office is currently located. All of the other offices are satellite offices.

In most cases the agents work out of their own homes. The Milan office could be vacated relatively easily. The interior has been upgraded to class A office space and since this is in short supply in Italy, it should be relatively easy to re-lease or sub-lease. The network of real estate agents throughout Europe that FRES has established would help in the event that FRES needed to leave the county.

III. Contingency Exit Strategy

See Initial Exit Strategy plan. The plan of exit would be simple to leave everything and leave the country.

IV. Conclusion

Employment restrictions in Italy will make it difficult to keep expanding. To have a reasonable exit strategy, FRES should move the headquarters to Sweden. The reason Sweden is more of an ideal location is due to the booming market and the favorable employment laws.

The other markets could be considered, but Russia would be difficult. Current employees would resist a move to Sweden. The United Kingdom does not have enough business. This is also true with the Netherlands. Spain might be a possibility for the home office. The company should not completely close the operation in Italy, but it should leave one or two agents, to continue the local market.

Refer to: International Real Estate Digest. Homepage. http://www.ired.com. U.S. Department of State. Homepage. http://www.state.gov.

U.S. Embassy. Homepage. http://usembassy.state.gov.

14. Selected References

CIA World Factbook. https://www.cia.gov/library/publications/the-world-factbook/index.html. http://www.ekormanyzat.hu/english. http://www.hungarytourism.hu/. http://www.ksh.hu/pls/ksh/docs/index_eng.ht ml. http://www.mfa.gov.hu/. "Termination of Employees in Italy." August 15,2002 (Retrieved September

22,2002). http://www.cmslegal.com/intelligence/cms_news/employita.htm. International Real Estate Digest. Homepage. http://www.ired.com.

Richard Ellis International Property Specialists. http://www.cbre.com. Time

Almanac. *TIME Almanac.* Boston: Information Please LLC.

U.S. Bureau of Census at http://www.census.gov.

U.S. Department of Commerce at http://www.stat-usa.gov.

U.S. Bureau of Economic Analysis at http://www.bea.gov. U.S. Department of

State. Homepage. http://www.state.gov. U.S. Embassy. Homepage. http://usembassy.st at e.gov. World Trade Centers Institute at http://www.wtci.org. World Trade Organization at http://www.wto.org.

See the Burns School Global Real Estate Web site at the UNIVERSITY OF DENVER at http://burns.daniels.du.edu

15. Glossary

Handelgesellschaft – notion of business corporations. Covers both corporations and partnerships.

Foldhivatal – the land office, all real estate must be registered at this office.

Comunione – Community property.

Conservatore dei Registri Immobiliari – Recorder of Mortgages.

Fedeazione Italiana Mediatori Agenti Affari – Trade association.

Imposta comunale sugli immobili – annual tax on income from real property based on property's assed value.

Societa in nome collettivo – General partnership.

Societa in accomandita semplice – Limited partnership.

About the Author

Kevin Sutton, graduate student of the Burns School of Real Estate and Construction Management, *Daniels College of Business,* UNIVERSITY OF DENVER.

India

INTERNATIONAL REAL ESTATE (GLOBAL REAL ESTATE)
Authored by *David Dinakar,* University of Denver;
Ramkumar Jayaraman, University of Denver and
Shamit Khemka; Dr. Mark Lee Levine, Editor

1. Geography

India is in located in Southern Asia, bordering the Arabian Sea and the Bay of Bengal, between Burma and Pakistan. India is a very large country, slightly more than one-third the size of the United States. Its total area is approximately 3,287,263 sq km. The land area is 2,973,193 square kilometers (sq km), and the water is 314,070 sq km.

There is 7,000 km of coastline in India. There are numerous border disputes involving Pakistan, China and Bangladesh. The climate varies from a sub-tropical monsoon in the south to being very temperate in the north.

India has numerous natural resources, including the fourth largest coal reserves in the world, iron ore, manganese, mica, bauxite, titanium ore, chromites, natural gas, diamonds, petroleum, limestone, thorium, barite, crude oil and arable land. Land area includes flat plain areas, deserts and mountains. Natural land uses include arable land of about 52.54% and meadows and pastures of only about 4.31%. Woodland and forests consist of almost one-fourth of the land in India.

The environmental issues include deforestation, soil erosion, overgrazing, desertification, air pollution from industrial effluents and vehicle emissions, water pollution from raw sewage and runoff of agricultural pesticides. Tap water is generally not potable throughout the country. There is a huge and growing population which overstrains the natural resources.

2. History and Overview

India has a very long and important historical position, with civilization dating back to 2,500 BC, where the inhabitants lived and developed an agricultural commerce trade. The British established outposts in India in the early 1600s at Madras, Bombay and Calcutta, among other locations.

The first British outpost in South Asia was established in 1619 at Suraton the northwestern coast. Later in the century, the East India Company opened permanent trading stations at Madras, Bombay, and Calcutta, each under the protection of native rulers. The British expanded their influence from these foot holds until, by the1850s, they controlled most of present-day India, Pakistan, and Bangladesh.

Beginning in 1920, Indian leader Mohandas K. Gandhi transformed the Indian National Congress political party into a mass movement to campaign against British colonial rule. The party used both parliamentary and nonviolent resistance, with non-cooperation, to achieve independence. On August 15, 1947, India became a dominion within the Commonwealth, with Jawaharlal Nehru as Prime Minister. Enmity between Hindus and Muslims led the British to partition British India, creating East and West Pakistan, where there were Muslim majorities. India became a republic within the Commonwealth, after promulgating its Constitution on January 26, 1950.

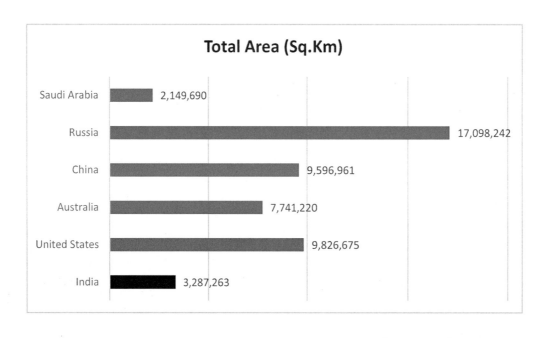

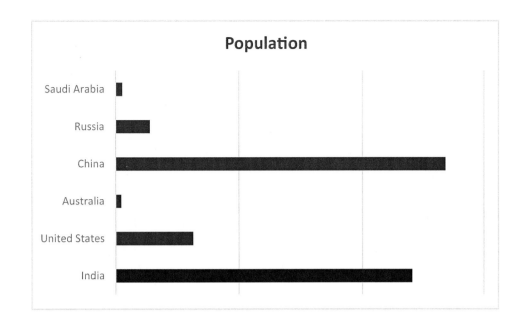

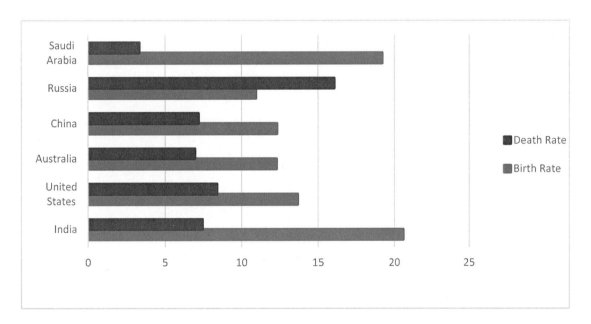

In April 1999, the BJP-led coalition government fell apart, leading to fresh elections in September. The National Democratic Alliance-a new coalition led by the BJP- gained a majority, to form the government with A.B.Vajpayee as Prime Minister in October 1999.

■ 3. People

India is a highly populated country of 1,236,344,631 people (2014). The age structure is 28.5% in the 0 to 14-year-old category, with 65.7% in the 15 to 64-year-old age category. India has a small populace, 5.8%, in the age 65 and older group, given the limited age expectancy of the total population.

Life expectancy for men is 66.68 years and 69.06 for women. Infant mortality is high, with approximately 43.19 deaths per 1,000. The birth rate is 19.89 per 1,000. The overall death rate is 7.35 per 1,000.

Ethnic divisions in India include the Indo-Aryan, which is about 72%.The Dravidian is 25% of the population. The balance is made up of a mix of people, including the Mongoloid (3%).

From a religious standpoint, India is made up of 80.5% Hindu, 13.4% Muslim, and the balance is comprised of Christians (2.3%), Sikhs (1.9%), and others unspecified. The many languages in India include Hindi, the national language and primary tongue of 41% of the people. India has 14 other official languages. There are also many other languages, each spoken by a million or more persons. The English language is very important in national and commercial developments in India. Literacy

is low in India, 61% overall, but official figures are questionable. The labor force in India is very large, with close to 502.2 million people (2014), yet India suffers from a highly uneducated population.

4. Government

According to its Constitution, India is a "sovereign, socialist, secular, democratic republic." Like the United States, India has a federal form of government. However, the central government in India has greater power in relation to its states. The central government is patterned after the British Parliamentary system.

The legal system is based on English common law, with limited judicial review of legislative acts. India accepts compulsory International Court of Justice (IJC) jurisdiction, with reservations. Suffrage for voting is 18 years of age. It is universal.

Branches of the government include an Executive Branch, a Legislative Branch, and a Judicial Branch (Supreme Court).

India maintains an Embassy in the United States in Washington, D.C., and consulates General in New York, Chicago, Houston, and San Francisco.

5. Economy

India's population continues to grow at about 1.25% per year (2014). While its Gross Domestic Product (GDP) of $2.048 trillion is low in dollar terms, it is the world's 4th-largest. Industrial and services sectors are growing in importance and account for most of the GDP, while agriculture contributes to about 25% of GDP. Less than 25% of the population lives below the poverty line. The inflation rate is 8% (2014). The GDP per capita is $5,800, and the GDP real growth rate is 5.6%. But a large and growing middle class now has available disposable income for consumer goods.

Significant liberalization of its investment regime since 1991 has made India an attractive place for foreign direct and portfolio investment. The U.S. is India's largest investment partner. Foreign investment is particularly sought after in power generation, telecommunications, ports, roads, petroleum exploration and processing, and mining. Exports include various commodities, e.g., clothing, chemicals, leather manufacturing, yarn, and other materials. Exports are mostly to the United States, United Arab Emirates (UAE), China, Singapore, United Kingdom and Hong Kong.

6. Currency

India's currency is the Indian *rupee* (INR). For a current examination of the exchange rate of the *rupee* with U.S. dollar, and other currencies, see the sources cited in the Burns School Global Real Estate Web site, Daniels *College of Business*, UNIVERSITY OF DENVER at http://burns.daniels.du.edu.

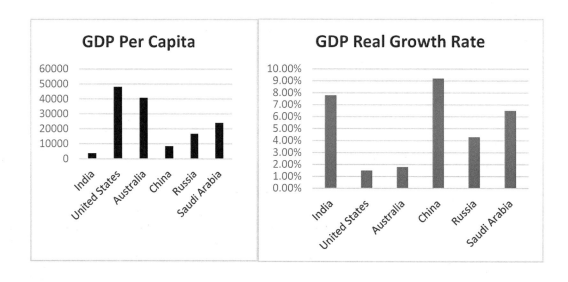

7. Transportation

India has 64,600 km of railroads. Highways total 4,689,842 km, including 79,116 km of expressways.

India has some navigable waterways, 14,500 km long. India has developed pipelines to transport crude oil, petroleum products and natural gas.

Several key shipping ports for many centuries include Chennai (Madras), Calcutta, Mumbai (Bombay), Kandla, Vishakhapatnam and Cochin.

India has 346 airports; 253 of them have paved runways (2013). Major cities have well-developed airports and fairly sophisticated equipment. India also has 45 heliports.

8. Communications

India has 31.08 million telephone main lines and 893.8 million mobile cellular lines (2013). *Doordarshan*, India's public TV network, operates 20 national, regional and local services, and more privately–owned TV cable and satellite service providers are permitted. The government controls AM radio; some privately-owned FM stations are permitted (2012). India has over 6.7 million Internet hosts (2014), with 61.338 million internet users (2009).

Local and long distance service are provided throughout all regions of the country, with services primarily concentrated in the urban areas. The major objective is to continue to expand and modernize long-distance networks to keep pace with rapidly growing number of local subscriber lines. A steady improvement is taking place, with the recent admission of private and private-public investors. Demand for communication services is also rapidly growing. Capacity for India to communicate within its country has been improved as a result of high technology, fiber optic cable, domestic satellite systems, Intel satellites, and other high-tech improvements.

9. Real Property Issues

The real estate and finance sector in India is more or less governed at state levels, not at the center of the federal government. The center does play an import ant role in finance for real estate, which includes new rules for foreclosure.

There were discussions in India, including a discussion about the formation (a few years back) of a real estate association. The position that the National Association of REALTORS® (NAR) has taken is to form a bilateral agreement between NAR, the National Real Estate Development Council (NAREDCO) and the Indian Institute of Real Estate (IRRE).

Forms of real estate ownership in India include tenancy in common, joint tenancy, and ownerships with entities, among others. Although there are means to legally undertake mortgages and other financing, the availability of the same for most of the population is fairly limited. Land use control acts include those under the Urban Land Ceiling and Regulation Act of 1976, which limits certain types of ownership. Such Act provides for some flexibility of ownership by the government, armed forces, certain banks, charities, etc.

Real estate transactions in India are conducted more or less in the unorganized manner. Real estate brokers range from local small-time vendors to big players, undertaking the estate agent's job in an organized fashion. However, the number of substantial parties is small. Most of the practitioners in the market operate on local levels, catering to small localities with a typical size of 5 sq km to 7 sq km. There are very few medium level real estate practitioners operating throughout a State. Even these players are dependent on the brokers of the localities for information. The extent of disorganization can be considered by the fact that, to become a real estate broker, one does not need to be educated in any manner. Sixty-five percent (65%) of the real estate practitioners in the Indian industry are people having sales of less than $500,000 a year. Out of those, 50% would not be educated past the 10th or 12th grade in school. The broker segment of this market receives most of their commissions and payments in an underhanded manner. The rates are negotiable, even after the deal is done.

The big-time players, who can be counted on one's fingertips, usually deal with only very big corporations and are content with doing a few high value transactions a year. Of late, a few international players have entered the market. Prominent amongst them are: Richard Ellis; Jones Lang LaSalle; Knight Frank; Brooks International; Meghraj Chesterton; and Colliers Jardine.

These international firms bring out monthly and quarterly newsletters, circulating them to corporate houses. They are also, for the moment, target only very large transactions. It looks as though most of them are trying to educate Indian consumers as to the benefits of dealing with these international firms.

Property titles in India are under two headings: Leasehold and Freehold. Leasehold properties are normally sold through an agreement to sell on power of attorney. The buyer usually checks for clear title or power of attorney in the seller's name, whether the land/property does or does not have all the required governmental clearances for the type of property. If the same are found to be in order, the transfer is registered in a court, after paying the stamps/court fees, which usually range from 6% to 14%.

Alternatively, of late, both the parties examine documents at the Registrar's office, verify everything, and sign the documents.

In 1990-1991 the National Association of REALTORS® (NAR) and National Association of Home Builders (NAHB) organized a visit to India and thus bought about the formation of the National Real Estate Development Council (NAREDCO) apart from other development plans for this unorganized sector.

The work of NAREDCO in India is equivalent to both these organizations in United States. NAREDCO is trying to play the same role in India now that both these organizations have played for the past 70 years in United States.

NAREDCO has already instituted a rating campaign for the developers and this is being undertaken in conjunction with The Credit Rating Information Services of India Ltd. (CRISIL). NAREDCO has created a training program for the REALTORS® and brokers and this may escalate to becoming a necessity in the future of real estate brokerage. It also proposes to rate real estate and other professionals in this industry as and when it is viable and enforceable.

10. Real Estate Trends

The real estate market is showing signs of maturity. Fueling this is the availability of financing for housing. Demand continues to outstrip supply, indicating better times for the real estate industry. Against the current demand of more than 200,000 houses per annum, the supply is less than one-third, at 60,000. The huge gap between demand and supply, and the easing of credit availability, has increased the business prospects. The housing shortage was estimated to be more than 40 million units in 2001.The commercial segment, which was showing a declining trend in the last six years, has now flattened. The retail segment is rising, showing very good growth.

The current number of active real estate offices and sales agents in the country cannot be provided as most of the brokers are very small time and are unorganized. They do not find the need to register themselves as property broker/estate agents. All in all, the figure could be about 5,000,000 registered brokers and more than 20,000,000 function as unregistered/part time brokers.

The commission rates vary from broker to broker, as they do from region to region and from transaction to transaction.

The average commission would be about 2% to 3% from each side, i.e., between 4% to 6 % for small deals, and between 1% to 2 % for large transactions. For rental commissions, this number is usually 15 days to1 month of rental equivalency, plus 2% of the initial non-refundable security deposit from each side.

As of date there are no specific licensing requirements for real estate agents in India.

They have to register their company. But, these laws are no different than those that require registering of a company for any other business.

11. Cultural Issues

Any nation's culture is complex and vibrant in its diversity.

While broad cultural characterizations such as those presented here can be generally accurate, following such generalities too strictly may be dangerously misleading. To conduct business effectively and profitably in a country, it is vital to have a thorough understanding of its culture's complexities.

Cultural issues are extremely important when undertaking business. This is true in any country. This is especially true in India, because there is a wide range of cultures that vary from state to state. Concerns with knowledge of cultural issues can be reflected in many business settings. Therefore, knowledge in this area is crucial. Traditions are somewhat unique. For example, Hindu women wearing a *bindi* or red dot on the forehead, can constitute a sign of femininity and gracefulness. (Women are increasingly becoming a dominant part of the work force. India is fast breaking away from the male, dominant past.)

Greetings include the traditional means of shaking hands, but other means, e.g., a slight bow and nodding, are also utilized.

12. Discussion Questions

1. What are some of the environmental issues in India and what affect do these issues have on its natural resources and its people?

2. Do the border disputes in India, with its neighbors, affect its ability to attract investors and capital?

3. India has a low percentage of educated people in its population. How does this impact India's economy and its ability to attract investment capital to India from abroad?

4. What is the impact on India's large below-poverty-level population on its real estate market?

5. What are some issues regarding religion and culture that are important when non-Indians want to invest in India?

13. Case Study

India Call Center (ICC) New Delhi, India

Memo

To: Board of Directors
From: Consultants
Re: XXwest Possible Bankruptcy

I. Problem

India Call Center (ICC) was opened in 2001, after extensive call center outsourcing in the United States. ICC opened a branch in New Delhi, India, because of the strong labor force and the low cost of doing business. ICC opened after it had secured a contract with XXwest to out source all of their call cent er operat ions toICC. thedeal agreement required that all of their call center needs would run through our office in New Delhi because of the high quality of customer service representatives there and the low cost. ICC purchased land and built a new call center for the operation. However, XXwest is being investigated by the SEC, detail. There is the possibility of a bankruptcy of XXwest. How will that impact ICC?

II. Initial Exit Strategy

The initial exit plan was to eventually sell the company to a local investor or possibly sell the operation to the government. The call center space could easily be transformed into office space for other businesses. The call center was built using cubicle furniture that can easily be reconfigured or torn out. There are only few hard-wall offices that might have to be changed to accommodate another business.

Unfortunately if ICC had to exit the market, ICC would have to lay off all of the employees who currently work in the New Delhi facility because relocation to the United States would be very unlikely and very costly for the Company.

When the operational part of the facility is shut down and the all the calls rerouted to another call center, then ICC could begin to show the office space. (ICC does not want to start showing the space until the operations have been shut down because of the employee morale. And brokers going through the space can have a negative effect on the productivity of employees.) One of the strategic firms in real estate would be hired to list and either sell the space or sublease it at a reasonable price. The cube furniture, switches, cable, additional HVAC, and other property would be included with the property, unless a new tenant would not want one of the above- mentioned items. (In that case, ICC would remove the item and attempt to sell it.) This would be the exit plan if time were not of the essence.

III. Contingency Exit Plan

With a brand new facility, a contingency exit plan is more difficult. The above exit plan would have to be implemented more quickly. There are not many shortcuts to the above-mentioned plan, but any that were reasonable and cost effective would be attempted.

Another option would be to peruse new accounts with renewed energy. One big account that might be feasible, because of the groundwork that has been undertaken by ICC, is the probable AX&X Broadband/Cratcast merger. Once this merger is completed, ICC could easily pursue Cratcast call centers. Cratcast is a company that is run by its markets, not by a headquarters. It could reduce overhead if the call centers were closed and the call center operations outsourced.

IV. Conclusion

The investment made into the new call center would not be something that ICC would want to walk away from, if there are good alternatives. It is the suggestion that in the United States ICC should take its best sales force and peruse new accounts. This option would give ICC the time to wait out the roller coaster ride that XXwest is experiencing, but it would also posture ICC to continue operations if XXwest were to go into bankruptcy and be liquidated. If, after a year, ICC was unable to secure any new contracts, implementation of the Initial Exit Strategy plan would be necessary.

Refer to: X-rates.com. Homepage. http://www.x-rates.com/.

U.S. Embassy. Homepage. http://usembassy.state.gov. U.S. Department of State. Homepage. www.state.gov.

14. Selected References

CB Richard Ellis International Property Specialists. http://www.cbre.com. Chesterton Meghraj.http://www.chestertonmeghraj.com.

Colliers Jardine. http://www.colliers.com. Indian Embassy. http://indianembassy.org/.

Jones Lang LaSalle. http://www.joneslanglasalle.com

Knight Frank.http://www.knightfrank.com

Time Almanac. *TIME Almanac.* Boston: Information Please LLC.

United States Department of State. *Background Notes: India*. United States Department of State http://www.state.gove/www/background_notes/india_0003_bgn.html. U.S. Bureau of Census at http://www.census.gov.

U.S. Department of Commerce at http://www.stat-usa.gov.

U.S. Bureau of Economic Analysis at http://www.bea.gov.

U.S. Embassy. Homepage. http://usembassy.state.gov. World Trade Centers Institute at http://www.wtci.org. World Trade Organization at http://www.wto.org.

World Bank. *Adult Illiteracy Rates*. X-rates.com. Homepage. http://www.x-rates.com/.

15. Glossary

Bindi – *A* red dot worn by women in the middle of the forehead.

Dravidian – *An* ethnic group in India.

ICJ – *The* International Court of Justice is the principal judicial organ of the United Nations (UN). Its seat is at the Peace Palace in The Hague (The Netherlands). It began work in 1946.

Indo-aryan – *An* ethnic group in India.

NAREDCO – National Real Estate Development Council.

About the Authors

David Dinakar resided in India and was Director of Systems and Technology, *Daniels College of Business,* UNIVERSITY OF DENVER, Denver, Colorado.

Ramkumar Jayaraman, Analyst Developer, PeopleSoft, Inc., Denver, Colorado.

Ireland

INTERNATIONAL REAL ESTATE (GLOBAL REAL ESTATE)

Dr. Mark Lee Levine, Editor

1. Geography

Ireland is part of Western Europe in the United Kingdom. It is located in the North Atlantic Ocean. It has 70,273 sq km (square kilometers) of area, and it is slightly larger than West Virginia.

The climate is temperate and has fairly mild winters and cool summers, being strongly overcast a good part of the year. Rolling hills and low mountains comprise most of Ireland.

Numerous natural resources include lead, petroleum, silver, peat, natural gas, zinc, gypsum, limestone, dolomite, and others. A number of environmental issues include water pollution and agricultural runoff problems.

2. History and Overview

From 1800 to 1921, Ireland was an integral part of the United Kingdom. Religious freedom was restored in 1829. But this victory for the Irish Catholic majority was overshadowed by severe economic depression and mass famine. The famine spawned the first mass wave of Irish emigration to the United States.

The turn of the century witnessed a surge of interest in Irish nationalism. The end of the war with the British brought the Anglo-Irish treaty of 1921, which established the Irish Free State of 26 counties within the British Commonwealth and recognized the partition of the island into Ireland and Northern Ireland, though supposedly as a temporary measure. Opposition to the treaty led to further hostilities–a civil war (1922-23), which was won by the pro treaty forces.

A new Irish constitution was enacted in 1937. The last British military bases were soon withdrawn, and the ports were returned to Irish control. Ireland was neutral in

World War II. The government formally declared Ireland a republic in 1948. However, it does not normally use the term "Republic of Ireland," which tacitly acknowledges the partition but refers to the country simply as "Ireland."[138]

3. People

Ireland has 4,832,765 people, 66.2% being in the 15-year to 64-year age category. The 0 to 14 year group has 21.4% of the population, with the balance being the minority, those 65 years of age or older at 12.4%.

The population growth rate is low at 1.2%. Birth rates are about 15.18 per 1,000. Death rates are 6.45 per 1,000. However, there is a net migration from the country of a little over 3.31 migrants per 1,000. Infant mortality is 3.74 per 1,000 live births. Life expectancy is fairly long in Ireland, with males at 78.28 years and females at 82.97. The average life expectancy is 80.56 years.

Ethnic groups are dominantly Celtic and English. Religions include almost 84.7% Roman Catholic, 2.7% Church of Ireland,

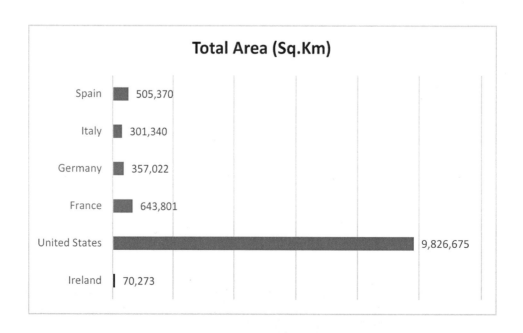

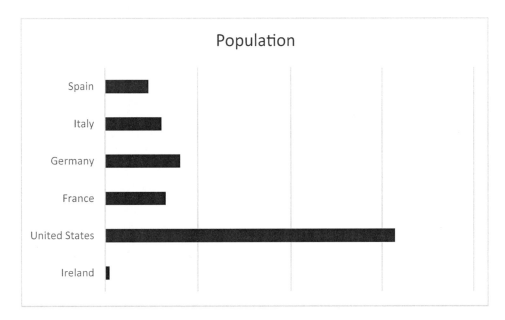

and a mix of others. The dominant languages are Irish (Gaelic) and English. Literacy is fairly high for those 15 years of age and older, at approximately 99%.

4. Government

Ireland is a republic, with the capital in Dublin. It has 28 counties. Ireland gained independence on December 6, 1921, from the United Kingdom. It celebrates its national holiday on St. Patrick's Day on March 17. The legal system is based on English common law, with some modifications. Voting is at 18 years of age for both male and female. The government consists of the Chief of State as the President, the head of government through the Prime Minister, and a Cabinet appointed by the President. The Legislative Branch includes the bicameral Parliament of the Senate and the House of Representatives. The Supreme Court is the highest court. The government of Ireland has an Ambassador for Ireland in Washington, D.C.; the U.S. Ambassador resides in Dublin.

5. Economy

The Gross Domestic Product (GDP) is approximately $245.8 billion (2014). The GDP per capita is about $46,800. The inflation rate is very low, at 0.3% (2014). Unemployment is high in the range of 11.3%, but has fallen in recent years. However, the GDP real growth rate is 3.60%.

6. Currency

Currency is the *euro* (it was the Irish *pound*). See the Burns School Web site for the UNIVERSITY OF DENVER at http://burns.daniels.du.edu for currency conversion rates.

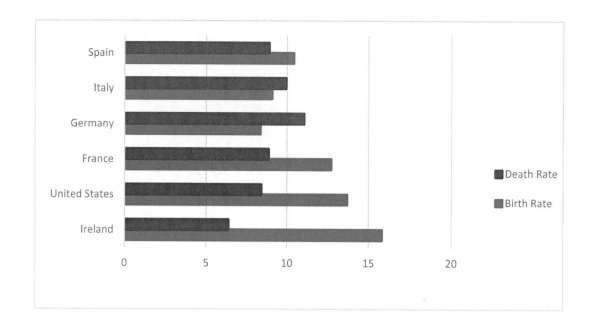

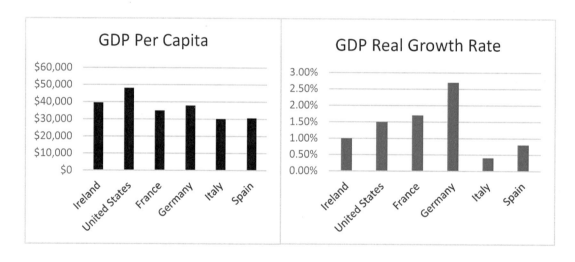

■ 7. Transportation

Ireland has a strong railroad system of 3,237 km (kilometers) of railways, along with 96,036 km of highways. Inland waterways, ports and pipelines are used for commercial transportation, among other uses. Ireland has 40 airports that serve in various capacities for passenger traffic as well as commercial use (2013).

■ 8. Communications

Ireland has 2.007 million main line telephones - disproportionately high for its population - and 4.906 million cellular telephones (2012). It has 4 public TV stations, and other broadcast stations are available. Ireland has 4 national radio stations, which allow for more sophisticated communication systems.

Around 1,387,000 Internet service provider hosts (2012) and 3,042,000 internet users.

■ 9. Real Property Issues

A significant portion of the costs for acquiring real property will rest with the Stamp Duty. The rates have recently been changed under the Finance Act of 2002. The rates apply to conveyances, transfers, and leases of residential property. The rates vary depending on the market value of the property and whether the buyer is a first-time owner and occupier. Properties that serve as the primary residence the stamp duty would be assessed based upon the site value or 25% of the full value of the property, whichever is higher.

Legal Property in Ireland may be registered or unregistered freehold. Title may also be leasehold and subject to a reserved ground rent payable to the superior titleholder. This type of lease allows most leaseholders to buy out the freehold title. The cost of buying the freehold can rise by a substantial amount as the purchase date approaches the reversion or expiration date.

Current legislation for residential leases could provide occupants who have leased for six consecutive months the right to lease up to four years. Rents would be adjusted to market levels on an annual basis. The landlord could recover possession in the case that the wishes to sell the property. When the four year period expires the landlord may reaffirm possession for no reason. The tenant must occupy for an additional 6 months before being eligible for another four-year lease.

The standard loan term in Ireland is 20 years. Most funds for the purchase of property in Ireland come from banks and building societies. Most will lend up to 92% of the sales price. Of course this rate can vary dramatically depending upon the purchaser and property.

Real Estate agents in Ireland are typically called *auctioneers* or estate agents. Estate agents are required to hold either an auctioneers license or a house agent's license. This is part of the reason for the title of auctioneer. There is no experience or academic requirement to hold the real estate license. The seller pays the commission in Ireland unless a buyer specifically retains an agent to act on his/her behalf.

10. Real Estate Trends

Several companies such as Jones Lang LaSalle (http://joneslanglasalle.com) and PriceWaterhoseCoopers (http://pwcglobal. com) provide detailed, current information on the latest real estate market trends. The real estate trade association in Ireland is the Irish Auctioneers and Valuers Institute (http://www.realestae.ie). For additional details in this area, see the Burns School Web site at the UNIVERSITY OF DENVER at http://burns.daniels.du.edu.

11. Cultural Issues

Any nation's culture is complex and vibrant in its diversity. While broad cultural characterizations such as those presented here can be generally accurate, following such generalities too strictly may be dangerously misleading. To conduct business effectively and profitably in a country, it is vital to have a thorough understanding of its culture's complexities.

While being well dressed in Irish business culture is important, little attention is given to designer labels and elaborate accessories. Fashions in general follow those of Europe. When conversing in Ireland, it is important to keep hand gestures to a minimum and maintain a comfort able distance between people. While this personal space is not as pronounced as in northern Europe, it is still important to maintain. Business is more commonly conducted during an afternoon meal rather than in the evening. Gifts are not necessary when conducting business. If compelled to give a gift, something nice but inexpensive could be given at the conclusion of a business deal.

12. Discussion Questions

1. How has Ireland's location in regard to Great Britain and Northern Ireland affected its ability to attract investors?

2. Is Northern Ireland's political situation troublesome to Ireland? Why or why not ?

3. How does Ireland's population growth rate affect the economy of Ireland today and in the future?

13. Case Study

Irish Bulldog Security (IBS) North King Street Smithfield, Dublin, Ireland

Memo

To: Board of Directors
From: Consultants
Re: Reduction of Offices within Ireland

I. Problem

Irish Bulldog Security (IBS) has been in business in Dublin for over 32 years. It has been in business in the U.S. for 45 years. IBS opened to help protect a building and high profile public figure. Specifically, after the violent summer of 1999, IBS has bodyguards and security guards for buildings, homes, apartments and any other facility that needs security. With the Good Friday Agreement (otherwise known as the Belfast Agreement that was signed in April 1998), the business of IBS has decreased. Especially in the last two years, since the violence has decreased, business also has declined.

II. Initial Exit Strategy

When the Company was started, it began with one bodyguard, who was hired by the government to protect high-profile individuals in the U.S. Thirteen years later after the violent summer of 1969 in Ireland, the owner decided to open a branch in Ireland. He is an Irish Immigrant to the US. This gave him the connections that were necessary to start the business and the ability to work through many hurdles, because he was from Ireland. At the time that Irish Bulldog Security expanded into Ireland, there was no exit plan.

III. Contingency Exit Strategy

The events in Ireland in the last four years have helped to reduce the violence and in turn have reduced the business. IBS must begin to look at downsizing its operation in Ireland and to consider possibly shutting down the branch. The building that IBS uses as its headquarters in Ireland is owned by IBS.

(The initial owner was able to purchase this property in Ireland because he was considered a "qualified person".) While IBS is downsizing, it would need to lease out the extra space in the building, until it is able to close the office and either sublease the building or attempt to sell the building by hiring a real estate agent who is familiar with the market.

IV. Conclusion

With the events in Ireland and the need to down size, the Consultants suggested that IBS begin to work on the Contingency Exit Strategy and attempt to close the offices in Ireland. This does not need to be completed immediately, but within the next year, when IBS should be completely out of Ireland.

Refer to: U.S. Embassy. Homepage. http://usembassy.state.gov. U.S. Department of State. Homepage. http://www.state.gov. X-rates.com. Homepage. http://www.x-rates.com/.

14. Selected References

CIA World Factbook at https://www.cia.gov/library/publications/the-world-factbook/index.html.

A variety of resources are available at Ireland Online at http://www.iol.ie/~discover/realestate.htm.

http://www.real-estate-european-union.com/english/ireland.html. Jones Lang

LaSalle, Ireland, http://www.joneslanglasalle.ie.

Price Waterhouse Coopers, http://www.pwcglobal.com.

Richard Ellis International Property Specialists. http://www.cbre.com. Time Almanac. *TIME Almanac.* Boston: Information Please LLC.

United States Department of St at e. *Background Notes: Ireland.* United States

Department of State (Online). Available:http://www.state.gov.

U.S. Bureau of Census at http://www.census.gov. U.S. Department of Commerce at http://www.stat-usa.gov. U.S. Bureau of Economic Analysis at http://www.bea.gov.

U.S. Embassy. Homepage. http://usembassy.state.gov. World Trade Centers Institute at http://www.wtci.org. World Trade Organization at http://www.wto.org. World Bank. *Adult Illiteracy Rates.* The Economist.

15. Glossary

Irish Auctioneers and Valuers – Trade Association.

Qualified Persons – only a "qualified person" can own land in Ireland. A qualified person must be(a) an Irish citizen or national member of E.U.,(b) Person continuously resident in Ireland during the last seven years, and(c) person acquiring land exclusively for purpose of industry other than agriculture, for private resident purposes where land does not exceed 5 acres.

About the Author

Dr. Mark Lee Levine *is the Editor of this Book.*

Israel

INTERNATIONAL REAL ESTATE (GLOBAL REAL ESTATE)
Authored by *Aytan A. Dove, CCIM;*
Ellen H. Levine, CCIM; Dr. Arie Avram

Dr. Mark Lee Levine, Editor

1. Geography

Located along the east edge of the Mediterranean Sea, Israel is in a geographic area considered as the crossroads between Europe, Asia and Africa. Israel is land- bordered to the north by Lebanon, Syria to the northeast, Jordan to the east, and Egypt to the southwest. Israel is part of the Middle East countries. Based on current negotiated agreements with the Palestinian Authority, the Gaza Strip is the largest population center along the Mediterranean Sea directly south of the Israeli border. There are other land areas along the West Bank (west side of the Jordan River that separates Israel and Jordan) that are under the administrative control of the Palestinian Authority.

The total land area of Israel, including that area currently under Palestinian self-government control, is approximately 22,072-square kilometers (Km²⁾, or approximately 8,522-square miles. A trip by car, from the northern to southern edges of Israel takes approximately six hours. The chart below shows the comparison of land area of Israel, in square kilometers, to neighboring Middle East countries.

Jerusalem, Israel's capital, is located toward the eastern, central section of the country, approximately 46km east of the Mediterranean Sea and the City of Tel Aviv. In the Year 2006, the population was reported at approximately 7.200.000, in 2008 at 7,112,359, and in 2009 7,233,701. A new census was done during 2009. According to the Central Bureau of Statistics in 2012 the Israeli **population** surpasses 7.5 million people, with 28% being under 14 years of age.

Israel's climate falls in a wide range from lower temperate to tropical, with plenty of sun shine. Two distinct seasons predominate: a rainy winter period from November to May, and a dry summer season, which extends through the next six months. Rainfall is relatively heavy in the north and center of the country, with much less in the northern Negev and negligible amounts in the southern areas. Israel's temperatures fall within a very wide range even though the country is very small. Typically, the range of temperatures in the northern region is from −1°C (31°F) in the winter months to 29°C (84°F) in the summer months. At the southern region the temperatures range from 21°C (70°F) in the winter to a very hot 40°C (104°F).

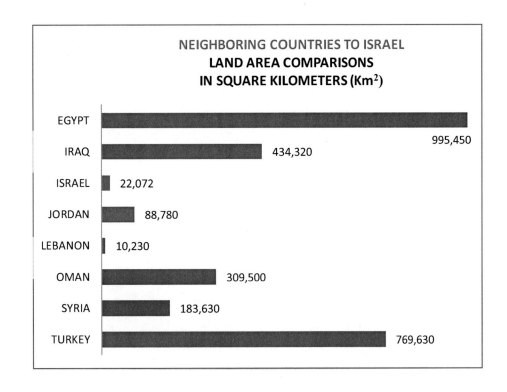

NEIGHBORING COUNTRIES TO ISRAEL
**LAND AREA COMPARISONS
IN SQUARE KILOMETERS (Km²)**

Country	Land Area (Km²)
EGYPT	995,450
IRAQ	434,320
ISRAEL	22,072
JORDAN	88,780
LEBANON	10,230
OMAN	309,500
SYRIA	183,630
TURKEY	769,630

For such a small country, Israel's geography presents some very dynamic challenges and unique contrasts. Most notably is the area around the Dead Sea, located southeast of Jerusalem. The Dead Sea is the lowest point on earth, at about 400 meters (m) below sea level. The waters of the Dead Sea are famous for having the highest level of salt content and overall water density in the world. There are companies from Israel and Jordan that are active in harvesting the rich minerals from this sea that includes; potash, magnesium bromine, table and industrial salts. Since the mid-1990s there has been a proposed project to link the Dead Sea with the Mediterranean Sea, by means of a canal and pipe system, which may help rest ore the Dead Sea to its natural dimensions and levels, which have been decreasing on an annual basis. During the last year a new plan for connecting the Red Sea with the Dead Sea was proposed by private entrepreneurs.

The country is long and narrow with almost half of its length having a coastline along the east end of the Mediterranean Sea. It would be accurate to describe Israel's geographic features by five distinct regions, which are: (1) the coastal plain, along the Mediterranean Sea; (2) the mountain ranges that run the length of the country from the Mount Hermon in the Golan Heights and descending to the Lower Galilee range of Mount Tabor; (3) the **Jezreel Valley,** the country's richest agricultural area; (4) the Negev, Israel's desert, represents almost half of Israel's land area but is inhabited by less than 11% of the total population; and (5) the Jordan Valley, an area that runs the length of the country in the east and is one of the most fertile areas of the country.

Agriculture in Israel: According to information available through the Ministry of Agriculture and Rural Development, Israel has been known, for over 60 years as a country "that can make the desert bloom and the swamps turn into agricultural wonders." Israel produces 95% of its own food requirements. Many food products imported are usually offset by the strong agriculturally related exports.

Most of Israel is considered arid in nature with the water supply being in a constant state of shortage. Rainfall, under normal weather conditions, occurs mostly between November and April and is very uneven as to distribution across the country. Since 1964, Israel completed and implemented a National Water Carrier system that brings water from the northern regions of the Jordan River to the central and southern regions.

Environmental Issues and Concerns: In a country with limited water supply and a consistent growth of population and tourism, the issue of water in Israel is central to environmental concerns over supply, demand, and pollution. Other key environmental concerns that in recent years have been given high priority throughout state and local government agencies and citizen groups include, but are not limited to, landfill management, air quality, light pollution, safe management of hazardous substance and nature conservation. During the last few years a large system of desalinization was constructed that provide the country with all its needs and lately offered surpluses to its neighbors.

■ 2. History and Overview

Biblical Israel has a long history that spans over 3,500 years. However, the State of Israel was created in 1948. Since then, it has continued to have border disputes. It has acquired other property from its neighbors, the result of various wars.

Eretz Yisrael, Land of Israel, is the birthplace and origination of the Jewish People, as a people, and as a nation. The first 1,000 years of the people and the land are well recorded in the Bible. Even though a majority of the people lived in forced exile, their physical presence in *Eretz Yisrael* has been unbroken and maintained until the establishment of the State of Israel on May 14, 1948. The following are general highlights of the chronology145 of key dates and world events in the history of the State of Israel:

Key Dates: 17th to 6th Century
World Events: Biblical Era (Patriarchs) (17th Century BCE); Exodus from Egypt (13th Century BCE); Settlement of the "Promised Land" by Israelites; First Temple destroyed, Exile to Babylonia (586);Persian & Hellenistic Period (536-142 BCE)

Key Dates: 63 BCE to 313 CE
World Events: Roman Rule – 2nd Temple destroyed 70 CE

Key Dates: 313-636 CE
World Events: Byzantine Rule

Key Dates: 636-1099
World Events: Arab Rule (Dome of the Rock built on Temple site)

Key Dates: 1099-1291
World Events: Crusader Domination (Latin Kingdom of Jerusalem)

Key Dates: 1291-1917
World Events: Mamluk Rule and 400 years of Ottoman Rule

Key Dates: 1917-1948
World Events: "Jewish National Home in Palestine", from the British Foreign Minister Balfour and beginning of British Rule

Key Dates: 1919-1948
World Events: Major Immigration to Israel

Key Dates: 1948
World Events: State of Israel Established

Key Dates: 1948-1952
World Events: Mass Immigration to Israel

Key Dates: 1956, 1967 & 1973
World Events: Three Arab-Israeli Wars resulting in Israeli Decisive Victories

Key Dates: 1979
World Events: Israel-Egypt Peace Treaty

Key Dates: 1994
World Events: Israel-Jordan Peace Treaty

Key Dates: 1993 to Present
World Events: On-going negotiations for Palestinian Self-Government and autonomy. The State of Israel is a democratic country with a President, Prime Minister, Parliament, and local governmental authorities. It became an independent state on May 14, 1948. Israel is one of the world's smallest nations, with the world's highest scientific and engineering ratio to general population on a per capita basis. It is also the home and cradle to three religions: Islam, Christianity, and Judaism.

Israel is a Jewish state where over 75% of the population is Jewish.

Viewing Tel Aviv Beaches from the east edge of the Mediterranean Sea, with the hills of the Galilei in the background. Photographer: Dana Friedlander; Courtesy of the Israeli Ministry of Tourism

▪ 3. People

As of September 11, 2012, Israel Central Bureau of Statistics, reported the population of Jerusalem as being 796,200, Tel Aviv Municipality 414,600, Haifa 269,300, Rishon LeZion (near Tel Aviv) 231,700, Petach Tikva (near Tel Aviv) 210,800, Holon (Tel Aviv) 182,000, B'nei Brak (Tel Aviv) 161,100, Beer Sheva 105,800, Ashdod 211,400, Eilat 47,700. The Tel Aviv Metropolitan area in Central Israel and located along the Mediterranean Sea, houses approximately 42% of the country's residents at approximately 3,464,100 residents within a 20-square mile area, or 52km².

According to the Israel Central Bureau of Statistics, as of January 2015, the State of Israel had a population of approximately **8,296,000** inhabitants. At the end of 2013, the population was reported at 8,059,000 for an overall increase of approximately 3.0% in two years. Approximately 6,229,600 of the total population are the Jewish population, or approximately 75.0%. The Arab population represents approximately 21.0% and the remaining populace representing approximately 4.0%. Israel is home to +/-43% of the total known Jewish population in the world.

The overall average age of the population in Israel is approximately 29.7 years. In 2013, the life expectancy was 80.3 years for men and 83.9-years for women. According to a report conducted in the summer of 2014, the Taub Center for Social Policy Studies that was titled as "Family Structure and Well-Being Across Israel's Diverse Population", Israel's birthrate is the *highest* in the *developed world* at 3.0 children per woman as compared to an international average of 1.7 children per woman. A strong influence on the higher number in Israel is due to its large Orthodox population.

Distribution by age in Israel is influenced by a wide scope of immigration, ethnic backgrounds and a changing, upward growth rate due to positive positions in the economy and the efforts of the peace process. Israel is still considered as one the "youngest" of the developed countries.

The Christian communities may be divided into four basic categories: Chalcedonian- Orthodox, Non-Chalcedonian Orthodox (Monophysite), Roman Catholic (Latin and Uniate) and Protestant.

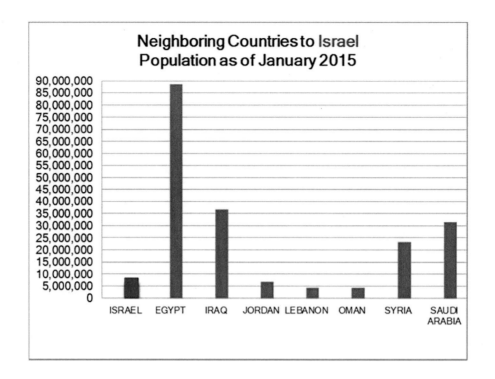

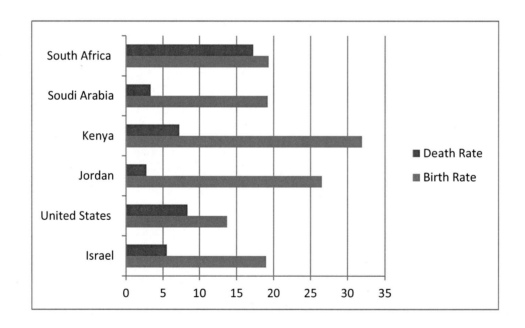

The Central Bureau of Statistics changed starting with the 1995 Census, due to the reporting and census data to reflect changes in definitions of religion and population groups. Up to the 1995 Census, tables include, as a rule, the population broken down by Jews, Moslems, Christians and Druze. Included with the Druze are members of other religions (such as: Buddhists, Hindus, Samaritans, etc.), who constitute only a few hundred in the population. Due to the arrival of many immigrants not listed as Jews in the Ministry of the Interior, the definitions of religion and population group were altered in the population estimate tables. Jews, Moslems, Christians total, Arab Christians, Other Christians, Druze and Not classified by religion.

The Arab citizens of Israel are usually defined collectively, but include the following Arab groups that have distinctive characteristics and cultural influences: Muslim Arabs, most of whom are Sunni and constitute 75% of the non-Jewish population; Bedouin Arabs, that comprise nearly 10% of the Muslim population; Christian Arabs that make up Israel's second largest minority group, who are affiliated with Greek Orthodox, Greek Catholic and Roman Catholic churches; the Druze, which have a separate cultural, social and religious community. According to the Ministry of Tourism, the Circassians are the smallest of the ethnic groups living in Israel that are a fascinating part of Israel's ethnic mosaic. They live in two Israeli villages, 3,000 in Kfar Kama in the Lower Galilee, and 1,000 in Rekhaniya in the Upper Galilee.

■ 4. Government

The Israeli government is a democracy. The capital is in Jerusalem. Many of the foreign embassies are located in Tel Aviv, since Jerusalem has yet to be accepted, worldwide, as Israel's capital. Israel's governmental structure is outlined in the following table:

Israeli Government Structure[149]

```
                HEAD OF STATE
                   President

   Legislative      Executive        Judiciary
   Speaker        Prime Minister     Court System
   Knesset         Government       Attorney General
   Committees      Ministries
   Mayors
                    State
                  Comptroller
   Council Heads

   Local Councils


   ELECTORATE
```

Israeli Government Structure149

The President is elected, by a simple majority, to a five-year term by the members of the *Knesset*, the Israeli Parliament. He can serve a second term. The Prime Minister and members of the *Knesset* are elected directly by the electorate.

Israel had general elections on March 17, 2015, with the new 120th Knesset being sworn in on March 31, 2015. As a result of these elections, with a high voter turnout of 71.8% the highest in past 16-years. The two largest parties include the Likud Party with 30 representatives, Zionist Union (Labor and Hatnuah Parties combined) with 24 representatives, followed by the Joint List (Arab Parties with 13 representatives. This election also resulted in a record number of 29 women a record for Israel's legislature.

Branches of government include an Executive Branch; the Chief of State is the President. The Prime Minister is the head of the government. The unicameral Legislative Branch, the *Knesset*, is otherwise known as the Parliament. A Judicial Branch is headed by the Supreme Court. Various ministries, committees, and other special governmental agencies as well as the various political parties existing in Israel, can be further researched and discovered through the *Israel Government Yearbook that*

appears to be the best and most current source about the Israeli government. See the Web site: http://www.knesset.gov.il.

Diplomatic representation of Israel with the United States exists with offices of an Ambassador in Washington, D.C. The United States maintains diplomatic representation with Israel by an Ambassador in Tel Aviv.

Israeli defense forces are in the form of army, navy and air forces, along with youth groups and other military or paramilitary support.

■ 5. Economy

The Israeli economy is a market economy with a history of strong government activity. During the five year from 2005-2009 Israel's economy went through a massive change to privatization. Israel has depended on many imports, such as oil, grains, raw materials and military equipment. However, because of recent changes in the laws, emphasis on less government, and more privatization, the trade deficit has been shrinking dramatically. Today, Israel's citizens enjoy a standard of living comparable to that of the United States and many West European countries.

Israel's economy has undergone a vast structural change that has exhibited a dynamic flair and one of resilience in both the shape and pace of its growth. Israel, for the first 40 years of its life as an independent state, has had a local economy based primarily on agriculture, limited commerce, and light industry. However, since 1993, Israel has become a major influence, internationally, with very competitive industries in key sectors of communications, electronics, information technology, biochemistry and agricultural technologies.

In May 1998, one of the most historic economic events occurred in Israel: All foreign-currency restrictions on households and the business sector were abolished, with certain exceptions. The removal of foreign-currency restrictions on Israeli residents, individuals and businesses enables residents to enjoy complete freedom to engage in transactions with nonresidents in both foreign and local currency. The change in the laws was designed to allow such free exchange to increase competition in financial services and therefore reduce financing costs. The State of Israel Ministry of Industry and Trade has an Investment Promotion Center with various staff members dedicated to attracting investment and business from other countries on a worldwide basis. The data available from this particular group on Israel's economy, investment opportunity and developments is one of the best sources available. Their web site is: http://www.tamas.gov.il (click on the Investment Promotion Center). (This site is shown in Hebrew, English and Arabic.)

As of the end of the Year 2013, the Israel Bureau of Statistics published the following employment numbers for the categories listed. These categories were revised in 2011 and are the most current.

Fueled by a steady increase in exports and by a high level of international investments, growth of the Israeli economy

EMPLOYED PERSONS BY INDUSTRY, AS OF 2013	
TOTAL ALL SECTORS	**3,429,520**
Agriculture, forestry and fishing	43,100
Manufacturing, Mining and Quarry	411,720
Electricity Supply	15,400
Water supply, sewage and waste management	16,100
Construction	165,750
Wholesale and retail trade and repair	402,660
Transportation, storage, postal and courier activities	146,600
Accomodations and food service activities	150,300
Information and communications	165,940
Financial and Insurance activities	118,540
Real Estate Activities	**28,200**
Professional, scientific and technical activities	236,970
Administrative and support service activities	147,680
Local, public and defence administration and social security	362,700
Education	413,200
Human health and social work activities	353,900
Arts, entertainment and recreation	61,420
Other service activities	69,400
Households as employers	64,140
Extraterritorial organizations and bodies	2,200
Unknown	53,600
TOTALS	**3,429,520**

Source: Israel Central Bureau of Statistics, Labor & Wages

has been largely expanding. Foreign direct investment (FDI) in Israel reached $4.4 billion in 2009. And by 2013, total foreign investment totaled $11.8 billion. (*Source: Central Bureau of Statistics*). Public Debt as a percentage of the 'Gross Domestic Product - GDP', which is the monetary value of all the finished goods and services in a specific time period and within a country's borders. The Israeli GDP has steadily declined from 102.0% in 2003 to 4.70% in 2007 to 69.80% in 2011 to a record low 67.00%, in 2013. Furthermore, unemployment continued to decline and sustained at 5.8% as of the 1st Quarter in 2014. In 2013, 32.60% of Israel's GDP was exported in the form of goods and services ($95.1 billion). In 2009, as most of the world experienced a decline in GDP, Israel experienced a 1.10% growth in its GDP. Its real GDP growth rate in in 2013 was 3.30%, while as of 1st Quarter in 2014 it stood at 2.90%. (Source: Israel Ministry of Finance).

Israel's economic growth is expected at 3.8% in 2013, after registering real GDP growth rates of 3.4% in 2012, 4.6% in 2011, and 5.7% in 2010, according to the IMF.

In October 2013, the country's unemployment rate dropped to 5.9% from 6.0% in September 2013 and 6.1% in August 2013, according to the CBS. There were about 218,000 unemployed in Israel in October 2013. Of the 3,704,000 employed Israelis aged 15 and over, 1,861,000 were men while 1,625,000 were women.

In September 2013, the country's annual inflation rate remained steady at 1.3% from the previous month, according to the CBS. The central bank's target rate of inflation ranges from 1.0% to 3.0%.

The GDP growth rate in Israel is also hampered by the lower participation of the Arab and Jewish ultra-Orthodox sectors. The additional problems of challenges in the field of education, dealing with bureaucracy and security issues, make the potential of higher employment participation by these groups more difficult. However, according to a wide variety of governmental published articles and proposals from the private sector, these problems are intensely being addressed, especially as a result of the 2015 Knesset Elections.

One of the key factors that is influencing the real estate environment, both residential and non-residential activities, is the explosion of the high-tech industries in Israel. A mere ten years ago the primary industries of Israel were centered around agricultural and textiles, until the 1990s. Since the late 1990s the high-tech, communications and science-oriented

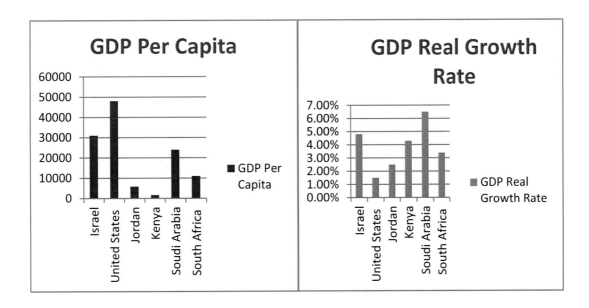

businesses provide the highest percentage of all of the sources for jobs, development, and education.

Taxes and Real Estate: Tax revenue is generally produced from income tax, gasoline taxes and value-added taxes. The Israeli tax system resembles models of Western Europe and the United States. On the whole, Israeli's over the age of 18 and working must file a tax return. The exception to this is for salaried employees whose taxes are withheld by the employers. Individual tax returns appear to be more advantageous than joint returns. Many of the "tax deductions" allowed in the U.S. and European tax return rules are not applicable in Israel (such as interest paid on mortgages, day care, and transportation expenses). The tax base is "progressive" ranging from 15% to 50%.

The Value Added Tax Rate (VAT) until September 1, 2012 was 16.0%, which was then raised to 17.0%. On June 2, 2013 the VAT was raised again to the current 18.0%. This number fluctuates and should be checked whenever considering doing business in the country. (See http://www.mof.gov.il.)

There are four types of taxation in Israel that are applicable to real estate this is bought, sold or held. These categories are 1) purchase tax; 2) capital gains tax; 3) property tax, and 4) income tax. These are subsequently discussed in the Real Estate Property issues section of this chapter. Other reliable sources for information the taxation in Israel these web sites are useful: *http://www.mof.gov.il* and the Hagshama Department of the World Zionist Organization at *http://www.wzo.org.il.*

6. Currency

The Israeli currency is known as the *New Israeli Shekel (ILS)* as of September 1985. One *shekel* equals 100 *agorot.* One agorah is equal to 10 *shkelim.*

One (1) new shekel is equal to 1000 shkelim. (The use of the shekel was first recorded in the Bible when Abraham negotiated a purchase of a field at Machpela, near Hebron. This currency was known as a unit of weight for payment in gold or silver.) Since 2007 most of the real estate transactions were based on the ILS (NIS). Once the transaction is completed and the price is translated to **ILS (NIS),** this price is usually annexed to the Israeli cost of living index, which is published on the 15th of every month for the previous month. See also the Burns School Global Real Estate Web site, Daniels *College of Business,* UNIVERSITY OF DENVER at http://burns.daniels.du.edu for currency conversions.

7. Transportation

The primary means of transportation in Israel is by motor vehicles. There are extensive rural, urban and major highway systems, the newest of which is Route 6, a north-south arterial. Public bus transportation is one of Israel's best transportation assets in that it provides inexpensive transportation to all areas of the country and Palestinian Authority.

There are 853 km of railways in Israel, including service between Jerusalem, Tel Aviv and Haifa and Beer Sheba. Other rail lines provide freight service between the port cities of Ashdod and Ashkelon, the area of Beer Sheva and Demona. Plans for rail lines are under development to many other cities, including connecting Haifa to Amman, Jordan. The Jerusalem Light Rail system (HaRakevet HaKala-in Hebrew), was completed and open for public use service began on August 19, 2011 initially free of charge. It became fully operational with affordable fares on December 1, 2011. The line is 13.9 kilometers (8.6 mi) long with 23 stops. This is one of Israel's newest and heavily used transportation systems in the Capital City of Jerusalem. The Light Rail connects to all other major and minor bus line stops and the Central Bus Station. Another form of light rail system has been approved for the Tel Aviv area and is scheduled to be completed in full operation in 2025. It is scheduled to have 33-stations, a total route length of 23 kilometers (14-miles). During the last several years the train system was extensively redeveloped and the total length in train lines in 2012 is more than 1,000 km. The seaports of Israel are located primarily along the Mediterranean coast, and another seaport in Eilat. The deep-water seaports are located in Haifa, Eilat, and Ashdod. A joint seaport project has been agreed between Jordan and Israel, near Eilat at Akaba. Israel has 48 airports (2010). The largest airport is Ben-Gurion International, located approximately 15 miles east of Tel Aviv. Other local commuter airports include the Dov Field in northern Tel Aviv, airports in Haifa, Jerusalem, Eilat and many other areas of the State. In addition to El Al, Israel's main airline, there are two commuter lines known as Arkia and Israair, which serve all of Israel and International locations in Europe, the Middle East and other nearby countries.

8. Communications

The communications system in Israel is highly developed and is considered by most as the most sophisticated in the Middle East even though it is not the largest telephone system in the region. As of 2010, there were approximately 3.276 million main line telephones in use by Israeli citizens. Mobile cellular telephones have increased rapidly to approximately 9,875,000 in 2010, which has reduced dramatically the need for most additional infrastructure. Israel relies on cable, satellites and other means of communication throughout the country. As of 2008, there were 23 AM radio stations, 15 FM stations and 2 short-wave stations. There were 17 television broadcast stations with an estimate of one-third of the population having televisions. Israel also has a cable and satellite system that provides television broadcasts from the United States, Western Europe, and neighboring Arab countries. Israel had approximately 100 stations and repeater stations operating (2008) including about

15 privately-owned radio stations. In 2011 there were about 2,179,000 Internet hosts (Internet service providers) and more than 4,515,000 Internet users.

9. Real Property Issues

The following is a select group of common real estate terms most often used in real estate basic and introductory discussions.

Basic Real Estate "Truisms"

Size of real estate units can be portrayed by "number of rooms", "square meters", "number of stories", and in some cases and areas by "number of families". Most often the terms for living areas are *"gross bruto"* and *"netto"* for net living area.

Number of Rooms, usually as applied to apartments, single-family dwellings, villas, cottages, condominiums, and the like, is based on either the *bruto* or the *netto*. The BRUTO method includes the bedrooms, kitchen, bathrooms, hallways, space in the closets and cupboards. The NETTO method includes only the number of bedrooms and living room. The kitchen and bathrooms are NOT included in the Netto method. For example: A three (3)-room apartment or house refers to two (2) bedrooms and one (1) living room.

Number of Stories, usually include the ground floor as "0" floor, the next level up is "Floor-1", the next level up is "Floor "2". The basement, or garage entrances have "minus" designations such as "-1", "-2", and etc.

Square Meters is based on the metric system. As pertains to land, one (1)-square feet is equivalent to ten (10)-square feet. Land is measured in Israel by the term "dunam". One (1) metric dunam consists of exactly 1,000-square meters. A *dunam* is equivalent to approximately 0.247105-acres, or approximately 10,760-square feet of land. There are approximately 4.04686 dunams to an acre.

As pertains to buildings, such as houses and apartments, the real problem is whether a home is measured gross (bruto) or net (netto) and what is included or excluded in these

Selected Dictionary of Israeli Real Estate Terms

ENGLISH	HEBREW (Transliteration)	HEBREW
APARTMENT	DIRAH	הריד
BUILDING	BINYAN	ןיינב
BUILDING CONTRACTOR	KABLAN	ןלבק
CAPITALIZATION	HIVUN	ןוויה
COMMISSION (FEE) CONTRACT	AMLAH, or D'MEI TEYOOCH CHOZEH	הלמע

DUNAM	LAND MEASUREMENT EQUIVALENT TO 1,000-SQUARE METERS, OR APPROXIMATELY 0.25-ACRES.	דונם
FLAT	DIRAH	דירה
FLOOR/ STOREY	KOMA	קומה
HOUSE	BAYIT	בית
LANDLORD	BA'AL BAYIT	בעל בית
LAND REGISTRY (OFFICE)	TABU – LISHKAT RISHUM M'KARKA'IN	טאבו
LAWYER	ORECH DEAN	עורך דין
MONEY	KESSEF	כסף
MORTGAGE	MISHKANTAH	משכנתא
MUNICPALITY	IRYA	עירייה
OFFICE	MISRAD	מסרד
PERMIT	ISHUR	אישור
PLOT, LOT, SITE	CHELKAT ADAMA	חלקת אדמה
POWER OF ATTORNEY	YIPUI KOACH	ייפוי כוח
PRICE	MECHIR	מחיר
PROPERTY-ASSET	(NICHSEI) M'KARKIN NECHASIM	נכסים
PROPERTY OWNER	NECHES	נכס
PROPERTY TAX	ARNONA	ארנונה
PURCHASE	KNEYYAH	קניה
PURCHASER/BUYER	KANYAAN	קניין
REAL ESTATE	NADLAN-M'KARKIN	נדל"ן-מקרקעין
REAL ESTATE AGENT	SOCHEN NADLAN	סוכן נדל"ן
REAL ESTATE OFFICE	MISRAD TIUCH NADLAN	מסרד טיוח נדל"ן
RENT	HASKARAH	השכרה
SALE	MECHIRAH	מכירה
SELLER	MOCHER/MOCHERET	מוכר/מוכרת
TAX	MAS	מס
TENANT	DAYAR/DAYERET	דייר
VILLA	Free standing house, or terraced apartment with a large balcony	וילה

measurements. "Gross" square meters is typically used for comparing properties that are for Sale and includes the exterior walls, interior walls of the property and a proportion of the common areas in an apartment building and offices buildings. "Net" square meters is calculated without the application to the interior or exterior walls. Most often, "Net" is used by the municipality to calculate the floor area of a property in order to calculate the levy for municipality taxes (ARNONA). What each municipality uses to quantify the "Net" varies from one municipality to another and therefore, must be carefully investigated for accuracy and current policies.

Typically, for purposes of ease and *rounding* a 3-bedroom apartment, 1.5-bathrooms, living room, kitchen, dining room and foyer that has a "Gross" square meters of 210, is equivalent to approximately 2,100-square feet gross floor area (210 x 10 = 2,100).

Types of Land Categories in Israel

The majority, approximately 93.0%, of the lands in Israel are owned by the State of Israel with a small portion still under private ownership, approximately 7.0%. Of the 93.0% State owned, Israel's basic law on real estate dictates that the lands of the State are jointly owned by the State of Israel at 69.0%, and the Development Authority at 12.0%, and the Jewish National Fund, also at 12.0%. The law prohibits transferring of the land by sale or other means. However, it does imply that long-term leases are permitted, which is the current practice.

In the beginning of 2014, the Central Bureau of Statistics (CBS) stated that "the Israel's housing market remains robust, amidst strong economic growth. Property demand continues to rise and the residential construction sector is picking up. The average price of owner-occupied dwellings in the country rose by 7.42% to ILS1,244,800 (US$355,522) during the year to Q3 2013, after annual increases of 7.58% in Q2 2013, 9.77% in Q1 2013, 5.82% in Q4 2012 and 4.99% in Q3 2012, according to the Central Bureau of Statistics (CBS). When adjusted for inflation,

Source: Central Bureau of Statistics (CBS)

house prices rose by 5.62% y-o-y to Q3 2013. Israeli house prices increased 2.39% (1.34% inflation-adjusted) during the latest quarter." (Source: Global Property Guide, January 5, 2014). The chart below shows the steady growth of housing prices in Israel through 2013. The price amounts are in NIS currency in 1,000's and are not represented in U.S. Dollars.

The number of apartment units is almost twice as many as single-family houses in Israel. This is largely because of Israel's small size and limited land areas for housing developments. Due to more favorable financing programs, an increase in home-ownership of single-family dwellings (houses, villas, cottages, etc.) has increased in 2013 and 2014. (Source: Global Property Guide, January 5, 2014).

Overall, the housing construction starts in Israel, as a whole, has been robust since the Year 2012, with a high acceleration in 2013 and a sharp decline in 2014 mostly due to the Gaza Conflict from June 16 through August 26, 2014. Beginning in January, 2015 the housing construction starts were encouraging but a recovery slowed by un-seasonal snows and extreme cold weather. By early Spring 2015, the Israel Central Bureau of Statistics projected that by the end of 2015, the housing construction environment may equal or exceed that of 2013. The graph chart below shows the Housing Construction Starts statistics as reported by the compiled by Trading Economics (www.tradingeconomics.com) and compiled by the Israel Central Bureau of Statistics (www.cbs.gov.il).

Dr. Noam Gruber, senior researcher, Taub Center for Social Policy Studies in Israel, wrote in the August 2014 publication of the *Policy Paper Series*, *The Israeli Housing Market*, for the Taub Center for Social Policy Studies in Israel,(www.taubcenter.org. il.), a comprehensive research report. In the opening page he wrote: *"Israeli housing prices have risen precipitously in recent years. The rising prices are due both to increased demand – driven mainly by low interest rates and preferential tax treatment – and to rigid supply, rooted in bureaucratic complications of the construction process, an inherent conflict of interest at the local level, and a high prevalence of condominium apartment living in Israel, which poses an obstacle to urban renewal."*

The graph below, as prepared by Taub Center for Social Policies as of January 2015, shows that between the years 2000 and 2008 that real estate housing prices were stable and even declining. After a sharp decline in interest rates in 2008, housing prices have steadily increased. Between the low rates in April 2007 and July 2013 increased by 53.0%, after inflation). Rental prices also followed a similar trend at a slower pace.

Various surveys of housing construction companies show that a lack of available land for construction and building permit delays as the two main reasons for an existing rigid housing supply. This in turn drives the increases in housing prices. This is further exasperated by the current fact that the overall process from "concept" to "owner/tenant occupancy" takes an average of 13 years. Of this period, the actual construction period is only two years and the rest devoted to bureaucratic procedures. There are new laws in the making, that will probably come to fruition in the immediate future, that will stream

ISRAEL CONSTRUCTION STARTS

SOURCE: WWW.TRADINGECONOMICS.COM | CENTRAL BUREAU OF STATISTICS, ISRAEL

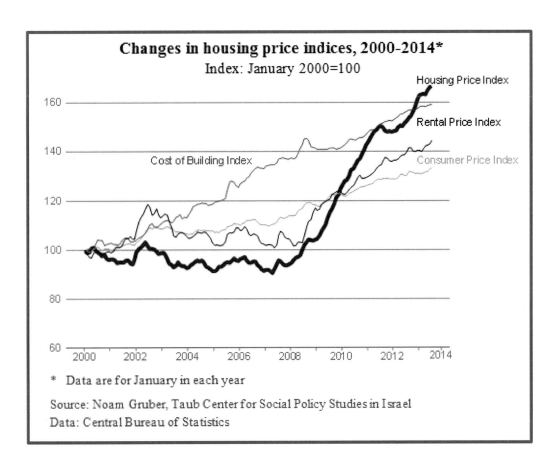

Changes in housing price indices, 2000-2014*

Index: January 2000=100

Housing Price Index

Rental Price Index

Cost of Building Index

Consumer Price Index

* Data are for January in each year

Source: Noam Gruber, Taub Center for Social Policy Studies in Israel

Data: Central Bureau of Statistics

line the process, country-wide, resulting in shorter process time and will in turn contribute to potential lower prices.

According to Noam Gruber, "Today, young and lower-income Israeli families are forced to choose between taking on larger mortgages or paying increasing rents and further delaying their hopes of home ownership."

About 150 projects were approved; *however, since this law passed only three (3) such projects as of 2011 were completed mainly due to a paralyzing bureaucracy.*

Real Estate Tax laws were changed in 2013 and went into effect on January 1, 2014. The new laws are more complex and in some areas more favorable for real estate investment. However, the complexities include the status of an individual such as a new Oley (Jewish Immigrant) to Israel, existing owners of real estate whether they own one or more than one properties, corporations, entities, religious groups, group investors, and the like. In 2018 the real estate tax laws will change again, and as to what extent, is not yet known. To summarize existing real estate tax laws in this Chapter may lead to potential confusion and unintended omissions, which could prove to be detrimental to potential buying, selling, leasing, and exchange strategies by others. It is imperative that under current real estate taxation laws in Israel that as with all transactions an experienced real estate lawyer should be consulted prior to the signing of any real estate related documents.

Real Estate Licensing Law of 1997:

As of April 1, 1999 the two-year transition period ended from the date the licensing laws were passed. The enforcement of the Real Estate Laws falls under the jurisdiction of the Minister of Justice; within the Ministry, it is under the Registrar of Real Estate.

The basic licensing requirements are as follows. The candidate must

1. Be a citizen,residentofIsrael,orforeignresident,withalegalw orklicenseinIsrael;
2. Be at least 18 years old;
3. Not have declared bankruptcy;
4. Have no infamous offenses in the previous five years;
5. Have no non-infamous offenses in the previous three years;
6. Pass a written examination; and
7. Complete approved continuing education courses for renewal every two years. The real estate examination is given twice a year. Courses required are usually presented through universities and private institutes. The examination covers matters on contractual law, real estate law, planning and construction laws, real estate tax laws, and parts of the Penal Code. All courses and exams are given in Hebrew. Land description is usually measured in the metric system. The land area is measured in *dunam*, or 1,000 square meters (sq m). There are approximately one four dunams in one acre of land. Square feet measurements, such as used for a size of an apartment (e.g., 1,200 square feet), is represented in *square meters*. A 1,200 square foot apartment is referenced as +/-120 square meters. If land is described by "frontage feet," it is translated as "meters of frontage and/or depth."

Rights and interests in land include those common in many Western countries, such as property taxes, eminent domain, government escheat, use of police power, zoning, and ownership interests that, where applicable, can constitute fee simple interests or leasehold interests.

Title insurance generally does not exist in Israel, as is true with most countries in the Middle East. However land is registered with the Israel Land Authority and that registration is similar to the recording of a deed. Matters such as rights-of-way, easements, encroachments, chain of title, and the like, are part of the registration process.

The contract form for real estate often follows the British and common law, as indicated. This is also true with mortgages and title work in general.

Listing Agreements:

An exclusive *right to sell listing agreement*, if used, is a relatively simple one-page or two-page agreement stating that the owner is obligated only to pay the listing broker the negotiated fee. The broker is not obligated to share the listing data with other brokers outside his or her office. Some of the larger brokerage houses have some form of exclusive contracts. While commonly used in the United States real estate industry, the use of an *exclusive right to sell agreement* is very limited in Israel as general practice.

Listing agreements are usually for a period of 90 days. The benefits to the seller of signing an *exclusive listing agreement* are based on the services the listing broker will provide, their reputation, office size, participation in some multiple listing service (MLS), and shortness of time in which they can produce a qualified buyer. The key factors for sellers to consider in the Israeli real estate market are two: (1) price, as compared to surrounding areas and competitive areas in other communities, and (2) flexibility in the time required selling and conveying possession.

The buyer's responsibilities include being properly represented by a broker and an attorney. Using a broker is not compulsory. As a matter of fact, less than 25% of residential property sales are done by brokers. As for commercial properties the number rises to about 80%. The development of the web during recent years and the possibility of advertising your own property without charge reduced the representation by brokers even more. Sellers have used the web many times to advertise not only their properties but also a few other virtual properties close to their locations, at higher prices, in order to raise the price of their properties. The buyer needs to be concerned with the clarity of title for the property being purchased. In a country where the state owns a majority of the land, and that country has had many years and various governments administrating real estate transactions, clear title is essential in all real estate transactions. The buyer is responsible for pre-settlement inspections and to verify guarantees that are provided by builders for newer properties. If there is an Association of tenants or owners, the buyer must be clear on all the rules and policies of the Associations, management contracts and maintenance agreements.

Most real estate professionals in the United States for example, prior to beginning to show prospective buyers residential properties, usually have the prospects go through a "pre-qualification" or "pre-approval" interview with a bank or mortgage company. If the buyer is buying for "cash", this pre-qualification step is avoided. By pre-approving the Buyer the search and financing experience is streamlined. When a Buyer does not know what he/she can afford, there is a strong possibility of looking out of a "qualified" price range and wasting a lot of time. Also by looking below a "qualified" price range there is a strong chance of not getting the right home that is desired. By starting off by getting a pre-approval, the Buyer can more easily sort by price, identify the right neighborhoods, and find the home they are looking for much faster, and most often with less stress.

In Israel, often Buyers find the neighborhood, find a home and find neighborhood amenities through the World Wide Web (Internet) which provides a tremendous choice of home possibilities. Some sign a purchase agreement subject to being approved for a loan and the appraised value. Since real estate contracts are prepared and, at times negotiated by attorneys, some of the idiosyncrasies connected to mortgages may be missed. As a result many transactions that were based on finding an acceptable mortgage "after the fact", are delayed, cause unexpected expenses or is lost.

Most professional real estate agents in Israel and good real estate attorneys will recommend that the "pre-qualification" or "pre-approval" for financing" be completed prior to looking for a home, neighborhood and municipality or district. Financing real estate in Israel is not difficult, but does follow basic standards and procedures.

All institutional financing of real estate in Israel require some level of a *down payment*. Financing arrangement from parents, relatives or individuals most often do not require down payments. This type of financing is more the exception than the rule. How much of a down payment is required to buy a home in Israel?

In Israel, in order to maintain the secure housing market, The Bank of Israel (Israel's Central Bank) is stricter about the down payment requirements. Currently, as of January 2015, there are three (3) basic categories for homebuyers. The key factor of these categories is whether a person looking to obtain a home mortgage, is or is not an Israeli citizen. Proof of being an Israeli Citizen is someone who was issued a *Teudat Zehutý*; which is the Israeli compulsory identity document, as prescribed in the Identity Card Carrying and Displaying Act of 1982.

If a homebuyer does NOT have a Teudat Zehut, a minimum of fifty (50.0%) percent down payment is required on the purchase price of the property. If the buyer IS an Israeli Citizen, then the down payment is thirty (30.0%) percent of the purchase price. Additionally, as a *first-time homebuyer and Israeli citizen*, then often a seventy-five (75.0%) percent loan can be negotiated which means a down payment of twenty-five (25.0%) percent. Currently there is a wide variety of mortgage packages, interest rates and terms from the various Banks who have home loans available.

However, the amount a prospective buyer can be qualified to pay on a house loan is based on the Buyer's MONTHLY NET income. This is calculated by taking the gross monthly income LESS taxes and results in Net Income. The Net Income must be at least three (3) times the monthly mortgage payment.

For example: If the monthly loan payment is 2,000 New Israeli Shekels (NIS), often referred to as the "nees", then the Net Monthly Income must be 6,000 NIS (2,000 NIS x 3). It is worth noting that this example is a "rule of thumb" and many other individual circumstances may weigh on the qualification process, terms and conditions of the house loan.

The third category of homebuyers is that of persons making Aliyah (Immigration) to Israel as new Israeli citizens (Olim). When mortgage rates were high, this benefit was very favorable to new Olim with substantially lower mortgage rates.

Under the current low mortgage rates (see chart below-Source: Bank of Israel, Data and Statistics, **http://www.boi.org.il/),** employing this benefit is not as favorable and is currently not often used.

The real estate transaction engages many professionals throughout the entire process. Understanding who these people are and their role in the transaction, before seeking a home location and financing is critical to assuring a less stressful and a more pleasant and profitable experience. These professions include, but not necessarily limited to:

- Attorneys who specialize in real estate transactions; In Israel it is legal for a single-lawyer to represent both the Buyer and the Seller. However, the potential of "conflict of interests" is high and each party (Buyer and Seller) should each have their own separate legal representation.
- Real Estate agents who are licensed and are in good standing with the Israeli Misrad HaMishpatim (Ministry of Justice);
- Engineers, whose job it is to check for structural problems, leaks, code compliance, and the like;
- Architects, actual physical structure is what appears in the records of the municipality, zoning plans and changes,

Effective Date of Interest Rates	More than 25 Years	From 20 to 25	From 15 to 20	From 10 to 15	From 5 to 10	Up to and including 5 Years	Average
March 11, 2015	2.84	2.79	2.54	2.24	1.85	2.12	2.29
February 11, 2015	2.87	2.79	2.58	2.24	1.85	2.37	2.44
January 12, 2015	2.89	2.77	2.54	2.14	1.81	2.17	2.30
December 11, 2014	2.94	2.79	2.63	2.14	1.61	2.01	2.21
June 11, 2014	3.25	3.08	2.81	2.28	1.65	1.96	2.23
January 12, 2014	3.54	3.36	3.17	2.57	2.07	2.18	2.49
December 11, 2013	3.60	3.46	3.30	2.73	2.03	2.27	2.54
June 11, 2013	3.36	3.23	2.69	2.17	1.79	2.02	2.07
January 11, 2013	3.72	3.48	2.96	2.40	2.13	2.37	2.42
December 11, 2012	3.65	3.44	3.09	2.51	2.13	2.39	2.43
June 11, 2012	3.63	3.57	3.20	2.53	2.46	2.64	2.67
January 11, 2012	3.92	3.87	3.53	3.00	3.05	3.17	3.19
December 12, 2011	3.88	3.87	3.60	3.11	3.23	3.30	3.31
August 11, 2011	4.13	3.80	3.65	3.12	3.09	3.01	3.08

additions and extensions made were by permit and not encroaching on neighboring properties, and what can and cannot be done as far as renovations, additions and improvements on a legal basis;

- Lenders, willing to give a preliminary approval and commit to a mortgage before a purchase contract is signed. There are two stages of approvals, 1) on the borrower and 2) on the property.
- When will the funds be available to the Buyer and in what form of currency. Most transactions are in NIS, but there are Sellers who have foreign currency account, such as the U.S. Dollar, the Euro, and others and insist that the funds be in a specified currency other than the NIS.
- Contractor/Owner of subdivision housing units, single-family house or apartments;
- Taxing Authority: There is a Purchase Tax in Israel that went in to effect in 2014. It is designed to help in limiting run-away inflation of home values. This tax formula is somewhat complex and should be clearly understood by the Buyer before any agreement is signed.

Municipality services, agencies and authorities: Before a contract is signed, knowing how the property is served and influenced by the local Municipality or District is a crucial step not always attended to by many Buyers. Often this detail, being overlooked, may cause many forms of unexpected fees, costs and restrictions, all of which could have been attended to with proper prior knowledge.

Settlement of a real estate transaction is subject to a multi-step system that includes the initial down payment of 10% to 25% and clarity of title, then final funds for settlement, from which approximately 25% to 35% is held for the final step (even though possession may have changed hands) to pay final taxes. Property taxes previously paid to the State of Israel have been eliminated in early 2000. Property taxes to local municipalities are still paid. There is a purchase tax of a rate that changes depending on the status of the buyer: for example, "new immigrant," the size of the apartment, and if it is the only property owned by the buyer. All these have an effect on the tax rate.[152]

For an examination in this area, see the sources noted below, such as Knight Frank, Jones Lang LaSalle, C. B. Richard Ellis and citations to International Real Estate

Digest, the National Association of REALTORS®, and the Burns School Global Real Estate Web site at the *Daniels College of Business*, UNIVERSITY OF DENVER at: http://burns.daniels. du.edu/.

For more information in this area, see the links to the real estate associations and other real estate organizations, along with larger real estate consulting firms and accounting firms noted in the Selected References section below.

■ 10. Real Estate Trends

The Israeli real estate trends are in a constant state of flux, as is true with many jurisdictions throughout the world. Recently,

brokers have been used for real estate sales, with commissions in the area of 2% for a transaction; however, in the new situation, as previously described, many brokers are charging only the buyers. In Israel, as in the entire world, the main factor in real estate value is the location. About 70% of the Israeli population lives along the coast. The most expensive properties are to be found in Tel Aviv (mainly in the northern part of the city) and in Jerusalem (mainly in the western part of the city).

Within the real estate industry, especially within the City of Jerusalem and surrounding area, there are a number of real estate companies, owners and staff, the Jerusalem Chamber of Commerce and other related businesses who are working to bring about a qualified and recognized level of real estate *professionalism* as exists with the United States National Association of Realtors, (NAR). Enthusiastic departmental leadership within NAR are working closely with the involved Jerusalem real estate brokers to generate a viable, credible and recognizable professional real estate image. Israel does not yet have a National Association, such as found in the United States. There are a number of U.S.A. National Franchise companies who are members of NAR that have franchise offices in Israel, also members of NAR.

The *commercial real estate* trends in Israel over the past 3-5 years has been encouraging and strong. High-rise offices, apartment buildings and hotels, under construction are seen in all the major cities such as Tel Aviv, Jerusalem and Haifa. Also, in many suburban communities within 10-20-minute drive to the city-commercial centers are also experiencing a robust increase in commercial development. The number of high-rise cranes, many decorative and lit at night, are so predominant in the skyline, that the joke is that these construction cranes are the official Israel bird. These cranes are also seen in the road projects, bridges, tunnels and many other infrastructure improvement programs all around the country.

Some of the current concerns include the following issues, briefly discussed.

1)   Office Building boom of construction. This is due to favorable financing for ownership instead of paying rent and tax advantages to own rather than to rent. With this has brought a current decrease in rental rates and therefore affecting overall value, downward, of the newer office buildings. This gluttony of office space is mostly around the Tel Aviv metropolitan area that represents over 40% of the total Israel population. In the other larger cities and peripheral areas, office space is in high demand with a combination of commercial and retail uses on the lower floors. Most of these buildings also have underground garages.

2)   The Israeli Railroad Company has been expanding rail service all over Israel and especially connecting Haifa, Tel Aviv and Jerusalem and other nearby communities. According to data provided by the Israel Land Authority, a contract between it and the Israel Railroad Company a plan for 30 new train stations all over the country is in process and all will have commercial centers at the train stations. All the income generated from retail, office, business and commercial leases will go directly to the Railroad Company.

3) Throughout the country there are many municipalities that are now demanding that apartment building owners renovate the facades of their buildings, at their own expense. Tel Aviv is reported to probably be the most aggressive municipality in this effort with noticeable results. Once the owner is asked to make the face-lift improvements, and does nothing, then the law allows the municipality to make the owner a "criminal". It begins with a letter from the Municipality declaring the facade of the building is neglected and needs a "face-lift". With the letter is a list of the work the Municipality states needs to be done. The apartment owners are asked to do the work with the supervision of an engineer. Should the apartment owners not comply then the municipality can do the work for them and send them the bill. This simplistic explanation of an aggressive program to clean-up does not provide the data on financing programs, enforcement, keeping contractors from gouging property owners and so forth.

4) A major commercial real estate trend that has the potential of creating a more affordable and owner-ship friendly market is the exemption from the Value Added Tax (V.A.T.) of 18.0% for certain purchasers acquiring apartments in new construction projects. This tax relief, if implemented, would not apply to projects where construction has already begun. Therefore, many potential buyers in such projects have held back their purchases until information as to the finality of this new law becomes known. Another proposed law will give construction companies an attractive discount on V.A.T. for construction services.

5) Only in the past few years has the New Israeli Shekel (NIS) not been linked ONLY to the U.S. Dollar. Real Estate transactions can now be completed using currencies from other countries. Because of its proximity to Israel the EURO has become an alternative currency favorite to the Dollar. The EURO is the single currency shared by 19 of the European Union's Member States, which together make up the euro area. Also traded is the British Pound, Japanese Yen and others.

The overall outlook for commercial real estate in Israel for the foreseeable future is "stability". In 1st Quarter of 2015, proved that Israel is recovering and weathering well the setbacks due to the Gaza Conflict in the summer of 2014. The backbone for this recovery appears to be due to the real estate market heavily influenced by Israel's world-class technology industry and relatively robust institutions.

■ 11. Cultural Issues

Any nation's culture is complex and vibrant in its diversity. While broad cultural characterizations such as those presented here can be generally accurate, following such generalities too strictly may be dangerously misleading. To conduct business effectively and profitably in a country, it is vital to have a thorough understanding of its culture's complexities.

Israeli customs and cultural issues are important and are distinguished from other countries. One of the primary reasons for a dramatically varied cultural "melting pot" and strong diversities in Israel is that Israel is composed mostly of foreign immigrants from all over the world, who bring with them their social and cultural practices as well as their particular Jewish religious practices, based on customs from their respective countries.

One of the most compelling cultural issues in Israel today is the issue of Judaism in Israel as to "Who Is a Jew?" and the role and acceptance among the various Jewish practices, such as Orthodox, Conservative and Reform. These are issues that pit the secular and the religious factions into heated debates, demonstrations and political upheavals.

The official language of Israel is Hebrew. The technical and business language is English. However many everyday signs, menus and instructions are in Hebrew, English and Arabic, with Yiddish, French and Russian also having dynamic influence in daily life. Talking often involves the use of hand gestures. Hebrew is a very guttural language. Often hand gestures, as well as exaggerated and animated body motions, are used when speaking. This is due to the influence of Mediterranean, Southern European and Asian immigration. A casual observer, unfamiliar with this cultural system of communication, may wrongfully interpret that people are always arguing and fighting. This is not the case. In almost every aspect of life in Israel, the cultural and social diversification is so vast and unique that the reader should explore the sources for ample and up-to-date information on this and related issues at the suggested sites described below.

The Web site at *http://www.israeliculture.about.com* is one of the most comprehensive, covering most aspects of Israeli Culture and related matters. The Ministry of Education, Culture and Sports is also another good overall source,

12. Discussion Questions

covering governmental involvement and responsibilities. (See http://www.mfa.gov.il and http://www.info.gov.il.) The daily newspapers provide a valuable source for additional information. See *The Jerusalem Post International* (http://www.jpost.com); *The Globes* (http://www.globes.

co.il); and *The HaAretz Internet English Edition* (http://www.haaretzdaily.com).

1. What is the impact of the terrorism in Israel on the economy of Israel, and what sector has been the hardest hit?

2. What are some of the environmental concerns in Israel?

3. What role does religion play in the cultural aspect of Israel, and what should a non-Israeli know about these issues in order to invest or conduct any kind of business in Israel?

13. Case Study

Key Criteria to Undertake Business in Israel

In addition to the Israeli Government Agencies that provide excellent information, consultation and services in order to bring commerce, industry, tourism and entrepreneur to Israel, one of the best sources available throughout the United States are the various offices of the American-Israel Chambers of Commerce.

Real estate information sources are available to real estate practitioners, investors, buyers, sellers and appraisers: the National Association of REALTORS®, the CCIM Institute, the Real Estate Management Institute, and almost every major national real estate franchise organization, just to name a few.

LEGAL ISSUES: The simplest rule to understand is that the real estate business, or any business to be conducted in Israel by an individual, a corporation or an entity must be legal in the United States and conduct activities in all legal matters pertaining to real estate activities, as well as finance, accounting, valuation, landlord-tenant rules, development and time-share opportunities. The Ministry of Justice is the government agency that is the governing authority for business legalities with additional support from all other ministries and agencies. It is worth noting

that the US-Israel business relationship based on sound legal principles and cooperation is recognized as one of the best international business cooperative environments in the world.

POLITICAL STABILITY: Political stability has been, and continues to be, one of the important recipes of success in the business relationship between Israel and many members of the international community. Israel is a democracy. The multi-party system is not that different from many countries throughout the world. Even though Israel has replaced the Prime Minister and cabinet more often than what is usual in other countries, such as the United States, such events have taken place through democratic means rather than by coupe-d'état or by military takeover. The integrity of business has never been at risk because of political changes in Israel since it became an independent nation 50 years ago.

ECONOMIC STABILITY: As reported by the Ministry of Industry and Trade, many business and real estate investors from almost every country with which Israel enjoys free trade agreements seek to invest both in the United States and Israel because they are strong models for market penetration and financial stability. Since the decline of the dot-coms on the U.S. stock exchange, Israel has had just an opposite experience and has not suffered major fluctuations in recent years

and has remained relatively stable against the U.S. dollar. Real Estate values have been depressed more as a result of unusually high price inflation during the mid-1990s. Subsequently, the real estate markets in residential and commercial enterprises have leveled off after a period of hard depression and lower than usual tourism and immigration. In the early part of 2002 these trends have shown a slow, but upward, revitalization.

PROFESSIONAL SERVICES: Many professionals such as doctors, educators, financial advisors, mental health professionals, nurses, engineers, programmers, and the like find fertile ground and welcome arms as professional practitioners in Israel. As in the United States, pre licensing, certifications and internships are part of the criteria for most professions. However, because Israel has over 150 American companies well established within its borders, transfers of these professionals into the company arena are relatively uncomplicated and beneficial.

A designated real estate practitioner with the Certified Commercial Investment Member (CCIM), Society of Industrial and Office Properties (SIOR), Certified Property Manager (CPM), and Member Appraisal Institute (MAI) designations can usually find a favorable environment within which to work and earn a living. But that practitioner would be required to meet Israel's licensing and certification laws, as previously discussed. The most cumbersome yet achievable certification is that of a real estate appraiser. Many universities and special schools offer comprehensive courses and preparation in order to meet the requirements set by the State of Israel. There are many successful real estate brokers, agents, and consultants in Israel who moved there from the United States, Russia, Eastern Europe, South Africa and South America. They came with their training and skills in various real estate endeavors and applied them to establish for themselves a place in their chosen profession.

LANGUAGE: The official language of Israel is Hebrew. The business language in Israel is English. This holds true for almost every aspect of the business and entrepreneurial world. Other languages often used and, in some areas, criteria for business success include Arabic, French, Spanish and German. Israel has one of the world's best short-term language school systems that provide newcomers with a strong basic Hebrew language foundation within a short 90-day period. In short, there are no measurable adverse issues that would negatively impact professional services or language criteria that would give cause to do business in Israel.

Key Criteria "Not" to do Business in Israel

A number of legal, political, and economic considerations might discourage doing business in Israel.

LEGAL ISSUES: Because Israel is a Jewish state, many laws revolve around religious rules and traditions. There is no separation of church and state as in the United States. Some businesses may have conflicting religious practices or times of operation and services that are opposite of the State sabbath and holiday laws. Those businesses may want to reconsider doing business in Israel.

POLITICAL STABILITY: The country's form of government creates coalitions between various small and large parties. These coalitions at times are formed with groups that are very extreme and radical in their thinking, policies and methodologies. Votes of "no confidence" in the Prime Minister and the consequent formation of new government leadership and party controls imposed on the population are ways of life in Israel. This is not an on-going occurrence, but does happen from time to time. If a business is sensitive to political party stabilities, this aspect of instability may be a concern.

ECONOMIC STABILITY: Israel is surrounded by antagonistic countries that are often quite open about their opposition to the Jewish state. Consequently, Israel's economy is influenced by the need to maintain and improve a defense force that could assure Israel's survival. Calls for boycotts against Israeli exports, against corporations that have a strong business foundation in Israel, and against emerging companies (high-tech and manufacturing) that are seeking to do business in and with Israel, may from time to time have a destabilizing influence on the economy. Through the past 38 years, since the1967 Six Day War, Israel has successfully been able to overcome many of these issues with companies such as Coca-Cola, PepsiCo, Avis, Hertz, Ben & Jerry's (Unilever), Dunkin' Donuts, Intel, Cisco Systems, IBM, Motorola, and many and many more. A list of all the companies that have opened in Israel and are doing business with Israel despite the threat of boycotts and repercussions from Arab countries can be found at www.inminds.com/boycott-us-companies.html.

Refer to: U.S. Embassy. Homepage. http://usembassy.state.gov. U.S. Department of State. Homepage. http://www.state.gov.

14. Selected References

CIA World Factbook. https://www.cia.gov/library/publications/the-world-factbook/index.html.

Richard Ellis International Property Specialists. http://cbre.com. Time Almanac.

TIME Almanac. Boston: Information Please LLC.

United States Department of State. *Background Notes: Israel.* United States Department of State (Online). Available:http://www.state.gov.

U.S. Bureau of Census at http://www.census.gov. U.S. Department of Commerce at http://www.stat-usa.

gov. U.S. Bureau of Economic Analysis at http://www.bea.gov.

U.S. Embassy. Homepage. http://usembassy.state.gov. World Trade Centers Institute at http://www.wtci.org. World Trade Organization at http://www.wto.org. World Bank. *Adult Illiteracy Rates.* The Economist. X-rates.com. Homepage. http://www.x-rates.com/.

15. Glossary

Agorot – 100 agorots equal 1 shekel.

Dunams – 1,000 square meters.

Knesset – A parliament of 120 members who are elected every four years.

Labor Party –One of the two largest political parties in Israel.

Likkud – One of the two largest political parties in Israel.

New Israeli Shekel – Israeli currency; the currency is known as a unit of weight for

About the Authors

Dr. Arie Avriam, Head of Management Program, Ashkelon Academic College in Israel.

Aytan A. Dove was a contributing author, with over 27 years of experience in the real estate and appraisal industry, including over half of those years devoted to developing and promoting more valuable means for American real estate professionals to interact and exchange real estate practices, opportunities, and development on an international basis. His competent and knowledgeable ties to Israel, Mexico, and other countries are a result of being actively involved in encouraging and advising career and ordinary investors to seek and successfully profit from investing in real estate in their own country and in the United States as well.

Ellen H. Levine, CCIM, resides in Denver, Colorado, and is a Colorado native. She has been involved in the real estate business for over 30 years in commercial properties and personal investments. Ellen graduated from the Executive Masters in Real Estate and Construction Management (XRCM) program at the Burns School of Real Estate and Construction Management, *Daniels College of Business,* UNIVERSITY OF DENVER.

Italy

INTERNATIONAL REAL ESTATE (GLOBAL REAL ESTATE)
Authored by *Kevin Sutton, graduate student, University of Denver*

Dr. Mark Lee Levine, **Editor**

■ 1. Geography

Italy is a peninsula located in Southern Europe, extending into the Mediterranean Sea, with approximately 301,340 sq km (square kilometers) of area, slightly larger than Arizona. It includes Sardinia and Sicily. Italy is bound by Austria, France, the Vatican, San Marino, Slovenia and Switzerland.

The climate is Mediterranean in nature, fairly balanced, except for colder portions in the far north and the dry, hot south. About 24.2% of the land is arable, with about 70% in meadows and pastures; forests and woodlands consist of nearly 22%. Environmental problems include air pollution, coastal inland polluter rivers and acid rain, among others. A number of natural hazards include landslides, earthquakes, volcanic eruptions, flooding, and others.

■ 2. History and Overview

Following the collapse of the Roman Empire, Italy became an oft-changing succession of small states, principalities, and king-doms, which fought among themselves and were subject to ambitions of foreign powers. The Renaissance brought with it a greater economy and an idea for a single Italian nationality. Italy became a nation in 1861.

Italy entered the World War II on the side of the Axis powers, only to renounce this alliance and support the Allies upon the Allies' invasion of Sicily in 1943.

The Roman Catholic Church's status in Italy was determined by a series of accords with the Italian government. The State of Vatican City is recognized by Italy as an independent, sovereign entity. While preserving that recognition, in 1984, Italy and the Vatican updated several provisions of the 1929 accords. Included was the end of Roman Catholicism as Italy's formal, state religion.[156]

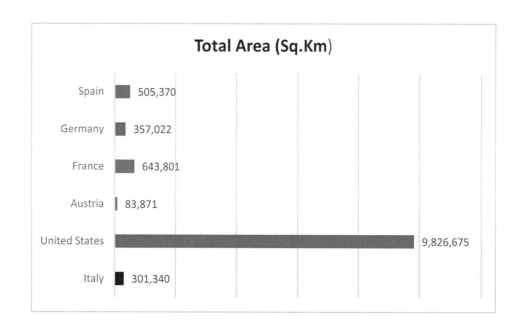

Total Area (Sq.Km)

Country	Total Area (Sq.Km)
Spain	505,370
Germany	357,022
France	643,801
Austria	83,871
United States	9,826,675
Italy	301,340

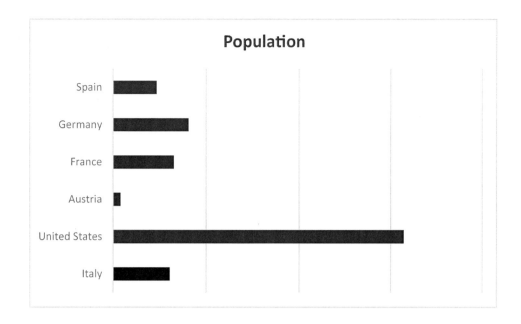

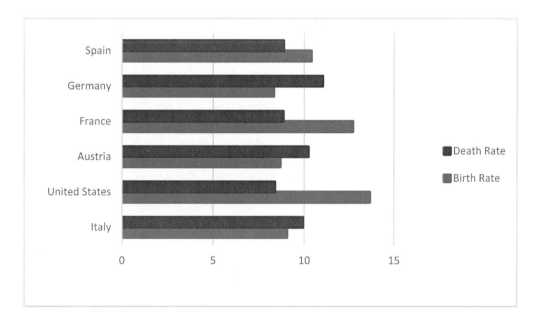

3. People

The Italian population is 61,680,122. Approximately 65.2% are in the 15-year through 64-year age group. The group of under 15 years of age is at 13.8%, and the group of over 64 years of age is at 21% as the remaining portion of the population.

The population growth rate was 0.03% (2014), consisting of 8.84 births per 1,000 in population. There are 10.1 deaths per 1,000. Net migration rate is about 4.29 migrants per 1,000. The infant mortality is 3.31 per 1,000. Life expectancy is overall 82.03 years, with 79.4 years for males and 84.82 years for females. The dominant ethnic population is Italian, with a mix of French, Germans, Sicilians and Sardinians. The clearly dominant religion is Roman Catholic at approximately 80%.

The Italian language is dominant, although a fair amount of German and French is spoken. Literacy is high at 98.4% for those reading and writing at age 15 and older. The labor force is 25.51 million (2014).

4. Government

The Italian government is a Republic, with the capital in Rome; it has 15 Regions. The Kingdom of Italy was formed on March 17, 1861, with final unification of the country occurring in 1870. The Italian legal system is based on civil law, with ecclesiastical law influences. Voting is at age 18 and is universal.

The Executive Branch of the government consists of a Chief of State, which is the President. The head of the government is the Prime Minister. The Cabinet is nominated by the President of the Council and is approved by the President of the Republic. The Legislative Branch is a bicameral Parliament, known as the *Parlamento*, consisting of a Senate and a Chamber of Deputies. The Judicial Branch is headed by the highest court, the Constitutional Court, known as the *Corte Costituzionale*.

Diplomatic representation consists of the Ambassador from Italy located in Washington, D.C.; the U.S. Ambassador to Italy is located in Rome.

5. Economy

The Gross Domestic Product (GDP) is $2.129 trillion (2014). The GDP real growth rate was -1.00% (2008), -5.00% (2009) and is currently at -0.2% (2014). The GDP per capita income is $34,500. Unemployment is about 12.5% (2014). Inflation was around 0.6% in 2009, and is currently around 0.1% (2014).

6. Currency

The currency was the Italian *lira* prior to its entrance into the Eurozone, and it currently uses the *euro*. See also the Burns School Global Real Estate Web site at the UNIVERSITY OF DENVER at http://burns.daniels.du.edu for currency conversions.

7. Transportation

Italy has 20,255 km (kilometers) of railroads, 487,700 km of highways, and several inland waterways. It has pipelines to transport crude oil, petroleum products and natural gas. Given the seaport location, Italy has numerous import and export ports; many are attractive locations for tourism. Supporting tourism and other activities, Italy has about 129 airports (2012).

8. Communications

Italy has 21,656,000 landline telephones (2012), and around 97.2 million mobile cellular telephones in use (2012). Italy has AM and FM radio stations as well as 1,300 commercial radio stations. Approximately 25,662,000 are internet hosts (2012) as internet service providers to 29,235,000 internet users.

9. Real Property Issues

Real property in Italy is referred to as *beni immobili*, immovables. Real property in Italy refers to the land, whatever is erected on it, along with trees, rivers, crops and springs. There are no restrictions on foreign ownership or sale of real property.

In general, the term of lease in Italy is not to exceed 30 years. The leasing agreement does not need to be in writing unless its term is in excess of nine years.

Title can be acquired through adverse possession as long as the property has been occupied for a continuous period of 20 years without fraudulent or violent means of acquisition. Real property and the rights associated with that property must be recorded in books of *Conservatore dei Registri Immobiliari*, Keeper of **Real Property** Records.

Taxes on real property are imposed by local municipalities in the form of an annual tax, *imposta comunale sugli immobili*, on income from real property based on the property's assessed value. The tax ranges from 0.1% up to 0.7%. and is not deductible. Capital gains taxes are assessed on transfers of real property. The rate varies between 5% and 30%. Real Estate companies which hold investment real estate are subject to gains tax on the appreciation of real estate portfolios. The tax is assessed every 10 years.

Registration tax is also levied on deeds and certain leases.

10. Real Estate Trends

Several companies such as Jones Lang LaSalle (http://www.joneslanglasalle.com), CB Richard Ellis (http://www.cbre.com),

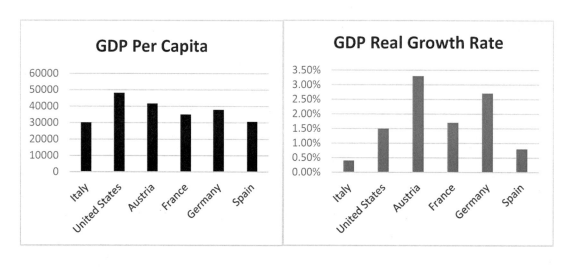

GDP Per Capita

GDP Real Growth Rate

and Colliers International (http://www.colliers.com) provide detailed, current information on the latest industrial, office, and retail real estate market trends.

For additional details in this area, visit the Burns School Global Real Estate Web site for the UNIVERSITY OF DENVER at http://burns.daniels.du.edu.

■ 11. Cultural Issues

Any nation's culture is complex and vibrant in its diversity.

While broad cultural characterizations such as those presented here can be generally accurate, following such generalities too strictly may be dangerously misleading. To conduct business effectively and profitably in a country, it is vital to have a thorough understanding of its culture's complexities.

Italians tend to dress in a very formal and stylish manner for both business and social situations. Appearance is interpreted as a reflection of an individual's status and achievement. Shorts are almost never worn in public except by tourists. Italians are very interested in accolades and assurances that they are dealing with someone of importance in the business environment. Business cards should include Italian translations on the reverse side along with relevant credentials. In Italy, conversations may be loud and animated. Interruptions are to be expected during the course of conversation. Travelers should be aware that the Roman Catholic Church remains a strong influence on Italian life.

12. Discussion Questions

1. What are some of the major industries in Italy and in what areas do you think Italy could benefit?

2. How does Italy's population growth rate affect its ability for economic growth?

3. What are some environmental issues that affect Italy?

4. Italy appears to be divided into two separate countries economically. What could be done to improve the economy in the less prosperous sector?

13. Case Study

Memo

To: Board of Directors
From: Consultants
Re: Downsizing

Fantasy Real Estate Sales (FRES)

Headquarters in Milan, Italy Offices in Italy, Sweden, Hungary, Spain, Russia, Netherlands, United Kingdom and Greece

I. Problem
Overview

Fantasy Real Estate Sales (FRES) was established in Greece in 1995. The idea behind the Company was drawn from a Greek real estate agent, XElvina Greeeelepis, owner of XXEGGG Realty. XElvina's real estate company had many different properties listed, including villas and private islands. The inspiration for FRES came from meeting XElvina. The Directors felt we would be able to help people find their "fantasy" pieces of real estate, such as castles, villas, ranches, winery's and any unique properties falling into the "fantasy" realm of real estate.

ITALY
Recently the headquarters of FRES, located in Milan, Italy, began to grow. It was doing so much business that it had seven full-time agents, and one office manager.

FRES needs to hire more people, but it is concerned with hiring too many, because if the Company has more than 15 employees, it will have to "take care of the employees" for a long time. This is based on the employment laws in Italy. See http://www.cmslegal.com/intelligence/cms_news/employment.htm.

RUSSIA
The Russian market is beginning to pick up new business. There are plenty of properties available, but FRES's target buyers are hesitant to purchase

property in Russia. (FRES is working on advertising the benefits of realty in Russia. FRES started doing overnight stays at the individual properties, so potential clients can see what it is like to be in Russia.)

HUNGARY

Currently, in Hungary, the Company has had a reduction in properties available for sale. FRES was been unable to secure properties for sale. It has also had two properties flood in the last two months.

NETHERLANDS

The market is booming. There seem to be enough "fantasy" properties at the current time.

UNITED KINGDOM (ENGLAND, SCOTLAND, WALES)

The United Kingdom, including the **England, Scotland and Wales** markets, has been relatively stable. These markets, for FRES, do not perform extremely well, but they do not go below projected income.

SPAIN

This market is just beginning to show the growth potential that was projected by FRES for the country. The market had a difficult time because prices were inflated. As such, it was not a good investment to purchase a fantasy property here; however, prices are beginning to come inline. Thus, with other European markets, the general market is beginning to pick up in sales.

SWEDEN

Currently the Swedish market is booming. The agents cannot keep up with the market.

II. Initial Exit Strategy

Exiting these countries would be relatively easy, except for Italy, where the headquarters office is currently located. All of the other offices are satellite offices. In most cases the agents work out of their own homes. The Milan office could be vacated relatively easily. The interior has been upgraded to class A office space and since this is in short supply in Italy, it should be relatively easy to re-lease or sub-lease. The network of real estate agents throughout Europe that FRES has established would help in the event that FRES needed to leave the county.

III. Contingency Exit Strategy

See Initial Exit Strategy plan. The plan of exit would be simple to leave everything and leave the country.

IV. Conclusion

Employment restrictions in Italy will make it difficult to keep expanding. To have a reasonable exit strategy, FRES should move the headquarters to Sweden. The reason Sweden is more of an ideal location is due to the booming market and the favorable employment laws.

The other markets could be considered, but Russia would be difficult. Current employees would resist a move to Sweden. The United Kingdom does not have enough business. This is also true with the Netherlands. Spain might be a possibility for the home office. The company should not completely close the operation in Italy, but it should leave one or two agents, to continue the local market.

Refer to: International Real Estate Digest. Homepage. http://www.ired.com. U.S. Department of State. Homepage. http://www.state.gov.

U.S. Embassy. Homepage. http://usembassy.state.gov.

14. Selected References

CIA World Factbook.https://www.cia.gov/library/publications/the-world-factbook/index.html.

Bank of Italy (Banca D'Italia),http://www.bancaditalia.it. Cmslegal.com."Termination of Employees in Italy." August 15,2002 (Retrieved Sept ember 22, 2002). http://www.cmslegal.com/intelligence/cms_news/employita.htm http://www.real-estate-european-union.com/english/italy.html.

International Real Estate Digest. Homepage. http://www.ired.com. http://www.mi.cnr.it /WOI/woiindex.ht ml.

Richard Ellis International Property Specialists. http://www.cbre.com. Time Almanac. *TIME Almanac.*

Boston: Information Please LLC. U.S. Bureau of Census at http://www.census.gov.

U.S. Department of Commerce at http://www.statusa.gov. U.S. Bureau of Economic Analysis at http://www.bea.gov.

U.S. Department of State. Homepage. http://www.state.gov. U.S. Embassy. Homepage.

http://usembassy.state.gov. World Trade Centers Institute at http://www.wtci.org. World Trade Organization at http://www.wto.org.

See the Burns School Global Real Estate Web site at the UNIVERSITY OF DENVER at http://burns.daniels.du.edu.

15. Glossary

Beni immobili – (immovable) real property.

Beni mobili – (movables) what ever is erected on land, trees, crops, rivers and springs.

Comunione – Community property.

Conservatore dei Registri Immobiliari – Recorder of Mortgages.

Fedeazione Italiana Mediatori Agenti Affari – Trade association.

Imposta comunale sugli immobili – annual tax on income from real property based on property's assed value.

Societa in nome collettivo – General partnership.

Societa in accomandita semplice – Limited partnership.

About the Author

Kevin Sutton, graduate student of the Burns School of Real Estate and Construction Management, *Daniels College of Business,* UNIVERSITY OF DENVER.

Japan

•

INTERNATIONAL REAL ESTATE (GLOBAL REAL ESTATE)
Authored by *Tokokazu (Kazu) Imazeki, Ph.D.*
and Dr. Mark Lee Levine, Editor

1. Geography

Japan is an island chain, located in eastern Asia, between the North Pacific Ocean and the Sea of Japan. It is approximately 377,915 sq km (kilometers), consisting of four major islands: Hokkaido, Honshu, Shikoku and Kyushu. The area for Japan is slightly less than that of California. Japan also includes Bonin Islands and over 3,000 minor islands. Japan's coastline is 29,751 km. The terrain is generally rugged, with mountainous areas.[162]

2. History and Overview

Japan has a history of dominating much of Asia. However, after World War II, Japan has had a strong relationship with the United States, as a democracy as well as an economically.

For several decades Japan has been the strong economic leader in Asia. Japan's rapid economic growth after World War II surprised even the Japanese, as well as the rest of the world. Within 25 years, Japan rose from the devastation of war to become the second largest industrial nation in the world. Japan will likely continue such economic dominance, although its minimal GDP growth rate suggests Japan's economic maturity largely explained by its increasing aging population. However, China, with its economic growth and size, will continue to gain on Japan as a major power in Asia. India is also strong in its physical size and population, adding another power to the Asian complex.

3. People

The population in Japan is **127,103,388** with an age structure of 61% in the 15- year-old to 64-year-old category. There are 25.8% in the category of 65+ years, with the balance, 13.2%, being in the 0 to 14-year-old category. Approximately 65,930,000 people are in the labor force.

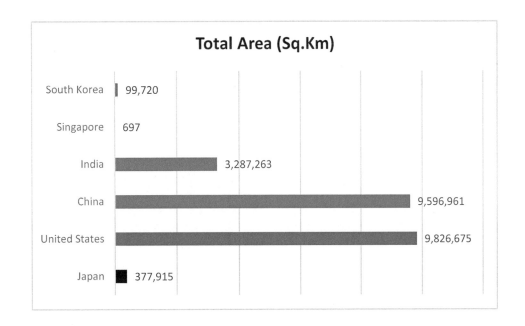

Total Area (Sq.Km)

South Korea	99,720
Singapore	697
India	3,287,263
China	9,596,961
United States	9,826,675
Japan	377,915

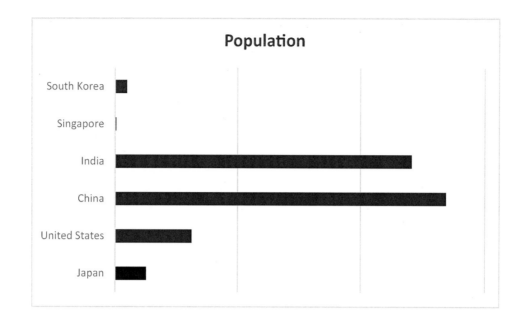

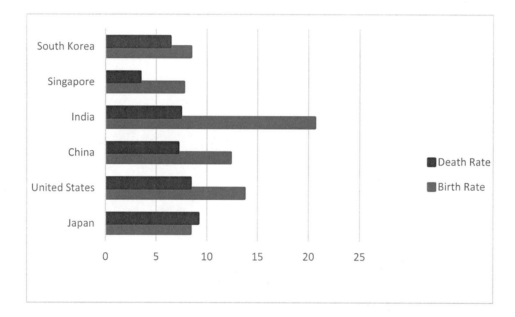

Japan's population growth is approximately -0.13% per year (2014). Birth rates are 8.07 per 1,000 population. Death rates are 9.38 per 1,000. The infant mortality rate is fairly low at 2.13 per 1,000. Life expectancy in Japan, overall, is 84.46 years, with 81.13 years for the male and 87.99 for the female.

Approximately 98.5% of the population is Japanese. The dominant language in Japan is Japanese. Japan has a highly literate population (over 99% of the population). Religions in Japan are mainly Shinto and Buddhist; these constitute about 84% of the population. The other religions are mixed, with about 10%. Of this 10%, about 2% is Christian. Also see ("Adult Illiteracy").

■ 4. Government

The defeat of Japan in World War II and the occupation of the country brought about fundamental changes in the whole structure of the government. This resulted in greater democratization in the government and greater decentralization in administration. Japan, today, is a state with a limited constitutional monarchy, with sovereign power residing in the people. The Emperor is merely the symbol of the state. Branches of the government include the Executive, Legislative and Judicial. Japan's capital is in Tokyo. It has 47 administrative divisions, sometimes labeled as *Prefectures*. Branches of the government are the bicameral *Diet* and *Kokkai*, which consists of the *Shugi-in*, the House of Representatives (the Lower House) and the *Shangi-in*, the House of Councillors (the Upper House), respectively. A number of political parties and political action groups exist in Japan.

The legal system is modeled after European, civil law, with English and American influence. The Judicial Branch is the Supreme Court, where the Chief Justice is appointed by the Emperor. The other just ices are appointed by the Cabinet.

Diplomatic representation exists with the United States, with an Ambassador in Washington, D.C. from Japan. U.S. diplomatic representation exists in Japan, via the Ambassador.

5. Economy

The Japanese economy has generally been strong since the end of World War II and rebuilding of Japan, with the help from Allied countries, especially the U.S. Japan's economy grew dramatically through the 1950s, '60s and '70s, culminating in the "bubble economy" period in the mid to late 1980s, and early 1990s. After the burst of the bubble economy in 1992, Japan has had economic difficulties with corporate bad debts and bankruptcies, sluggish economic growth and deflation. In addition, Japan now has a huge national debt and is facing higher costs for social welfare, due to its aging population. Japan has a modern economy, with a Gross Domestic Product (GDP) per capita of $37,800. The GDP real growth rate is 1.3% (2014).

6. Currency

Currency in Japan is the Japanese *yen.* See the Burns School Global Real Estate Website for the UNIVERSITY OF DENVER at http://burns.daniels.du.edu for currency conversions.

7. Transportation

Japan has a very sophisticated railroad system of 27,182 km (2014). Japan Railways (JR) operates many trains daily, including Shinkansen super-expresses on its nationwide system. In urban areas, rail companies besides JR also have an extensive rail network linking cities and towns. Within big cities, subways are also available for convenient intra-city transportation.

The highway system is also very sophisticated and developed; it has approximately 1,210,251 km (kilometers). Many of the highways are paved, toll roads.

Japan has many inland waterways and seagoing craft that support trade, fishing and recreational activities. Ports include Yokohama, Tokyo, Nagoya, Osaka, Kobe and others. Japan has a very advanced airport system, with approximately 175 airports (2012). Tokyo International Airport at Haneda mainly serves domestic flights. New Tokyo International Airport in Narita serves international flights.

8. Communications

Japan's communication system is highly sophisticated with the ratio of telephones to population being very strong. The number of hardwired telephones was 64.273 million and 138.363 million cellular mobile phones (2012). Its system is one of the strongest in the world, including many local and international services, earth stations and submarine cables to other areas, including those connecting to the United States, China and Korea, with many radio and television broadcast stations, shortwave radio stations. About 63,466,000 Internet service providers (hosts) provided service to 99,182,000 Internet users (2012).

9. Real Property Issues

The Japanese real estate market recorded robust growth for years in the mid-2000s, after the recovery from a decade long recession.

Growing demand for real estate increased commercial rent as well as the price. This upward trend in the market is called "fund bubble" since it was largely driven by private investment funds in both domestic and foreign origins. A part of this boom is also attributed to the bank of Japan's monetary policy maintaining the money supply extremely loose quantitatively in order to stimulate the economy. Excessive capital along with advanced securitization technique provided easy access to financing sources and reduced financing cost for investment. Steadily grown J-REIT market, established in 2001, also helped to improve the market transparency and to attract funds through public investment vehicles.

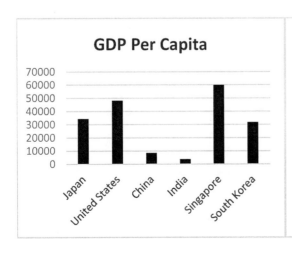

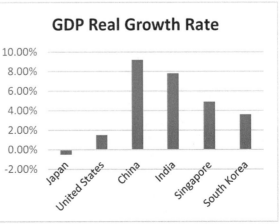

Uprising global recession changed the market condition dramatically in the late 2000s, and the industry faced significant difficulty. Financial institutions tightened loan for real estate including refinancing, and the lack of investment capital further declined the property value. Financially troubled real estate companies were forced to liquidate their assets and/or find financial partners although some of the financially weaker companies went bankrupt including a listed J-REIT company.

In the 2010s, the Japanese economy was under recovery from the Japan Earthquake and Tsunami (2011). In order to stimulate the economy, the Bank of Japan's easy money policy maintained the interest rate significantly low and made property financing accessible. Publicly assessed value of land suggested that the property market values were close to the bottom, particularly in urban areas, although the condition of the leasing market varies by property sectors.

There is no restriction on the purchase of land and buildings by foreign investors, if the investment is "validated" under Japanese law. Acquisition costs in Japan generally run about 10% to 15 % of the property price, including acquisition tax (4%), registration tax (2%), commissions (1% to 3%), and other miscellaneous expenses. A real estate brokerage license is required for agency services of property leasing and transactions in Japan.

The freehold is dominant type of property ownership in Japan. A land lease is granted only under the condition that the building is owned by an entity different from the actual land owner. In Japan, land is perceived and registered as a separate asset from buildings. Therefore, the term "land owner" is normally used instead of "property owner." Buildings can be owned by *strata title*.

Mortgage rights in Japan are created on specific property by agreements. Generally, the priority of mortgages on property is determined by the dates of formally registering the mortgage position on the public record. First in time generally prevails. Foreclosure of mortgages is enforced through the courts and through auction sales.

Property taxes exist on a local basis, such as a fixed asset tax, city planning tax, business office tax and corporate inhabitant tax. On the national level, there are corporate taxes, capital gain tax, consumption taxes, and so on.

Land use controls are generally administered through the Ministry of Land, Infrastructure, Transport and Tourism and each local government. The majority of urban area is classified by zoning, with regulation for proper use of land and total buildable floor area. Properties in Japan are measured in *tatami mats*. Standard size is 90 cm x 1q80 cm, or approximately 3 ft. x 6 ft.

■ 10. Real Estate Trends

Real estate trends in Japan can be best seen through specific links, noted below, including input from various real estate firms, such as Jones Lang LaSalle, Ikoma C.B. Richard Ellis, Sanko Estate, Japan Real Estate Institute, and numerous other firms. http://www.joneslanglasalle.co.jp/Japan/EN-GB/Pages/English.aspx. See also: http://www.cbre.co.jp/Pages/Default.aspx. http://www.cushwake.com/cwglobal/jsp/localHome.jsp?Country=Japan&Language =EN&. http://www.sankoestate.com. http://www.reinet.or.jp/en/index.ht ml.

For details in this area, see also the Burns School Global Real Estate Website: http://burns.daniels.du.edu.

■ 11. Cultural Issues

Any nation's culture is complex and vibrant in its diversity. While broad cultural characterizations such as those presented here can be generally accurate, following such generalities too strictly may be dangerously misleading. To conduct business effectively and profitably in a country, it is vital to have a thorough understanding of its culture's complexities.

Cultural practices in Japan are extremely important, given that it is difficult to enter the real estate market without being aware of cultural distinctions and the requirement to have introductions and personal contacts before business can reasonably be undertaken in Japan.

Personal appearance, types of greetings, use of business cards, polite and impolite gestures, rules as to visitation, eating habits, type of food that is eaten, and much more are crucial elements to understand *prior* to undertaking any business in Japan. a. See the links noted below for a detailed discussion of these areas relative to cultural issues. http://www.jetro.go.jp and http://www.visitjapan.jp/eng/top.html.

12. Discussion Questions

1. What are some cultural issues in Japan that could adversely affect a foreigner who is trying to do business in Japan?

2. How has Japan's location on the globe been beneficial to Japan's economic growth?

3. Why was real estate booming in the mid 2000s? What factors gave investors positive impacts on investment?

13. Selected References

CIA World Factbook.https://www.cia.gov/library/pub-lications/the-world-factbook/index.html.

Kawakami, Sumie, "Japan to Ease Bankruptcy Laws, "The *Japan Inc. Newsletter*.

(November 21, 2001). Retrieved September 18, 2002 at http://www.japaninc.net/newsletters/?list=jin&issue-158.

Richard Ellis International Property Specialists, http://www.cbre.com Time Almanac.

TIME Almanac. Boston: Information Please LLC.

United States Department of State. *Background Notes: Jordan*. United States Department of State (Online). Available:http://www.state.gov.

U.S. Bureau of Census at http://www.census.gov. U.S. Department of Commerce at http://www.stat-usa.gov. U.S. Bureau of Economic Analysis at http://www.bea.gov. U.S. Embassy. Homepage. http://usembassy.state.gov. World Trade Centers Institute at http://www.wtci.org.

World Trade Organization at http://www.wto.org/wto. (For unrestricted official World Trade Organization documents and texts.)

14. Glossary

Diet and Kokkai – Bicameral House of Representatives (Lower House) and House of Councillors (the Upper House).

Shinkansen – Super-express trains.

About the Author

Tokokazu Imazeki, *Ph.D.*, Chief Analyst, Sanko Estate Co., Ltd. Dr. Imazeki is the Chief Analyst of Sanko Estate as well as the Managing Director of Commercial Property Research Institute. Based in Tokyo, Dr. Imazeki analyzes major office markets across Japan and publishes their market reports periodically. Prior to joining Sanko Estate, he worked for LaSalle Investment Management and Jones Lang LaSalle (JLL) for over 7 years in total. At LaSalle, he was the Investment Strategist and a member of the Global Research team. He also participated in LaSalle's Asian Investment Committee regularly and covered the market analysis and forecasts for investments in Japan. At JLL, he was an Associate Director heading JLL Japan's research team. He received a Ph.D. in Real Estate from Georgia State University, an M.B.A. in Real Estate from the University of Denver and a Bachelor of Economics from Chuo University.

Jordan

INTERNATIONAL REAL ESTATE (GLOBAL REAL ESTATE)
Authored by *Samer I. Asfour and Dr. Mark Lee Levine,* Editor

1. Geography

Jordan, or the Hashemite Kingdom of Jordan, is known as a one of the Middle Eastern countries. Jordan presents an ideal gateway to the Middle East region and the rest of the world. It shares borders with six Middle Eastern countries; Iraq, Syria, Saudi Arabia, Israel, the Palestine National Authority territories and Egypt, with a total ground area of 89,342 square kilometers (sq km).

The multi-border characteristic of Jordan reinforces its accessibility, giving it competitive leverage over neighboring Middle East countries, such as those that possess less exposed boundaries.

Jordan's climate is mostly hot and dry in the summer; it is cool and wet in the winter. The weather in Amman (altitude 777 meters) (777 m) is hottest in August, with 17°C (63°F) as a minimum to 40°C (104°F) as a maximum. The coldest month is January; it is -3°C (27°F) as a minimum to 16°C (61°F) as a maximum. The driest months are May to August. The wettest month is February, with a 75.5 mm average rainfall.

Jordan is not well endowed with mineral resources, especially compared with its neighbors. It has a modest level of natural gas, which in 1998 was being produced from three wells in the Risha district near the Iraqi border. Crude oil exploration is also under way, although success has been extremely modest. Jordan's most exploit able natural resources have been its fertilizer minerals, which are considered as one of the main contributors to the national income. Potash is found in the Dead Sea and raw phosphates in the south at al-Hasa and Shidiya.

The gravest environmental challenge that Jordan faces today is the scarcity of water. This is likely to continue to be an important political issue as the population grows, given the country's limited water resources.

2. History and Overview

After the fieriest clashes between the Ottoman-Turkish army and Arab resistance forces during World War 1, and with the help of United Kingdom, the State of Jordan (then known as Transjordan) was created in 1921.

King Hussein's grandfather, Abdullah, became its head, establishing an immediate close relationship between Jordan and the West which continues today.

In 1946 Jordan obtained nominal independence from British mandate and assumed its current status as Hashemite Kingdome of Jordan. Five years later, King Abdullah was assassinated. After a brief two years reign, King Talal abdicated in favor of his son, Hussein Bin Talal who died of cancer in February, 1999. The current ruler of Jordan is King Hussein's oldest son, Abdullah the Second.

The first Arab-Israeli war occurred in 1948. Israel was able to control most of Palestine, except part of eastern Palestine which was then incorporated into Jordan and became known as the West Bank. As a result, the refugee out flow moved to Jordan, creating tensions, which were obviously felt in the 1970 conflict.

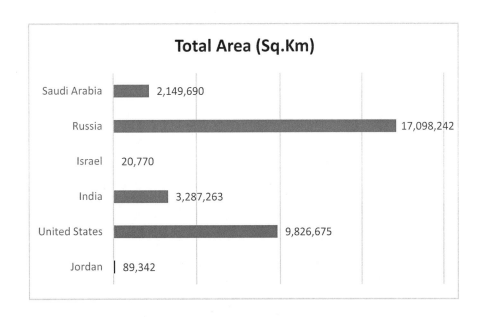

In 1967, there was the Second Arab-Israeli war. The whole West Bank was occupied, including east Jerusalem, and it came under Israeli control. Jordan proper suffered a further bout of turbulence with the arrival of more Palestinian refugees.

In 1990, Jordan was rocked by another regional crisis as Iraq invaded Kuwait. More than 300,000 refugees moved to Jordan, putting Jordan under more pressure.

In 1994, Jordan signed a peace treaty with Israel, concluding 45 years of war. The Jordan- Israeli Peace Treaty was signed on October 26, 1994, at the southern border crossing of Wadi Araba. The treaty guaranteed Jordan the restoration of its occupied land (approximately 380 sq km), and guaranteed the Kingdom an equitable share of water from the Yarmouk and Jordan rivers. Moreover, the treaty clearly defined Jordan's western borders.

Seeking to lay a firm foundation for a just, comprehensive and lasting peace, the treaty also outlined a number of areas in which negotiations would continue. To this end, Jordanian and Israeli negotiators have signed a series of protocols, establishing a mutually beneficial framework of relations in fields such as trade, transportation, tourism, communications, energy, culture, science, navigation, the environment, health and agriculture, as well as co operatory agreements for the Jordan Valley and the Aqaba-Eilat region.[169]

■ 3. People

The population of Jordan is **7,930,491.** The average population growth rate was 3.86% (2014). However, in 1990 to 1991, the growth rate was 8.05%, with the arrival of 300,000 people, more or less, after the Gulf crisis.

The population is almost completely Arab. The exceptions include small communities of Ciracassians and Chechens, who number in the tens of thousands. The population is overwhelmingly Sunni Muslim. The Christian population, which accounted for 2.2% of the total population in 2010, has been shrinking due to overall declining birth rates.

The bulk of the population is concentrated in the capital and other adjacent centers.

Greater Amman has grown rapidly over the years, largely because of successive refugee inflows, expansion of the public sector, growth in the services sector and rural-urban migration. Life expectancy in Jordan is 74.1 years, with approximately 75.5 years for females and 72.79 for males. The birth rate is 25.23 births per 1,000. The death rate is 3.8 deaths per 1,000. Infant mortality rate in Jordan is 15.73 per 1,000.

The official language is Arabic. English is a common second language. Literacy is high in Jordan at around 89.9%.

The labor force continues to grow and is mainly distributed in the following areas: social & administrative services 77.4%, agriculture 2.7% and industry 20%.

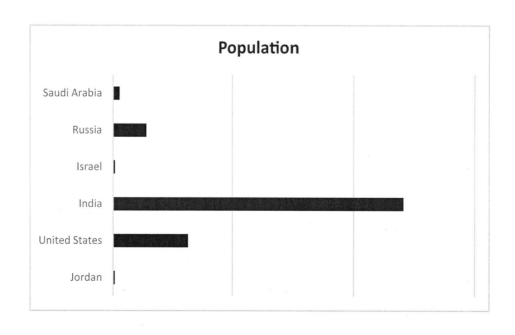

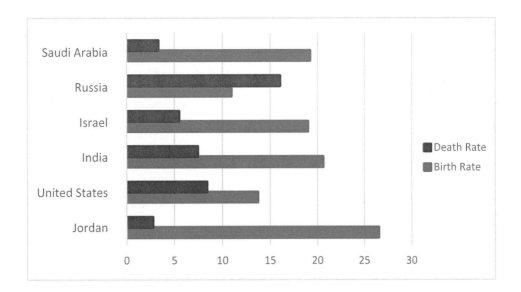

4. Government

Jordan is a constitutional monarchy based on the Constitution promulgated in 1952 during the brief reign of King Talal. Executive authority is vested in the king and his council of ministers. The King signs and executes all laws. His veto power may be overridden by a two-thirds vote of both houses of the National Assembly. He appoints and may dismiss all judges by decree. He approves amendments to the Constitution, declares war, and commands the armed forces. Cabinet decisions, court judgment s, and the national currency are issued in his name.

The council of ministers, led by a prime minister, is appointed by the King, who may dismiss other cabinet members at the prime minister's request. The cabinet is responsible to the Chamber of Deputies on matters of general policy and can be forced to resign by a two-thirds vote of "no confidence" by that body. Legislative power rests in the bicameral National Assembly. The 80-member Chamber of Deputies, Majlisal-Nuwaab, elected by universal suffrage to a four- year term, is subject to dissolution by the King. Of the 80 seats, 71 must go to Muslims and 9 to Christians. The 40- member Senate is appointed by the King for an eight- year term. The Constitution provides for three categories of courts-civil, religious, and special. Administratively, Jordan is divided into eight governorates, each headed by a governor appointed by the King. They are the sole authorities for all government departments and development projects in their respective areas. Despite the Constitution, King Hussein was the country's ultimate authority. He had achieved that by a combination of his personal qualities, the longevity of his rule and his manipulation of traditional tribal relations. His power was bolstered by a well-trained army and an efficient security and intelligence network. King Abdullah- the-Second is following the same practices espoused by his father.

The mandate over Transjordan ended on May 22, 1946. On May 25, 1946, the country became the independent Hashemite Kingdom of Transjordan. It continued a defense treaty relationship with the United Kingdom until 1957, when the treaty was dissolved by mutual consent.

Taxation is generally from income and profit tax, domestic transaction tax, foreign trade tax, additional tax, and value added tax.

Taxation of Companies and Businesses: All companies, local and foreign, operating in Jordan are subject to corporate income tax at the following rates: Mining, industry, hotels, hospitals, transportation, contracting and other sectors approved by the Council of Ministers is at 15%. Banks, financial and finance companies, exchange companies and brokerage companies (in case of banks, financial and insurance companies, the tax payable each year should not be less than 25% of their net income before any distributions are made) are at 35%. All other companies pay at 25%.

Taxation of Individuals: Salaries, wages and other income paid to Jordanian and foreign employees are taxable. The Income Tax Law gives a 50% exemption from tax on private sector employees' annual salaries up to Jordanian *dinar* (JD) 12,000 and a 25% exemption on amounts above JD 12,000. Foreign employees working for non-Jordanian companies are exempt from paying all income tax. In addition, there are personal and family exemptions given by the income tax law. In the public sector, 50% of the salaries and wages of employees are tax exempt.

5. Economy

Jordan has a market-oriented free economy, where ownership of business entities is largely private. Direct state ownership is relatively small; it is significant only in the mining sector (phosphate and potash) and in sectors of public utilities (electricity, water, communications, public bus transport, railway and air transport), which are all under the privatization program. Prices, except for a few subsidized goods, interest rates and wages are generally determined by market forces.

Jordan's economy is service-oriented. The services sector, which is comprised of financial services, trade, transportation, communication, construction, and education, contribute to the Gross Domestic Product (GDP) and employ two-thirds of the labor force.

A trade agreement signed with the European Union (EU) came into effect January 1, 1999. The agreement calls for a progressive liberalization of trade through 2010. In April, 2000, Jordan acceded to the World Trade Organization (WTO), a process which entailed extensive legislative and regulatory reform. The government has partially privatized the national telecommunications company and the state-owned cement firm, and it is in the process of privatizing the national airline.

Jordan and the United States were negotiating a Free Trade Agreement (FTA) to eliminate trade barriers between the two countries over a period of years. In 1999, the two countries signed a Trade and Investment Framework Agreement (TIFA), which seeks to remove impediments to trade and investment.

The U.S. and Jordan have a Bilateral Investment Treaty (BIT), which protects investors and establishes procedures for resolving investment disputes. Annual cash transfers from the U.S. Agency for International Development (USAID) are conditioned on the implementation of specific policy reforms aimed at speeding privatization, developing capital markets, and improving the investment climate. USAID supports a comprehensive set of economic reform and private enterprise development activities aimed at implementing policy reforms and improving the overall business climate for trade and investment.

Reforms to the customs, taxation, and investment laws have improved Jordan's business climate. Investors have shown interest in Qualifying Industrial Zones (QIZs), which are industrial parks that can export products to the United States, duty free, if 35% of the product's content comes from the QIZ, Israel, and/or the West Bank/Gaza. QIZ factories have created more

than 6,000 jobs. The number is expected to continue increasing rapidly.[172]

The government is also developing the port of Aqaba as a Special Economic Zone (SEZ), with low taxes, minimal bureaucracy, and investor-friendly policies. The Central Bank of Jordan lifted all restrictions on capital flows.

Major Economic Trends: Real GDP per capita is $11,900. The GDP real growth rate is 3% (2014).

Unemployment continues to be a major problem; unofficial estimates put the figure at 12.3% or more (2014). In 2000, a record number of young Jordanians, estimated around 120,000, joined the workforce. Foreign exchange reserves were at a record high of about $2.7 billion at the end of March 2000. This amount was equal to 8.3 months of imports. The exchange rate is fixed at 0.079 JOD per U.S. dollar (2008). Since mid-1999, the Central Bank of Jordan (CBJ) has been trying to relax monetary policy (i.e., lower interest rates) to jump-start the economy. However, banks have been slow in lowering their lending rates. CBJ's maneuvering room is limited by the need to keep a differential between U.S. interest and JD rates.

Exports, $8.556 billion (2014 est.), include clothing, fertilizers, potash, phosphates, agricultural products and pharmaceuticals.

Imports are $22.8 billion (2014 est.), including crude oil, machinery, transport equipment, iron, cereals and manufactured goods.

■ 6. Currency

Following a severe economic and financial crisis in Jordan in 1989, the Central Bank of Jordan was forced to devalue the *Jordanian dinar* (JOD). The exchange rate of the dinar was fixed against a basket of currencies, producing a stable exchange rate around JD 0.7 against the U.S. dollar. In 1995, the currency was officially pegged to the U.S. dollar, with an average exchange rate of 0.709 JOD to 1 U.S. dollar (2008). There is no restriction on converting the dinar or transferring money outside the

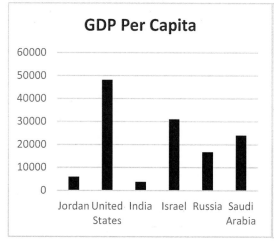

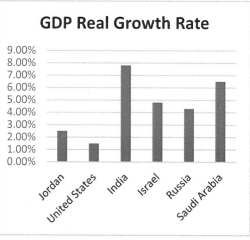

country. Most foreign currencies can be converted against the Jordanian dinar. Notes are issued in denominations of 0.5, 1, 5, 10, 20, and 50 dinar. For current conversion rates, see the Burns School Global Real Estate Website, Daniels *College of Business*, UNIVERSITY OF DENVER at http://burns.daniels.du.edu.

7. Transportation

The transportation sector, for the time being, is almost entirely state controlled. However, the government plans to turn over the majority of its operation to the private sector as part of the privatization program. In the area of land transportation, the Public Transportation Corporation provides car and bus service within the country. Jordan has an expanding network of roads and highways which is constantly being upgraded. It is now possible to reach every major tourist destination by a modern, hard-surfaced road. Signposts to tourist sites and urban areas are in both Arabic and English. There are 7,203 km of paved highways.

In the area of air transportation, Jordan has 18 airports (2013). In addition, Jordan has 507 km of railways.

The only seaport Jordan has is the seaport of Aqaba, which is located at the southern part of Jordan on the Red Sea.

8. Communications

The communication sector, like the transportation sector, is almost a completely state-controlled sector. Together, transportation and communication employ about 7% of the workforce and account for 5% of economic activity. Jordan Radio and Television Corporation (JRTV), the main government-owned station, transmits operates with other radio, television and satellite TV stations.

9. Real Property Issues

Most of the property in Jordan is owned by private owners and is leased on long-term leases. Reforms to the current property law are in process to control the relationships between the owner and the tenant.

Recently, brokers, who are not professional, have been used for real estate sales with commissions agreed upon between parties for each transaction. Professional real estate agencies are still not available in Jordan. Most real estate business is undertaken because of personal efforts and contacts. No license is required for brokerage work, or for appraisal/valuation work.

The regulatory body that attempts to control the real estate market, The Land & Property Department, is still not very active.

Ownership of real property is evidenced by title deeds. Real property records are kept manually and administered by designated notaries public who also register ownership and record

transfer of real property and real property mortgages. Land description is usually given under the metric system All real estate contracts are covered by the law. Each contract must be registered at the court and the Land & Property Department to be effective.

10. Real Estate Trends

Approximately 30% of the Jordanian population lives in the capital, Amman. Irbid comes after that with approximately 20%, 15% lives in Zarqa, and 3% in Aqaba. A considerable amount of Jordanian land is uninhabited, presenting space and room for expansion and for the establishment of new businesses. Land and building costs are cheaper outside the major cities.

Non-Jordanian investors are allowed to purchase real estate in Jordan. Prices of land for **commercial** use in western Amman ranges from U.S. $275 to U.S. $1,400 per square meter (sq. m.). Areas of land outside the capital are available at considerably lower prices than land located in the cities.

Business entities in western Amman are usually located in the commercial centers and downtown, Shemisani, Gardens St., Sweifieh and Al-Hussein. Office space is plentiful and the qualityishigh. Annualrent for office space in western Amman ranges from U.S. $60 per sq. m. to U.S. $140 per sq. m. Retail stores are available for rent in western Amman with an annual rent of U.S.$6,000 to U.S.$13,000,depending on location and the age of the building.

Real estate business is expected to rapidly improve since the government is in the process of establishing several Free and Industrial Zones.

The Jordanian Free Zone areas were established to promote export-oriented industries and transit trade. Commodities and goods of various origins and nature are deposited in the free zone areas for the purpose of storage and manufacturing, without having to pay the usual excise fees and other taxes, since they are treated as if they are goods outside Jordan. Jordan now is adopting a master plan for turning Aqaba into a "Special economic Zone" with custom free and law tax regulation. This plan will energize some gigantic and complicated schemes for relocating the main port and the grain ports to the south as well as establishment of several touristic and light industry activities.

Businesses in *Free Zones* are enjoying the following benefits: Exemption from income and social taxes on profits for 12 years; Exemption from income and social tax on non-Jordanian workers' allowances; Duty free imports; Exemption from all taxes on real estates; Exemption of custom duty on products to be marketed in Jordan market; 10% exemption on rental fees of land leased for industrial purposes; and Free movement and transfer of capital and profits.

Industrial Estates: Industrial estates are fully equipped with advanced Infrastructure facilities including road networks, modern utilities, maintenance facilities, sewage, and disposal treatment plants. Ancillary services include vocational training centers, banking services, private customs clearing centers, Ministry of Industry and Trade branch, Amman Chamber of Commerce branch, Jordan Export Development and Commercial Centers (JEDCO) branch, and free zone area, in addition to labor, insurance, advertising, auditing, and marketing offices.

Two industrial estates are currently in operation in the cities of Sahab and Irbid: Amman Industrial Estate (Sahab) and Al-Hassan Industrial Estate (Irbid).

Five other estates are under development in different parts of the country. Enterprises operating in industrial estates are exempted from income tax and social services tax for a period of two years from the date of the commencement of operations. Projects operating in industrial estates are exempted from land and building taxes throughout the life- span of the project.

Land and building facilities are available for purchase or rent at concessionary prices.

Construction Sector: There were more than 1,536 registered contracting companies in Jordan. During 1994, the value of construction contracts reached U.S.

$987 million, of which 70% was for private sector work and 30% for public sector work.

The construction industry is highly profitable in Jordan, with one of the lowest land and construction costs in the region. The availability of locally produced construction materials at competitive stable prices increases the profit appeal of this industry. St one is quarried locally, cement is produced locally and steel reinforcement bars are available locally as well as imported. Ceramic tiles, sanitary fixtures, kitchen cabinet s, timber joinery, air conditioning and heating equipment, electrical items, lifts, pipes and wires are all produced locally. They are available at competitive prices compared to imported substitutes, providing savings in customs duties and overseas transportation. Jordan's construction sector is of high caliber and expertise. There were more than 32,879 registered engineers and architects in Jordan by the end of 1994 in various fields, of which 37% were civil, 27% electrical, and 20% mechanical engineers. Approximately 20% of registered engineers graduated from Jordanian universities, and the remaining 80% graduated from academic institutions in other countries due to the limited capacity of local universities. Of the engineers who studied abroad, approximately 26% graduated from Arab countries, 30% from Europe and 12% from the United States.

Modern construction technology has been incrementally used including precast concrete, environmental control systems, and intelligent building management systems. Many joint ventures are being formed between international consultants, contractors and local firms in order to improve competitiveness and capitalize on the market. International firms are providing the special technical know-how local firms are contributing with their technical services. Encouraged by the prospect of peace, an increasing number of international consultants and contractors are showing interest in the region.

■ 11. Cultural Issues

Any nation's culture is complex and vibrant in its diversity. While broad cultural characterizations such as those presented here can be generally accurate, following such generalities too strictly may be dangerously misleading. To conduct business effectively and profitably in a country, it is vital to have a thorough understanding of its culture's complexities.

Jordan customs and cultural issues are import ant and distinguished from all other Arab neighbor countries. Jordanian men, not like other Arab Gulf Countries, wear western fashioned clothes, except in Badieh, where traditional *dishdasheh* is worn.

Greetings often use the word *Salam Alaikom,* which means "hello," and more specifically, "peace be upon you." Frequently, males, and females will follow the greeting by kissing each other's right and left cheeks. However; the relationship between the people determines the type of greeting. A casual Hello is *Marhaba.*

Embroidery is one of the most import ant traditional crafts of Jordanian women and one which has, in recent years, been incorporated into high fashion. Elegant gowns and jackets have been created using traditional needlework, together with rich, Middle-Eastern fabrics. These designer collections are frequently modeled on the catwalks of Jordan's hotels. Also they are exported to the United States and Europe through the Noor Al-Hussein Foundation.

The Bedouin people wove many practical items by hand, using sheep's wool, goat hair, and camel hair. Bedouin weaving served many purposes in the nomadic environment. These items included bedding-bags, rugs, saddle-bags, food containers and room dividers for the tents.

12. Discussion Questions

1. In what areas has Jordan benefited from its peace treaty with Israel?

2. What are some religious and cultural practices in Jordan that are important to know when doing business in Jordan?

3. What impact has the establishment of Jordanian Free Zone areas had on Jordan's economy?

13. Case Study

Construction Vocational Training (CVT) Amman, Jordan

Memo

To: Board of Directors
From: Consultants
Re: Lack of teachers

I. Problem

Newest satellite offices in Jordan and South Korea Construction Vocational Training (CVT) has entered a number of countries. It provides construction trade vocational training. CVT has established offices in Kenya, and has recently opened offices in South Korea and Jordan. Both locations we are having a difficult time finding teachers. Either they are unavailable in the country, or the teachers that CVT brings from another country decide to leave after a short term. Because of the lack of teachers, both sights must be reviewed for a possible closing.

II. Initial Exit Strategy

The initial exit strategy was never solidified. CVT rents a small office, with a classroom setting. CVT can exit both leases without too much difficulty or cost. CVT would need to finish the classes currently in session, through the end of the year. Once that has been completed, CVT would need to terminate its advertising. This can be accomplished within a month.

III. Contingency Exit Strategy

It would be difficult in either country to exit much more quickly than the initial exit strategy plan.

IV. Conclusion (ALTERNATIVE APPROACH)

At this time, it is suggested that CVT close the school with the least amount of activity. Then CVT could hire teachers for two-week periods, fly them in and pay for all of their expenses; and then fly them back. This way they will not be in the country long enough to want to leave. CVT can obtain a variety of professionals. CVT should give this plan six months, and then it should reevaluate the situation.

Refer to: X-rates.com. Homepage. http://www.x-rates.com/.

U.S. Embassy. Homepage. http://usembassy.state.gov. U.S. Department of State. Homepage. http://www.state.gov.

14. Selected References

Central Bank of Jordan, Annual Report, 1989, 1994,1998,1999 & 2000 at http://www.cbj.gov.jol/.

C.B. Richard Ellis International Property Specialists. http://www.cbre.com. CIA World Factbook.https://www.cia.gov/library/publications/the-world- factbook/index.html.

The Economist Intelligence Unit, *Country Profile 2000* (Quarter 1 & 2).

Export and Finance Bank, *Country Report,* 1999 at http://www.efbank.com.jo. IMF, International Financial Statistics.

International Real Estate Digest. Homepage. http://www.ired.com.

The Jordan Times Internet Edition. http://www.jordan-times.com/. (3-letter day of the week abbreviation).

The Jordan Times Internet Edition. "Tafileh Housing Survey Under Way,". http://www.jordant imes.com/Sun/homesnews/homenews8.htm.

Kamal Salibi, *The Modern History of Jordan,* IB Tauris, London, 1993. Library of Congress website at http://www.loc.gov/. Search for Jordan. The Peace Treaty between Jordan and Israel. http//:www.mideastinfo.com/documents/peace2.htm.

Time Almanac. *TIME Almanac.* Boston: Information Please LLC.

United States Department of State. *Background Notes. Jordan.* United States Department of State (Online). Available:http://www.state.gov. U.S. Bureau of Census at http://www.census.gov.

U.S. Department of Commerce at http://www.stat-usa.gov.

U.S. Bureau of Economic Analysis at http://www.bea.gov. U.S. Department of State. Homepage. http://www.state.gov. U.S. Embassy. Homepage. http://usembassy.state.gov.

Wilson, Rodney, *Politics and the Economy in Jordan*, Rout ledge, London, 1991. World Trade Organization at http://www.wto.org.

World Bank (Unknown). *Adult Illiteracy Rates*. The Economist. See also: American Business Bureau, American Embassy. Amman (August 2000).

Encyclopedia Britannica CD. Personal information, some field research. X-rates.com. Homepage. http://www.x-rates.com/.

15. Glossary

Free Zones – In Jordan, free zones enjoy the following benefits: exemption from income and social taxes on profits for 12 years; exemption from income and social tax on non-Jordanian workers' allowances; duty free imports; exemption from all taxes on real estates; exemption of custom duty on products to be marketed in Jordan market ; 10% exemption on rental fees of land leased for industrial purposes; and free movement and transfer of capital and profits.

Marhaba – A casual hello.

Salam Alaikom – Means hello, more specifically, peace be upon you.

About the Author

Samer I. Asfour, Chief Operating Officer of Design Jordan in Amman, Jordan. Mr. Asfour was the General Manager of the Amman World Trade Center in Amman, Jordan.

Kenya

INTERNATIONAL REAL ESTATE (GLOBAL REAL ESTATE)
Dr. Mark Lee Levine, **Editor**

1. Geography

Kenya borders eastern Africa, the Indian Ocean between the countries of Somalia and Tanzania, Ethiopia, Sudan and Uganda.

Kenya is 580,367 sq km (square kilometers) of area, with 569,250 sq km of that in land, and the balance in water areas. Kenya is slightly more than twice the size of the U.S. state of Nevada. Total coastline includes about 536 km. Several border disputes exist, especially with Sudan. The climate is mostly tropical, with arid interior areas.

Natural resources include gold, limestone, salt, rubies, wildlife and other important resources. Land use is approximately 30% for forest and woodlands, and about 37% for pastures. The rest is a mix of various uses, including arable land of 9.84%. Environmental concerns include especially water pollution from urban and industrial waste and degradation of water from increased use of fertilizers and pesticides. Other environmental issues result from soil erosion and deforestation.

2. History and Overview

Kenya was a former British colony, gaining independence from Britain on December 12, 1963. Kenya then became a Dominion within the Commonwealth, which recognized the British Queen as Head of State, and also as the Queen of Kenya. However, only one year later, Kenya became a Republic within the Commonwealth. The Constitution states that Kenya is a sovereign Republic.[177]

3. People

Kenya has **45,010,056** people. The age structure is dominated by the 15 to 64 age group at 55.1%, with 42.1% in the 0 to 14-year-old category. Only a small percentage, 2.8%, of the population is in the over 65 age range.

The population growth rate is substantial, at 2.11% per year. There are 28.27 births per 1,000. Death rates are 7 in 1,000. Infant mortality is high, at 40.71 per 1,000 live births. The total population has a life expectancy of only 63.52 years of age, with males at 62.06 and females at 65.01 years.

Ethnic groups include the Kikuyu group at 22%, Luhya at 14% and a mix of others, including Africans and non-Africans.

The dominant religion is Protestant, at 45%, followed by Roman Catholic at 33%, and indigenous traditions at 10% of the populace.

The official language is English, although Swahili is generally predominant. Many other languages are also spoken in Kenya. The literacy rate is fairly low, with only about 85.1% literacy for those in ages 15 and older who can read and write.

The work force is fairly low at approximately 17.7 million (2014), with unemployment very high at 40% (2014).

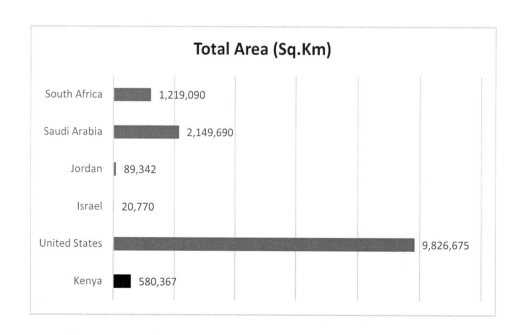

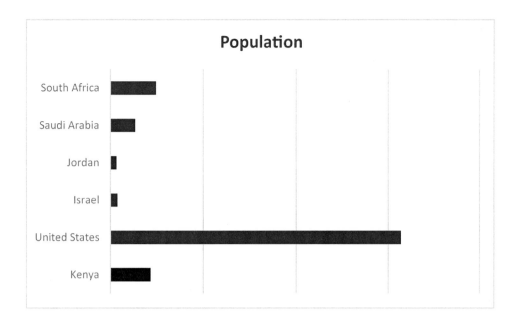

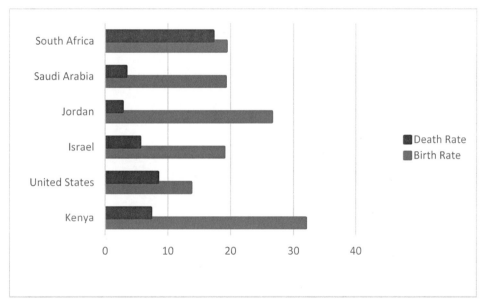

4. Government

The Kenyan government is a republic with the capital in Nairobi.

Seven (7) divisions or Provinces and other smaller areas administer the government. Independence was December 12, 1963, where Kenya gained its independence from the United Kingdom. Constitutions have been drafted over many years; the first Constitution was on December 12, 1963, but it was amended and reissued with numerous changes over many years.

The legal system is based on the English common law, amended or adjusted because of tribal laws and Islamic laws, which influenced the developing legal system.

The government includes an Executive Branch, with the President; the Legislative Branch is unicameral, through the National Assembly, sometimes called the *Bunge*; and the Judicial Branch. Numerous political parties include the Kenya-African National Union, or KANU, the Democratic Party of Kenya, as well as others. Diplomatic representation includes an Ambassador for Kenya in Washington, D.C. Likewise, the United States maintains its Embassy office in Nairobi.

5. Economy

Kenya, since about 1993, has worked to stabilize its economy and has received help from the International Monetary Fund (IMF), the World Bank and others.

Kenya exports many products such as tea, coffee, petroleum products and others. The Gross Domestic Product (GDP) of the country is $62.72 billion (2014). The GDP per capita is

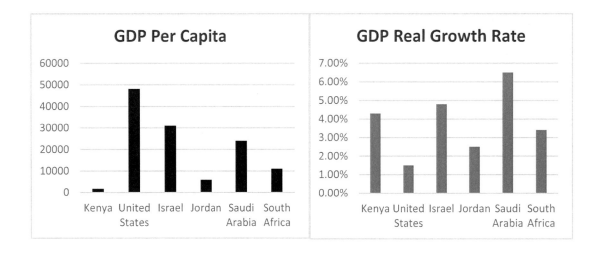

$3,100. Inflation is 7.2% (2014). The GDP real growth rate is 5.3% (2014).

■ 6. Currency

The currency is the Kenya *schilling*, known as KES, which equals 100 cents for each one Kenya *schilling*. See the Burns School Global Real Estate Web site at the UNIVERSITY OF DENVER at http://burns.daniels.du.edu for current conversions.

■ 7. Transportation

Transportation in Kenya utilizes railroads, with 2,066 km (kilometers) of line available. Highways are 160,878 km, but only 11,189 km are paved. There are also inland waterways, ports and airports for transportation. Petroleum products are exported from Kenya.

■ 8. Communications

Kenya suffers from a limited communication system. Only 251,600 landline telephones are in use (2012), and 30,732,000 mobile cellular telephones (2012). Kenya has state-owned and privately-owned television stations and radio stations. Approximately 3,996,000 million Internet users (2012) are serviced by 71,018 Internet service providers (hosts).

■ 9. Real Property Issues

Acquisition costs and other data on real estate transactions in Kenya are very limited, given limited control and development by the government. However, a program of consolidation of land registration activity was commenced in 1954 and has been developing. Land consolidation and adjudication is helping organize some ownership positions in Kenya. Land ownership is often held by individuals, tribes, clans and sections in families or other groups. Information on mortgages, financing, closings, appraisal and other real estate activities is not well documented. However, Web links are provided for subsequently in the Selected References section and they provide additional information in these areas.

■ 10. Real Estate Trends

Information on offices, retail, industrial, residential, etc., is difficult to collect because the available data is very limited, and the government has only limited activity in this area. Links to other sources, noted in the Selected References section, such as the Central Bank of Kenya along with real estate organizations, are very helpful for additional information.[181]

■ 11. Cultural Issues

Any nation's culture is complex and vibrant in its diversity. While broad cultural characterizations such as those presented here can be generally accurate, following such generalities too strictly may be dangerously misleading. To conduct business effectively and profitably in a country, it is vital to have a thorough understanding of its culture's complexities.

Dress and greetings in many activities in Kenya are similar to those in the United States, although most of these are shaped by the current activity and whether a business activity and whether a business activity or indigenous tribal population activity is involved. Greetings and general business activity is similar to the United States, including the use of handshakes, kiss on the cheek, and general greetings.

12. Discussion Questions

1. How does the low age of life expectancy affect Kenya's economy?

2. Is Kenya considered a strong economy in Africa?

13. Case Study

Memo

To: Board of Directors
From: Consultants
Re: Exporting Issues

I. Problem

INTERNATIONAL ANIMAL EXPORTS (IAE) NAIROBI, KENYA

International Animal Exports (IAE) has been in business for over 24 years. Recently the Company was left, by the sole owner, who died in a plane crash recently. The Company was left to Ms. XMelody ZRight, a young lady. Ms. X.Z. has been familiarizing herself with the Company. After through research, it has come to the attention of Ms. X.Z. that the Company is not following the proper procedures to export animals. IAE is not following C.I.T.E.S (Convention on International Trade in Endangered Species of Wild Fauna and Flora). IAE has not applied for the proper documentation in Kenya, nor in any of the countries where the animals have been exported. The Company's current Trade License is about to expire. And, after visiting the holding area, Ms.X.Z. has now questioned the treatment of the animals. **II. Initial Exit Strategy** There is not a current initial exit strategy plan in place.

III. Contingency Exit Strategy

To exit the business in Kenya, IAE would need to complete, at a minimum, the following: Transport the remaining animals in holding to the customer; Close our offices; and terminate the long-term land lease. These seem to be the important aspects to exiting the business. IAE could also attempt to sell the business to a competitor, but there is very little time to act.

IV. Conclusion

Because the license is about to expire, and Ms. X.Z. is not comfortable with the way the business has been run, Ms. X.Z. thinks that the Company is running too high risks by operating at the current standards. The consultants have suggested that the business be closed as quickly as possible, giving deference to the above-noted issues. The Company should cease to take any more orders. It should cancel all of the advertisements, immediately. IAE can hire an attorney to represent the Company to let the offices spaces and work out of the long-term leases.

Refer to: U.S. Embassy. Homepage. http://usembassy.state.gov. U.S. Department of State. Homepage. http://www.state.gov. X-rates.com. Homepage. http://www.x-rates.com/.

14. Selected References

CIA World Factbook at https://www.cia.gov/library/publications/the-world-factbook/index.html.

Central Bank of Kenya at http://www.cent ralbank. go.ke/.

Convention on International Trade of Endangered Species of Wild Fauna and Flora. Homepage. (Retrieved Sept ember 18, 2002). http://www.cit es.org/. International Real Estate Digest.

Martindale-Hubbell. Homepage. http://www.ired. com.

C.B. Richard Ellis International Property Specialists. http://www.cbre.com. Time Almanac. *TIME Almanac.* Boston: Information Please LLC.

United States Department of State. *Background Notes: Kenya.* United States Department of State (Online). Available:http://www.state.gov.

U.S. Bureau of Census at http://www.census.gov. U.S. Department of Commerce at http://www.stat-usa. gov. U.S. Bureau of Economic Analysis at http://www.bea.gov.

U.S. Department of State. Homepage. http://www.state.gov. U.S. Embassy. Homepage. http://

usembassy.state.gov. World Trade Organization at http://www.wto.org. World Bank. *Adult Illiteracy Rates*. The Economist.

X-rates.com. Homepage. http://www.x-rates.com/.

15. Glossary

Kikuyu – ethnic group in Kenya approximately 22%.

Luhya – ethnic group in Kenya approximately 14%.

Swahili – not the official language of Kenya, but the most predominant.

About the Author

Dr. Mark Lee Levine *is the Editor of this Book.*

South Korea

INTERNATIONAL REAL ESTATE (GLOBAL REAL ESTATE)
Authored by *Michael Sunoo, JD and Dr. Mark Lee Levine*, Editor

1. Geography

South Korea, officially known as Republic of Korea, is located in the southern half of the Korean peninsula in Eastern Asia, bordering the Sea of Japan and the Yellow Sea, south of North Korea. The total area of the peninsula is 219,020 square kilometers (km), similar in size to that of U.K, New Zealand, or Romania. At 99,720 sq. km, South Korea itself possesses 45% of the peninsula's total land mass, and North Korea has 120,540 sq. km, the remaining 55%. South Korea's coastline is 2,413 km long.

The country has a varied terrain, with about 70% of the peninsula being mountainous, particularly in the north and east. Most of the arable land lies in the west and south of the country. Along the southern and western coasts the mountains descend gradually towards broad coastal plains. About 15.64% of the land is arable, with only about 2.13% of the land is used as meadows and pastures. However, approximately 67% of the total land area is comprised of forests and woodlands. Most of South Korea's rivers have their tributaries on the north and east sides and flow into the Yellow and South Seas. There are four large rivers in Korea, the Apnok (Yalu) and the Tuman rivers

in North Korea, and the Naktong and the Han rivers in South Korea. Most arable land and major cities are located along these rivers. Along the southern and western coasts lie as many as 3,500 islands, of which by far the largest is Cheju.

The climate of Korea has four distinct seasons and is similar to that of the eastern United States. A pleasant spring is followed by a hot and humid summer with monsoon rains. Autumn is crisp and cool, and winters tend to be cold and dry. The Korean peninsula is generally protected from Southeast Asia's fall typhoons by the Japanese archipelago, and earthquakes are rarely experienced.

South Korea's main natural resources consist of coal, tungsten, graphite, molybdenum, lead, as well as hydropower, among others. Currently there are no known petroleum resources.

Environmental concerns consist of air pollution, water pollution, discharge of sewage and industrial fluids in major cities.

2. History and Overview

The first kingdom recorded in Korean history was Ko-Chosun (Ancient Chosun) established in B.C. 2333. Ko-Chosun lasted for about more than 2,000 years until China attacked it in B.C. 198. There then followed the "Three Kingdoms" period when the peninsula was split between Koguryo, Paekjae, and Shilla. The three kingdoms were eventually united under Shilla. However, the United Shilla again split into three kingdoms. It was in 935 A.D. that these three kingdoms were reunited under Koryo.

Around the 10th century, the Koryo Kingdom was engaged in trade as far away as the Middle East. The current English name for Korea is derived from this kingdom. The kingdom lasted until 1392 when the Chosun dynasty took power in a coup by Yi Song-Gye. The Chosun dynasty consolidated its power through a rigid and hierarchical social system based on neo- Confucianism.

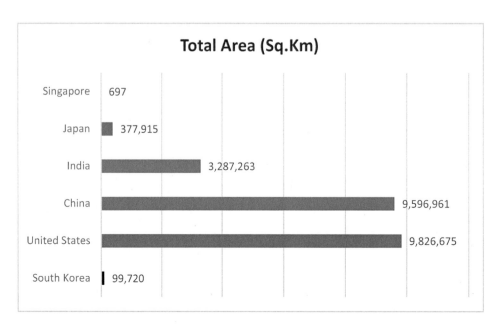

Total Area (Sq.Km)

Singapore	697
Japan	377,915
India	3,287,263
China	9,596,961
United States	9,826,675
South Korea	99,720

During the Chosun Dynast y, much social and cultural development took place. Movable type printing was invented. Under King Sejong the Great, the Hangul script was devised as the Korean alphabet, and is considered perhaps the most linguistically scientific writing system in the world. Confucian culture permeated the life of Korean people as the dynasty made neo-Confucianism its official code.

Throughout most of its history, Korea has been invaded, influenced, and fought over by its larger neighbors due to its strategic location. During the Chosun dynasty, Korea suffered numerous foreign invasions. Chosun dynasty lasted until the Japanese annexation in 1910. Japan ruled Korea from 1910 until its defeat in World War II. During the Japanese occupation, Japan attempted to impose cultural assimilation upon Koreans and mobilized Koreans forcibly in wartime. Korea became independent upon the Japanese surrender. However, the joy over the Japanese defeat was short-lived because Korea was split between American and Soviet occupation forces, and Koreans became deeply ideologically and politically divided. As a result, the Republic of Korea was declared on August 15, 1948 with Syng-Man Rhee as President in the area south of the 38th parallel and on September 3, 1948, the Soviet-influenced Democratic People's Republic of Korea was declared with Kim Il-Sung as its leader in the north. The UN General Assembly approved the Republic of Korea as the only legal government of the whole of Korea.

In 1950, North Korea launched a full-scale attack on South Korea. The United Nations (UN), declaring the invasion illegal, resolved to dispatch forces. Sixteen UN members including the United States, the United Kingdom, Turkey, France, and Canada dispatched troops to protect the newly established democracy. The internecine war dragged on for three years, leaving both sides devastated economically, and families separated even to this day. Armistice negotiations began in July 1951, but hostilities continued until 1953 with heavy losses on both sides. On July 27, 1953 the military commanders of the North Korean Army, the Chinese People's Volunteers, and the U.N. Commission (UNC) signed an armistice agreement at Panmunjom. Neither the United States nor South Korea is a signatory of the armistice per se, though both adhere to it through the UNC. No comprehensive peace agreement has replaced the1953 armistice pact; thus, both South Korea and North Korea are still technically at war. Though both Korean governments have repeatedly affirmed their desire for reunification of the Korean Peninsula, the two had no official communication or other contact until 1971. In 1988, two-way trade between North and South Korea was legalized. The trade between the two Koreas hit almost $1.82 billion in 2008 before declining sharply thereafter. Until recently, South Korea was North Korea's second-largest trading partner after China. Unfortunately, North-South economic ties were seriously damaged by escalating tensions following North Korea's torpedoing of the South Korean warship Cheonan in March 2010. In April 2010, North Korea seized five properties at Mt. Geumgang owned by South Korea's

Hyundai Asan. In September 2010, South Korea suspended all inter-Korean trade with the exception of the Kaesong Industrial Complex. In November 2010, North Korea attacked Yeonpyeong Island with artillery, further escalating tensions between the North and South. As of March 2012, economic ties had not seen signs of revival.

■ 3. People

The origins of the Korean people are obscure. Korea was first populated by a people or peoples who migrated to the peninsula from the northwestern regions of Asia, some of whom also settled parts of northeast China (Manchuria). Koreans are racially and linguistically homogeneous, with no sizable indigenous minorities, except for some Chinese (approximately 20,000).

South Korea's major population centers are in the northwest area and to the south of Seoul-Inch'on. The mountainous central and eastern areas are sparsely inhabited. The Japanese colonial administration of 1910-1945 concentrated its industrial development efforts in the comparatively under-populated and resource-rich north, resulting in a considerable migration of people to the north from the southern agrarian provinces. This trend was reversed after World War II as Koreans returned to the south from Japan and Manchuria. In addition, more than 2 million Koreans moved to the south from the north following the division of the peninsula into U.S. and Soviet military zones of administration in 1945. This migration continued after the Republic of Korea was established in 1948 and during the Korean War (1950-1953). About 10% of the people now in the Republic of Korea are of northern origin. With **49,039,986** people, South Korea has one of the world's highest population densities– much higher, for example, than India or Japan– while the territorially larger North Korea has substantially less people. Ethnic Koreans now residing in other countries live mostly in China (1.9 million), the United States (1.52 million), Japan (681,000), and the countries of the former Soviet Union (450,000).

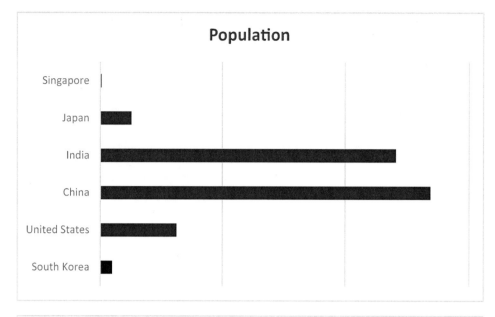

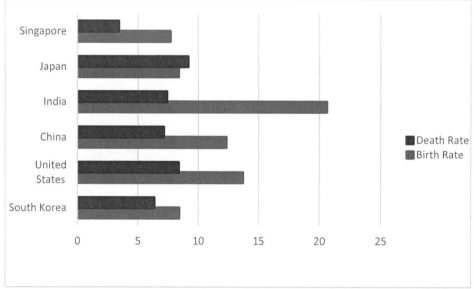

The population growth rate is 0.16% (2014 est.) Birth rates are 8.26 out of 1,000 population (2014 est.); death rate is about 6.63 per thousand in population (2014 est.) Infant mortality is almost 3.93 per 1,000 live births. Life expectancy is 79.8 years of age overall, with 76.67 years for males and about 83.13 years for females.

The age structure is dominated by approximately 73.2% in the 15 to 64 age category, with 14.1% in the 0 to 14-year range. The balance, 12.7%, is in the 65 years of age and older. The labor force is 26,430,000 (2014), a little under one-half of the total population. Of the total, 69.4% are in the service industry, with 23.6% in industry and 6.9% in agriculture, fishing, and forestry.

Religion: South Korea's traditional religions are Buddhism and Shamanism. Buddhism has lost some influence over the years, but is still followed by about 24.2% of the population.

Shamanism–traditional spirit worship–is still practiced. Confucianism remains a dominant cultural influence. Since the Japanese occupation, it has existed more as a shared base than as a separate philosophical/religious school. Some sources place the number of adherents of Chondogyo–a native religion founded in the mid-19th century that fuses elements of Confucianism and Christianity—make it significant in South Korea. Christian missionaries arrived in South Korea as early as the 16th century, but it was not until the 19th century that they founded schools, hospitals, and other modern institutions throughout the country. Christianity is now one of Korea's largest religions.

Language: Korean is the official language and is spoken throughout the country. All Koreans speak the same language with only minor regional variations.

Literacy is very high at 98% for those in the ages 15 and older who can read and write. Koreans place a strong emphasis on education, following Confucian philosophy. Education has been the essential basis for social advance and a major factor in Korea's fast economic development over the past three decades.

English is a common second language and is taught in middle and high schools.

Chinese and Japanese are widely taught at secondary schools.

■ 4. Government

The South Korean government consists of three major divisions: the Executive, the Legislative, and the Judicial. Executive authority in the Republic of Korea is in the hands of the President, who is elected by Korean citizens for a five- year term but may not be re-elected. The President is the chair of the state cabinet, which consists of the Prime Minister and the heads of the executive ministries. By order of the President, the Prime Minister is responsible for the overall co- ordination of the various ministries and agencies.

Legislative power is exercised by a unicameral national assembly under a multiparty system. The assembly's 299 members are directly elected by popular vote to four-year terms.

The Judiciary is independent. It functions on three levels: the Supreme Court, High Courts, and District and Family Courts. Another entity, the Constitution Committee, rules on constitutional and other questions, including impeachment referred by lower courts. The Supreme Court has final review of the constitutionality of statutes and the legality of administrative decrees. It also hears final appeals from lower courts and from military court martial. The legal system is a combination of European civil law, Anglo-American law and Chinese classical positions.

The Republic of South Korea is divided administratively into nine provinces and six main cities - Seoul, Pusan, Inch'on, Taegu, Kwangju, and Taejon – which have provincial status. South Korea celebrates its independence day in August 15, 1948. Suffrage is at 20 years of age and is universal.

South Korea has defense forces in the form of Army, Air Force, Navy, Marine Corps, and National Maritime Police (Coast Guard).

Diplomatic representation exists through the South Korean Ambassador located in Washington, D.C. and the U.S. Ambassador located in Seoul. ROK is a member of numerous international associations.

In August 1991, South Korea joined the United Nations (UN) along with North Korea, and since then has been active in most UN specialized agencies and many international organizations. The Republic of Korea has also hosted major international events such as the 1988 Summer Olympics and has co-hosted the 2002 World Cup (with Japan). South Korea became a member of the Organization for Economic Cooperation and Development (OECD) in 1996 and completed a term as a non-permanent member on the UN Security Council at the end of 1997.

South Korea maintains diplomatic relations with more than 170 countries and a broad network of trading relationships. Former President Roh's policy of Nordpolitik–the pursuit of wide-ranging relations with socialist nations and contact with North Korea–has been a remarkable success. The R.O.K. now has diplomatic ties with all the countries of Eastern and Central Europe, as well as the former Soviet republics. The R.O.K. and the People's Republic of China established full diplomatic relations in August 1992.

Since normalizing relations in 1965, Korea and Japan have developed an extensive relationship centering on mutually beneficial economic activity. Although historic antipathies have at times impeded cooperation, relations at the government level have improved steadily and significantly.

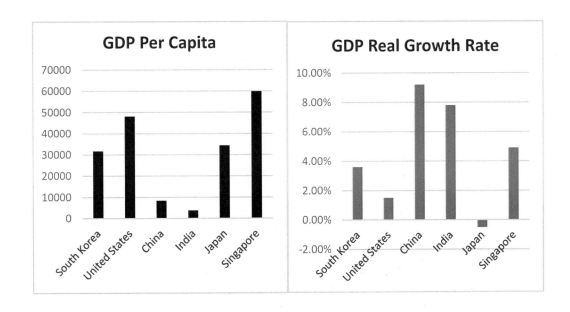

■ 5. Economy

Since the end of the Korean War in 1953, the Republic of Korea has achieved astounding economic growth. Under the leadership of President Park Chung-Hee, who took power through a coup in 1961, South Korea accomplished an incredible economic development. The Republic of Korea's economic growth over the past 30 years has been spectacular. Per capita GNP, only $100 in 1963, exceeded $10,000 in 1997, was $27,100 (2008), and was $35,400 in 2014. One of the world's poorest countries only a generation ago, South Korea is now the United States' seventh-largest trading partner and is the 14th largest economy in the world.

The Asian financial crisis, which began in 1997, has drastically affected South Korea's economy. In November 1997, Korea followed Thailand and Indonesia in suffering a loss of international confidence, resulting in a severe foreign exchange liquidity crisis. The South Korean *won* experienced a loss of over 50% of its value against the dollar by the end of 1997, and foreign currency reserves dropped to dangerously low levels. In December 1997, South Korea signed an enhanced $58 billion International Monetary Fund (IMF) package, including loans from the IMF, World Bank and the Asia Development Bank. Under the terms of the IMF program, South Korea agreed to accelerate the opening of its financial and equity markets to foreign investment and to reform and restructure its financial and corporate sectors to increase transparency, account ability and efficiency. Today, the Korean government is zealously restructuring the financial, corporate, and government sectors. The South Korean government is making efforts to internationalize its market. President Lee Myung-bak was elected in December 2007 on a platform that promised to boost Korea's economic growth rate through deregulation, tax reform, increased FDI, labor reform, and free trade agreements (FTAs) with major markets. The current administration has planned for one percent tax reduction in income for salary and self-employed people. To increase real estate sales transactions and relieve tax related burdens on families, the government plans to reduce capital gains and property holding taxes.

The U.S.-South Korea Free Trade Agreement:

In 2011, the U.S.-South Korea Free Trade Agreement (KORUS FTA) was ratified by both governments and went into effect on 3/15/2012. The KORUS FTA is the second-largest U.S. FTA (next to NAFTA). South Korea is the seventh largest trading partner of the United States, and the United States is South Korea's third-largest trading partner. The KORUS FTA covers a wide range of trade and investment issues and, therefore, could have substantial economic implications for both the United States and South Korea.

A primary objective of the United States was to gain access to South Korean markets in agricultural products, pharmaceuticals and medical equipment, some other high technology manufactured goods, and services, particularly financial and professional services—areas in which U.S. producers are internationally competitive but for which South Korean barriers seemed to be high. For South Korea, gaining a large increase in market access was not as critical a priority since South Korean exporters already have a significant presence in areas in which they have proved to be competitive—consumer electronics and autos, for example, and in which they already face only low or zero U.S. tariffs. However, South Korea arguably did seek to preserve its share of the U.S. market in the face of growing competition from emerging East Asian producers from Thailand, Malaysia, Vietnam, and possibly China. South Korea likely also aimed to improve its competitive position in the U.S. market vis-à-vis Japan where the elimination of even low tariffs might give South Korean exporters some price advantage.

Liberalization of direct foreign investment:

The Foreign Investment Promotion Act was passed to expand opportunities for international investors. All types of businesses will be opened to them. Furthermore, non-South Korean participation in equity transactions is now allowed even in large public enterprises and key industries through privatization measures.

In July 1998, all major restrictions on non-South Korean acquisition and use of real estate were removed. So, non-South Koreans are now allowed to purchase, rent, and sublet subdivide residential and non-residential buildings freely. Tax benefits of various kinds are provided for foreign investors. The tax concession period has been extended from the current eight years to ten years, and the range of tax exemptions was expanded to include high-tech and value- added service industries.

Local governments were granted greater autonomy in offering tax exemptions for non-South Koreans.

South Korea's Key Industries:
South Korean economic development was made possible by export-oriented strategies, highly skilled human resources, and effective industrial policies. Korea's five major industries are: (1) automobiles (fifth largest in the world); (2) semiconductors (third largest in the world); (3) iron and steel (Korea's iron & steel industry had grown to be the world's sixth largest by 1991); (4) petrochemicals (Despite its relatively short history, Korea's petrochemical industry has grown into the world's fifth largest, accounting for approximately 4% of Korea's aggregate production and 5.1% of worldwide ethylene production capacity.); (5) shipbuilding. (South Korea ranks top in the global shipbuilding industry. Hyundai, Daewoo, and Samsung are the three biggest ship builders in the world.)

Financial Institutions:
The financial institutions in Korea may be divided into three categories by function: a central bank, the Bank of Korea; banking institutions including commercial and specialized banks; and nonbank financial institutions including development, savings, investment, insurance, and other institutions.

The South Korean financial system has been undergoing substantial changes in the course of the implementation of a comprehensive financial reform program, which is a part of agreement with the IMF that the Korean government promised to pursue upon the signing of the financial aid package. These are broad measures designed to spur financial liberalization and internationalization. This has coincided with a shift from a government-orientated stance on economic policy towards a more market-oriented stance.

South Korea is becoming a very attractive country for investment, providing good investment opportunities for foreigners. It is situated as an ideal manufacturing and distribution center for a still highly dynamic region.

■ 6. Currency

The unit of Korean currency is the *won*. Coin denominations are 1, 10, 50, 100, and 500. Bank notes are 1,000, 5,000 and 10,000. The exchange rate fluctuates with market conditions. See the Burns School Global Real Estate Website, Daniels *College of Business*, UNIVERSITY OF DENVER at http://burns.daniels.du.edu for currency conversions.

■ 7. Transportation

South Korea has an increasingly sophisticated transportation system serving domestic and international travelers.

Civil Aviation: Although most interurban travel was either by express bus or by train, air service between major cities was increasingly available and popular, especially among business travelers. Korean Air, founded by the government in 1962 and privately owned since 1969, was South Korea's sole airline until 1988. A second carrier, Asiana Airlines, was established in 1988 to serve three domestic cities. Asiana now serves international cities. As of the end of 2004, the two carriers served 95 cities around the world ranking 5th in the world in annual cargo handling capacity and 12th in passenger transport. Until 2001, Seoul's main international airport was Kimp'o International Airport. It nearly doubled in size by 1989 (largely because of the Seoul Olympics) to accommodate the rapidly growing number of air travelers.

The new international airport was completed in 2001 in the city of Inch'on. All international airlines in the Kimpo International Airport moved to Inch'on International Airport when it officially opened in 2001, leaving Kimp'o Airport to serve only the domestic flights. Inch'on International Airport is projected to become the biggest air hub in the Northeast Asia with an annual capacity of 100 million passengers and 7 million tons of cargo by the year of 2020. With its strategic location, Inch'on International Airport is poised to become a leading logistics and transportation hub in Northeast Asia. Expansion plans for the airport area include establishing a Free Trade Zone, International Business District and Special Economic Zone. There also are international airports at Pusan and Cheju; another is planned for Ch'ongju. There are 111 airports (2013) and 466 heliports (2013).

Seaports: There are two major ports in South Korea: Pusan and Inch'on. These ports are linked to Seoul by double-track railroad lines. The annual cargo handling Whatcapability of Korea's ports in 2003 amounted to about 596 million tons.

Subways and Railroads: In 1990, subways were gradually replacing buses as the main means of transportation in Seoul. The Seoul subway, the first part of which opened in 1974, was operated by the Seoul Metropolitan Rapid Transit Company. In 1990 the subway had more than 200 kilometers (km) of track, enabling commuters to reach any station within the 45-km radius of the capital city within an hour. One line connected Seoul with Inch'on. Four subway lines served Seoul, in addition to the lines of the Korean National Railroad. In 2005 the system carried approximately 5,600,000 million passengers daily. Seoul's subway system is the eighth largest in the world. South Korea has an excellent railroad network. The first railroad, which linked Seoul and Inch'on, was opened in September 1899. Other major lines included lines originating in Mokp'o, Masan, and Pusan. These lines connected to Seoul and to Sinuiju in North Korea, where they were linked with the Trans-Siberian Railway. The railroad network was badly damaged during the Korean War, but it was later rebuilt and improved.

Throughout the 1970s and 1980s, the Korean National Railroad, a state-run corporation under the Ministry of Transportation, was in charge of all rails and continued electrifying heavily used tracks and laying additional tracks. As of 2005, the combined length of the country's railroad network was approximately 3,472 km, including approximately 1,361 km of electric railroads. Suburban lines were electrified and connected to the Seoul subway system.

The high-speed service linking Seoul with the southern port city of Pusan was launched in April 2004. The new bullet train service, dubbed Korea Train Express or KTX, will cut travel time from Seoul to Pusan to two hours and 10 minutes from four and a half hours when the entire project is finished in 2010. It is expected to help ease current traffic congestion on highways. There are currently 3,381 km of railways in South Korea (2014).

Roads: Domestic transportation improved greatly during the 1980s, and growth was evident in all sectors. The rapid improvement and extension of public roads and the increasing availability of motor vehicles contributed enormously to the mobility of the population. Approximately 104,983 km of roadways spanned the country in 2014, 83,199 km of which were paved. Express highways facilitated travel between major cities and reached a combined length of 3,779 kilometers in 2014, as compared to 86.8 kilometers in 1967.

8. Communications

Communications services improved dramatically in the 1980s with the assistance of international partners and as a result of the development of the electronics industry. The number of telephones in use in 2012 reached 30.1 million and mobile cellular telephones reached 53.625 million.

Radio, and in more recent years television, reached virtually every resident. The Japanese established a radio station in Seoul in 1927. By 1945 there were about 60,000 radio sets in the country. By 2002, there were approximately 47,500,000 radio receivers in use, and 61 AM and 150 FM radio stations, as well as 2 short wave radio stations, In 2014, there were multiple public and privately-owned radio stations. Transistor radios and television sets have made their way to the most remote rural areas.

Most city people and a significant number of rural families owned or had access to a television. Ownership of television sets grew to an estimated 15,900,000 sets in 2002, and 121 television stations were broadcasting (2002). There were approximately 15,900,000 television sets in 2002, and 121 television stations were broadcasting (2002). In 2008, there were 57 television broadcast stations, plus 103 cable operators and 119 relay cable operations). In 2010, there were multiple public and privately-owned television stations. In 2012 there were 315,697 Internet service providers (hosts) with an estimated 39,400,000 people using the Internet (2009). Although all mail is subject to postal inspection, mail service is reliable. International courier service is also available.

9. Real Property Issues

Property laws were significantly influenced by non-Korean countries. From 1910 through 1945, Korea was under Japanese occupation. Korea was heavily influenced by Japanese legal systems and adopted many Japanese laws. Japanese law was heavily influenced by European civil codes, especially with respect to property laws. When Korea was freed from Japanese occupation in 1945, the U.S. government had a major role in assisting the South Korean government's transition. Because U.S. property law was used as a model for some areas of property law in South Korea, it is, therefore, important to remember that real property law in Korea follows both U.S. and European law. South Koreans are very pragmatic people. This pragmatism and cultural context is apparent in the legal system. For example, both purchase contract and lease agreement documents in Korea typically encompass only a single page. Long complex documents are loathed by Koreans, who dislike the very concept of written contracts, and prefer to consummate deals only through handshakes. They like simplicity, not complication. In the Orient, common sense and tradition still dominates the contractual relationship. Written contracts are not looked upon as legally binding as in America. The country is aggressively modernizing and revising its systems. Therefore, it is important to keep in mind that materials presented in this section can change quickly.

In July 1998, a law was passed which allows non-South Korean individuals or companies to acquire Korean real estate the same as the South Korean people or South Korean companies. It removed and eased the limitations on purchases of land so that the market will be completely open to non-South Koreans. South Koreans abroad will now be able to purchase land or building under the same conditions as resident South Koreans. Non-South Koreans will not only be able to buy real estate for business reasons but also for non-business purposes.

Commercial Leases in South Korea

The typical lease period is one year and renewable at market rents. Leases of up to five years are obtainable but *key money* (earnest money/performance funds) and rentals would be subject to review annually. However, there is no specific guideline in writing for level of rent readjustment.

Floor Space Measurements: Floor space is generally measured on a gross basis. **Rent and Additional Rent:** Rent is usually charged separately from additional charges such as air conditioning, management charges, utilities and car parking. These are independently charged to the tenant's account. The normal practice of paying rent is by paying deposit money plus a monthly rental. The proportions vary with different landlords. Frequently, the tenant may pay only key money and no rental. The amount of the key money can be very substantial, but is normally fully refundable without any interest.

Rent Adjustment during the Lease: In accordance with the law, landlords are entitled to adjust the rent even within the fixed 1-year or 2-year lease period. However, landlords seldom exercise this right.

Incentives Offered by the Landlords: Very few incentives are offered by landlords. These days, discounts of about 20% would be granted for premises outside the central business district area where the market is much softer. It is quite common for units to be let with very few fittings, although a finished floor, painted walls, and lighting would be considered standard.

Tenant Improvements: The handling of tenants' improvements depends on the agreement reached between the two parties. In most cases, all improvement work normally paid for by the tenant has to be approved by the landlord. Plans need to be submitted and approval obtained prior to commencement of the work. At the end of the lease the property must be put back to the condition it was at the beginning of the lease with the exception of fair wear and tear at the cost of the tenant.

Options to renew the lease: It is common for tenants to be granted to renew their leases.

Residential Leases in South Korea

Advance Payment (Rent): The most common method in non-South Korean communities in Seoul requires advance payment of the total monthly rental for the entire lease term. The contract is usually signed for two years to three years. No money is returned at expiration of the lease. But prepaid rental is refundable prorated for the unexpired term of a lease, if the lease is terminated prior to expiration date. One of the merits of this method is that the landlord is responsible for maintenance during the lease period. Rent does not normally include utility cost s, such as electricity, water, gas and heating.

Monthly Rental (Wolsei): This method is a deposit plus monthly payment system. The deposit amount is about 10 times to 20 times the monthly payment. Usually 10% of the total amount is paid up front when signing the contract and the remainder plus one month's rental is paid at the time of actual move-in. The amount deposited is returned to the tenant upon expiration of the lease. The tenant is responsible for maintenance.

Traditional Lease (Chonsei): In this method about 40 to 80% of the value of the house is deposited with the owner for the lease period. The whole portion is returned upon expiration of the lease. The tenant may use the house for the duration of the contract without monthly payment. The interest on the deposit serves as rent. When the contract has expired, the deposit is returned to the tenant.

Common practice is that the landlord is not responsible for maintenance. Accordingly, the tenant is required to cope with all maintenance issues by himself or herself unless otherwise provided in the pertinent lease contract. For example, replacement of curtains or repapering of rooms will be on the tenant's expense. ***Standard Official Land Price:*** Land pieces which can serve as a standard for land prices of that area are chosen from among countrywide land masses, and are called *land samples* (450,000 land parcels nationwide, hereafter referred to as *sample lands*). It is the responsibility of the Minister of Construction and Transportation to survey such lands and notify the appropriate land price per unit width, won per square meter (m sq), on the first of January. It is, however, generally notified at the end of February.

Brokerage fee rates vary depending on the market price of the property involved in the transaction. The customary real estate brokerage fees in South Korea are outlined in the table below.

Taxation on the Acquisition of Real Property: When a company (individual) acquires real property, it must pay an acquisition tax on the items regardless of how it was acquired, e.g. purchase, inheritance, gift etc. The voluntarily reported price, i.e., actual acquisition cost, at the time of acquisition is the tax base for the acquisition tax. However, the value reported should be no less than the "standard value" determined by the local government every year unless the value can be verified by the company's books or judicial decisions. Thus, when a company acquires taxable assets, actual acquisition cost shall be the tax base since actual cost is verifiable on the books. The standard tax rate is 2% of the tax base. In case where business property is acquired in the Seoul Metropolitan Area (SMA) prescribed by the law for use of a company's head office, it will be subject to a 6% tax rate (three times the

Customary Real Estate Brokerage Fee Rate in South Korea

Type of Transaction	Market Price	Upper Limit of Rate(%)	Limit Price of Fee (Thousand won)
Buying, Selling, and Exchange	Under 50 million won	0.6	250
	Over 50 million won-Under 0.2 billion won	0.5	800
	Over 0.2 billion won-Under 0.6 billion won	0.4	Mutual Contract
	Non-residential building-Land and Buying and Selling Price is over 0.6 billion won		Mutual contract between client and broker within 0.2-0.9%
Leasing:	Under 50 million won	0.5	200
	Over 50 million won-Under 0.1 billion won	0.4	300
	Over 0.1 billion won- Under 0.3 billion won	0.3	Mutual contract
	Over 0.3 billion won		Mutual contract between client and broker within 0.2-0.8%

normal tax rate). Several items such as villa, golf course, non-business purpose land are subject to five times the standard taxation, i.e., 10%.

Registration Tax: A company (individual) is obliged to pay Registration Tax when it (one) officially registers the acquisition, transfer, alteration, or expiration of property rights or other titles subject to statutory registration laws. The tax base for the registration of real property and motor vehicles is the actual value at the time of registration. As in the case of the Acquisition Tax, the tax base should be voluntarily reported by the taxpayer and the value reported should be no less than the standard value determined by the local government. Tax rates vary depending on the reason of registration or the type of property that is registered.

Education Surtax: The purpose of the Education Tax is to secure funds for improvement of the educational environment. It is a surtax that should be paid when filing and paying the Registration tax, Property tax, and Aggregate Land Tax. **Stamp Tax:** Stamp Tax is levied on documents for establishing, transfer, or changing the ownership or rights on real property, such as contracts for sale, property leasing, loan property insurance, etc. Duty rates range from KW 100 to KW 350,000 depending on the type of documents.

■ 10. Real Estate Trends

Until recently, a major obstacle to non-South Korean investment in the country had been the myriad legal and regulatory provisions related to international investment. However, to boost investment, these have been coordinated and simplified in a single legal framework, the Foreign Investment Promotion Act (FIPA), which was passed by the National Assembly in September 1998. The FIPA provides international investors with a one-stop service based on centralized regulations, in sharp contrast to the previous web of complex procedures.

Office Market: The average annual office rental in Seoul CBD in 2008 was $54.96 per square foot. Despite the global financial crisis, demand for office spaces remains strong for the metropolitan areas of Seoul. Tenants are seeking more spaces in existing buildings due to a healthy economy driven by Korea's strong exports sector. Office vacancy is average 0.36%.

Residential Market: Residential market has seen healthy growth due to South Korea's strong economy, which has averaged 5.5% growth from 2001 to 2006.

During this period, especially in metropolitan areas of Seoul, owing to its proximity to employment, business, culture, and education, the residential real estate market experienced an average 70% increase in value appreciation. But in 2007, because of high property taxes, slow economy, and strict mortgage regulations, the residential real estate market softened.

Similar to the US, homeownership is regarded as the path to wealth and security.

Seoul and its surrounding areas are home to 20 million people out of the country's population of close to 49 million. With current administration's pro-business stance, the government is implementing policies to re-energize residential real estate market.

Title Insurance: One of the biggest complaints among foreign investors in Asia were over property titles. As with many other countries, South Korea uses land registry system which is similar to the Torrens Land Registration system used in the U.S.[188]

However, the land registry system used in South Korea has some major perils. The Korean government does not guarantee the validity, truth or accuracy of these Korean land registry records. Its main function is to make public the recorded land ownership and lien information for the benefit of third parties and interested parties. Also, Korean attorneys have not historically been involved in searching title and giving a certificate of title. The parties to the transaction were simply left to do their own title search and take their own risks, even for commercial deals.

Aside from the U.S. and few other countries, title insurance has not been widely adopted. However, since the opening of Korean real estate to the global market following the 1997 Asian financial crisis, which promoted the global flow of investment capital, and the introduction of REITs and debt securitization, title insurance is accepted as a necessary part of real estate transactions.

Although title insurance is still at its early stage in South Korea, the growth of its usage is expected to increase to satisfy foreign investors and to meet the global financial standards.

Real Estate Investment Trusts: After the 1997 Asian financial crisis, many Korean companies under corporate restructuring put their properties for sale on the market. The influx of real estate in the market caused a significant asset deflation. In order to lessen the asset deflation, the South Korean government introduced the asset-backed securities (ABS) system and the mortgage-backed securities (MBS) system in 1999. However, general securitization of real estate was not implemented until the enactment of the *Real Estate Investment Trusts Act* (REITs Act) in 2001, which is largely modeled on US REITs regulations. In 2005, an amendment was made to the REITs Act to facilitate increased usage of REITs and to protect investors. This amendment, which was designed to promote the use of REITs and the protection of investors, should encourage indirect investment in real estate by the public and institutional investors. With the introduction of REITs, considerable changes are expected in the capital market as well as real estate market in Korea. **Land Acquisition by non-South Koreans:** Until 1998, non-South Korean individuals or corporations were not allowed to purchase real estate except for restricted uses, such as plants, offices, warehouses and other auxiliary buildings, and employee's residences. The South Korean government has now liberalized land acquisition systems on a drastic scale, fully opening the domestic real estate market. Moreover, the present policy requiring approval will soon be shifted to one of granting permission upon notice. This opening of the domestic real estate market is expected to help stimulate international investments. This opening of domestic real estate market to foreigners is providing both efficiency and transparency to the South Korean real estate market.

New Laws Concerning Acquisition and Management by Foreigners: Regulations concerning the use and limiting the area of land acquired by non-South Korean corporations were abolished, putting them on an equal footing with South Korean corporations. In the case of mergers and acquisitions of this type, the non-business land of the South Korean company may be kept by the non-South Korean-invested corporation. When resident or nonresident foreigners acquire land properties, national treatment is applied. A simple notification system is adopted in the case of acquisition of land by a non-South Korean. While acquisition of land is liberalized, it does not include land set aside for military use, cultural heritage protection, or wildlife protection. Rule of Reciprocity is adopted. If acquisition of land is restricted in another country it will be restricted in South Korea.

Free Trade Area: The government has designated several free export zones for the bonded processing of imported materials into finished goods for export. The free export zones are specially established industrial areas where non-South Korean- invested firms can manufacture, assemble, or process export products using freely imported, tax-free raw materials, or semi-finished goods. Tax incentives are provided for foreign invested firms.

Foreign Investment Zone: The South Korean government also established an area as Foreign Investment Zone (FIZ). These areas are designated according to investor's preference. All foreign firms locating in a FIZ will be eligible for tax reductions, and financial support will be provided to foster FIZ development. Medical, educational, and housing facilities will be provided at discretion of the Foreign Direct Investment (FDI) committee.

■ 11. Cultural Issues

Any nation's culture is complex and vibrant in its diversity. While broad cultural characterizations such as those presented here can be generally accurate, following such generalities too strictly may be dangerously misleading. To conduct business effectively and profitably in a country, it is vital to have a thorough understanding of its culture's complexities.

Though Koreans have transitioned greatly into Western society, the traditional ways of thinking in many areas are still practiced. Korea still observes Confucian ethics based on a strong belonging to a group. Whereas an American may think in individual terms, i.e., "what is in my best interest?", the Korean oftentimes thinks in group terms, i.e., what is in the best interest of the group and how can I help to maintain harmony within the group? For this reason, the majority of Koreans are

intensely patriotic. To negotiate the close of a deal, persuasively put forth the benefits to the group, whether it is to the company or country.

Koreans have a great respect for the family and hierarchy. Koreans still have a great respect for anyone senior in age, and intuitively establish their hierarchical position relative to others based on age. When doing business, Americans should be sensitive to Korea's historical relationship with Japan, which made a virtual colony of the Korean peninsula. Because of the Japanese colonial period, Koreans have an emotionally intense reaction at times to things Japanese, though there is an admiration for Japanese business acumen. A business person should show great respect towards the Korean society. Any comparative mention of Japan versus Korea, where Japan has the upper edge, may harm a business deal.

For South Koreans, relationships are all important. "Cold calls" don't work. Introductions are crucial! South Koreans want to do business with people with whom they have formed a personal connection or whereby a mutual intermediary has made an introduction. Alumni contacts are a major source of networking in South Korea. Americans should be ready to mix business with social life as the South Koreans base their business relationships on personal ones.

The exchange of business cards is very important and a means by which South Koreans learn about the name, position and status of the other person. Koreans observe a very strict hierarchical code, where Koreans will generally meet to discuss business with persons of the same, parallel rank. Businesspersons should always have their preferably bilingual business cards at the ready and should treat the exchange of a counterpart's card with respect. For example, it is a sign of respect to receive and present items with both hands, followed in business etiquette by passing and receiving a card with the right hand. One should never give a card, or anything else for that matter, with the left hand as it shows disrespect). For historical reasons, Chinese characters, which South Koreans can generally understand, are regarded as more sophisticated. As such, a business card written in Chinese characters can serve for a business trip to South Korea, China, and Japan. Negotiating style is particularly important. South Koreans can prove subtle and effective negotiators, and a commitment to a rigid negotiating tact early on may work to the non-South Korean's disadvantage. Your offer may include the best price, technology and profit potential but still be turned down because the South Korean customer does not like your style.

An important point to keep in mind concerns the nature of reaching an agreement with a Korean firm. Westerners attach great importance to a written contract which specifies each detail of the business relationship. South Koreans, on the other hand, value a contract as a loosely structured consensus statement that broadly defines what has been negotiated but leaves sufficient room to permit flexibility and adjustment. The Korean Government has attempted to address this dual perception by formulating "model" contracts for licensing technology and other arrangements. Both parties must be assured the obligations spelled out in a negotiated contract are fully understood.

12. Discussion Questions

1. What are some environmental issues in South Korea?

2. What is the economic impact on South Korea as a result of its proximity to North Korea?

3. What cultural aspects of Korea should foreigners be aware of when conducting business in Korea; discuss topics that could be insulting to Koreans.

13. Case Study

Memo

To: Board of Directors
From: Consultants
Re: Lack of teachers

I. Problem

Construction Vocational Training (CVT) Amman, Jordan Newest satellite offices in Jordan and South Korea Construction Vocational Training (CVT) has entered a number of countries. It provides construction trade vocational training. CVT has established offices in Kenya, and has recently opened offices in **South Korea** and Jordan. Both locations we are having a difficult time finding teachers. Either they are unavailable in the country, or the teachers that CVT brings from another country decide to leave after a short term. Because of the lack of teachers, both sights must be reviewed for a possible closing.

II. Initial Exit Strategy

The initial exit strategy was never solidified. CVT rents a small office, with a class room setting. CVT can exit both leases without too much difficulty or cost. CVT would need to finish the classes currently in session, through the end of the year. Once that has been completed, CVT would need to terminate its advertising. This can be accomplished within a month.

III. Contingency Exit Strategy

It would be difficult in either country to exit much more quickly than the initial exit strategy plan.

IV. Conclusion (ALTERNATIVE APPROACH)

At this time, it is suggested that CVT close the school with the least amount of activity. Then CVT could hire teachers for two-week periods, fly them in and pay for all of their expenses; and then fly them back. This way they will not be in the country long enough to want to leave. CVT can obtain a variety of professionals. CVT should give this plan six months, and then it should reevaluate the situation.

Refer to: Trafficking in Persons Report. June 5, 2002, released by the Office to Monitor and Combat Trafficking in Persons. (Retrieved September 18, 2002). http://www.state.gov/g/tip/rls/tiprpt/2002/10653.htm.

International Real Estate Digest. Homepage. http://www.ired.com. U.S. Embassy. Homepage. http://usembassy.state.gov. U.S. Department of State. Homepage. http://www.state.gov. X-rates.com. Homepage. http://www.x-rates.com/.

14. Selected References

Breen, Michael. The Koreans: Who They Are, What They Want, Where Their Future Lies, rev. ed. New York: Thomas Dunne, 2004.

Cherry, Judith. *Cassell Business Briefings Series, Republic of Korea*. London; New York: Cassell, 1993.

CIA World Factbook at https://www.cia.gov/library/publications/the-world-factbook/index.html.

DeMente, Boye. Korean Business Etiquette: the Cultural Values and Attitudes That Make Up the Korean Business Personality. Boston, Mass.: Tuttle

Books, 2004. Dresser, Norine. Multicultural Manners: Essential Rules of Etiquette for the 21st Century. rev. ed. New Jersey: John Wiley & Sons, 2005.

Dunung, Sanjyot. *Doing Business in Asia: The Complete Guide*. New York, NY: *Lexington Books*, 1995.

Friedman, Thomas L. The Lexus and the Olive Tree: Understanding Globalization.

New York: *Anchor Books, 2000.* (see update book editions) Kim, Eung Young. A Cross-Cultural Reference of Business practices in a New Korea.

West port, Connecticut : Quorum Books, 1996.

Kohls, L. Robert. Learning toT hink Korean: A Guide toLiving and Working in Korea. Yarmouth,ME:Intercultural Press,2001.

Koo, John H and Andrew C. Nahm. ed. An Introduction To Korean Culture. Elizabeth, NJ: Hollym, 1997.

Facts about Korea. 2000 edit ion. Korean Information Service, Seoul, Korea. International Real Estate Digest. Homepage. http://www.ired.com.

Richard Ellis International Property Specialists. http://www.cbre.com. Time Almanac. *TIME Almanac.* Boston: Information Please LLC.

Trompenaars, Fons, and Charles Hampden-Turner. Riding the Waves of Culture:

Understanding Diversity in Global Business. 2d ed. New York: McGraw Hill 1998. Trafficking in Persons Report. June 5, 2002, released by the Office to Monitor and Combat Trafficking in Persons. (Retrieved September 18, 2002).http://www.state.gov/g/tip/rls/tiprpt/2002/10653.htm.

United States Department of State.Background *Notes: South Korea.United* States Department of State (Online).Available:http://www.state.gov. U.S. Bureau of Census at http://www.census.gov.

U.S. Department of Commerce at http://www.stat-usa.gov. U.S. Bureau of Economic Analysis at http://www.bea.gov U.S. Embassy. Homepage. http://usembassy.state.gov.

Walker, Danielle, Thomas Walker, and Joerg Schmitz. The Guide to Cross Cultural Success: Doing Business Internationally. 2d ed. New York: McGraw Hill, 2003. World Trade Centers Institute at http://www.wtci.org.

World Trade Organization at http://www.wto.org.

World Bank (Unknown). *Adult Illiteracy Rates*. The Economist. p.124. X-rates.com. Homepage. http://www.x-rates.com/

15. Glossary

Foreign Investment Zone – South Korean government has established an area that is designated according to investor's preference. All firms located in a FIZ will be eligible for tax reduct ions, and financial support will be provided to foster FIZ development.

Hangul – the Korean alphabet.

Key Money – earnest money/performance money.

Ko-Chosun – (Ancient Chosun) the first kingdom recorded in Korean history. This kingdom lasted more than 2000 years.

No-ray-bang – where a group of businesspeople go to an establishment to drink and sing along to a video machine playing music. As most no-ray-bang machines come equipped with songs in English, a businessperson may want to be prepared to sing at least one song in order to gain social favor with their Korean counterpart.

Oo-ri-na-ra – (our country).

Room salons – where Korean women serve food and drink to their patrons.

Won – the currency of Korea.

ORGANIZATIONS:

AfDB: The African Development Bank (ADB) is a development finance institution engaged in the task of mobilizing resources towards the economic and social progress of its Regional Member Countries (RMCs). http://www.afdb.org. **APEC:** The Asia-Pacific Economic Cooperation (APEC) forum is the primary international organization for the promoting open trade and economic cooperation among 21 member economies around the Pacific Rim.http://www.apec.org.

ARF: The ASEAN Regional Forum (ARF) was set up in 1994 as a regional security dialogue platform and forum for security co-operation in the Asia-Pacific region. **AsDB:** The Asian Development Bank (ADB) is a multilateral development finance institution dedicated to reducing poverty in Asia and the Pacific.

ASEAN: The Association of Southeast Asian Nations (ASEAN) Declaration states that the aims and purposes of the Association are: (i) to accelerate the economic growth, social progress and cultural development in the region through joint endeavors in the spirit of equality and partnership in order to strengthen the foundation for a prosperous and peaceful community of Southeast Asian nations, and (ii) to promote regional peace and stability through abiding respect for justice and the rule of law in the relationship among countries in the region and adherence to the principles of the United Nations Charter.

Australia Group: The Australia Group is an informal group of countries that are committed to combating the proliferation of chemical and biological weapons. The countries participating in the Australia Group are suppliers and/or trans-shippers of chemicals, biological agents and/or production equipment which could be used in chemical and/or biological weapons programs. http://www.australiagroup.net.

BIS: The BIS is an international organization that fosters cooperation among central banks and other agencies in pursuit of monetary and financial stability. http://www.bis.org.

CP: Cleaner Production (CP) refers to a mentality of how goods and services are produced with the minimum environmental impact under present technological and economic limits. By achieving economic, environmental and health/safety benefits, Cleaner Production provides a significant contribution to achieving sustainable production and consumption.

EBRD: The European Bank for Reconstruction and Development (EBRD) uses the tools of investment to help build market economies and democracies in 27 countries from central Europe to central Asia. http://www.ebrd.com.

ESCAP: The regional arm of the United Nations Secretariat for the Asian and Pacific region is the Economic and Social Commission for Asia and the Pacific (ESCAP). It promotes economic and social development through regional and sub-regional cooperation and integration.http://www.unescap.org.

FAO: The Food and Agriculture Organization (FAO) of the United Nations was founded in 1945 with a mandate to raise levels of nutrition and standards of living, to improve agricultural productivity, and to better the condition of rural populations. http://www.fao.org.

G-77: As the largest Third World coalition in the United Nations, the Group of 77 (G-77) provides the means for the developing world to articulate and promote its collective economic interests and enhance its joint negotiating capacity on all major international economic issues in the United Nations system, and promote economic and technical cooperation among developing countries.http://www.g77.org.

IAEA: The International Atomic Energy Agency (IAEA) serves as the global focal point for nuclear cooperation. IAEA assists its Member States, in the context of social and economic goals, in planning for and using nuclear science and technology for various peaceful purposes, including the generation of electricity, and it facilitates the transfer of such technology and knowledge in a sustainable manner to developing Member States. http://www.iaea.or.at.

IBRD: An institution of the World Bank Group, the International Bank for Reconstruction and Development (IBRD) provides important support for poverty reduction by providing its middle-income client countries access to capital in larger volumes, on good terms, with longer maturities, and in a more sustainable manner than the market provides. http://www.worldbank.org.

ICAO: The International Civil Aviation Organization (ICAO) was established to develop the principles and techniques of international air navigation and to foster the planning and development of international air transport in order to: encourage the development of airways, airports, and air navigation facilities for international civil aviation; meet the needs of the world wide population for safe, efficient, and economical air transport; promote flight safety throughout international air navigation; and promote the development of all aspects of international civil aeronautics. http://www.icao.int .

ICC: The International Commerce Commission (ICC) promotes an open international trade and investment system and the market economy.

ICFTU: The International Confederation of Free Trade Unions (ICFTU) organizes and directs campaigns on issues such as: the respect and defense of trade union and workers' rights; the eradication of forced and child labor; the promotion of equal rights for working women; the environment; education programs for trade unionists all over the world; encouraging the organization of young workers; sends missions to investigate the trade union situation in many countries. http://www.icftu.org.

ICRM: The International Red Cross and Red Crescent Movement (ICRM) promotes worldwide humanitarian aid through the International Committee of the Red Cross (ICRC) in wartime, and International Federation of Red Cross and Red Crescent Societies (IFRCS; formerly League of Red Cross and Red Crescent Societies or LORCS) in peacetime.http://www.icrc.org.

IDA: The International Development Association (IDA) seeks to accelerate broad- based growth through sound macroeconomic and sect oral policies, especially for rural and private sect or development; to invest in

people through strong support for the social sectors, including gender mainstreaming and efforts to counter the challenge and social impact of communicable diseases, especially HIV/AIDS; to build capacity for improving governance–including in public expenditure management–and combating corruption; to protect the environment for sustainable development; to foster recovery in post-conflict countries; and to promote trade and regional integration. http://www.worldbank.org.

IEA: The International Energy Agency (IEA) promotes cooperation on energy matters, especially emergency oil sharing and relations between oil consumers and oil producers; established by the OECD.http://www.iea.org.

IFAD: The International Fund for Agricultural Development (IFAD) was created to mobilize resources on concessional terms for *programmes* that alleviate rural poverty and improve nutrition. The Fund has a very specific mandate: to combat hunger and rural poverty in developing countries.http://www.ifad.org.

IFC: The International Finance Corporation (IFC) supports private enterprise in international economic development andIBRDaffiliates.http://www.ifrc.org.

IFRCS: The International Federation of Red Cross and Red Crescent Societies (IFRCS) exists to organize, coordinate, and direct international relief actions; to promote humanitarian activities; to represent and encourage the development of National Societies; to bring help to victims of armed conflicts, refugees, and displaced people; and to reduce the vulnerability of people through development programs.http://www.ifrc.org.

IHO: The International Hydrographic Organization (IHO) is an intergovernmental consultative and technical organization that was established to support the safety in navigation and the protection of the marine environment.http://www.iho.shom.fr.

ILO: The International Labor Organization (ILO) deals with world labor issues. http://www.ilo.org.

IMF: The International Monetary Fund (IMF) promotes world monetary stability and economic development. http://www.imf.org.

IMO: The International Maritime Organization (IMO) deals with international maritime affairs.http://www.imo.org.

Inmarsat: The International Mobile Satellite Organization provides worldwide communications for commercial, distress, and safety applications, at sea, in the air, and on land.http://www.inmarsat.org.

Intelsat: The International Telecommunications Satellite Organization develops and operates a global commercial telecommunications satellite system. http://www.intelsat.com.

Interpol: The International Criminal Police Organization promotes international cooperation among police authorities in fighting crime. http://www.interpol.int.

IOC: The International Olympic Committee (IOC) promotes the Olympic ideals and administers the Olympic Games.http://www.olympic.org.

IOM: The International Organization for Migration (IOM) facilitates orderly international emigration and immigration. http://www.iom.int.

ISO: The International Organization for Standardization (ISO) promotes the development of international standards with a view to facilitating international exchange of goods and services and develops cooperation in the sphere of intellectual, scientific, technological, and economic activity. http://www.ico.ch.

ITU: The International Telecommunication Union (ITU) deals with world telecommunications issues. http://www.itu.int.

MINURSO: The United Nations Mission for the Referendum in Western Sahara (MINURSO) was established in May 1991,to enable the people of Western Sahara to choose freely between integration with Morocco or independence.

NAM: The Non-aligned Movement (NAM) establishes political and military cooperation apart from the traditional East or West blocs.

NEA: The Nuclear Energy Agency promotes the peaceful uses of nuclear energy; associated with OECD. http://www.nam.gov.za.

NSG: The Nuclear Suppliers Group (NSG) establishes guidelines for exports of nuclear materials, processing equipment for uranium enrichment, and technical information to countries of proliferation concern and regions of conflict and instability. http://www.nuclearsuppliersgroup.org.

OAS: The Organization of American States (OAS) promotes regional peace and security as well as economic and social development. http://www.oas.org.

OECD: The Organization for Economic Cooperation and Development (OECD) plays a prominent role in fostering good governance in the public service and in corporate activity. It helps governments to ensure the responsiveness of key economic areas with sectorial monitoring. By deciphering emerging issues and identifying policies that work, it helps policy makers adopt strategic orientations. It is well known for its individual country surveys and reviews.http://www.oced.org.

OPCW: The Organization for the Prohibition of Chemical Weapons (OPCW) enforces the Convention on the Prohibition of the Development, Production, Stockpiling and Use of Chemical Weapons and on Their Destruction; provides a forum for consultation and cooperation among the signatories of the Convention. http://www.opcw.org.

OSCE: The Organization for Security and Cooperation in Europe (OSCE) fosters the implementation of human rights, fundamental freedoms, democracy, and the rule of law; acts as an instrument of early warning, conflict prevention and crisis management; and serves as a framework for conventional arms control and confidence building measures. http://www.osce.org.

PCA: The Permanent Court of Arbitration (PCA) facilitates the settlement of International disputes. http://www.pca-cpa.org.

UN: The United Nations (UN) maintains international peace and security and to promote cooperation involving economic, social, cultural, and humanitarian problems. http://www.un.org.

UNCTAD: The United Nations Conference on Trade and Development (UNCTAD). http://www.unctad.org.

UNESCO: The United Nations Educational, Scientific, and Cultural Organization (UNESCO).http://www.unesco.org.

UNHCR: The United Nations High Commissioner for Refugees (UNHCR) ensures the humanitarian treatment of refugees and finds permanent solutions to refugee problems. http://www.unhcr.ch.

UNIDO: The United Nations Industrial Development Organization (UNIDO) is a specialized agency that promotes industrial development especially among the members.http://www.unido.org.

UNU: The United Nations University (UNU) conducts research in development, welfare, and human survival and tot rain scholars. http://www.unu.edu.

UPU: The Universal Postal Union (UPU) promotes international postal cooperation. http://www.upu.int.

WHO: The World Health Organization (WHO).http://www.who.int.

WIPO: The World Intellectual Property Organization furnishes protection for literary, artistic, and scientific works. http://www.wipo.int.

WMO: The World Meteorological Organization (WMO). http://www.who.ch.

WToO: The World Tourism Organization (WTO) promotes tourism as a means of contributing to economic development, international understanding, and peace. http://www.world-tourism.org.

WTrO: The World Trade Organization (WTO) provides a means to resolve trade conflicts between members and to carry on negotiations with the goal of further lowering and/or eliminating tariffs and other trade barriers.http://www.wto.org

ZC: The Zangger Committee (ZC) establishes guidelines for the export control provisions of the Nonproliferation of Nuclear Weapons Treaty (NPT).

About the Author

C. *Michael Sunoo, J.D., M.A.,* an attorney and a licensed real estate broker in Colorado and California. He has lived and studied for many years in Japan, South Korea, and the United States and, as a result, has a thorough understanding of cultural nuances and business protocols of Asian peoples and American society. Mr. Sunoo is also an Adjunct Professor at the Franklin L. Burns School of Real Estate and Construction Management, Daniels *College of Business,* UNIVERSITY OF DENVER.

México

(United States of Mexico)

INTERNATIONAL REAL ESTATE (GLOBAL REAL ESTATE)
Authored by *Bernardo Noriega,* **CIPS,** *Ari Feldman,* **CCIM, SIOR, CIPS, ALC, FIREC, Dipl. FIABCI** and *Dr. Mark Lee Levine,* **Editor**

1. Geography

The United Mexican States are often referred to as "Middle America." They are a federation comprising thirty-one states and a federal district, the capital **Mexico City,** whose metropolitan area is one of the world's most populous. It borders the Caribbean Sea, the Gulf of Mexico and the Pacific Ocean, between Belize, Guatemala and the United States.

Mexico has a total area of 1,964,375 sq km (square kilometers) (761,606 square miles), with approximately 1,943,945 sq km of land area. Mexico is slightly less than three times that of the state of Texas in the United States. The coastline is approximately 9,330 kilometers in length.

By reason of its latitude and topography, Mexico has a wide diversity of climates, ranging from hot, with annual medium temperatures of over 26 C (79°F), to cold climates with temperatures lower than 10°C (50°F). Nevertheless, 93% of the national territory fluctuates between temperatures of 10°C and 26°C (79°F). These percentages include hot sub-humid climates in 23% of the territory; it is dry in 28% of the area; and, it is very dry in 21% of the land.

The terrain includes high, rugged mountain areas with low coastal plains, some plateaus and desert areas.

Mexico is rich with many resources, e.g., petroleum, silver, copper, gold, zinc, lead, natural gas and timber. Land use is approximately 26% forests, 39% meadows and pasture, 13.2% in arable land of approximately 12%, and a mix of others, including permanent crops of about 1.1%. Environmental issues include limited water in certain areas, heavy water pollution, poor air quality in urban centers such as Mexico City, and concerns with other pollutants. Due to its geographical setting, Mexico is in a privileged position by being adjacent to the United States, one of the most powerful global economic motors. Additionally, Mexico is considered the best alternative to making the North American market accessible to the European Union.[192]

2. History and Overview

Mexico has a strong and rich history of various cultures, including Mayas, Aztecs and other cultures that existed prior to the Spanish Conquest. The Spanish explorer, Hernan Cortes, arrived at what is now the city of Veracruz and conquered Mexico in the1500s founding the colony of New Spain, which endured for approximately 300 years. Independence from Spain as a result of war occurred on Sept ember 16, 1810. In 1821 a Treaty was signed that provided for Mexican independence from Spain establishing a Constitutional monarchy. In 1822, the monarchy failed and a republic was proclaimed and formally established in 1824. Mexico has had many conflicts for independence, including in 1836 when Texas declared itself independent. Between 1846 and 1848, Mexico was at war with the United States and with France during the Franco-Mexican War (1861-1867). During this period, the Hapsburg monarchy under Emperor Maximilian I (1864-1867) was also evident as a ruling authority.

From 1858 through 1871, Benito Juarez, a native Zapotec Indian served five terms as an elected president. He was the first full-blooded indigenous national to lead a country in the

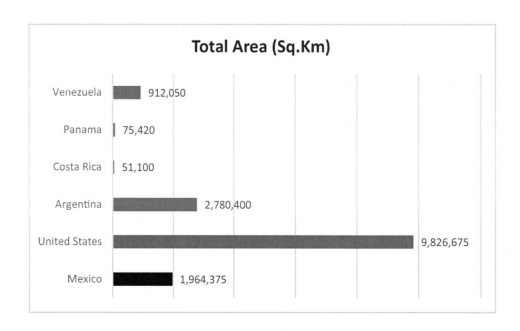

Total Area (Sq.Km)

Venezuela	912,050
Panama	75,420
Costa Rica	51,100
Argentina	2,780,400
United States	9,826,675
Mexico	1,964,375

Western Hemisphere in over 300 years. Porfirio Díaz Mori ruled Mexico from 1876 to 1880 and from 1884 to 1911. He was considered one of the most controversial figures in the history of Mexico. The term Porfiriato refers to the years when Díaz ruled. His reign ultimately ended in a severe Revolution lead by Francisco Madero (1911-1913) **which lasted from 1910 to 1920, culminating in a 1917 Constitution** crafted by then president Venustiano Carranza (president 1915 to 1920). Under a succession of names — for more than 70 years (1929–1999) Mexico was ruled by the "state party" PRI (Institutional *Revolutionary Party*) founded by Plutarco Elí as Calles (president 1924 to 1928) **until, the elections held on July 2, 2000, in which, Vicente Fox was elected Constitutional President. He was the candidate of the National Action Party, *Partido Accion Nacional,* (PAN) representing the center-right sector of the Mexican population.** This new tendency for change continued in the 2006 elections, when another PAN candidate, Felipe Calderon Hinojosa, was elected for a term ending in 2012.

Mexico, throughout its history, has passed through many stages; from being the main power of all America into a country with serious social and economic problems in the1800's. It entered a development period during the 1900's, and fully entered the world scene in the early Twenty-first Century. Until the beginning of the 21st century it was Latin Americas leading economy.

Generally speaking, political and economic development has been a painful process that has generated instability and a low-quality economic environment for the general populous,. This economic instability is the reason for serious illegal migration problems between Mexico to the United States that throughout the years has created frictions between the governments of both nations.

Many Mexicans who are unable to find well-paying job opportunities venture north for better opportunities with their neighbors. There they meet serious cultural and economic problems but also find better opportunities for their personal and economic development.

■ 3. People

The population in Mexico is **120,286,655** people (July 2014 est.) The age structure is approximately 27.9% ages 0 to 14; 15 to 64 constitute the largest populace segment at 65.5%., with only 6.6% of the population 65 or older, reflecting difficult economic and health problems.

The population growth rate is 1.21% (2014), with a birth rate of approximately 19.02 per 1,000 population (2014 est.) The death rate is 5.24 per 1,000. Life expectancy in Mexico is 75.43 years, with males living to 72.67 years, and females to

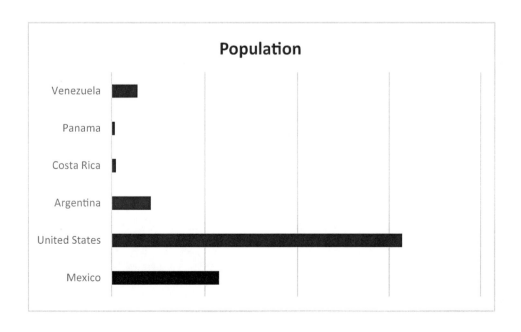

Population

- Venezuela
- Panama
- Costa Rica
- Argentina
- United States
- Mexico

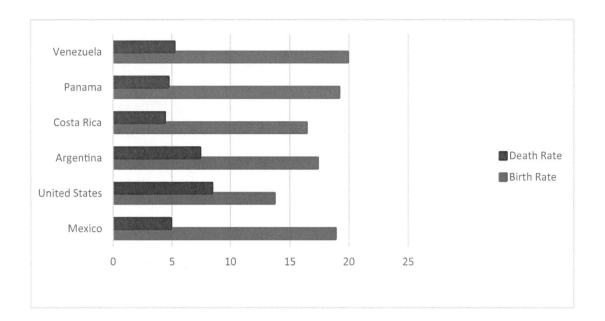

78.32. The Mexican population is increasingly urban, with close to 78% living in cities.

Ethnic divisions in **Mexico** include *Mestizos*, who are a combination of Amerindian and Spanish, and make up 62% of the population. The Amerindian population is 21%. Caucasians are 10%. The balance of the population is a mix of other ethnicities.

The dominant religion is Roman Catholic, about 82.7% of the population; 5% of the population is Protestant, with a mix of others.

The primary language is Spanish, (spoken by 92.7%); 0.8% of the population speaks an indigenous language (native dialects). Mexico has the largest Spanish-speaking population in the world, with more than twice as many Spanish-speaking people as the second largest Spanish-speaking country. Almost one-third of all Spanish, native speakers in the world live in Mexico. Literacy is approximately 86.1% of the population being able to read and write at age 15 and older. The labor force is approximately 52,900,000 people (2014). Mexico has the second largest defense budget in Latin America, with annual military expenditures of US$6 billion or about 0.59% GDP (2012) and includes 503,777 total personnel. It is primarily devoted to civil defense and service but also has devoted forces to fight the growing problems related to drug cartel activities. The inhabited part of Mexico is made up of approximately 22 million dwellings. The states that present the largest occupancy per dwelling are: Guanajuato, Tlaxcala, Chiapas, Puebla, Aguascalientes, Querétaro, Guerrero, and San Luis Potosí. Chihuahua, the Federal District, Baja California Sur, and Tamaulipas are the states that have fewer inhabitants per dwelling.

Of these 22 million existing inhabited dwellings, 78.2% of them are connected to sewer service, 88.1% have piped water, and 94.5% are connected to the electrical grid. In Mexico, personal relationships as well as business relationships are considered important. It is common that different types of business are concluded during meals or in informal gatherings. Typically, Mexicans honor their word. After signing a contract for the buying or selling of a property, to a certain extent, most Mexicans will attempt to honor the letter of the contract.

◼ 4. Government

The government is a federal republic, operating under a centralized government format, with the capital in Mexico City (Federal District), and with many administrative divisions. Independence from Spain was declared Sept ember 16, 1810; this date is Mexico's Independence Day. The current Constitution was ratified February 5, 1917. The legal system is a mix of U.S. Constitutional theory and civil law. There are judicial reviews of legislative acts as well as international reviews with the International Court of Justice (ICJ), with some reservations. Voting in Mexico is at 18 years of age. In 2008, president Calderón proposed a major reform of the judicial system, which was approved by the Congress of the Union, that included oral trials, the presumption of innocence for defendants, the authority of local police to investigate crime —until then a prerogative of special police units—and several other changes intended to speed up trials. Branches of the government consist of the Chief of State, the legislative Branch, and a Judicial Branch, with a Supreme Court of Justice, *Suprema Corte de Justicia*. There are multiple political parties with political pressure often asserted by various organized bodies, including workers' unions and the Roman Catholic Church. Diplomatic representation exists between Mexico and most other countries. For information about the Mexican government, see: http://www.presidencia.gob.mx/en, where it links to both the centralized and decentralized federal government, to state governments, and to the Republic's Presidency.

5. Economy

The economy of Mexico is the12th largest in the world. As an overview, Mexico has a free-market economy with a mixture of both modern and outmoded industrial and agricultural practices. During the last several years, Mexico has had a number of economic issues (often referred to as *crises*), banking problems, bad-debt and inflation concerns. These facts have often resulted from investors' mistrust of the economic future of Mexico. Nonetheless, starting with the PRI President, Ernesto Zedillo's government (1994-2000), the Mexican economy's essential principles have changed to become one of the most open economies in the world, achieving Free Trade treaties with the main world markets. NAFTA, involving Mexico, the United States of America and Canada, as well as the agreement signed with the European Community, put Mexico at the center of commercial transactions between Europe and America, consequently introducing Mexican products in significant markets. Since the implementation of the North American Free Trade Agreement (NAFTA) in 1994, Mexico's share of U.S. imports has increased from 7% to 12%, and its share of Canadian imports has doubled to 5%. Mexico has free trade agreements with over 50 countries, including Guatemala, Honduras, El Salvador, the European Free Trade Area, and Japan – putting more than 90% of trade under free trade agreements. After the economic crisis in 1994 (official currency devaluation), Mexico reorganized its public and private external debt by implementing private investment, fostering economic principles, currency exchange freedom (floating currency exchange), tributary system reorganization, current public expenditure reductions, and increases in infrastructure investment; these factors have generated an economic stability with an annual Gross Domestic Product (GDP) growth rate of 3% to – 5% during the last years. For the year 2009, there is an estimated economy growth of 1.3% due to the international financial crisis. After almost 8 years, where the currency ranged between 10 & 11 pesos to the US dollar, the peso sank to 14 to 1 at the end of January 2009. The Central Bank infused $400 million dollars to maintain stability.

A dramatic reduction in remittances received from Mexican nationals working abroad ($19 billion 2007) has had a profound impact on small market village's local economies. Mexico's GDP plunged 6.2% in 2009 as world demand for exports dropped, asset prices tumbled, and remittances and investment declined. GDP posted positive growth of 5.4% in 2010 and 3.8% in 2011, with exports – particularly to the United States - leading the way. In 2007, the Mexican Gross Domestic Product (GDP) was $1.353 trillion; participation of the main economic sectors on GDP was Primary Sector: 28%; industrial: 21.5%, where manufacturing constitutes 74.7% of its value; and the service sector, 50.5%. Commerce, restaurants and hotels are the most significant with 30.9%. In 2014 the GDP was $1.296 trillion (2014). In 2014 GDP (purchasing power parity) was $2.143 trillion. The Gross Domestic Product (GDP) per capita is $17,900 (2014 est.) In 2000, the federal entities with the highest GDP per capita in Mexico were the Federal District (US $17,696), Campeche (US $13,153) and Nuevo León (US $13,033); the states with the lowest GDP per capita were Chiapas (US $3,302), Oaxaca (US $3,489) and Guerrero (whose only significant income source is Acapulco US$4,112).While the northern city of Monterrey and the capital, Mexico City enjoy a Human Development Index (HDI) similar to European countries Metlatonoc in the state of Guerrero, equals a HDI similar to Malawi in Africa. During the current decade, inflation was not a problem for Mexico, but in some instances during previous decades, it was in the 20% to 30% range, and averaged 3.8% (2014 est.) After a recovery from the global crisis of 2008, GDP posted positive growth of 5.4% in 2010 and 2.4% in 2014, with exports – particularly to the United States – leading the way.

Mexico has an official unemployment rate of 4.7% (2014 est.), with both significant underemployment and an historic large underground economy.

Mexico traditionally exports crude oil and oil products, along with cotton, silver and coffee. Major imports to Mexico include machinery, electrical equipment, car parts and other mechanical parts (including aircraft parts). In the last 10 years, Mexico has had success in the manufacturing for the

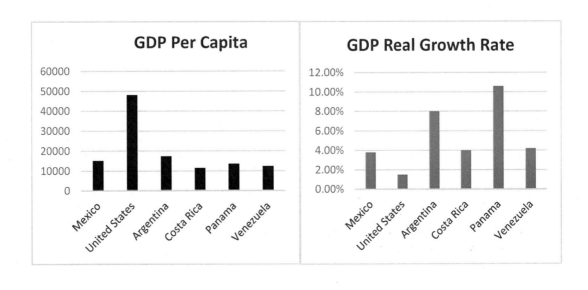

international market. The northern part of the country has attracted inbound industries (maqiladoras), which assemble a variety of products for the textile, electronic and the motor vehicle industry. This has been an important factor in increasing the amount of manufacturing exports. A clear example of this advance is the motor vehicle industry, in which Mexico has become one of the main car exporters at a world-wide level. Industries focus on food and beverage, tobacco, petroleum, motor vehicle production and assembly and tourism. To find Mexico's economic information, look for the Mexican Central Bank, Banco de Mexico, at: http://www.banxico.org.mx, where among other items, historic information about the Mexican *peso* rate exchange against American dollar can be found as well as price indexes, Gross Domestic Product (GDP) and relevant economic information.

6. Currency

The Mexican *peso* contains 100 *centavos*. The Mexican peso was very volatile position in the last decade of the 20th century, with varying increases and decreases, many substantial. In the first years of the new millennium, the Mexican peso and the Mexican economy have gained strength, averaging $12.39 pesos per the dollar in the last several years. See the Burns School Global Real Estate Web site for the UNIVERSITY OF DENVER at http://burns.daniels.du.edu for currency conversions.

7. Transportation

Mexico has about 17,166 (2010) km (kilometers) of railroad lines. Mexico's 377,660 km of highways include 137,544 km of paved roadways, including multi-lane freeways or expressways, many of which were toll ways. Many railroads and highways are in need of repair, although the principal highways in the country are made of concrete and remain in very good condition.

Since 1998, a Mexican highway privatization process started as well as railroad lines and airports; this has generated huge benefits to infrastructure in these issues. Mexico has some inland waterways, although fairly limited, with about 2,900 kilometers of navigable rivers and coastal canals. Pipelines transport crude oil and petroleum products. Some of the ports in Mexico include Veracruz, Lazaro Cárdenas, Acapulco, La Paz, Manzanillo, Mazatlan, Salina Cruz and Tampico. Mexico has 1,714 airports (2014). The Mexico City International Airport remains the largest in Latin America and the 44th largest in the world. México has paved runways generally near the major cities and resorts. For more information about communications and transportation in the Mexican Republic, look for Communication and Transportation Department, (SCT) *Secretaria de Comunicacionesy Transportes,*at http://www.sct.gob.mx.

8. Communications

Mexico has about 20.22 million (2012) landline telephones, with use of microwave radio relay links; these were privatized in 1990 in Mexico.

Also in use are satellite earth stations as well as newer technologies to enhance the telephone system, although the general infrastructure is behind that of more developed countries, such as the United States and Western Europe. Nevertheless, the telecommunications sector is now reasonable, even in local markets, for telephones as well as long distance. In respect to cellular telephones, Mexico contracts with various private companies which render this service. Mexico, as of 2012, had 100.786 million cellular phones in operation, almost five times the number of landlines. There are more than 1,500 radio broadcast stations and many television stations (excluding repeaters). Television, via satellite, was introduced in Mexico several years ago. Today it is well developed, providing a great number of channels and parallel services such as SKY and a number of cable TV companies. Televisa— the largest Spanish media company in the Spanish- speaking world is headquartered in Mexico City.

Mexico has three telecommunication satellites in orbit, which guarantee communication throughout the country and abroad. These satellites are Solidaridad 2, Satmex 5 and Satmex 6. They distribute communications like telephones, television, radio paging, radio and a great number of additional services.

Regarding the Internet, Mexico's use is among the highest of countries in Latin America with more than 31,020,000 users (2009), almost 80% of which have broadband service and 16,233,000 individual hosts (service providers) as of 2012.

9. Real Property Issues

Mexico is a federal, democratic, representative republic with representative districts. Generally speaking, the separate areas are free and sovereign, subject to a united position for the Federation under its constitution. Additionally, states have their own Constitutions. As a result of a 1989 revision to Mexican law (foreign investment act updated 1997) relative to investments, a more relaxed legislation now allows foreign investment and ownership by non-Mexican citizens in Mexican real estate. Mexico is home to the largest number of U.S. citizens living outside the U.S. (estimated at one million two hundred fifty thousand) and represents 25% of all U.S. citizens abroad.

Acquisition costs generally involve the commissions paid, as well as legal fees and other closing cost. Commissions range 5% - 7%, with legal fees running 2% to 4% of the purchase price. Information on property ownership can be located in the Public Registry of Property in each city. The Public Registry of Property, *Registro de la Propiedad,* contains information relative to each property in its jurisdiction, where all transactions are registered, including sales, mortgages and embargoes (liens) with judicial order. Thus, those interested in buying property can have a high degree of safety. Notwithstanding the above, Title Insurance can be obtained in México from U.S. based Title Warranty firms. Transaction information on sales is generally collected by private firms; however, such information does not approach the disclosure rules and the volume of information for real estate transactions that exists in the United States.

Mexico has real estate trade associations in various locations throughout the count ry. The largest organization is the *Asociacion Mexicana de Profesionales Inmobaliarios,* (AMPI) where members include 2,000 professionals throughout the country and maintains a bi-lateral agreement with the National Association of Realtors® USA (NAR).There is also the Mexico Chapter of FIABCI, the International Real Estate Federation. Some Mexican real estate brokerage companies and individuals are registered members of the National Association of REALTORS® (NAR) in the United States. The first class of Mexican real estate professionals graduated and obtained the Certified International Property Specialist (CIPS) designation in 2000.In 2001 a chapter of the CCIM Institute was formed in Mexico City and there are now several CCIM throughout the country. A number of Mexican nationals have active membership in both SIOR, RLI and ULI as well as U.S. engineering and architectural associations. Mexico requires real estate brokers to register with the government, but currently there is no legal requirement for licensing.

Eminent domain as a concept exists in Mexico; the constitution provides for reasonable compensation is to be paid in such cases. Escheat exists, whereby property can flow back to the government, if there are no beneficiaries of the deceased. Although, this is uncommon, because if the deceased died intestate, a civil hearing usually takes place, during which the family members in direct line to the deceased owner execute their rights to the estate of the deceased.

Police power is important regarding control of real estate and it has similar characteristics to those that exist in the United States. Forms of ownership include separate property, joint tenancy, partnerships, limited partnerships, corporations as well as other entities. Property ownership in Mexico consists of a bundle of rights similar to those in the United States of America. These rights includes right to own, to mortgage, lease, to hold in name, and to sell. All of these rights are protected by Mexican law, since they are considered the cornerstones of private property ownership and a market economy. Real estate on the Mexican coastline, such as Acapulco, Los Cabos, Cancun and other similar cities have defined limitations for foreigner nationals taking direct title, according to Articles 27 in the Mexican Constitution. But the legal concept of a Beneficial Trust (Fideicomiso) can be used, where four out of the five essential rights of the bundle of rights are present, excluding the right to "hold it in ones own name." This limitation has a provision under law so a buyer can use this beneficial trust where title is held by a bank acting for the foreign national trustor or taking title to the real estate in the name of a corporation wholly owned by non-Mexicans. Transfer of title is generally by written deed (Escritura). Positions of adverse possession and general claims to real estate are in concept similar to those that

exist in other western countries, such as in the United States, although the time frame for proof of adverse possession varies from other countries that follow such doctrine. Mexican adverse position passes in 5 years. Transfer or modification of ownership or possession of real estate, although not required, is registered to protect the interests of the parties. Contracts for purchase of real estate must be in writing, as is true with most contracts for leasing of real estate in Mexico. Special benefits inure to leases of longer than 10 years. Notaries in Mexico are quasi-governmental officials and accredited attorneys who are specially trained in the area of contracts and transfer of real estate title. They are responsible for validating title allowing for transfer (notary's do not warrant tit le), collecting taxes on capital gains, acquisition taxes and recording of documents. Closing in escrow is generally handled by the notary, who is paid for such services. Notary's are the only attorneys in Mexico entitled to create a document for recordation in the Public Registry.

Mexico has ad valorem property taxes (Impustos *Sobre la Renta*). These are levied, annually, by the government and may only represent.^{025}% of the property value. Acquisition transfer taxes are also paid by buyer when property is transferred. This acquisition tax is equal to between 2 and 3.5% percent of the recorded price of the transaction Zoning and use permits (Uso *de Suelo*) in Mexico can be difficult, especially in the larger cities, such as Mexico City. Before purchasing a nonresidential property, one must be sure of the use, to determine if the intended use is authorized in the zone. There are zones clearly identified as exclusively residential, and others in which there can be additional uses, such as commercial. Industrial uses are delimited and restricted in cities. Also, there have developed strict regulations regarding ecological matters, which companies and individuals must meet. In Mexico City, due to overpopulation, special regulations have been imposed in specific areas of the city where uses cannot be modified for at least 15 years. In rapidly increasing areas of the coast specific environmental studies and permits are required as well as minimum lot sizes for individual ocean front properties.[196]

■ 10. Real Estate Trends

After the economic crisis suffered by the currency devaluation in Mexico at the end of 1994, the real estate market experienced a signification retraction, triggered by inflation and interest rates at levels of 55% per annum, a total lack of mortgage credit for real estate purchases, a pronounced decrease in demand, and an increased supply with little regard to absorption.

These problems reduced economic activity in this sector to 70% of the levels reached in 1992. This situation continued until 1999, during which macroeconomic indicators and actual sales showed a recovery. Restrictive policies in government expenditures, the fostering of productivity in the manufacturing field, free flotation of the Mexican peso, and opening of markets by means of NAFTA and the European Union Agreement generated in 1999 a peaceful economic prosperity unprecedented at a worldwide level. This earned the confidence of international investors. In the January through June 2000 period these investors placed more than $6.6 billion dollars in Mexico.

Reduction of inflation to 8.5% and the confidence gained by the international markets reactivated credit flows and movement of the Mexican real estate market for the year 2000. The present Mexican real estate market has the absorption capacity of more than 2,000,000 residential dwellings per year. This demand for housing is growing all over the country, but primarily in the larger cities. As of 2008, the Mexican market was fully recovered, with an abundant supply of mortgages at an interest rate averaging 11% annually generating in a huge Real Estate market investment climate, including several billion Euros coming from Spain and other EU investors, revitalizing the second home and tourism properties in cities such as Cancun, Los Cabos and Puerto Vallarta. Significant mega developments were constructed along the Caribbean coast of Mexico, along the Gulf of Mexico side of the Yucatan peninsula, the Pacific coast north and south of Puerto Vallarta and the coastal areas of the Sea of Cortez (Gulf of California).

Within the commercial area, the growth of the Mexican economy has encouraged the creation, growth and implementation of a significant number of national and international firms that require working space to facilitate their activities; this explains the large number of real estate offices involved in planning and construction in selective parts of the country. Mexico has received a large number of franchises of all types for commercial business, from the food industry, clothing, furniture, services, and other consumer goods, all of which have generated development. The cities with movement in this market are almost any city with a population greater than 500,000. In the first years of the 21st. century, a large number of retail spaces and malls have beginning to emerge in every medium to major city in the country, anchored by many of the recognized international retail firms. The manufacturing sector has shown strong growth, generating an increase in demand for industrial and warehouse distribution space. By tradition, industrial plants were located on the northern part of the country. But they are now beginning to gravitate towards the central region of México, creating another market for industrial residential and commercial real estate. The cities of León, Aguascalient es, Hermosillo, Torreón, Puebla, and Guadalajara; and, of course, Monterrey, have reported higher growth rates. This development has also generated the need for large distribution centers, which have been built in most major city across the country. The tourist industry makes an important contribution to the improvement of the real estate and the construction industry in Mexico. Mexico is the eighth most visited country in the world (with over 23 million tourists a year). The developments located in the southeast state of Quintana Roo, – Cancun, Playa del Carmen, Tulum, the Riveria Maya and the islands of Isla Mujeres and Cozumel – has been one of the favored destinations for European tourism in Mexico, which has seen expansion in a spectacular fashion. Groups of Mexican real estate professionals, such as the *Asociación Mexicana de Profesionales Immobiliaros (AMPI)*, the Mexican Association of Real Estate

Professionals, already use their own Internet addresses, where they share with their associates and the public, in general, information regarding a multiple listing type service.

There already exist in Mexico a series of portals that provide significant information about real estate markets. Another useful tool to investigate the Mexican real estate market is the *International Real Estate Digest* at http://www.ired.com, where many Mexican real estate brokerage companies are registered, as well as the most generally used MLS in Mexico, which is http://www.metroscubicos.com.mx.

Trends regarding the cost of space for lease or sale can be most easily determined by looking at the links in the Selected References section contained here, that includes, among others, office, retail, industrial, residential and multi-family property. Also cited are links to major real estate brokerage companies, law firms and consulting firms that practice in Mexico. http://www.lomelin-colliers.com.mx,   http://www.joneslanglasalle.com.mx, and http://www.cushwake.com.mx http://www.stewart.com.mx/ http://www.martindale.com/c- Mexico-law-firms-city.htm.

■ 11. Cultural Issues

Any nation's culture is complex and vibrant in its diversity. While broad cultural characterizations such as those presented here can be generally accurate, following such generalities too strictly may be dangerously misleading. To conduct business effectively and profitably in a country, it is vital to have a thorough understanding of its culture's complexities.

If cultural distinctions and issues are not addressed, real estate transactions may not gain a foothold at inception. One can likely not even enter the potential of a real estate purchase, sale or lease arrangement without a proper introduction that meets formal Mexican cultural requirements. Greetings in Mexico are traditional handshakes and nodding of the head. It is also quite common to see a kiss on the cheek between men and women and children. Men familiar with each other often shake hands, embrace, pat the back twice, and shake hands again when meeting or departing. "No" might be indicated by a vocal sound, as well as by indicating shaking the hand from side to side, with the index finger extended, and palm outward. A "thumbs up" gesture is often utilized for approval of a position. Gesturing towards others is never done with the pointed finger. A beckoning signal is the palm pointed downward with the hand opening and closing. Much conversation in Mexico can take place with hand signals only.

Mexicans generally are very hospitable. It is common to invite visitors home to have refreshments, dinner, etc. It is considered generally impolite to refuse such refreshments. Unannounced visits are an accepted custom. It is not unusual to see large groups of young and older people at restaurants and hotels.

Supper is often served later than is traditional in the United States (9:00 p.m.), often with a hiatus, or gap from working in the morning at 10 a.m. and again in the afternoon for long lunches that begin at 2:30 and end at 4:00pm or later. These gaps in the workday may generate a later working day and, thus in turn, the later dinner. Eating in a formal setting involves both hands kept on or above the table, as opposed to in the lap, the latter being more common in the United States. It is not uncommon to see elbows rested on the table.

12. Discussion Questions

1. How does Mexico's proximity to the United States help/hurt the economic conditions in Mexico?

2. How has the creation of NAFTA affected Mexico's economy?

3. What are some environmental issues facing Mexico?

4. What are some of the important cultural issues that affect doing business in Mexico?

13. Case Study

Memo

To: Board of Directors
From: Consultants
Re: Resignation of X.Y.

I. Problem

REAL ESTATE FOR VAIL (REV)
MEXICO CITY , MEXICO

Real Estate for Vail (REV) was first opened in Mexico in 1985. It focused on selling second homes and providing vacations rentals to Mexicans. Through the eighties and early nineties, REV had plenty of business. However, in the late nineties, business started to slow down. In the most recent years it has stabilized.

The key employee, X William Yemder has lived and worked in Mexico for 10 years, operating the office, solely on his own. It has been a great experience, but Mr. X.Y. is now moving back to the United States, to attend the UNIVERSITY OF DENVER to obtain an advanced degree in real estate.

II. Initial Exit Strategy

Currently REV has small office space located in downtown Mexico City. The lease expires in March, next year. The current landlord has agreed to a buyout clause. The current clients' files can all be transferred to the Colorado office. REV would be able to continue to take care of their needs through email and phone. The list of prospective new clients can also be transferred to the Colorado office. A trip, once per month, to Mexico City, should be enough to continue working the relationships. Advertising should remain in place, but there will be a change in the contact information. Once the office and clients are cared for, not only would REV reduce its overhead, but it would also be able to operate from Colorado.

III. Contingency Exit Strategy

There should be no need for a contingency exit strategy. Mr. X.Y. will stay in place to follow through on the Initial Exit Strategy plan. Once that is complete, Mr. X.Y. will be moving. If REV wants to keep the office in Mexico, Mr. X.Y. will stay on for one month, while REV looks for a replacement. If REV decides to not accept the Initial Exit Plan, Mr. X.Y. will be open to discuss the plans.

IV. Conclusion

The suggestion is to close the office in Mexico City and continue to operate the Mexico activity from the Colorado office.

Refer to: International Real Estate Digest,. Martindale-Hubbell, Homepage. http://www.ired.com U.S. Embassy. Homepage. http://usembassy.state.gov.

U.S. Department of State. Homepage. http://www.state.gov. X-rates.com. Homepage. http://www.x-rates.com/.

14. Selected References

CIA World Factbook.https://www.cia.gov/library/pub-lications/the-world-factbook/index.html. http://en.wikipedia.org/wiki/Mexico. http://en.wikipedia.org/wiki/Economy_of_Mexico. http://www.ampi.org/.

http://www.ampidf.com.mx. http://www.inegi.gob.mx. http://met roscubicos.com.mx. http://www.ired.com.

http://www.joneslanglasalle.com.mx. http://www.cushwake.com.mx. http:// www.lomelin-colliers.com.m x. http://www.presidencia.gob.mx. http://www.sct.gob.mx.

International Real Estate Digest. Martindale-Hubbell. Homepage. http://www.ired.com Organization of American States at http://www.oas.org.

Richard Ellis International Property Specialists. http://www.cbre.com.

Time Almanac. *TIME Almanac.* Boston: Information Please LLC. U.S. Bureau of Census at http://www.census.gov.

U.S. Department of Commerce at http://www.stat-usa.gov.

U.S. Bureau of Economic Analysis at http://www.bea.gov. U.S. Embassy. Homepage. http://usembassy.state.gov.

United States Depart ment of St at e. *Background Notes: Mexico.* United States Department of State (Online).Available:http://www.state.gov.

World Trade Center Institute at http://www.wtci.org. World Trade Organization at http://www.wto.org. X-rates.com. Homepage. http://www.x-rates.com/.

15. Glossary

Asociacion Mexicana de Profesionales Inmobaliario – real estate trade association.

Beneficial Trust – This term is used where four out of the five essential rights making up the Bundle of Rights are present, excluding the right to "hold in your own name" This limitation has a very simple solution: by using the Beneficial Trust or buying the real estate under the name of a corporation, in which the foreigner could be the sole owner.

Bundle of Rights – similar to those of the United States. Right to own, to mortgage, to lease, to have it in your name, and to sell it.

Middle America – Mexico is sometimes referred to as Middle America.

Public Registry of Property – information on property in each city of Mexico. **Bernardo Noriega, CIPS.**

About the Authors

Prof. *Ari Feldman*, CCIM, SIOR, CIPS, ALC, FIREC, Dipl FIABCI, Mayan Mayan Properties / Trafalgar Advisors LLC. Ari Feldman is a prominent international real estate consultant who over the last three decades has specialized in discreet services and has participated in consult at ion, listing, sales, leasing or development of shopping centers, industrial properties and resort hotels in five countries on four continents. A problem solver and non-conventional thinker dedicated to the total success of his client base, he has had been involved in hundreds of transactions. In addition to private individuals, he has assisted many of the top 500 global corporations. The recipient of many awards and honors and author of numerous papers, his skill set encompasses acquisition, operating, financial and investment modeling, demographic analysis, strategic planning, and audit, appraisal, project management, legal consulting and witness services as well as consult ant facilitating between lenders, owners, buyers, and sellers. Born and educated in the United States, he attended Antioch College and the University of Dayton Law School, earning advanced real estate designations in international commercial, industrial and land studies. He is a senior affiliate of Trafalgar Advisors LLC / Trafalgar Global Partners and heads the Mexican office. Since 1993 he has lived in Mexico and is fluent in Spanish.

Netherlands

INTERNATIONAL REAL ESTATE (GLOBAL REAL ESTATE)

Dr. Mark Lee Levine, **Editor**

■ 1. Geography

The Netherlands is located in Western Europe between Belgium and Germany, bordering the North Sea, at the mouths of the Rhine, the Maas and the Schelde rivers. Total area is fairly small at 41,543 sq km (square kilometers), which is a little less than twice the size of New Jersey in the United States. The coastline is 451 km. The climate is temperate and generally has cool summers and mild winters.

Land use involves approximately 1.06% for permanent crops, 29.98% for arable land, 10% for forest and woodlands, and the balance in various other uses. Natural resources include natural gas, petroleum and very fertile soil.

Environmental concerns exist with organic compounds, soil nutrients, air pollution, and acid rain, among others. Natural hazards include using many dikes and dams to protect the land area in the Netherlands. Numerous environmental protective steps are being undertaken by the Netherlands to avoid problems such as air pollution, endangered species, hazardous wastes, marine dumping, nuclear tests, etc.

■ 2. History and Overview

The Dutch won their independence from Spain in 1648. Prosperity was built in large part from trade, especially with England. During this time the Netherlands became a great sea and colonial power. The countries importance declined however with the gradual loss of Dutch technological superiority and after wars with Spain, France, and England. Following Napoleon's defeat in 1813, the Netherlands and Belgium became known as the "Kingdom of the United Netherlands" under King Willem I. The Belgians then withdrew from the alliance in 1830 to form their own kingdom.

The Netherlands were neutral in World War I. Although The Netherlands attempted to be neutral in World War II, Germany overran the country, claiming almost 250,000 lives from the Dutch, many Jews and other ethnic groups living in the area.

World War II was very devastating to The Netherlands.

Remnants of the Netherlands' global empire were granted either full independence or nearly complete autonomy following World War II. Currently the five islands of the Netherlands Antilles and Aruba are integral parts of the Netherlands realm but enjoy a large degree of autonomy.[200]

■ 3. People

The Netherlands has a fairly small population of **16,877,351.** The population in the 14 and under category is 16.9%; 65.5% in

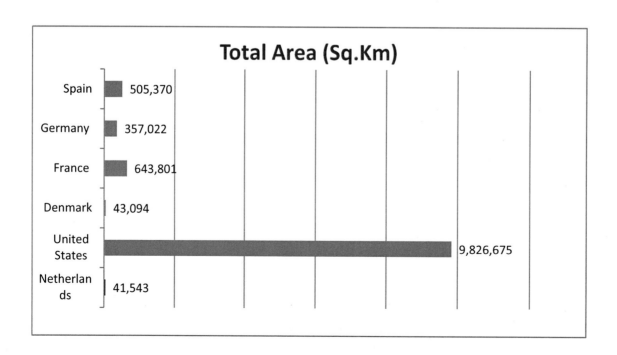

Total Area (Sq.Km)

Spain	505,370
Germany	357,022
France	643,801
Denmark	43,094
United States	9,826,675
Netherlands	41,543

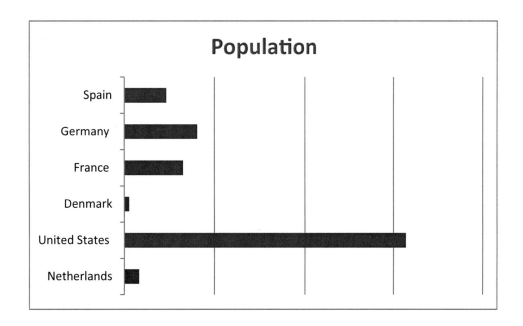

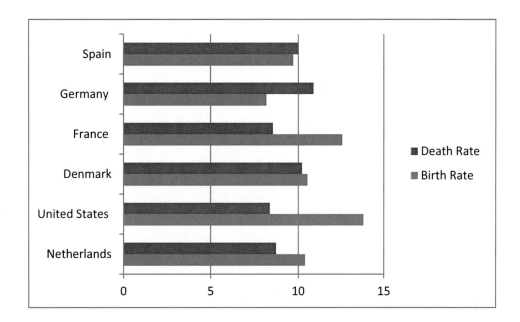

the 15-year-old to 64-year-old category; and the balance, 17.6%, is in the 65 years of age or older category.

There is a fairly high standard of living for the Dutch, which results in a life expectancy, overall, of 81.12 years, including 79.02 years for males and 83.34 years for females (2014). There are 10.83 births per 1,000 population, and there are 8.57 deaths per 1,000 population. Religions consist of 28% Roman Catholics, 19% Protestants, and a mix of other religions for the balance. (Approximately 42% of Netherlanders claimed to be "unaffiliated.")

The official and dominant language is Dutch, although English is fairly popular. The Dutch are literate, with approximately 99% of the population able to read and write at age 15 or older.

◼ 4. Government

The Netherlands is a constitutional monarchy, with its capital in Amsterdam. The Hague is the seat of the government. Administrative divisions consist of 12 groups or areas. The Dutch received their independence in 1579 from Spain. Their national holiday is the Queen's Day, which started on April 30, 1938. The legal system is based on incorporation of part of the French penal position and influenced by other civil law positions.

The government consists of the Executive Branch, the royal house or *Koninklijik Huis*, with the Chief of State as being the Queen and the Prime Minister as head of government. The Legislative Branch is bicameral (the first chamber, *Eerste Kamer,* and the second chamber, *Tweede Kamer).* The Judicial Branch, which has a Supreme Court known, is known as the *De Hoge Raad.* There are a number of political parties in the Netherlands.

Diplomatic representation exists with the United States maintaining an Embassy in The Hague. The Dutch maintain an office for their Ambassador in Washington, D.C.

■ 5. Economy

The Dutch economy is extremely strong. The Dutch are very aggressive in investing throughout the world. The Dutch rank third world wide in agricultural exports. The Gross Domestic Product (GDP) per capita is $47,700 (2014).

While the GDP is $880.4 billion, the GDP real growth rate is 0.6%. Unemployment is 7.2% (2014); the economy continues to show strong signs. It has viable exports in machinery and equipment, chemicals, fuels, agricultural products and other areas.

■ 6. Currency

Currency is the *euro* (it was the *guilder).* See the Burns School Global Real Estate Web site for the UNIVERSITY OF DENVER at http://burns.daniels.du.edu for currency conversion rates.

■ 7. Transportation

Heavy use is made of railroads in the Netherlands with 3,013 km (kilometers) of rail lines. The Dutch also use 139,295 km of highways to transport goods and services. Pipelines transport natural gas, oil and refined products. Major ports include Amsterdam and Maastricht, among others. The Netherlands has 29 airports (2013).

■ 8. Communications

A highly sophisticated telephone system is widely used throughout the country, relying on microwave, cable, satellite earth stations and other high-technology applications. Numerous radio stations and television broadcast stations are utilized. The Netherlands has approximately 13,699,000 Internet hosts (service providers) and 14,872,000 Internet users.

■ 9. Real Property Issues

The Dutch have a fairly sophisticated real estate system in which commissions are generally paid by the seller for residential and commercial transactions, where a broker is employed. These rates vary, but they can often be 2% to 3% of the sales price of the transaction. There are commission fees or charges paid for commercial leases. As is true in much of Europe, a notary, a specialized area of legal practice, is paid a percentage for handling a real estate transaction. Registration fees are also paid for real estate transactions.

Real Property in the Netherlands is deemed as everything growing on or that has been built on land. It includes everything permanently affixed to, or destined for permanent service of the land. Transfer of property is executed through a notarial deed. The property is registered with the title and mortgage register for the district where the property is located. This register also holds the description of land parcels and maps, *kadaster.* The Buyer is typically responsible for the notarial fees. The additional bundle of rights associated with a property is transferred through the notarial deed. These additional rights may include *erfdienstbaarheid (easements* and servitudes), erfpacht (long lease), *opstal* (right to own buildings etc. on other person's land), and *vruchtgebruik* (usufruct, right to use and to enjoy fruits of other person's property).

Municipalities in the Netherlands may have preemptive rights over real property in some areas. There is strict legislation

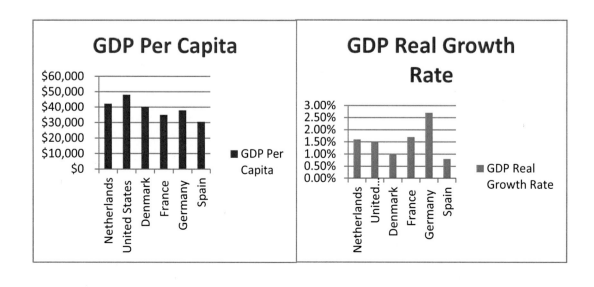

regarding construction and the need to obtain permits. Real property is also subject to a number of environmental regulations. There are no restrictions on the ownership of Dutch land by non-Netherlanders.

A mortgage must be executed before a notary. The mortgage must describe the property, detail the debt in nature and quantity, indicate parties, and any specific stipulations by the mortgagee. For validity the mortgage must be recorded with the Title and Mortgage registry for the appropriate district. Mortgage ranking is based upon date of entry. Creditors with claims secured by the mortgage have priority over other creditors and before taxes, with the exclusion of property taxes. In the case of foreclosure a public auction is held in the presence of the notary.[204]

10. Real Estate Trends

The Dutch continue to acquire sophistication in the real estate field, including activities within and outside the Netherlands as to real estate transactions. For an overview of various areas or markets in the real estate field, including office, general commercial, investments, multi-unit, residential, vacant land and retail, see the links cited below in the Selected References section. Several companies such as Jones Lang LaSalle (http://joneslanglasalle.com) and CB Richard Ellis (http://www.cbre.com) provide detailed, current information on the latest real estate market trends in the Netherlands.

11. Cultural Issues

Any nation's culture is complex and vibrant in its diversity.

While broad cultural characterizations such as those presented here can be generally accurate, following such generalities too strictly may be dangerously misleading. To conduct business effectively and profitably in a country, it is vital to have a thorough understanding of its culture's complexities.

The Netherlands operates on a highly sophisticated Western level of undertaking business. Cultural issues are very important. Generally speaking, the Dutch are warm and hearty, often greeting with a handshake and the popular phrase of "Dag" ("Hello"), or "Hoe *gaat het?*" ("How are you?") in the Dutch language. Gestures are similar to those in the United States and many Western cultures.

Three meals a day are usually served, similar to that in the United States, with dinner being earlier than most other western, European countries. Many meals include staples, such as bread and cheese.

12. Discussion Questions

1. What are the environmental concerns in the Netherlands?

2. What is one of the Netherlands most important exports?

3. Is the location of the Netherlands a factor in attracting foreign investors?

13. Case Study

Memo

To: Board of Directors
From: Consultants
Re: Downsizing

I. Problem

OVERVIEW
Fantasy Real Estate Sales (FRES)

Headquarters in Milan, Italy Offices in Italy, Sweden, Hungary, Spain, Russia, Netherlands, United Kingdom and Greece Fantasy Real Estate Sales (FRES) was established in Greece in 1995. The idea behind the Company was drawn from a Greek real estate agent, XElvina Greeeelepis, owner of XXEGGG Realty. XElvina's real estate company had many different properties listed, including villas and private islands. The inspiration for FRES came from meeting XElvina. The Directors felt we would be able to help people find their "fantasy" pieces of real estate, such as castles, villas, ranches, winery's and any unique properties falling into the "fantasy" realm of real estate.

ITALY

Recently the headquarters of FRES, located in Milan, Italy, began to grow. It was doing so much business that it had seven full-time agents, and one office manager. FRES needs to hire more people, but it is concerned with hiring too many, because if the Company has more than 15 employees, it will have to "take care of the employees" for a long time. This is based on the employment laws in Italy. See http://www.cmslegal.com/intelligence/cms_news/employment.htm.

RUSSIA

The Russian market is beginning to pick up new business. There are plenty of properties available, but FRES's target buyers are hesitant to purchase property in Russia. (FRES is working on advertising the benefits of realty in Russia. FRES started doing overnight stays at the individual properties, so potential clients can see what it is like to be in Russia.)

HUNGARY

Currently, in Hungary, the Company has had a reduction in properties available for sale. FRES was been unable to secure properties for sale. It has also had two properties flood in the last two months.

NETHERLANDS

The market is booming. There seem to be enough "fantasy" properties at the current time.

UNITED KINGDOM (ENGLAND, SCOTLAND, WALES)

The United Kingdom, including the **England, Scotland and Wales** markets, has been relatively stable. These markets, for FRES, do not perform extremely well, but they do not go below projected income.

SPAIN

This market is just beginning to show the growth potential that was projected by FRES for the country. The market had a difficult time because prices were inflated. As such, it was not a good investment to purchase a fantasy property here; however, prices are beginning to come inline. Thus, with other European markets, the general market is beginning to pickup in sales.

SWEDEN

Currently the Swedish market is booming.The agents cannot keep up with the market.

II. Initial Exit Strategy

Exiting these countries would be relatively easy, except for Italy, where the headquarters office is currently located. All of the other offices are satellite offices. In most cases the agents work out of their own homes. The Milan office could be vacated relatively easily. The interior has been upgraded to class A office space and since this is in short supply in Italy, it should be relatively easy to re-lease or sub- lease. The network of real estate agents throughout Europe that FRES has established would help in the event that FRES needed to leave the county.

III. Contingency Exit Strategy

See Initial Exit Strategy plan. The plan of exit would be simple to leave everything and leave the country.

IV. Conclusion

Employment restrictions in Italy will make it difficult to keep expanding. To have a reasonable exit strategy, FRES should move the headquarters to Sweden. The reason Sweden is more of an ideal location is due to the booming market and the favorable employment laws. The other markets could be considered, but Russia would be difficult. Current employees would resist a move to Sweden. The United Kingdom does not have enough business. This is also true with the Netherlands. Spain might be a possibility for the home office. The company should not completely close the operation in Italy, but it should leave one or two agents, to continue the local market.

Refer to: International Real Estate Digest. Homepage. http://www.ired.com. U.S. Department of State. Homepage. http://www.state.gov.

U.S. Embassy. Homepage. http://usembassy.state.gov.

14. Selected References

CIA World Factbook. https://www.cia.gov/library/publications/the-world-factbook/index.html. http://www.dnb.nl/english/. http://www.minbuza.nl/default.asp?CMS_ITEM=MBZ257570. http://www.real- estate-european-union.com/english/netherlands.html. Jones Lang LaSalle, Netherlands, http://www.joneslanglasalle.com.

Price Waterhouse Coopers, http://www.pwcglobal.com.
Richard Ellis International Property Specialists. http://www.cbre.com. Time Almanac. *TIME Almanac.* Boston: Information Please LLC.
United States Department of State. Background *Notes: Netherlands. United* States Department of State (Online). Available:http://www.state.gov.

U.S. Bureau of Census at http://www.census.gov. U.S. Department of Commerce at http://www.stat-usa.gov. U.S. Bureau of Economic Analysis at http://www.bea.gov. U.S. Embassy. Homepage. http://usembassy.state.gov. World Trade Centers Institute at http://www.wtci.org. World Trade Organization at http://www.wto.org. World Bank. *Adult Illiteracy Rates*. The Economist. X-rates.com. Homepage. http://www.x-rates.com/.

15. Glossary

Besloten vennootschap met beperke aansprakelijkheid – (B.V.) private company with limited liability.

Eetsmakelijk – eat deliciously, used in same way as bon -appetite.

Hold Thesum Certificate – Required for a real estate license.

Naamloze venrotschap – (N.V.) public company.

Nederlandse Verninging Van Makelaars in Onroerende Goedren – Dutch Association of Real Estate Agents.

About the Author

Dr. Mark Lee Levine is the Editor of this Book.

Panama

INTERNATIONAL REAL ESTATE (GLOBAL REAL ESTATE)
Authored by *Dr. Mark Lee Levine* and *Kathy Shahani*

Dr. Mark Lee Levine, Editor

1. Geography

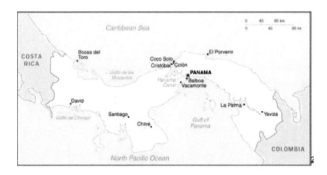

Panama is located in Central America, sometimes referred to as Middle America, bordering the Caribbean Sea and the Pacific Ocean, between Colombia on the south and Cost a Rica on the north. Panama has about 75,420 sq km (square kilometers) of area, with 2,490 km of coastline.

The climate is tropical, mostly hot and humid, with many rainy days during May to January. Many rugged mountains and coastal areas comprise Panama. Limited resources in the form of forests, copper, shrimp and several other minor resources are harvested by Panama. Arable land in Panama is 7.2%, with about 2.56% in permanent crops, and the balance 90.79% includes woodlands and pastures. Deforestation of its rain forest and misuse of its land are environmental concerns, as well as the issue of water pollution.

2. History and Overview

Panama's history has been shaped by the evolution of the world economy and the ambitions of great powers. Shortly after its discovery, Panama was seen as the path between the seas, and it quickly became the crossroads and market place of Spain's empire in the New World. Panamanian fortunes fluctuated with the geopolitical importance of the isthmus.

The treaty granted rights to the United States "as if it were sovereign" in a zone roughly 10 miles wide and 50 miles long. In that zone, the U.S. would build a canal, then administer, fortify, and defend it "in perpetuity." From 1903 until 1968, Panama was a constitutional democracy dominated by a commercially oriented oligarchy. In October of 1968, the military ousted the current president and established a military junta government. The Panama Defense Forces (PDF) continued to dominate Panamanian political life behind a facade of civilian government. By this time, Gen. Manuel Noriega was firmly in control of both the PDF and the civilian government.

The United States froze economic and military assistance to Panama in the summer of 1987 in response to the domestic political crisis and an attack on the U.S. embassy. On December 20, the U.S. military entered Panama to protect U.S. lives and property, to fulfill U.S. treaty responsibilities to operate and defend the Canal, to assist the Panamanian people in restoring democracy, and to bring Noriega to justice. Panama worked quickly to restore its government. In what was considered a free and fair election, Mireya Moscoso took office on Sept ember 1, 1999. During her administration, she has attempted to strengthen social programs, especially for child and youth development, protection, and general welfare. Education programs have also been highlighted. More recently, Moscoso was focused on bilateral and multilateral free trade initiatives with the hemisphere. Moscoso's administration successfully handled the Panama Canal transfer and has been effective in the administration of the Canal.[208]

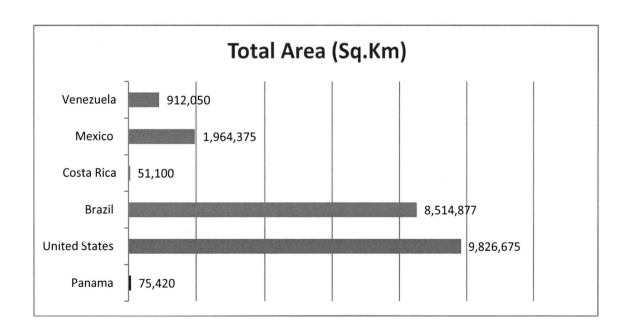

■ 3. People

Panama has **3,608,431** people. The population in the 15-year to 64- year category is 64.8%, and 27.4% in the 0 to 14-year age group. The balance is in the 65 years of age or older group, 7.8%. This major portion of the population, almost 1/3 in the younger category, is very unusual when compared with most countries.

The population growth rate is fairly strong at almost 1.35% (2014). Birth rates are about 18.61 per 1,000; death rates are about 4.77 per 1,000. The infant mortality rate is 10.7 per 1,000 live births. The life expectancy is fairly high at 78.3 years overall, with females at 81.22 years, and males at 75.51 years.

Ethnic dominance belongs to the *Mestizo*, a mix of European and Amerindian ancestry, making up 65% of the population. The balance of the populace comes from West Indian, white and other Indians, among others. In Panama, 85% of the people are Roman Catholic, and most of the balance are Protestants. The official language in Panama is Spanish, although English is spoken by about 14% of the population. The literacy rate is 91.9% for those who are 15 years of age or older.

■ 4. Government

The government of Panama is a constitutional democracy, with its capital in Panama City. The national Independence Day is in November. The Panama legal system is based on civil law, with some judicial review of legislative acts. Voting is compulsory and universal at 18 years of age. The government consists of an Executive Branch as the Chief of State and head of the government, as the President, and with the Cabinet, appointed by the President. The Legislative Branch is unicameral in the form of a legislative assembly known as the *Asamblea Legislativa. The Judicial Branch, the highest* court, is the Supreme Court of Justice. Diplomatic representation includes the Panama Ambassador located in Washington, D.C.; the U.S. Ambassador is located in Panama City.

The flag of Panama is divided into four equal rectangles, with the top quadrants white, with a blue 5-pointed star in the center, and plain red. The bottom quadrants are plain blue on the hoist side, and white with a red 5-pointed star in the center.

Panama has defense forces including the national police force, maritime force, national air service, and a Judicial Branch technical police.

■ 5. Economy

The Gross Domestic Product (GDP) is $44.69 billion (2014). The national GDP per capita income is $20,300. The GDP real growth rate is 6.6%.

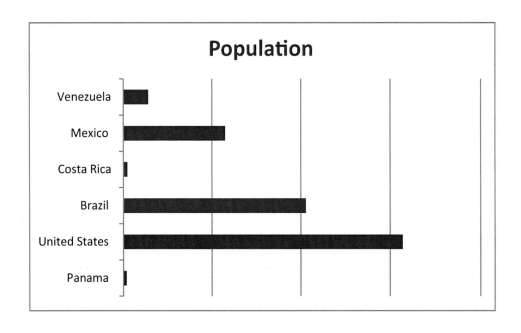

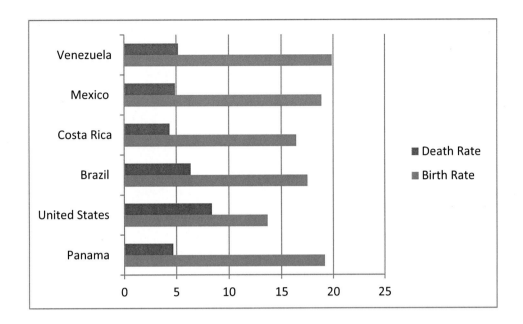

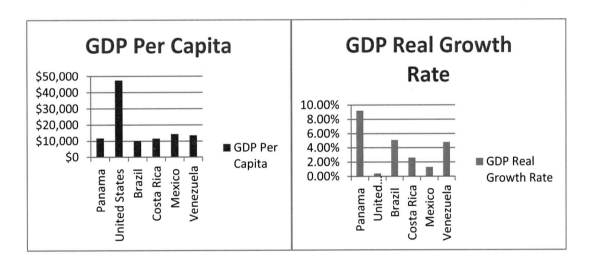

Reported inflation is 2.9% (2014). Unemployment seems to be fair at 4.5% (2014).

A well-developed service sector accounts for three-fourths of the Panamanian Gross Domestic Product (GDP) and includes the Panama Canal, banking, the Colon Free Zone, insurance, container ports, flagship registry, and tourism. In 2000 and 2001, there was a slump in the Colon Free Zone and in agricultural exports that, when coupled with the global slowdown and the withdrawal of U.S. military forces, slowed economic growth. To compensate for the economic slump and to stimulate growth, the Panamanian government planned public works programs, new regional trade agreement, and tax reforms.

■ 6. Currency

The currency is the *balboa*, equaling 100 *centesimos*. See the Burns School Global Real Estate Web site for the UNIVERSITY OF DENVER at http://burns.daniels.du.edu for currency conversions.

■ 7. Transportation

In Panama, 76 km (kilometers) of railroads are in use, with 15,137 km of highways. Panama has navigable inland waterways and the famous Panama Canal, which has *PANAMA* now been turned over to Panama. Panama boasts some pipelines that transport crude oil. It has ports, given the strategic shipping location, as well as 117 airports (2013).

■ 8. Communications

Panama has fairly limited communication systems, given that the population has only about 640,000 telephones (2012) and

6.77 million mobile cellular telephones. Connection through coaxial submarine cables and some Intel satellite positions help. Radio and television stations support its communication systems.

9. Real Property Issues

Distinctions of real and personal property in Panama are nearly identical to those used in the United States. The owner of real property owns the surface and subsoil and whatever exists below grade with exception to any restrictions from easements, mining laws, the law of waters, and police regulations. The sale of real property is binding once the buyer and seller have agreed upon the item being sold, the price, and the execution of a public instrument. The sale of real property must be recorded immediately. Conditional sales are permitted provided that the property is easily identifiable and the contract is recorded with the Public Registry Office. The public registry office contains different subdivisions for property registration and mortgage registration. Transfer of title must be by deed. The deed must contain a true statement of consideration, a true description of the property including bounds, the material of a constructed building on the property. Grant or and grantee must sign the deed simultaneously with two witnesses and before a notary public. The deed then has to be recorded with the Public Registry Office.

Mortgages are also executed before a notary public and recorded at the public registry office. Mortgages from a foreign country, made on property in panama are valid if recorded in the public registry. Gains in sale of **real estate** are considered income, but computed on separate basis for tax purposes. There are exemptions from **real estate** tax applicable to land and buildings of export zone. Scale (tariff) of taxes on real property was as follows: (1) 1.75% on any amount exceeding U.S.

$20,000 on assessed value of money to be taxed and up to U.S. $50,000; (2) 1.95% on assessed value in excess of U.S. $50,000 up to U.S. $75,000; (3) 2.10% on assessed value over and above U.S. $75,000. For purpose of taxation, rural **real estate** is valued at minimum of U.S. $30 per hectare.[212]

10. Real Estate Trends

Several companies, such a CB Richard Ellis (http://www.cbre.com), Price Waterhouse Coopers (http://www.pwcglobal.com), and the *Asociacion Panamena de Corredoresy Promotores de Bienes Raices* (ACOBIR) (http://www.acobir.com), provide detailed, current information on the latest real estate market trends in Panama.

11. Cultural Issues

Any nation's culture is complex and vibrant in its diversity.

While broad cultural characterizations such as those presented here can be generally accurate, following such generalities too strictly may be dangerously misleading. To conduct business effectively and profitably in a country, it is vital to have a thorough understanding of its culture's complexities. Panamanians, in general, are a very social people. Conversations often taken place with people sitting or standing close to one another. Visiting another's home is very common place for friends and relatives. It is considered a form of flattery, whether planned or not.

Along with being highly social there is a more informal atmosphere in regard to appearance. The climate has a significant impact on this aspect as well. Wearing shorts and lighter weight clothing are more common. Wearing formal attire (including suits) is rare.

12. Discussion Questions

1. Is the weather a factor in Panama as to attracting investors from abroad?

2. Has the location of Panama been a factor in the development of the economy in Panama?

3. What is the strength of Panama's economy?

13. Case Study

Memo

To: Board of Directors
From: Consultants
Re: Closing in Panama

I. Problem

American Hot Dog Stand (AHDS) Panama 5, Republic of Panama

American Hot Dog Stand (AHDS) has stands all over the world. It specifically targets foreign countries with a high concentration of American Citizens. In Panama, AHDS was reaching all of its project ions, until the turnover of the Panama Canal to Panama in December, 1999. AHDS knew then that sales might drop, but it felt it was beneficial to continue for a period of two years. The restaurant has done marginal for the last two years to test the market. This last year sales have dropped, dramatically.

II. Initial Exit Strategy

The lease for the restaurant was structured so that would expire in March of 2000, three months after the transfer of the Panama Canal. This gave AHDS three months to observe sales and make a decision at the end of the three-month period. The sales actually increased in these three months. Thus, the Company signed another lease, with the clause that it could exit at the end of any year in December, with three months notice.

III. Contingency Strategy

The country was relatively safe, and there was no contingency plan in place.

IV. Conclusion

Due to the drop in sales and the lack of target customers in Panama, it is in the Company's best interest to close the shop. AHDS can give three months of advance notice and exit the lease at the end of the year. It can close the shop at the end of November. This gives the Company one month to dispose of the assets within the restaurant. The Landlord, at one time, expressed his interest, in attempting to re-lease the property with the fixtures, to buy the fixture. The Company should pursue this avenue to see whether the Landlord wants the assets. Most of the assets are not easily moved. The inventory has been monitored. Any new order would need to be placed in November, to be certain that there is not much in inventory. The advertising can be terminated with one month's notice. One of the Company's representatives should go to Panama to follow through. This should be someone with the authority to make decisions, should any problems arise. This will make the transition out of Panama smooth.

Refer to: International Real Estate Digest, Martindale-Hubbell, Homepage. http://www.ired.com. U.S. Embassy. Homepage. http://usembassy.state.gov. U.S. Department of State. Homepage. http://www.state.gov. X-rates.com. Homepage. http://www.x-rates.com/.

14. Selected References

CIA World Factbook.https://www.cia.gov/library/publications/the-world- factbook/index.html. http://www.latinworld.com/centro/panama/economy.com. http://www.panoramapanama.com.

International Real Estate Digest.Martindale-Hubbell. Homepage. http://www.ired.com.

Organization of American States at http://www.oas.org.

Richard Ellis International Property Specialists. http://www.cbre.com. Time Almanac. *TIME Almanac.* Boston: Information Please LLC.

U.S. Bureau of Census at http://www.census.gov.

U.S. Department of Commerce at http://www.statusa.gov. U.S. Bureau of Economic Analysis at http://www.bea.gov. U.S. Embassy. Homepage. http://usembassy.state.gov.

United States Department of St at e. *Background Notes: Panama.* United States Department of State (Online).Available:http://www.state.gov.

World Trade Centers Institute at http://www.wtci.org. World Trade Organization at http://www.wto.org. X-rates.com. Homepage. http://www.x-rates.com/.

15. Glossary

Abrazo – hug.

Association de Corredores y Promotores de Bienes Raices –

(ACOBIR) Real Estate Trade Association.

Camisillas – Male workers wear open-necked shirts.

About the Author

Dr. Mark Lee Levine *is the Editor of this Book.*

Kathy Shahani contributed to part of this material. She is a practicing broker and investor in Panama. She is very involved with the FIABCI Organization.

Russia

INTERNATIONAL REAL ESTATE (GLOBAL REAL ESTATE)
Authored by *Samer Ismail Asfour and Dr. Mark Lee Levine. Editor*

■ 1. Geography

Russia, also called the Russian Federation, is the world's largest country, stretching over a vast expanse of Eastern Europe and northern Asia. Russia covers almost twice the territory of either the United States or China. It is located in northern Asia bordering the Arctic Ocean, between Europe and the North Pacific Ocean. Its total area is 17,098,242 square kilometers (sq km). Russia is bounded on the west by Finland, Estonia, Latvia, Lithuania, Belarus, and Ukraine (with the western exclave of Kaliningrad *oblast* [province] touching Poland). And, it is bounded on the south by Georgia, Azerbaijan, Kazakhstan, Mongolia, China, and North Korea. It faces the Baltic and Black Seas on the west, the Arctic Ocean and conjoined seas on the north, and the Pacific Ocean and conjoined seas on the east. Russia has a total of 20,241 km of land boundaries with the following countries: Azerbaijan 284 km, Belarus 959 km, Southeast China 3,605 km, South China 40 km, Estonia 290 km, Finland 1,313 km, Georgia 723 km, Kazakhstan 6,846 km, North Korea 17.5 km, Latvia 292 km, Lithuania 227 km, Mongolia 3,441 km, Norway 196 km, Poland 432 km, and Ukraine 1,576 km.

The multi-border characteristic of Russia reinforces its accessibility, giving it competitive leverage over neighboring European and Asian countries which possess less exposed boundaries.

■ 2. History and Overview

The defeat of the Russian Empire in World War I led to the seizure of power by the communists and the formation of the Union of Soviet Socialist Republics (USSR). The brutal rule of Josef STALIN (1924-53) strengthened Russian dominance of the Soviet Union at a cost of tens of millions of lives. The Soviet economy and society stagnated in the following decades until General Secretary Mikhail GORBACHEV (1985-91) introduced *glasnost* (openness) and *perestroika* (restructuring) in an attempt to modernize communism, but his initiatives inadvertently released forces that by December 1991 splintered the USSR into 15 independent republics. Since then, Russia has struggled in its efforts to build a democratic political system and market economy to replace the strict social, political, and economic controls of the communist period. During Peter the

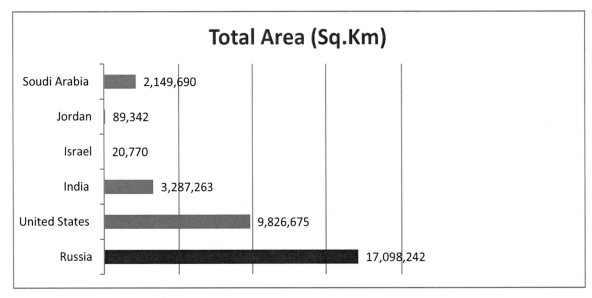

Total Area (Sq.Km)

Country	Total Area (Sq.Km)
Soudi Arabia	2,149,690
Jordan	89,342
Israel	20,770
India	3,287,263
United States	9,826,675
Russia	17,098,242

Great's reign (1689-1725), Russia burst into European and world consciousness, and European influences spread throughout Russia in ways still manifesting themselves in the history and current fortunes of Russia and its neighbors. He created Western style military forces, subordinated the Russian Orthodox Church hierarchy to the czar, reformed the entire governmental structure, and established the beginnings of a Western-style education system. His introduction of European customs generated nationalistic resentments in society, and a philosophical duality of "Westernizers" and nationalistic "Slavophiles" emerged over the next centuries. This dualism manifested itself in various ways over time and since the dissolution of the Soviet Union in 1991 has re-emerged as a key dynamic of current Russian social and political thought.

During the 19th century, which saw great social, economic, and political change in the rest of Europe, the Western Hemisphere, and Asia, the Russian Government sought to suppress repeated attempts at reform from within as well as in such neighboring states as Hungary and Poland. Its economy failed to compete with those of Western countries, and pressures for social and political change continued to build under the weight of agrarian traditions, the feudal serf system, and untrammeled and wasteful privilege among the aristocracy. Russian cities were also growing but did not have an industrial base to generate employment. This shortfall was especially acute after the emancipation of serfs in 1861. Countering these reactionary pressures politically was dynamic expansion across Siberia until the port of Vladivostok was opened on the Pacific coast in 1860. Great accomplishments such as the Trans-Siberian Railroad opened vast frontiers to development late in the century but did not solve fundamental problems of economic opportunity and prosperity for the majority of Russian people. Centuries of successful imperialistic expansion ended with the defeat in the unpopular Russo-Japanese war in 1905. Subsequent disaffection fueled the successful Revolution of 1905 and spurred Czar Nicholas II tactically to grant a constitution. However, hopes for reform were short-lived. Brutal suppressions by the government grew into programs of police terror, and manipulations of popular anger were channeled into anti-Semitic pogroms and other actions against national groups. State abuses contrasted with official attempts at conciliation, such as land reform.

1917 Revolution and the Ussr

Ultimately, both approaches failed, and the ruinous effects of the World War I, combined with internal pressures, sparked the March 1917 revolution. Alexander Kerenski became Premier. On November 7, 1917, the Marxist-Leninist Bolshevik party, led by Vladimir Lenin, seized control and established the Russian Soviet Federated Socialist Republic. Civil war broke out in 1918 between Lenin's "Red" forces and Kerenski's "Whites" and lasted until 1920, when, despite foreign interventions, the Bolsheviks triumphed. After the Red Army conquered Ukraine, Belorussia, Azerbaijan, Georgia, and Armenia, a new nation was formed in 1922. This became known as the Union of Soviet Socialist Republics (USSR).

The USSR lasted 69 years; for more than half that time, it ranked as a nuclear superpower. In the 1930s, tens of millions of its citizens were collectivized under state agricultural and industrial enterprises and millions died in political purges and the vast penal and labor system or in state-created famines. During World War II, as many as 20 million Soviet citizens died. The USSR's chief political figures were Lenin, leader of the Bolshevik party and head of the first Soviet Government, who died in 1924. In the late 1920s, Joseph Stalin emerged as General Secretary of the Communist Party of the Soviet Union (CPSU) amidst intraparty rivalries and maintained complete control over Soviet domestic and international policy until his death in 1953. His successor, Nikita Khrushchev, served as Communist Party leader until he was ousted in 1964. Aleksey Kosygin became Chairman of the Council of Ministers, and Leonid Brezhnev was made First Secretary of the CPSU Central Committee in 1964. But in 1971, Brezhnev rose to become "first among equals" in a collective leadership. Brezhnev died in 1982 and was succeeded by Yuriy Andropov (1982-84), Konstantin Chernenko (1984-85), and Mikhail Gorbachev, who resigned as Soviet President on December 25, 1991. On December 26, 1991, the USSR formally was dissolved.

The Russian Federation

The Russian Federation's independence dates from August 24, 1991. After the December 1991 dissolution of the Soviet Union, the Russian Federation became its largest successor state, inheriting its permanent seat on the United Nat ions Security Council, as well as the bulk of its foreign assets and debt. Almost all of the former Soviet republics agreed to retain a vehicle for mutual discussion and cooperation– the Commonwealth of Independent States (CIS). Georgia joined the CIS in late 1993. Boris Yeltsin was elected President of Russia by popular vote in June 1991. By the fall of 1993, politics in Russia reached a stalemate between President Yeltsin and the parliament. The parliament had succeeded in blocking, overturning, or ignoring the President's initiatives on drafting a new constitution, conducting new elect ions, and making further progress on democratic and economic reforms. In a dramatic speech on Sept ember 21, 1993, President Yeltsin dissolved the Russian Parliament and scheduled national elections for December 12, 1993. After an armed insurrection by opposition supporters failed on October 3, Yeltsin ordered the army to take over the parliament building (called the White House) in Moscow.

Two houses of the new Russian Parliament were elected in December 1993—the upper Federation Council (170 members) and the lower State Duma (450 members). Half of the new Duma members were elected from party lists and the other half in single-seat races in individual election districts. Pro-reform groups won a total of 112 Duma seats. Independents won 135 seats, while representatives from other parties gained 15 seats. The opposition, a diverse group, aimed for a unified posit ion, but remained divided over key political and economic issues. They also had to resolve if they should participate in mainstream politics. Fifty-four percent (58 million) of the registered voters participated in the December 12, 1993 elections. A new constitution took effect the same day.[216]

3. People

The population of Russia is **142,470,272** (2014). The average population growth rate is approximately −0.03% (2014 est.)

Russians, constituting 77.7% of the total population of Russia, have played the leading role in the political, economic, and cultural life of the Russian Empire and the Soviet Union for centuries. They speak a language belonging to the eastern branch of the Slavic language group. Members of more than 60 other ethnic groups also live in Russia, and about 25 of these minorities have their own autonomous republics within the Russian Federation. Broadly, the main divisions within the population are (1) the Slavic group, consisting mainly of Russians, Ukrainians, and Belarusians living chiefly in the west but also widely dispersed throughout the expanses of the country; (2) the Altaic group, speaking mainly Turkic, Manchu- Tungus, and Mongolian languages and found mostly in Central Asia; (3) the Uralic group, speaking Uralic languages and widely dispersed throughout the Eurasian forest and tundra zones; (4) the Caucasus group, speaking various languages and living in the North Caucasus region of Russia; and (5) the Paleosiberian groups, speaking a variety of languages and living across far- eastern Siberia.

Religions are also diverse, the Slavs being mostly Orthodox Christian (Russian Orthodox especially), the Turkic speakers being predominantly Muslim, and the Mongolians being

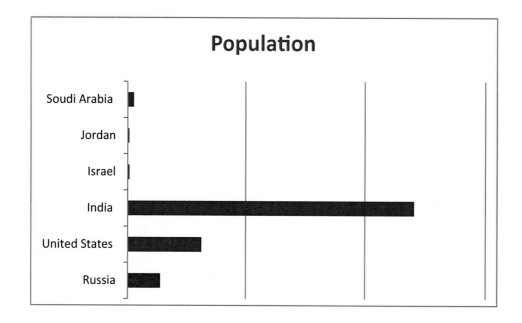

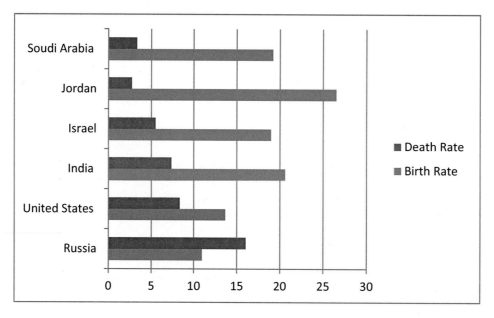

mostly Buddhist. Examining the major ethnic divisions: Russian is 77.7%; Ukrainian is 1.4%; Bashkir is 1.1%; Chuvash 1%; and the balance is spread among other groups. Life expectancy in Russia is 70.16 years, with approximately 76.3 years for females and 64.37 for males. The birth rate is 11.87 births per 1,000 of population. The death rate is 13.83 deaths per 1,000 of population. Infant mortality rate in Russia is around 7.08 per 1,000 live births.

The official language is Russian. English is becoming a common second language. Literacy is very high in Russia at 99.4% of those 15 years and older.

■ 4. Government

In the political system established by the 1993 Constitution, the President wields considerable executive power. There is no vice president, and the Legislative branch is far weaker than the Executive branch. The president nominates the highest state officials, including the Prime Minister, who must be approved by the Duma. The president can pass decrees without consent from the Duma. He also is head of the armed forces and of the national Security Council. Russia is a federation, but the precise distribution of powers between the central government and the regional and local authorities is still evolving. The Russian Federation consists of 89 components, including two federal cities, Moscow and St. Petersburg. The Constitution explicitly defines the federal government's exclusive powers, but it also describes most key regional issues as the joint responsibility of the federal government and the Federation components. In the past few years, the Russian government has begun to reform the criminal justice system and judicial institutions, including the reintroduction of jury trials in certain criminal cases. Despite these effort s, judges are only beginning to assert their constitutionally mandated independence from other branches of government. The Duma passed a Criminal Procedure Code and other judicial reforms during its 2001 session. These reforms helped make the Russian judicial system more compatible with its Western counterparts. These are seen by most as an accomplishment in human rights.[219]

The Russian Federation Cabinet, or Ministries of the Government, is composed of the Premier and his deputies, ministers, and other agency heads. All are appointed by the President. There is also a Presidential Administration (PA) that provides staff and policy support to the President, drafts presidential decrees, and coordinates policy among government agencies. A Security Council also reports directly to the President.

Elections are held every four years in the Russian Federation. The President is elected by popular vote for a four-year term. A Presidential election was held on March 26, 2000, and was expected in 2004. Because there is no vice president, if the President dies in office or he/she cannot exercise the Presidential Powers, because of ill health, is impeached, or resigns, the Premier succeeds him. The Premier serves as acting President until a new Presidential election is held, which must be done within three months. The Premier is appointed by the President with the approval of the Duma.

The Russian Legislative branch has two parts. The first is the bicameral Federal Assembly, *Feralnoye Sobraniye*, consisting of the Federation Council, *Soviet Fderatsii*.

As of July 2000, it seats 178 members who are appointed by the top Executive and Legislative officials in each of the 89 federal administrative units—oblsts, krays, republics, autonomous okrugs and oblasts, and the federal cities of Moscow and Saint Petersburg. Federal Assembly members serve four- year terms. The second part is the state Duma, *Gosudarstvennaya Duma*. The Duma has 450 seats. Half of its members are elected by proportional representation from party lists winning at least 5% of the vote. Another half comes from single-member constituencies; these members are elected by direct popular vote to serve four-year terms.

The Judicial branch consists of the Constitutional Court, the Supreme Court, and the Superior Court of Arbitration. Judges for all courts are appointed for life by the Federation Council; on the recommendation of the President.[220]

■ 5. Economy

A decade or more after the implosion of the Soviet Union in December 1991, Russia is still struggling to establish a modern market economy and achieve strong economic growth. Its trading partners in central Europe were able to overcome the initial production declines that accompanied the launch of market economy reforms within three to five years. Russia, on the other hand, saw its economy contract for five years because the government's Executive and Legislature branches dithered over the implementation of many of the basic foundations of a market economy. Russia achieved a slight recovery in 1997, but the government's stubborn budget deficits and the country's poor business climate made it vulnerable when the global financial crisis swept through in 1998. The crisis culminated in August 1998, with the depreciation of the ruble, a debt default by the government, and a sharp deterioration in overall living standards. The economy subsequently has rebounded, growing by an average of more than 6% annually in 1999 through 2001 on the back of higher oil prices and a weak ruble. This recovery and renewed government efforts in 2000 and 2001 to advance lagging structural reforms have raised business and investor confidence over Russia's prospects. Yet, serious problems persist. The Russian economy remains heavily dependent on commodities exports, particularly oil, natural gas, metals, and timber. Because over 80% of Russia's exports are commodities, Russia is extremely vulnerable to swings in world prices.

Compounding its export problem, Russia's industrial base is increasingly dilapidated and must be replaced or modernized if the country is to achieve sustainable economic growth. Other problems include widespread corruption, lack of a strong legal system, capital flight, and brain drain.[221]

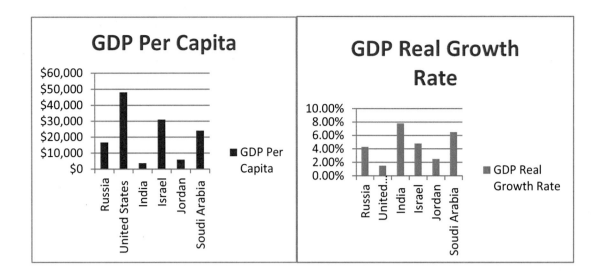

The Russian Federation's economic problems are reflected in its Gross Domestic Product (GDP) per capita at $24,800. It is about one-third of the per capita GDP in European Union countries. Russia's GDP real growth rate is 0.5%, and its GDP is $2.057 trillion (2014).

■ 6. Currency

Russia's currency is the Russian *ruble*. For current conversion rates, see the Global Real Estate Web site at the Burns School, Daniels *College of Business*, UNIVERSITY OF DENVER at http://burns.daniels.du.edu.

■ 7. Transportation

Russia has 1,218 total airports (2013).

Russia's railways total 87,157 km, with 86,200 km in common carrier service and 30,000 km in the service of specific industries, and, thus, unavailable for common carrier use; 40,300 km of the railways in common carrier use are electrified. Russian highways total 1,283,387 km, of which 927,781 km are paved (including 39,143 km of expressways). Russia's unpaved roads total 355,666 km. These roads are generally made of unstabilized earth and can be difficult to negotiate in wet weather (2012).

Russian Federation waterways run 102,000 km (total routes in general use), of which 72,000 km include European Russia links the Baltic Sea, White Sea, Caspian Sea, Sea of Azov, and Black Sea (2012).

Extensive pipelines in Russia deliver a variety of products: condensate 122 km; gas 163,872 km; liquid petroleum gas 1,378 km; oil/gas 80,820 km; and refined products 13,658 km (2013).

Among the most active ports and harbors in Russia are: Arkhangel'sk, Astrakhan, Kaliningrad, Kazan', Khabarovsk, Kholmsk, Krasnoyarsk, Moscow, Murmansk, Naklhodka, Nevel'sk, Novorossiysk, Petropavlovsk-Kamchatskiy, Saint Petersburg, Rostov, Sochi, Tuapse, Vladivost ok, Volgogrfad, Vost ochnyy, and Vyborg.

Moscow

Russia is heavily dependent for freight transport on its railways. The hub of this network is the capital, Moscow.

St. Petersburg

St. Petersburg is one of Russia's most important hubs of transportation. Its port, the nation's largest, is of international significance.

Ukraine

The city is a focus of rail routes, with trunk lines radiating to Helsinki, Finland, and Warsaw as well as to Moscow and other major Russian cities. The flat relief of most of Ukraine presents few obstacles to transportation. Although by European standards the density of the country's hard-surface road network is low, asphalt- paved highways connect all the regions and large industrial centers.

Ukrainian ports on the Black Sea and the Sea of Azov are found at Odessa, Illichivsk, Mykolayiv, Kherson, Feodosiya, Kerch, and Mariupol.

Kiev is connected by air with all the regional centres of the country and with major cities throughout Europe and Asia, as well as with New York City, Los Angeles, Toronto, and Sydney (Australia). International airports in Ukraine include Boryspil near Kiev and those at Kharkiv, Lviv, and Odessa. The exploitation of petroleum and natural gas in Ukraine has necessitated the creation of an extensive pipeline transport system. The transportation system makes Ukraine's mineral, industrial, and agricultural products available to the entire region. Recent conflicts have developed between Russia and the Ukraine.

8. Communication

Throughout the history of the Soviet state, the communications media were controlled by the government and the Communist Party. With the coming of democratization in the 1990s, however, the Russian media were released from most state controls. In Russia, there are 42.9 million telephone main lines in use (2012) and 261.9 million mobile cellular telephones. The telephone system has undergone significant changes in the 1990s. There are many companies licensed to offer communication services. Access to digital lines has improved, particularly in urban centers, and Internet and e-mail services are improving. Russia has made progress toward building the telecommunications infrastructure necessary for a market economy. However, a large demand for main line telephone service remains unsatisfied. At home, cross-country digital trunk lines run from Saint Petersburg to Khabarovsk, and from Moscow to Novorossiysk. The telephone systems in 60 regional capitals have modern digital infrastructures. Cellular services, both analog and digital, are available in many areas. In rural areas, the telephone services are still out dated, inadequate, and low density. Internationally, Russia is connected by three undersea fiber optic cables. Digital switches in several cities provide more than 50,000 lines for international calls. Satellite earth stations provide access to Intels at, Intersputnik, Eutelsat, Inmarsat, and Orbita systems. Russian radio broadcast stations include 323 AM, 1,500 FM, and 62 shortwave (2004). There are 7,306 television broadcast stations. Internet service providers (hosts) total 14.865 million (2012), and Internet users total 40.853 million (2012).

9. Real Property Issues

Commissions on real estate transactions vary greatly depending on the company providing the services. Western companies frequently require higher fees because they usually offer better service. Some typical commission rates are: landlord representation, 7% to10% (Western companies) and 3.5% to4% (Russian companies); tenant representation, U.S. $30 to $50 per leased sq m for big clients and 1 month rent for small clients. Sale commissions range from 2% to 3%. There is a 12% or more transfer tax paid by the seller. Public registry is $10 to $250, split between the buyer and seller. The attorney/notary fee is a 1.5% split. Official valuation, if required, is $50 or more, split. There is no central land registry that would guarantee title to a land/property purchaser.

There is also currently no land code that sets up the framework for overall land reform and sale in Russia. The new constitution gives Russians the right to own, inherit, lease, mortgage, and sell real property. Free sale and purchase of land by Russians and joint ventures with non-Russian companies' participation is allowed according to Decree #1767 on land for October 1993.

In addition, an investor should be careful about property taxes in Russia. The residential rate is 1% of real estate value, and all other property types are 2.5% of real estate value. All tax returns are paid in rubles. Non-Russian legal entities without a permanent establishment in Russia are not liable to Russian profit tax. In such cases, rental income from letting a property located in Russia is normally subject to withholding a tax at a rate of 20% of the gross rent.

10. Real Estate Trends

Office: For the city of Moscow, the total supply of office space is 2.2 million sq m with 40% considered to be international quality space. Demand in 2000 for offices was within an average lease requirement of 400 to 500 sq m, and 320,000 sq m of office space were either leased or sold in that year. This figure represents an increase of 50% over the previous year. The vacancy rate was on average 8%. Lease term was between 3 years and 5 years. Operating expenses were around $100 per sq m per year. Typical space size is around 500 to 900 sq m. Prices range between $400 to $650 per sq m per year.

Retail: For the city of St. Petersburg, the retail market depends on tourist activity, per capita income, and local consumption. The retail market is relatively stable across the country. The vacancy rate in St. Petersburg is now around 8%. In 1998, the sale prices for retail space dropped by 25% to 30% and reached $37 to $177 per sq m. In 1998, department store prices were $28 to $37 per sq m per year. Lease rates based on new construction or reconstruction of more than 50 sq m in a prime location were $42 to $120 per sq m per month in Moscow, and $20 to $80 per sq m in other cities. Sale prices range from $1,200 to $7,000 per sq m in Moscow and $600 to $2,400 in other cities.

Residential: The residential market for both new and resale properties is brisk in the major cities of Moscow and St. Petersburg, less so in smaller cities and rural areas. The larger brokerage firms are generally owned and managed by those who have absorbed Western style marketing methods from visits and attendance at training programs in the United States and England. The Russian Guild of REALTORS@ strives to bring a higher level of ethical standards to real estate practice in Russia.

11. Cultural Issues

Any nation's culture is complex and vibrant in its diversity.

While broad cultural characterizations such as those presented here can be generally accurate, following such generalities too strictly may be dangerously misleading. To conduct business effectively and profitably in a country, it is vital to have a thorough understanding of its culture's complexities.

Russian clothing styles are the same as those in Europe, but they are not as sophisticated, in most instances. Jeans are popular among most age groups, except older women. In winter, people wear *ushanki* (fur hats). Shorts are becoming popular among the younger generation. The older generation dresses more conservatively.

When meeting, Russians shake hands firmly and might say *Zdravstvuyte*, pronounced sdrav- STVUH-teh, it means "Hello", *Dobry dien*, Good day, or *Privet*, a casual "Hello." Some women prefer not to shake hands, but it is impolite for a man not to offer his hand. Friends and family often kiss on both cheeks. Because the question, *Kak dela?*, How are you?, is taken literally, Russians answer in detail and at length. Asking the question without waiting for a full response is rude. *Kak dela?* is not used as a formal greeting. Titles, such as *Gospodin*, Mr., and *Gospozha*, Mrs., *were not* used under the communists, but they are being revived. In addressing an older or respected person, one uses the given name and a patronymic (possessive of father's first name). However, surnames are preferred in formal greetings. It is considered inappropriate for a younger person or subordinate to address an elder or superior in a causal manner. Pointing with the index finger is improper, but commonly practiced. It is impolite to talk (especially to an older person) with one's hands in the pockets or arms folded across the chest. To count, a Russian bends (closes) the fingers rather than opening them. Russians like to visit and have guests.

Sitting around the kitchen table and talking for hours is a favorite pastime. Shoes are sometimes removed upon entering a home. Refreshments are usually offered, but guest may decline them. Friends and family may visit anytime without prior arrangement. They make themselves at home and can usually expect to be welcomed for any length of time. Visits with new acquaintances are more formal and require prior notice.

Giving gifts is a strong tradition in Russia. Almost every event (birthdays, weddings, holidays, etc.) is accompanied by presents. For casual visits, it is common (but not required) for guests to bring a simple gift (flowers, food, and vodka) to their hosts. What is given is less import ant than the friendship expressed by the act. Flowers are given in odd numbers; even numbers are for funerals. If a bottle of vodka (which means "little water") is opened, custom dictates it be emptied by those present. Eating with the fork in the left hand and the knife in the right is standard, but many people use only a fork. Hands are kept above the table and not in the lap. Most Russians like to eat a large breakfast whenever possible. Soup is common for lunch or dinner. Traditionally, a popular feature of any meal is zakuski (appetizers). There are many different kinds of zakuski; eating too many may spoil an appetite. Russians put more food than they can eat on the table and leave some on the plate to indicate there is abundance (whether true or not) in the house. Guests who leave food on the plate indicate they have eaten well. Russians generally do not go to lunch in cafés or restaurants, because the few that exist are fairly expensive. Instead, people eat at cafeterias, where they work or bring food from home.

For details in this area, see the Burns School Global Real Estate Web site for the University of Denver at http://burns.daniels.du.edu.

12. Discussion Questions

1. What are several factors that you think are important in Russian culture which could affect the relationships between foreigners and Russian citizens?

2. How has Russia sought to strengthen its economy since the dissolution of the Soviet Union? Is it succeeding?

3. Russia has borders with many countries. Do these borders play any significant role in the development of Russia's economy?

4. 4. Do you see anything that alerts you regarding Russia's land size and its population compared to smaller countries (land size and population) with regard to GDP and other economic factors?

13. Case Study

Memo

To: Board of Directors
From: Consultants
Re: Downsizing

I. Problem

OVERVIEW
Fantasy Real Estate Sales (FRES)

Headquarters in Milan, Italy: Offices in Italy, Sweden, Hungary, Spain, Russia, Netherlands, United Kingdom and Greece. Fantasy Real Estate Sales (FRES) was established in Greece in 1995. The idea behind the Company was drawn from a Greek real estate agent, XElvina Greeeelepis, owner of XXEGGG Realty. XElvina's real estate company had many different properties listed, including villas and private islands. The inspiration for FRES came from meeting XElvina. The Directors felt we would be able to help people find their "fantasy" pieces of real estate, such as castles, villas, ranches, winery's and any unique properties falling into the "fantasy" realm of real estate.

ITALY

Recently the headquarters of FRES, located in Milan, Italy, began to grow. It was doing so much business that it had seven full-time agents, and one office manager.

FRES needs to hire more people, but it is concerned with hiring too many, because if the Company has more than 15 employees, it will have to "take care of the employees" for a long time. This is based on the employment laws in Italy. See http://www.cmslegal.com/intelligence/cms_news/employment.htm.

RUSSIA

The Russian market is beginning to pick up new business. There are plenty of properties available, but FRES's target buyers are hesitant to purchase property in Russia. (FRES is working on advertising the benefits of realty in Russia. FRES started doing overnight stays at the individual properties, so potential clients can see what it is like to be in Russia.)

HUNGARY

Currently, in Hungary, the Company has had a reduction in properties available for sale. FRES was been unable to secure properties for sale. It has also had two properties flood in the last two months.

NETHERLANDS

The market is booming. There seem to be enough "fantasy" properties at the current time.

UNITED KINGDOM (ENGLAND, SCOTLAND, WALES)

The United Kingdom, including the **England, Scotland and Wales** markets, has been relatively stable. These markets, for FRES, do not perform extremely well, but they do not go below projected income.

SPAIN

This market is just beginning to show the growth potential that was projected by FRES for the country. The market had a difficult time because prices were inflated.

As such, it was not a good investment to purchase a fantasy property here; however, prices are beginning to come inline. Thus, with other European markets, the general market is beginning to pickup in sales.

SWEDEN

Currently the Swedish market is booming. The agents cannot keep up with the market.

II. Initial Exit Strategy

Exiting these countries would be relatively easy, except for Italy, where the headquarters office is currently located. All of the other offices are satellite offices. In most cases the agents work out of their own homes. The Milan office could be vacated relatively easily. The interior has been upgraded to class A office space and since this is in short supply in Italy, it should be relatively easy to re-lease or sub-lease. The network of real estate agents throughout Europe that FRES has established would help in the event that FRES needed to leave the county.

III. Contingency Exit Strategy

See Initial Exit Strategy plan. The plan of exit would be simple to leave everything and leave the country.

IV. Conclusion

Employment restrictions in Italy will make it difficult to keep expanding. To have a reasonable exit strategy, FRES should move the headquarters to Sweden. The reason Sweden is more of an ideal location is due to the booming market and the favorable employment laws. The other markets could be considered, but Russia would be difficult. Current employees would resist a move to Sweden. The United Kingdom does not have enough business. This is also true with the Netherlands. Spain might be a possibility for the home office. The company should not completely close the operation in Italy, but it should leave one or two agents, to continue the local market.

Refer to: International Real Estate Digest. Homepage. http://www.ired.com. U.S. Department of State. Homepage. http://www.state.gov.

U.S. Embassy. Homepage. http://usembassy.state.gov.

14. Selected References

Bertaud, Alain. *Cities Without Land Markets: Lessons of the Failed Socialist Experiment.* World Bank. Washington D.C.: 1994.

Bromley, Daniel W. *Environment and Economy: Property Rights and Public Policy.* Blackwell. Oxford, UK; Cambridge, USA: 1991.

CIA World Factbook.https://www.cia.gov/library/publications/the-world-factbook/index.html.

CIPS Materials. National Association of Realtors.

Culturgrams®. Kennedy Center Publications. Brigham Young University, Provo, UT : 1995. *Refer to Encarta Encyclopedia.* ©MicroSoft, Inc. 1995. *Encyclopedia Britannica* (1999). Ernst and Young. *Doing Business In Russia.* Ernst and Young International: 1995.

Firestone, Jamison. *The Moscow Times.* "Real Estate Firms Awash in a Sea of Regulations." June 27, 1995. No. 740.

Hines, Mary Alice. *Global Corporate Real Estate Management: A Handbook for Multinational Businesses and Organizations.* Quorum Books. New York: 1990. *International Estate Planning: Principles and Strategies.* Section of Real Property, Probate and Trust Law, Section of International Law and Practice, American Bar Association. Chicago, IL: 1991.

International Property Investment Journal - Quarterly. Harwood Academic Publishers, POB 786, Cooper St at ion, New York, NY 10276.

International Trade Reporter. "Foreign Investors in Moscow Now May Acquire Leases to Land." June 14, 1995. Vol. 12, No. 24; Pg. 1041.

Jaffe, Austin J., and C.E. Sirmans. *Real Estate Finance.* "Real Estate Research Around the World." Fall 1994. V. 11, N.3, Page 16.

Madalena, Jesus A. *International Property Investment.* World Peace Law Cent er. Washington, D.C.: 1981

Martindale Hubbell International Law Digest. Reed Einsliver Inc.: 1995.

Mozolin, V.P. Property *Law in Contemporary Russia.* International Law Institute. Washington, D.C.: 1993.

National Real Estate Investor. "Industrial Developments International." February 1, 1996. V. 38, N. 2. Page 32.

National Real Estate Investor. "Risks and Rewards of Going Global." June, 1995, Vol. 37; No. 6; Page 74.

New Grollier Encyclopedia. Multimedia Edition: 1994.

Price Waterhouse. *Doing Business with Russia.* Price Waterhouse Lt d.: 1995. Renard, Vincent and Rodrigo Acosta (edit ors). *Gestion Fonciereet Operations Immobilieres en Europe de L'Est.* (Land Tenure and Property Development in Eastern Europe.) ADEF: Pirville-CNRS. Paris: 1993.

Russia (Federation). *Business and Commercial Laws of Russia: Translations with Expert Commentary.* John P. Hubb, general edit or; translations by Russia Information, Inc. Shepard's McGraw-Hill. Colorado Springs, Colorado, 1993. Tolkacheva, Julie. *The Moscow Times.* "Moscow Legalizes Sale of Land Leases." June 6, 1995. No. 726.

Williams, Carol J. *Los Angeles Times.* "Russia; Milit ary Housing Now Hot Property." September 29, 1995. Friday, Home Edit ion, Par A; Page 5. For details in this area, see the Burns School Global Real Estate Web site for the University of Denver at http://burns.daniels.du.edu.

Int ernat ional Real Estate Digest. Homepage. www.ired.com. U.S. Bureau of Census at http://www.census.gov. U.S. Department of Commerce at http://www.stat- usa.gov. U.S. Bureau of Economic Analysis at http://www.bea.gov. U.S. Department of State. Homepage. http://www.state.gov. U.S. Embassy. Homepage. http://usembassy.state.gov. World Trade Centers Institute at http://www.wtci.org.

World Trade Organization at http://www.wto.org. World Bank. *Adult Illiteracy Rates.* The Economist X-rates.com. Homepage. http://www.x-rates.com/. Personal information; field research

15. Glossary

Presidential Administration – Provides staff and policy support to the president, drafts. Presidential decrees, and coordinates policy among government agencies.

Zdravstvuyte – (pronounced Sdra – STVUH – the) meaning hello.

Dobry dien – (Good day).

Privet – a casual hello. **Gospodin** – Mr. **Gospozha** – Mrs.

About the Author

Samer I. Asfour, Chief Operating Officer of Design Jordan in Amman, Jordan. Mr. Asfour was the General Manager of the Amman World Trade Center in Amman, Jordan.

Saudi Arabia

INTERNATIONAL REAL ESTATE (GLOBAL REAL ESTATE)
Authored by *Samer Ismae Asfour* and
Travis McCain Dr. Mark Lee Levine, Editor

1. Geography

The Kingdom of Saudi Arabia, a country occupying most of the Arabian Peninsula, is west of the Persian Gulf and east of the Red Sea. Saudi Arabia is bordered by Jordan, Iraq, and Kuwait on the north; by Qatar, the United Arab Emirates, and Oman on the east; by a portion of Oman on the southeast; and by Yemen on the south and southwest. It is separated from Egypt, the Sudan, and Ethiopia by the Red Sea on the west; from Bahrain by the Gulf of Bahrain on the east; and from Iran by the Persian Gulf, also on the east. Saudi Arabia has an area of 2,149,690 sq km. The capital and largest city is Riyadh. Saudi Arabia is mostly desert, although a major mountain range extends northwest to southeast along the western edge of the country.

Climatically, Saudi Arabia is almost entirely a desert. There are three predominant climatic zones: a small area of humid and mild temperature conditions in Asir near the Yemen border, with annual rainfall that can average more than 480 mm (19 inches); a step along the western highlands, less than 160 km (100 miles) wide in the north and widening to nearly 480 km (300 miles) near Mecca; and arid and semiarid desert, which constitutes more than 95 percent of the total land area. In Rub' Al-Khali a decade may pass with no rain at all. Temperatures

nationwide tend to be cooler during the winter months (between 14° C [58° F] and 23° C [74° F]) and extremely hot in the summer, with temperatures from June to August exceeding 38° C (100° F) and frequently reaching 54° C (129° F). Humidity is low, except along the coasts, where it can be high and very oppressive.

2. History and Overview

261 Except for a few major cities and oases, the harsh climate historically prevented much settlement of the Arabian Peninsula. People of various cultures have lived there over a span of more than 5,000 years.

The Dilmun culture, along the Gulf coast, was contemporaneous with the Sumerians and ancient Egyptians, and most of the empires of the ancient world traded with the states of the peninsula.

The Saudi state began in central Arabia in about 1750 A.D. A local ruler, Muhammad bin Saud, joined forces with an Islamic reformer, Muhammad Abd Al-Wahhab, to create a new political entity. Over the next 150 years, the fortunes of the Saud family rose and fell several times as Saudi rulers cont ended with Egypt, the Ottoman Turks, and other Arabian families for control on the peninsula. The modern Saudi state was founded by the late King Abd Al-Aziz Al-Saud (known internationally as Ibn Saud). In 1902, Abd Al-Aziz recaptured Riyadh, the Al-Saud dynasty's ancestral capital, from the rival Al-Rashid family. Continuing his conquests, Abd Al-Aziz subdued Al-Hasa, the rest of Nejd, and the Hijaz between 1913 and 1926. In 1932, these regions were unified as the Kingdom of Saudi Arabia. Boundaries with Jordan, Iraq, and Kuwait were established by a series of treaties negotiated in the 1920s. The Saudi-Kuwaiti neutral zone was administratively partitioned in 1971, with each state continuing to share the petroleum resources of the former zone equally. Tentative agreement on the partition of the Saudi-Iraqi neutral zone was reached in 1981, and partition was finalized by 1983. The country's southern boundary with Yemen was partially defined by the 1934 Treaty of Taif, which ended a brief border war between the two states. It remains

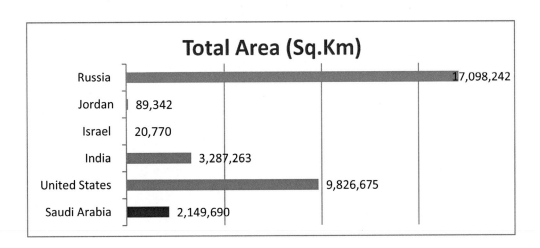

undefined in many areas. The border between Saudi Arabia and the United Arab Emirates was agreed upon in 1974. Boundary differences with Qatar remained unresolved.

The mid-1960s experienced external pressures generated by Saudi-Egyptian differences over Yemen. When civil war broke out in 1962 between Yemeni royalists and republicans, Egyptian forces entered Yemen to support the new republican government, while Saudi Arabia backed the royalists. Tensions subsided only after 1967, when Egypt withdrew its troops from Yemen.

Saudi forces did not participate in the Six-Day (Arab-Israeli) war of June, 1967, but the government later provided annual subsidies to Egypt, Jordan, and Syria to support their economies. During the 1973 Arab-Israeli war, Saudi Arabia participated in the Arab oil boycott of the United States and Netherlands. A member of the Organization of Petroleum Exporting Countries (OPEC), Saudi Arabia had joined other member countries in moderate oil price increases beginning in 1971. After the 1973 war, the price of oil substantially rose, dramatically increases beginning in 1971. After the 1973 war, the price of oil substantially rose, dramatically increasing Saudi wealth and political influence.

In 1975, King Faisal was assassinated by a nephew, who was executed after an extensive investigation concluded thathe acted alone. Faisal was succeeded by his half-brother Khalid as King and Prime Minister. Their half-brother Prince Fahd was named Crown Prince and First Deputy Prime Minister. King Khalid empowered Crown Prince Fahd to oversee many aspects of the government's international and domestic affairs. Economic development continued rapidly under King Khalid, and the kingdom assumed a more influential role in regional politics and international economic and financial matters. In June 1982, King Khalid died, and Fahd became King and Prime Minister in a smooth transition. Another half-brother, Prince Abdullah, Commander of the Saudi National Guard, was named Crown Prince and First Deputy Prime Minister. King Fahd's brother, Prince Sultan, the Minister of Defense and Aviation, became Second Deputy Prime Minister. Under King Fahd, the Saudi economy adjusted to sharply lower oil revenues resulting from declining global oil prices. Saudi Arabia supported neutral shipping in the Gulf during periods of the Iran-Iraq war and aided Iraq's war-strained economy. King Fahd played a major part in bringing about the August, 1988 cease-fire and in organizing and strengthening the Gulf Cooperation Council (GCC), a group of six Arabian Gulf states dedicated to fostering regional economic cooperation and peaceful development.

In 1990-91, King Fahd played a key role before and during the Gulf war. It was his early, formal request to President Bush for military assistance on August 6, 1990, that allowed U.S. troops to deploy in time to avert possible moves by Iraq's Saddam Hussein into Saudi Arabia. King Fahd's action also consolidated the coalition of forces against Iraq and helped define the tone of the operation as a multilateral effort to reestablish the sovereignty and territorial integrity of Kuwait. Acting as a rallying point and personal spokesman for the coalition, King Fahd helped bring together his nation's GCC allies, Western allies, and Arab allies, as well as non- aligned nations from Africa and the emerging democracies of Eastern Europe. He used his influence as Custodian of the Two Holy Mosques to persuade other Arab and Islamic nations to join the coalition.

Upon King Fahd's death on August 1, 2005, Crown Prince Abdullah assumed the throne as King. Prince Sultan, Minister of Defense and Aviation, became Crown Prince and the First Deputy Prime Minister.[227]

■ 3. People

The total population of the Kingdom during 2014 was estimated at 27,345,986, with an annual growth rate of 1.49%.

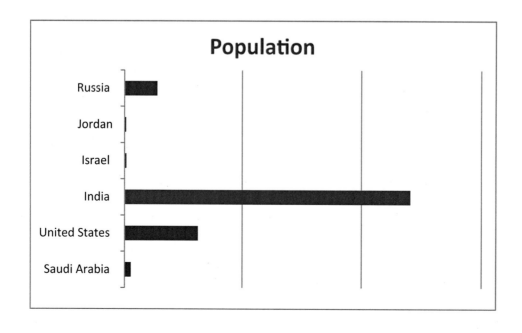

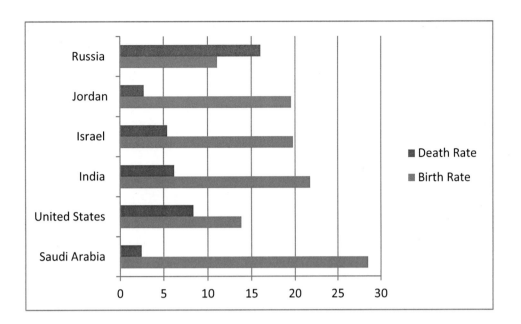

The age group between 0 and 14 years constituted 27.6% of the total population.

The age group between 15 to 64 years is 69.2%. The 65 years of age and older group is only 3.2%. The greatest percentage of the population is centered on the capital city of Riyadh. Jeddah has a large population of residents, followed by Makkah.[229]

The life expectancy in Saudi Arabia is 74.82 years, with 76.94 years for females and 72.79 years for males (2014). The birth rate is 18.78 births per 1,000. The death rate is 3.32 per 1,000.

The fertility rate is estimated to be about 2.17 children per woman. The infant mortality rate in Saudi Arabia is 14.58 per 1,000 live births (2014).

The official language is Arabic. English has become a common second language as a result of the large expatriate population. Literacy is 78.8%. However, this percent is rapidly increasing in the last decade as a result of the government's concern to improve the level of education.

At an unemployment rate of 11.2% among Saudi males (2014), the labor force continues to grow. See the U.S. Department of State Web site regarding Saudi Arabia's Labor Regulations at http://www.state.gov/e/eeb/ifd/2006/62029.htm.

Foreign Investment: Leading up to its recent agreement with the World Trade Organization (WTO) in December 2005, Saudi Arabia began taking steps towards a more conducive foreign investment environment by passing laws for its capital markets, insurance, intellectual property rights sectors, as well as revisions to the tax code which reduced the taxes on foreign-owned capital.

1969 Labor and Workman Regulations

Although in actuality the typical percentage of Saudi workers in a firm is much less, the *1969 Labor and Workman Regulations* states 75 percent of a firm's work force and 51 percent of its payroll must be Saudi unless the firm was given an exemption from the Ministry of Labor. Foreign firms and investors are under constant pressure to employ more Saudis, in 1996 the Saudi Government established a new quota that called for any company employing over 20 workers to increase the total number of Saudis by 5 percent per year. Under the quota system each company would have attained a 45 percent Saudi workforce, however a revision to the Labor law came in 2005 which now requires any firm to establish a workforce containing 75 percent Saudi Nationals. Over the course of the new quotas, very few firms have been able to meet the requirements. Any company that does not meet the minimum personnel rule is not given visas for expatriate workers.

■ 4. Government

The government is based on the *Shari'ah,* or Islamic law. The King serves as both a religious and governmental leader, and also holds the title of Prime Minister. There is a crown prince; he is at the same time the First Deputy Prime Minister. The Cabinet is a Council of Ministers appointed by the King, and includes royal family members.

A 90-member Consultative Council is appointed for four years by the King but has no legislative powers. The basic law that articulates the government's rights and responsibilities was introduced in 1993. Administratively, Saudi Arabia is divided into thirteen provinces, governed by Princes or close relatives of the royal family. All governors are appointed by the King. The Gulf Cooperation Council (GCC) is a group of six Arabian Gulf states dedicated to fostering regional economic cooperation and peaceful development.

5. Economy

Long-range economic development is directed through the implementation of five-year plans.[231] Saudi Arabia has an oil-based economy with strong governmental controls over major economic activities.[232]

The Gross Domestic Product (GDP) per capita is estimated to be $52,800. The GDP real growth rate is 3.6%. The total GDP was $777.9 billion (2014).

6. Currency

The unit of currency is the *Saudi riyal (SAR)* which is divided into 100 *halalahs*. Notes are issued in denominations of 1, 5, 10, 50, 100 and 500 riyals.

There are also riyal coins. Officially, the Saudi Riyal (SR) is pegged to the International Monetary Fund's Special Drawing Rights. Since 1981, however, the Saudi Arabian Monetary Authority has instead chosen to peg the SR to the U.S. dollar. To minimize exchange risks for the private sector, to facilitate long term planning and to encourage repatriation of capital from abroad, the Saudi Government had maintained the exchange rate at SAR 3.75 per U.S. $1.00 since 1987. There is no restriction on converting the riyal or transferring money outside the country. Most foreign currencies can be converted against the Saudi *riyal*.

7. Transportation

Saudi Arabia has an expanding network of roads and highways, which is constantly being upgraded. Total length of highways in 2012 was 221,372 km, but only 47,529 km of highways are paved. Signposts are both in Arabic and English in most of the Kingdom. Of Saudi Arabia's 214 airports, only 82 are paved. In the area of railway transportation, the Kingdom has 1,378 km of railroads (2010). In the area of maritime transport, the Kingdom has several main ports: Ad Dammam, Al Jubayl, Jiddah, and Yanbu'al Sinaiyah.

8. Communications

The communication sector in Saudi Arabia includes a telephone system with 4.8 million main lines in use (2012) and 53 million mobile cellular telephones in use. Saudi Arabia's telephone system has been modernized to include extensive domestic microwave radio relay and coaxial and fiber optic cable systems as well as international microwave radio relay to Bahrain, Jordan, Kuwait, Qatar, UAE, Yemen, and Sudan; coaxial cable to Kuwait and Jordan; submarine cable to Djibouti, Egypt, and Bahrain; satellite earth stations - - 5 Intelsat (3 Atlantic Ocean and 2 Indian Ocean), 1 Arabsat, and 1 Inmarsat (Indian Ocean region). The Saudi state controls radio and television networks. The Internet has increased rapidly in Saudi Arabia after 1998. In 2012 there were 145,941 Internet service providers (hosts) and an estimated 9,774,000 Internet users (2012).[235]

9. Real Property Issues

Most of the property in Saudi Arabia is owned by Saudi citizens. (See the Burns School Global Real Estate website for updated information)[236]

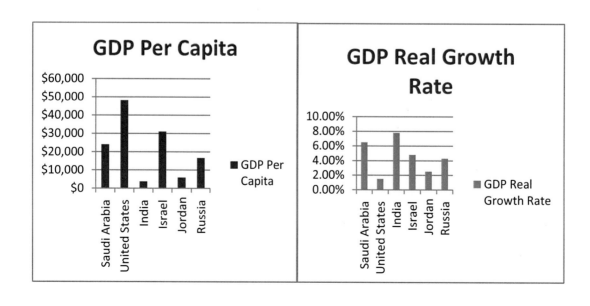

■ 10. Real Estate Trends

(See the Burns School Global Real Estate website for updated information at http://burns.daniels.du.edu.)[237]

■ 11. Cultural Issues

Any nation's culture is complex and vibrant in its diversity.

While broad cultural characterizations such as those presented here can be generally accurate, following such generalities too strictly may be dangerously misleading. To conduct business effectively and profitably in a country, it is vital to have a thorough understanding of its culture's complexities. Saudi customs and cultural issues are very important and more distinguished from other Gulf countries. Men wear the *ghotra* (headdress) and *thobe* (ankle-length shirt, usually white, that covers long pant s). A *mishlah* (cloak) is often worn over the thobe. A third piece which is not seen is the *tagia*, a small white cap that keeps the *ghotra* from slipping off the head The *ghotra* is not removed in public. Some men have adopted western dress for some occasions, but the majority of men retain the customary clothing. A *ghotra* is usually either red checkered or completely white. It is held in place by an *iqual* (braided black cord). The white *ghotra* is usually made of lighter fabric and may be seen more often in the summer.

Depending on the location, women in public have veiled faces and wear an *abayah* (a black robe that covers the entire body). The *abayah* is often worn over beautifully tailored dresses. Modesty is of utmost importance. Even visit ors are expected to dress conservatively; tight fitting or revealing clothing is unacceptable. Women's fashions do not stop with the abayah; although one is male, that is all the male would be likely to see. Beneath the black cloak, Saudi women enjoy fashionable clothing and take great pride in their appearance. They enjoy bright colors and lavish material. Non-Muslim women living in Saudi Arabia often wear the *abayah* as a sign of respect for local customs.

Greetings often use the word *Salam Alaikom*, which means "hello," and more specifically, "peace be upon you." Frequently, males will follow the greeting by kissing each other's right and left cheeks. Women, do not shake hands with men in public, nor do they speak to foreigners (not "relatives").

Saudi's national dish is known as *Kabsah*. This is a whole rice dish with meat, cooked with a hot red sauce and served on a big plate.

The preparation, serving and drinking of *gahwa*—Arabian coffee—are each individual rituals derived from Bedouin hospitality. These are traditions that are still bound today by the same ceremony and etiquette which have ruled for centuries.

Public care of one's teeth is perfectly acceptable in Saudi Arabia, and is done with the *miswak*, a natural toothbrush-cum-toothpaste. This multi-purpose stick cleans the mouth, whitens the teeth and sweetens the breath, and is widely used throughout the Arab world. Muslims use it on the recommendation of the Prophet Mohammed, who used it during fasting and also advised its use as a breath freshener before prayer. By contrast, with the conventional plastic toothbrush, the *miswak* can be used anytime, anywhere. It completely dispenses with the need for toothpaste squeezing, vigorous brushing, foaming at the mouth or spitting. Dental research has discovered interesting information about the *miswak*. Chemical analysis revealed that it contains a total of 19 natural substances which are beneficial to dental health. Its natural antiseptics have a bactericidal action, killing harmful microorganisms in the mouth. The tannic acid it contains has astringent qualities which protect the gums from disease. Its aromatic oils increase salivation. Because of its built-in antiseptics, the *miswak* needs no cleaning. Because its bristles are parallel to the handle rather than perpendicular, it can reach more easily between the teeth, where a conventional toothbrush often misses.

12. Discussion Questions

1. What is Saudi Arabia's largest item of export? Import?

2. Discuss why it is important for a visitor to have knowledge of Saudi Arabia's customs, culture and religious way of life, and what are some of these?

3. Can anyone who is not a Saudi citizen own real estate in Saudi Arabia?

13. Case Study

Human Trafficking Investigation (HTI) Riyadh, Saudi Arabia

Memo

To: Board of Directors
From: Consultants
Re: Closing the office

I. Problem

Human Trafficking Investigation (HTI) is a non-profit organization, working toward the eradication of human trafficking. HTI responds to missing persons. It helps to provide housing, legal services, jobs and other services to victims and those involved. The office in Saudi Arabia has been open for over six months. HTI has been trying to establish safe havens and other services, but it has so far been unable. HTI is considering closing the office, until it can obtain the connections needed to continue to support trafficking victims. Part of the reason it has trouble is because, apparently, the government does not acknowledge the problem, even though Saudi Arabia falls into a Tier 3 category,

as defined by the Trafficking in Persons Report.

A Tier 3 country is defined as: The governments of countries in Tier 3 do not fully comply with the minimum standards and are not making significant efforts to bring themselves into compliance. Some of these governments refuse to acknowledge the trafficking problem within their territory. On a more positive note, several other governments in this category are beginning to take concrete steps to combat trafficking. While these steps do not yet reach the appropriate level of significance, many of these governments are on the path to placement Tier 2. (See http://www.state.gov)

The government of Saudi Arabia has not completed efforts to meet all duties under the Act.

II. Initial Exit Strategy

Initial exit strategy was to stay until the funds ran out, or there was an eradication of human trafficking in Saudi Arabia.

III. Contingency Exit Strategy

Exiting Saudi Arabia would not be too difficult. The lease expires at the end of this year, as long as HTI gives notice. Since foreigners are not allowed to own land, HTI did not purchase any property when it entered the country. HTI can easily relocate its staff to either France or Singapore, whichever office it will keep open.

IV. Conclusion

Exiting Saudi Arabia at this time is not the ideal situation. But, because of the lack of cooperation and the lack of networks, HTI must move the office. HTI can attempt to work from out side of the country as well. Hopefully it will be able to help others in a more positive way.

Refer to: International Real Estate Digest. Homepage. http://www.ired.com. U.S. Department of State. Homepage. http://www.state.gov.

U.S. Embassy. Homepage. http://usembassy.state.gov.

14. Selected References

CIA World Factbook https://www.cia.gov/library/publications/the-world-factbook/index.html.

International Monetary Fund (IMF), Int ernat ional Financial Statistics. International Finance Corporation at www.ifc.org.

The Economist Intelligence Unit, Country Profile 1999.

Energy Information Administration at www.eia.doe.gov.

Meed Magazine. Library of Congress website.

International Real Estate Digest. Homepage. http://www.ired.com. U.S. Bureau of Census at http://www.census.gov.

U.S. Department of Commerce at http://www.stat-usa.gov.

U.S. Bureau of Economic Analysis at http://www.bea.gov. U.S. Department of State. Homepage. http://www.state.gov.

U.S. Embassy. Homepage. http://usembassy.state.gov. World Trade Centers Institute at http://www.wtci.org. World Trade Organization at http://www.wto.org.

See also: Personal information, some field research. X-rates.com. Homepage. http://www.x-rates.com/.

15. Glossary

Abayah – a black robe that covers the entire body.

Ghotra – headdress men wear.

Gulf Cooperation Council – (GCC) a group of six Arabian Gulf states dedicated to fostering regional economic cooperation and peaceful development.

Kabasah – national dish which includes whole rice and meat cooked with hot red sauce.

Mishlah – cloak is often worn over the thobe.

Miswak – a toothbrush-cum-toothpaste, public care of one's teeth is acceptable.

OPEC – Organization of Petroleum Exporting Countries.

REDF – (Real Estate Development Fund) was est ablished toprovide healt hy and modern houses for citizens

Riyadh – the largest city and the capital of Saudi Arabia.

Salam Alaikom – means hello.

Saudi Riyal – thecurrency, which is made up of 100 halalahs.

Sharia – thegovernment is based on Sharia, which is Islamic Law.

Tagia – a small white cap that is not seen that is used to prevent the ghotra from slipping.

Thobe – ankle-length shirt, usually white, that covers long pants.

About the Author

Samer I. Asfour, Chief Operating Officer of Design Jordan in Amman, Jordan. Mr. Asfour was the General Manager of the Amman World Trade Center in Amman, Jordan.

Travis McCain, graduate student, Burns School of Real Estate and Construction Management, *Daniels College of Business,* UNIVERSITY OF DENVER.

Singapore

INTERNATIONAL REAL ESTATE (GLOBAL REAL ESTATE)
Dr. Mark Lee Levine, **Editor**

■ 1. Geography

Singapore is located in Southeast Asia. It is comprised of islands between Malaysia and Indonesia. It has approximately 687 sq km (square kilometers) of land area, slightly greater than 3.5 times the size of Washington, D.C., with about 193 km of coastline.

0.9% of the land is arable, with 5% being forests and woodlands. There are border disputes between Singapore and its neighbor, Malaysia, particularly over several islands. The climate is hot, humid and tropical, with a great deal of rain. Thunderstorms occur almost 40% of the year. The terrain is generally comprised of lowlands, with water and nature preserves. Singapore has limited natural resources, comprised mainly of fish and deepwater ports. Environmental problems include pollution of industrial, air, water, and vehicle emissions are of pollution.

■ 2. History and Overview

In 1824, the British purchased Singapore Island, and by 1825, the city of Singapore had become a major port. In 1826, Singapore, Penang, and Malacca were combined as the Straits Settlements to form an outlying residency of the British East India Company. In 1867 the Straits Settlements were made a British Crown Colony, an arrangement that continued until 1946.

The opening of the Suez Canal in 1869 and the advent of steamships launched an era of prosperity for Singapore as transit trade expanded throughout Southeast Asia. In the 20th century, the automobile industry's demand for rubber from Southeast Asia and the packaging industry's need for tin helped make Singapore one of the world's major ports.

In 1959, Singapore became self-governing. In 1963, it joined the newly independent Federation of Malaya, Sabah, and Sarawak (the latter two former British Borneo Territories) to form Malaysia. After a period of friction, between Singapore and the Central Government in Kuala Lumpur, Singapore separated from Malaysia on August 9, 1965, and became an independent republic.[241]

■ 3. People

The population of Singapore is **5,567,301** with 78.1% of the population within the 15-year to 64-year age range and 13.4% in the 0 to 14 year age group.

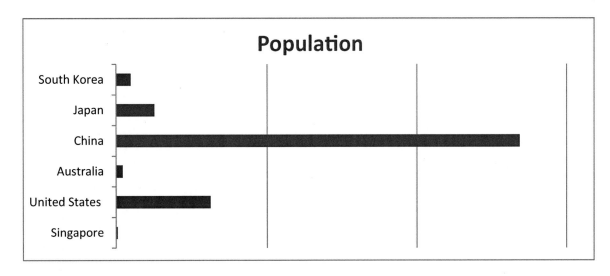

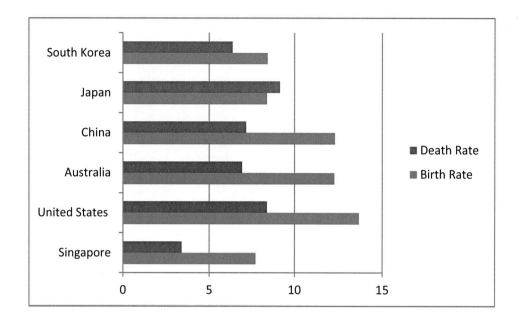

The balance of the population, 65 years of age or older, make up 8.5% of the total population.

The population growth rate is 1.92% according to 2014 estimates, with 8.1 births per 1,000. There are 3.42 deaths per 1,000. The infant mortality rate is about 2.53 deaths per 1,000 live births. Life expectancy is generally 84.38 years, with males at about 81.86 years, and females at 87.07 years.

Singapore's ethnic profile includes 74.2% Chinese, 13.3% Malayas, 9.2% Indians, and a mix of others. The dominant religions are Buddhist and Muslim, with other religions. There are four official languages, Mandarin at 36.3%, English at 29.8%, Malay at 11.9%, and Hokkien at 8.1%, although the main language is Chinese, and about 4.1% speak Cantonese. The literacy rate for Singporeans over 15 years of age is 92.5%. The labor force is 3.557 million, with an unemployment rate at 1.9% (2014).

4. Government

The government is a parliamentary republic within the Commonwealth. The capital is Singapore. Independence from Malaysia occurred on August 9, 1965. The legal system is based on the English common law. Suffrage for voting is 21 years of age and is universal and compulsory. The government consists of the Executive Branch, through the Chief of State as the President, the head of government being the Prime Minister, and a Cabinet that is appointed by the President. The Legislative Branch is unicameral, with a Parliament. The highest Judicial Branch is the Supreme Court. Diplomatic representation with the U.S. consists of the Singapore Ambassador being located in Washington, D.C., and the U.S. Ambassador located in Singapore.

5. Economy

The Gross Domestic Product (GDP) is $307.1 billion. The GDP per capita is $81,300, which is extremely high within Asia. The GDP real growth rate is 3%. Inflation has been higher than usual, until recent years, mainly due to economic turmoil in many parts of Asia. However, inflation had been fairly low, at 1.5% (2014). Unemployment is low at 1.9% (2011).

6. Currency

Currency is the Singapore *dollar*. See the Burns School Global Real Estate Web site for the UNIVERSITY OF DENVER at http://burns.daniels.du.edu for currency conversion rates.

7. Transportation

Singapore has strong railway and highway systems, with 3,425 km of paved roadways. One of the finest ports in the world for importing and exporting through Asia is in the city of Singapore, along with other ports. Singapore has 9 airports.

8. Communications

Singapore has sophisticated communications systems through its approximately 1.99 million mainline telephones and 8.063 million mobile telephones. The state controls broadcast media including radio and television stations (2012).

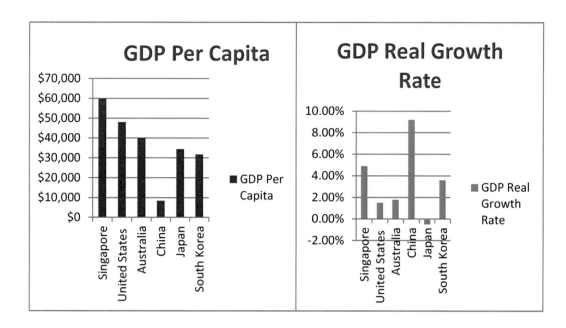

■ 9. Real Property Issues

Real property law, in general, is similar to that of pre-1925 English Law apart from the registration system. English legal concepts and instruments such as licenses, easements and profits, restrictive covenants, mortgages and covenants are applicable. There are three common types of land grants, namely estates in fee simple, estate in perpetuity, and leases. Temporary occupation leases also exist, but they are not commonly encountered in everyday practice. There are two types of registration, those governed by Registration of Deeds Act and those governed by Land Titles Act. The Registration of deeds act provides registration of deeds of conveyances, assignments, memorandum of charges and discharges, deeds of consent to discharge of trustee, private acts, and orders of court certificates of appointment of trustee in bankruptcy. In order to be effective, leases greater than seven years have to be registered. Instruments to be registered are given priority based upon the date of registration and not by date of instruments or of their execution. The Land Titles Act is based upon the Torrens system in South Australia. Registration of instrument is necessary to protect one's legal interest in property. Instruments are ineffectual until registered. Proprietor of registered land holds the land free of all encumbrances, liens, estates and interests except those in the land-register. Priority is given in order of registration or notification irrespective of dates of instruments. The Conveyance and Law of Property Act states that legal mortgages can only be created by way of deed in English language. The form of mortgage will be conveyance for freehold estates, or assignment for leasehold estates by mortgagor of his interest in land to mortgagee with proviso for redemption when mortgage debt is repaid in the future. Registration is required for protection under Registration of Deeds Act.[245]

■ 10. Real Estate Trends

Real estate trends in Singapore, like in most countries, are continually evolving. Several companies such as CB Richard Ellis (http://www.cbre.com), Jones Lang LaSalle (http://www.joneslanglasalle.com) and the Institute of Estate Agents (http://www.iea.org.sg) provide detailed, current information on the latest industrial, office, and retail real estate market trends in Singapore.

■ 11. Cultural Issues

Any nation's culture is complex and vibrant in its diversity.

While broad cultural characterizations such as those presented here can be generally accurate, following such generalities too strictly may be dangerously misleading. To conduct business effectively and profitably in a country, it is vital to have a thorough understanding of its culture's complexities.

When out in public it is important to note that there is no physical contact between the opposite sexes. Same sex contact is considered normal and a sign of friendship. Do not maintain direct eye contact for extended periods of time. Vary the gaze so as not to appear to be staring or glaring. Gift giving is very acceptable among friends, but because of strict bribery laws, public officials will almost never accept gifts. Gifts will often be refused three times, before accepting, so as not to appear greedy. Punctuality is import ant. Never keep a Singaporean business person waiting. Business attire tends to be more informal due to the temperature and humidity in Singapore. Jackets are not often worn. It is best to dress conservatively and then remove jackets, ties, etc. when it seems appropriate.

For additional information in this area see the Burns School Global Real Estate Web site for the UNIVERSITY OF DENVER at http://burns.daniels.du.edu.

12. Discussion Questions

1. For such a small country what do you think are some of the reasons why Singapore has such a strong economy?

2. How much of a role do you think religion plays in the conducting of business in Singapore?

3. What is the effect on Singapore being in such close proximity to Malaysia and Indonesia?

13. Case Study

Human Trafficking Investigation (HTI) Singapore

Memo

To: Board of Directors
From: Consultants
Re: Closing the office

I. Problem

Human Trafficking Investigation (HTI) is a non-profit organization working toward the eradication of human trafficking. HTI responds to missing persons, and it helps provide housing, legal services, jobs and other services to those who have been trafficked. Recently it opened an office in Singapore, with two employees. The current situation has not provided enough work for any employees, much less two. HTI has not been able to make the connections necessary to help. The Office to Monitor and Combat Trafficking in Persons considers Singapore a Tier 2 country, according to the Trafficking in Persons Report released.

Tier 2 Definition: The governments of countries in Tier 2 do not yet fully comply with the Act's minimum standards but are making significant efforts to bring themselves into compliance with those standards. Some are strong in the prosecution of traffickers, but provide little or no assistance to victims. Others work to assist victims and punish traffickers, but have not yet taken any significant steps to prevent trafficking. Some governments are only beginning to address trafficking, but nonetheless have already taken significant steps towards the eradication of trafficking.[246]

II. Exit Strategy

Initial exit strategy was to stay until the funds ran out, or there was an eradication of human trafficking in Singapore.

III. Contingency Exit Strategy

A contingency plan would be to vacate the hotel that HTI is currently operating from Singapore. Because of the difficulty to obtain the proper networks,

HTI has had to leave some countries. Thus, for the initial stage of operation, HTI can operate out of a hotel. HTI is still in that stage in Singapore; thus, transferring employees and closing the office would be simple.

IV. Conclusion

The office in France is considering closing and moving to another country. HTI should evaluate Singapore for re-location of the office. Singapore is considered a Tier 2 country. This would be where HTI would want to have its headquarters influence people within the country.

For additional resources, see:

Trafficking in Persons Report. June 5, 2002, released by the Office to Monitor and Combat Trafficking in Persons. (Retrieved September 18, 2002). http://www.state.gov/g/tip/rls/tiprpt/2002/10653.htm.

U.S. Embassy. Homepage. http://usembassy.state.gov. U.S. Department of State. Homepage. http://www.state.gov.

14. Selected References

*CIA World Factbook.https://www.cia.gov/library/publications/the-world-*factbook/index.html.

Richard Ellis International Property Specialists. http://www.cbre.com. Time Almanac. *TIME Almanac.* Boston: Information Please LLC.

United States Department of State. *Background Notes: Singapore.* United States Department of State (Online).Available:http://www.state.gov.

U.S. Bureau of Census at http://www.census.gov. U.S. Department of Commerce at http://www.stat-usa.

gov. U.S. Bureau of Economic Analysis at http://www.bea.gov.

U.S. Embassy. Homepage. http://usembassy.state.gov. World Trade Centers Institute at http://www.wtci.org. World Trade Organization at http://www.wto.org.

World Bank (Unknown). *Adult Illiteracy Rates.* The Economist. X-rates.com. Homepage. http://www.x-rates.com/.

15. Glossary

Malay – a national and official language of Singapore along with Chinese.

Sari – wraparound skirt worn by women.

About the Author

Dr. Mark Lee Levine is the Editor of this Book.

South Africa

INTERNATIONAL REAL ESTATE (GLOBAL REAL ESTATE)

Dr. Mark Lee Levine, Editor

1. Geography

South Africa is on the southern tip of the African continent. The land area is 1,219,090 sq km (square kilometers). It includes the Prince Edward Islands (Marion Island and Prince Edward Island). Total land is slightly less than twice the size of Texas.

South Africa borders Botswana, Lesotho, Mozambique, Namibia, Swaziland and Zimbabwe. South Africa is divided into nine Regions or Provinces.

The coastline totals 2,798 km. Border disputes between South Africa and Swaziland are prevalent. The terrain is comprised of plateaus, rugged hills and narrow coastal plains South Africa's national resources include gold, diamonds and other gems, copper, salt, natural gas and other natural resources.

Land use is approximately 0.34% for permanent crops, about 9.89% arable, and approximately 89.77% include forests and woodlands and a mix of other uses. Numerous environmental issues exist, especially since the governmental focus has been more on economic issues, growth concerns, political questions, apartheid, and other matters, rather than environmental concerns.

Recent environmental actions taken by the government include the Antarctic Treaty, Endangered Species treaties, Hazardous Waste treaties, and other attempts to reduce river pollutants, acid rain, and soil erosion.

2. History and Overview

South Africa has been inhabited for thousands of years. Most of today's black South Africans belong to the Bantu language group that, apparently, migrated south from central Africa.

The Portuguese were some of the first Europeans to reach the Cape of Good Hope, arriving there in 1488. The Dutch (the Netherlands) became involved in the Dutch East India Company in 1652 in South Africa. By 1780, the European settlements extended through the southern part of the Cape and through the eastern part toward the "Great Fish River." The British gained control of the Cape of Good Hope in the 18th century. Many other political positions were maintained by various governments throughout the years. However, by May of 1910, the Republics then in South Africa and the British colonies formed the Union of South Africa, which was a self-governing dominion out of the British Empire.

Many events since that time affect the political shape of South Africa. One of the most important events occurred in 1984, with a new constitution where some ethnic groups were allowed a governmental role. However, power generally remained mostly in the hands of the white populace.

In 1976 and in 1985 there was some activity through the National Party. However, in February, 1990, the state President (then Mr. DeKlerk) announced an anti- apartheid position. Shortly thereafter, Nelson Mandela was released from prison. A new constitution was formed in December, 1993. Eventually Mr. Mandela was installed as President in May, 1994.250

3. People

South Africa has a population of **48,375,645.** Age structure is dominated by those under 65 years of age, with 28.3% in the 0 to 14-year category, 65.4% being in the 15- year-old to 64-year-old range, and 6.3% in the 65 and older age range.

The birth rate is approximately 18.94 per 1,000 members of the total population (2014). The death rate is approximately 17.49 in 1,000. Life expectancy is low at 49.56 years of age; this

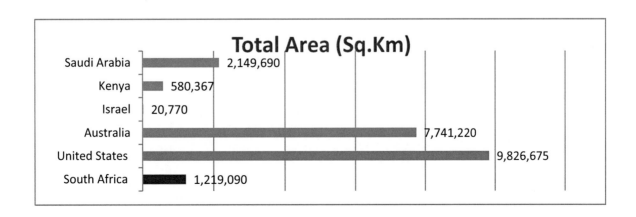

Total Area (Sq.Km)

Country	Total Area (Sq.Km)
Saudi Arabia	2,149,690
Kenya	580,367
Israel	20,770
Australia	7,741,220
United States	9,826,675
South Africa	1,219,090

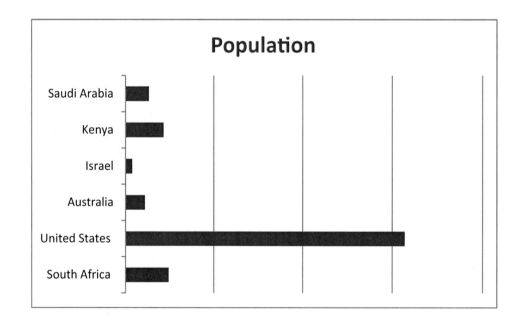

is primarily because of the spread of AIDS, with males at 50.52 years and females at 48.58 years.

The ethnic divisions are 80.2% black, 8.4% white, with a mix of others. The dominant religion is Christianity at over 57%, Muslim at 1.5% and others. The balance is a mix of other religions. A number of "official" languages are spoken; there are 11 in South Africa, including Afrikaans, English, Swazi and others. Literacy is fairly low, at approximately 86.4%.

▪ 4. Government

The government of South Africa is a republic, with its administrative capital at Pretoria. However, the legislative capital is at Cape Town; and, the judicial capital is at Bloemfontein. Nine (9) administrative Divisions are in South Africa. Independence from the United Kingdom came on May 31, 1910 from the

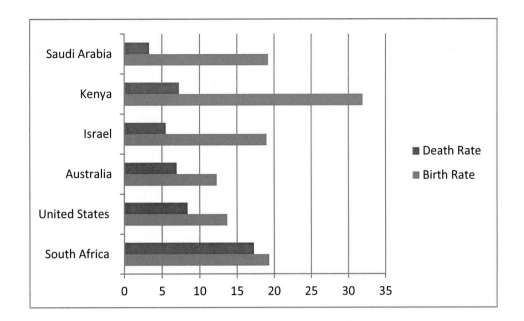

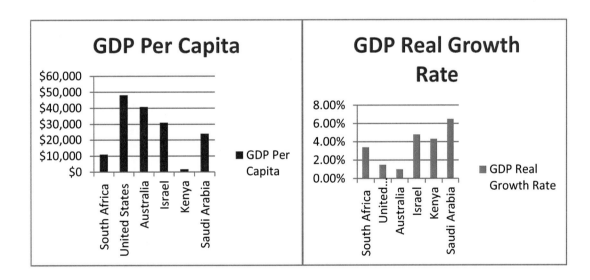

United Kingdom; this date is the major holiday. The Freedom Day is April 27, 1994. The Constitution was amended many times; the most notable, recently, was April 27, 1994, with the elimination of apartheid.

The legal system is based on the Roman-Dutch law, with a strong sprinkling of English common law. The government consists of an Executive Branch headed by the President, the Legislative Branch, which is a bicameral Parliament, and a Judicial Branch that includes the constitutional court, Supreme Court of Appeals, and other lower courts. Numerous political parties in South Africa developed, especially after the elimination of apartheid.

Diplomatic relationships exist with the U.S. Embassy office in Pretoria. South Africa's Ambassador maintains its office in Washington, D.C.

■ 5. Economy

The South African economy has been influenced by health issues, unemployment, changes in the political settings resulting from the elimination of apartheid, and numerous other external factors. The Gross Domestic Product (GDP) per capita is $12,700. Unemployment is fairly high at 25% (2014). The GDP real growth rate is 1.4%.

Exports include gold and other minerals, machinery and equipment.

■ 6. Currency

The South African currency is the *rand (ZAR)*. One *rand* equals 100 cents. For the current rate of exchange for the rand, see the CIA World Fact book Web site https://www.cia.gov/library/ publications/the-world-factbook/index.html, and Burns School Global Real Estate Web site for the UNIVERSITY OF DENVER at http://burns.daniels.du.edu.

■ 7. Transportation

Modern transportation is fairly limited in South Africa, although 20,192 km (kilometers) of railways are utilized. Highways run for 747,014 km, but only about 158,952 km are paved. Very limited inland waterways exist. Pipelines transport crude oil and petroleum products, along with natural gas.

The major ports for shipping include Cape Town, Durban, East London and Port Elizabeth. South Africa has a number of airports with paved runways.

■ 8. Communications

Adverse effects from economic turmoil and high crime rate have resulted in an underdeveloped economic communication infrastructure.

However, one of the most developed African telephone systems is in South Africa, with 4.03 million main telephone lines and 68.4 million mobile cellular telephones in use (2012). South Africa has numerous radio and television stations as well.

■ 9. Real Property Issues

Economic and political changes in South Africa have resulted in changes relative to real property issues, ownership of real estate, documentation and control of the transfer of real estate. A very limited amount of information is available for South African real estate, although the government is attempting to provide additional information, a stronger surveying

system and control system. All titles for land are registered. There is a formal recordation or registering process in South Africa for the transfer of real estate. Many controlling acts or laws in South Africa relative to the transfer of real estate are required. See the Credit Agreement Act No. 75, the Usury Act, the Alienation of Land Act, and numerous other Acts as noted in Martindale-Hubbell *International Law Digest*, noted below. Most of the land control laws are based on the English common law and Roman-Dutch law.

■ 10. Real Estate Trends

Only a limited amount of information is available in this area. South Africa has signed the General Agreement on Tariffs and Trade (GATT Treaty). For more information, see the Web sites noted in the Selected References sect ion.[254] Several companies, such a CB Richard Ellis (http://www.cbre.com), Knight Frank (http://www.knightfrank.com), and Colliers

International (http://www.colliers.com) provide detailed, current information on the latest real estate market trends in South Africa.

■ 11. Cultural Issues

Any nation's culture is complex and vibrant in its diversity.

While broad cultural characterizations such as those presented here can be generally accurate, following such generalities too strictly may be dangerously misleading. To conduct business effectively and profitably in a country, it is vital to have a thorough understanding of its culture's complexities. Dress throughout most of South Africa's Western-style clothing. General business greetings and dealings include the normal salutations of "Good morning," shaking of hands and typical Western-style greetings.

12. Discussion Questions

1. There has been a good deal of recent discussion in the news about the epidemic of AIDS in various parts of Africa, the high death rate and the young age at which Africans die. What is the effect of this on South Africa in terms of attracting foreign investment?

2. What are some areas that have influenced South Africa's economy?

3. What affect, if any, does South Africa's location have on its ability to trade with the rest of the world?

13. Case Study

Low-Income Housing Builders (LIHB)
Pretoria, South Africa

Memo

To: Board of Directors
From: Consultants
Re: Lack of Business

I. Problem

Low-Income Housing Builders (LIHB) has branch offices in the United States. LIHB expanded to South Africa last year, with the hope that it would be able to obtain financing to help build much-needed housing. LIHB has been operating in the United States for the last 30 years. It also has a commercial construction side.

LIHB was originally granted a contract to build an office building. While in South Africa, the need for low-income housing was brought to the attention if LIHB's Board of Directors. Members of the Board felt that LIHB would be able to possibly help the situation and make a profit at the same time. (LIHB has already established some good connections during the commercial project.)

II. Initial Exit Strategy

This is still in the process. LIHB is still working on market studies and trying to determine

III. Contingency Exit Strategy

the workings of the South African housing market.

LIHB has come to realize that there might not be as much opportunity in South Africa as first thought. There is a lack of readily available funds. The difficulty of cutting through red tape is also a major issue. The "exit strategy" would be to not enter the South Africa market.

IV. Conclusion

It has come to the attention of LIHB that there is an OPIC (Overseas Private Investment Corporation), the U.S. government organization that arranges financing and risk insurance for sustainable development projects. This agency will provide $15 Million for loan guarantee to construct 90,000 homes. "Watson said he hoped the OPIC initiative would help address 2.2 million unit shortage of low-income housing in South Africa by also stimulating local commercial lenders to expand their home-building financing nationwide." (See "To Help Finance Low-Income Housing in South Africa," by Jim Fisher-Thompson, at http://usinfo.state.gov/regional/af/trade/a2090301.htm.)

If LIHB can utilize this information and successfully, work with local subcontractors, and in the process provide a project management apprenticeship, LIHB might be able to maximize profits while helping set up the construction industry in South Africa for growth. It is suggested by the Consultants that each Board member of LIHB move slowly on its decision to do business in South Africa, and read the entire article: "U.S. To Help Finance Low- Income Housing in South Africa," by Jim Fisher-Thompson, at http://usinfo.state.gov/regional/af/trade/a2090301.htm.

Refer to: Convention on International Trade of Endangered Species of Wild Fauna and Flora. Homepage. http://www.cites.org/.

U.S. Embassy. Homepage. http://usembassy.state.gov.

U.S. Department of State. Homepage.(http://www.state.gov. X-rates.com.

Homepage.(Retrieved September 16,2002).http://www.x-rates.com/.

14. Selected References

CIA World Factbook https://www.cia.gov/library/publications/the-world-factbook/index.html.

International Real Estate Digest. Martindale-Hubbell. Homepage. http://www.ired.com.

C.B. Richard Ellis International Property Specialists. http://www.cbre.com. Time Almanac. *TIME Almanac.* Boston: Information Please LLC.

United States Department of State. Background *Notes: United* States Department of State (Online). Available:http://www.state.gov.

U.S. Bureau of Census at http://www.census.gov. U.S. Department of Commerce at http://www.stat-usa.gov. U.S. Bureau of Economic Analysis at http://www.bea.gov. U.S. Department of State. Homepage. http://www.state.gov. U.S. Embassy. Homepage. http://usembassy.state.gov. World Trade Organization at http://www.wto.org. World Bank. *Adult Illiteracy Rates.* The Economist. X- rates.com. Homepage. http://www.x-rates.com/.

15. Glossary

Alienation of Land Act – deals with installment payments and sale of land.

Credit Agreement Act No 75 – certain credit must be given to a credit receiver before the contract has begun.

Howzit – English speaking young people use this as slang for how are you?

Rand – South African currency, one rand equals 100 cents.

Sawubona – Zulu and Swazis greet each other, it literally means I see you.

Usury Act No. 73 – deals with leasing and money lending transactions.

Yebo – yes.

About the Author

Dr. Mark Lee Levine is the Editor of this Book.

Spain

INTERNATIONAL REAL ESTATE (GLOBAL REAL ESTATE)
Dr. Mark Lee Levine, Editor

1. Geography

Spain is located in the western part of Europe, southwest of France. It borders the Bay of Biscay, Mediterranean Sea, North Atlantic Ocean, and the countries of Andorra, France, Gibraltar and Portugal. Border disputes include Gibraltar, along with other countries.

Spain has a total area of 505,370 sq km (square kilometers). Coastline is 4,964 km long. The climate in Spain is quite temperate, with fairly clear and hot summers and cold winters.

Natural resources include coal, lignite, iron ore, zinc, lead, copper, hydro power and others. Arable land is about 24.89% of total land in Spain, with approximately 9.14% for permanent crops and 61.97% for forests, woodlands and a mix of other uses.

A number of environmental issues include concern with air pollutants, pollution of the Mediterranean Sea, raw sewage, some droughts in certain areas, and loss of wetlands.

2. History and Overview

During the 16th century, Spain became the most powerful nation in Europe, due to the immense wealth derived from its presence in the Americas. But a series of long, costly wars and revolts, capped by the defeat by the English of the "Invincible Armada" in 1588, began a steady decline of Spanish power in Europe. The 19th century saw the majority of Spanish colonies revolting and asserting their independence. During the 20th century, the monarchy was briefly ousted and the first republic was established. Spain experienced a dictatorial rule from 1923 to1931 that was then followed by the second republic. Political polarization began to increase leading added tension eventually resulting in the Spanish Civil War in 1936. Following the victory of his nationalist forces in 1939, Gen. Francisco Franco ruled a nation exhausted, politically and economically. Spain was officially neutral during World War II, but followed a pro-Axis policy. The victorious Allies isolated Spain at the beginning of the postwar period. The country did not join the United Nations (EU) until 1955. In 1959, under an International Monetary Fund (IMF) stabilization program, the country began liberalizing trade and capital flows, particularly foreign investment. Despite the success of the economic liberalization, Spain remained the most closed economy in Western Europe. The pace of reform slackened during the 1960s as the state remained committed to guiding the economy.

In the 1960s and 1970s, Spain was transformed into a modern industrial economy with a thriving tourism sector. Its economic expansion led to improved income distribution and helped develop a large middle class. Social changes brought about by economic prosperity and the inflow of new ideas helped set the stage for Spain's transition to democracy during the latter half of the 1970s.

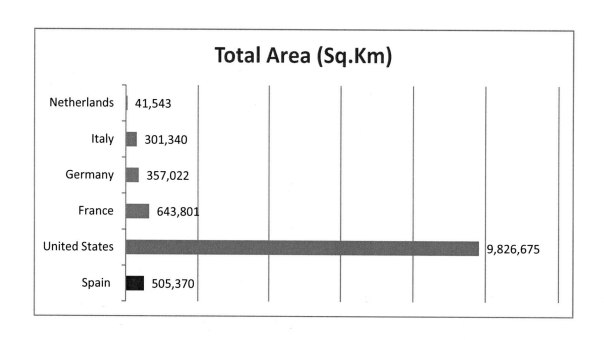

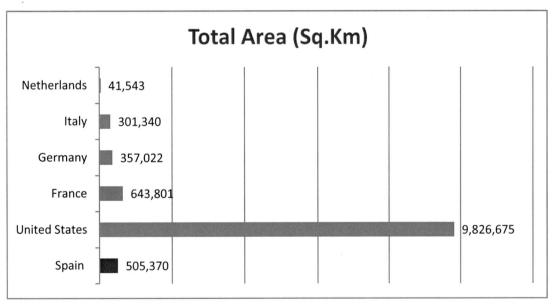

Spain gained full membership in the European Community (EC) in 1986 and has undertaken a strong program to integrate within the European Union (EU).[258]

■ 3. People

Around **47,737,941** people reside in Spain. The age structure is dominated by 67% in the 15-year to 64-year-old category, and a fairly even balance of the other age groups, that is, 0 to 14 years of age at 15.4%, and 17.6% over 64 years old.

The birth rate is 9.88 in 1,000 people (2014). The death rate is 9 in 1,000. Therefore, absent substantial changes in migration, which is fairly unusual, the population is generally stable. Life expectancy in Spain, overall, is 81.47 years, with males at 78.47 and females at 84.67 years.

The dominant religion in Spain is Roman Catholic, with 94% of the population. There is a mix of other religious groups sprinkled throughout the populace.

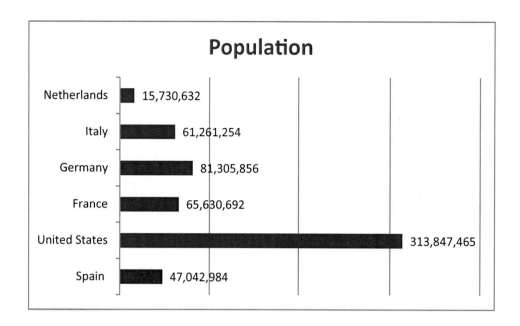

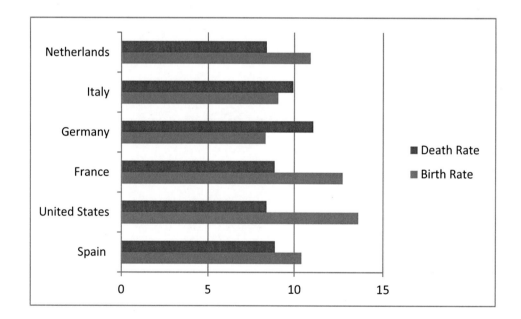

The dominant, official language is Castilian Spanish at 74%, although other forms of Spanish are also spoken. Literacy is fairly high at approximately 98.7% being able to read and write.

■ 4. Government

The government in Spain is a Parliamentary monarchy with its capital in Madrid. Seventeen (17) autonomous communities divide Spain.

Spain obtained independence in 1492 by expulsion of the Moors and its unification within Spain. The national holiday is October 12. Spain operates on a Constitution that was effective in 1978 with a civil law system.

Branches of government include the Executive Branch with the Chief of State, the King, the Legislative Branch, which is bicameral, and a Judicial Branch, headed by the Supreme Court. Numerous political parties operate within Spain. Its diplomatic representation in the U.S. is in Washington, D.C. The U.S. maintains its Embassy office in Madrid. United States.

■ 5. Economy

The Spanish economy is a mix of capitalism and governmental influences. The Gross Domestic Product (GDP) is approximately $1.4 trillion, with the GDP per capita at $33,000 (2014). The GDP real growth rate is 1.3%. Inflation is at -0.1%, although unemployment over the last number of years has been high at around 24.3% (2014).

6. Currency

Currency is the *euro (it* was the *peseta,* with 100 centimos in 1 *pesenta).* There are seven different denominations in the *euro* banknote series, ranging from the 5 to 500 *euro* note.

See the Burns School Web site for the UNIVERSITY OF DENVER at http://burns.daniels.du.edu for currency conversion rates.

7. Transportation

Spain operates a number of railroads, with 15,293 km (kilometers) of rail lines (2012). Extensive highways are used, with 683,175 km paved. Pipelines are used to transport crude oil, petroleum products and natural gas. Spain is very active in shipping, with major ports at Barcelona, Bilbao, Las Palmas and other locations. Spain has 150 airports, of which 99 are paved (2012).

8. Communications

The Spanish communication system is adequate, with a modern telephone system relying on hard cable and earth stations, satellite communications, microwave and other high-technology capacity, including AM radio, FM radio and shortwave radio stations, as well as television broadcast stations.

9. Real Property Issues

Real estate commissions in Spain often range between 3% to 5%. Commissions also exist at about 10% for leases, although this amount varies on the transaction. In general, the fees for property acquisition total to approximately 10% of the purchase price. This can include fees for stamp duty, land registry, notary etc. There is also a tax on the increased value of the land since it was last sold. All property taxes are based upon the official registered price not the actual purchase price. It is possible and somewhat common for sellers to understate the purchase price. This allows both the seller and buyer to save on certain taxes and fees. You could then be liable for capital gains tax on profit once the true price is revealed. Many real estate agents are also attorneys. There is extensive use of notaries, known as *natarios,* which is a specialized area of attorneys who are involved in almost all real estate transactions. Notaries are responsible for preparing all contract documents and assuring that they comply with Spanish regulations. Real estate trade associations include the *Junta Central de Los Colegios Oficiales.* See the sites in the Selected References section for additional information about trade organizations.

Rights and interests in real estate are controlled by specific laws relative to recording ownership in Spain. Various forms of ownership interests include partnerships, corporations, joint ventures, sole ownership posit ions, and ot hers. Transfer of title is controlled by the notary who is involved in the real estate transaction. The documents are often recorded in transfer offices.

10. Real Estate Trends

Numerous laws impact real estate transactions, such as ad valorem taxes, transfer taxes, income taxes and taxes on non-residents.

Coastal areas are very popular real estate purchases in Spain. To find property at reasonable prices, however, it is advisable to look inland. Barcelona and Madrid offer an urban feel with stunning historical and contemporary architecture.

See various links in the Selected References section and their Web sites for current real estate rates for purchases and leases involving residential and commercial properties.

11. Cultural Issues

Any nation's culture is complex and vibrant in its diversity.

While broad cultural characterizations such as those presented here can be generally accurate, following such generalities too strictly may be dangerously misleading. To conduct business effectively and profitably in a country, it is vital to have a thorough understanding of its culture's complexities.

The Spanish are very concerned with in vogue dress and western-style dress.

Most greetings are western style, including handshakes, kiss on the cheek with the women, and normal greetings of "Good day," "Good evening," and "Hello."

Formal titles are often used in business settings, which may reference "the don" to show proper respect.

12. Discussion Questions

1. What are some environmental issues that affect Spain?

2. In addition to its location, what are some reasons that Spain has been isolated?

3. What are some areas to check if a foreign investor has an interest in purchasing real property in Spain?

13. Case Study

Fantasy Real Estate Sales (FRES)

Headquarters in Milan, Italy Offices in Italy, Sweden, Hungary, Spain, Russia, Netherlands, United Kingdom and Greece.

Memo

To: Board of Directors
From: Consultants
Re: Downsizing

I. Problem

OVERVIEW

Fantasy Real Estate Sales (FRES) was established in Greece in 1995. The idea behind the Company was drawn from a Greek real estate agent, XElvina Greeeelepis, owner of XXEGGG Realty. XElvina's real estate company had many different properties listed, including villas and private islands. The inspiration for FRES came from meeting XElvina. The Directors felt we would be able to help people find their "fantasy" pieces of real estate, such as castles, villas, ranches, winery's and any unique properties falling into the "fantasy" realm of real estate.

ITALY

Recently the headquarters of FRES, located in Milan, Italy, began to grow. It was doing so much business that it had seven full-time agents, and one office manager. FRES needs to hire more people, but it is concerned with hiring too many, because if the Company has more than 15 employees, it will have to "take care of the employees" for a long time. This is based on the employment laws in Italy. See http://www.cmslegal.com/intelligence/cms_news/employment.htm.

RUSSIA

The Russian market is beginning to pick up new business. There are plenty of properties available, but FRES's target buyers are hesitant to purchase property in Russia. (FRES is working on advertising the benefits of realty in Russia. FRES started doing overnight stays at the individual properties, so potential clients can see what it is like to be in Russia.)

HUNGARY

Currently, in Hungary, the Company has had a reduction in properties available for sale. FRES was been unable to secure properties for sale. It has also had two properties flood in the last two months.

NETHERLANDS

The market is booming. There seem to be enough "fantasy" properties at the current time.

UNITED KINGDOM (ENGLAND, SCOTLAND, WALES)

The United Kingdom, including the **England, Scotland and Wales** markets, has been relatively stable. These markets, for FRES, do not perform extremely well, but they do not go below projected income.

SPAIN

This market is just beginning to show the growth potential that was projected by FRES for the country. The market had a difficult time because prices were inflated.

As such, it was not a good investment to purchase a fantasy property here; however, prices are beginning to come inline. Thus, with other European markets, the general market is beginning to pickup in sales.

SWEDEN

Currently the Swedish market is booming. The agents cannot keep up with the market.

II. Initial Exit Strategy

Exiting these countries would be relatively easy, except for Italy, where the headquarters office is currently located. All of the other offices are satellite offices. In most cases the agents work out of their own homes. The Milan office could be vacated relatively easily. The interior has been upgraded to class A office space and since this is in short supply in Italy, it should be relatively easy to re-lease or sub-lease. The network of real estate agents throughout Europe that FRES has established would help in the event that FRES needed to leave the county.

III. Contingency Exit Strategy

See Initial Exit Strategy plan. The plan of exit would be simple to leave everything and leave the country.

IV. Conclusion

Employment restrictions in Italy will make it difficult to keep expanding. To have a reasonable exit strategy, FRES should move the headquarters to Sweden. The reason Sweden is more of an ideal location is due to the booming market and the favorable employment laws. The other markets could be considered, but Russia would be difficult. Current employees would resist a move to Sweden. The United Kingdom does not have enough business. This is also true with the Netherlands. Spain might be a possibility for the home office. The company should not completely close the operation in Italy, but it should leave one or two agents, to continue the local market.

Refer to: International Real Estate Digest. Homepage. http://www.ired.com. U.S. Department of State. Homepage. http://www.state.gov.

U.S. Embassy. Homepage. http://usembassy.state.gov.

14. Selected References

CIA World Factbook.https://www.cia.gov/library/publications/the-world-factbook/index.html.

http://www.real-estate-european-union.com/english/spain.html.

http://www.sispain.org/.

Jones Lang LaSalle, Ireland, http://www.joneslanglasalle.ie. PriceWat erhouseCoopers, http://www.pwcglobal.com.

Richard Ellis International Property Specialists. http://www.cbre.com. Time Almanac. *TIME Almanac.* Boston: Information Please LLC.

United States Department of State. *Background Notes: Spain.* United States Department of State (Online). Available:http://www.state.gov.

U.S. Bureau of Census at http://www.census.gov. U.S. Department of Commerce at http://www.stat-usa.gov. U.S. Bureau of Economic Analysis at http://www.bea.gov. U.S. Embassy. Homepage. http://usembassy.state.gov. World Trade Centers Institute at http://www.wtci.org. World Trade Organization at http://www.wto.org. World Bank. *Adult Illiteracy Rates.* The Economist. X- rates.com. Homepage. http://www.x-rates.com/.

15. Glossary

Junta Central de Los Colegios Oficiales – Real estate trade association.

Natarios – notaries, there is an extensive use of notaries in Spain, specialized area of attorneys who are involved in almost all real estate transactions.

About the Author

Dr. Mark Lee Levine is the Editor of this Book.

Sweden

INTERNATIONAL REAL ESTATE (GLOBAL REAL ESTATE)
Dr. Mark Lee Levine, Editor

1. Geography

Sweden is located in northern Europe, bordering the Baltic Sea, Gulf of Bothnia and Skagerrak, between the countries of Finland and Norway.

Sweden is a fairly small country of 450,295 sq km (square kilometers), similar to the size of the state of California. Sweden has a coast line of 3,218 km long.

The climate is fairly temperate, but cold as a result of its northern location. Terrain is generally flat or rolling lowlands, with some mountains in the west.

Natural resources include zinc, iron ore, lead, copper, silver, timber, hydropower and other resources. Land use consists extensively of forests and woodlands of about 68%. Arable land is about 7%. There is a mix of other uses for the balance of the land. Environmental problems include concern with acid rain, damage to soil and lakes, pollution of the North Sea and the Baltic Sea, and natural hazards, such as ice. Sweden is active in ozone-layer protection, protection of timber and wetlands, protection of whaling and other resource protection.

2. History and Overview

Around the 1500s, Sweden, Denmark and Norway were united under Danish rule. The Swedes revolted and eventually gained their independence. After the Napoleonic Wars, Denmark was ceded to Sweden, until 1905, when Norway became independent.

Sweden attempted to remain independent in both World War I and World War II, although it was very involved in both wars. Sweden joined the European Union (EU) in 1995.

3. People

Sweden is a fairly small country, with a population of **9,723,809.** The age structure is dominated by 63.3% in the 15-year-old to 64-year-old category. The balance of the population is either younger, 0 to 14 years at 16.9%, or is in the 65- year-old or older category at 19.8%.

The birth rate is 11.92 in 1,000. The death rate is 9.45 in 1,000. Life expectancy is very high in Sweden, at 81.89 years, with 80.03 for males and 83.87 years for females.

Religion in Sweden consists mainly of 87% Lutheran, and 13% of other religions including Roman Catholic, Muslim, Jewish and Buddhist, as well as other groups. The dominant language in Sweden is Swedish, with English, Finnish, and other languages being spoken. The Swedes are very literate, with

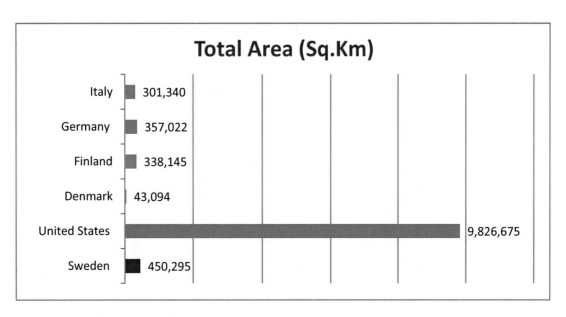

Total Area (Sq.Km)

Italy	301,340
Germany	357,022
Finland	338,145
Denmark	43,094
United States	9,826,675
Sweden	450,295

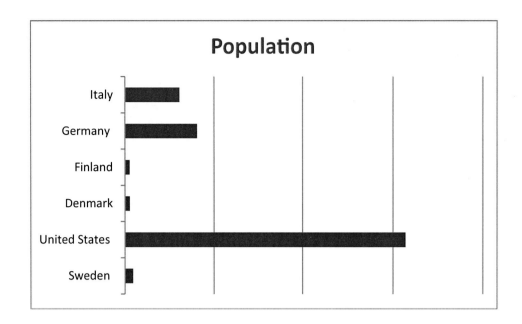

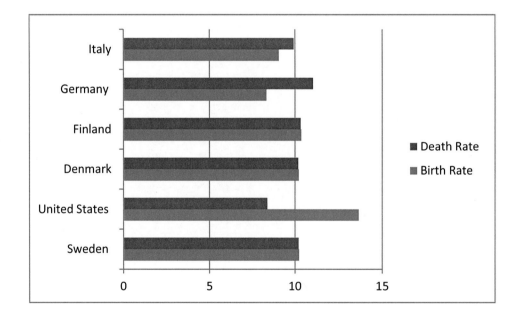

approximately 99% of the population who can read and write in the age group of 15 and older.

4. Government

The government of Sweden is a constitutional monarchy with its capital in Stockholm. There are 21 administrative counties in Sweden. Independence Day is June 6, 1523, when Gustav Vasa was elected king. The national holiday is June 6. The Constitution was formed and became effective on January 1, 1975. The legal system is influenced by civil law, with a compulsory International Court of Justice (ICJ) jurisdiction. Branches of government include the Executive Branch, headed by the

Prime Minister, or *Statsminister*, the Legislative Branch, or *Riksdag*, which is unicameral, and the Judicial Branch, which is the Ministry of Justice, which is headed by the Supreme Court, or *Hogsta Domstolen*. Diplomatic representation in the United States exists by Sweden maintaining an office for its Ambassador in Washington, D.C. The United States maintains an office in Stockholm at its Embassy.

5. Economy

Recently Sweden has been very strong economically, continuing to increase its domestic and international economic position. The Gross Domestic Product (GDP) per capita income is high

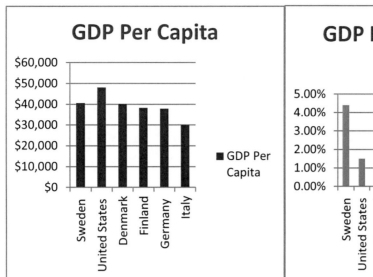

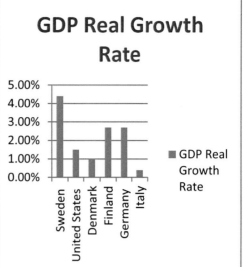

at $44,700. The GDP real growth rate is 2.1%. Inflation is -0.1% (2014), and unemployment has been higher at 7.9% (2014).

Sweden is involved in exporting numerous items, including machinery, mot or vehicles, paper product s, iron and steel products and chemicals, among others.

6. Currency

Sweden uses the Swedish *kronor* (SEK) with 100 *öere* equaling 1 Swedish *kronor*. See the Burns School Global Real Estate Web site for the UNIVERSITY OF DENVER at http://burns.daniels.du.edu for currency conversion rates.

7. Transportation

Sweden utilizes a series of railroads throughout the country, with 11,633 km (kilometers) of rail lines. Highways run 579,564 km including 1,913 km of expressways (2014). Inland waterways and pipelines are utilized. Major ports include Goteberg, Halmstad, Stockholm and numerous others. Sweden has 231 airports, including 149 with paved runways (2013).

8. Communications

Domestic and international communications are excellent, with approximately 4.321 million telephones and 11.643 million mobile cellular telephones, including microwave, TV channels, coaxial cables, and other sophisticated high-tech equipment. Sweden has publicly-owned and privately- owned radio stations and shortwave radio stations, as well as television broadcasting stations.

9. Real Property Issues

Real estate agents for both the buyer and seller are used. The seller normally pays commissions on real estate transactions. Commissions are often 4% to 6%. Property ownership is registered and controlled, with a registration system to reflect ownership, claims on property, easements, etc. Real estate salespeople are required to hold a license to undertake real estate transactions for a commission. Extensive training is required for such licensing. Forms of ownership are similar to that in the United States. Ownership by non- Swedes sometimes requires proper registration with the National Board of Trade, the *Kammerskollegium*. Titles are properly registered in the Land Registrar office. For more information on such activities in Sweden, including for real estate agents, land registration and control relative to real estate transactions, see the Association of Swedish Real Estate Agents in the Selected References section below.

10. Real Estate Trends

Real estate activity has been very heavy recently. For information on pricing of office space for rentals and sale of retail, industrial, investment, residential, multifamily, among others, see the Web sites noted in the Selected References section below, such as for Jones Lang LaSalle, CB Richard Ellis, etc.

11. Cultural Issues

Any nation's culture is complex and vibrant in its diversity.

While broad cultural characterizations such as those presented here can be generally accurate, following such generalities too strictly may be dangerously misleading. To conduct business effectively and profitably in a country, it is vital to have a thorough understanding of its culture's complexities. Cultural behavior is highly westernized in Sweden. The Swedes dress fairly conservatively, being neat and clean, although more casual in business undertakings when compared to the U.S.

Greetings are similar to those that we find in many western countries. They include "Good day" and "Good morning" greetings. Gestures are similar to those used in the United States, e.g., use of the handshake. The Swedish society is fairly homogenous and well organized. Generally speaking, the Swedish attitude is toward hard work, regular hours, and less overtime. Quality and balance are important within the Swedish economy and culture.

---

12. Discussion Questions

1. What are the positive and negative implications of Sweden being part of the Scandinavian Block?

2. What does the more socialistic position in Sweden indicate to you as to changes that must take place when doing business in Sweden, as opposed to undertaking activity in the United States, if there are such differences?

3. Do you think the development of more single family homes would be a wise investment in Sweden? Why or why not?

---

13. Case Study

Memo

To: Board of Directors
From: Consultants
Re: Downsizing

FANTASY REAL ESTATE SALES (FRES)
Headquarters in Milan, Italy Offices in Italy, Sweden, Hungary, Spain, Russia, Netherlands, United Kingdom and Greece

I. Problem

OVERVIEW
Fantasy Real Estate Sales (FRES) was established in Greece in 1995. The idea behind the Company was drawn from a Greek real estate agent, XElvina Greeeelepis, owner of XXEGGG Realty. XElvina's real estate company had many different properties listed, including villas and private islands. The inspiration for FRES came from meeting XElvina. The Directors felt we would be able to help people find their "fantasy" pieces of real estate, such as castles, villas, ranches, winery's and any unique properties falling into the "fantasy" realm of real estate.

ITALY
Recently the headquarters of FRES, located in Milan, Italy, began to grow. It was doing so much business that it had seven full-time agents, and one office manager. FRES needs to hire more people, but it is concerned with hiring too many, because if the Company has more than 15 employees, it will have to "take care of the employees" for a long time. This is based on the employment laws in Italy. See http://www.cmslegal.com/intelligence/cms_news/employment.htm.

RUSSIA
The Russian market is beginning to pick up new business. There are plenty of properties available, but FRES's target buyers are hesitant to purchase property in Russia. (FRES is working on advertising the benefits of realty in Russia. FRES started doing overnight stays at the individual properties, so potential clients can see what it is like to be in Russia.)

HUNGARY
Currently, in Hungary, the Company has had a reduction in properties available for sale. FRES was been unable to secure properties for sale. It has also had two properties flood in the last two months.

NETHERLANDS
The market is booming. There seem to be enough "fantasy" properties at the current time.

UNITED KINGDOM (ENGLAND, SCOTLAND, WALES)

The United Kingdom, including the **England, Scotland and Wales** markets, has been relatively stable. These markets, for FRES, do not perform extremely well, but they do not go below projected income.

SPAIN

This market is just beginning to show the growth potential that was projected by FRES for the country. The market had a difficult time because prices were inflated. As such, it was not a good investment to purchase a fantasy property here; however, prices are beginning to come inline. Thus, with other European markets, the general market is beginning to pickup in sales.

SWEDEN

Currently the Swedish market is booming. The agents cannot keep up with the market.

II. Initial Exit Strategy

Exiting these countries would be relatively easy, except for Italy, where the headquarters office is currently located. All of the other offices are satellite offices. In most cases the agents work out of their own homes. The Milan office could be vacated relatively easily. The interior has been upgraded to class A office space and since this is in short supply in Italy, it should be relatively easy to re-lease or sub- lease. The network of real estate agents throughout Europe that FRES has established would help in the event that FRES needed to leave the county.

III. Contingency Exit Strategy

See Initial Exit Strategy plan. The plan of exit would be simple to leave everything and leave the country.

IV. Conclusion

Employment restrictions in Italy will make it difficult to keep expanding. To have a reasonable exit strategy, FRES should move the headquarters to Sweden. The reason Sweden is more of an ideal location is due to the booming market and the favorable employment laws. The other markets could be considered, but Russia would be difficult. Current employees would resist a move to Sweden. The United Kingdom does not have enough business. This is also true with the Netherlands. Spain might be a possibility for the home office. The company should not completely close the operation in Italy, but it should leave one or two agents, to continue the local market.

Refer to: International Real Estate Digest. Homepage. http://www.ired.com. U.S. Department of State. Homepage. http://www.state.gov.

U.S. Embassy. Homepage. http://usembassy.state.gov.

14. Selected References

Certain items in this Section have been drawn from Jones Lang LaSalle, Quarterly *Investment Reports,* with permission from the publisher. All rights reserved. For additional information, see the following:

CIA World Factbook.https://www.cia.gov/library/publications/the-world-factbook/index.html.

http://www.real-estate-european-union.com/english/sweden.html. http://www.riksbank.se. http://www.sverigeturism.se/smorgasbord/index.html.

http://www.sweden.se/si/67.cs. http://www.visit-sweden.com/.

Richard Ellis International Property Specialists. http://www.cbre.com

Time Almanac. *TIME Almanac.* Boston: Information Please LLC.

United States Department of. *Background Notes: Sweden.* United States Department of State (Online). Available:http://www.state.gov

U.S. Bureau of Census at http://www.census.gov

U.S. Department of Commerce at http://www.stat-usa.gov U.S. Bureau of Economic

Analysis at http://www.bea.gov. U.S. Embassy. Homepage.

http://usembassy.state.gov. World Trade Centers Institute at http://www.wtci.org. World Trade Organization at http://www.wto.org.

World Bank. *Adult Illiteracy Rates.* The Economist.

X-rates.com. Homepage. http://www.x-rates.com/.

15. Glossary

Aktiebolag – (AB) only form of limited liability company in Sweden.

Fast Egendom – real estate.

God dag – Good day.

Halla – hello, used when answering the phone.

Handelsbolag – (HB) all partners have unlimited liability. **Inskrivnings-och-fastighetsregister** – computerized title and property register.

Kommanditbolag – (KB) one or more partners have unlimited liability.

Los egendom – personal property or chattels.

klarsamfundet – Association of Swedish Real Estate Agents.

About the Author

Dr. Mark Lee Levine is the Editor of this Book.

United Kingdom

INTERNATIONAL REAL ESTATE (GLOBAL REAL ESTATE)
Authored by *Tyler Elick Dr. Mark Lee Levine*, Editor

■ 1. Geography

The United Kingdom is in Western Europe, including islands that cover the northern 1/6th of Ireland, located between the North Atlantic Ocean in the North Sea; the United Kingdom is northwest of France. The United Kingdom has 243,610 sq km (square kilometers) of area, with 12,429 km of coastline. Numerous border disputes abound with various European countries. The climate is fairly temperate; however, more than one-half of the days are overcast. England's natural resources include natural gas, iron ore, petroleum products, lead, salt and other minerals. Arable land consists of about 25.68%, permanent crops 0.19%, and forests and woodlands.

The United Kingdom is concerned with numerous emissions from power plants that pollute the air and rivers as well as from disposable waste.

■ 2. History and Overview

The legislative union of Great Britain and Ireland was completed on January 1, 1801, under the name of the United Kingdom. However, armed struggle for independence continued sporadically into the 20th century. The Anglo-Irish Treaty of 1921 established the Irish Free State, which subsequently left the Commonwealth and became a republic after World War II. Six northern, predominantly Protestant, Irish counties have remained part of the United Kingdom.

Foreign trade has been a cornerstone of national policy of the UK and has guided their heavy presence in a number of locations worldwide. Control over its empire gradually began to lessen during the interwar period. During this period, Ireland,

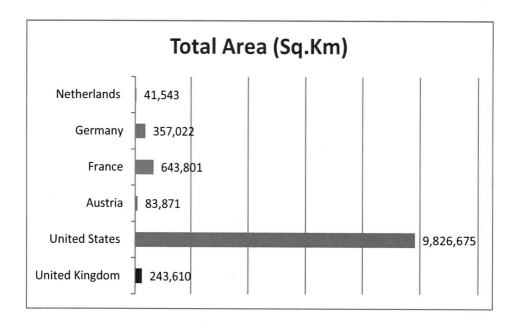

Australia, Canada, and New Zealand were granted autonomy, with Pakistan and India following in 1947. Most of Britain's former colonies belong to the Common wealth, and the United Kingdom has a voice in matters concerning these developing countries. In addition, the Commonwealth helps preserve many institutions deriving from British experience and models, such as parliamentary democracy, in those countries[271]

■ 3. People

The United Kingdom has **63,742,977** people. Approximately 65.2% of the populace is 15 to 64 years of age, with 17.3% from 0 to 14 years of age, and 17.5% in the 65 years of age and older range.

Life expectancy for the male population is 78.26 years. The female life expectancy is 82.69 years. The population growth rate is 0.54% and is fairly stagnant. Birth rates are about 12.22 per 1,000, and death rates about 9.34 per 1,000. The infant mortality rate is about 4.44 deaths per 1,000 live births.

Ethnic divisions are comprised of 83.6% English, 8.6% Scottish, and a mix of the balance of Irish, Welsh, Ulsters, West Indians, and others. The Anglican Christian religion dominates the approximately 71.6% of the Christian population. Approximately 4.4% of the population is made up of Muslims in the United Kingdom, with a mix of other religious groups (2012). (The United Kingdom does not include a question on religion in its census; therefore, the data is somewhat questionable.) The dominant language throughout the United Kingdom is English, with a fair amount of Welsh and Scots being spoken. The literacy rate is strong, at about 99% literate for those who

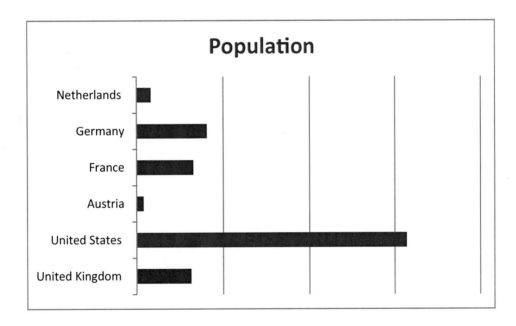

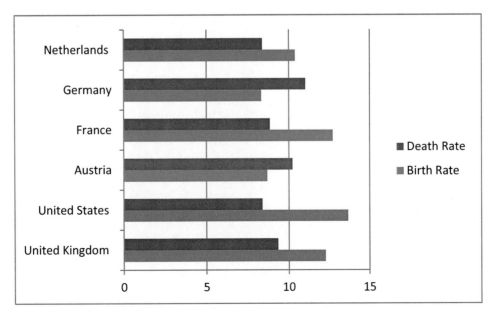

can read and write at the age of 15 and older. The labor force consists of approximately 32.59 million in the United Kingdom.

4. Government

The government is a Constitutional monarchy, with the capital in London. The United Kingdom consists of 47 Boroughs, 29 London Boroughs, 36 Counties, 12 metropolitan cities, 10 Districts and 9 Regions as well as 3 island areas. Independence Day is January 1, 1801, the day the United Kingdom was established. The legal system is based on the common law, with early Roman and modern Continental influences. Voting is 18 years of age and is universal.

The government consists of an Executive Branch through the Chief of State. The Prime Minister appoints a *Cabinet of Ministers*. The Legislative Branch is a bicameral *Parliament* in the form of a *House of Lords*, a 618-member body, as well as a *House of Commons*, with 646 seats since 2005. The Judicial Branch is the *House of Lords*. Diplomatic representation with the United States consists of the U.S. Ambassador located in London, with the United Kingdom Ambassador located in Washington, D.C. The United Kingdom has defense forces in the form of an Army, Royal Navy (which include their Marines) and a Royal Air Force.

5. Economy

The Gross Domestic Product (GDP) real growth rate is 3.2% (2014 est), and the GDP is $2.848 trillion (2014 est.) The national GDP per capita is $37,700. Inflation has generally been in the 1.6% range, with unemployment higher at 5.7% (2014).

6. Currency

Currency is the British pound *(GBP)*. See the Burns School Global Real Estate Web site for the UNIVERSITY OF DENVER at http://burns.daniels.du.edu for currency conversions.

7. Transportation

The United Kingdom has 16,454 km. of railroads and 394,428 km. of highways, as well as inland waterways and pipelines to transport crude oil, petroleum products and natural gas. A number of ports include London, Liverpool, Aberdeen, etc. the United Kingdom's 460 airports help the transportation system (2013).

8. Communications

The United Kingdom has 33.01 million telephones composed of land lines, submarine cables, and fiber-optic systems. There are 82.109 million mobile cellular service subscribers. The UK has well developed public and commercial television and radio broadcasting systems. There are 8.107 million Internet service providers (hosts), and 51.444 million (over one-half of the population) are Internet users.

9. Real Property Issues

In English common law theory, the monarchy is the ultimate "owner" of all land. However, an entity can be granted an estate in land, which is what is owned. There are 2 Ownership types

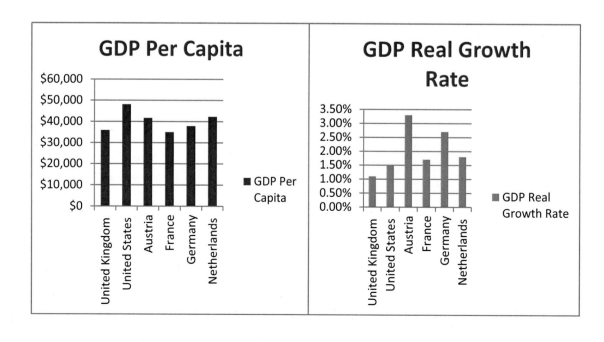

in the United Kingdom, freehold and leasehold. Freehold is also called a "fee-simple title" or "estate in fee simple" and is the right to own a property for an indefinite amount of time. A leasehold estate is a form of limited tenure, which allows exclusive possession of real estate for a specified period of time.

Almost all real estate in the United Kingdom is registered and titled with the Land Registry. The title includes 3 sections: a property register (identifies property and ownership type), a proprietorship register (identifies the owner and quality of title), and a charges register (contains details of any third party rights or covenants).

Real estate brokers in the United Kingdom are called Estate Agents. Estate Agents are mainly involved in the marketing and solicitation of property, and a Solicitor is used to prepare and exchange contracts. Estate Agents do not have a standardized licensing process, yet legitimacy can be established through membership in regarded associations such as: Royal Institution of Chartered Surveyors (RICS), and the National Association of Estate Agents (NAEA). The NAEA also has a listing service like the MLS. United Kingdom tax issues that are relevant to a real estate transaction are: Stamp Duty Tax, Value Added Tax, Capital Allowances, Capital Gains Tax, With holding taxes on rent s, and tax treatment of interest on related loans. More information on these current tax rat es can be found at the United Kingdom's government website http://www.direct.gov.uk.

Other useful links include: British Property Federation - http://www.bpf.org.uk. National Association of Estate Agents - http://www.naea.co.uk. Royal Institution of Chartered Surveyors – http://www.rics.org. Housefund.co.uk – http://www.housefund.co.uk.

10. Real Estate Trends

The most recent addition to the UK's real estate market is the establishment of Real Estate Investment Trusts (REITs) which will have an ongoing effect on the investment property market and economic sector as a whole. Some great sources for current real estate trends in the United Kingdom can be found listed by the British Property Federation (http://www.bpf.org.uk) and the European Property Federation (http://www.epf- fepi.com). For an overview of various areas or markets in the real estate field, including office, general commercial, investments, multiunit, residential, vacant land, and retail, see the links cited in the Selected Resources section or at http://burns.daniels.du.edu.

Several companies, such as Jones Lang LaSalle (http://www.joneslanglasalle.com) and CB Richard Ellis (http://www.cbre.com) provide detailed, current information on the latest real estate market trends in the United Kingdom.

11. Cultural Issues

Any nation's culture is complex and vibrant in its diversity.

While broad cultural characterizations such as those presented here can be generally accurate, following such generalities too strictly may be dangerously misleading. To conduct business effectively and profitably in a country, it is vital to have a thorough understanding of its culture's complexities. The United Kingdom has a strong cultural belief in individuality, emphasizing the rights of the individual and their place in society. The United Kingdom is a much more formal atmosphere and titles, honorary or hereditary, and last names are used to show respect. The respect for elders is extremely important and loud talking or disruptive behavior is seen as unacceptable. Good manners are very important and offence is taken to early familiarity or nonchalance. Handshakes are a standard greeting for men and women, and personal space is important. One should maintain a wide physical space while conversing and eye contact is rarely kept. Punctuality is very important in any meeting and small talk or icebreakers are not necessary. Meetings can quickly proceed from introductions to business matters, yet the decision making process is slower, and it is considered rude to rush a decision or conclusion. Gifts are not usually given in doing business. Often times, ordinary vocabulary can differ between Queen's English and American English (which is perceived as too casual).

An offensive gesture to avoid is the "V" for Victory sign (with your palm facing yourself). The terms "British" and "English" are not interchangeable. "British" refers to that of Great Britain (England, Scotland, and Wales) whereas "English" refers to solely that of England.

See the Burns School Global Real Estate Web site for the UNIVERSITY OF DENVER at http://burns.daniels.du.edu.

12. Discussion Questions

1. Do you think that Great Britain's high literacy rate has a bearing on its economic performance? What other factors contribute to Great Britain's success?

2. What, if any, affect does Great Britain's climate and location have on its ability to pursue and attract investment by foreigners?

3. Are there cultural influences in Great Britain that might affect the way business is conducted between Great Britain and foreigners?

13. Case Study

Memo

To: Board of Directors
From: Consultants
Re: Downsizing

I. Problem

OVERVIEW
Fantasy Real Estate Sales (FRES)

Headquarters in Milan, Italy Offices in Italy, Sweden, Hungary, Spain, Russia, Netherlands, United Kingdom and Greece Fantasy Real Estate Sales (FRES) was established in Greece in 1995. The idea behind the Company was drawn from a Greek real estate agent, XElvina Greeeelepis, owner of XXEGGG Realty. XElvina's real estate company had many different properties listed, including villas and private islands. The inspiration for FRES came from meeting XElvina. The Directors felt we would be able to help people find their "fantasy" pieces of real estate, such as castles, villas, ranches, winery's and any unique properties falling into the "fantasy" realm of real estate.

ITALY

Recently the headquarters of FRES, located in Milan, Italy, began to grow. It was doing so much business that it had seven full-time agents, and one office manager.

FRES needs to hire more people, but it is concerned with hiring too many, because if the Company has more than 15 employees, it will have to "take care of the employees" for a long time. This is based on the employment laws in Italy. See http://www.cmslegal.com/intelligence/cms_news/employment.htm.

RUSSIA

The Russian market is beginning to pick up new business. There are plenty of properties available, but FRES's target buyers are hesitant to purchase property in Russia. (FRES is working on advertising the benefits of realty in Russia. FRES started doing overnight stays at the individual properties, so potential clients can see what it is like to be in Russia.)

HUNGARY

Currently, in Hungary, the Company has had a reduction in properties available for sale. FRES was been unable to secure properties for sale. It has also had two properties flood in the last two months.

NETHERLANDS

The market is booming. There seem to be enough "fantasy" properties at the current time.

UNITED KINGDOM (ENGLAND, SCOTLAND, WALES)

The United Kingdom, including the **England, Scotland and Wales** markets, has been relatively stable. These markets, for FRES, do not perform extremely well, but they do not go below projected income.

SPAIN

This market is just beginning to show the growth potential that was projected by FRES for the country. The market had a difficult time because prices were inflated. As such, it was not a good investment to purchase a fantasy property here; however, prices are beginning to come inline. Thus, with other European markets, the general market is beginning to pickup in sales.

SWEDEN

Currently the Swedish market is booming. The agents cannot keep up with the market.

II. Initial Exit Strategy

Exiting these countries would be relatively easy, except for Italy, where the headquarters office is currently located. All of the other offices are satellite offices. In most cases the agents work out of their own homes. The Milan office could be vacated relatively easily. The interior has been upgraded to class A office space and since this is in short supply in Italy, it should be relatively easy to re-lease or sub- lease. The network of real estate agents throughout Europe that FRES has established would help in the event that FRES needed to leave the county.

III. Contingency Exit Strategy

See Initial Exit Strategy plan. The plan of exit would be simple to leave everything and leave the country.

IV. Conclusion

Employment restrictions in Italy will make it difficult to keep expanding. To have a reasonable exit strategy, FRES should move the headquarters to Sweden. The reason Sweden is more of an ideal location is due to the booming market and the favorable employment laws. The other markets could be considered, but Russia would be difficult. Current employees would resist a move to Sweden. The United Kingdom does not have enough business. This is also true with the Netherlands. Spain might be a possibility for the home office. The company should not completely close the operation in Italy, but it should leave one or two agents, to continue the local market.

Refer to: International Real Estate Digest. Homepage. http://www.ired.com. U.S. Department of State. Homepage. http://www.state.gov.

U.S. Embassy. Homepage. http://usembassy.state.gov.

14. Selected References

For additional information, see the following:

*CIA World Factbook,*https://www.cia.gov/library/publications/the-world-factbook/index.html

British Property Federation,http://www.bpf.org.uk. European Property Federation,http://www.epf-fepi.com. Housefund.co.uk,http://www.housefund.co.uk.

Jones Lang LaSalle, http://www.joneslanglasalle.com.

National Association of Estate Agent s, http://www.naea.co.uk. *Richard Ellis International Property Specialists.* CB Richard Ellis (http://www.cbre.com).

Royal Institution of Chartered Surveyors, http://www.rics.org. Time Almanac. *TIME Almanac.* Boston: Information Please LLC. United Kingdom's government website,http://www.direct.gov.uk.

United States Department of State. *Background Notes: United Kingdom.* United States Department of State (Online).Available:http://www.state.gov.

U.S. Bureau of Census at http://www.census.gov. U.S. Department of Commerce at http://www.stat-usa.gov. U.S. Bureau of Economic Analysis at http://www.bea.gov. U.S. Embassy. Homepage. http://usembassy.state.gov.

UNIVERSITY OF DENVER Global Real Estate Web site (Burns School) at http://burns.daniels.du.edu.

World Trade Centers Institute at http://www.wtci.org. World Trade Organization at http://www.wto.org. World Bank. *Adult Illiteracy Rates.* The Economist.

15. Glossary

National Association of Estate Agents – Real Estate Trade Association.

Crofters Act of 1886 – established rights of tenancy.

About the Author

Tyler Elick, graduate student, Burns School of Real Estate and Construction Management, *Daniels College of Business,* UNIVERSITY OF DENVER.

United States

INTERNATIONAL REAL ESTATE (GLOBAL REAL ESTATE)
Bill James, MAI, Co-Author (Appraisal) and
Dr. Mark Lee Levine, Co-Author and Editor

■ 1. Geography

The United States is located in North America, bordering the North Atlantic Ocean on the east, and the North Pacific Ocean on the west, between Canada to the north, and Mexico to the south. The capital is in Washington, D.C. The United States is comprised of 50 states. The United States has about 9,826,675 sq km of land area, with 19,924 km of coastline.

A temperate climate permeates throughout most of the United States, with a tropical climate in some areas to the south, Hawaii and Florida; arctic temperatures exist in the north, especially in the state of Alaska. Terrain varies throughout the United States, from flat lands to rugged, high mountains.

The United States is concerned with air pollution, resulting in acid rain, carbon dioxide, water pollution from pesticides, and other major environmental issues.

Natural hazards include volcanoes (Hawaii and the west coast of the United States), earthquakes (in California and other regions), mud slides (especially in California), frost in Alaska, etc.

■ 2. History and Overview

The American Revolution

In the early 1770's, serious disagreements arose between the British colonies and the British government. While colonists could not be elected to the British Parliament in London, Parliament passed many taxes that colonists had to pay. The Colonists called this "taxation without representation." Because they had paid to defend the colonies in the French and Indian War, the British believed that they had every right to tax the colonists. On the other hand, the British government did not understand colonial life or the hardships brought about by heavy taxation. Instead of giving the colonists more independence, the British government passed even more laws. War broke out. The 13 colonies successfully revolted against the British, and the United States of America was born.

Abolitionists, Slaves and the Civil War

By 1850, few people in the United States could talk calmly about slavery. White Southerners, slave owners or not, saw slavery as a way of life, without which they could not function economically. Northerners argued that it was wrong for one human being to own another and some began to speak out against slavery. Called "abolitionists," they wanted to abolish, or end, slavery.

The Civil War

The Civil War was a defining era for the U.S. and it changed the nature of the American government. An underlying issue was the relationship of the states with regard to the national government (in this case, it can be argued, the power of the states

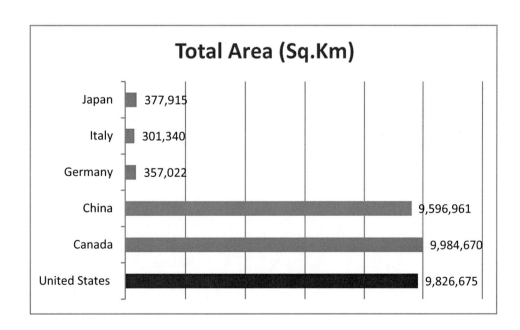

to preserve slavery as a legal institution). Both sides claimed the principles of the American Revolution as their own. The North prevailed and the slaves were freed. The first sweeping civil rights laws, in particular the 14th and 15th Amendments to the Constitution were passed in the immediate postwar period.

The Golden Age

By the early 1900's, the United States was one of the richest nations in the world.

Every year thousands of ships left ports like New York and New Orleans loaded with steel, machinery, and other goods for delivery to all parts of the world. Americans were also starting businesses in other countries. As trade and industry grew overseas, the United States found itself more involved in events in distant lands. Americans liked taking a leading role in world affairs; they did not like the thought that of being dragged into quarrels in other parts of the world. That concern grew in 1914. On a Sunday afternoon in June, two young students from the small country of Serbia in Eastern Europe shot and killed the nephew of the Emperor of Austria. When Americans read of the event on Monday morning, few dreamed it would lead to a world war. Yet within a few years, 30 countries were drawn into World War I, including the United States. Eventually, Germany, among other countries, was defeated.

The Great Depression and World War II

The Great Depression that slowed business during the 1930s brought hard times to the whole world. People desperately turned to leaders who promised to bring power and prosperity to their country. Germany, especially hard hit by the depression, was also hurt by the treaty that ended World War I. The treaty took land and resources away from Germany. Germany also had to pay for the damage it had done during the war. Germany turned to Adolf Hitler to solve its problems. Hitler's power-mad approach culminated in World War II, one of the most brutal wars in history. Germany was defeated by the Allied forces on May 8, 1945, and Japan surrendered on Sept ember 2, 1945.

The Cold War and After

In February of 1945, the Allies agreed to hold open, democratic elections in every country they had freed from Nazi domination. From the start, the Soviet Union ignored that agreement and set up communistic controls in one eastern European country after another. President Truman and later U.S. Presidents set out to keep the Soviet Union from taking over any more countries. The struggle that followed between the United States and the Soviet Union was labeled the "Cold War," a battle fought with words and money, not with guns or bombs. At the same time, each side prepared for a war it hoped would never come. By 1949, the Soviets had their own atom bomb, triggering a deadly arms race. Each country was determined to produce more weapons, and more destructive power, than the other. The competition took ideological forms, too, as each tried to win other countries to its point of view. Eventually the U.S.S.R. failed in its mission, and many of its controlled countries became independent, leaving only the United States as a world superpower.

■ 3. People

The United States has a population of **318,892,103** of which 19.4% are in the 0 to 14 year-old category, 66.1% are in the 15-year-old to 64-year-old category. The balance in the 65+ years of age and older range, at 14.5%, is growing rapidly.

The population growth rate is 0.77%, with birth rates at 13.42 per 1,000 and death rates at 8.15 per 1,000. Life expectancy in the United States is 79.56 years, with 77.11 years for males and 81.94 years for females. The ethnic division is about 79.96% White (including 15.1% Hispanic), 12.85% Black, 4.43% Asian, 0.97% Amerindian and Alaska native, 0.18% Pacific Islander, and 1.61% of additional races.

The dominant religious denomination in the United States is Protestant at 51.3%, with 23.9% Roman Catholic, 1.7% Mormon, 1.6% other Christian, 1.7% Jewish, 0.7% Buddhist, 0.6% Muslim and a mix of other religions. The dominant language is English at 79.2%, with some Spanish spoken, especially in

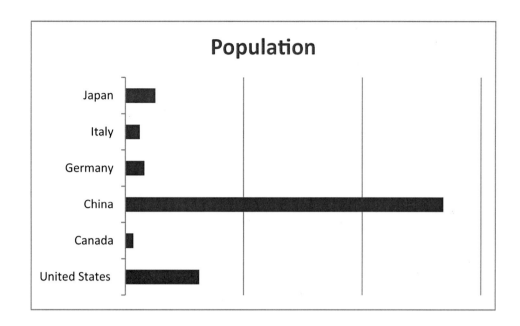

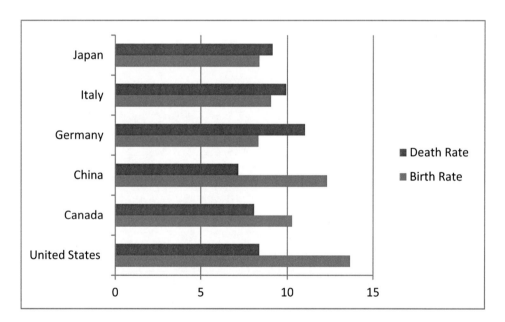

California, Florida, and the Southwest. Literacy is about 99% for 15 years of age and older.

■ 4. Government

The United States consists of a federal republic, with a strong democratic base. The capital is Washington, D.C. Administrative divisions consist of 50 states and 1 District (Washington, D.C.). A number of other dependent areas, such as Puerto Rico, have special protection or relationships with the United States. Independence was July 4, 1776, which is the national holiday. The U.S. law is based on a Constitution, which became effective March 4, 1789. The legal system is based on English common law, with judicial review under the structure of the judicial system acting as a check on the legislative acts. Suffrage in the United States is generally 18 years of age and is universal. Government branches consist of the Executive Branch by the Chief of State and head of government as the President. A cabinet is appointed by the President, with approval in most areas by the Senate. The Legislative Branch is bicameral, consisting of a Senate and a House of Representatives. Defense forces in the United States consist of an Army, Navy (including the Marines), Air Force, and National Guards within the states.

■ 5. Economy

The Gross Domestic Product (GDP) grew from $14.82 trillion (2010) to $17.42 trillion (2014). The GDP per capita increased

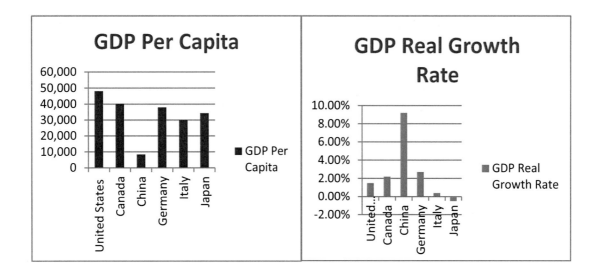

from $47,800 (2010) to about $54,800 (2014). The inflation rate in the U.S. increased from 1.6% (2010) to 2.0% (2014). Unemployment decreased from 9.6% (2010) to 6.2% (2014). The Gross Domestic Product (GDP) real growth rate increased from 2.1% (2007) to 3.0% (2010), then to 2.4% (2014).

The United States has the most technologically powerful, diverse, advanced, and largest economy in the world. In this market-oriented economy, private individuals and business firms make most of the decisions. The government buys needed goods and services predominantly in the private marketplace. U.S. business firms enjoy considerably greater flexibility than their counterparts in Western Europe and Japan in decisions to expand capital, lay off surplus workers, and develop new products. At the same time, they face higher barriers to entry in their rivals' home markets than the barriers to entry of non-U.S. firms in the U.S. markets. U.S. firms are at or near the forefront in technological advances, especially in computers and in medical, aerospace, and military equipment, although their advantage has narrowed since the end of World War II. The onrush of technology largely explains the gradual development of a "two-tier labor market." Those at the "bottom" lack the education and the professional/technical skills of those at the top; and more and more fail to obtain pay raises, health insurance coverage, and other benefits. The educated "top" fare better. The years 1994 through 2000 witnessed increases in real output, low inflation rates, and a drop in The years 1994 through 2000 witnessed increases in real output, low inflation rates, and a drop in unemployment to below 5%. However, long-term problems included inadequate investment in economic infrastructure, rapidly rising medical costs of an aging population, sizable trade deficits, and stagnation of family income in the lower economic groups. Softening of the economy that began in 2001 was accelerated by the terrorism incidents of 9/11. The economy grew slowly since then, but went into recession in 2008 in response to the collapse of credit markets in the United States and worldwide that originated with the collapse of the U.S. subprime residential mortgage industry. The continued economic problems of Japan, Russia, Indonesia, Brazil, and many other countries, including the United States itself, cloud the outlook for the future.

6. Currency

Currency in the United States is the U.S. *dollar*, which equals 100 cents. See the Burns School Global Real Estate Web site, *Daniels College of Business*, UNIVERSITY OF DENVER at http://burns.daniels.du.edu for currency conversions.

7. Transportation

The United States has a strong rail system, with nearly 224,792 kilometers (km) of main routes, along with 6,586,610 km of highways.

About 41,009 km of inland waterways in the United States are also used. Pipelines are utilized to transport petroleum, natural gas, and certain other chemicals. Numerous ports on the east and west coasts, as well as inland ports via waterways, such as Chicago and Houston, all support the export and import of goods. Also supporting the transportation system are 13,513 airports (2014).

The U.S. has ports in Anchorage, Baltimore, Boston, Charleston, Chicago, Duluth, Hampton Roads, Honolulu, Houston, Jacksonville, Los Angeles, New Orleans, New York, Philadelphia, Port Canaveral, Portland (Oregon), Prudhoe Bay, San Francisco, Savannah, Seattle, Tampa, and Toledo, among other key locations.

8. Communications

The United States has one of the strongest communication systems in the world, utilizing 139 million main telephone lines plus 310 million cellular phones (2014), and fiber optic cables, microwave, coaxial cables, and satellites. The United States bolsters communication system with nearly 15,000 radio stations operating, including AM radio, FM radio and shortwave radio broadcasting stations, and thousands of television stations. The international system consists of ocean cable systems and satellites in use. There are approximately 505 million Internet hosts (service providers) and 245 million Internet users (2012).

■ 9. Real Property Issues

Property law is generally the same from state to state.

The following discussion illustrates basic principles of real estate law found in most states in the United States.[282]

A. Definition of Property

1. Property signifies dominion or right of use, control, and disposition, which one may lawfully exercise over things or objects.
2. Property involves relationships, e.g., one distinction of relationships included in the "Restatement of Property" is: "§ 1.Right:.a legally enforceable claim of one person against another, that the other shall do a given act or shall not do a given act.
    "§ 2. *Privilege:* a legal freedom on the part of one person as against another to do a given act or a legal freedom not to do a given act.
    "§ 3. *Power:* an ability on the part of a person to produce a change in a given legal relation by doing or not doing a given act.
    "§ 4.Immunity: a freedom on the part of one person against having a given legal relation altered by a given act or omission to act on the part of another person.[283]

B. Grouping of Property Types in General

Property can be grouped in many ways. The following are only a few:

Real Property versus Personal Property: One of the most basic classifications is *real property,* as opposed to *personal property.* The extremes on the continuum, as is true with most demarcations, are easy to define. Thus, a piece of raw land is easily placed in the "real property" area. Likewise, a pencil is easily placed in the "personal property" classification. A significant problem arises when there is an attempt to distinguish property which has the characteristics of both groups, such as leases or fixtures.

Tangible Property versus Intangible Property: Another basic property classification involves those types of property interests which have physical substance, referred to as "tangible property." There is an overlap of property noted in the first classification above. Both real and personal property may be in either the tangible group or the intangible group. Thus,

an easement is included in the intangible group (intangibles in the real estate area are often referred to as "incorporeal interests"). Tangible property includes interests in property (rights, etc.) that are capable of physical possession. Thus, ownership of a pencil or fee simple is a tangible interest. (The physical assets, which are capable of actual physical or symbolic livery of seis in, are often referred to as "corporeal interests.") *Future Interests versus Present Interests:* These groups are basically "reversionary interests," "remainder interests" and "executory limitations," among others.

Real Property; Freehold versus Non-freehold Interests: In addition to the classifications noted above, there are further sub classifications within many of the earlier-noted groups. For example, there is the sub classification of "freehold interest" versus "non-freehold interest." This distinction is of extreme importance in many states.

C. Grouping of Property Types Freehold Interests

The classes of "freehold interests" often include:

"Fee Simple" or "Fee Simple Absolute": This interest is the largest and greatest estate in the land. Technically, where land is free from all ownership rights, it should be referred to as a "fee simple absolute" (FSA), not "fee simple." However, note the subsequent discussion of the Colorado statute applicable to the use of the words "fee simple."

The "fee simple," or "fee simple absolute" may be inherited. Further, if the fee is not otherwise limited, it is deemed by some states to be a "fee simple absolute."

However, the fee can, of course, be limited. Thus, the fee could be followed by some limitation, a few examples of which are noted and discussed subsequently. Thus, one may own a fee "subject to" a special limitation.

Life Estate: In addition to the "fee simple" discussed above, there can also be a grant, and, thus, an ownership in real property, which is referred to as a "life estate." Thus, if A gives his A property for his life, and then to B, A would own a (real property) "life estate" interest. The interest would exist for the remainder of A's life. Further, if X conveys Black acre to Y for life, Y will own a life estate, which will cease upon Y's death, and X has retained vested "fee simple" (not "absolute"), which is referred to as a "reversion." Upon Y's death, the reversion vests in "possession." (We say "vests in possession" since the estate of X is already vested, as to other rights.) The life estate and reversion are transferable.

Life Estate, Per Autre Vie: In addition to the above example, there may be a life estate created for the duration of the life of another. D could convey a life estate to E, but the life estate for the benefit of E could end on the life of D, or the life of someone else in addition to the life of E. Thus, if the life estate would end with the death of D, the party making the

conveyance, then even though E died, E's interest would pass to his heirs, since the life estate would remain until the death of D.

Curtesy and Dower Abolished:
Under some state statutes the concepts of curtesy and dower *i.e.*, rights in property to a spouse, on the death of a spouse, have been abolished. Therefore, the concept of a life estate in certain property to the spouse as existed under common law no longer exists.

Fee Tail:
The concept of fee tail is only briefly covered here because it has been abolished in many states. Some states' abolition of this estate, however, is not a complete denial of its existence but rat her somewhat of a slight modification. For example some states provide that a person who is seized in fee tail of any land, that is, receives a grant of a fee tail interest, is deemed to be seized of the land only for a life estate with a remainder in fee simple absolute to the person or persons to whom the estate would pass on the death of such first grantee, according to the course of the Common Law. Thus, in effect the statute says that one who receives an interest by means of a grant as a fee tail will be deemed to hold only a life estate, and a person who would take from him under Common Law, will take a fee simple absolute.

Under **Common Law,** *the* person who would take from the grantee would be the oldest son because the rule of "primogeniture" applies at least if the language of the statute is taken literally primogeniture would apply). This interpretation is open to question. However, some authorities argue that rather than applying the rule of primogeniture (that is, the position that the oldest son takes all property, as opposed to dividing the property among all children), the courts would probably attempt to apply the Statute of Descent and Distribution. However, again the literal reading of the statute requires the primogeniture application.

Defeasible Fee, Special Limitations, and Condition Subsequent:
There are also types of fee simple estates which are limited, due to events which may occur which should reduce or increase estates. "Future Interests" included grants of a fee simple subject to a special limit at ion. *For example*, where A receives a grant of land, with a restriction that said land can never be used for purposes of serving alcoholic beverages, and if in the event the same is served, the interest to A will immediately terminate and re-vest in the grant or; A's interest is a fee simple subject to a special limit at ion. Likewise, there may be other limit at ions on the grant, such as a fee simple subject to a condition subsequent.

D. Grouping of Property Types Types of Non-Freehold Estates

In addition to the conveyance of the freehold estates earlier mentioned, there may be conveyance of property which is not of sufficient importance to be classified as a "freehold estate." Under Common Law the non-freehold interests were often referred to as "chattels real." Chattels real, as that term was used under the Common Law, are treated as real property under some state statutes. Therefore, under that type of statute they may be inherited and are also devisable by will. As such, they are also freely transferable during life, except as otherwise limited by statute or contract among the parties. Generally, non-freehold interests are leases. In most states, there are four general groups of leases. Before proceeding to the types of leasehold estates, it is worthwhile to note some basic points. First, where land is leased, there is no limit as to the period of time it may be leased, and it still constitutes a lease so long as the interest is less than a life estate. Even though the conveyance is for 100 years (unless the courts would construe this as an actual grant of the fee, which is usually not the case),it is a non-freehold estate, even though it might last longer than most life estates. Where a lease involves a period in excess of one year, most states require a writing to be able to enforce the lease.

The four types of tenancies or non-freehold interests regarding leases include:

1. **Tenancy *for a Period*:** A tenancy for a set period of time expires under the given period, without a requirement to give notice, at least under most state laws.

   If the tenant remains in possession past the stated period of time, the tenant is deemed a tenant at sufferance, and, therefore, may be ejected through proper statutory means unless the landlord recognizes that the tenant as a tenant from period to period, or a continuing tenant. The tenancy that may be created by the recognition by the landlord of the hold-over tenant at sufferance may be for a period equal to the original term of the prior lease, or it may be a tenancy at will, or the period-to-period tenancy. The decision would depend upon the circumstances and upon statute. Most courts favor a period-to-period tenancy. What period this will be, when the period-to-period tenancy is employed, would depend on the facts but is often a period equal to the prior period.

2. **Tenancy at Sufferance:** A tenancy at sufferance is not truly a tenancy, but is a situation where there is a limbo state. For example, as noted above, where a tenant for a fixed period holds over improperly, he is a tenant at sufferance until the landlord elects to eject the tenant or create a new period-to-period tenancy.

3. **Tenancy from Period to Period:** This tenancy, which is usually employed with rental of apartments or many other short rental periods, involves a rental from year to year, month-to- month, or so forth. This type of tenancy results in an *automatic* renewal for the given period, such as year to year, unless otherwise terminated as may be provided in the contract or as provided in statute. Where this type of tenancy exists, the landlord or the tenant must terminate the tenancy in the manner provided by statute, unless otherwise agreed. Under many statutes notice must be given to terminate the tenancy.

Such notice is often as follows:

PERIOD OF TENANCY: For less than one week

AMOUNT OF NOTICE: One day

PERIOD OF TENANCY: For one week or longer, but less than one month or a tenancy at will.

AMOUNT OF NOTICE: Three days

PERIOD OF TENANCY: For one month or longer, but less than six months

AMOUNT OF NOTICE: Ten days

PERIOD OF TENANCY: For a year or longer

AMOUNT OF NOTICE: Three months 284

4. **Tenancy *at Will*:** Where the landlord and tenant agree that there is a tenancy, as opposed to a tenancy at sufferance, but the period of time is indefinite, it is a tenancy at will. In this case, either the landlord or tenant may terminate the agreement at any time providing that the statutory notice is given. Most states provide that no notice is required for termination of a tenancy for a set period.

E. Ownership by Multiple Parties

In addition to the simple ownership of land by one individual, there are many types of ownership of land which involve multiple parties. For example, a "tenancy **in common**" involves an undivided interest in the ownership in property by multiple parties. It exists, generally, whenever two or more parties own, simultaneously, concurrent interests in the identical property, and the property is not otherwise classified as provided hereunder.

Rights and Liabilities Connected with Owning Land: In the tort area, there are certain rights given to the landowner, which he may employ to seek compensation where his property or use of the property has been damaged. For example, trespass to property may be abated by an action in tort. A loss of land as a result of an improper taking of possession or a holding over may be remedied by a forcible entry and detainer action (FED). Actions involving condemnation, actions involving damage to property and encroachments, may also be maintained.

F. State Condominium or Horizontal Property Acts

In many states, condominium ownership is becoming increasingly popular. Many state statutes provide for fee simple absolute ownership in the individual air space, such as the apartment unit, and an undivided tenancy in common interest with the other tenants with regard to the common space. The common elements would include such areas as the common parking spaces, common grass and recreational areas, hallways and corridors. The individual air space is defined under the statute as the enclosed room or rooms of the given contemplated building.

G. Licenses

A license is not an interest in land and, therefore, is distinguished from the easement concept noted. A license involving real estate involves a consent by the owner of the land to allow someone to occupy the land or otherwise use the land in a manner which, absent the license, would constitute trespass. An ineffective easement is often construed to be a license. As indicated, licenses are generally revocable at the election of the party giving the license. They are generally no assignable, personal in nature, and destructible by death of the licensee. One exception to this is a license coupled with an interest. If one has a license coupled with an interest to enter upon land and remove a given substance, such as minerals or crops, the license is often treated by the courts as irrevocable by the grantor of the license.

H. Acquisition of Real Property by Other Than Purchase or Grant Acquisition in General

Patent: Most ownership in real property is evidenced by a grant from the federal government via a patent. The patent may be granted as a result of compliance with homestead rules or under other special statutes. Most property which is owned by individuals was initially derived from a grant from the United States, since title to the public property was vested in the United States (except as otherwise conveyed to the states).

I. Enabling Acts

As far as state land is concerned, enabling acts, which allowed the state admission to the United States, also allowed the state land, which was granted by Congress to the particular state. Obviously, although each state has boundaries, the state does not own all of the real estate. Sections 16 and 36 in each township were granted by the United States to the state to be used for schools and other governmental purposes. There is also "in **lieu of land**"; this is additional land conveyed to the state by the United States where, before the state becomes a state, part of Sections 16 and 36 of a given township had been previously conveyed by the United States to a private party. Where this occurred, the additional land conveyed to the state to compensate for the lost land is referred to as "in lieu of land."

J. Basic Real Property Principles

1. Sovereign: Land may (generally) not be acquired, as against a sovereign, such as the United States or a state, by means of adverse possession. As far as states are concerned, part of the sovereign immunity doctrine has been eliminated.

2. Titles: In addition to grants from the United States, foreign governments in territories, which were previously under their control and jurisdiction, made grants. Certain types of grants or patents are not total; a reservation may be maintained. Many patents contain reservations whereby the United States reserves the right for miners to seek a proprietary interest in a vein or lode. There may be a

reservation by the United States of rights-of-way for canals and future ditches.

Adverse Possession:

In addition to acquisition of land by a "normal" grant or patent, real property may also be acquired by adverse possession. Adverse possession is the concept whereby one takes property and uses it as against the true owner; after the requirements of the statute are met, that party acquires the ownership.

The requirements of adverse possession are sometimes referred to as the *Cohen* Rule. This rule is derived from the statute requiring the land to be held continuously, openly, *hostilely*, exclusively, and notoriously for the period of time required by law. These requirements are:

1. **Continuous**: The requirement of continuous occupancy does not mean the land cannot be left for a given period of time if there is an intention to retain the control and use of the land. The continuous requirement is terminated when an outside person takes possession of the property without permission.

2. **Open *and Notoriously:*** The requirement that the property be held openly and notoriously is such that the immediate community would know that the adverse possessor is attempting to claim title. The fact that the actual owner did not receive actual knowledge of the same is not required. If there is an attempt to *conceal* the adverse nature of ownership, the requirement is not met.

3. **Exclusive**: The use must be exclusive in nature. What "exclusive" means depends on the nature or general use of the land. It could be "exclusive" in nature where the land is used only for part of the year, *e.g.*, where the land is pastureland and that is the "normal" use,

4. ***Hostile:*** The use must be hostile in nature as against the true owner. Use of land under lease or under a contract allowing permission for use, or as a co-tenant, or otherwise deriving the land under the express or implied consent of the true owner is not hostile. This does not mean that one cannot claim adverse possession where he is a lessee, co-tenant, or otherwise uses the land with permission. (He specifically gives notice of his position and disclaims the relationship to claim adverse possession.)

5. ***Title:*** A further requirement is possession under claim of title. The possessor of the land must claim it under claim of title and not merely for temporary use. There is a distinction between a claim of title and a claim of right. The latter is not required. The party taking possession may claim there is a better title, so long as he does not claim that his title derives from such better title (and thus is subordinate to said title), and so long as he asserts his title as against all other claims.

   There is a special advantage under some state laws where claim of title is made and ***color of title*** exists. Under one state statute, where there is a claim of title and it is made under color of title, that is, a claim that the possessor has title to the property, made in good faith, with the *paying of taxes for a seven year consecutive period*, the seven years will apply for adverse possession (as opposed to the normal period which is often much longer, as noted subsequently).

6. **Time *Period:*** The required number of years of occupancy to meet the time period requirement for adverse possession differs from state to state. The statutory periods range from as few as 5 years in some states to as many as 30 years in others.

Constructive Adverse Possession:

Where there is actual possession of *part* of the land, constructive adverse possession may be maintained for *additional* adjacent land. However, the constructive adverse possession portion of the land may not be of a substantially disproportionate nature to the area actually occupied. For example, occupancy of a farm area may allow constructive adverse possession to adjacent pasturelands, even though they were not actually used. However, the amount of the pasture may not be substantially more than the farm. Some state statutes provide that a person not in possession of real estate may sell it even though another is in adverse possession.

Limitation on Adverse Possession:

Adverse possession only applies against persons who would have a cause of action against the adverse possessor as a result of his action to attempt to control the land. The adverse possession doctrine does not apply against holders of future interests where the future interests are not yet **possessory.**

Tacking:

Where one is an adverse possessor, meeting all the requirements previously diseu8sed, and that adverse possessor has held the land, at least in some states, for 15 years, his period of holding may be tacked to a subsequent purchaser from the adverse possessor.

Taxes:

In addition to the methods earlier discussed, title to property may be acquired by a tax deed. Thus, where an owner of real property fails to pay his taxes, the property may be levied on and sold. A treasurer's deed will eventually be issued to the purchaser, absent a redemption. It is established that tax title is deemed original title. Therefore, a tax title can be an advantage; it may clear up previous ambiguities or uncertainties in the title. Title under a Treasurer's deed is usually to the property where it is assessed and sold. Care must be exercised to see that there is complete ownership, including the mineral interests, since, under some state laws, the tax deed would not be sufficient, based upon the general description of the land, to convey the mineral interests where there had been a previous reservation of the same.

Other General Methods for Acquiring Ownership in Land:

The other methods of acquiring ownership in land are more the exceptions rather than the general rule.

The methods discussed subsequently herein are those which are sometimes referred to as derivative titles. That is, the title is derived from a former owner. The transfer may include the normal grant or conveyance by sale, a transfer by death, whether testamentary or intestate, foreclosures, levy and execution, dedication to the public, abandonment, acquisition from insolvency proceedings or court decree, gifts, or in other manners.

K. Principles of Real Property Conveyance

Normal Conveyance: The most typical example of a transfer of land is by deed from the record owner. Usually, any person, association, body politic or corporate, can convey real property by deed. Some state statutes provide that except in cases where water rights are represented in the form of stock, they are conveyed as real estate; thus, title may pass under an appurtenant clause in a deed if the circumstances establish the intent. Livery of seis in is often not necessary. (Under general principles, consideration is not necessary. Under some statutory deed forms, there is a *statement of* consideration. Therefore, it is often uncertain whether a deed is valid without the statement of consideration. It is the author's opinion that such deed would be valid, notwithstanding the lack of the recitation of consideration. Apparently the statute, as earlier cited, is only a permissible means of making the conveyance, not a required form for making the conveyance; however, most deeds include a statement of consideration. Most conveyances carry the right of possession. It is an immediate right of possession unless a future day of possession is specified. Even though the executory contract post pones possession, the contract might merge into the deed.

1. ***Required Elements of a Deed:*** Aside from the *consideration* element, there are other items, which must be included in a deed to make it valid. There must be a designation of the *grantor*, a *description* which is sufficiently clear to identify the property, *signature* of grantor (to avoid the problem of the Statute of Frauds), *delivery* of the deed, and in some states certain other requirements (*e.g.,* Words of Conveyance).
2. ***Description:*** Land must be conveyed by sufficient description so it may be identified. A deed without any description, or a deed which does not sufficiently identify the property, does not "close," is not sufficient to "convey" property. To be marketable, as opposed to being a good conveyance, the land must be sufficiently described from the deed itself.
3. ***Delivery:*** A deed to be effective must be delivered. Delivery requires the overt *act* and manifestation of the *present intention* to make the conveyance. The transfer of the deed must be meant to transfer the property as opposed to temporary possession of the deed or review of the same. Delivery is also effective where the deed is put in escrow, providing it is beyond the control of the grantor for recall of the deed. That is, the escrow agent cannot be an agent who is subject to complete control of the grantor. For the escrow to be effective, the deed should be required

to be transferred to the grantee upon the happening of the condition upon which the deed was placed in escrow. Properly prepared, an escrow creation can often be effective even though the conditions occur subsequent to the death of the grantor, or even where the death of the grant or is a condition precedent to physical possession of the property.

4. ***Grantor Identified:*** The grantor must be specifically designated in the body of the deed. Capacity is often presumed to exist for a natural person; unless the contrary appears, capacity is not the same as it is with an unnatural person. Capacity is not, of itself, required. Therefore, as in the case of a corporation, the certificate of incorporation should be shown of record.
5. ***Signature of Grantor:*** The grantor must sign the conveyance. To avoid technical defects, the grantor should sign the deed in the *same name* he received it when he was the grantee. This is discussed subsequently under the concept of marketable title.

   Where a corporation is involved, the corporate officer should sign. The proper officer to sign depends on state statute. In many states the statute requires a single signature of the executive officer, even though the general form used will provide for signature places for the president and the secretary. If there is an attorney-in- fact involved acting for the record owner, the attorney should sign the name of the owner for him as attorney-in-fact. The power of attorney should, of course, be recorded for reference. Some states provide that powers of attorney must be recorded. If an instrument is executed under a power of attorney, the power of attorney must be properly acknowledged and recorded in the county in which conveyance is required to be recorded.
6. ***Other Elements Usually in the Deed:*** Another requirement in the deed is that the grantee be clearly identified. If a deed is delivered in blank because the grantor is uncertain as to the grantee or for other reasons, the deed is ineffective at that point in time.
7. ***Seals.*** In most states, seals are not required for the valid execution of a deed. Seals are utilized by corporations; this often has the effect of creating a *prima facie* case for the position that the same was executed properly by the corporate officer under the theory that the seal would not be on the deed unless it was proper.

L. Acknowledgment

Acknowledgments in a deed are not normally required to create a valid deed. The appearance before a notary is not usually a necessary element to a valid deed. The acknowledgment usually creates a *prima facie* case for the authenticity of the deed and often makes it admissible in Courts of record without further evidence of the proper execution by the grant or. If the deed is properly acknowledged and properly recorded, it usually creates a *prima facie* case that in fact it was delivered. As stated, acknowledgments are not usually necessary for a *valid* deed; however, it is often a necessary element to have a *market-able* deed.

M. Recording

Generally under most state laws, deeds, mort gages, and other in- cumbrances on property along with other instruments *may* be recorded. It is not normally a requirement to have the deed recorded to make it valid. Where the statute allows the recording, it is generally provided that such instrument is valid as against any person who is charged with constructive notice; that is, notice which appears of record. Placing an instrument of record will not accomplish the purpose of constructive notice unless the statute authorizes the recording of the instrument and gives it the effect of constructive notice. Many states provide for the recording of tax levies, sheriff's certificates of purchase, **lis pendens,** and other types of instruments.

In most states recording is of extreme importance. It is of particular importance if the state is a modified "race" statute state. That is, the first grantee to record his instrument, assuming he is without notice of any prior unrecorded interest, will prevail, as opposed to another person, even though the other person took title prior in time. Many state statutes protect not only a *purchaser*, that is, one paying value, but also any good faith class of persons with *any kind* of interest.

One receiving a gift or devise can prevail, as opposed to an earlier unrecorded purchaser's interest. Recording is generally only valid as against other interests, which could have been recorded. The interests of an adverse possessor in property cannot be recorded; therefore, those interests will not be terminated or cut short by a sale by the actual owner {record owner) to a bona fide purchaser for value.(Most title policies exclude coverage as to parties in possession.)

N. Other Restrictions of Record

Where an instrument is of record and it refers to another instrument and the subsequent instrument is not of record, it is usually not sufficient to result in constructive notice.

Often statements contained in the deed or other instrument which affect title to real property, where that instrument has been of record in the Clerk and Recorder's Office of a given county for a set period of time, *e.g.*, 20 years or more, constitutes *prima facie* evidence of the facts recited. Anyone attempting to oppose those facts has the burden of rebutting the *prima facie* case. Many statutes provide that any instrument, which refers to the grantee in a fiduciary capacity, will not be notice of the fiduciary capacity unless the instrument shows the name of the beneficiary represented and defines the trust or other document involved. Reference to the trust or other document is usually sufficient if the deed refers to another document and incorporates it by reference or otherwise identifies it where that instrument is of record.

O. Title Insurance

In addition to reviewing the record for instruments recorded which affect title, title protection may also be assured by means of title insurance, which is of course an insurance policy issued by an insurance company which attempts, except for exclusions and other limitations, to insure either the mortgagee or the owner-mortgagor, or both, that the title is as stated in the commitment and insurance policy. The insurance policy, if it covers the given insured, only protects up to the purchase price, as a general rule. Such insurance generally does not cover the profit element where a purchaser acquires property at a reduced price and could sell it for a substantial gain, but there is a title defect.

P. The Torrens System

In addition to the recording system mentioned earlier and title insurance, title might be held in a different manner and the ownership and marketability delivered in another manner. This is under the Torrens system, which applies in some states. The registration system developed from an individual who worked with the registration of ships. The thought was, rather than having all the complicated title questions that exist under the normal recording system, possibly one could register land similar to registering ships and keep a better, more accurate record. A parcel of land may be registered, except for a tax tit le, which has certain limit at ions under the statute, by applying certain steps. The applicant applies to the court for registration. The court will decree title to be registered, assuming basic registration requirements are met and proof of title is shown. The registrar then registers the title according to the court decree and holds the original certificate in the registrar's office. A duplicate of the registration certificate is issued to the landowner and also to the holder of the lien, if one is involved.

Once registration is accomplished, the registered title cannot be conveyed or otherwise transferred or encumbered except by noting the encumbrance upon the registration certificate of title. Where registered land is to be conveyed, the duplicate certificate is surrendered to the registrar who issues a new certificate to the new grantee. If the certificate is lost or otherwise destroyed, the duplicate certificate must be obtained by order of the court.

The value of the registration method is that the subsequent recipient of the certificate of title will take title, assuming he is a good faith purchaser for value, with no notice, free and clear from all encumbrances except those noted on the certificate of title, except for certain rights of appeal under the Registration Act, certain rights or claims existing under the Constitution or statutes which do not appear of record, certain public highways and other easements, ditches, special tax or other assessments for which a sale of land has not yet occurred prior to the time of the registration, existing leases not exceeding three years, and certain other limitations. One important advantage of the registration system, as opposed to the normal recording system; is that the registered property cannot be lost by adverse possession. Registered titles are not normally subject to a general judgment lien as is the case with recorded titles. Recording of most documents will not affect registered title. Exceptions to this are the recording of a Treasurer's deed, which can initiate a new title, which will be paramount to the registered title. A federal tax lien can be valid against a registered title.

Q. Encumbrances Upon Real Estate

1. ***Mortgages and Deeds of Trust:*** One of the most common methods of creating an encumbrance upon real property is by a deed of trust.

    Only the mortgagee may release a mortgage. Deeds of trust utilize either a public or private trustee. If a private trustee is used, it is treated similar to a mortgage. If it is a public trustee, a release is by the public trustee but certain documents, such as a cancelled note and request for release, must be executed by the creditor-beneficiary under the deed of trust. A mortgage or deed of trust lien often expires 15 years after the last due date of the final principal payment. The 15-year period may often be extended for an additional 15-year period by an instrument in writing signed by the beneficiary or creditor-owner of the indebtedness.

2. ***Judgments:*** A judgment usually becomes a general lien upon all the real property of the judgment debtor within the county where the creditor records the transcript of judgment. Judgment liens of a general nature and liens of levy and execution expire six years after entry of the judgment. The judgment lien can usually be released by recording with the, Clerk and Recorder of the county in which the judgment is located a statement to the effect that the judgment has been satisfied or by recording of the instrument which releases the property. The latter instrument is executed by the judgment creditor or the assignee from the judgment creditor.

    The general judgment lien can usually be destroyed by the execution upon such judgment and levy against the property. The levy will be destroyed by release, by order of court, or by satisfaction of the judgment by the debtor. The levy is often valid for six years or more after its recording.

3. ***Mechanics Liens:*** Most states allow a lien for mechanics where they supply services or materials in the construction or improvement of property. Under many state laws a mechanic's lien may be created by a material man, contractor, subcontractor, builder, a mechanic, and all other persons of every class who perform labor upon or furnish materials to be used in the construction or improvements or for value of services rendered or labor done or materials furnished, etcetera. The lien is not usually automatic. The mechanic claiming the lien must file a statement, signed and sworn to by the claimant or his agent, which sets forth the material required by statute. Liens for labor must often be filed within a given period, e.g., two months after the completion of the building, structure, or other improvement.

    a. ***Time Period:*** Liens for labor must often be filed within a given period, *e.g.*, two months, after the completion of the building, structure or other improvement.

4. ***Foreclosure:*** Where foreclosure is required involving a trust - deed, the public trustee may generally foreclose the deed of trust. The creditor completing a notice of election and demand for sale and presenting the same to the public trustee initiates the foreclosure by public trustee. The public trustee then causes the property to be advertised and sold in compliance with the statute.

5. ***Redemption:*** Redemption periods vary from state to state in most standard real estate forms used by real estate brokers and salesmen, there is reference to having a good and marketable title. It is generally thought that a title is marketable if it can be derived of record from the United States or the State and the same is free from any liens or other defects or encumbrances which would lead a reasonable man, who desires to buy the property, to refuse to purchase the land without a reduction in price due to some defect or restriction on title.

R. Marketibility

Marketability concepts were earlier discussed, although not specifically labeled as such. Thus, the previous discussion on mortgages and other encumbrances are restrictions on marketability as noted in the above definition. Additional concepts and restrictions on marketability are noted hereafter. Generally, each successive record holder within a given chain of title, that is, a given ownership from the grantor to the grantee, to grantor to grantee, and so forth, is presumed to be a bona fide purchaser for value without notice of outstanding claims. A conveyance or encumbrance from a person who is not, at that point in time in the chain of title—that is, he is not a record holder—may be ignored unless such person subsequently acquires title to the questioned property. Sheriff's deeds, public trustee's deeds, court decrees, and certain other types of deeds concerning title and other official acts which have been of record for nine years in the county where the land is located, and where no action has been commenced to avoid such title, are very difficult to oppose. Where land is under option, such option ceases to be notice of the potential purchaser's right to an interest under said option one year after the date for which the conveyance was noted in the option where no conveyance took place arid no action was brought to enforce or procure the conveyance. No action can be brought to enforce the conveyance of any real estate under a bond for deed or agreement for the sale and purchase of real estate, unless the action is brought within a given statutory period from the day upon which the conveyance was due, unless the purchaser was in possession of the property.

An unbroken chain of title must be maintained. Thus, from the inception, such as the patentee to every subsequent owner of record, there must be sufficient identification tracing ownership from one to the next. Names, which are pronounced somewhat alike, or substantially alike are referred to as ***idemsonans.*** They are often presumed to be the same person, notwithstanding the difference in spelling. However, surnames, although pronounced alike, which are spelled sufficiently different so that they will not be indexed in the same section of the Recorder's indices will produce a break in the chain of title. The surname Cohen and Kohen illustrates this type of situation. Where identical names are used, such as the grantee then becomes the grantor; they are often presumed to be the same person unless contrary evidence is illustrated. Likewise, use of nicknames or abbreviations of the common name will not destroy the presumption of identity. The same is true with titles, prefixes, suffixes, and the like. The use of Mr. or Miss illustrates this issue. These are not part of a name, and their use or omission from the record will not normally affect the presumption of identity unless they are inconsistent in the *subsequent use*, such as the use of Miss Smith and the subsequent use of Mr. Smith. Notwithstanding the above, it has been held that the middle initial or middle name are a material part of the name. Under some state statutes, after a given period, variances between names of the grantee and subsequent grantor, involving anyone of the following three variations, will not destroy the presumption of identity which would otherwise exist:

1. If one instrument contains middle initial and the other instrument contains no middle initial.
2. Where one instrument contains a name with the full Christian name and another instrument contains a name with only the initial of such Christian name.
3. If one instrument contains the full middle name and the other instrument contains only the initial of the middle name.

S. Constructive Notice

All parties acquiring interest in property are on notice of all instruments, which are necessary to their own chain of title whether or not they are of record. They are also of notice of any rights of any person in possession of or making actual use of the property they are acquiring, even if the instrument is not of record. They are also on notice as to all matters, which they have actual knowledge of, or matters which may require them to make inquiry, which could derive the notice in question.

Homestead: Some states (and federal law) allow a homestead interest not to exceed a specified amount. This homestead interest is exempt from certain executions and attachments arising from any debt, contract, or other obligation.

The creation of a homestead can often occur in one of three ways:

1. The owner who has title to the home may record an instrument in writing which describes the property, sets forth the nature and source of the owner's interest in the property, and states that the owner is claiming a homestead in the property.
2. The clerk may, assuming it is feasible, permit the owner or spouse, in lieu of recording the above statement, to make what is referred to as a "marginal homestead entry" upon the deed itself, which is presently of record.

3. It may be created automatically, by Statute. *Homestead* refers to occupancy of the home for use as the residence. Therefore, it often only applies so long as the home is occupied in that manner. It will, however, normally extend to the widow, widower, or minor children. The homestead allowance is in addition to the allowances allowed to a widow and orphans under many of the probate statutes. To convey or otherwise encumber or destroy the homestead interest, the husband and wife, jointly, assuming marriage exists, must normally execute the conveyance or conveyances. A separate instrument may be executed, which releases the interest in the homestead rights, signed by the husband and wife or other parties who are involved in the homestead interest. A conveyance of the property in question from one spouse to the other spouse usually does not destroy the homestead.

A creditor is normally entitled to levy upon homestead property, but only the excess of the sales price over the homestead allowance, plus costs and expenses, is available to the creditor. If there is no surplus, often statutes provide that the property cannot be sold. The parties entitled to the homestead may sell the property and segregate the proceeds from the sale. If the same is invested, in some states, within one year of the date of the sale, and if within a given number of days from the date of the purchase of a new home, there is recorded an instrument reflecting the homestead, the new property will carry the benefit of the old homestead exemption

T. Overview History of the Law

1. **THE LAW:** "Law" is a word that is used often by everyone in common parlance, but it is something that is very nebulous. Many courts have said that "Law" is an order for methods or rules, which we follow to organize our lives. Dictionaries have said that law is a rule of conduct or action prescribed or formally recognized as binding or enforced by the controlling authority.
2. **ORIGIN OF THE LAW:** The function and creation of the law is tied to man but is also affected by so many other sources operating *on* mankind.

   EXAMPLE: Man needed laws and regulations with regard to firearms only at the time that firearms were created. In recent times, we have developed "law" with regard to hijacking of airplanes because skyjacking is of relatively recent origin. Likewise, other laws must be *developed* within the total structure of law and the legal framework. For example, someday there must be regulations as to ownership of right of ways in space, rights *to* occupy planets, division of planets, division of other resources on other planets, controlled interplanetary space travel, control over rocket ships and hijacking of them, and regulations as to transporting goods in space. Therefore, to ask for the history of the law is to ask for man's evolution. It *develops as man develops*. To be somewhat more concrete, we might examine briefly a few of the basic principles, which form the basis of our current legal system in the United States.

3. ***ORDER OF THE AUTHORITY IN THE LAW:*** Most people have read the papers or heard a newscast whereby a statement is made that "the lower court was *bound* by the earlier position of the Supreme Court." However, the question should be raised as to why the lower court was "bound by the higher court." The establishment of the concept of precedence underlies this point of law. A precedent simply means something that came beforehand and sets a general guideline. Whether a precedent or a prior position is controlling depends upon the order of the law.

One basic classification of authority is (1) **primary authority; (2) secondary authority; (3) third or tertiary authority.**

   a. *Primary Authority:* The primary authority category is that type of authority, which is binding on the court in question. Thus, a lower court hearing a case for which the Supreme Court in the same state has previously decided the matter would be "bound" by the higher authority. Statutes can be declared unconstitutional because they are in conflict with the Federal Constitution. This is another way of saying there is primary or higher authority than the statute. The primary authority group is that authority which, when it exists, is binding if not in conflict with another authority which is higher than it within the same classification. For example, the genesis for law in the United States is that of the United States Constitution (and Common Law). All statutes, cases, laws, treaties, or other matters must be consistent with the Federal Constitution. Likewise, the State Constitution must not be in opposition to the Federal Constitution because the Federal Constitution declares in Article 6, Section 2, under the Supremacy Clause, that it is the "supreme law of the land." Therefore, it is a type of primary authority. There are other types of "primary authority," using the earlier definition, meaning that type of authority that is binding upon the court. For example, a statute passed by a given state in question which is relevant to the question at hand before the court would be binding upon the court; i.e., the court *must follow* it unless it can show there is some other type of authority which is of a higher nature. Again, if the United States Constitution is in conflict with a statute, whether the statute be state or Federal, the statute would fail as being "unconstitutional."

4. ***COMMON LAW:*** In addition to the sources of law indicated, namely under the constitution, statutes, treaties, or so forth, there is also the Common Law. The Common Law is referred to as that body of law derived mainly from England. The English Common Law was the main source of law in the United States because, as most people know, the United States was settled in its initial form as colonies, and the settlers needed some basic form of legal system

to operate under until a new approach could be undertaken. Therefore, the colonies, and subsequently, most states, generally accepted the proposition that the law in the given colony or state should be the law as it existed under the Common Law, i.e., in England, unless otherwise specifically modified by statute or other law. This concept is generally followed today; thus, the Common Law applies in the United States in most jurisdictions, unless otherwise specifically changed by statute or other interpretation. Exactly what is the "Common Law" is difficult to determine because the Common Law includes unwritten custom, trade practice, and informal rules. In summary, the Common Law developed sometime after the Norman Conquest; therefore, the time period for Common Law is usually fixed at around 1067 A.D. or thereafter.

5. ***DEMARCATIONS IN THE LAW:*** There are many ways to classify or group the law.

For example, there is "statutory *law,*" that is, law which is formed by statutes. There is "case *law;*" that is, law which develops as a result of interpretations from a case-by-case (*ad hoc*) approach. In addition, there are other divisions or ways to classify the law. There is "civil *law*" (where one party opposes another party), as opposed to "criminal *law,*" (the State or the "People" versus a given defendant or defendants).

6. THE ***CONCEPT OF STARE DECISIS: Stare decisis*** is a principle, which is strongly connected with the concept of ***precedent.*** As discussed earlier, *precedent* is a position, which is binding or at least has some authority to direct the court toward a conclusion on the case before it. Thus, if the court is hearing a case on whether a tenant is entitled to remove carpeting which he laid in the apartment during the time of his residency, the court might be guided by other prior cases or decisions which have discussed and reviewed this issue. This is referred to as precedent. The concept of following prior decisions, i.e., precedent, in the form of *cases*, is referred to as ***stare decisis.***

Appraisal: Appraisal is often called "valuation" and is often, in the United States, defined by the Uniform Standards of Professional Appraisal Practice (USPAP) as, "the act or process of developing an opinion of value; an opinion of value." Typically, there are three approaches to estimating value:

1. The ***Market Approach*** uses prices of similar properties which have sold recently as indicators in estimating the value of the subject property.

2. The ***Cost Approach*** combines the cost of construction of the building and other improvements, minus depreciation, with the value of land to estimate the value of the subject property.

3. The ***Income Approach*** considers the amount of net income and appreciation, which can reasonably be expected to accrue in the future, and discounts these to a present value. The approach that is used depends on the characteristics of the real property and its market. Approaches

are reconciled into a market value appraisal, based on their relative reliability. In applying the approaches, the appraiser considers the "highest and best use" of the subject property, which is generally the use that produces the most economic benefit to the owner. Highest and best use is dependent on land use controls, physical characteristics of the real estate and local economic and real estate market conditions. Appraisals are frequently used to assist in underwriting financing secured by the subject, determine a sale or purchase price, or to settle a dispute involving the real property. Of prime importance is the unbiased objectivity and expertise of the appraiser. The field of appraisal developed as a profession in the USA during the early 20th century in an effort by brokers and lenders to assist their clients to buy, sell and finance their real properties. The American Institute of Real Estate Appraisers was created by the National Association of REALTORS® and was established the MAI designation for primarily commercial/investment appraisers. The savings and loan industry created the Society of Real Estate Appraisers, which established the SRA designation for single-- family residential appraisers. The need for these credentials and the professional discipline associated with them became most apparent during the Great Depression in the 1930s. In 1990, these two organizations combined to form the leading professional association for appraisers in the United States, the Appraisal Institute. (The United States has many other appraisal organizations, such as the Royal Institution of Chartered Surveyors, an organization that is very active in Europe and throughout the world.) During the late 1980s, U.S. real estate markets experienced a severe downturn in real estate finance and investment. This resulted in part from the earlier deregulation of the savings and loan industry. As a result, in 1989, the US Congress passed the Financial Institutions Reform, Recovery and Enforcement act (FIRREA), creating mandatory requirements for real estate appraisals in federally related transactions as well as federal standards for certification of appraisers. This established nationwide licensing of appraisers by individual states and created USPAP as the rules of the profession, based primarily on the professional standards of the Appraisal Institute. As real estate markets become less government controlled around the world, real estate lenders, investors and regulators in other countries are increasingly looking to the US for viable valuation methodologies, standards, policies and procedures for real estate assets in conjunction with economic growth. See the Burns School Global Real Estate Web site for the UNIVERSITY OF DENVER at http://burns.daniels.du.edu.

■ 10. Real Estate Trends

Real estate trends in the United States, as is true with other countries, vacillate as other markets change.

Prior to the Great Recession, which began in 2008 the most recent US real estate market downturns were in the mid-1970s, late 1980s, and in the early 2000s, all followed by strong upward trends. In the mid-1970s, hotel and resort properties were affected the most.

The late 1980s market downturn was severe with greatest effect on the office market. It was caused by a general economic recession and aggravated by the 1986 Tax Reform Act. The Act eliminated many real estate tax advantages created in 1981 that allowed investors to take large tax write-offs based on deductions for depreciation, interest, and other accounting items. The savings and loan debacle that resulted, in part, from deregulation of the savings and loan industry also in 1986 added to the problem.

The economic expansion of the 1990s stimulated demand for all types of real estate, which resulted in vastly improved market conditions by the mid and later years of the decade. Real estate market conditions improved steadily in the 1990s and stabilized in the early 2000s with the office and apartment markets experiencing substantial vacancy after the September 11 terrorist attacks. Most real estate markets recovered slowly with strong residential market growth stimulated until the mid-2000s by low mortgage interest rates. As demand accelerated, sale prices of many investment-grade properties reached replacement cost once again encouraging speculative development. Markets generally remained in a healthy balance until the local and national economies fell into recession in 2001 exacerbated by the terrorism events of that year.

During the downturn in the early 2000s all categories of real estate, except single-family residential, assisted by low interest rates, were adversely affected, but then they slowly recovered. By mid-2002, all categories of real estate once again experienced higher vacancy rates, stable or declining effective rental rates, and a reduction in new development. But with an absence of additional terrorism events and reduced interest rates, real estate markets began a slow recovery. The market for single family residences and condominiums, particularly sensitive to the availability of financing, benefited from reductions in interest rates. But the residential market was severely softened by the subprime mortgage industry collapse which began in early 2007 generating the Great Recession.

Because of the financial crisis initiated in the subprime residential mortgage industry in 2007, all real estate market segments experienced a downturn, however the apartment and single family residential markets have improved considerably, with more moderate growth of the industrial market.

The "credit crunch" created by the subprime debacle made transactions more difficult because institutional investors, the source of much real estate capital became much more cautious. Now capital is slowly being released to real estate and other markets, but most of it is still risk averse. As the economy and real estate markets recover and cost effectiveness stimulates construction of mass transit systems, significant mixed use and transit oriented real estate is being developed, often including apartments, many of them subsidized and affordable.

In the area of family homes and condominiums, generally the price structure differential is important to focus on. Lower-priced homes, depending on the part of the country, may be priced under $300,000 in major U.S. cities, or under $200,000 in smaller U.S. cities. Mid-priced homes generally would range in somewhere between $200,000 and $450,000, keeping in mind that this range will be impacted by the size of the U.S. city. More expensive-priced homes are generally above the mid-price range; however, many pockets of very expensive homes exist in almost every major U.S. city.

Real Estate Categories: **Real** estate categories are generally described in the United States as "residential" or "commercial." "Commercial" generally covers all property that is not a single-family dwelling, or the condominium/townhome type of structure, including investments in residential-use properties, such as apartment buildings. In some areas, a further demarcation from that of the generic term of "residential" and "commercial" may exist. There some "commercial" groupings might be "unimproved land," "farm land," "development land," "special-use-type property" such as golf courses, nursing homes, hospitals, etc. Also, the categories of "shopping centers," "industrial use properties," and "resort-type properties," "hotels" and "motels," and other sub-categories within the label of "commercial" property. Because of the weakness in the stock market over the last few years, and the continued concern with the same, along with lower interest rates reflected in the bond market, the real estate market has had greater impetus in real estate investments. This trend appears to continue, with some adjustments taking place because of absorption of inventory, limited additional production adding to "supply," placing of other firms in new facilities, and so forth. It appears that development of new projects, and trends for the same, are favored when the market is weaker, and governments react to it by more favorable laws and flexibility in timing and activities for new developments. However, the reverse is also true: When the market is stronger, and more supply of new product, it appears that governmental officials often tighten the strings to prevent inflation and other economic problems, such as foreclosures and bankruptcies. Cultural differences, and expansion of more immigrants to the United States, has called for different types of real property uses, especially in reacting to the needs of cultural and ethnic groups as they immigrate to the U.S. This may include a desire for a different type of structure, such as a residential structure that can facilitate multiple generations living within or around the same structure. New trends continue to develop and cause concern in some areas, such as legal issues involving toxic waste and developments that were in areas previously contaminated. Other concerns involve changes in legal development, restraints on legal development, and potential exposure for developers because of legal issues. Events from September 11, 2001 are also of concern in real property issues, which may necessitate additional security. Shopping centers, office buildings, industrial complexes, resort complexes and special-use properties usually provide more security regarding especially potential terrorist attacks and other considerations. A major issue that has developed in the residential field, and may spread to the commercial field as well, has been regarding mold and other toxic items that may create additional liability for those connected with real estate.

■ 11. Cultural Issues

Any nation's culture is complex and vibrant in its diversity. While broad cultural characterizations such as those presented here can be generally accurate, following such generalities too strictly may be dangerously misleading. To conduct business effectively and profitably in a country, it is vital to have a thorough understanding of its culture's complexities. The United States is a Constitutional Republic. References to the Constitution of the United States of America, which in the Bill of Rights expresses the positions of freedom of religion, freedom of the press, freedom of assembly, freedom from unreasonable searches and seizures, right to counsel (attorney), rights to due process and protection under the law, the right to be compensated for property that is taken from an individual by the government, and similar concerns influence the culture and openness of U.S. society. The United States stresses these freedoms, and, in turn, those instill cultural differences that may not exist in many other countries, especially those that do not follow a democratic form of government. The United States is known as a "transparent society" or community. U.S. citizens and residents have more availability to information and knowledge relative to governmental positions and officials than citizens of other countries. For example, one important law in the United States, the Freedom of Information Act, allows its citizens and residents to be aware of important information that might be secret or denied to residents and citizens in many other countries. The United States of America is generally thought to be open, friendly and casual in undertaking business relationships. Although attorneys are used more often in real estate transactions, and longer, more detailed contracts are utilized, such formality is not normal when undertaking many business transactions. Addressing an individual in a more casual nature is more common in the United States than is true with many other countries, such as those in Asia or in Latin America. Transactions for real estate often involve formal documentation, and calculations for property are often equal to, or more important, than many personal relationships that might otherwise be present. That is, often properties are purchased without a buyer or a seller ever meeting each other. This is quite common in residential transactions, and is also common in some commercial transactions. Usually in the United States a broker representing the buyer tenders an "offer to purchase real estate" to a broker representing the seller. (In the United States, individuals and companies often have their own brokers, and such brokers operate ONLY for that individual or entity, not all of the parties in the transaction, at least in many circumstances. To have one person operate for everyone creates in the United States what is often thought to be a "conflict of interest" and something that is improper in many circumstances.)

Greetings in the United States are fairly casual and often involve a first-name basis, in a short-term meeting. Greetings by shaking hands and references to "Hello" or "How are you?" are quite common.

Business: Business is sometimes undertaken in the U.S. by soliciting through what is referred to as "cold call," via phone calls without a prior introduction, or by personal solicitation without a prior introduction, as well as sending materials without a prior introduction. Such approach is unheard of in many societies, such as some of those in South Korea or Japan. However, in the United States in real estate transactions, there is less concern with the individual parties involved, and more concern with the calculation of the numbers involved that produce, for example, the Net Operating Income (NOI) from the property, as opposed to concern of who owns the property in question.

Individuality vs. Group: There is a strong feeling of support for the "individual" within the United States, as opposed to the "group." As such, individuals tend to want to own their own property, whether that be a piece of real estate for the residence, investments, automobile and so forth. It is common for individuals to seek their "own space," with an opportunity to be alone, to have time to contemplate and think individually, as opposed to that of "group thinking" or "group activities." While interactions within a business setting, such as the workplace, are still very important in the United States, more emphasis is placed, as compared with Latin American and Asian countries, on the "individual," not the "group."

12. Discussion Questions

1. The United States has a very strong economy, but it can be affected by many factors. Name several of these factors and explain why these could become problematic.

2. What cultural issues that are prominent in the U.S. may be seen by other countries as troublesome?

3. What is unique about the U.S. government compared to other governments in the world? Does the government influence the way business is conducted in the United States?

13. Case Study

U.S.A. Now

(Located outside of the United States)

USA NOW undertakes the exportation and selling of specialty food products which are not normally available in the United States, thus appealing to specific ethnic groups within the U.S. who have a yearning for such foods. One example of such food is the DRAGON FRUIT, a fruit found in Vietnam and certain other Asian countries, with only limited import in to the United States. USA NOW has recently favored locating in smaller strip centers in communities normally attracted to such specialty foods and related products. USA NOW has developed ten of these specialty stores in the New York area and has considered expanding into other U.S. cities.

The company's current concern is a potential backlash that apparently they have faced in New York from certain individuals who may not have a long history of living in the United States. Since increased resistance by the U.S. government to issue Visas and other permits for individuals (whether students or otherwise) to enter into the United States, the Board of Direct ors is generally concerned that exporting goods to the U.S., to market mainly in the U.S., may not be well received, especially following the 9/11/01 terrorism acts in New York, Washington, D.C. and Pennsylvania, as well as other recent tragedies. The Board of Directors is looking to you, as a Consultant, to advise as to whether you feel the business will be adversely impacted to the level that they should possibly now consider exiting all activities within the United States. Do you anticipate that their concern should only be temporary, and that their business should continue to grow? What are key signs to indicate that the Company should consider terminating business in the United States? The Company has done very well in the New York area, aside from events recently, as noted. USA NOW had anticipated expanding their operations into New Jersey and surrounding areas in the Northeast of the United States. What would be your recommendations to the Board of Directors on this issue?

SOLUTIONS, DISCUSSION

The Board of Directors for U.S.A. NOW has stated that the Company has done very well thus far. Given the mix of populations in the United States from various ethnic backgrounds, it is likely that the company will continue to be well received.

The company's concern with being involved in Muslim-type food products might be of greater concern, as opposed to other non-Muslim-type foods and products. The Company might adjust their product line to allow for a reduction in Muslim-type foods and products, due to the recent resistance. Issues, which might alarm the Board of Directors, could include a significant drop in sales, specific actions directed adversely against the company or any of its stores or employees, additional terrorism activities that might target other ethnic groups, and changes in laws or governmental positions that might impact the company's activities.

USA NOW should continue its business, being alert and vigilant for abrupt changes, as noted. The company might carefully consider expansion toward non-controversial ethnic groups. Consider the impact of whether USA NOW was located in Europe, or Central or South America, or the Middle East, or Asia.

Refer to: X-rates.com. Homepage. http://www.x-rates.com/.

U.S. Embassy. Homepage. http://usembassy.state.gov. U.S. Department of State. Homepage. http://www.state.gov.

14. Selected References

CIA World Factbook, https://www.cia.gov/library/publications/the-world-factbook/index.html

Organization of American States at http://www.oas.org.

Richard Ellis International Property Specialists. http://www.cbre.com. Time Almanac. TIME Almanac. Boston: Information Please LLC.

United States Department of State. Background Notes: United States. United States Department of State (Online). Available: http://www.state.gov.

U.S. Department of Commerce at http://www.stat-usa.gov. U.S. Bureau of Economic Analysis at http://www.bea.gov. U.S. Embassy. Homepage. http://usembassy.state.gov. World Trade Centers Institute at http://www.wtci.org. World Trade Organization at http://www.wto.org.

World Bank. Adult Illiteracy Rates. The Economist.

X-rates.com. Homepage. http://www.x-rates.com/.

15. Glossary

Cost Approach – Combines the cost of construction of the building and other improvements, minus depreciation, with the value of land to estimate the value of the subject property.

Income Approach – Considers the amount of net income and appreciation, which can reasonably be expected to accrue in the future, and discounts these to a present value.

Market Approach – Uses prices of similar properties, which have sold recently as indicators in estimating the value of the subject property.

About the Authors

William M. James, MAI, CCIM, president of James Real Estate Services, Inc., in Denver, Colorado. He began his appraisal career in 1973 with the commercial and investment appraisal firm of Shorett and Riely in Seattle, Washington, and opened the company's first branch office in Anchorage, Alaska. In Denver since 1976, he earned an MBA degree from the UNIVERSITY OF DENVER in Real Estate and Construction Management in 1979. Over the years, while conducting appraisals and market studies on a wide variety of semi-rural, residential, general, and special purpose commercial and investment properties, he has managed rezoning, development and redevelopment projects, and instructed appraisal courses. Bill is a Certified General Appraiser (former member of the Colorado Appraisal Board) and licensed Real Estate Broker in Colorado.

Dr. Mark Lee Levine is the Editor of this Book.

Venezuela

INTERNATIONAL REAL ESTATE (GLOBAL REAL ESTATE)
Authored by *Jose Ramirez Dr. Mark Lee Levine*, Editor

1. Geography

Venezuela is located in the northern part of South America. It occupies most of the northern border of South America. It borders Colombia to the west, Guyana and the Atlantic Ocean to the east, and Brazil to the south.

Venezuela's area is 912,050 square kilometers (km) and is approximately twice the land size of California. Coastlines consist of 2,800 km on the Caribbean Sea and the Atlantic Ocean.

Border disputes exist on the western side of the Esequibo River, along with other disputes with Colombia, relative to the Gulf of Venezuela.

The Venezuelan climate is typically tropical, hot and humid, with warm days and cool nights. The temperature varies according to the altitude, from 0°C (32°F) or less in the highest Andean crests to more than 34°C (93°F) in the lower zones of the coast. The average temperature in Caracas is 25°C (77°F).

Terrain includes the Andes Mountains, Maracaibo Lowlands, West-Central Range, Coastal Range, Plains Elevations, Orinoco Delta and Guiana Highlands in the southeast. Venezuela has natural resources in the form of petroleum, natural gas, coil, hydroelectric power, iron ores, aluminum, and other minerals. Still, Venezuela's number one export is petroleum, which accounted for over 90% of its total exports in 2011.

Venezuelan arable land use is approximately 2.85% and about 0.71% in land for permanent crops. The balance is in other uses, including meadows and pastures, forests and woodlands.

Environmental issues include sewage pollution in the "*Río Güaire*" (Caracas), "*Playas del Estado Vargas*", and "*Lago de Valencia*", oil and urban pollutants in the "*Lago de Maracaibo*", and deforestation and soil degradation in the "*Estado Bolívar*", resulting from mining operations. . Conservation efforts are present relative to nuclear test bans; ozone protection; desertification; biodiversity; endangered species and marine life conservation; and pollution relative to wetlands and other areas. Venezuela is prone to natural hazards such as earthquakes and flooding.

2. History and Overview

Venezuela's independence was declared on July 5, 1811. On December 17, 1819, in the "*Congreso de Angostura*", under Simón Bolívar, "El Libertador", Venezuela joined the new Republic of Colombia, "*La Gran Colombia*", along with the Departments of Nueva Granada (presently Colombia) and Quito, until January 29, 1830. On January 29, 1830 the final decision to separate Venezuela from "*La Gran Colombia*" was taken. On May 6, 1830, Venezuela's new Congress is installed in Valencia, Venezuela. The separation became official, however, on September 22, 1830, when a new Constitution was approved. Then, Venezuela separated and became a sovereign country. From that moment until 1958, Venezuela was submersed in hegemonic governments and dictatorships. On January 23, 1958, the last dictator, Marcos Pérez Jiménez was overthrown. A .Government Junta

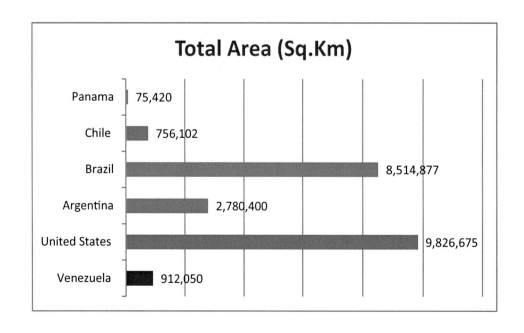

Total Area (Sq.Km)

Panama	75,420
Chile	756,102
Brazil	8,514,877
Argentina	2,780,400
United States	9,826,675
Venezuela	912,050

occupied the presidency until February 13, 1959, when Rómulo Betancourt is sworn into office as Venezuela's president elected. After that, Venezuela experienced somewhat calm democratic periods for roughly 40 years, until 1999, when Hugo Chávez took office. From that point forward, a series of confrontations in Venezuela have resulted in a series of elections to attempt to reform the leadership. The country has undergone substantial economic and political changes in the late 1900s and into the 21st Century, including the creation of a new Constitution in 1999 that changed Venezuela's official name from "República de Venezuela" to "República Bolivariana de Venezuela." After Hugo Chávez dead, his protégé, Nicolas Maduro, was sworn into the office to finalize Hugo Chávez presidential period. Nicolas Maduro was later elected president for the period that started on April 19, 2013, amid elections fraud, abuse of power, and human rights protest in the country.

Most Venezuelans come from areas in Europe and Africa. A good number of Venezuelans have a background from Spanish, Italian and Portuguese following World War II emigration. Most of the population, close to 85%, lives in urban areas, along the coastline, and in the Andes Mountains. As is true with many other large countries, such as Australia, Venezuela has much of its population in a very small area. In Venezuela, almost half of the land is south and east of the Orinoco River. But, only about 5% of the population dwells there. The most densely populated area in Venezuela is located in the Coastal Range, which only covers 3% of its total area, but contains three import ant cities: Caracas, Valencia and Maracay.

■ 3. People

Venezuela has **30,620,404** (2015 est.) people, with an age structure of 27.1% in the 0 to 14-year-old category; 66.4% of the population is in the 15- through 64-year-old category; and 6.5% in the 65 years of age and older group.

Life expectancy for the male population is 72.18 years (2015, est.) The female life expectancy is approximately 78.26 years (2015, est.) The population growth rate has been fairly strong, at approximately 1.42% (2014, est,). Birth rates are about 19.42 in 1,000 of population (2014, est.) The death rate is 5.27 in 1,000 (2014, est.)

Ethnic divisions in Venezuela include the Spanish, Italian, Portuguese, Arab, German, African, and indigenous persons. The dominant religion is Roman Catholic at 96%, with about 2% Protestant, and a mix of others. The dominant language is Spanish as the official language. Native dialects also are spoken in the remote interior. Literacy is approximately 95.5%, which is lower than in many of the developed countries.

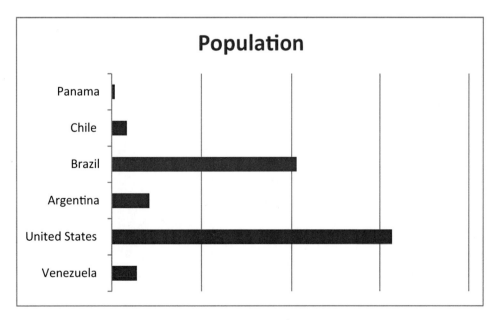

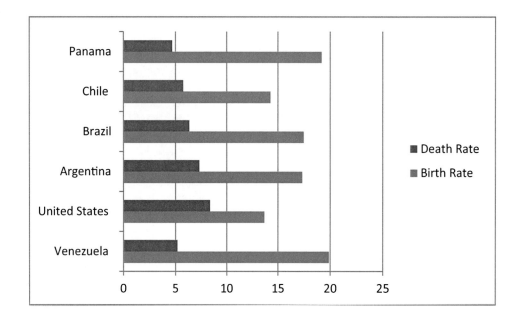

4. Government

Venezuela is a federal republic, with the capital located in Caracas. There are 23 states of administrative-type divisions known as *Estados*, one Federal District, *Distrito Federal*, and one Federal Dependency, *Dependencias Federales*, which is comprised of 72 individual islands, grouped in 11 federal controlled island groups. Venezuela gained its independence from Spain on July 5, 1811. This date is their national holiday of independence. The current Constitution was formed on December 30, 1999. The legal system in Venezuela follows the Napoleonic Code with an open, adversarial court system. The government consists of the Executive, Legislative, Judicial, Citizen, and Voters Branches (1999 Constitution).

The Executive Branch consists of a President, a Vice President, and a council of ministers, appointed by the President. The Legislative Branch is a unicameral assembly, *Asamblea Nacional Constituyente*. The Judicial Branch consists of the Supreme Court of Justice, or Tribunal *Supremo de Justicia*, and other lower-level courts. The Citizen branch is represented by the People's Defense Officer, *Defensor del Pueblo*, Republic General Public Prosecutor, *Fiscal General de la República*, and Republic General Controller, *Contralor General de la República*. The Voters Branch is represented by the National Voters Council, *Consejo Nacional Electoral (CNE)*.

Diplomatic representation exists with the United States with Venezuela's office located in Washington, D.C. The U.S. diplomatic representation exists with an Embassy in Caracas.

5. Economy

The Venezuelan economy is dominated by the petroleum sector, with approximately one-third of the Gross Domestic Product (GDP), about 96% of its export earnings, and about 45% of the central government revenues. Therefore, petroleum is the key and controlling economic factor in Venezuela.

The Gross Domestic Product (GDP) per capita earning is $14,414.8 Venezuela GDP growth rate is 1.3% (2013, est.) The inflation rate on consumer prices was 18.7% (2006), was extremely high at 30.4% (2008), was 27.6% (2011), and, again, was extremely high at 40.6% (2013, est.) The unemployment rate at 7.5% (2013, est.) has also been fairly high in the last few years, leading to increased disparity in income equality.

Industries, in addition to petroleum, include iron ore, construction materials for production, food processing, textiles, steel and other production activities, including mot or vehicle assembly plants. Venezuela exported, in 2011, a total of $91.338 billion. In 2011, Venezuela imported $36.388 billion, mostly in medicaments, transmission apparatus incorporating reception apparatus, for radio-telephony, radio-telegraphy, radio-broadcasting or television, vessels, incl. warships and lifeboats, live bovine animals, and Oil-cake and other solid residues. Venezuela's major trading partners for exports are United States at 27.90%, China at 11.97%, Brazil 8.63%, Colombia 4.18% and Mexico 4.08% (2011).

6. Currency

Currency is the *bolivar fuerte* (VEB), consisting of 100 cents in one (1) bolivar. This replaced the original bolivar in early 2008 (Bs.F. 1 = Bs. 1,000 (*original bolivares*). See the Burns School Global Real Estate Web site for the UNIVERSITY OF DENVER, Daniels *College of Business,* at http://burns.daniels.du.eduforcurrencyrateconversions.

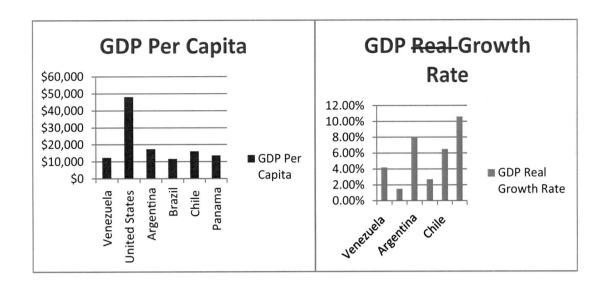

7. Transportation

Venezuela has approximately 806 kilometers (km) of railroad lines and 96,155 km of highways, including 32,308 km of paved highways. There are inland waterways in Venezuela that can accept larger vessels for shipping. With petroleum being an import and export product, pipelines are very important to transport crude oil and other petroleum product s, along with natural gas. Venezuela has numerous ports for shipping, including those such as Amuay, Bajo Grande, Puerto Cabello, Puerto La Cruz, and other ports.

Venezuela has 409 airports, including 129 airports with paved runways, and many of the airports are able to handle major jets (2010).

8. Communications

In 2012, Venezuela had approximately 7.65 million main telephone lines in use and 30.52 million mobile cellular telephones. Current expansion includes satellite earth stations, coaxial cables, and interurban fiber optic network (2010). Venezuela has numerous state-run and private radio stations and television broadcasting stations.

9. Real Property Issues

Property ownership information can be obtained from the Office of the Registrar, *Oficina del Registro*, located in the area where the property is situated. In Venezuela, on the one hand, the buyer is required to pay a commission to the financial institution. This is not always true for the legal fees, which may not be included in the commission paid to the financial institution. Clarifying this issue with the institution in advance is recommended. The legal fees may vary depending upon the selling price of the real estate. In general, savings and loan associations, *entidades de ahorroy préstamo*, include legal fees in their commissions.

The buyer also has to pay the registry fee to record the title. To register the property, the buyer has to pay a fee based on the selling price of the real estate. In addition, the buyer has to pay for witnesses, stamps, photocopies, dispatch, and to "expedite" the process. (These payments have to be made in cash; the buyer receives no proof of payment.) On the other hand, the seller pays a brokerage commission that is normally within the range of 3% to 5% of the price for land and improvements. To protect against losses, lenders may require personal, hazard and earthquake insurance. Insurance companies usually require the owner to pay one year in advance. Property owners typically desire additional insurance coverage for personal liability and other risks, such as earthquakes and vandalism. Tenants can insure contents. There are multiple-listing service (MLS) companies that are widely available through the Internet. One of the most well known real estate trade magazines is Inmobilia (*http://www.inmobilia.com*).

Real estate trade associations include the Venezuelan Real Estate Chamber, *Cámara Inmobiliaria de Venezuela (http://www.camarainmobiliaria.org.ve)*, and Venezuelan Construction Chamber, Cámara *Venezolana de la Construcción (http://www.cvc.com.ve)*.

A recommended source to find detailed information about real estate organizations in Venezuela is http://www.inmuebles.com. This Web site also includes a section called *Biblioteca* (library),which contains online current copies of Venezuela's Leasing Law and Apartment Law. There are no license requirements to practice real estate in Venezuela, but there is political pressure to write and implement such a law and to improve the level of professionalism within the industry. Appraisers are licensed by *Sociedad de Ingenieria de Tasación de Venezuela* (SOITAVE) (http://www.soitave.com), Venezuelan Society of Engineers and Appraisers, and are typically used in connection with a mortgage. This organization regulates the amount of the commission paid to its members based on the value of the appraisal (http://www.soitave.org/seccion.php?mira=149&b=1&tot=99). This Web site also includes a section called *Leyes* (Laws), which contains too on-line current copies of Venezuela's Leasing Law and Apartment Law. The land description system utilized in Venezuela resembles that of the United States as to the metes-and-bounds description. (There is no formal land survey system used in Venezuela.) Similar to the United States, Venezuela will recognize the transfer of title by delivery of a deed, conveyances by representatives after death, and the use of adverse possession in some settings. Most deeds are hand written, as opposed to type written transfers. Generally speaking, mortgages will have no effect unless they are properly recorded for notice relative to the property. There are numerous types of mortgages in Venezuela, such as what is labeled as legal, judicial and conventional mortgages. Contracts for the sale of real property or for an interest in real property must be in writing. In addition to the requirement that contracts be in writing, there are five essential elements for the contract to be valid.

1. The contract must include key elements: First and last name, profession, and address of both parties (buyer and seller); a complete description and address of the real property; selling amount; date and payment plan and description.
2. All parties to the contract must be legally competent.
3. There must be mutual agreement or "a meeting of the minds," which is a mutual willingness to enter into a contract.
4. The contract must be for a lawful purpose, i.e., not contrary to law.
5. The contract must be supported by consideration, i.e., something of value must be given, e.g., money, a promise, property or services.

When a contract is breached, the wronged party may choose to accept partial performance, rescind the contract, or sue for specific performance, damages or both. It is common for real estate contracts to contain a provision for liquidated damages in case of default by a purchaser and specific performance in cases of default by a seller. Land ownership in Venezuela does not have any restriction on non- Venezuelans. They are allowed to own land on an equal basis to that of the nationals (Decree 2095). They, in general, are allowed to repatriate their capital. Profits are not taxed. They are not required to have the approval of Venezuela's government officials to invest in real estate. Also, they have total access to local financing. Local private financing mortgage annual percentage rates, for the acquisition of primary residences, to Venezuelan citizens and permanent residents, vary from 4.66% to 10.66%, for 30-year term loans. The loan-to-value of these loans is usually 75% of the sale price or appraised value, with a cap on the amount subject of financing. The mortgage annual percentage rates are established based on the monthly family income and how this compares with the minimum wage. Families with monthly income greater than 3 minimum wages and less than 15 minimum wages may apply to these mortgages. Otherwise, mortgage annual percentage rates are as high as 24%, as these are not regulated by the Venezuelan government (as of March 2015).

A number of strong Web site links help to acquire information in Venezuela, especially the National Association of REALTORS® web site and the Miami Association of REALTORS. See also the Global Real Estate Web site at the UNIVERSITY OF DENVER, *Daniels College of Business*, Burns School of Real Estate and Construction Management (Burns School) at http://burns.daniels.du.edu.

■ 10. Real Estate Trends

Recently there has been a strong push on building malls and retail buildings. Over ten large malls were constructed in the last few years in Venezuela, as well as a series of retail outlets. Questions exist over whether this expansive construction of malls can be reasonably supported. For real estate trends, see the Web sites at Jones Lang LaSalle, C.B. Richard Ellis, CORFAC International, Colliers International, DTZ International Property Advisors, Knight Frank, and the National Association of REALTORS® Web site (http://www.realtor.com). See the Global Real Estate Web site at the UNIVERSITY OF DENVER, *Daniels College of Business*, Burns School of Real Estate and Construction Management (Burns School) at http://burns.daniels.du.edu.

■ 11. Cultural Issues

Any nation's culture is complex and vibrant in its diversity.

While broad cultural characterizations such as those presented here can be generally accurate, following such generalities too strictly may be dangerously misleading. To conduct business effectively and profitably in a country, it is vital to have a thorough understanding of its culture's complexities. Venezuelans are very fashionable and current on European styles. Greetings are often with full embrace, patting one on the back; and, with women, often there is a kiss on the cheek. Handshakes are commonly used. Much activity for visiting, gestures, and social eating are similar to those customs used in the United States.

12. Discussion Questions

1. How could the economy of Venezuela become impacted by the border disputes with Colombia?

2. What issues, relative to the environment, face Venezuela?

3. How can Venezuela improve the level of professionalism in the real estate industry?

4. What is the US$ sale value of a property being offered in Venezuela? What exchange rate would apply?

13. Case Study

Wines of the World (WOW) Caracas, Venezuela

Memo

TO: Board of Directors
From: Consultants
Re: Exiting strategy for Blight Eaten Vineyards in Venezuela

I. Problem

Wines of the World (WOW) purchased a vineyard in Venezuela last year. This was the first purchase of what would have been many vineyards all over the world. The vineyard in Venezuela had been owned by the same family for over 100 years. The father died the prior year before WOW acquired it. The children did not want to run the vineyard. The last three years, prior to WOW taking over the vineyard, had been produced three good crops of grapes, according to the sellers and the accounting records. (A real estate agent was used in the purchase of the business.) This last season no crop was harvested. The grapes were eaten by "Blights," insects that can destroy a vineyard in no time at all. The goal of the company was to find existing functioning wineries' in other parts of the world, including, but not limited to, Brazil, Italy, France and the U.S. Venezuela was the first country on the list for expansion, because WOW found that the winery was available and because of the favorable price.

II. Initial Exit Strategy

The initial exit strategy was to place the vineyard up for sale after 10 years to 20 years of production. WOW wanted this to be a winery to make a mark on the wine world. Once the winery had been well established, internationally, it would be placed up for auction, by an international auction house. This would provide prestige when selling. This would give WOW the opportunity to require a minimum bid, to hope that the name and the prestige would bring a higher price.

III. Contingency Exit Strategy

Due to the loss of an entire crop from the Vineyard, WOW must look at exiting the wine business altogether. WOW needs to liquidate all of the assets and then put the winery up for sale, using a qualified broker who has access marketing and who would be able to sell the business as soon as possible. If WOW is unable to sell the land, WOW could possibly develop the land, if it could get the property re-zoned. This option would take more money and effort, but might be a possibility if WOW has no choice.

IV. Conclusion

Because of the destruction of the grapes, WOW has lost an entire year of profits. If WOW can possibly hold on through the year, existing on the sales from the last year and reserve capital, the Consultants suggest that WOW try to hold onto the business. The vineyard is in a perfect location, not only to attract tourists, but also to produce quality wine. The Consultants also suggest that WOW bring in an expert, who can suggest a plan of action to possibly save any grapes that are left and to provide planning for the next year's crops. Once this proposal has been evaluated, the Consultants suggest that WOW work on a new marketing campaign, target markets, work to improve the winery and its processes, while it waits for next year's crop.

   Refer to: International Real Estate Digest . Homepage. http://www.ired.com. X-rates.com. Homepage. http://www.x-rates.com/.

   U.S. Embassy. Homepage. http://usembassy.state.gov. U.S. Department of State. Homepage. http://www.state.gov.

14. Selected References

Central Bank of Venezuela (2000). *Macroeconomic Indicators*. Central Bank of Venezuela (Online).Available: http://www.bcv.org.ve.

CIA World Factbook. https://www.cia.gov/library/publications/the-world-factbook/index.html.

Commerce and Industry Ministry (1997).Legal *Aspects Related to Investments*. Commerce and Industry Ministry (Online).Available: http://www.mic.gov.ve. Congress of the Republic of Venezuela/SAIL (2000). *History*. Congress of the Republic of Venezuela (Online).Available:http://www.internet.ve/sail/ev/historia.html.

CONINDUSTRIA (2000).Annual *Inflation in Caracas Metropolitan Area 1988-2000*.

CONINDUSTRIA (Online). Available: http://www.conindustria.org.

Hodgson, Cullinan and Campbell (1999)."Land *Ownership and Foreigners – A Comparative Analysis of Regulatory Approaches"*. Food and Agriculture Organization of the United Nations (Online).Available:http://www.fao.org.

Official Tourist Agency: CORPOTURISMO (Unknown). *Venezuela: A Jewel for the World*. Caracas: CORPOTURISMO.

Venezuelan Real Estate Chamber (2000).Guide *to Sell and Purchase Real Estate in Venezuela*. Inmuebles.com (Online). Available: http://www.inmuebles.com. Venezuelan Presidential Ministry (2000). *Venezuela en Internet*. Venezuelan Presidential Ministry (Online). Available: http://www.venezuela.gov.ve. Time Almanac. *TIME Almanac*. Boston: Information Please LLC.

Burns School Global Real Estate Web site for the UNIVERSITY OF DENVER at http://burns.daniels.du.edu.

International Real Estate Digest. Homepage. www.ired.com. Organization of American States at http://www.oas.org. U.S. Bureau of Census at http://www.census.gov. U.S. Department of Commerce at http://www.stat-usa.gov. U.S. Bureau of Economic Analysis at http://www.bea.gov. U.S. Department of State. Homepage. http://www.state.gov. U.S. Embassy. Homepage. http://usembassy.state.gov. World Trade Centers Institute at http://www.wtci.org. World Trade Organization at http://www.wto.org. X-rates.com. Homepage http://www.x-rates.com/.

Instituto Nacional de Meteorología e Hidrología, Estadísticas Básicas de Precipitación, Temperatura y Humedad, http://www.inameh.gob.ve/pestadistico.php

United Nations Data, Country Profile: Venezuela, https://data.un.org/CountryProfile.aspx?crName=Venezuela (Bolivarian Republic of) Gobierno Bolivariano de Venezuela, Sistema Nacional de Control Fiscal, Contraloría General de la Fuerza Armada Nacional Boivariana, Nace la Gran Colombia, http://www.congefan.mil.ve/index.php/component/content/article/83-principal/242-nace-la-gran-colombia?showall=1&limitstart=

Gobierno Bolivariano de Venezuela, Ministerio del Poder Popular para la Defensa, Guardia Nacional Bolivariana, Noticias, 29 Enero: Separación de Venezuela de la Gran Colombia, http://www.guardia.mil.ve/index.php/noticias/operativos/47-tal-d%C3%ADa-como-hoy/414-separaci%C3%B3n-de-venezuela-de-la-gran-colombia.html

República Bolivariana de Venezuela, Asamblea Nacional, Secretaría, Dirección de Archivos y Biblioteca, El Poder Legislativo en la Historia, http://monitorlegislativo.net/wp-content/uploads/2014/11/historiaAN.pdf

History, Hoy en la Historia, Venezuela se Independiza de la Gran Colombia: 22-09-1830, http://mx.tuhistory.com/hoy-en-la-historia/venezuela-se-independiza-de-la-gran-colombia

World Statesmen.org, Nations and Territories: Venezuela, http://www.worldstatesmen.org/Venezuela.html

Wikipedia,Presidente de Venezuela,http://es.wikipedia.org/wiki/Presidente_de_Venezuela#Presidentes_de_Venezuela

Ministerio del Poder Popular de Planificación, Instituto Nacional de Estadística, Demográficos - Proyecciones de Población: Venezuela. Proyección de la población, según entidad y sexo, 2000-2050 (año calendario), http://www.ine.gov.ve/index.php?option=com_content&view=category&id=98&Itemid=51

Estimaciones y Proyecciones de la Población en la República de Panamá, por Provincia. Comarca Indígena, Distrito y Corregimiento, Según Sexo: Años 2000-2015, Boletín No. 10, https://www.contraloria.gob.pa/inec/Archivos/P2391Boletin10.pdf

Boletín No. 10, https://www.contraloria.gob.pa/inec/Archivos/P2391Boletin10.pdf Instituto Nacional de Estadísticas, Chile, Demográficas y Vitales,

Demografía, Población, País y Regiones. Actualización Población 2002-2012 y Proyecciones 2013-2020, http://www.ine.cl/canales/chile_estadistico/demografia_y_vitales/demografia/pdf/poblacion_sociedad_enero09.pdf

Instituto Brasileiro de Geografia e Estatística (IBGE), Diretoria de Pesquisas. Coordenação de População e Indicadores Sociais. Gerência de Estudos e Análises da Dinâmica Demográfica, http://www.ibge.gov.br/home/estatistica/populacao/projecao_da_populacao/2013/default_tab.shtm

Ministerio del Poder Popular de Planificación, Instituto Nacional de Estadística, Demográficos - Proyecciones de Población: Esperanza de Vida al Nacer por Sexo, según año, 2000-2050 (año calendario): http://www.ine.gov.ve/index.php?option=com_content&view=category&id=98&Itemid=51

World Bank, World Integrated Trade Solution, Trade Stats by Country, Venezuela GDP per Capita (Current US$) 2009-2013, http://wits.worldbank.org/CountryProfile/Country/VEN/StartYear/2009/EndYear/2013/Indicator/NY-GDP-PCAP-CD

The World Bank, Research, Global Economic Prospects, Country and Region Specific Forecasts and Data, http://www.worldbank.org/en/publication/global-economic-prospects/data?region=LAC

The World Bank, Data, Inflation, Consumer Prices (Annual %), http://data.worldbank.org/indicator/FP.CPI.TOTL.ZG?display=default

United Nations Data, Country Profile: Venezuela (Bolivarian Republic of), https://data.un.org/CountryProfile.aspx?crName=Venezuela (Bolivarian Republic of) The World Bank, Data, Unemployment, Total (% of Total Labor Force), http://data.worldbank.org/indicator/SL.UEM.TOTL.ZS/countries

World Bank, World Integrated Trade Solution, Trade Stats by Country, Venezuela Trade Summary 2011 Data, http://wits.worldbank.org/CountryProfile/Country/VEN/Year/2011/Summary

Banco Mercantil, Persónas, Créditos, Créditos Hipotecários, Crédito Ley Especial de Protección al Deudor Hipotecario de Vivienda, http://www.bancomercantil.com

Banesco, Personas, Créditos, Créditos para la Vivienda, Crédito Hipotecario para Adquisición de Vivienda Principal, http://www.banesco.com

Banco de Venezuela, Personas, Financiamiento, Credi-hipotecario, http://www.bancodevenezuela.com/

15. Glossary

Cámara Inmobiliaria de Venezuela – Venezuelan Real Estate Chamber.

Contralor General de la República – Venezuela's Comptroller General.

Defensor del Pueblo – Venezuela's ombudsman, from the Citizen Branch.

Fiscal General de la República – Venezuela's Attorney General.

Oficina del Registro – Office of the Registrar; property ownership information can be obtained from this office.

SOITA VE – Society of Engineers and Appraisers; appraisers are licensed by this group.

About the Author

José F. Ramirez was born in Caracas, Venezuela, where he earned a degree in civil engineering at the Universidad Central de Venezuela. He later earned a, in the United Stated, a diploma in business administration from the University of California – Berkeley; a master's in real estate and construction management from the Burns School of Real Estate and Construction Management, *Daniels College of Business,* UNIVERSITY OF DENVER; and, in Australia, a Master of Construction Law from the University of Melbourne. At the beginning of his career, he actively appraised residential real estate in Venezuela. A few years later, he actively participated in the design and development of commercial real estate in that country. More recently he has provided consulting construction and real estate services for commercial real estate in Colombia, United States and Venezuela. He currently works as a consultant for the construction and real estate development industries in the United States.

APPENDICES

Appendix A

Country Comparison Chart

Country	Total Area in Sq Km	Population	Birth Rate	Death Rate	National Product Per Capita	National Product Real Growth Rate
Afghanistan	652,230	30419,928	39 30	14 59	$1 000 00	7 10%
Argentina	2.780.400	42.192.494	1734	736	$17.400 00	800%
Australia	7.741.220	22 015.576	12 28	694	$40 800 00	1 80%
Austria	83.871	8219.743	8 69	1023	$41 700 00	3 30%
Brazil	8.514877	205,716.890	17 48	638	$11 600 00	2 70%
Canada	9.984.670	34 300.083	10 28	809	$40 300 00	2 20%
Chile	756,102	17067 369	14 28	579	$16 100 00	650%
China	9.595.961	1.343 239.923	1231	7 17	$8 400 00	9 20%
Costa Rica	51,100	4 636,348	16 40	438	$11.500 00	400%
Czech Repub	78.867	10,177.300	862	1094	$25 900 00	1 80%
Denmark	43.094	5 543.453	1022	1019	$40 200 00	1 00%
Finland	338,145	5 262 930	1036	1033	$38 300 00	2 70%
France	643,801	65630.692	12 72	885	$35 000 00	1 70%
Germany	357,022	81 305.856	833	11 04	$37 900 00	2 70%
Hingary	93,028	9958.453	9 49	1270	$19 600 00	1 40%
India	3,287,263	1.205073.612	20 60	7 43	$3 700 00	780%
Ireland	70.273	4 722.028	15.81	638	$39 500 00	100%
Israel	20.770	7 590.758	18 97	550	$31 000 00	480%
Italy	301,340	61 261,254	906	993	$30 100 00	0 40%
Japan	377.915	127.368 088	8 39	915	$34 300 00	-0 50%
Jordan	89.342	6508.887	26 52	274	$5 900 00	2 50%
Kenya	580,367	43013.341	31 93	7 26	$1.700 00	430%
South Korea	99.720	48 860.500	8 42	638	$31.700 00	360%
Mexico	1,964.375	114.975,406	18 87	490	$15.100 00	380%
Netherlands	41.543	16730.632	10 89	8 39	$42 300 00	160%
Panama	75.420	3510 045	1917	4 69	$13 600 00	1060%
Russia	17,098.242	138.082.178	1094	16 03	$16 700 00	4 30%
Saudi Arabia	2.149,690	26534,504	1919	3 32	$24 000 00	650%
Singapore	697	5353494	7 72	341	$59 900 00	490%
South Africa	1,219.090	48 810.427	19 32	1723	$11.000 00	340%
Spam	505.370	47 042 984	10 40	888	$30 600 00	080%
Sweden	450.295	9.103 788	10 24	1021	$40 600 00	4 40%
United Kmgd	243,610	63 047,162	12 27	9 33	$35.900 00	1.10%
US (of Amer)	9.826.675	313.847 465	1368	8 39	$46100 00	1 50%
Venezuela	912.050	28 047.938	19 88	52	$12 400 00	4 20%

Appendix B

Case Studies

Case Study 1

Expanding into Europe: Does it Make Sense?

Examining Finland, Germany, Sweden, Denmark, and Russia

By Walter S. Clements, Leslie A. Kramer, Suzanne Miller, Gary M. Ralston, and Ira D. Warshauer *An analysis is being performed by a Board of Directors or other decision makers to evaluate the possibility of a U.S. firm expanding its U.S. construction operation to a country (or countries) outside the United States. Also involved in the examination is the possibility of considering investing in real estate outside the United States, with or without connections to real estate construction. This analysis covers the countries of **Denmark, Finland, Germany, Russia,** and **Sweden** and was conducted in 2001.*

The analysis follows a format designed to help weigh many facets when making decisions on whether to operate outside the United States. An attempt to compare financial issues, such as the rate of return on investment, is only one of many considerations that must be weighed when venturing outside of the United States. Many factors, such as the country's economic, political, cultural, and stability conditions, are absolute necessities when evaluating potential expansion into international markets, as reviewed and analyzed in this Case Study #1.

Preface

With the end of the Cold War and the crumbling of the Berlin Wall, the prevailing international system, globalization, has provided new opportunity for expansion into markets outside the United States. The modern phenomenon of the shrinking world, caused by advances in communications and media, transportation, and technology, has influenced virtually everyone's domestic politics, commerce, environment, and international relations. With the end of communism, the concept of free markets has spread throughout the world and has challenged the historical roots of many societies. The old adage "If you can't beat them, join them!" is now a prevailing attitude throughout the world. As a result, many countries are now struggling to balance their identity, home and community with the need to modernize, streamline, and privatize their economies in order to thrive in the globalized system. The forces of culture, geography, and tradition are at odds with the forces of our new electronic global economy, as globalization has replaced the Cold War system by integrating capital, technology, and information.

Note to reader: The numbers in this Case Study #1 may differ from the text information as this Case Study was undertaken in 2001.

Introduction

Realty & Construction, LLC (REACON) is a medium-size company that is doing extremely well in the United States in both construction and real estate investment. The principals of the company have determined that with the new global economy, geographic diversification made sense, and consequently it chose a region of Europe for expansion opportunity. Scandinavian countries (Denmark, Finland, and Sweden), Germany, and Russia were all considered. The principals of REACON had been assigned the task of determining which specific country presented the best opportunity for investment. On projects in the United States, the company's hurdle rate (opportunity cost) is 20% before tax and 12% after tax. To adjust for risk on an international project, it was determined that the company would require a 25% return before tax and a 15% return after tax. But calculating a return on investment was the easy part. REACON's challenge was to establish the actual criteria for determining the highest and best opportunity abroad.

REACON's principal established that the following four areas and their application to real estate investment, relative to the United States, were of paramount importance:

1. Communications
2. Cross-culture issues
3. Creativity
4. Ethics and values:

    Additionally, the company established that the following specific factors needed to be examined and understood when looking at an international arena:

    a. Explore broad-scope coverage of the country and its political and economic systems.
    b. Discover broad-scope basic real estate concepts within the country. (For example, is there fee simple ownership? Who controls the ownership of real estate and is it private or public?)
    c. Determine what regulatory bodies exist in the real estate area and how difficult is it to work within those regulatory bodies for necessary approvals, such as zoning, permits for building, etc.
    d. Consider basic real estate legal issues, such as interest in land, legal description, use of contracts, deeds, evidence of tit le, etc.
    e. Examine the present appraisal and valuation problems.
    f. Consider special interest areas in real estate. These may include, for example, water interests, mineral interests, and sale of air rights.

g. Examine special leasing issues, terms of the lease, who negotiates the lease, whether brokers are involved, and so forth.

h. Because agency rules are normally a major area of concern in any country, consider the agency rules.

i. Because the acquisition or disposition of property is dependent on contracts, examine contractual issues relating to real estate.

j. Financing issues are always of concern, whether it involves the purchase of a small residence or a major piece of real estate. Examine how much financing exists and what are its costs. Also, examine economic considerations that are present, such as inflation, among other issues.

k. Determine what encumbrances exist and how encumbrances are supported through a mortgage, deed of trust, note, and so forth.

l. Find out if formal property management companies, asset management companies, and similar entities exist.

m. Ascertain whether a brokerage system exists and how sophisticated that system is, including multiple-listing services, databases, etc.

n. Examine specialized brokerage areas and development of specialized knowledge, designations, and similar considerations. Are there MAIs, CPMs, CCIMs, CIPS, and other specialized individuals within the market?

o. Find out if special tax rules about property tax, income tax, value added tax, and similar taxes are in force.

p. Consider any related areas of the law the impact real estate. For example, are there mobile homes, mineral interests, water laws, and special certifications and approvals?

q. Consider other national, regional, and local laws, including treaties or other agreements for international activities between or among countries and citizens in those countries. In an effort to organize the aforementioned specific factors, the company used a number of factors, for example:
1. **Geography**
2. **History and Overview**
3. **People**
4. **Government**
5. **Economy**
6. **Currency**
7. **Transportation**
8. **Communications**
9. **Real Property Issues**
10. **Real Property Trends**
11. **Cultural Issues**

Denmark: Market Situation

A permanent link between Denmark and Sweden shall be established with the completion of the Ø resund project. This project has been described as the biggest economic and social development in Scandinavia in the early 21st century. It will integrate Copenhagen metropolitan area and southern Sweden. Copenhagen is Denmark's capital city as well as its largest urban area. The section of southern Sweden integrating with greater Copenhagen includes the industrial city of Malmo, the university city Lund, and the port and industrial city of Helsingborg. They will be joined through the construction of a bridge and tunnel system. The 5- mile (7.8 km) bridge and the 10-mile (16 km) tunnel is expected to create a new metropolitan area with some 3.2 million people, which is almost double the size of the second largest metropolitan area in the region, Stockholm. The integration of this region will be further supported by infrastructure spending on the Copenhagen highway system, the Copenhagen airport, and the public railway transport that will link downtown Copenhagen and Malmo, as well as locations throughout the region, and will cost more than U.S. $10 billion. Once completed, the new city of Orestad will have created 50,000 jobs in its total area of 765 square miles. Currently, Denmark has a home ownership rate of 52%. Denmark allows the interest on any loan, including mortgages, to be deducted from income taxes. The Danish government is trying to limit this, but any change is likely to be insignificant. There is no capital gain's tax on the sale of one's home. This is very significant in a country with a 60% marginal income tax rate. The remaining 48% of Danes who live in rented accommodations benefit from rent control, which makes rented housing comparatively inexpensive.

Economy

The unemployment rate in greater Copenhagen was 6.4% in 1998. Average income has increased 33% since 1990. The rate of inflation was 1.3% in 1998. The Gross Domestic Product (GDP) growth rate has ranged from 3.1% to 3.6% from 1994 to 1997. Business investments increased 8.8% in 1997.

Snapshot of Denmark

Population (1999): 5,314,000
Language Spoken: Danish
Land Area: 16,640 square miles (43,095 sq km)
Largest City: Copenhagen
Cities with Population over 100,000: Copenhagen, Odense, Alborg, and Arhus
Monetary Unit: Danish *krone* (DK)
Average Annual Inflation Rate (1990-1999): 1.3%
GDP (Gross Domestic Product) per Capita (1997): U.S. $30,565 (DK $212,124)

Real Estate Practices

The national government of Denmark requires real estate practitioners to obtain a license before conducting real estate transactions. To obtain a license, an examination must be passed. In addition, a college education is required, as are four years of evening business courses and two years of experience in the industry. Once the license has been obtained, no continuing education is required to keep it. Commissions are not regulated by the government and are paid by the seller. Typically, commission is 2% to 4% of the sale price. The buyer is responsible for paying a transfer tax that amounts to 1.2% of the sale price (excludes residential transactions). Real estate practitioners represent either the buyer or the seller but not both. Multiple-listing systems (MLS) exist in Denmark. The National Association of Real Estate Practitioners in Denmark operates an Internet- based MLS. Denmark has a very high rate of loan-to-purchase financing. Typically, 60% to 85% of a home purchase is financed. The financing of both private and commercial real estate purchases in Denmark generally comes from the Danish mortgage bond credit system. These mortgage bonds are judged to have roughly the same level of security as Danish government bonds. Real estate mortgages are recorded in the public registers of the local authority in which the purchase was made. All sectors of the Danish economy operate under a high tax burden, and property ownership is no exception. Besides the high initial transfer tax of 25%, the imputed rent of owner-occupied homes is included in the base for the income tax paid to the central government, counties, and municipalities. The imputed rent is calculated as a percentage of the property's assessed value. Other annual taxes on property include a Land Tax, on unimproved land and on improvements to land, and a Service Tax, on commercial and government buildings. These latter two taxes are for the benefit of local governments and are not the significant taxes in terms of generating revenue.

Land Rights and Usage

The government in Denmark has the right to levy property taxes, the right of *escheat*, and the right to control the use of private property through the exercise of police power and zoning. A real estate transaction is closed by a notary. The notary is responsible for preparing the title deed, *skoeder*, recording the deed, and arranging the final settlement between the parties. In order to be valid, deeds and mortgages are registered. Denmark bases its title records system on the German Title Registry system. The Danish title registry maintains and consistently updates an inventory of properties in the country. In this inventory, all properties can be identified by what is known as their *cadastral* parcel numbers. Private surveyors provide the subdivision plans and measurements from their work to the registry, which then updates maps and assigns plots a cadastral parcel number. The cadastral number is needed when completing the mandatory reporting of the transfer of property at the registry. Further information on the property transfer, such as the sale price and mortgage details, must be reported to the valuation authority. A high degree of information on any property is publicly available and reliable.

In Denmark, real estate practitioners must obtain a wide variety of information from the local government before closing on a sale. They must find out details on the property such as from unpaid bills, outstanding taxes, status of utility connections, and any environmental issues. Normally, up to six to eight separate departments of the local government must be consulted to a mass all of the required information. Dragsholm Kommune, a municipality of about 213,500 people, has developed a system that now transfers the inquiries into electronic forms. This allows the different departments to work on an overall request at the same time. This system has cut the time in half that it normally takes for Danish real estate practitioners to get the information they need to legally conclude a sale. The next step is to allow the real estate practitioners to submit both their requests and payments electronically. This model is being followed in other local authorities and has the potential to greatly ease a significant bureaucratic time burden on Denmark's real estate sector.

Non-Dane Ownership

Non-European Union citizens and companies that have been located in Denmark for less than five years, can purchase real estate only after applying to and receiving permission from the Danish Department of Justice, the *Justits ministeriet*. It commonly takes four weeks to obtain approval for a purchase. Restrictions are also placed on non-Danish European Union citizens who want to purchase vacation homes. This derives from a general unease throughout Scandinavia about the purchase of second homes by mainly German citizens. It is uncertain how long these restrictions against European Union citizens will remain legally enforceable under European Union law.

Real Estate Trends

Copenhagen has an inventory of office space totaling just over 10 million sq m. Vacancy levels are approximately 2%. Despite the strong market and high demand for office space, Copenhagen rents are still fairly inexpensive relative to other European capital cities as rates average between U.S. $22 to U.S. $24 per square foot per year. Industrial inventory is just over 16.6 million sqm as of 1997, and vacancy for the Copenhagen area is approximately 5% as of 1999. Average rents are 400 to 500 DKK per square meter per year. Public investment in the residential market has been on the increase in recent years. In 1997, 91.5 billion sq ft, in 17,500 new housing units, were constructed. The retail market is expanding in Denmark as many international retail chains are trying to establish a shop on the main shopping street in a city, *Stroget*. Typically, there is little vacancy on *Stroget* in the large cities in Denmark. As a result, rents have increased to their highest level ever. In general, hotel occupancy rates have increased since 1996. In 1998, hotels in greater Copenhagen were at an 80% occupancy rate.

Real Estate Issues

More than 80% of real property transactions in Denmark involve real estate professionals. Denmark's real estate trade association is called The Danish Association of Chartered Estate Agents, Dansk *Ejendonsmaeglerforehing*. The *Dansk Ejendonsmaeglerforehing* was founded in 1912 and has approximately 1,800 individual members. Real estate license requirements are regulated by the Ministry of Trade and Commerce. Danes obtain loans from commercial banks and mortgage banks. Interest rates are typically adjustable and loan-to-value ratios range between 60% and 80%.Appraisals and property insurance are typically required by lenders to secure a loan. Speculative building is uncommon, except where the building is significantly preleased. Corporations are exempt from paying *ad valorem* property taxes. A stamp duty is paid on deeds, mortgages, and real property leases. The stamp duty fee ranges from 0.3% to 4% of the property value. All signatories to the transaction are responsible for the payment of the stamp duty. Central business districts throughout Denmark are subject to stringent land use controls.

Conclusions

According to a survey, conducted by Transparency International, Scandinavian Countries – Denmark, Finland, and Sweden – are perceived as the least corrupt countries as seen by businessmen, while some African, Southeast Asian, and Lat in American countries are perceived as extremely corrupt.

The economy in Denmark has grown significantly since 1990. The rate of inflation was 1.3% in 1998.

And business investments have been steadily increasing with the completion of the Ø resund project, the potential for real estate investment and construction.

■ Finland

Market Situation

Finland is a country located in northwestern Europe, consisting of approximately 305,470 sq km (130,500 square miles) or about the size of Montana. It is the fifth largest country in Europe with a population of just over 5,000,000. Its population is highly educated, with a literacy rate of 100% for people over 15 years old. It is also a fairly mature society with more than 60% between the ages of 15 and 67 years old. Finland is keenly situated as a prime transportation hub. It is close to Stockholm, St. Petersburg, Moscow, Tallinn, Riga, Copenhagen, and Hamburg. It has 78,000 km of excellent roads. Two international highways crisscross the country. It also has 6,000 km of rail lines that are the same gauge as Russian rail lines, and 21 airports. Finland also has a highly sophisticated satellite tracking system to permit real time tracking of shipments. The International Monetary Fund (IMF) ranks the Finnish infrastructure as number two in the world. Finland is a republic with a President who is elected to a six-year term and a Prime Minister who is the head of the Cabinet, called the Council of State, the *Valtioneuvosto*, that is made up of 200 members. The stability of the government and the currency reduces the risk associated with investing in Finland. While Finnish and Swedish are the national languages, the most common second language is English. Therefore, U.S. investors would have little difficulty conducting business in Finland. Finland has pioneered many energy saving programs increasing the efficiency of domestic energy use by 30% to 40% in the past decade. They have also increased the use of nuclear powered energy plants to cut their dependence on foreign imports of fossil fuel. Other national resources consist of timber, copper, zinc, iron ore, and silver, but only 8% of the land is used for agriculture, and 76% is woodland.

Economy

Finland's economy was characterized by economic nationalism up until the late 1980s, and all restrictions on non-Finnish direct investment were lifted by 1993. In an era of global competition, Finland has been a leader in the deregulation of capital movement and technological development in the area of information and technology. While Finland does not give non-Finnish owned companies special incentives or tax relief, it does not penalize them either, treating these companies the same as nationally owned companies. The concentration of non-Finnish foreign-owned firms is in knowledge- intensive industries, rather than manufacturing industries. Finland, by the way, is the only country in Europe to have paid off its World War II debt. Finland is the wireless capital of the world. The Helsinki Wireless Virtula Village is part of a $1 billion development project. Helsinki will soon host the first wireless community in the world, where wireless devices will be used for everything from shopping to advanced broadband portal service. Finland was one of the first countries to open its telecommunications market to free competition. It was the first country to grant licenses to third generation mobile networks. With Nokia as Finland's largest company, more than 70% of the population uses cell phones, and they are adapting quickly to the trend of mobile networks toward broadband mobile networks toward broadband mobile phones with multimedia services. Engineering and electronics represent 46% of their exported goods. The 11-country formation of the European Union (EU) with its single currency will have the most dramatic positive effect on the growth of any one country joining the EU. And by the very nature of its positive effect on its members, it will have a similarly negative effect on the countries that are excluded. The most positive effect will come as the result of the stability of the single currency and the reduction of costs associated by businesses needing to convert wages, benefits, and sale and purchase transactions to various currencies and trying to hedge the market exchange rates. It will be much easier to finance transactions and to budget investments with fairly stable inflation and interest rates. The transition period will be through the end of 2001, with all Finland national currency being exchanged by the end of February 2002.

Snapshot of Finland

Population (2000 est.): 5,167,486
Language Spoken: Finnish, Swedish, English
Land Area: 130,500 square miles (305,470 sq km)
Largest City: Helsinki
Cities with Population over 100,000: Helsinki, Espoo, Vantaa, Tampere, Turku
Monetary Unit: *Markka* (FMk) or *Finmark, Euros*
Exchange Rate (as of January 2000): *Euros* per U.S.$1 = 0.9386:
Average Annual Inflation Rate (1990-1999): 1%

GDP (Gross Domestic Product) per Capita (1999 est.): $21,000; 3.5% growth rate

Real Estate Practices

Finland has a nationwide MLS, and *Suomen innteistonvalittajain Liitto* of Helsinki is the real estate trade organization in Finland. Licensed real estate agents handle approximately 60% of all property transactions. Many of the recent commercial developments have been centered in Espoo, which is only a 15-minute drive from Helsinki. The quality of life combined with the highly educated and motivated work force has been a magnet for high-tech companies. The largest new business development in the region is the construction of the telecommunications research center in Ruohalahti, a former wasteland that is being transformed into a high-tech wonderland. The Helsinki High-Tech Center consisting of four eight-story towers, a total of 387,700 sq ft (34,893 sq m) will be opening for business later in 2001.

Land Rights and Usage

It is customary to negotiate the sale of real estate through a written contract, but a person's word is also binding. The transfer of title is handled through a registry, and there are two types. The Land Register, the *Kiinteistörekisteri*, is used to record the location of the land. The Property Register, the *Fastighets register*, is used to record the ownership interest. Attorneys and licensed real estate agents are used in the majority of transactions.

Non-Finnish Ownership

In some cases ownership of land by either non-Finnish investors or companies may be restricted, but it is not prohibited. Land is transferred by written contracts, with evidence of title being recorded at the Land Registry for the description and the Property Registry for the owner's name. Property taxes are assessed based on the value of the property and range from 0.2% to 0.8%.

Real Estate Trends

Low interest rate mortgages and efforts to improve housing conditions for the working class were emphasized with the passage of the Housing Corporation Act and the Housing Mortgage Bank in 1920. As *Arava* legislation, providing for government-subsidized housing, was passed in the mid-1950s, there was a huge surge in construction for the next two decades. Approximately 75% of all housing in Finland was built during this time, approximately 48,000 units annually. Up until the 1980s, two-thirds of the housing being built was apartments, with the rest single family. After the 1980s the percentage was reversed. Nearly 75% of these structures were built with indoor plumbing, hot water, and central heat. However, the housing program's most serious failure was in its boring and sterile design with a dormitory feel, which lead to social problems.

Real Estate Issues

Over half of the real estate transactions are done with real estate agents, who have to be licensed and meet age and citizen requirements. The service cost of buying real estate is somewhat higher than in the United States. In addition to sales commissions that range from 4% to 8% of the purchase price, there is also a 1% notary fee and a 6% stamp duty fee.

Conclusions

A growing number of companies that wanted to invest in Russia are choosing Finland instead because of its easy access to Russia with lower risk. Finland has a very low crime rat e, stable economy, active outdoor lifestyle, and highly educated work force. Of the students receiving a college degree, 25% receive an engineering degree. This is the highest percentage in the world. With little besides timber and wood products to export, the true natural resource of Finland is its people. With rugged individualism similar to the rugged geographic features of their landscape, the Finns have successfully managed their lives while enjoying their rugged outdoors. During the winter solstice, Helsinki has less than six hours per day of sunlight with temperatures averaging 16°F. The summer temperatures average in the mid-60s (60°F).

Most Finns speak English as a second language. Finland would be an excellent place for investment for a small-sized to mid-sized company. The country has more than adequate transportation lines to move people and products throughout the country and to other surrounding countries. The people of Finland are its greatest asset. They are highly educated and are transforming their education system to include more computer and technology courses. The Finns will be an asset to any company, with their rugged individualism and ability to overcome hardship, all with a sense of humor. Their biggest advantage, however, is their inclusion in the European Union (EU), which will add additional stability to a country that already has a stable government, currency, and work force.

■ Germany

Market Situation

Germany is Western Europe's richest and most populous nation. The real estate market is defined by powerful historic influences. The commercial real estate market exhibits areas of focused and well-publicized "booms." These boom-and-bust fluctuations have been brought about by the reunification of Western and Eastern Germany and the centrality of the country in the new European Monetary Union or "Euro Zone" and by the economic recession that has plagued the country for most of the 1990s. The positive developments in the German commercial real estate market are concentrated in the three major urban engines of the national economy: Frankfurt, Munich, and Berlin. Each city owes its own distinctive growth to different factors pressing on the German economy.

Berlin has been the largest urban construction site in Europe for the past decade in preparation for its position as the capital of the newly unified Germany.

Frankfurt is Germany's financial center and also the headquarters of the European Central Bank, the institution that sets monetary policy for Euroland. Many believe that during this decade Frankfurt will overtake London as the headquarters of the European financial services sector and emerge as Europe's financial capital. Frankfurt has also become the location of choice for the European headquarters of many American and other international corporations.

Munich is the traditional economic powerhouse metropolis of Germany and is repositioning it self in the global economy through mergers. Munich's strong real estate market is attributable to its position as a major administrative center as well as an international center for the automobile and electronics industries. Currently, Germany has a home ownership rate well below North American standards – 40% in Western Germany and only 27% in Eastern Germany. There is a fairly uniform mortgage industry requirement of a 20% down payment, which serves somewhat as a barrier to entry for first-time homebuyers. Another explanation for the low home ownership rates is the stringent tenants' rights laws and government rental controls, which provide Germans in the rented sector a feeling of security in tenancy that is somewhat comparable to ownership in the United States. Germany's real estate market is not intrinsically difficult to operate in. Transfer taxes payable on acquisition of 3.5% are some of the lowest in Europe, and it is possible to structure deals to avoid local taxes on income and capital gains. Leverage is also attractive with 5-year money currently available at about 5%. Last year's huge reduction in the main rate of German corporate tax from 40% to 25% is one of the reasons Germany is merging as the top property investment market in Europe. Several international companies have identified Germany as a top property investment market in Europe, based on their examination of **cyclical factors:** current economic position, property cycle position, and currency risk; and **structural factors:** transparency, landlord's obligations, and exit liquidity. A new provision from the German government that took full effect in 2002 allows for sale of stakes in corporations to be tax exempt and encourages a focus on shareholder value which should result in the untangling of the web of cross-holdings of major groups, particularly banks. This provision, combined with the fact that German corporations are adopting international accounting standards should result in significant focus on asset-heavy corporate balance sheets. Because German corporations own about 70% of the real estate they occupy – compared with about 20% in the United States – there should be substantial corporate dispositions of property.

Economy

Germany is Europe's largest economy. Gross Domestic Product (GDP) growth averaged 1.5% from 1995 to 1999 but is forecast to average 2.8% for 2000 to 2004 (consistent with the European average). German properties are poised for significant rental growth for the first time in ten years.

Snapshot of Germany

Population (1999): 82,797,408
Language Spoken: German
Land Area: 151,750 square miles (393,040 sq km)
Largest City: Berlin
Cities with Population over 500,000: Berlin (3.34M), Hamburg (1.7M), Munich (1.3M), Cologne (962K), Frankfurt (652 K), Essen (603K), Dortmund (593K), Stuttgart (582K), Dusseldorf (568K), Bremen (543K), Duisburg (523K), Hannover (516K).
Monetary Unit: *Deutsch Mark* (DM)
Average Annual Inflation Rate (1992-1998): 2.6%
GDP (Gross Domestic Product) per Capita (1998): U.S.$25,080 (DM 45,800).

Real Estate Practices

Residential real estate practitioners in Germany face a marketplace with a low percentage of buyers in comparison to the country's wealth. Most transactions are direct sales without the use of a real estate practitioner. The mortgage market is well organized and structured – albeit somewhat inflexible. The industry standard requirement of a minimum 20% down payment serves somewhat as a barrier to home ownership. The mortgage banks issue mortgage-backed bonds, *pfandbriefes*, to fund first loans of up to 60% of house values. The mortgage banks and savings institutions offer a contract savings plan for prospective buyers which, when completed, guarantees them a second (usually 20%) mortgage. The purchase of a property is affected through the conclusion of a sales agreement – which includes an exact description of the property and the encumbrances relating thereto. In addition, an agreement on the transfer of legal title must be concluded, and this has to be entered in the land register, *Grundbunch*. Prior to the registration of transaction of title, the tax authorities must issue a clearance certificate confirming payment of real estate transfer tax. Both agreements and all additional agreements legally relating thereto must be notarized. The purchase of property in the new federal states requires the approval of the city of municipal administration.

Land Rights and Usage

There are four main types of property ownership in Germany:

1. Absolute Ownership, *Eigentum*, is equivalent to the common law concept of fee simple ownership. An absolute owner has the right to sell, lease, will, or give the property away.
2. Condominium Ownership, Wohnugseigentum, is ownership of a self-contained residential unit in a multiunit building. Part ownership, Teileigentum, is ownership of a self-contained unit in a nonresidential building.

3. Hereditary Building Right, *Erbbaurecht*, is a legal estate in land. It is somewhat equivalent to the common law concept of a free holding. The owner has the right to build and use the improvements on the site and sometimes controls the entire site. The land is not owned, and the hereditary building right usually lasts for 99 years or the life of the improvement.

4. Long-Term Leases, *Dauernutzungsrechte*, are leases of over 30 years and are recorded as land encumbrances. Short-term leases are not recorded and do not give rise to leasehold interests.

The four powers of the state over property are: (1) taxation; (2) eminent domain; (3) police power; and (4) *escheat*.

Non-German Ownership

Investors wishing to invest in German real estate have various options in terms of the best way to structure the acquisition. Basically, the choice is between a direct acquisition of assets and an indirect acquisition, i.e., through a purchase of shares in a company owning the targeted assets. Germany also provides a number of interesting instruments such as open- end real estate funds and closed-end funds in the form of partnerships for investors who wish to obtain a return on real estate through pure financial instruments.

Real Estate Trends

The German economy is very reliant on its manufacturing industries. In the year 2000 there were clear indications of a sustained economic revival with manufacturing growth driving business confidence to new highs. Overseas orders have surged, aided by the weak Euro. Domestic demand is improving as a result of a more favorable employment market and the introduction of tax reforms which will increase disposable income. The German economy grew by about 2.8% in 2000, and similar levels are expected for the foreseeable future. In Germany, the property market has lagged behind the rest of Europe for a number of years (returns have been about 5% for the past several years) but is now poised for enhanced performance. Investors should expect to achieve capital growth through growing rents.

Office: Reflecting improved economics; all five major German cities underwent an increase in demand for office space over the past two years. The Munich area was the most active, followed by Frankfurt, which experienced one of the highest absorption levels on record. Vacancy levels have decreased, as there has not been sufficient new development to compensate for demand. This has put an upward pressure on rents, particularly in Frankfurt.

Retail: Consumer spending remains fairly cautious, although there was noticeable improvement in 2000, making the end of seven disappointing years of somewhat flat retail rents. Continued strengthening of domestic demand should assist the retail market. Sunday trading continues to be an issue as well as the resolution of various matters at several major retailers. Profit margins are being squeezed due to competition of ever-expanding international retailers.

Industrial: In recent years, *Öffentliche Wirtschaftsförderungsgesellschaften*, public economic assistance agencies, have been active in the development of industrial parks. If an entrepreneur is interested in buying a plot of land, he normally inquires directly from the municipalities. It is not common to hire a broker or a real estate agency for searching. If a potential buyer wants to insure thathe or she is being asked a fair market price, the potential buyer can get information from the independent *Gutachterausschüsse*, local valuation committees. Usually the public space (streets, green spaces) remains in the ownership of a municipality. Because of the competition between municipalities, the offered prices are usually low, and most municipalities, therefore, take a loss.

Residential and Multifamily: Investment yields for prime properties in Germany are quite low. Most cities range between 5% and 5.5%. Investment yields on industrial properties are also low, usually in the 7% to 8.25% range. The German real estate market is best described by examining the five major cities: Berlin, Dusseldorf, Frankfurt, Hamburg, and Munich.

Real Estate Issues

Most residential real estate transactions are direct and are conducted without the use of professional real estate practitioners. Commercial leases are typically ten years in duration with adjustments in rental rates based on changes in Consumer Price Index (CPI) or market. Appraiser valuation is based on federal statutes that detail the information to be gathered, the factors to be considered, and the framework of the appraisal process.

Conclusions

Economic growth and tax reform will boost the German economy. The German real estate market is poised for growth, matching the nation's strong economic growth (current GDP growth rates are nearly twice the level of the past few year). The real estate markets are only now recovering from overbuilding in the early 1990s and are poised to show significant rental growth for the first time in ten years. German open-end funds – which have dominated the real estate market – are not receiving capital flows at the same levels as in recent years because tax reform has reduced their historic tax shelter benefits. Therefore, the domestic competition for assets will be weaker than in the past. The previous focus by the funds on tax benefits allowed them to accept lower yields on real estate investments. Because tax reform will return German real estate to economic yield levels, investors should expect the asset class to follow the total return characteristics of the U.S. market in the mid-1990s. Corporate rationalization will provide a number of large deals well suited to investors who can identify value. These opportunities include the return to the public market of large blocks of both corporate and multifamily properties. With changes in the German tax code, less available supply, and corporate dispositions of property, this is the time for real estate investors to follow the lead of institutional investors into German real estate.

▪ Russia

Reasons to Invest in Russia

Since Russian privatization of real estate began in the early 1990s, the real estate markets in the large cities in Russia started experiencing rapid escalation in value. The economy was overheating. The economic crises of 1998 put an immediate halt to that escalation of values, and prices plummeted. Beginning in 2000, with some stabilization and more experience in the housing and office markets, U.S. business is starting to venture into Russia with housing and manufacturing. The opportunity now exists to invest ahead of the curve. According to an April 2000 U.S. Department of Commerce report, some companies are exploring joint-venture opportunities to build panelized building system factories in target regions in Russia. If the negotiations go well, these factories will produce prefabricated housing components that would be shipped to a building site where a home would be constructed. Other firms are exploring real estate development opportunities to serve as design and project management specialists in partnership with local counterparts. The focal point for a decision to be made about investing in Russia with a real estate construction company depends largely on the ability to not only assess the situation of doing business today in Russia, but more importantly the ability to assess Russia's ability to mitigate the risks and make it safer as well as more profitable for capital to flow into the country in the form of investment. Today the real estate sector remains largely underdeveloped. Real estate agents, title companies, and law firms are still in their developing stage. In addition, the lack of a central land registry, which would guarantee title to a land/property purchaser, is another obstacle to the natural development of the real estate sector. Currently, there is no land code that sets up the framework for overall land reform and sale in Russia.

However, a mention of that land reform becoming priority in 2000 has been speculated about since Vladimir Putin became Acting President. Delta Credit, a U.S.-Russian investment fund's residential mortgage finance program, was introduced in mid-1999 with about $100 million in capital. The fund runs its programs with 11 selected Russian banks. Mortgage financing standards have sparked a surge in demand in Moscow and St. Petersburg where partner banks offer home loans.

The main issue of interest is the political scene as it relates to foreign investment. Russia is a country of symbols. One of them is St. Petersburg itself. It has historically symbolized the openness of Russia to Western ideas and technologies. Putin needs Western capital. His population, on the other hand, needs to know the direction the country is moving. If Putin chooses to move his state Westward, the most elegant way of showing this to the entire population and to the entire world would be by increasing the importance of St. Petersburg in the Russian political life. So the eventual increase of the political influence of the second biggest city could easily move prices of properties upward from their current levels of $400 to $450 per sqm. Moscow is the most important city because it is the largest in Russia. However, in the early 1990s before the great economic crisis of the Asian currency deflation in 1998, the largest corporations in Russia were relocating to Moscow to be close to the political power. Since December of 1999 real estate prices in Moscow have gone down by 5% and in July were about $680 per sq m. The experts do not foresee any revolution in the real estate market in Moscow in the following months.

Russia could be the real "country of unlimited possibilities" depending completely on Putin's ability to accomplish some very difficult things that put them in a near "catch 22" position. They need to attract Western capital to become stronger militarily to position themselves against those countries from whom they need capital. They also need to attract more foreign investment while at the same time reduce the amount they have to pay on current overseas obligations. And finally, corrupt business practices have to be regulated to provide an arena of "fair play." From the above-mentioned moves by the manufactured housing industry, it appears the profit potential is making it worth the risks for some. Russia could be the land of opportunity if our investments are down with the proper joint-venture partners and coupled with one of the lenders who take equity positions. The potential for growth in such a raw capitalistic environment is now, not when the problems are solved.

▪ Sweden

Sweden is located in northern Europe, between Finland and Norway, and is in close proximity to Germany and many other countries. It is approximately 450,000 sq km in area (174,000 square miles) and is about the size of California. Summers are mild, and winters usually have below-freezing temperatures and moderate snowfall. The far north has long, cold winters and bright summers of moderate temperatures.

Market Situation

The current population is 8,876,744 people and is not expected to growth significantly, with a projected population in 2010 of 9,084,000. Due to this slow growth rate, the population is relatively old. Approximately 43% of the population is 45 years of age or older. The people of Sweden are fairly homogenous – over 86% of the residents are Swedish and Lutheran. The official and predominant language is Swedish. The literacy rate is 100%. A fair number of Swedes also grow up with England as a second language.

Economy: Sweden's location is prime because it is at the center of the Baltic region both geographically and financially. Access into and out of the country is made easy by nearly 13,000 km of rail, 211,000 km of mostly-paved highways, 2,000 km of navigable waterways, and a plethora of airports. In addition, the almost-completed *Øresund Bridge* will link Malmö to Copenhagen and Sweden to the entire European continent. Sweden is also a significant contributor to the high-tech sector. Sweden invests a greater percentage of its Gross Domestic Product (GDP) in information technology and telecommunication than the United States, United Kingdom, Finland, and Germany.

Many initial public offerings are expected in the next few years. Sweden has followed some familiar patterns also seen in the United States. The country experienced a hot real estate market in the mid-1980s to late 1980s and then a downturn in the early 1990s. It is now in its upswing and has been showing consistently strong growth over the last several years. GDP is projected to increase again in 2001 at 3.3%, inflation at only 0.4%, and unemployment is reported at only 5.5%. As the leading financial center of the Baltic region, Sweden is in a prime position for investment opportunities. In the capitol of Stockholm, where 25% of the population resides, vacancy rates in both residential and commercial units are almost nonexistent. Detached single-family homes have appreciated approximately 20% in the least year alone.

Why Germany?

Each of the five countries we explored as possible investment markets for REACON do have profit potential for various reasons. However, as a combination of variables, Germany proves to be the best fit at this time. Note that 80% of the countries we are considering in Western Europe have great access to each other via rail, sea, highway, and air. These countries are also benefiting from their recent membership in the European Union (EU).Germany has the added benefit of hosting the site of the European Central Bank, located in Frankfurt. Germany also provides the benefit of a larger market, as Germany boasts the richest and most populous nation in Western Europe. Each market studied does have some regulated real estate professional association with use of these professionals varying from 60% to 80% of all transactions. At a commission rate ranging from 3% to 8% of purchase price, depending on the country, this could be a significant expenditure. In Germany, however, the majority of transactions bypass the use of a professional, potentially saving a great deal of money. In addition to the use of real estate professionals, Finland, Denmark, and Sweden have "stamp duty" fees, notary fees, and/or transaction fees of up to 25%, which could provide prohibitively expensive. Here, again, Germany requires less in the way of fees, requiring only a 3.5% transaction fee and providing opportunities to avoid local and capital gains taxes, allowing more dollars to hit our bottom line. Although international investment has become easier since Germany became members in the European Union (EU), Denmark, Finland, and Sweden still do have some restrictions. On

a relative basis, it is much easier, as an international entity, to invest in Germany. All the markets investigated do have growth potential, but it is concentrated more in outlying areas than in the more desirable central business districts. Berlin is an exception and it, in fact, has been the largest urban construction site in Europe for the last decade. Germany is the top property investment market,. based on examination of both cyclical and structural factors. One of the most striking benefits of investing in Germany is its low corporate tax rate. Recent reforms there have slashed this rate significantly to only 25% – the lowest of the five countries reviewed. Each of the countries investigated does show promise for real estate investment. Indeed, it is possible that slight adjustments in market conditions could provide another country to be a more favorable market. Currently, however, the economic growth and tax reform in Germany provide the most compelling reasons for investment there. These points will allow for market characteristics similar to those seen in the U.S. market in the mid-1990s. We all know what great successes there were in the United States then – we cannot pass up an opportunity for similar successes in Germany.

About The Authors

Walter S. Clements, Senior Vice President and principal at Coliers Turley Martin Tucker in Kansas City, Missouri. He has been in the brokerage business since 1971 and received his CCIM designation in 1975. He has participated in exchanging, syndications, and development, including marinas, mini storage, and fast food restaurants. He is also a principal in a development company that is developing four shopping centers and an office park. He received his certificate in real estate from the University of Michigan and has a BS in Business Administration from Central Michigan University and recently completed a Master's degree in Real Estate and Construction Management from the UNIVERSITY OF DENVER, Burns School of Real Estate and Construction Management.

Leslie A. Kramer, director of sales and marketing for Ryland Homes-Inland Empire Division. She provides marketing support of each division by coordinating national programs, advertising, sales and Ryland's Internet-based marketing efforts. She is instrumental in creating Ryland's national marketing strategies and promotions. Ms. Kramer holds a BS degree in entrepreneurship and small business management from the University of Colorado, Boulder, and is pursing a master's degree in Real Estate and Construction Management from the UNIVERSITY OF DENVER, Burns School of Real Estate and Construction Management.

Suzanne Miller has served as Vice President of Asset Management for Commercial Net Lease Realty, Inc., since July 2001. Ms. Miller has over 20 years of commercial real estate experience including the management, leasing, and construction management of more than 15 million square feet of office, retail, and industrial properties. She is a number of the International Council of Shopping Centers (ICSC), Commercial Investment

Real Estate Institute (CIREI), and earned the CCIM professional designation (Certified Commercial Investment Member). Ms. Miller has a master's degree in Real Estate and Construction Management from the UNIVERSITY OF DENVER, Burns School of Real Estate and Construction Management.

Gary M. Ralston, President, Chief Operating Officer, and a member of the Board of Directors for Commercial Net Lease Realty, Inc., a real estate investment trust. He is responsible for overseeing the overall operations of the trust and has guided the company's growth from less than $20 million in real estate assets to its current level of nearly $1.5 billion. Mr. Ralston holds the CCIM, SIOR, SRS, CPM, and CRE designations, and is also a Florida licensed real estate broker and certified building contractor.

■ Case Study 2

Real Estate and Construction Investment Analysis: Comparing Germany & Hungary By David Gibson, Don Cape, Mike Elliot t, Kyler Knudsen, Scott Schraiberg, and Adam Berszenyi Similar to Case Study #1, involving the same type of factual setting, Case Study 2 considers those factors that should be weighed and the criteria to be used when deciding whether or not to expand internationally in the areas of real estate construction and/or real estate investments. This Case Study differs from the first Case Study in part because of the weight given to these participants (proposed directors of a firm to be formed) as compared with those directors in the first Case Study. *Case Study #2 was conducted in February 2001 and covers the countries of Germany and Hungary.*

Introduction

As discussed in the previous stockholder meeting, our firm will embrace the spirit of "globalization" by diversifying its holdings to include foreign real estate. Our real estate development and construction company is most interested in investing in European real estate. Our firm has done several feasibility studies on most of the major European nations and we have narrowed our search to two promising countries, Germany and Hungary. Each country has strengths and weaknesses. In order to quantify our analysis, we have identified and weighted the criteria we feel most relevant to this decision process. As requested by the board of directors, our carefully selected group has conducted a thorough analysis of Germany and Hungary. Our research revealed that Germany provides a better climate for construction and real estate investment than that of Hungary and therefore we recommend investment in the German real estate and construction markets. The primary basis for our recommendation is founded upon Germany's population trends, the availability of skilled laborers, favorable governmental and legal conditions, their favorable economic status, the highly developed transportation network, and the current and projected health of the real property market there.

Historical Background: Often, an understanding of a country's history can provide valuable insight to the economic and cultural development of a region. Although we did not include the history as a critical criterion in our analysis, we felt it necessary to provide this brief overview to the board. Germany enjoys a history as Western Europe's richest and most populous nation. Today, Germany remains a key member of the continent's economic, political, and defense organizations. European power struggles immersed the country in two devastating World Wars in the first half of the 20th century. In 1945, this resulted in the country being broken into four zones and an occupation by the United States (U.S.), United Kingdom (U.K.), France, and the Soviet Union. During the beginning of the Cold War, two German states were formed in 1949: the western Federal Republic of Germany (FRG) and the Eastern German Democratic Republic (GDR). The democratic FRG embedded it self in key western economic and security organizations, the European Community and the North Atlantic Treaty Organization (NATO). Meanwhile, the communist GDR was on the front line of the Soviet-led Warsaw Pact. The decline of the U.S.S.R. and the end of the Cold War allowed for German unification in 1990. Since then, Germany has expended considerable funds to bring eastern productivity and wages up to western standards. In January 1999, Germany and ten other E.U. countries formed a common European currency, the Euro Dollar. We believe despite the challenges associated with standardizing the monetary system; this standardization will strengthen European markets and economies in the long term.

Hungary's history goes back more than 1,100 years. The Magyars settled the region known as Hungary in 895 A.D. Since the Hungarian area lies between Europe and Asia, along historically key trade routes, Hungary has known its fair share of war and struggle. Hungary was once part of the Austro-Hungarian Empire, until it collapsed during World War I. In recent history, Post World War II, Hungary fell under Communist rule. In 1956, the spirited Hungarian people unsuccessfully tried to thwart Russian control. Later, under the more flexible rule of Gorbachev, Hungary led the movement to dissolve the Warsaw Pact. In the early 90's, after the fall of the U.S.S.R., Hungary began to align themselves more politically and economically with Western Europe. Although Hungary's future looks much brighter now they are not restrained by communism, the country still suffers from over 50 years of inadequate investments in infrastructure development and maintenance. Although Hungary is no longer under Communist control, ideals associated and experienced by much of the population have developed a culture circumspect to property ownership. As capitalism flourishes and Communist ideals are expunged, opportunities will increase exponentially.

Course of Action Selection

As discussed in previous board meetings, we have identified seven possible courses of action (COAs). These COAs are as listed:

COA 1- Pursue only construction in Germany.
COA 2- Pursue real estate only in Germany.

COA 3- Pursue construction and real estate in Germany.
COA 4- Pursue only construction in Hungary.
COA 5- Pursue only real estate in Hungary.
COA 6- Pursue construction and real estate in Hungary.
COA 7- Do not pursue any business in either country, stay within the United States.

Due to economies realized through regionally consolidated efforts, we narrowed our options to three primary courses of action. The scenarios we deemed most viable to consider included COAs three, six and seven. These scenarios will further be recognized as COAs one, two, and three respectively.

Selection of Criteria

The criteria analyzed in our research and compared within our decision matrix includes:

1. Population and population trends;
2. Availability of skilled labor force;
3. Government type and favorable legal environment;
4. The countries' economic situation;
5. Condition of transportation network; and
6. The real property market

We think it is important to note why inflation was not included in our criteria. Although inflationary risks can present considerations, we believe inflationary risks are minimal in real estate. This belief is based upon the reasoning that historically, inflation has been comparable between Germany and Hungary (eight and ten percent respectively). Historically, there has been a relatively low level of inflation risk for real estate investments because inflation tends to increase the replacement cost of properties (Fisher, Mart in, 1994).

Population and Population Trends

Population is an important factor to consider. A country's population serves as an indicator for the market size and helps us scope potential consumers of our products and services. Ostensibly, growth rates can serve as indicators or benchmarks for potential growth when considered in conjunction with additional criteria. Our data comes from two secondary data sources, the Central Intelligence Agency and the United States' State Department web sites (http://cia.gov and http://www.state.gov). Germany's population (2000 est.) is 82,797,408 or roughly eight times that of Hungary's. Their current growth rate is 0.29% compared to Hungary's 0.33%. It is also important to note the German birth rate is higher (9.35 per 1,000 vs. 9.26 per 1,000) and the infant mortality rate is lower (4.77 deaths per 1,000 vs. 9.15 per 1,000) when comparing Germany's rates to those of Hungary's.

These trends reflect both a better standard of living in Germany and manifest the larger, continually growing market in Germany.

Investment in construction efforts would not prove feasible if we could not staff operations. For this reason it is imperative to note the availability of laborers. As alluded to with population rates and trends, the German market again proves favorable. The majority of Germany's population (68%) is between the ages of 15 and 64. This comes to approximately 56,302,237 people compared to Hungary's 706,413 for the same pool of potential laborers. The U.S. Government estimates the German labor force at 40.5 million compared to Hungary's 4.2 million. Despite the variance in our comparisons, our conclusion remains constant.

Government and Legal Considerations

Governmental and legal implications can prove extremely beneficial or they could be devastating. When considering the stability and functionality of a country's government, our primary consideration was corruption. We made a subjective assessment of the level of corruption within each country's government. We believe the regulatory process and laws currently in affect are irrelevant if they can be circumvented through corrupt practice. There are a number of conditions that contribute to the functionality of a government and their legal system. Germany's current government type is classified as a Federal Republic, although this system is new to many regions within Germany. As mentioned, Germany was divided in four zones of occupation, during World War II in 1945, then two zones in 1949 and finally achieved unification after the Cold War in 1990. Germany established a basic law system under their 1949 Constitution and continues to use this as their legal system. Despite the historical challenges Germany has endured with territorial and governing divisions, their current system remains virtually corruption free. This may be a result of their economic achievements and political affiliations. Since World War II, Germany has worked closely with the U.S., the U.K. and other European countries, in order to build governmental and economic relations. For more information on Germany's government, see Appendix B.

Hungary has experienced similar challenges with their succession from the U.S.S.R and Communist rule. Hungary operates a Parliamentary Democracy form of government as outlined in their 1949 Constitution but modified in 1972, 1989 and 1997. Modifications include revisions to allow constitutional checks on the prime minister and an establishment of parliamentary oversight. Their final revision included an amendment to streamline their judicial system. Despite continual improvements, we believe corruption is still more prevalent in the Hungarian system. The preponderance of Hungary's corruption can be explained by difficult economic conditions and remnants of communist influence. For more information on Hungary's government, see Appendix C.

The German and Hungarian Economy

The economic status of country candidates is a critical factor. In fact, we have identified economic stability as one of the two most important selection criteria (the other being transportation). Our analysis revealed that the German economy is clearly stronger and more stable than the Hungarian economy. Although our confidence remains in the German economy,

Hungary continues to demonstrate strong economic growth and to continue to work towards accession to the European Union. Over 85% of Hungary's economy has been privatized. Foreign ownership and investment in Hungarian firms has been widespread with cumulative foreign direct investment. This investment totaled $21 billion by 1999. Hungarian sovereign debt is now rated investment grade and GDP growth of four percent in 1999 will likely be matched or even exceeded in 2000. Inflation, while diminished, is still high at ten percent. Economic reform measures include regional development, encouragement of small and medium-size enterprises, and support of housing. Hungary's primary industries include: mining, metallurgy, construction materials, processed foods, textiles, chemicals (especially pharmaceuticals), and the production of motor vehicles.

The German economy is much more powerful than that of Hungary's. Germany possesses the world's third most technologically advanced economy, after the U.S. and Japan, but its capitalistic economy has started to struggle under the burden of generous social benefits. Germany's high rate of social contributions (such as high wage assistance) makes unemployment a long-term, not just cyclical, problem. Meanwhile Germany's aging population has pushed social security outlays to exceed contributions from workers.

On 1 January 1999, the E.U. introduced a common currency that is now being used by financial institutions in some member countries. The exchange rate from the German deutsche mark to Euro Dollar was 2.09988 as of February 2001. The Euro is scheduled to replace the local currency in consenting countries for all transactions in 2002. Germany is currently a member of the European Union, however Hungary presents itself as a fore-runner for future membership. The integration and upgrading of the eastern German economy remains a costly, long-term problem, with annual transfers from the west amounting to roughly $100 billion. Growth slowed to 1.5% in 1999, largely due to lower export demand and still-low business confidence. Recovering Asian demand, a push for fiscal consolidation, and newly proposed business and income tax cuts, if passed, are expected to boost growth trend rates back to around 2.5% in 2000 and beyond. The adoption of a common European currency, and the general political and economic integration of Europe, will bring major changes to the German economy in the early 21st century. German industries are among the world's largest and most advanced producers of iron, steel, coal, cement, chemicals, machinery, vehicles, machine tools, electronics, food, beverages, shipbuilding, and textile production. Overall, the German economy appears fundamentally stable.

Transportation Networks

We have selected transportation as one of the two most critical criteria and weighted it accordingly in our decision. Our ability to transport materials is critical to overall success. The construction industry is extremely competitive and continues to experience reduced profit margins. Due to increased pressure for cost savings, effective supply chain management has become more and more critical. Delayed transport of materials, logistical logjams or other kinks in the supply chain cannot be remedied with technology if the transportation networks are inadequate. Hungary's lack of infrastructure investment and maintenance leaves the majority of their networks in sub-adequate condition. Hungary is clearly disadvantaged in comparison to Germany. For more specific information on the Hungarian and German transportation network, see Appendix D.

Real Property Considerations

We have weighted real property considerations the same as population and access to labor. After careful consideration, we have decided that Germany has a more favorable real property environment. This is because the Hungarian people have not had much access to real property for a period of more than 40 years. Communism did not allow for either private citizens or corporations to actively participate in any of the four major real estate sectors (residential, office, warehouse, and retail). Hungary's foreign ownership restrictions are much more severe than those of Germany. Hungary requires foreigners to obtain permits from the local Public Administrative Office. Germany has no such legislation. Obviously, for an American firm investing overseas, Germany's lack of restrictions is an advantage.

Finally, the Hungarian system of recording land is inferior to that of Germany. Hungary follows the old Austrian system of land recording from the Hapsburg times. The system is not completely computerized and does not include the sales price. Germany's recording system is computerized and includes all necessary information. We prefer Germany's system so that we can track the history of prices over time. For more information on German and Hungarian real property, see Appendix E.

Conclusion

In conclusion, we recommend investment in Germany for expansion of both our real estate and construction efforts. All selected criteria indicate more favorable conditions in the German market. These indications, coupled with the corporate goal of global growth reflect both a favorable market and a great deal of potential. Reward does not come without risk. Despite more favorable conditions for some criteria in the U.S. market, we feel this market is the most mature of those compared. In order to participate in emerging growth trends abroad, we believe investment in the German market provides a strategic location to initiate business while positioning our firm for potentially favorable markets in other European markets. Furthermore, Germany is already a member of the European Union, whereas Hungary is still hoping to be accepted. This must be taken into considerations since we believe acceptance in the European Union will provides increased access to markets and will have a substantial affect on real estate values.

Below we have provided our decision matrix (See Appendix A), which quantifies our analysis. Note that population, access to labor, and real property considerations were weighted equally, while favorable economic and transportation issues were more heavily weighted. Although we believe the countries' governmental structure and the legal environment are sufficiently important to place in our selection criteria, we deemed these systems were both sufficiently favorable and therefore slightly less important than other criteria. Therefore, this criterion was weighted the least.

■ Appendix A - Decision Matrix

Decision Matrix

Criteria	Weight	COA-1	COA-2	COA-3
Population	3	3	2	1
		9	6	3
Access to Labor Force	3	3	2	1
		9	6	3
Government & Legal	2	3	2	1
		6	4	2
Economy	4	2	1	3
		8	4	12
Transportation	4	2	1	3
		8	4	12
Real Property Issues	3	2	1	3
		6	3	9
TOTAL		61	36	53

■ Appendix B - Government-Germany Government Type: federal republic.

Administrative divisions: There are 16 states throughout the country, they are as follows:

1. Baden-Wuerttemberg
2. Bayern
3. Berlin
4. Brandenburg
5. Bremen
6. Hamburg
7. Hessen
8. Mecklenburg-Vorpommern
9. Niedersachsen
10. Nordrhein-Westfalen
11. Rheinland-Pfalz
12. Saarland
13. Sachsen
14. Sachsen-Anhalt
15. Schleswig-Holstein
16. Thueringen

Unification: West Germany and East Germany united on October 3,1990 to form one country known as Germany, under the Constitution of the United German.

Legal system: German civil law system

Executive branch:

Chief of state: President Johannes RAU (since 1 July 1999)

Head of government: Chancellor Gerhard SCHROEDER (since 27 October 1998) **Cabinet:** The Cabinet is appointed by the president on the recommendation of the chancellor

Elect ions: The president is elected for a five-year term by a Federal Convention including all members of the Federal Assembly and an equal number of delegates elected by the Land Parliaments. The Chancellor is elected by an absolute majority of the Federal Assembly for a four-year term.

Legislative branch: bicameral Parliament or Parliament consists of the Federal Assembly of 656 seats (currently 669 seats for the 1998 term).

The Assembly is elected by popular vote under a system combining direct and proportional representation. A party must win five percent of the national vote or three direct mandates to gain representation.

Members serve a four-year term The Federal Council or Bundesrat consists of 69 votes: State governments are directly represented by votes with three to six votes depending, on population of the state. Elections: There are no elections for the Bundesrat. The composition of the Bundesrat is determined by the composition of the state- level governments and has the potential to change any time when one of the 16 states holds an election

Judicial Branch: Federal Constitutional Court or Bundesverfassungsgericht, Judges are elected half by the Bundestag and half by the Bundesrat.

■ Appendix C - Government-Hungary Administrative divisions

19 counties:

Bacs-Kiskun

Baranya

Bekes

Bekescsaba Borsod-Abauj-Zemplen Budapest

Csongrad Debrecen Dunaujvaros Eger

Fejer

Gyor Gyor-Moson-Sopron Hajdu-Bihar

Heves

Hodmez ovasarhely Jasz-Nagykun-Szolnok Kaposvar

Kecskemet

20 urban counties:

Komarom-Esztergom Miskolc

Nagykaniz sa

Nograd

Nyiregyhaz a
Pecs
Pest
Somogy
Sopron Szabolcs-Szatmar-Bereg Szeged
Szekesfehervar Szolnok Szombathely
Tatabanya Tolna
Vas Veszprem Zala

One capital city:

Z alaegersz eg

Legal system: Based on the Western rule of law model. Elections: The National Assembly elects the president for a five-year term

Prime Minister is elected by the National Assembly on the recommendation of the president

Legislative branch: Unicameral National Assembly or Orszaggyules (386 seats)

Members are elected by popular vote under a system of proportional and direct representation to serve four-year terms

Elections Date:

Last held on 10 and 24 May 1998 Next to be held May/June 2002

Judicial branch: Constitutional Court, judges are elected by the National Assembly for nine-year terms

■ Appendix D - German and Hungarian Transportation Network Hungarian Transportation includes: Railways: 16,524 km. Highways: 188,203 km.

Waterways: 1,373 km
Ports and harbors: Budapest and Dunaujvaros
German Transportation includes: Railways: 40,826 km
Highways: 656,140 km
Waterways: 7,500 km

Ports and harbors: Berlin, Bonn, Brake, Bremen, Bremerhaven, Cologne, Dresden, Duisburg, Emden, Hamburg, Karlsruhe, Kiel, Lubeck, Magdeburg, Mannheim, Rostock,and Stuttgart.

■ Appendix E - Real Property Considerations Real Property Issues

Hungarian Market Statistics

Residential real estate market

Number of resident ial r/e all over the country 1949: 2,467,000 1970: 3,122,000 1980: 3,542,000 1990: 3,853,000 1996: 3,991,000

Number of residences in Budapest in 1996: 807,104 Number of new construction:

1970 - 1979: 80,000 – 100,000 per year
1980 – 1989: 50,000 - 90,000 per year
1992 - 1999: 21,000 – 28,000 per year (19,287 in 1999)
Number of homes per 1000 inhabit ant s: 400 (In EU: 450)
Number of needed new construction:
40,000 per year Number of vacant flats:200,000
Average area of residences: 49 sqm
Average area of new construction:
1971 - 1980: 64 sqm 1980 - 1990: 79 sqm 1991 - 1999: 96 sqm
Technology of construction:
780.000 flats: large pre-fabricated concrete slabs and modern industrial technology The rest of the four million flats: traditional technology
Private ownership
1980: approx. 50 % 1990: 74 %
1999: approx. 92 %
Mobility: one-two times during the lifetime after marriage
Income necessity for home purchasing: Income of seventen years Housing expenditure / income ratio:
1980 -1990: 10-15 % 1996 -1999: 30-35 %
Home purchasing credit interest rate: 17.5 %
Special interest rate subsidiary for new construction with lower than 100,000 USD sales price: 8.5% Apartment sales prices (new, normal): $367-1167 per sqm Apartment rental prices: $ 3- 11 per sqm

Office market

Total surface area of quality (Class A and B) office space in Budapest at present excluded pre- 1989 office space: approx. 800,000 sqm

Annual average absorption in 1990 - 1999: 50,000 – 80,000 sqm
Estimated new office space in:
1999: approx. 120,000 sqm
2000: approx. 230,000 sqm
Number of quality office buildings in Budapest : 80
Vacancy rate in Budapest:15-16% (2000)
Rental fee in 2000 outside the city-center of Budapest: 20-33 DEM per sqm in the inner- city:32 - 45
DEM per sqm (in 1992- 1993 :55-50 DEM per sqm) Yield rate:9-12 %

Retail market

Total surface area of retail space (malls, hypermarkets) built in 1996-1999 in Budapest: approx.
400,000 sqm
Number of built shopping centers in Budapest and environs: 25
Sales price: 1700 - 3700 USD per sqm (Budapest)
Rental fee: 20 - 160 DEM per sqm per month (Budapest)

Industrial and warehousing market (1999)

Rentable modern warehousing capacity in Budapest and environs: 2,500 sqm (approx. 170,000 sqm in midst 2000)

Total surface area of modern warehousing capacity is approximately 40,000 sqm (approx. 250,000 sqm in midst 2000).

Total surface area of old, not adequate industrial warehousing supply in Budapest: approx. 450,000 sqm

Estimated surface area demand at present and in the near future for modern industrial and warehousing capacity: approx. 300,000 sqm

Industrial and warehousing projects under development in Budapest: 200,000 sqm in a site of 500,000 sqm

Sales price of old establishments: 300 - 500 USD per sqm

Rental fee of old warehousing capacity: three-nine DEM per sqm modern warehousing capacity: 7 - 13 DEM per sqm

Industrial parks

Number of industrial parks in the country: 112 (operating: 60)

Hotels

There is intensive new development. In Budapest 20 four and five stars hotels with 3,000 rooms will be built between 2000-2002.

German Market Statistics
Market volume:

Two indicators provide information about the German property market: - The total stock of real estate - Details of transaction sizes

In 1995 the Federal Republic of Germany registered a stock of residential properties to the value of about 7.852 trillion marks. Of this amount roughly 5.09 trillion was attributable to the value of the buildings and 2.76 trillion to the value of the land. The major portion of this property, valued at about 7.3 trillion marks, was in the hands of private householders, and the value of assets held by German households in foreign real estate amounted to 0.13 trillion marks.

A closer look at residential properties shows that the above stock is divided as follows: 64 percent single-family houses and duplexes, 33 percent multiple dwellings (share of freehold apartments).

Sales Volume

The sales value of real estate in the Federal Republic, what is known as the property transaction volume, reached 349 billion marks in 1999, the second highest volume recorded since the peak of 1994. That means that every year between four and five percent of the total real estate value is traded, leading to the conclusion that, on average, property is held for a period of more than 20 years. In 1997 the number of transactions was around 950,000, real estate brokers facilitated about half of them, the other half being effected without their help. By extrapolating from the land transfer tax statistics and the comparative analysis drawn up by the RDM (Association of German Real Estate Brokers), we see that the more than 4,700 RDM member companies broker real estate transactions worth 60 to 70 billion marks per year.

Homeownership Rates

The homeownership rate in the Federal Republic of Germany, i.e. the proportion of households living in their own property, is about 40 percent (44 percent in the old west states and 26 percent in the new federal states of the east); that is a very low figure compared with the rest of Europe. Neighboring European countries, such as France, Great Britain, Italy or Spain have homeownership rates from about 60 to over 80 percent. Major causes for the low homeownership rate in Germany were displacement, with 12 million refugees streaming westwards between 1944 and 1950 and the former German Democratic Republic, whose communist legacy still affects the country today.

Housing Stock

What is particularly noticeable about Germany's housing stock is that multifamily dwellings with three or more units dominate. More than half of all 36.8 million dwellings are in this type of house. Taking an average dwelling size of 85 square metres, every citizen has, theoretically, 39 square metres at his disposal. Owner-occupied dwellings average 110 square metres, whereas the average rented dwelling is only 68 square metres in size.

Hungarian Real Estate Practices
1. Relationship of practitioner to buyers and sellers:

In Hungary the R/E brokerage is licensed due. The licensing is regulated by a separate government decree. The decree defines the content and competence of the brokerage activity but the details of the practice are free, they are not regulated. Generally the obligations between the practitioner and the party are defined in written contract, but a written form is not mandatory. The ethical code of the Hungarian Real Estate Association requires a written contractual relationship between the practitioner and the party. Membership in the Hungarian Real Estate Association is voluntary. Practitioner may represent the interest of seller or buyer or both of them, but the practitioner shall accept any compensation from more than one client only if each of them consents it in writing prior to closing.

In Hungary only approx. 20-25 % of the residential r/e transactions are carried out by brokers, the rest of the residential properties are sold directly by the owners. The brokerage activity was reborn in 1990. In the past decades of the communist regime only one state-owned company and the lawyers were entitled to intermediate in selling and buying. The public has begun to use the service of the brokers again ten years ago. Slowly more and more clients do it but the tradition is still thin.

Due to this circumstance the overwhelming majority per approx. 90 % of the residential property listings are not exclusive (In case of commercial R/E transactions the proportion is almost on the contrary.)

2. Services:

There is no any legal regulation regarding the services to provide to the clients. The most essential task of a practitioner is procuring a buyer, tenant or searching for a property adequate to the requirement of the client. Generally the practitioner provides the services as follows.

He/she signs a contract with the client (listing), detailing in it the property to be sold, rented or found, expiring date of the contact, price limit of the property, commission and some other specifications (e.g. type of listing, way of marketing).

He/she inspects the property, assists to determine the price of the property, in case of specific requirement takes responsibility of compiling an appraisal report, procures the documents relating to the property, takes charge of marketing, assists to prepare the deed and provides advises.

3. Remuneration:

No law or decree regulates the commission. It is agreed in writing and varies depending upon the type, price of property, time limit of selling, complexity of service or any special condition. Generally the amount of commission is in case of:

- Selling:1 - 3 - 5 % + VAT of the selling price, - Buying:1 - 3 % + VAT of the selling price - Renting:8 - 15 % + VAT of one year's rent.

In most cases the seller or landlord pays the commission. Commission due upon signing the deed.

4. Entrance /Statutory/ Licensing Requirements:

The 49/1982 regulates the brokerage activity. (X.[7].) MT and the 13/1988 (XII.[27].)ÉVM decrees. The main stipulations of these decrees are as follows.

Brokerage activity comprises:

Mediation of selling and buying and changing of buildings and plots (real estates), Meditation of renting of buildings and plots, Searching real estates, Appraising real estates, Collecting and preparing the documents needed to the transaction.

Every economical organizations and natural persons possessing professional license are entitled to brokerage. Lawyers don't need to have professional license to operate ad brokers except appraisal activity (they are not allowed to appraise any R/E). Natural persons must be entered on a list of names and have an official certificate of no criminal record. Economical organizations should employ at least one employee possessing professional license, official certificate of no criminal record and entered on a list of names. The requirements to obtain license are regulated by the 8/1995.(V.[25].)

BM (Interior Ministry) Decree. (It is the last decree, the previous one had been cancelled.)

The broker candidates having a certificate of final examination in a secondary school-as a minimum school qualification – have to participate on a professional course and take a written, *oral* and practical exam. (Number of class hours and subjects are free, only the exam is determined by the decree. The most successful course has 500 class hours.) On the written and oral exam the candidates should give a proof of knowledge on:

- Technical subjects (e.g. architectural structure)
- Legal subjects (e.g. concept of R/E, parts of civil law, registration of R/E, rules of buying, selling, changing, tax of R/E.)
- Economical subjects (e.g. credit subsidies for purchasing R/E, rules of accountancy).
- Brokerage practice (e.g.- duties on selling, buying and changing: preparation of contact, financial constructions, determination of tax and financial conditions, procedure of registration, listing, searching on demand and offer, methods to determine the selling price, searching for partners; appraisal: characteristics of the settlement, collecting information on the R/E from different institutions, authorities, on site, determine technical parameters of the R/E; possessing skills on: informing clients on financial constructions, taxation, equipment, state, value of r/e.)

On the practical exam the candidates should defend their thesis, which subject is determined by the Interior Ministry (The licensing decree has been issued by this ministry.) A real estate license does not need to be renewed.

5. Marketing system:

There is no centralized marketing system. The majority of the brokers is working individually even the multinational agencies. The whole market is free for every licensed practitioner. There is no local or regional restriction. From day to day appears more and more web based market ing syst ems. Part of them are simple advertisements or databanks, others are MLS- All of them are privately owned by individuals or companies. The market is free to operate any marketing system of any kind. The most important MLS are:

- http://www.dunaholding.hu/(free access)
- www.ingatlan-buda.hu (free access)
- web-cei.com (Databank for member's association of 13 European countries).

6. Arbitration:

Members of the above mentioned MLS and the Hungarian Real Estate Association set tle their dispute according to the ethical code of the relative organization. In case of controversies arisen members may appeal to the ethical commission of the concerning organization.

7. Referral System:

Referrals are not frequent. Referral system works mainly among the members of MLS. Each MLS has its own regulation. Generally the commission is spitted into 50-50 % between the listing broker and referring broker. Most companies are locally based and they are not involved in other business activities in addition to real estate.

8. Foreign Ownership:

The Government Decree 7/1996.(I.¹⁸.) regulates in detail the acquisition of real estate by foreigners. Foreigners in possession of a permit obtained from the local Public Administration Office may acquire a right to real estate, except for arable land or land located in protected nature reserves.

Foreigners by right of inheritance may acquire the ownership right to real estate without permission. Companies registered in Hungary (even if they are fully foreign-owned) may purchase also without permission real estate necessary to operate their business activity. The permission shall be denied, if the acquisition of the real estate by the foreigner does interfere, according to the mayor's declaration, with a municipal interest.

The authorization to purchase r/e may be refused, if the state, of which the foreigner is a citizen, does not provide the same treatment for Hungarian citizens and Hungarian legal entities on the basis of an international treaty or reciprocity as it does for its own residents. If the purchasing of R/E does not interfere with any municipal or other public interests, permission shall be granted in some cases, e.g. if the foreigner has received an immigration permit, or the foreigner exchanges the real estate he/she owns in Hungary to another piece of R/E in Hungary, etc.

The application for the authorization shall be submitted to the head of the local Public Administration Office, attaching several documents, e.g. a copy of the contract on the acquisition of the R/E, a duplicate copy of the ownership sheet from the real estate registry (title), not older than three months, etc.

9. Land Registration System:

The Hungarian land registration system has many years of history and is as old as the Habsburg Empire and still is working reliably, continuously up to modern times. (In the nineties it has been computerized countrywide.) It is based on the Austrian Grund Buch system, which consists of a cadastre combined with a land registry.

The legal description of land is recorded by a cadastral map, which is drawn in scale. Parcels reflected on the cadastral map are cross-referenced to a land registry, which consists of a three-page record:

Page 1 of the land registry describes the parcel itself, its size, location and the permitted use.

Page 2 sets forth ownership in format ion, included the ownership history.

Page 3 provides information with respect to liens, easements and other similar claims or restrictions regarding the property.

There is no record of selling price!

The information set forth in the land registry is guaranteed by the state. To the extent that there may exist unrecorded claims, Hungarian law provides that a bona fide purchaser who acquires property without knowledge of such claims nevertheless acquires clear title. The transfer of property right must put down in a written, authentic form (deed), which has to be countersigned by a lawyer or a notary. The deed has to be submitted to the Land Registration Office in 30 days after it's signing. Titles are accessible to everybody in the Land Registration Office.

10. Other professions:

Brokers are entitled persons to intermediate in a transaction between the parties. They manage every details of selling or buying, except the contract on transfer of property ownership. This must be done by the collaboration of a lawyer or notary. Lawyer's fee is negotiable, generally approx. one percent of the sales price. Notary's fee is fixed, it varies according to the value of the property, it is approx. less than one percent. Lawyers are allowed to perform a task of a broker – without possessing a brokerage license.

11. Discipline/Code of Ethics:

There is no Code of Ethics mandatory for all of the brokers of the country. Members of the Hungarian Real Estate Association (a nationwide organization) are obliged to respect the ethical rules of HREA. These rules is the summary of the ethical attitude norms, which states how the members shall carry their activity made possible by the law and what consequences shall follow any irregular activity.

The ethical code regulates the members' attitude concerning clients and regarding among each other.

An ethical committee is responsible for the enforcement of the ethical rules.

In case of violation of the ethical rules the following coercive measures are taken:

- Rigorous and last warning, informing the members and make the facts public.
- Exclusion of the member who violated the ethical rules and making the exclusion public. The code of ethics of the Hungarian Real Estate Association entered into force in 1992.

German Real Estate Practices
1. Relationship of Practitioners to Buyers and Sellers:

The German Civil Code defines the legal obligations between the practitioners and the party, the buyer and/or the seller. The practitioner is a property agent. There are contracts with the buyer and/or the seller. Those contracts are typically written. Contracts are mandatory. Yes, there are other types of relationships between real estate practitioners and the consumer that are not agency based, per example property managing based, facility management based.

2. Services:

Services are primarily to assist in sale as well as in rental. The services provided by the real estate practitioners to sellers and buyers are:

- Information about all market conditions round the object, especially the real market price-situation

- Round-about-service regarding the object itself
- All services to give advice on law and taxes to sellers and buyers.

3. Remuneration:

Remuneration is paid either by the seller or by the buyer or by each of them per half. The method of payment of commission and/or fees is money-transfer just after signing the contract at the Notary public. Payment occurs at the time of a successful conclusion of a real estate contract signed by a notary public. The Notary public controls the funds in real estate transactions. Yes, there are any statutory restrictions on remuneration by the German Civil Code Law.

4. Entrance/Statutory/Licensing Requirements:

The entrance requirements for real estate practitioners are the license given by the State. Education, courses, certifications etc. are not required, but they are required by the RDM for membership. Mandatory continuing education is necessary for RDM-members only.

Yes, a practitioner can market properties anywhere in the country. There are no regional/local restrictions. A non-resident cannot market properties. The German law, the industrial control, regulates the industry, the trade supervised office. A license is necessary. Licenses will not be renewed, but the German law knows the revocation of license if the practitioner is unworthy of keeping it.

5. Marketing System:

Yes, a marketing system exists. It is manual as well as computerized. Local/regional/national markets in scope. Marketing systems are web based. All types of properties are included, residential, commercial etc. Sale and rental as well these systems are proprietary. Access to these systems has the RDM-members and the consumers to look in web sites. The RDM Germany is operating a special marketing system.

6. Arbitration:

Yes, it is a mechanism to adjudicate remuneration disputes between real estate practitioners by the RDM own arbitration-rules-system.

7. Referral System:

No, there is not a national referral system. Referrals are not commonplace. Most companies are locally based and national. These companies are not very much involved in other business activities in addition to real estate. Referrals are not regulated in any manner.

8. Foreign Ownership:

There is no legislation that restricts foreign investment.

9. Land Registration System:

The registration of property ownership is mostly computerized. The land registration in Germany, the district land registrations run it. The real estate practitioners have access to it, if they are entitled to look in it.

10. Other Professions:

Yes, there are other professions directly involved with and being paid for the sale/rental of properties, that means the credit banking institutes and saving banks and their daughters. Lawyers can sell properties as well. Lawyers, notaries and other professionals are mostly not required to be involved to complete real estate transactions.

11. Discipline/Code of Ethics:

Yes, a Code of Ethics exists. It's the Code of Ethics of the RDM Germany. Yes, it is an internal discipline process. Responsible for its enforcement is the national board and the managing directory.

Hungarian and German Overview

The ten years of transition has altered the context of investing and building in the region known as Central-East-Europe – comprising the countries of Poland, Czech Republic, Slovakia and Hungary – to a great extent. With sustained direct foreign investment as a result of the privatization of state owned enterprises and numerous greenfield developments there is a strong demand – mostly in and around capital cities and metropolitan areas of sizable population – for office, retail, hotel and industry/ warehousing accommodation. Cities, like Budapest, once studied by experts of the World Bank as "cities without land markets" are showing the structural tendencies (both good and bad) of western capitals: off center office boulevard developments, regional shopping centers, sub-urbanization of jobs and housing.

Hungarian Office sector

In Hungary the most visible real estate developments occurred in the office and retail sectors. With the arrival of international corporations there was a strong demand for modern, quality office space. Multinational financial institutions and business service companies own approximately 65% of the banking and 80% of the insurance industry. With strong growth in the telecommunication sector another sizeable jump for corporate office space is expected.

In 1989 – 1999 some 700,000 square meters office space was developed in Budapest alone. A yearly production of 50,000 – 80,000 m2 or 6-10 large project developments. Rents showed a sharp increase from DM 25 per square meters per month (in 1990) to DM 45 (in 1995) – the period of pioneers - but now settled around DM 40 in central locations and DM 30 in off centre locations. Class A properties are still yielding 10% to 12% but expected to decline to a 7.5% to 8.5% range within the next five years.

Graph depicts new office supply in Budapest.

German Office sector

In inner-city centers the improved economic climate has, according to a market analysis conducted by the Ring Deutscher

Makler (RDM), led to surging rents for offices. The continued market growth in the second half of the year is due both to re-locating companies and new start-ups as well as the demand for different or larger premises.

The strong surge in office rentals noted by the RDM market research division is currently limited to large cities with more than half a million inhabitants. Here the last 12 months have produced average rent increases of just below eight percent (prior year five percent) both for standard space and for the most sought-after properties. The rise was larger in the cities with the highest office rents in Germany, which are, apart from Frankfurt and Munich, Hamburg, Berlin and Düsseldorf. Here the increase in rent was around nine percent (prior year eight percent).

In Germany's major cities the best sites can command monthly square meter prices of between 50 and 80 DM. The turnover of floor space in the country's largest office centers, such as Frankfurt, Munich, Berlin and Hamburg, was between 400,000 and 600,000 square meters in 1999, with the ratio of unleashed property averaging 5 percent. Due to continued optimism in German business circles, the RDM expects to see further office rent rises in the economic centers. In the new Federal states rents for office space declined once more, falling by 4 percent. Compared with the nearly 9 percent drop last year, one may speak of a slight improvement in stability. The average rent for office space in East Germany is currently about 40 percent below prices in West German cities.

Hungarian Retail sector

Retail development started later but had a fast development curve, both in Budapest and now in provincial cities above 100,000 inhabitants. Between 1996 and 1999 seven new shopping malls were opened in Budapest, with the additional development of hypermarkets (Cora, Auchan, Tesco, InterSpar) in a suburban areas. Retail rents average between DM 30 to 60/m2/month.

Retail is about "shopping formulas" and the consumer goods starved Central European economies were a fertile ground for the rapid penetration and expansion of international retailers. The leading business area is the food sector, with the neighborhood-centered supermarkets and discount shops with somewhat larger catchments area. With some 90% of the housing stock in private ownership retailing chains (building material, gardening and hand held tools) were also quick to take market position with a spread strategy for the secondary towns. The "hypermarket formula", combining discount prices with wide variety of choice of products across the food, clothing and recreation consumer goods, is another strong retail entry. Hypermarkets gained a 17% market share of the retail spending in Hungary in merely three years, demonstrating the viability of larger shopping formulas. Because of the strong bulk purchasing and logistical power of hypermarket chains they arguably contributed to the reduction of inflation and the shrinking share of the gray economy.

New retail supply Budapest:

German Retail Sector

The market for shop space in urban centers currently underlines the difficult competitive situation in which the German retail trade finds itself. Only for superior quality property in the one hundred percent locations can a definite increase in rents be observed. For the other top sites in large cities first signs are recognizable that the six-year price slide is coming to a standstill. In particularly sought-after sites in cities of more than half a million inhabitants, shop rents have shown their first definite increase since the recession that started in the mid- nineties and are about three percent up. This increase is mainly limited to smaller shops (up to 100 square metres) and is the result of keen competition for the very best sites in the city. Here the flagship stores of the international fashion, jewelry and designer elite determine the prices. Rents for attractive, small shop space in top city locations are around 350 DM per square meter in Munich, 320 DM in Düsseldorf and Dortmund. In Frankfurt the prices are around 300 DM, in Hamburg and Berlin 200 DM per square meter and month.

Hungarian Warehouse Sector

Due to its small domestic market the Hungarian economy is strongly export oriented, hence the need for logistic and warehousing space. German, Dutch and U.S. developers focus on the creation of industrial and logistic parks, mainly around Budapest and the export industry region of the western region. This market was largely dormant till 1998 when the first speculative development was initiated. In 1999 additional projects got off from the ground and by the year 2000 – 2002 some 300,000-m2 light industrial, warehousing and logistical complexes are expected to be completed most of the new supply is being built as "built to suit" projects, as the expanding multinational companies out grow the old industrial buildings and warehousing facilities that they acquired when purchasing Hungarian companies during the privatization process. The growth of demand for logistical facilities signals the emergence of the Budapest agglomeration as a gateway location for distribution functions towards East Europe and the Balkan. New industrial/warehousing supply Budapest.

Hungarian Residential Sector

The "looser" of the transition and take off period was the housing sector. During the 1980s the average annual output was 60,000 units compared to current output of 20,000 – 25,000 newly built homes per year. As the real value of construction and mortgage interest rate subsidies diminished during the high inflation period of 1989-1995 their impact on stimulating new construction has decreased. A new subsidy stimulus in 1995 gave rise to new housing construction again, but as inflation remained high the real value decreased thorough the years. It is expected that the new financial regime of deep (three percent) interest subsidy and long term (30 years) mortgage instruments will induce a growth for the next five years (approximately 25 – 30,000 units per year). As a result of strict inflation control policies imposed by the E.U. accession progress there will be a longer value retaining impact of these subsidies than in the previous five years.

Per capita housing construction and granted building permits in Budapest and the rest of the country:

German Retail Sector

In the old states we can observe price rises of between 1.4 and 2.8 percent for building land. In the owner-occupied housing sector (detached houses and row houses) price rises of between 0.9 and 1.6 percent may be observed. The year 2000 has not yet seen the condominium market turn around, a sect or in which the RDM has registered a drop in prices of between one and 1.4 percent. In the new states, all sectors have seen prices fall by between 0.5 and three percent this year, despite signs that the decline is bottoming out. Prices for building plots in the old federal states range, on average, according to desirability of the site, from 360 to660 DM per square meter; prices in the Capital, Berlin, area reach up to 1,700.

For single-family houses (incl. garage and land) the RDM has found prices averaging between 370,000 DM and 890,000 DM, depending on residential area. In the Bavarian capital of Munich, the price in excellent residential areas can be as high as 1.8 million marks. The national average price per square meter for condominiums is between 1,850 and 4,000 DM. In large cities this price can be between 6,000 and 7,000 marks for sought-after sites. On the German market for rented accommodation, a five year decline in the rents for new lease agreements is slowing down in pace. The RDM's latest market analysis shows that rental charges in new leases signed during the last 12 months are now only 0.1 to 0.5 percent lower. In the cities, rents for new property being let for the first time are, by contrast, rising noticeably, by between one and two percent. Over the rest of the year, however, the RDM expects to see the market for rented accommodation become more st able. The rental price of accommodation, taking the net rent per square meter, exclusive of ancillary charges, for a 3 room, 70 square meter dwelling, averages between 8 and 11 marks in the old states. New properties being let for the first time command average prices of between 12 and 13 marks per square meter. Rental prices can be as much as 20 marks per square meter in large cities such as Hamburg, Munich, Cologne, Frankfurt or Düsseldorf.

Hungarian Investment Outlook

Although the cities of Central Europe are now firmly on the international real estate market there are still some "pioneering" opportunities with high risks and high rewards. There is a lack of financial intermediaries focusing on the needs of the property market. There are still limited projects in the leisure/ entertainment/tourism sector. The rental-housing sector is unexplored. More opportunities can be developed with the "built to suit" projects and "sale and lease back" financing instruments. For many of the market players' real estate is now a transparent and complementary investment opportunity in addition to bonds and equity markets. But moving development projects successfully from conception to realization requires sizeable equity, skill, experience and creditworthiness with lending institutions. In our view only multinational development companies will be able to master all these credentials in the Hungarian property market. As a conclusion our medium tem forecast for the major real estate market segments in the Budapest metropolitan area is the following:

Office sector

Temporary oversupply of new construction, with absorption catching up in two 2-3 years time stable rents and low vacancy rate in the financial district, soft rent in the off-center office locations. There is a growing supply of landscaped office park sites for medium size corporate headquarters. Still there are few investment grade properties.

Retail sector

Strong "brands" competition among hypermarket chains, a likely evolution towards "edge of town power centers". Although the anticipated sustained–three growth of incomes and purchasing power will justify the further development of city centre or mid-town shopping centres there will be a pressure on the existing shopping centres to upgrade their quality, improve tenant mix, and add more leisure elements. The already existing shopping centres will be of investment grade once these additional quality and attraction improvements are made.

Warehousing and logistics

Strong expansion opportunities around Budapest and the other export producing regions of the country. There will be a need to develop integrated warehousing, light manufacturing and R&D locations, although the majority of building projects will be "built to suit" type. Developers with multinational production and logistical clients will take the lead.

Residential

Recovery of the housing sector, more even regional demand and more demand for developer built housing. Besides the suburban luxury demand there will be opportunities in Budapest for city core luxury products. Few investment grade rental project catering for the expatriate management sect or and young, high income start up families.

German Investment Outlook

On balance the RDM takes a positive view of the future growth opportunities on the German property market. The tax reforms, which have just passed through parliament, should have a beneficial effect on the demand for property. A further boost to demand is a renewed increase of real incomes, a steady gentle rise in the number of people in employment and greater confidence in the economy. In view of this, it is generally expected that people will be more inclined to spend money, which will stabilize the rental situation on the market for commercial property. Finally the RDM believes that there is pent-up demand for owner-occupied housing, following several years of reluctance to buy. Therefore slight increases in the price of single-family dwellings may be expected in the west. In the east, the RDM reckons with a gradual stabilization of prices, which are still tending to fall at present.

Volume

In the Federal Republic, what is known as the property transaction volume, reached 349 billion marks in 1999, the second highest volume recorded since the peak of 1994. That means that every year between four and five percent of the total real estate value is traded, leading to the conclusion that, on average, property is held for a period of more than 20 years. In 1997 the number of transactions was around 950,000, real estate brokers facilitated about half of them, the other half being effected without their help. By extrapolating from the land transfer tax statistics and the comparative analysis drawn up by the RDM (Association of German Real Estate Brokers), we see that the more than 4,700 RDM member companies broker real estate transactions worth 60 billion to 70 billion marks per year.

Homeownership Rates

The homeownership rate in the Federal Republic of Germany, i.e. the proportion of households living in their own property, is about 40 percent (44 percent in the old west states and 26 percent in the new federal states of the east); that is a very low figure compared with the rest of Europe. Neighboring European countries, such as France, Great Britain, Italy or Spain have homeownership rates from about 60 to over 80 percent. Major causes for the low homeownership rate in Germany were displacement, with 12 million refugees streaming westwards between 1944 and 1950 and the former German Democratic Republic, whose communist legacy still affects the country today.

Housing Stock

What is particularly noticeable about Germany's housing stock is that multifamily dwellings with three or more units dominate. More than half of all 36.8 million dwellings are in this type of house. Taking an average dwelling size of 85 square metres, every citizen has, theoretically, 39 square metres at his disposal. Owner-occupied dwellings average 110 square metres, whereas the average rented dwelling is only 68 square metres in size.

Bibliography

Jeffrey D. Fisher and Robert S. Martin, Income Property Valuation (Dearborn Trade Publishing. 1994, 2004).

Background Notes: Germany. Retrieved January 21, 2001 from the World Wide Web: http://www.state.gov

Background Notes: Hungary. Retrieved January 21, 2001 from the World Wide Web: http://www.state.gov

CIPS Network, Country Profile, Market Situation. Retrieved January 21, 2001 from the World Wide Web: http://www.cipsnetwork.com

Mitropolitski, S. (2000), Perspective: Hungary. Retrieved January 21, 2001 from the World Wide Web:http://www.ired.com/news/mkt/hungary.htm,

The Currency Site: Currency Converter. Retrieved January 21, 2001 from the World Wide Web: http://www.oanda.com/converter/classic,

The World Factbook 2000-Germany. Retrieved January 21, 2001 from the World Wide Web: http://www.cia.gov

ABOUT THE AUTHORS

Donald E. Cape, Jr. has worked with the Thermo Companies in Denver, Colorado. He received his Masters of Real Estate and Construction Management from the Burns School of Real Estate and Construction Management, Daniels College of Business, UNIVERSITY OF DENVER.

Michael B. Elliott has over ten years of diversified national real estate experience including acquisitions, asset management, redevelopment, development, REIT /Fund development, investment, teaching, and real estate appraisal and brokerage. He is the principal of Requity Real Estate Group, LLC, in Denver, Colorado, and is also an Adjunct Professor in the Burns School of Real Estate and Construction Management, Daniels College of Business, UNIVERSITY OF DENVER.

David R. Gibson received his Masters of Real Estate and Construction Management from the Burns School of Real Estate and Construction Management, Daniels College of Business, UNIVERSITY OF DENVER. He also holds MPA and MBA degrees.

Kyler W. Knudsen, real estate appraiser with Home State Bank in Loveland, Colorado.

Scott Schraiberg received his Masters of Real Estate and Construction Management from the Burns School of Real Estate and Construction Management, Daniels College of Business, UNIVERSITY OF DENVER.

Adam Berszeny also worked on this Case Study 2.

■ Case Study 3

Real Estate Investment Opportunities in the British Isles and Europe:

An In-Depth Look at Niche Markets in Scotland, Norway, France, Ireland, and Netherlands By J. Matthew McMullen, AIA, NCARB, LEED-AP

PREFACE

In the summer of 2006, J. Matthew McMullen, partner in the architectural, design/build and real estate development firm of.AM Build visited the British Isles and other selected countries in Europe as part of the Global Perspectives In Real Estate course offered by the Daniels College of Business at the UNIVERSITY OF DENVER. Matt had been looking for international opportunities to present to his partners in the firm, and this whirlwind trip of 7 countries in 10 days was an opportunity to get a quick glimpse of the real estate markets in each country. Required reading for the class prior to the cruise included both The Lexus and the Olive Tree, and The World Is Flat by Thomas L. Friedman. In both of these books, the author Friedman asserts that we are currently in a time of rapid globalization of the world's economy and that the defining measurement of this new globalization system is speed, pure and simple. Friedman further asserts that innovation will replace tradition and that either the present or the future will replace the past, and the fact that nothing that came before will matter as much as what will come next. The only way that what will come next can arrive is if what is here and now in the present is overturned.

While accepting the basic premise of the arguments that Friedman puts forth, Matt and his partners have accumulated wealth in real estate development in the continental United States by seeing opportunity and changes in the urban fabric before others recognized the same opportunities: in other words, the proverbial "hole in the donut." This part of the speed and overturning equation was congruous with AM Build's thinking. Where a departure from Friedman's thinking occurred for Matt and AM Build was in the core belief that as speed is occurring in the global economy, there is an underlying yearning by the masses for a reconnection to a simpler time and a reconnecting to community as discussed in the book The Third Place by Ray Oldenburg. This thinking was to become the 'pinpoint' in the 'whole in the donut' that AM Build would seek to exploit internationally in order to compete with the large multinational and international real estate development funds and firms. Friedman addressed this very concept in The Lexus and The Olive Tree in Chapter 2, 'Information Arbitrage'. On Page 22, Friedman states, "You have to learn how to arbitrage information from these disparate perspectives and then weave it all together to produce a picture of the world that you would never have if you looked at it from only one perspective. That is the essence of information arbitrage." That is also the essence of what a master architect /developer does, pinpoints changes in the urban fabric in concept before they occur in reality.

This concept of yearning for a connection to community, place and the known is best described by Friedman as The Olive Tree. On page 31, he states, "Olive Trees are important. They represent everything that roots us, anchors, us, identifies us and locates us in this world. Olive Trees are what give us warmth of family, the joy of individuality, the intimacy of personal rituals, the depth of private relationships, as well as the confidence and security to reach out and encounter others." Conversely, on page 32 Friedman describes the Lexus as representing "an equally fundamental age-old drive, the drive for sustenance, improvement, prosperity and modernization. The Lexus represents all the burgeoning global markets, financial institutions and computer technologies with which we pursue higher living standards today." The real estate investor and developer that are able to blend both of these factors into his/ her development will truly achieve financial success and community-building satisfaction. It is the search for this successful blend that the rest of this case study will be devoted.

OPPORTUNITIES: When Matt and AM Build began its analysis of the countries visited during the cruise (Great Britain, Ireland, Scotland, Norway, the Netherlands, Belgium, and France), they quickly narrowed the potential candidates for international investment down to the following countries: Scotland, Norway, France, Ireland and the Netherlands. This first pass was informed by these two sources: "Demographics and Destiny: The real estate investment implications of global demographics," by M. Leanne Lachman, Urban Land Magazine, pp. 49-53 (July 2006), and "Global Demographics and Their Real Estate Investment Applications," by M. Leanne Lachman, in Urban Land Institute (ULI) Issues Paper series, http://www.uli.org/policypapers/issues. In both the condensed article and the more comprehensive paper on the ULI site, Ms. Lachman makes a very bold assertion that seems to be supported by her demographic study of countries actively competing in the global economy. This is an underlying assumption:

"The most startling was that all real estate sectors in continental Europe will evolve into 'replacement markets' over the next couple of decades. Replacement demand results only from one of three factors:

1. demolition of old buildings
2. fires that devastate structures
3. physical and functional obsolescence.

In a stagnant economy, neither job growth nor an increase in household numbers generates new demand, so replacement needs are the only justification for new construction. That (scenarios) results in very modest activity-akin to treading water." This assumption became the core driver behind AM Build's international investment strategy. Look for existing development and structures that are experiencing physical and functional obsolescence and re-position those assets for a new economic life through either recognizing a higher and better use for that existing property, or purchasing an asset at a distressed price and repositioning that property to take advantage of a greater and more stable revenue stream.

In the search for a higher and better use, AM Build looked very closely at the following industry sectors that would fit nicely within its individual partner and collective partners' skill- sets.

RETAIL

While AM Build cut its teeth on retail in the continental United States, the demand for additional Retail in Europe did not appear to be supportable, other than auto-oriented retail. AM Build is rapidly building its reputation for mixed-use pedestrian retail. The core value of creating walk able pedestrian places for retail vs. auto-centered retail eliminated this category. This thinking was further supported by this excerpt from the Lachman article:

"**For** retail properties, demand growth relies on income gains, total population increase, or both. Continental Europe's total population will decline more slowly than the labor force, so weak demand for store space will not be noticeable as quickly as the lack of office demand. Also, Europe wants additional modern, automobile-oriented shopping facilities, so retail development is likely to continue for some time. Nonetheless, older people do not spend as much on consumer goods, a fact or to keep in mind when considering investment in countries with an aging population."

Office

AM Build's forte has never been speculative office space development, as a large downturn in the Denver metro area home market in the early 2000's greatly tempered enthusiasm for any speculative office ventures, much less one overseas. Lachman addresses this industry sector in the following quote:

"A structural transition to replacement demand is already visible in some European office markets, particularly in Germany. When office job growth is limited or nonexistent, any development of additional inventory produces higher vacancy rates and weaker rents. Outsourcing will have the effect of further erosion of office demand. Labor force reduction has a devastating impact on office markets. For people investing in European and Japanese office buildings, this is a critical point: new development must be accompanied by removal of at least an equal amount of high-quality space. Without net new demand, though, there cannot be additional supply - only replacements."

Adaptive Re-use

AM Build was very comfort able with this industry sector and building type having repositioned several buildings within Colorado and Los Angeles. One example that was particularly successful was the adaptive re-use of a 1930's glass-blowing factory. into an independent production studio for one of the former producers of a popular TV show and movie franchise. Given its history of success, AM Build felt that this would be a successful niche that would capture the historical nature of Europe and blend the two core principles of Friedman's globalization, the Lexus and the Olive Tree. This idea was further supported by an additional Lachman quote:

"Europe will continue to need state-of-the-art logistics facilities at crucial transportation hubs.

Tourism will receive more and more government support because it brings in foreign exchange, is able to employ older people, and uses in-place infrastructure; this means hotel investments will be fine. Targeted retail - a proxy for highly selective locations and types of stores, and probably heavily oriented to the tourist market - will also be a sound investment." A retail development in Boulder, Colorado includes a niche boutique hotel designed to cater to the uniqueness and wired, high-tech nature of Boulder's visitor population. Adaptive re-use of an existing structure that could be transformed into a hotel/restaurant-bar concept could be particularly appealing. Matt visited. in New York. a boutique hotel with a restaurant, bar and gift shop on the main level that once housed .cruise line administrative offices. Perhaps this concept could be replicated in other European locations.

Competition by U.S. Based International Real Estate Investors

A final opportunity seemed to be defined by the following headline: "U.S. Losing Steam as Top Europe Invest or," Commercial Property News (August 2006). Since 1997 the proportion of investment by the United States has been on a steady decline, with a large bump occurring in 2000. This slowdown was even further accelerated by the dot-com bubble burst and the 9/11 attacks. The United Kingdom and Ireland in particular are feeling the brunt of this drop in investment as a result of the diminishing perceived risks of international investment in Eastern Europe. A second factor is the relocation of companies relocating to low-cost markets like China and India. In AM Build's opinion this seems to set up an opportunity in the British Isles to take advantage of an overheated market as capital moves towards other international destinations.

Introduction to the Firm: AM Build. is a medium size company. AM Build is in business to provide a one-point source of responsibility for quality design, construction and real estate development. Our mission is to provide quality award-winning sustainable design, construction and development in an ethical manner to visionary for-profit clients and investors located locally, nationally, and internationally, resulting in beautiful animated environments to live, work and play. The immediate, mid-range and long-range goals for the business are to develop a profitable international organization that will work in the new global economy to combat the inconsistencies of local, regional and national economies. The firm is positioning itself to develop a series of projects with an ownership and equity position to maximize profit and create new markets for services. The recognition garnered by producing quality .design and construction work could result in being named The American Institute of Architects (A.I.A.) and The Associated General Contractors (A.G.C.)

Colorado Firms of the Year in the near future.

The business is structured as a LLC with one major shareholder and two other managing members. The management philosophy for AM Build is to allow the head of each of the three Divisions, Architecture/(Design), Construction/(Build), and Real Estate Investment/(RE) to manage their respective areas of specific expertise and corresponding arm of the business. Each manager was specifically selected and placed in his or her role to optimize his or her strengths and career background. Below each of the management heads is an incredibly visionary and talented support staff giving unique talents and passion to each of our client's and investor's projects. The result of this integrated teamwork approach to design, building and development is the firm's numerous design and construction awards and publication in various media.

A final compliment to the in-house staff is the top-notch level of qualified outside service providers that the firm has gathered together to ensure that each client and investor receives the maximum amount of customer service, the highest level of design and quality construction and the maximum return on their investment. Our firm's philosophy is that in order to reach the highest echelon of the industry, we must gather the best of the best around us as advisors, team partners, craftsmen and financial backers. Management capability is the conduit through which client and investor service flows, and our firm will continue to refine and improve the workability of the management structure. AM Build has established the following investment parameters in order to move forward with any international project.

1. 26% return before tax 2.15% return after tax.

C. Decision Parameters:
The Managing Members of AM Build have established that the four following areas in their application to real estate investment, relative to operations in the United States, are the primary factors to consider in the "go" or "no go" decision for international investment:

1. Communications
2. Cross-cultural issues
3. Creativity
4. Ethics and values.

In addition, the Managing Members of AM Build established the following factors for examination and consideration when a decision is made whether to pursue a real estate investment opportunity in an international country:

a. Investigate broad-scope coverage of the specific international country and its political and economic systems.
b. Define the broad-scope coverage of the basic real estate concepts within the country. (For example, is there fee simple ownership? Who controls the ownership of real estate, i.e., is it public or private? Government controlled?)
c. Determine the regulatory bodies that exist in the real estate arena and how difficult it is to work within those regulatory bodies for necessary approvals, such as zoning, building permits, special use permits, etc. Is the government your partner in business?
d. Consider basic real estate issues, beginning with interest in land, legal description, use of contracts, deeds, evidence of title, etc.
e. Examine the current appraisal and valuation issues in the country.
f. What are the special interest areas in the country, i.e., water interests, mineral interests and sale of air rights?
g. Consider any special leasing issues, terms of leases, who negotiates the lease, whether there is broker involvement, and any other special issues.

h. What are the agency rules in the country?
i. Close examination of contractual issues relating to real estate.
j. What financing exists? Costs of financing? Economic considerations, such as inflation, must be examined.
k. What encumbrances exist? How are these encumbrances supported through a mortgage or a deed of trust or note?
l. Do formal property management companies exist? Are there asset management companies as well?
m. Does a brokerage system exist and what is the sophistication of that system? Is there a system comparable to the MLS or property databases?
n. What are areas of specialized brokerage that exist within the country? is there an existing system of specialized knowledge with corresponding designations, i.e., MAI, CPM, CCIM, CIPS, and others?
o. What special tax rules exist, i.e., property tax, income tax, value added tax (VAT) and similar taxes?
p. Consider other areas of the country's law that impact real estate, i.e., mobile unit s, mineral interests, water law, special certification, and approvals.
q. Consider other national, regional and local laws, including treaties or other agreements for international activities between or among countries and citizens in those countries. As a way of grouping this information, AM Build uses the following matrix as developed by the Burns School of Real Estate and Construction Management (Burns School) at the *Daniels College of Business,* UNIVERSITY OF DENVER, and posted on the Burns School Global Real Estate Web Site at http://burns.daniels.du.edu:
1. GEOGRAPHY
2. HISTORY/OVERVIEW
3. PEOPLE
4. GOVERNMENT
5. ECONOMY
6. CURRENCY
7. TRANSPORTATION
8. COMMUNICATIONS
9. REAL PROPERTY ISSUES (with detailed support)
10. REAL ESTATE TRENDS (with detailed support)
11. CULTURAL ISSUES.

I. The European Economy and Investment Climate

The following assessment of the European Capital Market is gleaned from the following publication, European Capital Markets Bullet in 2006 HI, Jones Lang LaSalle (August, 2006).

Transaction volumes set a new record at 95 billion euro for the first half of 2006. This reflected a 30% increase over the same period in 2005. Three-quarters of this volume was concentrated in the United Kingdom (UK), Germany and France. UK transactions dominated @ 35% (down from 45% in 2005), with Germany in 2nd place @ 20% (up from 13%), and France in

3rd place at 15% (doubling from 8%). The Netherlands, meanwhile, only accounted for 2% of transactions. There may be a window here as not as much capital is flowing into the country, representing lesser competition for AM Build.

The UK also has the largest share of cross-border transactions, with Germany and France right behind. In contrast, Ireland represented only 2% of European cross border transactions. This could lead to an overheated closed reinvestment market that AM Build may be able to exploit. Having said this, Ireland did have a relatively huge share of cross-border purchase volumes at 10%. This is a large amount for such a small country and perhaps represents that Irish investors may be realizing the over-extended nature of the market and are starting to diversify.

British investors lead in both selling and buying @ 27% for both, while the Germans are the largest net sellers (25% of sales, 7% of purchases). More than half of this record volume came in office with a quarter of the volume in retail. Hotel transactions rose from 3% to 12%, a key statistic for AM Build to track. Most of this volume (56%) occurred in the UK. British investors were the biggest sellers at 62% of sales with the largest volume from hotel operators at 45% and unlisted vehicles at 23%. Unlisted vehicles led the purchase volume at 38% with private investors at 11%, showing that the private investor sector is starting to become very active. There was continuing yield compression and convergence, and interest rates had little impact on volumes or yields in this first half. Indirect vehicles, either listed or unlisted, accounted for two-thirds of the purchase volume.

The following Market transparency discussion is summarized from the following publication, Real Estate Transparency Index 2006, Jones Lang LaSalle (2006). Market transparency, one of Friedman's key markers for investment in a country, continued to rise in the first half. In the 2006 EMEA Transparency Index, which tracks Investment Performance Indices, Market Fundamentals Data, Financial Reporting Regime, Regulatory and Legal Environment, Professional Standards and the Transaction Process, the UK (1.25), Netherlands (1.37) and France (1.40) were ranked 5th, 7th and 9th in the Index and part of the highest transparency level, while Ireland (1.85) at 15th and Norway (1.96) at 20th closely followed in the second tier at the high transparency level. The United States and Australia led the Index at 1.15. Countries that are part of the European Union (EU) have higher real estate market transparency. This highest and high transparency leads directly to the security and return of investment for outside foreign investors, as opposed to a disadvantage versus local investors. However, as mentioned earlier, with yields converging investors will need to seek less-transparent markets to exceed core returns. The investor must ask whether these higher returns in less-transparent markets will represent sufficient reward vs. the higher risk being taken.

The future outlook for the second half of 2006 includes the following assertions: Transaction volumes for the year should approach 200 billion euro.

Yields should hit the floor in many office and retail markets.

Investors will move up the risk curve by investing in high vacancy buildings and development situations in search of higher returns. AM Build will be well positioned through its design, construction and investment expertise to provide finished product for resale or partnership opportunities with equity capital.

Investors will move further into non-traditional property types. Again, AM Build will be well positioned with its experience in adaptive re-use.

Where yields are reaching new lows, thinner levels of bidding will occur in core markets. International investors will increasingly focus on continental Europe, with a large amount of the interest from Australian Listed Property Trusts. Increased volumes of capital will also flow in from the Middle East with an emphasis on trophy properties.

All of the above prognostications for the second half of 2006 set up well for AM Build's investment

strategy. AM Build will proceed to look for vacant properties or undeveloped land to re-position into assets that can be spun off to a variety of investment capital sources, domestic and international. Next, let's look at the specific niche market of hotel opportunities, specifically condo hotel.

A. Hotel/Condominium Hotel: Hotel Ownership Outlook

In a look at Hotel Ownership, the following publication is referenced: The Hotel Ownership, Pendulum in Motion 2006, by Jones Lang LaSalle Hotels.

Private equity firms will have an advantage in the hotel sector given that private equity firms will take advantage of cheap debt and higher levels of leverage, up to 95% vs. REITs that are restricted to 60% leverage. United States REITs, in particular, typically leverage up to 40%-45% because of investors' lower appetite for risk. REITs are also required to distribute up to 95% of taxable income to shareholders. This leaves little income flow to invest in growth or to pay for the capital expenditure requirements so common in hotels. Private equity firms, in comparison, can infuse capital for improvements, implement aggressive asset management and improve a hotel's trading performance to increase the enterprise value of the property.

AM Build plans on using this specific strategy to separate itself from institutional firms/capital and re-position its investment properties to attract this same institutional investment capital on the flip. This strategy should fit in very well with the large REIT's aversion to risk. In concurrence with this strategy, private equity firms are typically seeking an IRR of 20% or greater. Their holding period may be as short as 18 months, but usually falls within the 3-year to 5-year range. During this holding period they seek to achieve these returns through a combination of cash flows and capital growth. While an excellent market exists for hotel properties with private and public companies entering the arena of hotel ownership, high net worth individuals are also becoming increasing strong players.

If the hotel trading outlook becomes uncertain, a backup exit strategy is the following. AM Build could remove any hotel assets it acquires from the market and convert those assets to condominiums. This could include full conversion or merely arranging for the planning permission and business case for this conversion. AM Build can sell the idea along with the assets to developers for execution of the strategy. AM Build will need to look closely at this scenario, however, as this skill- set lies in-house, and too much money may be left on the table by divesting too early in the game. AM Build is working with several other companies that are excellent end-user targets for an asset the AM Build chooses to develop.

In Europe, hotel ownership and real estate are closely linked, while in the UK and Nordic countries the separation of operations and real estate is more common. This may lead to an opportunity for AM Build to provide either a long-term lease to an operator or a leaseback arrangement to further reduce risk.

In the current market, buyers are drawn to hotels due to lack of available project in traditional real estate classes and the availability of capital to invest. The low cost of debt at this point finds opportunistic investors looking to match hotel seller's pricing expect at ions. Private equity firms dominated the market in 2005 with 41% of the total transacted volume. Traditionally, investment in the European hotel market has been soured in Europe, but in 2005 the United States was responsible for approximately $6.8 billion, with $1.5 billion from Asia and approximately $1 billion from the Middle East. European ownership is becoming increasingly global.

The future of European hotel ownership looks to single asset deals keeping the market active. There should be increased activity from private equity firms and high new worth individuals, particularly Middle Eastern investors who are eager to diversity their portfolio outside of the Middle East and spread their risk. Given strong competition for hotel assets in the major cities, many investors will start to divert their focus to secondary cities. Due to a lack of competition, higher returns should be found in these locations.

Hotel Investment Outlook

Delving further into the Hotel investment sector and outlook, AM Build referenced the following publication: Hotel Investment Outlook 2006, Jones Lang LaSalle Hotels. The following European Markets are markets to watch in the hotel market cycle. In both Dublin and Paris, the RevPAR growth is slowing, with Dublin quickly approaching a falling RevPAR cycle. In the Amsterdam city centre, and the Scottish regions, the RevPAR is in a rising cycle. Both Amsterdam and Paris are rated a strong buy, while Dublin is on the watch list. Dublin's status is mainly due to its quickly slowing RevPAR.

Condominium Hotels

Due to the positive outlook for the hotel industry in general and mostly favorable outlook in AM Build's selected markets, the following publication was referenced to study the niche sector of condominium hotels: Focus on Condominium Hotels-Europe's Latest Hotel Phenomenon April 2006, Jones Lang LaSalle Hotels.

Approximately 16 billion euro of hotel real estate was transacted in 2005. The condo hotel investment market structure in Europe is highly fragmented, highly diverse and somewhat opaque. As mentioned earlier, a more diverse product structure exists within the hotel sector with leaseback or manage-back options. Within the condo hotel slice, product quality is rated midscale to luxury. The destination focus is either resort or within the city centre. The real estate interest consists of a single letting unit. The economic benefit includes income returns plus limited opportunity cost and benefit of use. Liquidity prospects are good and are underpinned by real estate values and income returns. There looks to be great growth potential in both the investor base and in city centre locations in particular.

Condo hotels offer ownership of a hotel room as a branded product. It is structured as a hotel/hospitality operating unit which is sold to individual equity investors, each of whom acquires a room or suite. The entire enterprise is managed as a hotel preparation under a single brand. A single operator-manager is appointed to supervise room lettings (rentals), payment of operating costs, implementation of maintenance and administration and distribution of profits. The individual unit owner has a predetermined number of weeks or days for their personal use. The units are rented out by the manger for the unused time with a profit-sharing arrangement between the owner and the management company. The individual unit owners can either occupy the unit full-time or participate in this rental pool. Unlike the United States, there are no securities issues with the rental pool arrangement. This financial investment vehicle can be made with or without income guarantees. Where foreign ownership is not allowed, a unit trust may be formed. In this arrangement investors buy shares in a fund and in return receive an ownership interest in land. Profits from assets are distributed to investors by dividend. As mentioned earlier, the product is in the mid-range to upscale-range with amenities and services to match. Flexible owner usage is allowed in daily periods.

Price point is usually greater than $200,000. Condo hotel is poised for success with increasing consumer sophistication and demand patterns changing. Timeshare and other similar concepts are past their prime.

In order to crease a successful condo hotel, the following factors should be in place:

1. The operation must be a cohesive and efficient hotel business, not an assembly of individual condo ownerships.
2. Maximize earnings potential through the design and configuration of the building and the public areas (i.e., front office, lobby, public toilet and restaurants).
3. Allow owners to have an allocation for predetermined days for personal use. Group these days in daily or weekly periods. In this way the hotel operator can manage the weekly demand cycle for the hotel successfully.
4. The individual condo owners can assign daily management to a branded hotel management company or a well-branded niche operator. The advantage of a branded management company is their reservation and global distribution systems that allow the individual to maximize revenue. Niche operators will usually be able to manage

small hotels and will agree to a long-term lease contract for fixed rent.

5. Create a transparent and fair remuneration structure for both the owners and the operator by either having rental paid from the operator to the owner or payment of management fee, based on revenue proportion, from owners to operator. The latter option includes a higher base fee for the operator and is paid out of total room revenues (profit sharing of room revenue-net operating profit). The operator usually retains all profit from food and beverage operations.

AM Build was particularly encouraged by the inclusion of a case study in the publication. In this case study, a luxury 20-room boutique hotel was purchased for 235,000 British pounds in Notting Hill, London (England). Investors were given usage rights for 52 days or less annually at a cost of 10 British *pounds* per night. The development company was experiencing a capital gain of 10%, and income returns of 6.5%. Secured debt is available for the individual owner. No restrictions were placed on resale. The investor/developer retains all freehold rights. The profit sharing agreement with the management company was structured to give 50% of the revenue from each guest room (including operating and management costs) to management. Investors are paid the remaining 50% with a fixed final deduction for FF&E reserve. The developer receives the initial capital payments during the pre-opening stage and spreads the risk of operations to the pool of investors.

Other international hotel brands believe that the European hotel landscape is ripe for condo hotel development, where the development itself includes self-contained hotel operations, fully self- contained condos or the development is included as part of a mixed use scheme. The inclusion of well-known hotel brands may increase overall sales value of adjacent residential components with available hotel services.

Within the condo hotel sector, AM Build has identified the following opportunities:

Design, entitlement, development and construction of condo hotel with leaseback structure with guaranteed returns. Management contract opportunity with upside potential based on historical hotel trading levels that remain profitable even in downturn cycles. With these two combined opportunities in mind, AM Build has set up the following investment model:

Investment Model Assumptions

75% room occupancy
100 British pound room rate
27,375 BP/year total room revenue
34,218 BP/year total revenue (includes 20% food and beverage and other) 17,108 BP/year net operating profit at 50%
13,687 BP/year owner's return (50% of room revenue)
230,000 BP owner's purchase price
6% owner's return on cost

3,421 BP/year manager-operator's return = 10% revenue.

As Operator, AM Build receives: Management fee of 50% of room revenues All other revenue from condo hotel guest Responsibility for all operating costs of operation = residual profit of 10% does not include development fee and entitlement fee for new product.

As Owner, AM Build receives

Net profit of 50% of room revenue = 6% ROI

The combination of these two profit centers equals the low end of AM Build's profit targets on an existing asset and will exceed the16% hurdle rate, with the inclusion of a development and entitlement fee on a newly developed and constructed condo hotel asset. While the returns for this niche market sector seem to meet the minimum profit hurdle rate, AM Build is also aware of the following advantages and disadvantages of the Condo Hotel sector:

Advantages for Owner

Lower price point for entry into hospitality sector.

Legal real estate interest that can be re-sold in total or individually Flexibility of usage and rental options to meet varying needs of different consumers Management is aligned to optimize operational performance and margins Ability to secure debt financing for acquisition Favorable tax and pension plan treatment in France and UK for individual condo owner.

Disadvantages to Owner

Establishing a fair and equitable procedure to reconcile multiple opinions on operations and divestment of the asset. Improving knowledge to understand the complexities of hotel management and operations Challenges of securing debt at optimal rates and LTVR Secondary market undeveloped Transparency and adequacy of paying for and managing capital expenditure or improvement of the asset Lack of cash to cover debt service or situation where hotel produces a loss, what is strategy?

Issues of legal, tax and exchange rates for investment outside investor's home country.

Advantages for Operator

Significantly higher fee potential and profit sharing as compared to a conventional hotel. Can generate revenue and can receive significant food and beverage and other revenues.

Disadvantages for Operator

Much of the potential upside of the transaction, including debt terms and financial return, depends on ability to sell units fast

With individual condo owners, managing multiple owners as guests. Challenge of exchange programs given the variations in unit prices.

Armed with favorable research regarding development and investment in the Condo Hotel sector, a workable condo hotel template that meets its minimum investment hurdle rate and an awareness of the advantages and disadvantages of acting as owner and operator of the condo hotel asset, AM Build was now ready to look at the investment climate and opportunities in each of the selected countries.

About the Author

J. Matthew McMullen, AIA, NCARB, LEED-AP, licensed architect, registered in Colorado, California and Texas. He is a licensed real estate broker associate in Colorado and holds a Masters of Science in Real Estate and Construction Management from the Burns School, *Daniels College of Business,* UNIVERSITY OF DENVER. He is currently completing a $20 million design build residence and developing a $150 million retail entertainment center in Boulder, Colorado.

■ Case Study 4

BOBCO Potential Expansion to the British Isles & Neighbors
  By Bob Behrens, CCIM
  Prepared by the BOBCO Board of Directors

Preface and Assumptions Set

BOBCO is a middle-sized, private owned company based in Denver, Colorado. The CEO and majority stockholder has led the company from a start-up company to its current status 15 years later. BOBCO is highly regarded in the Rocky Mountain region as a firm that has enjoyed success in the construction/development community and has made prudent investment transactions. BOBCO has evolved into a two Division Company with both Divisional Vice Presidents reporting directly to the CEO. Currently, BOBCO has resources to deploy in that several construction projects have been completed and the investment portfolio has been streamlined to only properties that are performing with strong cash flow. Others in the investment portfolio were sold the last 18 months as the peak of the investment market in the region. BOBCO is extremely liquid at this time. Business is booked on the horizon in the region where BOBCO thrives doing commercial construction/development. Because of the extremely liquid position from the sale of properties from the company investment portfolio, the Board of Directors has asked for this white paper on the possible expansion to the British Isles. Both Divisions of BOBCO are to be considered for this possible expansion into the global arena.

The CEO/Majority Stockholder is a *protégé* of a very successful entrepreneur. During his time with this industry legend, the CEO of BOBCO learned invaluable lessons. In particular, a lean and mean organizational structure has been maintained throughout the life of BOBCO thanks to this upbringing. Another hallmark of the heritage passed on to the CEO by his mentor was the insistence of rapid decision making. By keeping a decision-making process that resembles an entrepreneurial model rather than a more cumbersome, traditional, and slower moving Board of Directors model, BOBCO has enjoyed a competitive advantage similar to the mentor's firm. Arguably,

BOBCO is in an implementation mode months ahead of the competition that has a more cumbersome decision-making matrix. The CEO of BOBCO, like his mentor, truly believes in "Ready, Fire and Aim."

The countries being considered for expansion by BOBCO's Divisions are Belgium, France, Ireland, Netherlands, Norway and Scotland. For baseline comparison purposes, the United States will be used. Because of BOBCO's Western success, expansion elsewhere in the United States is another option to the company. For the purposes of this White Paper, the six countries will be narrowed to two. At that time, the "go" or "no-go" decision and Executive Summary will be prepared.

The White Paper is being prepared by a Vice President of BOBCO. The CEO trusts this officer and has delegated other visioning assignments to this member of the management team. The Vice President preparing this report for the Board has a marketing background, and is a competent and respected human resources manager. The officer has, in the past, been successful in gaining consensus in the Board Room and is willing to allow credit for success to be shared with colleagues. The CEO has indicated to this Vice President that if global expansion occurs, this individual would be promoted to the head of a new International Division for BOBCO. This Vice President earned his Masters in Real Estate from UNIVERSITY OF DENVER. As luck would have it, the Burns School, *Daniels College of Business,* UNIVERSITY OF DENVER, was offering an offshore trip to the countries in question that completed the tour in time for conclusion of this White Paper.

The Vice President joined the Delegation without hesitation and will state his findings from his first-hand travels in the decision-making portion of the White Paper.

Methodology for Initial Market Comparisons

General data will be compiled on all of the prospective countries. This information will be primarily retried from this Paper's Appendix. The Appendix is comprised of information gathered from the CIA World Factbook, the Burns School Global Real Estate Web site at the *Daniels College of Business,* UNIVERSITY OF DENVER at http://burns.daniels.du.edu, and Wikipedia (http://www.wikipedia.com). Other information gleaned from personal visits during this UNIVERSITY OF DENVER Delegation to the countries in this comparison will be interspersed as appropriate. Initial ranking of the prospective countries will be done using a matrix of common denominators. Of course, consideration of "deal killers" also will be analyzed as general data is gathered relating all of the prospective countries and wound into the decision making early on in the process.

Once general data is distilled, the initial group can be then reduced to two candidates. At this time, final criteria for specific risk/reward considerations in line with BOBCO's current hurdles adjusted for regional and country risk, along with congruence with BOBCO's Mission Statement, will be analyzed with specific global expansion opportunities in the remaining two countries. BOBCO currently ha a minimum return criteria that it will not deviate from under any circumstances. A minimum of 18% before-tax rate of return and 11% after tax is a sacred "go" or "no-go" hurdle. There will be a recommendation at the time of "go" or "no-go" for an appropriate hurdle for the global markets that BOBCO would consider entering.

Conclusion and Recommendations

The Vice President will have a fairly short report for the Board of Directors, as timing is a critical issue in moving into the global market place. Other than in Ireland, there was very limited commercial development/building occurring from what was observed on the Delegation's tour stops. The opportunities for the BOBCO Development/Construction Division witnessed on this tour with the Delegation were nil. Time could change this position. However, now this Division of BOBCO should seek additional business in the United States until other global opportunities with appropriate risk/reward, and volume of activity would give a new player a fair chance to gain a foothold. In the short run, BOBCO should spend some time and resources in exploring known opportunities in Mississippi and Louisiana rebuilding in the aftermath of Hurricane Katrina. What about Ireland? BOBCO would have had a great run if they would have entered this global marketplace 10 or 12 years ago with both Divisions. At a presentation at the Royal Surveyors office in Dublin, Royal Institution of Chartered Surveyors (RICS) (http://www.rics.org/) with the Delegation, two comments anchored the fact that BOBCO missed the market swing. Even the sophisticated and competent Royal Surveyors could not explain what was driving this market upwardly out of control. They accept this good fortune, but between the lines, unstated, they are concerned with no apparent economic factors driving this upward spiral of value.

The second comment was stated in a presentation by one of our hosts describing a graphic I have tried to duplicate below. An offhand comment by one of our hosts gives the clue to a market ready to implode because of out-of-control optimism and contracted cash flows diminishing for several years.

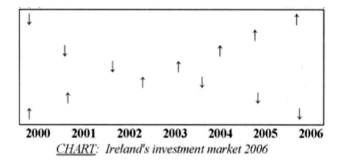

CHART: Ireland's investment market 2006

Investment Value due to appreciation/projected reversion values depicted by the LINES pointing UPWARD

Decreasing rental cash flows per square meter depicted by the LINES pointing DOWNWARD. This is a market headed for trouble!

The opportunity for BOBCO's Investment Division is two-fold. First of all, a member of the Investment Division or new International Division should be placed in Dublin and open an office. Relationships should be made and expertise offered subtlety regarding expertise in real estate-owned scenarios, workouts of non-performing loans and a source of ownership investment capital when revenues justify a price value once again. Timing is a key with a strategy like this one, but millions of dollars will be made after this market collapses and betrays many greater fools who are in title of a lot of property in Ireland now. Optimism is not enough to hold a market like this together. Cash flow is the one thing that will bring reality back. There is pain for a lot of investors in Ireland on the horizon, and BOBCO can help as well as get positioned to invest at the bottom of the next market swing.

Secondly, here is where the Netherlands may be of interest to BOBCO. In the meetings with the hosts in the Netherlands, their recovering market was referenced a number of times. Returns are currently in the 3.5% to 4% area. Investors from the Netherlands have been active in investing in North America in the past. BOBCO's Investment Division should seek to develop relationships with Dutch brokers in control of investors and/or pension fund money. BOBCO's spec buildings and investment holdings may be appropriate for Dutch investors. Additionally, funds are being put together by one of the hosts for an off-shore investment fund. BOBCO should contact suppliers and find out what product types they will be shopping for once the fund is fully funded. So, it appears that BOBCO can have a path into the global marketplace from what was learned on this Delegation tour. Not a strategy of the usual BOBCO pizzazz, but a workable strategy that is within budget, on target with long-range visioning/planning and allows for the engine of BOBCO, the Construction/Development Division, to stick to the knitting with the possible expansion to the South. Key result areas cannot be ignored. One small step for Globalization, but one giant step for BOBCO. Larger steps for BOBCO's Globalization efforts are on the very near horizon.

About the Author

Robert L. Behrens, CCIM, CRP, President of RE/MAX Commercial in Denver, Colorado, and was the 2004 President of the CCIM Institute.

Behrens was the founding Director of RE/MAX International's Commercial Investment Division, where he worked for more than 14 years before forming his own company, BEHRENS & ASSOCIATES. He rejoined RE/MAX in 2002 in his current position. He served as Treasurer of the Denver Metropolitan Commercial Association of REALTORS® in its inaugural year and has been active nationally with the National Association of REALTORS®. He has served on numerous committees of the CCIM Institute and was the Colorado/Wyoming CCIM Chapter President in 1995. Behrens received theRE/MAX Int ernat ional Dist inguished Service Award in 2005.

Behrens also is a Certified Relocation Professional, board member of the Finance Department at Metro State College in Denver, and board member of the West side Community

Builders group, which provides housing for low-income families. Behrens is a licensed aircraft pilot and an avid golfer.

LINEAR MEASURE: 7.92 inches = 1 link 12 inches = 1 foot
3 feet = 1 yard
25 links = 1 rod
100 links = 1 chain 16-1/2 feet = 1 rod 5-1/2 yards = 1 rod 40 rods = 1 furlong 8 furlongs = 1 mile 66 feet = 1 chain 80 chains = 1 mile 320 rods = 1 mile 8,000 links = 1 mile 5,280 feet = 1 mile 1,760 yards = 1 mile

SQUARE MEASURE:
144 sq. in. = 1 sq. foot
9 sq. feet = 1 sq. yard

30-1/4 sq. yards = 1 sq. rod 16 sq. rods = 1 sq. chain
1 sq.yard = 272-1/4 sq.ft.
1 sq.chain = 4,356 sq.ft.
10 sq. chains = 1 acre
160 sq. rods = 1 acre
4,840 sq. yards = 1 acre 43,560 sq.ft.= 1 acre
640 acres = 1 sq. mile
1 sq.mile = 1 section
36 sq. miles = 1 township
6 miles square = 1 township 1 sq. mile = 2.59 sq. kilometer
1 sq. meter = 10.76 sq. ft.

Appendix C

Unit Conversions

■ Table Of Land Measurement Metric System

Most of the world does its measuring in meters. The metric system in use today is called the International System of Units, IS for short, and it has been accepted as the measurement standard in nearly all countries of the world. The United States is moving toward the metric system. In the future, licensees may have to be conversant with the metric system in order to handle legal descriptions and land descriptions. The metric system progresses logically in units of 10. In the metric system, prefixes have the same meanings whether measuring length, volume, or mass. The most common prefixes are micro (millionth), milli (thousandth), centi (hundredth), deci (tenth), mega (1,000,000 times the base), kilo (1,000 times the base), hecto (100 times the base), and deka (10 times the base).

To convert between the units in the metric system, move the decimal point to the right or left. The basic dimension of the metric system is the meter, which equals approximately 3.3 feet. All dimensions of length can be expressed as variations of a meter: millimeter (mm), centimeter (cm), meter (m), or kilometer (km). Conversions between these measurements are simple decimal locations based on factors of 10. The basic metric unit of land measurement is the hectare (abbreviated as ha), a square with each side 100 meters long, covering an area of 10,000 square meters. A hectare is equivalent to 2.471 acres.

Myriameter	mym	10,000	6.2 miles
Kilometer	km	1,000	.62 miles
Hectometer	hm	100	109.36 yards
Decameter	dkm	10	32.81 feet
Decimeter	dm	1	3.94 inches
Centimeter	cm	.01	.39 inches
Millimeter	mm	.001	.04 inches

LENGTH: U.S. TO METRIC
1 inch = 25.4 millimeters (mm) 1 foot = 0.3 meters (m)
1 yard = 0.9 meters (m)
1 mile = 1.6 kilometers (km)
LENGTH: METRIC TO U.S.
1 millimeter (mm) = 0.04 inch 1 meter (m) = 0.28 feet
1 meter (m) = 1.09 yards
AREA: U.S. TO METRIC
1 sq.inch = 6.5 sq.centimeters (cm2) 1 sq.foot = 0.09 sq.meter (m2)
1 sq. yard = 0.08 sq. meter (m2)
1 acre = 0.4 hectare (ha)

1 sq.mile = 2.6 sq.kilometers (km2)
LENGTH: METRIC TO U.S.
1 sq. centimeter = 0.16 sq. inch 1 square meter = 10.76 sq. feet
1 square meter = 1.2 sq. yards 1 hectare = 2.471 acres
1 sq. kilometer = 0.39 sq. mile
LENGTH Unit Myriameter **Abbreviation** mym
Number of Meters
10,000
Approximate U.S. Equivalent
6.2 miles **Unit** Kilometer **Abbreviation** km
Number of Meters
1,000
Approximate U.S. Equivalent
.62 miles **Unit** Hectometer **Abbreviation** hm
Number of Meters
100
Approximate U.S. Equivalent
109.36 yards **Unit** Decameter **Abbreviation** dkm
Number of Meters
10
Approximate U.S. Equivalent
32.81 feet **Unit** Decimeter **Abbreviation** dm
Number of Meters
1
Approximate U.S. Equivalent
3.94 inches **Unit** Centimeter **Abbreviation** cm
Number of Meters
.01
Approximate U.S. Equivalent
.39 inches **Unit** Millimeter **Abbreviation** mm
Number of Meters
.001
Approximate U.S. Equivalent
.04 inches **LENGTH: AREA Unit**
Square Kilometer
Abbreviation
sq. km or km2
Number of Meters
1,000,000
Approximate U.S. Equivalent
.3861 square miles
Unit Hectare **Abbreviation**
ha
Number of Meters
10,000
Approximate U.S. Equivalent
2.471 acres
Unit Are **Abbreviation** a
Number of Meters
100
Approximate U.S. Equivalent
119.6 square yards
Unit Centiare **Abbreviation** ca
Number of Meters
1
Approximate U.S. Equivalent

10.76 square feet

Unit

Square Centimeter

Abbreviation

sq. cm or cm2

Number of Meters

.0001

Approximate U.S. Equivalent

.155 square inches

AREA:

The above charts can be used to convert different units of measurement between the English and Metric systems. These "Units *of Measurement and Conversion*" charts, in part, are reprinted with permission from the "Real Estate Manual," State of Colorado, Colorado Real Estate Commission (2002).

Appendix D

Decision-Making Criteria

■ Afghanistan

a. **Legal for Foreign Firm to Conduct Business?:** Yes
b. **Economic Stability/Instability:** Very unstable
c. **Currency Issues/Monetary Stability:** Newly founded/tied to dollar
d. **Safety/Risk to Individual:** Many rebel factions
e. **Difficulties in Ownership Interests:** Ownership rights are in a state of constant flux
f. **Accessibility for People & Goods:** Roads are damaged, and supplies only get through about 50% of the time
g. **Rate of Return:** Potential very high, but risk may offset potential gains
h. **Risk/Reward Consideration:** Very high risk with uncertain reward
i. **Other Factors:** Newly implemented government with many opposing groups

■ Argentina

a. **Legal for Foreign Firm to Conduct Business?:** Yes
b. **Economic Stability/Instability:** Somewhat unstable, with high susceptibility to fluctuations and recession
c. **Currency Issues/Monetary Stability:** Lacks stability
d. **Safety/Risk to Individual:** Safety risks are minimal, common-sense precautions recommended **e. Difficulties in Ownership Interests:** Rights protected under National Constitution. Disputes can be resolved in international court s
f. **Accessibility for People & Goods:**
g. **Rate of Return:** Potential very high, but risk may offset potential gains
h. Risk/Reward Consideration: Very high risk
i. **Other Factors:** Fiscal and legal reformation may be necessary in order to create more incentive for foreign investment

■ Australia

a. **Legal for Foreign Firm to Conduct Business?:** Yes
b. **Economic Stability/Instability:** Very stable
c. **Currency Issues/Monetary Stability:** Independent monetary policy to specifically target inflation
d. **Safety/Risk to Individual:** Minimal safety risk
e. **Difficulties in Ownership Interests:** Acquisition in excess of certain amounts may be subject to government scrutiny
f. **Accessibility for People & Goods:** Highly developed system commensurate with demographic pattern
g. **Rate of Return:** Stable
h. **Risk/Reward Consideration:** Low risk
i. **Other Factors:** Stable

■ Austria

a. **Legal for Foreign Firm to Conduct Business?:** Yes
b. **Economic Stability/Instability:** Very stable
c. **Currency Issues/Monetary Stability:** Stability with the Euro
d. **Safety/Risk to Individual:** Crime rate extremely low
e. **Difficulties in Ownership Interests:** Some barriers and governmental regulation; however, privatization is helping to reduce these obstacles
f. **Accessibility for People & Goods:** Highly developed system
g. **Rate of Return:** Stable
h. **Risk/Reward Consideration:** Low risk
i. **Other Factors:** Stable

■ Brazil

a. **Legal for Foreign Firm to Conduct Business?:** Yes
b. **Economic Stability/Instability:** Fairly stable, but many tariffs and barriers still exist
c. **Currency Issues/Monetary Stability:** Fairly stable;" now" stable
d. **Safety/Risk to Individual:** Concerns are milder in urban areas while along border countries; risk is slightly increased
e. **Difficulties in Ownership Interests:** Foreign ownership is allowed but subject to government approval
f. **Accessibility for People & Goods:** Rail and roads are insufficient and often in poor condition. Gas prices are very high.
g. **Rate of Return:** Some Concern
h. **Risk/Reward Consideration:**
i. **Other Factors:** Government is committed to stabilizing economy and negotiating for the Free Trade area of the Americas. Court systems lack of enforceability is a concern

■ Canada

a. **Legal for Foreign Firm to Conduct Business?:** Yes
b. **Economic Stability/Instability:** Very stable
c. **Currency Issues/Monetary Stability:** Stable
d. **Safety/Risk to Individual:** Some crime in urban areas, but violent crime is rare
e. **Difficulties in Ownership Interests:** Investments may be subjected to foreign review board; but few barriers exist
f. **Accessibility for People & Goods:** Highly developed system with the exception of remote areas in North
g. **Rate of Return:** Stable
h. **Risk/Reward Consideration:** Low risk
i. **Other Factors:**

Chile

a. **Legal for Foreign Firm to Conduct Business?:** Yes
b. **Economic Stability/Instability:** Fairly stable, experiencing highest growth in Latin America and avoiding economic crisis
c. **Currency Issues/Monetary Stability:** Stable
d. **Safety/Risk to Individual:** Some concern over terrorist activity in tri-border area, but no credible threats
e. **Difficulties in Ownership Interests:** No restrictions on rights of private ownership
f. **Accessibility for People & Goods:** Modern and reliable with continued improvement
g. **Rate of Return:** Stable
h. **Risk/Reward Consideration:** Low to medium risk
i. **Other Factors:** One of the more open Latin American markets

China

a. **Legal for Foreign Firm to Conduct Business?:** Yes
b. **Economic Stability/Instability:** Growth has been stable and exceeding government project ions despite global slowdown
c. **Currency Issues/Monetary Stability:** Fairly Stable
d. **Safety/Risk to Individual:** Safety risks and crime are low, common sense precautions recommended
e. **Difficulties in Ownership Interests:** Individuals do not own land; however, long-term lease agreements are available as the economy continues to open
f. **Accessibility for People & Goods:** Infrastructure investment continues to grow and improve current system
g. **Rate of Return:** Stable, but concern with growth rate
h. **Risk/Reward Consideration:** Low to medium risk
i. **Other Factors:** Needs Consistent and clear set of laws to reduce business risk

Costa Rica

a. **Legal for Foreign Firm to Conduct Business?:** Yes
b. **Economic Stability/Instability:** Continual growth, but mounting deficits provide for concern
c. **Currency Issues/Monetary Stability:** Fairly Stable
d. **Safety/Risk to Individual:** Crime is of some concern, particularly for foreigners in popular tourist locations
e. **Difficulties in Ownership Interests:** Only a few sectors are regulated or disallowed for investment. Ownership rights are protected, but the system results in many discrepancies
f. **Accessibility for People & Goods:** Lack of recent investment has resulted in insufficient infrastructure
g. **Rate of Return:** Stable
h. **Risk/Reward Consideration:** Medium risk

i. **Other Factors:** Well-educated and productive work force, favorable tax and duties regime in Free Trade Zones, and central location makes investment attractive

Czech Republic

a. **Legal for Foreign Firm to Conduct Business?:** Yes
b. **Economic Stability/Instability:** Continue invested and consumer demand have helped growth, but lack of foreign demand has been a hindrance
c. **Currency Issues/Monetary Stability:** Current deficit issues prevent conversion to the Euro until later in the decade, but currency fairly stable
d. **Safety/Risk to Individual:** Civil disorder is rare, and crime is fairly low
e. **Difficulties in Ownership Interests:** Existing legislation protects property rights. Individuals may not hold land, but registered companies in the country may acquire property
f. **Accessibility for People & Goods:** Below European standards, but current investment is creating improvement
g. **Rate of Return:** Stable
h. **Risk/Reward Consideration:** Low to medium risk
i. **Other Factors:** Rising costs of labor and integration into EU have begun economic focus away from manufacturing

Denmark

a. **Legal for Foreign Firm to Conduct Business?:** Yes
b. **Economic Stability/Instability:** Very unstable
c. **Currency Issues/Monetary Stability:** Currency remains stable in relation to the Euro
d. **Safety/Risk to Individual:** Minimal safety risk and low crime rate
e. **Difficulties in Ownership Interests:** Foreign ownership is allowed with a few exceptions
f. **Accessibility for People & Goods:** One of the highest-rated infrastructures in the world. Highly efficient
g. **Rate of Return:** Stable
h. **Risk/Reward Consideration:** Low risk
i. **Other Factors:** Stable

Finland

a. **Legal for Foreign Firm to Conduct Business?:** Yes
b. **Economic Stability/Instability:** Has recovered well from early 90's recession. Still has experienced some quarterly volatility
c. **Currency Issues/Monetary Stability:** Stable
d. **Safety/Risk to Individual:** Minimal safety risk and low crime rate
e. **Difficulties in Ownership Interests:** Foreign participation is relatively unrestricted

f. **Accessibility for People & Goods:** Highly developed and on same rail configuration as Russia, providing for easy access to the neighboring country
g. **Rate of Return:** Stable
h. **Risk/Reward Consideration:** Low to medium risk
i. **Other Factors:** Only EU country bordering Russia

■ France

a. **Legal for Foreign Firm to Conduct Business?:** Yes
b. **Economic Stability/Instability:** Moderate growth and inflation projected with a heavy dependence on global economic recovery
c. **Currency Issues/Monetary Stability:** Stable
d. **Safety/Risk to Individual:** Relatively low crime rate and few incidences of violent crime
e. **Difficulties in Ownership Interests:** Government maintains selected legal monopolies that create some agitation among the private sector. Foreign investment is treated equally with local
f. **Accessibility for People & Goods:** Advanced technology and substantial investment make infrastructure among the world elite
g. **Rate of Return:** Stable
h. **Risk/Reward Consideration:** Low risk
i. **Other Factors:** Stable

■ Germany

a. **Legal for Foreign Firm to Conduct Business?:** Yes
b. **Economic Stability/Instability:** Country has enjoyed economic stability, but slow growth, high unemployment, and mounting debt are causes for concern
c. **Currency Issues/Monetary Stability:** Stable
d. **Safety/Risk to Individual:** Minimal safety risk and low crime rate
e. **Difficulties in Ownership Interests:** Almost no discrimination toward foreigners investing in property
f. **Accessibility for People & Goods:** Modern and reliable, with costs slightly above average
g. **Rate of Return:** Stable
h. **Risk/Reward Consideration:** Low to medium risk
i. **Other Factors:** Stable

■ Hungary

a. **Legal for Foreign Firm to Conduct Business?:** Yes
b. **Economic Stability/Instability:** Trade openness, strong foreign investment, and export- driven growth have resulted in tremendous growth for the country; however, the changing global economy and changing policy could alter this pattern

c. **Currency Issues/Monetary Stability:** Stable
d. **Safety/Risk to Individual:** Street crime rate has been increasing, but violent crime is still very low
e. **Difficulties in Ownership Interests:** Law states that foreign entities may only hold property required for its economic activities, however loose interpretation of the rule has allowed foreigners to engage in property development
f. **Accessibility for People & Goods:** Relatively well developed, with significant government backing for future improvements. Less populated regions still lack adequate infrastructure
g. **Rate of Return:** Stable
h. **Risk/Reward Consideration:** Low to medium risk
i. **Other Factors:** Hungary will become a member of the EU in May 2004.Central location provides easy access to nearly all European markets

■ India

a. **Legal for Foreign Firm to Conduct Business?:** Yes
b. **Economic Stability/Instability:** Country has shown continued growth and tremendous potential and a near immunity to global slowdowns
c. **Currency Issues/Monetary Stability:** Stable
d. **Safety/Risk to Individual:** Some concern over terrorist activity in certain regions, but no reliable pattern has been found
e. **Difficulties in Ownership Interests:** Foreign investment remains relatively controlled with equity limits and governmental approval required for many types of investments
f. **Accessibility for People & Goods:** Current transportation infrastructure hampers growth significantly; privatization efforts have begun to have a positive impact
g. **Rate of Return:** Stable
h. **Risk/Reward Consideration:** Medium to high risk, with potential for large reward
i. **Other Factors:** Corruption is of major concern and is prevalent in many industries

■ Indonesia

a. **Legal for Foreign Firm to Conduct Business?:** Yes
b. **Economic Stability/Instability:** Not yet fully recovered from economic recession; fiscal improvement have not translated into economic growth
c. **Currency Issues/Monetary Stability:** Conservative fiscal and monetary policies have resulted in lower interest rates and a strengthening of the rupiah; but political issues exist.
d. **Safety/Risk to Individual:** Significant concern over terrorist activity; crime rates are very high
e. **Difficulties in Ownership Interests:** Foreigners do not have freehold rights in land. Long- term leases with the government or local parties are used to provide land use

f. **Accessibility for People & Goods:** Infrastructure is in need of significant improvement, particularly in automotive transportation. Congestion and pollution are major fact ors being addressed by the government

g. **Rate of Return:** Concern with political issues

h. **Risk/Reward Consideration:** High risk

i. **Other Factors:** Structural reforms are needed to improve the legal system, reduce corruption, and encourage investors to return.

■ Ireland (U.K.)

a. **Legal for Foreign Firm to Conduct Business?:** Yes

b. **Economic Stability/Instability:** Irish economy has experienced recent slowdown. Despite this fact; the economy has appeared fairly resilient to global downturns

c. **Currency Issues/Monetary Stability:** Stable

d. **Safety/Risk to Individual:** Violent crime rate has been low but is rising; the frequency of petty theft is quite high

e. **Difficulties in Ownership Interests:** Secured interests in property are enforced by a reliable legal system. This system allows for virtually equal access by foreign investors

f. **Accessibility for People & Goods:** Development of Ireland's inadequate physical infrastructure must be accelerated and sustained if robust growth levels are to be achieved in the medium and long- term

g. **Rate of Return:** Stable

h. **Risk/Reward Consideration:** Low to medium risk

i. **Other Factors:** Majority of growth has resulted from foreign-owned enterprises; domestic demand appears to be softening

■ Israel

a. **Legal for Foreign Firm to Conduct Business?:** Yes

b. **Economic Stability/Instability:** In the midst of an economic downturn resulting in a significant drop in standard of living

c. **Currency Issues/Monetary Stability:** Stable

d. **Safety/Risk to Individual:** Heavy security and questioning occurs for entry and exit of the country. There have been incidents of terrorism; moderate crime rate

e. **Difficulties in Ownership Interests:** Secured interests in property are recognized and enforced by the Israeli judicial system. A reliable system of recording exist s, such as security interests.

f. **Accessibility for People & Goods:** Numerous large scale infrastructure projects are underway

g. **Rate of Return:** Stable

h. **Risk/Reward Consideration:** Medium risk

i. **Other Factors:** Stable but concern with Mideast conflict

■ Italy

a. **Legal for Foreign Firm to Conduct Business?:** Yes

b. **Economic Stability/Instability:** Structural impediments in the economy seem to discourage investment and job creation, leading to slow economic growth

c. **Currency Issues/Monetary Stability:** Stable

d. **Safety/Risk to Individual:** Violent crime rate is low, with petty crimes being a significant problem

e. **Difficulties in Ownership Interests:** Laws governing physical property are adequate and enforced. The legal system protects and facilitates acquisitions and disposition of all property right s, such as land, buildings and mort gages

f. **Accessibility for People & Goods:** Government has focused on a ten-year infrastructure improvement plan designed to reduce bureaucratic obstacles

g. **Rate of Return:** Stable

h. **Risk/Reward Consideration:** Low to medium risk

i. **Other Factors:**

■ Japan

a. **Legal for Foreign Firm to Conduct Business?:** Yes

b. **Economic Stability/Instability:** The country has experience little or no growth in recent years, but significant corporate and structural reform have begun to combat these issues

c. **Currency Issues/Monetary Stability:** Stable

d. **Safety/Risk to Individual:** Petty and violent crime rates are very low

e. **Difficulties in Ownership Interests:** There are no significant barriers to foreign investment, and the country has liberalized most restrictions regarding specific industry sectors

f. **Accessibility for People & Goods:** Fully developed physical infrastructure with continued improvements being planned

g. **Rate of Return:** Stable

h. **Risk/Reward Consideration:** Low to medium risk

i. **Other Factors:** Contrast between serious economic situations and tremendous opportunity for investment abound

■ Jordan

a. **Legal for Foreign Firm to Conduct Business?:** Yes

b. **Economic Stability/Instability:** Economy has continued to grow in recent years despite global economic slowdown

c. **Currency Issues/Monetary Stability:** Fairly stable

d. **Safety/Risk to Individual:** Crime rates are generally very low, with some concern in urban areas. Terrorism and violence in the region is of significant concern

e. **Difficulties in Ownership Interests:** Property acquisition is allowed and enforced through reliable legal processes.

There are restrictions on percentages of foreign investment in certain industries

f. **Accessibility for People & Goods:** Road conditions are good but underdeveloped by Western standards
g. **Rate of Return:** Stable
h. **Risk/Reward Consideration:** Medium risk
i. **Other Factors:**

Kenya

a. **Legal for Foreign Firm to Conduct Business?:** Yes
b. **Economic Stability/Instability:** Growth has been far below potential, with decreasing foreign investment
c. **Currency Issues/Monetary Stability:** Concerns in Africa
d. **Safety/Risk to Individual:** Threat of indiscriminant terrorist activity is high, along with a high crime rate
e. **Difficulties in Ownership Interests:** Obtaining title is often a long and corrupt process. Large acquisitions may require governmental approval
f. **Accessibility for People & Goods:** Best in Africa but has deteriorated due to lack of regular maintenance and repair
g. **Rate of Return:** Concerns in Africa
h. **Risk/Reward Consideration:** High
i. **Other Factors:** Government has attempted reforms to stabilize the economy and create growth. Corruption is still an issue

Korea (South)

a. **Legal for Foreign Firm to Conduct Business?:** Yes
b. **Economic Stability/Instability:** Economic growth has slowed, with decreasing consumer demand and continued slumping of local and foreign investment
c. **Currency Issues/Monetary Stability:** Stable
d. **Safety/Risk to Individual:** Safety risks and crime are low; common sense precautions are recommended
e. **Difficulties in Ownership Interests:** Recent legislation has granted equal rights to foreigners in the acquisition of property
f. **Accessibility for People & Goods:** Transportation is in need of expansion. Government has allocated significant funds toward this end over the next 15 years
g. **Rate of Return:** Stable
h. **Risk/Reward Consideration:** Medium
i. **Other Factors:** Excellent market for goods and services across almost every sector

Mexico

a. **Legal for Foreign Firm to Conduct Business?:** Yes
b. **Economic Stability/Instability:** Seasonally adjusted economic indicators have shown the country moving into economic recovery. However, there is still a great deal of uncertainty and high dependence on U.S. economic recovery
c. **Currency Issues/Monetary Stability:** Foreign direct investment has aided the peso in recent years. Invest or confidence is still fairly high; stable
d. **Safety/Risk to Individual:** Crime rates in the country are very high and often violent
e. **Difficulties in Ownership Interests:** Ownership is fairly open and encouraged by the government. Significant restrictions apply, especially toward the petroleum industry.
f. **Accessibility for People & Goods:** Infrastructure has improved significantly in recent years but still lags behind actual needs in many regions of the country
g. **Rate of Return:** Stable
h. **Risk/Reward Consideration:** Low to medium risk
i. **Other Factors:** Foreign direct investment is among the highest for developing countries in the world

Netherlands

a. **Legal for Foreign Firm to Conduct Business?:** Yes
b. **Economic Stability/Instability:** Global slow-down has had tremendous impact on the economy, dropping growth well below previous trends. Despite global recovery project ions, outlook for the Dutch economy is not as strong
c. **Currency Issues/Monetary Stability:** Stable
d. **Safety/Risk to Individual:** Visitors to large urban centers may be at risk for petty theft, but crime rates as a whole are very low
e. **Difficulties in Ownership Interests:** Trade and investment policies are among the most open in the world. Air transport is one of the few sectors with restrictions and regulations regarding foreign investment
f. **Accessibility for People & Goods:** Access is good through most areas of the country. Current governmental plans for improvements will continue to strengthen these systems
g. **Rate of Return:** Stable
h. **Risk/Reward Consideration:** Low to medium risk
i. **Other Factors:**

Panama

a. **Legal for Foreign Firm to Conduct Business?:** Yes
b. **Economic Stability/Instability:** Reduced trade and investment, due to the regional and worldwide economic slowdown as well as contraction of domestic demand that have had negative impacts. However, growth in tourism, telecommunications, and maritime sectors indicates potential growth and recovery in the near future.

c. **Currency Issues/Monetary Stability:** Dollar-based economy offers low inflation and little foreign exchange risk; stable

d. **Safety/Risk to Individual:** Crime in urban areas is moderate but growing. Certain regions of the country should be avoided due to drug trafficking and terrorist activity

e. **Difficulties in Ownership Interests:** Unique areas of Panamanian law make local legal counsel essential. Expansion and modernization of property registry is underway

f. **Accessibility for People & Goods:** Infrastructure is fairly well developed. Roads are well maintained. Improvements are planned for further expansion and capacity

g. **Rate of Return:** Stable

h. **Risk/Reward Consideration:** Low to medium risk

i. **Other Factors:** Stable

■ Puerto Rico

a. **Legal for Foreign Firm to Conduct Business?:** Yes

b. **Economic Stability/Instability:** The country has experienced reduced growth in conjunction with world economic slowdowns. Job loss to foreign countries has been significant, especially due to relocation U.S. manufacturers. The country is highly dependent upon U.S. success and investment

c. **Currency Issues/Monetary Stability:** Stable

d. **Safety/Risk to Individual:** Most violent crimes are confined to poor urban regions; however, petty theft occurs in many tourist locations

e. **Difficulties in Ownership Interests:**

f. **Accessibility for People & Goods:** Transportation is improving due to better fiscal management and heightened demand for such improvements

g. **Rate of Return:** Stable

h. **Risk/Reward Consideration:**

i. **Other Factors:** Benefits from US federal funds, offers tariff-free access to the US market for manufacturers, and has a bi-lingual population.

■ Russia

a. **Legal for Foreign Firm to Conduct Business?:** Yes

b. **Economic Stability/Instability:** The country is working toward dramatic economic growth in the next ten years. Consistent grow has been achieved over the last five years, but certain industry sectors must improve to meet desired goals

c. **Currency Issues/Monetary Stability:** Stable

d. **Safety/Risk to Individual:** There are some risks of crime and security in Russia. Certain regions are particularly dangerous. Common-sense precaution is highly recommended

e. **Difficulties in Ownership Interests:** Legislative gaps and ambiguities impede the general exercise of the rights to own, inherit, lease, mort gage, and sell real property

f. **Accessibility for People & Goods:** Infrastructure has suffered significantly due to neglect over the last decade. Recent plans have been developed to address these problems. Economic success has turned some of these plans into reality

g. **Rate of Return:** Previous underfunding and significant potential for growth could produce high rewards; stable

h. **Risk/Reward Consideration:** Medium risk

i. **Other Factors:** Tremendous economic potential, but has received minimal direct foreign investment in recent years

■ Saudi Arabia

a. **Legal for Foreign Firm to Conduct Business?:** Yes

b. **Economic Stability/Instability:** The economy is highly dependent upon the export of petroleum products and their pricing. Country is also significantly intertwined with the U.S. Country has shown continual growth over recent years

c. **Currency Issues/Monetary Stability:** Stable, but Mideast tension

d. **Safety/Risk to Individual:** Terrorist activity has increased lately. Crime is relatively low, but persons not observing local customs could be subject to harassment and violence

e. **Difficulties in Ownership Interests:** The Saudi legal system protects and facilitates acquisition and disposition of private property, consistent with Islamic practice respecting private property. Non-Saudi corporate entities will be allowed to purchase real estate in Saudi Arabia according to the new foreign investment code, although it is unclear how this policy is being implemented

f. **Accessibility for People & Goods:** Solid distribution network exists. Long distance between major population centers encourages air travel rather than over ground transportation

g. **Rate of Return:** Stable, but political concerns

h. **Risk/Reward Consideration:** Low to medium risk

i. **Other Factors:** Concerns with Mideast crises, corruption, etc.

■ Singapore

a. **Legal for Foreign Firm to Conduct Business?:** Yes

b. **Economic Stability/Instability:** The country is in the midst of recovery from recession. Outlook is very strong due to open-trade economic policies which have helped to compensate for land labor and resource constraints

c. **Currency Issues/Monetary Stability:** Stable

d. **Safety/Risk to Individual:** Crime rates are very low, with occasional occurrences of petty theft in tourist areas

e. **Difficulties in Ownership Interests:** Under the Residential Property Act, foreigners may purchase freehold condominiums but are not permitted to own landed homes (houses) and apartments in buildings of fewer than six stories, unless approval is first obtained from the Minister of Law. There are no restrictions on commercial and industrial property

f. **Accessibility for People & Goods:** Transportation is fairly strong, with the country boasting one of the largest and most efficient ports in the world

g. **Rate of Return:** Stable

h. **Risk/Reward Consideration:** Low to medium risk

i. **Other Factors:** Gateway to the Asian region. Recovery of key markets relative to Singaporean exports is essential to economic recovery

■ South Africa

a. **Legal for Foreign Firm to Conduct Business?:** Yes

b. **Economic Stability/Instability:** Growth has outpaced world averages in recent years, and structural reform have created booms in the service and manufacturing industries

c. **Currency Issues/Monetary Stability:** Concerns in Africa

d. **Safety/Risk to Individual:** There are some risks of crime around tourist areas. Petty theft can be common. More violent acts do occur occasionally so general caution is recommended

e. **Difficulties in Ownership Interests:** Volatile

f. **Accessibility for People & Goods:** Most advanced transportation network on the continent and among the best with regard to developing countries. Recent budgetary cuts have put strain upon the existing roadway network

g. **Rate of Return:** Concern

h. **Risk/Reward Consideration:** Higher risk

i. **Other Factors:** Many socio-economic challenges along with lack of job creation, high unemployment, labor market rigidities, and slow rates of foreign direct investment; volatile

■ Spain

a. **Legal for Foreign Firm to Conduct Business?:** Yes

b. **Economic Stability/Instability:** Spain remains as one of the fastest-growing members of the EU. The country has placed recent emphasis toward a balanced budget and labor reforms to reduce a high unemployment rate

c. **Currency Issues/Monetary Stability:** Currency remains stable in relation to the Euro

d. **Safety/Risk to Individual:** Spain has a moderate crime rate with relatively few incidences of violent crime

e. **Difficulties in Ownership Interests:** Spanish law permits foreign investment of up to 100 percent of equity, and capital movements have been completely liberalized. Property protection is effective in Spain, although the system is slow.

The Spanish legal system fully recognizes property rights and facilitates acquisition and disposition.

f. **Accessibility for People & Goods:** Upgrades in infrastructure are necessary to help develop and modernize Spain, particularly in rural regions, in relation to the rest of the EU. Future developments will focus on the continued improvement of the highway system, modernization of airports, railroads and ports

g. **Rate of Return:** Stable

h. **Risk/Reward Consideration:**

i. **Other Factors:**

■ Sweden

a. **Legal for Foreign Firm to Conduct Business?:** Yes

b. **Economic Stability/Instability:** The country is expecting slow growth rates over the next few years and, thus, a modest economic recovery. Inflation still remains low and stable

c. **Currency Issues/Monetary Stability:** Swedish currency has risen against the US dollar. Exporters to Sweden have reduced expenses, and Swedish citizens enjoyed increased purchasing power

d. **Safety/Risk to Individual:** Minimal safety risk and low crime rate

e. **Difficulties in Ownership Interests:** Foreign investment has grown significantly over the last decade due to structural changes. Swedish law adequately protects property rights.

f. **Accessibility for People & Goods:** Fully developed physical infrastructure with continued improvements still being planned

g. **Rate of Return:** Stable

h. **Risk/Reward Consideration:** Low to medium risk

i. **Other Factors:**

■ United Kingdom

a. **Legal for Foreign Firm to Conduct Business?:** Yes

b. **Economic Stability/Instability:** Growth has slowed in conjunction with global slowdowns. This is expected to improve in the coming years. Current economic aims include reform of the National Health Service, education reform, trade liberalization and productivity improvement.

c. **Currency Issues/Monetary Stability:** The pound is very stable, and the current government is considering adoption of the Euro

d. **Safety/Risk to Individual:** Safety risks and crime are low, common sense precautions recommended

e. **Difficulties in Ownership Interests:** There are only restrictions on foreign ownership in a few industry segments. Generally foreign and local investment is treated on an equal basis

f. **Accessibility for People & Goods:** Systems are adequate

g. **Rate of Return:** Stable

h. **Risk/Reward Consideration:** Low risk

i. **Other Factors:** The UK government's economic policies generally seek to sustain job creation. Specific measures have included tax reform; privatization of state-owned industries and utilities; deregulation of financial services, telecommunications and transportation; and labor law reforms

■ United States

a. **Legal for Foreign Firm to Conduct Business?:** Yes

b. **Economic Stability/Instability:** The economy has experienced slowdowns in conjunction with global conditions. The economy appears ready for recovery and has shown signs of growth in recent quarters

c. **Currency Issues/Monetary Stability:** The US dollar has continued to slide against other currencies, particularly the Euro

d. **Safety/Risk to Individual:** Crime rates are moderate. Recent terrorist activities have created additional concern around major cities and landmarks

e. **Difficulties in Ownership Interests:** Foreign ownership is relatively unrestricted. The legal system treats foreign and native investors on an equal basis

f. **Accessibility for People & Goods:** Transportation systems are highly efficient and well maintained

g. **Rate of Return:** Stable

h. **Risk/Reward Consideration:** Low risk

i. **Other Factors:**

■ Venezuela

a. **Legal for Foreign Firm to Conduct Business?:** Yes

b. **Economic Stability/Instability:** The Venezuelan economy contracted significantly over the past year. A dramatic reduction has occurred in foreign direct investment as a result of economic and political uncertainty.

c. **Currency Issues/Monetary Stability:** Some concern

d. **Safety/Risk to Individual:** Definite safety concerns along the Colombian border. Petty theft and resulting violence have known to occur in tourist areas

e. **Difficulties in Ownership Interests:** Foreign investors may pursue property claims through Venezuela's legal system. There are problems of lengthy procedures, uneven judgments and allegations of corruption

f. **Accessibility for People & Goods:** Fiscal restraints have impeded the infrastructure improvement process.

g. **Rate of Return:** Some concern

h. **Risk/Reward Consideration:** High risk

i. **Other Factors:** The country contains large untapped resources of natural gas.
   ORGANIZATIONS:

Appendix E

Internet Resources

AfDB: The African Development Bank (ADB) is a development finance institution engaged in the task of mobilizing resources towards the economic and social progress of its Regional Member Countries (RMCs). http://www.afdb.org.

APEC: The Asia-Pacific Economic Cooperation (APEC) forum is the primary international organization for the promoting open trade and economic cooperation among 21 member economies around the Pacific Rim.http://www.apec.org.

AsDB: The Asian Development Bank (ADB) is a multilateral development finance institution dedicated to reducing poverty in Asia and the Pacific.

Australia Group: The Australia Group is an informal group of countries that are committed to combating the proliferation of chemical and biological weapons. The countries participating in the Australia Group are suppliers and/or trans-shippers of chemicals, biological agents and/or production equipment which could be used in chemical and/or biological weapons programs. http://www.aust ralia-group.net.

BIS: The BIS is an international organization that fosters cooperation among central banks and other agencies in pursuit of monetary and financial stability. http://www.bis.org.
Burns School: Burns School of Real Estate and Construction Management, *Daniels College of Business*, UNIVERSITY OF DENVER. Burns School Global Real Estate Web sit e: http://burns.daniels.du.edu.

EBRD: The European Bank for Reconstruction and Development (EBRD) uses the tools of investment to help build market economies and democracies in 27 countries from central Europe to central Asia. http://www.ebrd.com.

ESCAP: The regional arm of the United Nations Secretariat for the Asian and Pacific region is the Economic and Social Commission for Asia and the Pacific (ESCAP). It promotes economic and social development through regional and sub regional cooperation and integration.http://www.unescap.org.

EU: The European Union (EU) is a family of democratic European countries, committed to working together for peace and prosperity. It is not a state intended to replace existing states. Its Member States have set up common institutions to which they delegate some of their sovereignty so that decisions of specific matters of joint interest can be made democratically at a European level. http://europa.eu.int.

Euro: The euro is the currency of 12 European Union (EU) countries: **Belgium, Germany, Greece, Spain, France, Ireland, Italy, Luxembourg, the Netherlands, Austria, Portugal,** and **Finland. Euro** banknotes and coins have been in circulation since January 1, 2002. http://europa.eu.int /euro.

FAO: The Food and Agriculture Organization (FAO) of the United Nations was founded in 1945 with a mandate to raise levels of nutrition and standards of living, to improve agricultural productivity, and to better the condition of rural populations. http://www.fao.org.

G-77: As the largest Third World coalition in the United Nations, the Group of 77 (G-77) provides the means for the developing world to articulate and promote its collective economic interests and enhance its joint negotiating capacity on all major international economic issues in the United Nations system, and promote economic and technical cooperation among developing countries.http://www.g77.org.

IAEA: The International Atomic Energy Agency (IAEA) serves as the global focal point for nuclear cooperation. IAEA assists its Member States, in the context of social and economic goals, in planning for and using nuclear science and technology for various peaceful purposes, including the generation of electricity, and it facilitates the transfer of such technology and knowledge in a sustainable manner to developing Member States. http://www.iaea.or.at.

IBRD: An institution of the World Bank Group, the International Bank for Reconstruction and Development (IBRD) provides important support for poverty reduction by providing its middle- income client countries access to capital in larger volumes, on good terms, with longer maturities, and in a more sustainable manner than the market provides. http://www.worldbank.org.

ICAO: The International Civil Aviation Organization (ICAO) was established to develop the principles and techniques of international air navigation and to foster the planning and development of international air transport in order to: encourage the development of airways, airports, and air navigation facilities for international civil aviation; meet the needs of the world wide population for safe, efficient, and economical air transport; promote flight safety throughout international air navigation; and promote the development of all aspects of international civil aeronautics. http://www.icao.int .

ICC: The International Commerce Commission (ICC) promotes an open international trade and investment system and the market economy.

ICFTU: The International Confederation of Free Trade Unions (ICFTU) organizes and directs campaigns on issues such as: the respect and defense of trade union and workers' right s; the eradication of forced and child labor; the promotion of equal rights for working women; the environment; education programs for trade unionists all over the world; encouraging the organization of young workers; sends missions to investigate the trade union situation in many countries.http://www.icftu.org.

ICJ: The International Court of Justice (ICJ) is the principal judicial organ of the United Nations (UN). Its seat is at the Peace Palace in the Hague (The Netherlands).It began work in 1946.http://www.icj-cij.org.

ICRM: The International Red Cross and Red Crescent Movement (ICRM) promotes worldwide humanitarian aid through the International Committee of the Red Cross (ICRC) in wartime, and International Federation of Red Cross and Red Crescent Societies (IFRCS; formerly League of Red Cross and Red Crescent Societies or LORCS) in peacetime.http://www.icrc.org.

IDA: The International Development Association (IDA) seeks to accelerate broad-based growth through sound macroeconomic and sect oral policies, especially for rural and private sector development; to invest in people through strong support for the social sectors, including gender mainstreaming and efforts to counter the challenge and social impact of communicable diseases, especially HIV/AIDS; to build capacity for improving governance–including in public expenditure management–and combating corruption; to protect the environment for sustainable development; to foster recovery in post-conflict countries; and to promote trade and regional integration. http://www.worldbank.org.

IEA: The International Energy Agency (IEA) promotes cooperation on energy matters, especially emergency oil sharing and relations between oil consumers and oil producers; established by the OECD.http://www.iea.org.

IFAD: The International Fund for Agricultural Development (IFAD) was created to mobilize resources on concessional terms for *programmes* that alleviate rural poverty and improve nutrition. The Fund has a very specific mandate: to combat hunger and rural poverty in developing countries. http://www.ifad.org.

IFC: The International Finance Corporation (IFC) supports private enterprise in international economic development andIBRDaffiliates.http://www.ifrc.org.

IFRCS: The International Federation of Red Cross and Red Crescent Societies (IFRCS) exists to organize, coordinate, and direct international relief actions; to promote humanitarian activities; to represent and encourage the development of National Societies; to bring help to victims of armed conflicts, refugees, and displaced people; and to reduce the vulnerability of people through development programs. http://www.ifrc.org.

IHO: The International Hydrographic Organization (IHO) is an intergovernmental consultative and technical organization that was established to support the safety in navigation and the protection of the marine environment.http://www.iho.shom.fr.

ILO: The International Labor Organization (ILO) deals with world labor issues. http://www.ilo.org.

IMF: The International Monetary Fund (IMF) promotes world monetary stability and economic development.http://www.imf.org.

IMO: The International Maritime Organization (IMO) deals with international maritime affairs.http://www.imo.org.

Inmarsat: The International Mobile Satellite Organization provides worldwide communications for commercial, distress, and safety applications, at sea, in the air, and on land.http://www.inmarsat.org.

Intelsat: The International Telecommunications Satellite Organization develops and operates a global commercial telecommunications satellite system. http://www.intelsat.com.

International Real Estate Digest: See the *International Real Estate Digest* (Mart indale- Hubbell) home page at http://www.ired.com.

Interpol: The International Criminal Police Organization promotes international cooperation among police authorities in fighting crime. http://www.interpol.int.

IOC: The International Olympic Committee (IOC) promotes the Olympic ideals and administers the Olympic games. http://www.olympic.org.

IOM: The International Organization for Migration (IOM) facilitates orderly international emigration and immigration. http://www.iom.int.

ISO: The International Organization for Standardization (ISO) promotes the development of international standards with a view to facilitating international exchange of goods and services and develops cooperation in the sphere of intellectual, scientific, technological, and economic activity.http://www.ico.ch.

ITU: The International Telecommunication Union (ITU) deals with world telecommunications issues. http://www.itu.int.

NEA: The Nuclear Energy Agency promotes the peaceful uses of nuclear energy; associated with OECD. http://www.nam.gov.za.

NSG: The Nuclear Suppliers Group (NSG) establishes guidelines for exports of nuclear materials, processing equipment for uranium enrichment, and technical information to countries of proliferation concern and regions of conflict and instability. http://www.nuclearsuppliersgroup.org.

OAS: The Organization of American States (OAS) promotes regional peace and security as well as economic and social development. http://www.oas.org.

OECD: The Organization for Economic Cooperation and Development (OECD) plays a prominent role in fostering good governance in the public service and in corporate activity. It helps governments to ensure the responsiveness of key economic areas with sectorial monitoring. By deciphering emerging issues and identifying policies that work, it helps policy makers adopt strategic orientations. It is well known for its individual country surveys and reviews.http://www.oced.org.

OPCW: The Organization for the Prohibition of Chemical Weapons (OPCW) enforces the Convention on the Prohibition of the Development, Production, Stockpiling and Use of Chemical Weapons and on Their Destruction; provides a forum for consultation and cooperation among the signatories of the Convention.http://www.opcw.org.

OSCE: The Organization for Security and Cooperation in Europe (OSCE) fosters the implementation of human right s, fundamental freedoms, democracy, and therule of law; acts as an instrument of early warning, conflict prevention and crisis management; and serves as a framework for conventional arms control and confidence building measures. http://www.osce.org.

OverseasPropertyOnline.com: European real estate Web site at http://www.real- estate- european-union.com/english.sitemap.html.

PCA: The Permanent Court of Arbitration (PCA) facilitates the settlement of internationaldisputes.http://www.pca-cpa.org.

UN: The United Nations (UN) maintains international peace and security and to promote cooperation involving economic, social, cultural, and humanitarian problems. http://www.un.org.

UNCTAD: The United Nations Conference on Trade and Development (UNCTAD). http://www.unctad.org.

UNESCO: The United Nations Educational, Scientific, and Cultural Organization (UNESCO).http://www.unesco.org.

UNHCR: The United Nations High Commissioner for Refugees (UNHCR) ensures the humanitarian treatment of refugees and finds permanent solutions to refugee problems. http://www.unhcr.ch.

UNIDO: The United Nations Industrial Development Organization (UNIDO) is a specialized agency that promotes industrial development especially among the members.http://www.unido.org.

UNU: The United Nations University (UNU) conducts research in development, welfare, and human survival and tot rain scholars. http://www.unu.edu.

UPU: The Universal Postal Union (UPU) promotes international postal cooperation. http://www.upu.int.

U.S. Bureau of Census: Homepage at http://www.census.gov.

U.S. Bureau of Economic Analysis: Homepage at http://www.bea.gov.

U.S. Department of Commerce: Homepage at http://www.state-usa-gov.

U.S. Department of State: Homepage at http://www.state.gov.

WCO: The World Customs Organization (WCO) promotes international cooperation in customs matters.http://www.wcoomd.org.

WHO: The World Health Organization (WHO).http://www.who.int.

WIPO: The World Intellectual Property Organization furnishes protection for literary, artistic, and scientific works. http://www.wipo.int.

WMO: The World Meteorological Organization (WMO). http://www.who.ch.

The World Factbook by the CIA: Web site at : http://www.cia.gov/cia/publications/factbook/.

World Trade Centers Institute: Web site at http://www.wtci.org.

WToO: The World Tourism Organization (WTO) promotes tourism as a means of contributing to economic development, international understanding, and peace. http://www.world-tourism.org.

WTrO: The World Trade Organization (WTO) provides a means to resolve trade conflicts between members and to carry on negotiations with the goal of further lowering and/or eliminating tariffs and other trade barriers. http://www.wto.org.

References

1 "The World Fact book," 2012, Central Intelligence Agency.[7] Now Updated to the current year.

2 "The World Factbook."[7]

3 M.L. Levine, The Global Real Estate Project: A Global Knowledge Exchange, 2012, University of Denver Franklin L. Burns School of Real Estate.

4 U.S.D.o.State,U.S. Department of State - Country Background Notes,2012,Available: http://www.state.gov.

5 Levine, The Global Real Estate Project: A Global Knowledge Exchange.

6 Levine, The Global Real Estate Project: A Global Knowledge Exchange.

7 Levine, The Global Real Estate Project: A Global Knowledge Exchange.

8 USAID, Strengthening the Economy. (Washington: USAID United States Agency: International Development, 2006).

9 Private Investments Law, Article 21.See http://www.commerce.gov.af.

10 B.o.C. Affairs, International Travel: Afghanistan (Washington: Travel.State.Gov United States Department of State,2012).

11 Affairs, International Travel: Afghanistan.

12 "The World Factbook."[7]

13 "The World Factbook."[7]

14 La Nacion, Buenos Aires, May 2002, Section 2 (pages 1-2) and The Wall Street Journal, May 28, 2002) p. A15.

15 Levine, The Global Real Estate Project: A Global Knowledge Exchange.

16 Levine, The Global Real Estate Project: A Global Knowledge Exchange.

17 Levine, The Global Real Estate Project: A Global Knowledge Exchange.

18 Levine, The Global Real Estate Project: A Global Knowledge Exchange.

19 La Nacion, Buenos Aires (May 2, 2002), Sec. 2, Page 1.

20 C.M.L. Mallet-Prevost, Martindale-Hubbell Law Digest: Argentina (New York: LexisNexis Martindale-Hubbell,2003).

21 Mallet-Prevost, Martindale-Hubbell Law Digest: Argentina.

22 Property Register: Argentina. (Washington: U.S. Department of State, 1999).

23 "The World Factbook."[7]

24 "The World Factbook."[7]

25 Levine, The Global Real Estate Project: A Global Knowledge Exchange.

26 U.S. Department of State, *Country Background Notes*. http://www.st at e.gov

27 Levine, The Global Real Estate Project: A Global Knowledge Exchange.

28 Levine, The Global Real Estate Project: A Global Knowledge Exchange.

29 Levine, The Global Real Estate Project: A Global Knowledge Exchange.

30 Mallet-Prevost, Martindale-Hubbell Law Digest: Argentina.

31 "The World Factbook."[7]

32 "The World Factbook."[7]

33 Levine, The Global Real Estate Project: A Global Knowledge Exchange.

34 Levine, The Global Real Estate Project: A Global Knowledge Exchange.

35 Levine, The Global Real Estate Project: A Global Knowledge Exchange.

36 Levine, The Global Real Estate Project: A Global Knowledge Exchange.

37 Certain items in this Section have been drawn from Jones Lang LaSalle, *Quarterly Investment Reports*, with permission from the publisher. All rights reserved.

38 "The World Factbook."[7]

39 "The World Factbook."[7]

40 Levine, The Global Real Estate Project: A Global Knowledge Exchange.

41 U.S. Department of State – Country Background Notes,http://www.state.gov.

42 Levine, The Global Real Estate Project: A Global Knowledge Exchange.

43 Levine, The Global Real Estate Project: A Global Knowledge Exchange.

44 Levine, The Global Real Estate Project: A Global Knowledge Exchange.

45 "The World Factbook."[7]

46 "The World Factbook."[7]

47 Levine, The Global Real Estate Project: A Global Knowledge Exchange.

48 State,U.S. Department of State - Country Background Notes.

49 Levine, The Global Real Estate Project: A Global Knowledge Exchange.

50 Levine, The Global Real Estate Project: A Global Knowledge Exchange.

51 Levine, The Global Real Estate Project: A Global Knowledge Exchange.

52 C.M.L. Mallet-Prevost, Martindale-Hubbell Law Digest: Canada (New York LexisNexis Martndale- Hubbell,2003).

53 "The World Factbook."[7]

54 "The World Factbook."[7]

55 Levine, The Global Real Estate Project: A Global Knowledge Exchange.

56 Levine, The Global Real Estate Project: A Global Knowledge Exchange.

57 "RepublicofChile:AGuidetothe20thCentury,"(NA),HistoricalText Archive:Chile, <http://www.historicaltextarchive.com.>.[7]

58 State,U.S. Department of State - Country Background Notes.

59 Levine, The Global Real Estate Project: A Global Knowledge Exchange.

60 Levine, The Global Real Estate Project: A Global Knowledge Exchange.

61 R. Lira, "Pension Funds and Housing Finance in Chile: A Question of Social Efficiency," Journal of Housing Research 5.2 (1994).

62 "Land Ownership and Foriegners - a Comparative Analysis of Regulatory Approaches," Food and Agriculture Organizations of the United Nations (1999),<www.fao.org>.

63 "The World Factbook."[7]

64 "The World Factbook."[7]

65 Levine, The Global Real Estate Project: A Global Knowledge Exchange.

66 Levine, The Global Real Estate Project: A Global Knowledge Exchange.

67 Levine, The Global Real Estate Project: A Global Knowledge Exchange.

68 UNICEF, China St at ist ics, 2003, United Nat ions Children's Fund, Available: http://www.unicef.org/infobycountry/china_statistics.html.

69 Levine, The Global Real Estate Project: A Global Knowledge Exchange.

70 C.M.L. Mallet-Prevost, Martindale-Hubbell Law Digest: China (New York: LexisNexis Martindale- Hubbell,2003).

71 "The World Factbook."7

72 "The World Factbook."7

73 C.R.A.C.o.C.(AMCHAM),Doing Business in Costa Rica,2011,Costa Rican-American Chamber of Commerce, Available: www.amcham.co.cr.

74 Levine, The Global Real Estate Project: A Global Knowledge Exchange.

75 B.o.C. Affairs, International Travel (Washington: Travel.State. Gov United States Department of State,2012).

76 Levine, The Global Real Estate Project: A Global Knowledge Exchange.

77 Levine, The Global Real Estate Project: A Global Knowledge Exchange.

78 Levine, The Global Real Estate Project: A Global Knowledge Exchange.

79 (AMCHAM), Doing Business in Cost a Rica.

80 "The World Factbook."7

81 "The World Factbook."7

82 Levine, The Global Real Estate Project: A Global Knowledge Exchange.

83 State,U.S. Department of State - Country Background Notes.

84 Levine, The Global Real Estate Project: A Global Knowledge Exchange

85 Levine, The Global Real Estate Project: A Global Knowledge Exchange.

86 Levine, The Global Real Estate Project: A Global Knowledge Exchange.

87 Mat erial from this section was partly created by Jan Boruvka, Secret ary General, Association of Real Estate Offices of the Czech Republic.

88 "The World Factbook."7

89 "The World Factbook."7

90 Levine, The Global Real Estate Project: A Global Knowledge Exchange.

91 State,U.S. Department of State - Country Background Notes.

92 Levine, The Global Real Estate Project: A Global Knowledge Exchange.

93 Levine, The Global Real Estate Project: A Global Knowledge Exchange.

94 Levine, The Global Real Estate Project: A Global Knowledge Exchange.

95 "The World Factbook."7

96 "The World Factbook."7

97 Levine, The Global Real Estate Project: A Global Knowledge Exchange.

98 State,U.S. Department of State - Country Background Notes.

99 Levine, The Global Real Estate Project: A Global Knowledge Exchange.

100 Levine, The Global Real Estate Project: A Global Knowledge Exchange.

101 Levine, The Global Real Estate Project: A Global Knowledge Exchange.

102 "The World Factbook."7

103 "The World Factbook."7

104 Levine, The Global Real Estate Project: A Global Knowledge Exchange.

105 State,U.S. Department of State - Country Background Notes.

106 Levine, The Global Real Estate Project: A Global Knowledge Exchange.

109 Levine, The Global Real Estate Project: A Global Knowledge Exchange.

110 Richard,Keith,"France May Limit Prostitution," August 11,2002,page A20,Washington Post (September16,2002).http://www. washingtonpost.com/wp-dyn/articles/A3846- 2002Aug10.html.

111 B.o.P.A. The Office of Website Management, What Is Modern Slavery?, 2012, The U.S. State Depart ment. Also see Trafficking in Persons Report. June 5, 2002, released by theOffice to Monitor and Combat Trafficking in Persons. http://www.state.gov/g/tip/rls/ tiprpt/2002/10653.htm.

112 "The World Factbook."7

113 "The World Factbook."7

114 Levine, The Global Real Estate Project: A Global Knowledge Exchange.

115 Levine, The Global Real Estate Project: A Global Knowledge Exchange.

116 Levine, The Global Real Estate Project: A Global Knowledge Exchange.

117 "Destatis Statistisches Bundesamt," 2012,Statistisches Bundesamt,<www.destatis.de>.7

118 F.M.o.D. (BMVg), 2012, The Press and information Office of the Federal Government, Germany Available:http://eng.bundesregier- ung.de/frameset/index.jsp.

119 Levine, The Global Real Estate Project: A Global Knowledge Exchange.

120 For more in this area, see theMartindale-Hubbell International Law Digest, among other sources.See the information noted in below in this Selected References section and the Web sitesnotedthereforad- ditionalresources.Alsosee"Immoportal.De:IeImmobilienwirtschaft Im Internet," 2012,Schulz & Low Consulting GmbH,<www.immoportal. de>.7

121 We thank **Dr. Karl-Werner Schulte** of theEuropean Business School, Germany, for contributing to this Chapter.

122 "The World Factbook."7

123 "The World Factbook."7

124 Levine, The Global Real Estate Project: A Global Knowledge Exchange.

125 U.S. Depart ment of St at e—Country Background Notes, Hungary. http://www.st at e.gov.

126 Levine, The Global Real

127 Levine, The Global Real

128 Levine, The Global Real

129 "The World Factbook."7

130 "The World Factbook."7

131 Levine, The Global Real

132 Levine, The Global Real

133 Levine, The Global Real

134 Levine, The Global Real

135 "The World Factbook."7

136 "The World Factbook."7

137 Levine, The Global Real Estate Project: A Global Knowledge Exchange. Estate Project: A Global Knowledge Exchange. Estate Project: A Global Knowledge Exchange. Estate Project: A Global Knowledge Exchange. Estate Project: A Global Knowledge Exchange. Estate Project: A Global Knowledge Exchange. Estate Project: A Global Knowledge Exchange. Estate Project: A Global Knowledge Exchange.

138 State,U.S. Department of State - Country Background Notes.

139 Levine, The Global Real Estate Project: A Global Knowledge Exchange.

140 Levine, The Global Real Estate Project: A Global Knowledge Exchange.

141 Levine, The Global Real Estate Project: A Global Knowledge Exchange.

142 "The World Factbook."7

143 "The World Factbook."7

144 "The World Factbook."7

145 See the detailed chronology at http://www.mfa.gov.il/mfa.

146 "The World Factbook."7

147 "The World Factbook."7

148 For more information, see http://www.mfa.gov.il. The Demographics Center; Ministry of Labor and Social Affairs Cent ral Bureau of St at ist ics, Office of thePrime Minist er, Cent ral Office of Information,Publications Service,Ministry of Education,Culture,and Sports.

149 I.M.o.F. Affairs, Facts About Israel: Political Structure, 2010, The State of Israel, Available: http://www.mfa.gov.il/MFA/Facts+About+Israel/State/THE+STATE-+Political+Structure.htm.

150 "The World Fact book."7 and "Israel Labor Force Dist ribut ion," 2012, theState of Israel, <http://www1.cbs.gov.il/reader/cw_usr_view_Folder?ID=141>.7

151 Levine, The Global Real Estate Project: A Global Knowledge Exchange.

152 For more informat ion, see Knight, Frank; Jones Lang LaSalle; CB Richard Ellis; and cit at ions to *International Real Estate Digest*, the National Association of REALTORS®, and the Burns School Global Real Estate Web site, *Daniels College of Business*, UNIVERSITY OF DENVER, at http://burns.daniels.du.edu/.

153 "The World Factbook."7

154 "The World Factbook."7

155 Levine, The Global Real Estate Project: A Global Knowledge Exchange.

156 State, U.S. Department of State - Country Background Notes.

157 Levine, The Global Real

158 Levine, The Global Real

159 Levine, The Global Real

160 "The World Factbook."7

161 "The World Factbook."7

162 Levine, The Global Real

163 Levine, The Global Real

164 Levine, The Global Real

165 Levine, The Global Real

166 "The World Factbook."7

167 "The World Factbook."7

168 Levine, The Global Real

169 For more information http://www.kinghussein.gov.jo/documents.html.

170 Levine, The Global Real Estate Project: A Global Knowledge Exchange.

171 Levine, The Global Real Estate Project: A Global Knowledge Exchange.

172 For more information about Qualifying Industrial Zones, see http://arabia.com.

173 Levine, The Global Real Estate Project: A Global Knowledge Exchange.

174 "The World Factbook."7

175 "The World Factbook."7

176 Levine, The Global Real Estate Project: A Global Knowledge Exchange.

177 State, U.S. Department of State - Country Background Notes.

178 Levine, The Global Real Estate Project: A Global Knowledge Exchange.

179 Levine, The Global Real Estate Project: A Global Knowledge Exchange.

180 Levine, The Global Real Estate Project: A Global Knowledge Exchange.

181 Levine, The Global Real Estate Project: A Global Knowledge Exchange.

182 "The World Factbook."7

183 "The World Factbook."7

184 Levine, The Global Real Estate Project: A Global Knowledge Exchange.

185 Levine, The Global Real Estate Project: A Global Knowledge Exchange. Estate Project: A Global Knowledge Exchange. Estate Project: A Global Knowledge Exchange. Estate Project: A Global Knowledge Exchange. Estate Project: A Global Knowledge Exchange. Estate Project: A Global Knowledge Exchange. Estate Project: A Global Knowledge Exchange. Estate Project: A Global Knowledge Exchange. about thepeace treaty bet ween Jordan and Israel, see

186 Levine, The Global Real Estate Project: A Global Knowledge Exchange.

187 Levine, The Global Real Estate Project: A Global Knowledge Exchange.

188 A system under which, upon the landowner's application the court may, after appropriate proceedings, direct the issuance of a certificate of title. With exceptions, this certificate is conclusive as to applicant's estate in land. The Torrens system of registration is the title itself; it differs from a title insurance policy, which is only evidence of title.

189 "The World Factbook."7

190 "The World Factbook."7

191 Levine, The Global Real Estate Project: A Global Knowledge Exchange.

192 To obtain all information about Mexico's geography, look *for Instituto Nacional de Estadistica, Geograffia e Informática INGEI* (Statistics, Geography, and Informatics National Institute) at http:/www.ingei.gob.mx.

195 Levine, The Global Real Estate Project: A Global Knowledge Exchange.

196 For more information on real estate issues and legal issues that overlap in this area, see the sources cited in *Martindale-Hubbell International Law Digest,http://www.ired.com.*

197 "The World Factbook."7

198 "The World Factbook."7

199 Levine, The Global Real Estate Project: A Global Knowledge Exchange.

200 State, U.S. Department of State - Country Background Notes.

201 Levine, The Global Real Estate Project: A Global Knowledge Exchange.

202 Levine, The Global Real Estate Project: A Global Knowledge Exchange.

203 Levine, The Global Real Estate Project: A Global Knowledge Exchange.

204 For more information about real estate transactions in the Netherlands, see Nederlandse Verninging Van Makelaars in Onroerende Goedren, Dutch Association of Real Estate Agents, the National Association of REALTORS®, and the Burns School Global Real Estate Web site, UNIVERSITY OF DENVER http://burns.daniels.du.edu.

205 "The World Factbook."7

206 "The World Factbook."7

207 Levine, The Global Real Estate Project: A Global Knowledge Exchange.

208 State, U.S. Department of State - Country Background Notes.

209 Levine, The Global Real Estate Project: A Global Knowledge Exchange.

210 Levine, The Global Real Estate Project: A Global Knowledge Exchange.

211 Levine, The Global Real Estate Project: A Global Knowledge Exchange.

212 Material from this section was partly created by Kathy Shahani.

213 "The World Factbook."7

214 "The World Factbook."7

215 Levine, The Global Real Estate Project: A Global Knowledge Exchange.

216 State, U.S. Department of State - Country Background Notes.

217 Levine, The Global Real Estate Project: A Global Knowledge Exchange.

218 Levine, The Global Real Estate Project: A Global Knowledge Exchange.

219 State, U.S. Department of State - Country Background Notes.

220 State, U.S. Department of State - Country Background Notes.

221 "The World Factbook."7

222 Levine, The Global Real Estate Project: A Global Knowledge Exchange.

223 "The World Factbook."7

224 "The World Factbook."7

225 Levine, The Global Real Estate Project: A Global Knowledge Exchange.

226 1 U.S. Department of State – Country Background Notes

227 State, U.S. Department of State - Country Background Notes.

228 Levine, The Global Real Estate Project: A Global Knowledge Exchange.

229 "The World Factbook."7

230 Levine, The Global Real Estate Project: A Global Knowledge Exchange.

231 See Information about Saudi Arabia's economy was derived, in part, from theLibrary of Congress Count ry St udies at http://lceb2.loc.gov/frd/cs (click on Saudi Arabia).

232 "The World Factbook."7

233 Levine, The Global Real Estate Project: A Global Knowledge Exchange.

234 "The World Factbook."7

235 "The World Factbook."7

236 Levine, The Global Real Estate Project: A Global Knowledge Exchange.

237 State, U.S. Department of State - Country Background Notes.

238 "The World Factbook."7

239 "The World Factbook."7

240 Levine, The Global Real Estate Project: A Global Knowledge Exchange.

241 State, U.S. Department of State - Country Background Notes.

242 Levine, The Global Real Estate Project: A Global Knowledge Exchange.

243 Levine, The Global Real Estate Project: A Global Knowledge Exchange.

244 Levine, The Global Real Estate Project: A Global Knowledge Exchange.

245 C.M.L. Mallet-Prevost, Martindale-Hubbell Law Digest: Singapore, Real Property (LexisNexis Martindale-Hubbell,2003).

246 Trafficking in Persons Report, (Washington: United States Department of State, 2002). Also see http://state.gov/g/tip/rls/tiprpt/2002/10682.htm.

247 "The World Factbook."7

248 "The World Factbook."7

249 Levine, The Global Real Estate Project: A Global Knowledge Exchange.

250 State, U.S. Department of State - Country Background Notes.

251 Levine, The Global Real Estate Project: A Global Knowledge Exchange.

252 Levine, The Global Real Estate Project: A Global Knowledge Exchange.

253 Levine, The Global Real Estate Project: A Global Knowledge Exchange.

254 Also see J. Fisher-Thompson, "U.S. To Help Finance Low-Income Housing in South Africa," The Washington File (2006), <http://usinfo.state.gov/regional/af/trade/a2090301.htm>.

255 "The World Factbook."7

256 "The World Factbook."7

257 Levine, The Global Real Estate Project: A Global Knowledge Exchange.

258 State, U.S. Department of State - Country Background Notes.

259 Levine, The Global Real

260 Levine, The Global Real

261 Levine, The Global Real

262 "The World Factbook."7

263 "The World Factbook."7

264 Levine, The Global Real

265 Levine, The Global Real

266 Levine, The Global Real

267 Levine, The Global Real

268 "The World Factbook."7

269 "The World Factbook."7

270 Levine, The Global Real

271 State, U.S. Department of State - Country Background Notes.

272 Levine, The Global Real Estate Project: A Global Knowledge Exchange.

273 Levine, The Global Real Estate Project: A Global Knowledge Exchange.

274 Levine, The Global Real Estate Project: A Global Knowledge Exchange.

275 "The World Factbook."7

276 "The World Factbook."7

277 Levine, The Global Real Estate Project: A Global Knowledge Exchange.

278 "Land Ownership and Foriegners - a Comparative Analysis of Regulatory Approaches."

279 Levine, The Global Real Estate Project: A Global Knowledge Exchange.

280 Levine, The Global Real Estate Project: A Global Knowledge Exchange.

281 Levine, The Global Real Estate Project: A Global Knowledge Exchange.

282 M.L. Levine, Real Estate transact ions, tax Planning and Consequences (St. Paul: thomas- West (The West group), 2012). Also see

283 M.L. Levine, Real Estate Fundament als (St. Paul: West Publishing Company, 1976). Also Estate Project: A Global Knowledge Exchange. Estate Project: A Global Knowledge Exchange. Estate Project: A Global Knowledge Exchange. Estate Project: A Global Knowledge Exchange. Estate Project: A Global Knowledge Exchange. Estate Project: A Global Knowledge Exchange. Estate Project: A Global

Knowledge Exchange. Estate Project: A Global Knowledge Exchange. see M.L.a.K. Levine, Handbook of Real Estate Law (Denver: PP& E, 1978).

284 Levine, The Global Real Estate Project: A Global Knowledge Exchange.

285 "The World Factbook."7

286 "The World Factbook."7

287 Levine, The Global Real Estate Project: A Global Knowledge Exchange.

288 Levine, The Global Real Estate Project: A Global Knowledge Exchange.

289 Levine, The Global Real Estate Project: A Global Knowledge Exchange.

290 Levine, The Global Real Estate Project: A Global Knowledge Exchange.